# THE LEGAL RIGHTS
# OF HANDICAPPED PERSONS

# THE LEGAL RIGHTS OF HANDICAPPED PERSONS

Cases, Materials, and Text

*1983 Supplement*

by
**Robert L. Burgdorf Jr., J.D.**
and
**Patrick P. Spicer, J.D.**

with a chapter by
**Christopher G. Bell, J.D.**

·P·A·U·L·H·
BROOKES
PUBLISHING C<u>O</u>

Baltimore · London

**Paul H. Brookes Publishing Co.**
Post Office Box 10624
Baltimore, Maryland 21204

Pages 13–14: Breslin, E., "Backlash Against the Disabled," 4 *Mental Disability Law Reporter* 345, Sept./Oct. 1980, reprinted with permission from the Commission on the Mentally Disabled.
Pages 14–19: Postlewaite, J., "Reviewing the '70s—A Decade of Extraordinary Gains? Or Paper Victories?" 5 *Amicus,* No. 3 & 4, p. 42, May/Aug. 1980; and Soskin, R., "Handicapped Advocacy: A Last Hurrah?" 5 *Amicus,* No. 3 & 4, p. 69, May/Aug. 1980, reprinted with permission from the National Center for Law and the Handicapped, Inc.
Pages 19–20: Milk, L., "Editorial: Beating the Backlash," 5 *Mainstream,* No. 4, p. 6, July/Aug. 1980, reprinted with permission from *Mainstream,* Inc.
Pages 207–208: "Accessibility Complaints Drop by 54 in FY '81," *Handicapped Rights and Regulations,* July 13, 1982, reprinted with permission from Business Publishers, Inc.

Typeset by The Composing Room of Michigan, Inc. (Grand Rapids)
Manufactured in the United States of America by The Maple Press Company
(York, Pennsylvania)

**Library of Congress Cataloging in Publication Data**

Burgdorf, Robert L., 1948–
    The legal rights of handicapped persons.

    Includes index.
        1. Handicapped—Legal status, laws, etc.—United
States—Cases.   I. Spicer, Patrick P.   II. Bell, Christopher
G. (Christopher George), 1951–      .   III. Title.
KF480.A7L43 Suppl.       346.7301'3        83-2471
ISBN 0-933716-31-1        347.30613

# PREFACE

Were we to capsulize the developments thus far in the 1980s regarding the legal rights of handicapped persons, we would summarize the situation as two steps forward, one step back. More cynical observers might argue for the converse—that the setbacks for handicapped people in this decade have outstripped advances. It is true that strong initiatives have developed to restrict or deny some of the hard-fought gains of legal rights of handicapped persons in areas such as education, employment, and transportation. Generally, however, redoubled efforts by handicapped citizens and their advocates have rebuffed most attempts to eliminate or reduce legal protections. Organized, outspoken advocacy efforts were recently able, for example, to repel attempts of the current federal administration to substantially rewrite and withdraw important provisions of regulations under the Education for All Handicapped Children Act and Section 504 of the Rehabilitation Act of 1973. The handicapped constituency is increasingly becoming aware of its political clout and ways in which that clout may best be wielded to promote the elimination of discrimination on the basis of handicaps.

Some court decisions, particularly by the United States Supreme Court, have disappointed handicapped persons. The *Davis, Rowley, Parham,* and *Pennhurst* decisions included in this volume are examples of cases in which the Supreme Court was less than fully sympathetic to the cause of handicapped litigants. And yet the overall effect of these decisions has not been devastating to the civil rights movement of handicapped people. Moreover, the Court's decision in *Youngberg* v. *Romeo* appears to be a major advance toward recognition of the long-debated constitutional right to treatment or habilitation for involuntarily confined mental health and mental retardation patients. And a number of decisions of other courts hold great promise for expanding recognition of handicapped persons' legal rights in regard to such issues as employment, transportation, and parental rights. Despite occasional lapses, courts have generally continued to enforce strong Congressional, state, and constitutional mandates for nondiscrimination toward handicapped people.

The struggle for legal equality for handicapped individuals continues at all administrative and judicial levels. As this book is going to press, the U.S. Supreme Court has agreed to hear the case of *LeStrange* v. *Consolidated Rail Corporation* in which it may resolve the question of a private right of action for employment discrimination under Section 504 of the Rehabilitation Act. The *Pennhurst* case, decided in favor of the handicapped residents by the Third Circuit Court of Appeals based upon state law, is again before the High Court.

History teaches that other minority groups and women had to overcome many decades of unfavorable court decisions before their causes were ultimately vindicated by the judiciary. In this context, given its relatively short duration, the civil rights movement for handicapped persons has been extraordinarily successful.

This volume is written as a supplement to the casebook *The Legal Rights of Handicapped Persons: Cases, Materials, and Text,* and presents decisions and materials that have been forthcoming since the publication of the parent volume. Cross-references are provided to describe where the more recent material fits into the original casebook material. The scope of the material included is generally coextensive with the casebook, although a few new section headings have been added to particular chapters. As in the original volume, cases and articles have been edited to remove extraneous and duplicative material, and footnotes, except those of particular pertinence, have been deleted.

Robert L. Burgdorf Jr.

# TABLE OF CONTENTS

# TABLE OF CASES

Principal cases are in *italic type.*

*To my parents, Patricia and Robert L. Burgdorf.*

*RLB*


*To my mother, Mrs. Lorraine Spicer; my sister, Cindy Spicer; and friends Tim and Michelle O'Brien.*

*PPS*

# The Legal Rights
## of Handicapped Persons

# I

# WHO ARE "HANDICAPPED" PERSONS?

Robert L. Burgdorf Jr.

## D. LEGAL AND GOVERNMENTAL DEFINITIONS OF HANDICAPS

p. 19—INSERT at the end of Note 2:

COURTS IN AT LEAST THREE STATES have given more narrow interpretations of the term *handicapped* as used in their state antidiscrimination laws. In *Lyons* v. *Heritage House Restaurants,* 89 Ill. App. 3d 163, 59 Ill. Dec. 686, 432 N.E.2d 270 (1982), a woman was dismissed from her job because she had developed an early form of cancer of the uterus. The Supreme Court of Illinois adopted as a definition of *handicap* that it is "a class of physical and mental conditions which are generally believed to impose severe barriers upon the ability of an individual to perform major life functions." At 432 N.E.2d 273. Applying this definition, the court held that cancer victims are not handicapped persons protected by the Illinois Fair Employment Practices Act. The *Lyons* court cited with approval two Illinois Court of Appeals decisions which had ruled that certain other conditions did not constitute handicaps: *Advocates for the Handicapped* v. *Sears, Roebuck & Co.,* 67 Ill. App.3d 512, 24 Ill. Dec. 272, 385 N.E.2d 39 (1978) (chronic kidney ailments and kidney transplant); *Kubik* v. *CNA Financial Corp.,* 96 Ill. App.3d 715, 52 Ill. Dec. 320, 422 N.E.2d 1 (1981) (malignant tumor in colon). In *Burgess* v. *Joseph Schlitz Brewing Co.,* 298 N.C. 520, 259 S.E.2d 248 (1979), the Supreme Court of North Carolina ruled that an individual who had been denied employment because of an employer's express policy against hiring persons with glaucoma was not a "handicapped person" under a state statute guaranteeing employment rights, because the glaucoma did not currently interfere with the individual's vision. Similarly, in *Providence Journal Co.* v. *Mason,* 116 R.I. 614, 359 A.2d 682 (1976), the court held that a woman who was discharged from her job because she had incurred a "whiplash" injury did not qualify as having a "physical handicap" under the Rhode Island Fair Employment Practices Act. The court interpreted a list of conditions constituting "physical handicaps" under the statute as exhaustive even though the statutory language defined the term *physical handicap* to "include, but not be limited to" the listed conditions. R.I. Gen. Laws Sec. 28-5-6(H). How consistent are these results with the legislative intent underlying the enactment of nondiscrimination provisions?

p. 29—INSERT after the Note on this page:

## E. E. BLACK, LTD. v. MARSHALL

*United States District Court for the District of Hawaii, 1980*
*497 F. Supp. 1088*

Decision and Order

SAMUEL P. KING, Chief Judge.

### I. Facts

This case of first impression involves the construction and interpretation of several sections of the Rehabilitation Act of 1973, 29 U.S.C. § 701 *et seq.* (1976 & Supp. III 1979), and appurtenant regulations. Section 503 of the Act, 29 U.S.C. § 793 (Supp. III 1979) (as amended) reads in pertinent part:

> Any contract in excess of $2,500 entered into by any Federal department or agency for the procurement of personal property and non-personal services (including construction) for the United States shall contain a provision requiring that, in employing persons to carry out such contract the party contracting with the United States shall take affirmative action to employ and advance in employment qualified handicapped individuals as defined in section 706(7) of this title.

29 U.S.C. § 706(7) (Supp. III 1979) reads in pertinent part:

> (A) Except as otherwise provided in subparagraph (B), the term "handicapped individual" means any individual who (i) has a physical or mental disability which for such individual constitutes or results in a substantial handicap to employment and (ii) can reasonably be expected to benefit in terms of employability from vocational rehabilitation services . . .
>
> (B) [T]he term "handicapped individual" means . . . any person who (i) has a physical or mental impairment which substantially limits one or more of such person's major life activities, (ii) has a record of such an impairment, or (iii) is regarded as having such an impairment.

Pursuant to the Act, and Executive Order No. 11558, the Secretary of Labor issued regulations governing procedures for enforcing the Act, and also supplementing and defining certain of the terms contained in the Act. 41 C.F.R. § 60-741.2 defines a handicapped individual as any person who:

> (1) has a physical or mental impairment which substantially limits one or more of such person's major life activities, (2) has a record of such impairment, or (3) is regarded as having such an impairment. For purposes of this Part, a handicapped individual is "substantially limited" if he or she is likely to experience difficulty in securing, retaining or advancing in employment because of a handicap.

Appendix A to 41 C.F.R. § 60-741 includes employment in its definition of "major life activities." That Appendix also provides:

> The phrase "*substantially limits*" means the degree that the impairment affects employability. A handicapped individual who is likely to experience difficulty in securing, retaining or advancing in employment would be considered substantially limited.

* * *

*"Is regarded as having such an impairment"* refers to those individuals who are perceived as having a handicap, whether an impairment exists or not, but who, because of attitudes or for any other reason, are regarded as handicapped by employers, or supervisors who have an effect on the individual securing, retaining or advancing in employment.

George Crosby is a thirty-one year old man who entered the apprenticeship program of the United Brotherhood of Carpenters in Honolulu in September 1973. The program involved on-the-job training and schooling designed to teach the basic carpentry skills necessary to become a journeyman. The job of carpenter's apprentice requires frequent bending, twisting and heavy lifting. The apprenticeship program required 8,000 hours of work in the field. Prior to starting the program, Mr. Crosby had worked packing and moving furniture and had also worked in the carpenter's union summer program. In high school Mr. Crosby had been active in basketball, cross-country and varsity football. He also played football for the University of Hawaii, and after college tried out for several professional football teams.

As an apprentice carpenter, Mr. Crosby worked for several construction contractors between September 1973 and May 1976. By May 1976, he had accumulated over 3600 hours of on-the-job training. During this time he had suffered two back-related problems. In March 1974 he strained his back while attempting to carry a load of lumber. The pain occurred in his lower left back around the beltline. He was treated for this injury for several months and collected $400 in workers' compensation benefits. In 1975, while attempting to put a concrete form in place, Mr. Crosby "felt a little discomfort" in his back. When he reported the incident he was sent to a doctor who examined and X-rayed his back, but could find nothing wrong. Mr. Crosby returned to work the same day.

On May 20, 1976, Mr. Crosby and several other apprentice carpenters were referred by the union to defendant E. E. Black, Ltd. (Black), a general construction contractor. Black required all apprentice carpenter applicants to take pre-employment physical examinations. Mr. Crosby had X-rays taken of his back, and Dr. George Henry, who read the X-rays, detected a congenital back anomaly, a partially sacralized transitional vertebra (also referred to as an "anomalous joint" or a "lumbosacral anomalous joint"). Dr. Henry told Black that because of this condition Mr. Crosby was a poor risk for heavy labor. Black denied Mr. Crosby employment on the basis of his pre-employment physical.

On June 4, 1976, Mr. Crosby was examined by Dr. Masao Takai, an orthopedist, who took X-rays, and found in addition to the anomaly mentioned above, a spina bifida occulta and a mild rotoscoliosis.[1] Dr. Takai concluded, after the examination, that Mr. Crosby's condition did not prevent him from performing the job of apprentice carpenter, and wrote a letter addressed "to whom it may concern" stating that if Mr. Crosby kept his back and abdominal muscles in good tone, "he should be able to

---

[1]Spina bifida occulta is an anomaly characterized by the defective closure of the bony encasement of the spinal cord. Rotoscoliosis is an anomaly which involves a narrowing of the disc space caused by a slight rotation of the spine.

perform whatever he prefers." Though Mr. Crosby showed the letter to Black, he was never recalled for an apprentice carpenter position.

Mr. Crosby testified at a hearing before an Administrative Law Judge that after the Black incident, the union would not refer him to any jobs that had pre-employment physicals. During the period between 1976 and 1978 Mr. Crosby worked at several construction jobs. He testified before the Administrative Law Judge that because of the incident with Black he had had great difficulty obtaining employment as a carpenter's apprentice, and had been unable to get the on-the-job training hours required to become a journeyman.

In July 1976, Mr. Crosby filed a complaint with the State of Hawaii Department of Labor, which complaint was referred to the defendant United States Department of Labor. Mr. Crosby alleged that he had been refused employment as an apprentice carpenter by Black because of a congenital abnormality in his back.

\* \* \*

Mr. Crosby's complaint was investigated by the Office of Federal Contract Compliance Programs (OFCCP) of the Department of Labor. That office found that Black had violated the Act and its implementing regulations, and on July 13, 1977 issued an administrative complaint.

\* \* \*

A hearing was held in Honolulu in April 1978 before Chief Administrative Law Judge H. Stephan Gordon. At the hearing the parties were afforded the opportunity to be heard, to introduce relevant evidence and to examine and cross-examine witnesses. A great deal of medical evidence was presented. In September 1978 Judge Gordon issued his decision. He first commented that "a review of [the medical] evidence reveals a sharp conflict among medical authorities on the relationship of unilateral sacralization of lumbar vertebra to low back injuries. However . . . this condition, as it exists in Mr. Crosby, in no way impairs his present ability to perform all the physical functions of a carpenter's apprentice. The medical dispute in this case is focused solely on whether this condition will tend to lead to back pain and injury in the future."

The Judge noted that the term "impairment" is nowhere defined in the Act or regulations, but he interpreted it as meaning "any condition which weakens, diminishes, restricts, or otherwise damages an individual's health or physical or mental activity." The Judge found that the Department had proved that Mr. Crosby was perceived to have an impairment, and that he experienced difficulty in obtaining employment because of this. However, the Judge found that the Department had not proved that the perceived impairment substantially limited a major life activity of Mr. Crosby—in this case, employment. Hence, the Judge found that Mr. Crosby was not a handicapped individual and was not protected by the Act. *U.S. Dept. of Labor* v. *E. E. Black, Ltd.,* No. 77-OFCCP-7R (U.S. Dept. of Labor, Sept. 13, 1978), [hereinafter Administrative Law Judge's Decision].

The Judge determined that Congress was not attempting to protect people with *any* impairment, "merely the most disabling." He concluded that the Department had to demonstrate that Mr. Crosby's impairment was so severe as to limit employment generally. "To prove this, Plaintiff must demonstrate that the impairment, as of the time of the alleged discrimination, impeded activities relevant to many or most jobs."

The Judge determined that since it had not been demonstrated that Mr. Crosby's perceived impairment had any present functional significance, ". . . it follows *a fortiori* that this impairment was not perceived as impeding activities indigenous to many or most jobs or as limiting any of Mr. Crosby's major life activities." The Judge went on to hold, however, that even if future functional significance was relevant in establishing that employment was substantially limited, the Department "still would not have met its burden in this case."

> . . . Dr. Henry perceived Mr. Crosby's impairment as disqualifying him only for jobs involving heavy labor. While many jobs exist which could be classified as heavy labor, they are relatively few when measured as a percentage of all jobs available in the labor force. Accordingly, an impairment which disqualifies a person from performing heavy labor would not necessarily affect his ability to perform the vast majority of jobs. Yet it is only persons with impairments impeding their ability to perform many or most jobs (measured against the full spectrum of possible employments) who are likely to experience difficulty in securing, retaining, or advancing in employment because of handicaps. Therefore, since Mr. Crosby's impairment was perceived as limiting his access only to a relatively few jobs, it cannot be considered severe enough to qualify under the statutory definition.
> *Id*. at 14.

The Judge also found that the pre-employment physical examination, used only for carpenter apprentice and laborer positions—both involving heavy labor—did not tend to screen out qualified handicapped individuals. He found that the job requirement bore a reasonable relation to jobs involving strenuous physical activity, and was consistent with business necessity and safe job performance. He did not discuss, however, whether screening out individuals with Mr. Crosby's specific problem was permitted. No doubt this was because he felt that as he had already concluded that Mr. Crosby was *not* a handicapped individual, it could not possibly have been a violation of the Act and regulations for Black to have screened him out. The Judge recommended that the complaint be dismissed in its entirety.

The OFCCP filed exceptions to the Recommended Decision and Order with Donald Elisburg, Assistant Secretary of Labor, Employment Standards Administration. After denying a motion to disqualify the Secretary of Labor, the Department of Labor and himself, the Assistant Secretary issued a Decision and Order on February 26, 1979. *U.S. Dept. of Labor* v. *E. E. Black, Ltd.*, No. 77-OFCCP-7R (U.S. Dept. of Labor., Feb. 26, 1979). Though his view of the facts was almost identical to that of the Administrative Law Judge, his view of the law was different. He agreed with the Judge that the term "impairment" as used in the Act and regulations means "any condition which weakens, diminishes, restricts, or otherwise damages an individual's health or physical or mental activity." However, he took a much more expansive view of the meaning of "substantially limits one or more . . . major life activities." He found that coverage under the Act did not require a showing that the impairment impeded activities relevant to many or most jobs, but rather that protection "under the Act is extended to every individual with an impairment which is a current bar to employment which the individual is currently capable of performing. . . . It is sufficient that the impairment is a current bar to the employment of one's choice with a federal contractor which the individual is currently capable of performing." He also overruled the Judge's finding that since Mr. Crosby's handicap was perceived as having no present functional significance, it could not possibly have been perceived as impeding activities indigenous to many or most jobs. He found that since the perceived impairment prevented Mr. Crosby from securing the job he wanted, Mr. Crosby was a handicapped individual under the definitions set forth in the Act and regulations. He further found that since Mr. Crosby, at the time he was denied employment, was currently capable of performing the job, he was a qualified handicapped individual as that term is used in 41 C.F.R. § 60-741.2.[4] Thus he found that Mr. Crosby was covered by the Act.

The Assistant Secretary also found that Black's affirmative action obligations were applicable to the job and contract for which Mr. Crosby was rejected. The Assistant Secretary determined that Black had violated 41 C.F.R. § 60-741.6, by applying physical job requirements that 1) tended to screen out qualified handicapped individuals and 2) were not related to the specific job of apprentice carpenter. He, unlike the Administrative Law Judge, viewed the job requirement not as the pre-employment physical, but as Black's requirement that Mr. Crosby not have the back condition he did. He agreed with the Administrative Law Judge that in the abstract the requirement of a healthy back bears the needed relation to the job, but found that the key question was whether the disqualifying condition "evaluated Mr. Crosby's current capacity to perform the work of an apprentice carpenter." Since Mr. Crosby's condition, according to the Assistant Secretary, had at best only a potential for future significance, it could not be used to disqualify Mr. Crosby from the job. The Assistant Secretary also noted that even the judgment "of possible future significance was contradicted by other testimony and by medical studies containing scientific data and statistics supporting an opposite conclusion." He also rejected Black's argument that hiring someone with a great risk of future back injury was justified by business necessity because of the very high potential workers' compensation costs. "A policy of excluding potential employees to reduce an employer's costs shifts the financial burden to the rejected handicapped individual. This is contrary to the intent of protective statutes such as the Act." Black also argued that forcing it to ignore its doctors' recommendations made it violate its O.S.H.A. obligations. The Assistant Secretary found, however, that Black's "safety and health obligations . . . are not violated by the employment of an impaired individual who is capable of performing the particular job."

The Assistant Secretary ordered Black to offer Mr. Crosby a job as an apprentice carpenter, and also ordered it to stop using "non-job related physical qualification requirements which tend to screen out qualified handicapped individuals for the job of apprentice carpenter." There were various other provisions in the Order, and certain back pay and other matters were remanded to the Administrative Law Judge. Black was ordered to comply or be debarred from all government contracts.

On March 16, 1979, plaintiffs Black, the Hawaii Employers Council and the General Contractors Association of Hawaii, Inc. filed this action for judicial review of

---

[4]That section reads: " 'Qualified handicapped individual' means a handicapped individual as defined in § 60-741.2 who is capable of performing a particular job with reasonable accommodation to his or her handicap."

the Assistant Secretary's decision. The case is now before the Court on cross-motions for summary judgment.

## II.   The Law

Plaintiffs' motion for summary judgment contains three major prongs: 1) 29 U.S.C. § 706(7)(B)(iii) and the related regulations, as construed and applied by the decision and Order of the Assistant Secretary, are unconstitutionally vague; 2) Congress limited the benefits of the Act to those handicapped individuals who encounter substantial difficulty in obtaining employment generally, and did not intend to protect job applicants who are denied a particular job because of a perceived impairment or because of the risk of future injury and 3) the defendants' imposition of burdens of proof on contractors to establish "reasonable reliance on valid expert opinion that there is imminent risk of serious injury" or "current inability to perform the tasks of the job" (a) conflicts with applicable regulations, (b) is inconsistent with federal statutory policy to promote worker safety and to encourage preventive medicine and (c) impinges upon the employer's right to due process of law. Defendants ask the Court to uphold the decision of the Assistant Secretary.

*A.   The Definition of "Impairment" and "Regarded as Having an Impairment"*

Plaintiffs argue that the definition of "handicapped individual" contained in the Act and the regulations is unconstitutionally vague. They also argue that since the meaning of the Act and the regulations was impossible to determine in 1976, at the time the decision not to hire Mr. Crosby was made, it would be an unconstitutional deprivation of due process to, in effect, retroactively sanction Black for not knowing what the Department of Labor and the courts were going to say the statute meant in 1979. The Court rejects plaintiffs' contentions.

29 U.S.C. § 706(7) defines a handicapped individual as a person who "(i) has a physical or mental impairment which substantially limits one or more of such person's major life activities, (ii) has a record of such an impairment, or (iii) is regarded as having such an impairment." Both the Administrative Law Judge and the Assistant Secretary, after determining that "impairment" is nowhere defined in the Act or the regulations, defined it as "any condition which weakens, diminishes, restricts, or otherwise damages an individual's health or physical or mental activity." The "is regarded as having an impairment" language was interpreted consistently with Appendix A to 41 C.F.R. § 60-741:

> Is regarded as having such an impairment refers to those individuals who are perceived as having a handicap, whether an impairment exists or not, but who, because of attitudes or for any other reason, are regarded as handicapped by employers, or supervisors who have an effect on the individual securing, retaining or advancing in employment.

Congress amended the statute in 1974, adding the "is regarded as having such an impairment" language. Their intent was to protect people who are denied employment because of an employer's perceptions, whether or not those perceptions are accurate. It is of little solace to a person denied employment to know that the employer's view of his or her condition is erroneous. To such a person the perception of the employer is as important as reality. As was stated in the Senate Report accompanying S. 4194, the bill that in 1974 added the language discussed above:

> [T]he new definition clarifies the intention to include those persons who are discriminated against on the basis of handicap, whether or not they are in fact handicapped, just as Title VI of the Civil Rights Act of 1964 prohibits discrimination on the ground of race, whether or not the person discriminated against is in fact a member of a racial minority. This subsection includes within the protection of sections 503 and 504 those persons who do not in fact have the condition which they are perceived as having as well as those persons whose mental or physical condition does not substantially limit their life activities and who thus are not technically within [the first clause] in the new definition. Members of both of these groups may be subject to discrimination on the basis of their being regarded as handicapped.

S.Rep. No. 93-1297, 93rd Cong., 2d Sess., reprinted in [1974] U.S. Code Cong. & Admin. News, pp. at 6389–90.

While the definition of impairment adopted by the Administrative Law Judge and the Assistant Secretary (taken from Webster's Third International Dictionary, unabridged, 1967) is broad, that does not mean that it is either improper or unconstitutionally vague. The Court's examination of the Act and the legislative history convinces the Court that Congress wanted the statute to have broad coverage and effect.

In § 301 of the White House Conference on Handicapped Individuals Act (the Act adding the amendments discussed above), Act of December 7, 1974, Pub.L. No. 93-516, 88 Stat. 1631–34 (codified at 29 U.S.C. § 701 note), it was stated:

> The Congress finds that:
>
> * * *
>
> (2) the benefits and fundamental rights of this society are often denied those individuals with mental and physical handicaps;
>
> (3) there are seven million children and at least twenty-eight million adults with mental or physical handicaps;
>
> (4) it is of critical importance to this Nation that equality of opportunity, equal access to all aspects of society and equal rights guaranteed by the Constitution of the United States be provided to all individuals with handicaps;
>
> * * *
>
> (7) all levels of Government must necessarily share responsibility for developing opportunities for individuals with handicaps. . . .

The Court believes that Congress wanted those individuals who either had or were perceived as having physical or mental conditions that disqualified them from employment to be considered as either impaired or regarded as impaired.

Given the legislative history of the Act, persons of common intelligence should have had fair warning that the term impairment meant "any condition which weakens, diminishes, restricts, or otherwise damages an individual's health or physical or mental activity." That is a broad, but entirely logical way of viewing the meaning of the term. And the phrase "is regarded as having an impairment" is almost self-explanatory given the meaning of impairment.

The Court sees no basis for the plaintiffs' contention that all impairments must be defined by reference to the American Medical Association Guides to the Evaluation of Permanent Impairment. Words are not precise symbols and statutory definitions are often unable to precisely define and cover all possible situations. Congress was not required to spell out in detail every possible condition or abnormality that could constitute an impairment. It is clear that Congress was trying to protect a large number of people in a broad range of situations. In *Southeastern Community College* v. *Davis*, 442 U.S. 397, 99 S.Ct. 2361, 60 L.Ed.2d 980 (1979), the Supreme Court, after setting out the definition of handicapped individual, noted:

> This definition comports with our understanding of § 504. A person who has a record of, or is regarded as having, an impairment may at present have no actual incapacity at all. Such a person would be exactly the kind of individual who could be "otherwise qualified" to participate in covered programs. And a person who suffers from a limiting physical or mental impairment still may possess other abilities that permit him to meet the requirements of various programs. Thus, it is clear that Congress included among the class of "handicapped" persons covered by § 504 a range of individuals who could be "otherwise qualified."

442 U.S. at 405–06 n.6, 99 S.Ct. at 2367. Congress was not required to define impairment any more precisely than it did, and the definition adopted by both the Assistant Secretary and the Administrative Law Judge is neither unconstitutionally vague nor otherwise improper.

Even if in some difficult cases the definition in the Act could be said not to furnish fair warning of its meaning, the Court believes Black had to have had fair warning that Mr. Crosby would be considered impaired or regarded as impaired. Black discovered what it considered a physical abnormality in Mr. Crosby, and it determined that that abnormality disqualified Mr. Crosby absolutely from the job of apprentice carpenter. Black should not have been misled as to the meaning of impairment in relation to Mr. Crosby.

B. *Definition of "Substantially Limited" and "Substantial Handicap to Employment"*

As noted, 29 U.S.C. § 706(7) partially defines a handicapped individual as one who "has a physical or mental disability which for such individual constitutes or results in a substantial handicap to employment. . . ." That section also provides that a handicapped individual is one who "has a physical or mental impairment which substantially limits one or more of such person's major life activities. . . ." 41 C.F.R. § 60-741.2 provides that "a handicapped individual is 'substantially limited' if he or she is likely to experience difficulty in securing, retaining or advancing in employment because of a handicap." The Administrative Law Judge determined that in order for plaintiff to prove that he was substantially limited and thus covered by the Act, he had to show that the impairment "impeded activities relevant to many or most jobs." The Assistant Secretary reversed the Administrative Law Judge on this point and found that an individual is substantially limited if "the impairment is a current bar to the employment of one's choice with a federal contractor which the individual is currently capable of performing." He found that the only impaired individuals not protected by the Act are those who are not capable of fulfilling a contractor's valid job requirements, and those whose impairment did not serve as the basis for the discrimination.

The Court believes that the Assistant Secretary's interpretation of the Act and the regulations is overbroad. He includes within the coverage of the Act any individual who is capable of performing a particular job, and is rejected for that particular job because of a real or perceived physical or mental impairment. Thus, for example, a worker who was offered a particular job by a company at all of its plants but one, but was denied employment at that plant because of the presence of plant matter to which the employee was allergic, would be covered by the Act. An individual with acrophobia who was offered 10 deputy assistant accountant jobs with a particular company, but was disqualified from one job because it was on the 37th floor, would be covered by the Act. An individual with some type of hearing sensitivity who was denied employment at a location with very loud noise, but was offered positions at other locations, would be covered by the Act. The Court does not believe this was the result intended by Congress. If it were, Congress would not have used the terms *substantial* handicap or *substantially* limits—they would have said "any handicap to employment" or "in any way limits one or more of such person's major life activities." The Assistant Secretary's definition ignores the word substantial. Such a definition contravenes the statutory language and is therefore invalid.

However, the Court believes that the definition adopted by the Administrative Law Judge is also invalid. He found that in order to be a "qualified handicapped individual," an individual would have to have an impairment "likely to affect his employability *generally*." The Court believes that this type of definition drastically reduces the coverage of the Act, and undercuts the purposes for which the Act was intended. A person, for example, who has obtained a graduate degree in chemistry, and is then turned down for a chemist's job because of an impairment, is not likely to be heartened by the news that he can still be a streetcar conductor, an attorney or a forest ranger. A person who is disqualified from employment in his chosen field has a substantial handicap to employment, and is substantially limited in one of his major life activities. The definitions contained in the Act are personal and must be evaluated by looking at the particular individual. A handicapped individual is one who "has a physical or mental disability *which for such individual* constitutes or results in a substantial handicap to employment . . ." (emphasis added). It is the impaired individual that must be examined, and not just the impairment in the abstract.

The Administrative Law Judge was concerned that focusing on particular jobs or particular fields rather than on employability in general would lead to anomalous results.

> . . . To further illustrate: a person may have as his life's dream employment as a running back with the Dallas Cowboys. He may be denied this employment solely on the basis of his inability to run 100 yards in 10 seconds or less. This person would then have an "impairment" (condition lessening physical ability) which actually prevented his obtaining particular, desired employment. Yet this person would not be considered "handicapped" within the meaning of the statutory definition since this particular impairment is not *likely* to impact adversely on his employability (since few jobs require this particular talent). The same point could be illustrated by a concert pianist with too-short fingers, or a 5'5" basketball star. These individuals have conditions which may actually affect their ability to obtain a particular job. But they are not "handicapped" within the meaning of the statutory definition because their respective impairments are not *likely* to affect their employability *generally*, measured against the full spectrum of possible employments.
>
> Administrative Law Judge's Decision, at 12.

The Judge's concerns are misplaced. It is true that the individuals he discusses would not be protected by the Act, but the reason is not because their impairment did not substantially limit employability. The individuals he discusses are not "capable of performing a particular job" and hence are not "qualified handicapped individuals" within the meaning of 60 C.F.R. § 60-741.2. An individual who is 5'5" is not capable of performing the job of center on the New York Knicks. An individual with extremely short fingers is not capable of performing the job of concert pianist. An individual who runs the 100 in 27 seconds is not capable of performing the job as running back for the Dallas Cowboys. Thus, what appears to be a major rationale for the definition adopted by the Administrative Law Judge disappears.

The Court believes that the real focus must be on the individual job seeker, and not solely on the impairment or the perceived impairment. This necessitates a case-by-case determination of whether the impairment or perceived impairment of a rejected, qualified job seeker, constitutes, for that individual, a substantial handicap to employment. Employers such as Black may argue that such an individualized, case-by-case inquiry places them in a precarious position—they do not know in advance who is covered by the Act. However, before they come to that precarious position, they must already be dealing with a person who has (or is perceived as having) a physical or mental impairment, who is capable of performing a particular job and who is rejected for that job because of the impairment. These facts alone should put federal contractors on notice that they may be dealing with a person covered by the Act.

Factors that are important in the case-by-case determination are the number and types of jobs from which the impaired individual is disqualified. And the focus cannot be on simply the job criteria or qualifications used by the individual employer; those criteria or qualifications must be assumed to be in use generally. The reason for this is that an employer with some aberrational type of job qualification (people with straight hair are inferior, and thus I require all job applicants to have curly hair) that screens out impaired individuals who are capable of performing a particular job, should not be able to say: "No one else has this job requirement, so the impairment does not constitute a substantial handicap to employment, and the applicant is not a qualified handicapped individual." If such an approach were allowable, an employer discriminating against a qualified handicapped individual would be rewarded if his reason for rejecting the applicant were ridiculous enough. In evaluating whether there is a substantial handicap to employment, it must be assumed that all employers offering the same job or similar jobs would use the same requirement or screening process.

Predicting whether the Act provides coverage in certain difficult or close cases may be hard for an employer. Yet, the Court believes that Congress intended the coverage of the Act to be broad in scope and intended that questions as to that coverage be answered on a case-by-case basis. Both of these intentions would be defeated if the coverage of the Act were reduced because of narrow definitions of "substantially limits" and "substantial handicap to employment."

C.  *Applicability of These Definitions to This Case*

There is no doubt that Mr. Crosby either had an impairment or was regarded as having an impairment. The back problem that Black perceived in Mr. Crosby was a condition that "weakens, diminishes, restricts, or otherwise damages an individual's health or physical or mental activity." Black's perception was that the back problem weakened, diminished *and* restricted Mr. Crosby's physical activity. Black found that Mr. Crosby was unsuited for jobs involving heavy labor. Thus, he was clearly impaired or regarded as impaired.

Mr. Crosby's impairment constituted, for him, a substantial handicap to employment. Black's rejection was related solely to Mr. Crosby's physical condition. He was disqualified from all Black's apprentice carpenter positions because of the heavy lifting involved. Had all firms offering similar positions involving heavy lifting used the same criteria as Black, Mr. Crosby would have been disqualified from all such jobs. The apprentice program required 8,000 hours in the field, and at the time of the incident Mr. Crosby had accumulated over 3,600 hours. There is no dispute that in order for him to have completed the 8,000 hours, Mr. Crosby would have had to have obtained jobs similar to the one he applied for with Black, involving heavy lifting. If all firms offering positions similar to the one offered by Black had used the same criteria as Black, Mr. Crosby would have had great difficulty completing the apprentice program and becoming a journeyman carpenter. The task might have been impossible, but in any case a large roadblock was placed in Mr. Crosby's path. He was substantially limited in his goal of becoming a journeyman.

The Court noted earlier that there might be cases where it is difficult to decide if disqualification from a particular job constitutes a substantial handicap to employment, especially if similar positions or similar fields remain open. However, being disqualified from becoming a journeyman carpenter (or having great difficulty in obtaining such a position) is not such a case. There has been no showing that similar positions would have been available to Mr. Crosby had all firms used Black's criteria, and, in fact, the Court doubts that there are any such positions available in Hawaii.

Black contends that the definition of substantially impaired that was adopted by the Assistant Secretary is unconstitutionally vague. Yet, as noted above, before the "substantially limited" question even comes up, it must first be determined that the applicant is impaired (or regarded as impaired) and capable of performing the job. It is not unconstitutional to tell employers that if such an applicant is rejected because of his impairment, they should be on notice that he could be protected by the Act. And, men of common intelligence would not be shocked to find out that a person is substantially impaired in finding employment if he is disqualified from pursuing the profession of his choice. That is certainly a reasonable interpretation. The Court believes that the definition and method of determination it has adopted is in line with the intent of Congress. Neither the Act nor the regulations are unconstitutionally vague.

That the definition of the Assistant Secretary has been rejected does not require that this case be remanded. The result he arrived at was the same result this Court arrived at, and, in addition, the factors this Court believed were not covered by the Assistant Secretary's definition are not relevant in this case. The criteria Black used were not related to a particular job location, but were related to the job itself. The position for which Mr. Crosby was disqualified was not very similar to a position he could have obtained had Black's criteria been in general use.

Black also contends that Congress did not intend to protect job applicants

denied employment based on risk of future injury. The Court believes that this statement is irrelevant in this case. Mr. Crosby was denied employment because of either an
impairment he had or an impairment Black believed he had.

Black also contends that it is unfair and unconstitutional to, in effect, retroactively sanction it for conduct it could not possibly have known was proscribed when it
rejected Mr. Crosby. It is true that defendants have, at times, sent out conflicting
signals as to the meaning of the Act. It is also true that in some close cases interpretation of the Act may be difficult. However, the Court does not believe that this is a close
case. As noted above, the Court believes that Black was or should have been on notice
at the time it rejected Mr. Crosby that Mr. Crosby was a handicapped individual within
the meaning of the Act and the regulations.

The Court finds from the uncontradicted evidence that Mr. Crosby was capable
of performing the job of apprentice carpenter at the time he was rejected. This is the
only relevant inquiry in determining whether a rejected applicant is a qualified handicapped individual. Non-imminent risk of future injury may possibly be a reason for
rejecting an applicant, but it does not make an otherwise capable person incapable.

Thus, the Court finds that Mr. Crosby was a qualified handicapped individual
as that term is used in § 503 of the Act, 29 U.S.C. § 793 (Supp. III 1979), and as that
term is defined in other sections of the Act and the regulations.

* * *

NOTE

The court rules that the Assistant Secretary of Labor's interpretation of the phrase
"substantial handicap to employment" is overbroad because it includes any individual
capable of performing a particular job who is rejected for that particular job because of
a real or perceived handicap. Examine the examples the court uses to illustrate the
invalidity of the Assistant Secretary's interpretation. Are these examples pertinent? Is
the court confusing "coverage of the Act" in terms of the definition of handicaps with
entitlement to relief under the Act? Where does the concept of "otherwise qualified"
enter into the analysis? Consider also the effect of the addition to the Act's coverage of
the "is regarded as having an impairment" category. Does this affect the court's
criticism of the Assistant Secretary's interpretation?

p. 52—ADD a new section to the end of Chapter 1:

## H.  ADVANCES AND SETBACKS

### Breslin, E., "Backlash Against the Disabled"

*4* Mental Disability Law Reporter *345 (1980)*

This election year, with tax cuts and austerity the familiar themes in the political rhetoric of many candidates, the progress that has been made by handicapped
individuals is particularly vulnerable to erosion. Large segments of the American
population are becoming increasingly resentful of what they perceive to be unreason-

able demands by special interest groups to gain favor in the distribution of federal dollars. Unfortunately, the few interest groups who most need special services are also the ones who are least able to resist the effects of economic retrenchment. Perhaps the most vulnerable segment of society is made up of individuals with mental and physical disabilities.

Only in the last 10 years have federal and state governments begun to seriously address discrimination against the handicapped in employment, community housing, transportation, education and medical services. Legislation such as section 504 of the Rehabilitation Act of 1973, the Developmental Disabilities Act, the Education for All Handicapped Children Act (P.L. 94-142), and the Architectural Barriers Act, as well as a national policy shift toward deinstitutionalization of the mentally disabled, foreshadowed significant progress. Yet, as is so often the case with social programs, the initial expectations far outstripped the actual achievements.

The promises that signaled new opportunities and better treatment for handicapped persons lie largely unfulfilled—undercut by poor government administration or local resistance. More disturbing, the advances that have been achieved are now coming under attack.

In the area of mass transit, section 504 regulations mandating full accessibility to the nation's rail and bus systems are threatened with repeal in the House of Representatives by critics who declare them economically unfeasible.

Organizations throughout the country that are involved in community-based housing for mentally disabled persons report stiff resistance in the form of exclusionary zoning, nuisance suits from local homeowners, and even outright violence.

The Bureau of Education for the Handicapped (BEH), created to assure an education for every handicapped child, is weakened by questionable administration and the reluctance of local officials to fully carry out special education programs. The bureau is now under investigation by Congress and the Department of Education for its handling of the implementation of P.L. 94-142.

In each of these three examples, advocates for handicapped persons portray the problem in terms of civil rights long denied and attribute the delay or resistance to prejudice or misunderstanding. Their opponents, on the other hand, talk of hard economic realities and the importance of the common good over the rights of any minority.

### Postlewaite, J., "Reviewing the '70s—A Decade of Extraordinary Gains? Or Paper Victories?"

*5 Amicus, No. 3 & 4, May/August, 1980, p. 42*

Consider for a moment the handicapped of the late '60s—pre-DD Act, pre-Rehabilitation Act and pre-Education for all Handicapped Children Act—all potent pieces of legislation, mandating enormous changes in all areas of our society.

The institutionalized in that era had little protection from physical and mental abuse and few advocates to assert their rights to receive treatment, to be placed in the least restrictive environment, to refuse drugs, etc. Community residences were practically nonexistent, and schools were totally unprepared and unwilling to integrate the mentally retarded into regular classrooms.

The physically disabled, also, had no established legal basis to demand their right to use physical structures as readily as the ablebodied, to be included in school functions, including athletic and social programs, and to use public transportation systems.

It was primarily as a result of a '60s-style militancy of the disabled, themselves, demanding civil rights protections similar to those established for racial minorities and women, that the legal foundations were formed, giving support to the handicapped.

Now that the legal framework has been constructed, what benefits have derived? How have conditions for the disabled improved since the legal void was filled? Consider the disabled in 1980:

With the Education For All Handicapped Children Act, mandating a "free, appropriate public education," the odds are better–though not assured–that mentally retarded children will receive a public school education. School administrators though, still resent the high costs involved and the extra burdens of formulating an appropriate program, and teachers, also, feel unprepared to cope with special needs. Regression frequently sets in during the summer recess and there is no guarantee of further education past the age of 21. Schools are not required to provide for vocational or social needs. With a supportive family and social service network, skills can be learned which will prepare the mentally retarded to live and work in the community; if not, it might be right back to the institution for them.

The physically disabled now have the security of laws such as the Architectural Barriers Act, enacted in 1968, but not enforced until 1973, and the Department of Transportation's implementing regulations to Section 504 of the Rehabilitation Act, both requiring accessibility of facilities and transportation systems. But for the physically disabled, lack of mobility still remains a serious restraint. Educational and employment opportunities have expanded greatly, but the country's generally mediocre and inadequate rail and bus systems remain largely inaccessible. The public schools are slow to integrate the physically disabled in all school activities and resent the cost of creating accessible facilities.

Certainly, these examples show that the disabled in 1980 fare far better than in the 1960s. Recent studies, though, make it clear that a few landmark cases and headline-making legislation have not brought about anticipated results. The federal government was exceedingly slow to issue its guidelines for Section 504 of the Rehabilitation Act which, when they did appear, evoked alarm and confusion. Reports show, furthermore, that because the regulations for Section 504 and P.L. 94-142 are not being enforced, thousands of children are still on school waiting lists, are institutionalized, and denied services; public buildings are still in effect closed to the physically disabled, and fewer than half of colleges and universities have made their programs accessible.

One could argue that the 1970s certainly brought the needs of the handicapped before the general public, due to organized efforts by the disabled themselves and their advocates; however, this exposure has also produced a backlash of protest. We are now experiencing counter-movements, such as the attempt in Congress to overturn the Department of Transportation's requirement that bus and subway systems be made accessible to people in wheelchairs. Also, despite the movement toward deinstitutionalization, money still pours in to maintain institutions. Community alternatives are in short supply, due to lack of funds, zoning restrictions and community opposition.

These issues are all discussed in the articles in [a special report in *Amicus*] written by experts in their fields. The authors review the legal gains made in the '70s and offer a preview of the '80s. They all conclude that litigation alone is insufficient to mold the law, that in order to make a real impact on the lives of the disabled, enforced legislation, community-based advocacy, and personal persuasion will prove most effective.

In other words, the excitable push that began in the 1970s will have to turn to sustained commitment in the 1980s if we are to avoid a reversal of rights that are at the very least paper victories and yet hold the promise for real progress. The landmark decisions are exciting headline-catchers, but, as *Brown* v. *Board of Education* and *Wyatt* v. *Stickney* have shown us, they are not particularly effective tools for social change. The sustained, quiet persuasion of knowledgeable, concerned advocates at the grass roots level, as well as strong government support and leadership will provide the quickest, surest victories.

### SOSKIN, R., "HANDICAPPED ADVOCACY: A LAST HURRAH?"

*5 Amicus No. 3 & 4, May/August, 1980, p. 69*

The National Center for Law and the Handicapped came into existence in 1972 at the infancy of the handicapped legal rights movement. After peak years of activism and hope, it struggles for survival while the movement may well face its darkest times as the eighties and a changing national mood and commitment unfold.

. . . [T]he seventies were a period of great successes and of fundamental changes in the area of handicapped rights. It was also a period where legal advocacy blossomed. However, I submit that a careful analysis of this advocacy will demonstrate the tenuous underpinnings of the movement and will illustrate how easily the advocacy movement can be unravelled.

Advocacy developed in many forms throughout the seventies. Among the most committed have been private attorneys (such as David Ferleger of Philadelphia, the attorney in *Bartley, Institutionalized Juveniles, Pennhurst*) who on miniscule private funds have pushed advocacy to its limits. Outside of a small number of dedicated private practitioners, however, little can be said for the private bar. The American Bar Association committed itself to advocacy with the Commission on the Mentally Disabled. After a rough start (e.g. an advocacy program at Norristown State Hospital in Pennsylvania), several worthwhile projects, including a legislative reform project and the *Mental Disability Law Reporter,* came into fruition. Despite rough financial times, the *Reporter* has flourished and survived, but it is the only component of the ABA Commission to be functioning currently.

The seventies also saw the advent of public interest law firms. Groups such as the Mental Health Law Project, PILCOP, Western Law Center for the Handicapped, Maryland D.D. Law Project, and NCLH, to name a few, were extremely active. However, no group has emerged as a representative legal advocacy group for all handicapped persons, nor has any group been able to coordinate and structure the advocacy strategies. Rather, public interest groups have developed, focusing on specialized disability groups (deaf or mentally retarded, for example) and within limited geographic areas. While the advent of a multitude of advocacy groups is certainly positive, numerous problems have developed as a result of the diversity which hamper the movement.

Lacking a coherent civil rights strategy, such as that developed by the NAACP Legal Defense Fund in the forties and fifties as it attacked racial segregation, the handicapped rights movement has seen uneven litigative and legislative thrusts. Often one disability group accomplishes its self-interest at the expense of another group. Unfortunately, some specialized interest groups fail to understand the need for cooperation and establishment of national civil rights principles to apply to all fellow handicapped persons. The right to education, to deinstitutionalization, to employment, to accessibility and to equal treatment should be available to all handicapped groups, regardless of mobility, IQ or genetics, yet this is not the way it is always advocated by certain groups.

Tragically, the public interest attorneys, themselves, dedicated to furthering the rights of handicapped persons, have found themselves caught up in the rivalries and inconsistencies of the movement. Rather than sustained and cooperative advocacy efforts, advocates find themselves battling for survival, with one's survival often meaning another advocate's demise. Thus, we see ten advocates fade to five, then to one and, ultimately, to none.

### Responsibility for Dissension

The reason for this intensive in-fighting at the expense of the movement is unclear. A prime responsibility, easily identifiable, must rest with the federal government. If one were to devise a scenario in which a government could promise support of advocacy yet undermine it simultaneously, one could not improve upon the federal government's performance in this area. Besides its obvious irrationalities of policy, such as promoting deinstitutionalization via the Developmentally Disabled Assistance and Bill of Rights Act while supporting the renovation of institutions via massive Title XIX funds, the government has maneuvered its funding of advocacy so as to pit advocates against each other for scarce resources. Thus, while the government takes the credit for the support of advocacy, the reality of advocates spending all too precious time seeking money, writing and rewriting grants, exercising political persuasion, and undermining fellow advocates is rarely perceived on a widespread basis.

Even the creation of a network of advocacy through state protection and advocacy systems does not change this perspective. These advocates, while working hard and obviously well-intentioned, are under the same constraints as others—uncertainties of funding and future existence. The effectiveness of any system must come into question when its first consideration, prior to committing itself to advocacy in a particular case, is the political and fiscal ramifications to its operation. Yet this occurs all too frequently. In addition, the P&As represent, once again, a fragmented approach to advocacy, as they are limited to advocacy for developmentally disabled individuals.

As a result, cases which have the potential for a major impact on handicapped rights (i.e. §504) are sometimes avoided or ignored by P&As because the plaintiff, while handicapped, is not developmentally disabled.

Unfortunately, the blame for less than 100 per cent effective advocacy cannot rest solely upon government. As anyone recognizes after awhile in this movement, dedication to public interest does not purify the human character. No matter how committed advocates are to their cause, individual egos and status often become motivating factors. The harsh reality of dealing with persons in the competitive atmosphere of private industry or the bureaucracies of government or universities is not that different in scope from the reality of public interest practice. To have major cases conducted in which counsel for two plaintiff parties with similar interests are barely on speaking terms is not exactly the ideal means for maximizing effectiveness and certainly stains the image of the self-sacrificing public interest attorney.

Another advocacy resource, not primarily geared towards handicapped persons but beginning to become more active in handicapped rights issues, is the Legal Services Corporation. While many offices are still inaccessible to the handicapped and other offices are unskilled in or lack concern for handicapped rights, the potential for advocacy with Legal Services is certainly great. Recently, there have been signs that the Corporation, itself, is focusing on developing a policy for handicapped rights advocacy, and some individual offices have become deeply immersed in handicapped cases with several specialized handicap units created. Until now, the Legal Services Corporation has appeared to be the advocacy network with the soundest fiscal stability and the rosiest political future; thus, the development of strong handicapped advocacy within legal services appeared to be the safest long-term approach.

### Gloomy Future Predicted

The radical political change which occurred in this nation as a result of the November 4th elections may alter the entire perspective of public interest law. The self-defeating propensities of advocacy groups and the government's clear ''carrot/stick'' tactics may become irrelevant. The political vote reflects a philosophical change within this nation which does not bode well for the handicapped or for any other minority groups. It reflects a conservative fiscal attitude, reliant upon the states and private sector for implementation and enforcement of programs and policies. We can expect relatively few federal resources diverted to advocacy groups or to federal enforcement of broad-ranging civil rights statutes. Can the states then be expected to assume those functions or will the private sector assume the responsibility for a larger role of self-policing? One's answers can merely be speculative.

\* \* \*

As the backlash to the effectuation of handicapped rights grows, evidenced by cutbacks of funds, proposed modifications to statutes, and resistant communities, it will be crucial to prevent advocacy groups from folding under the pressures. Whether groups will resist such pressures cannot yet be ascertained. A few observations of recent developments are not encouraging. In one state, a local advocacy group supports the state's efforts to establish villages for institutional residents—in effect a segregated community on the outskirts of town. In other states, state chapters of associations for retarded citizens endorse mini-institutions as meaningful deinstitutionalization or are hesitant to support any litigation against state institutions. On the national scene, the associations for retarded citizens, under heavy pressure from pro-institutional parent groups, falters over support of an *amicus* brief written on its behalf because it too broadly condemns all institutions. Finally, a leading legal advocacy group files an *amicus* brief in a federal court of appeals in opposition to the mainstreaming and integration thrust of P.L. 94-142, based upon the belief of one disabled group that they are different and that segregation is desirable.

The advocacy movement, though often perceived as united and strong, is in reality extremely vulnerable to changing times. The underpinnings of the movement, both consumer and legal, are dependent for their existence on funds of which distribution is beyond their control. We now enter a period in which that distribution may well be curtailed. The strength and the ultimate existence of a handicapped advocacy movement hangs in the balance.

### MILK, L., "EDITORIAL: BEATING THE BACKLASH"

*5* Mainstream *No. 4, July/August, 1980, p. 6*

"The age of the advocate is past," [former] Education Secretary Shirley Hufstedler recently told a disabled advocate. Her message is being echoed everywhere as commentators and Congress say they are tired of the constant clamor of competing interest groups calling for more and more for their own constituents.

This backlash has reached alarming proportions for disabled advocates. There is real fear that the combination of economic recession and mass emotional depression could cause the general public to reject the concept of handicapped rights. The current congressional amendment on accessible mass transit is a case in point. Suddenly, some in Congress and the press are calling for the end to all rights to mass transportation for disabled and elderly people.

Handicapped people have reason to fear the overreaction characterizing the current political climate. Today it affects transportation. Tomorrow, rights to education, health care or employment could be in jeopardy. Once mass hysteria overcomes sensible debate, it is easy for good people to make bad decisions, and bad people to speed the process along.

It is time to get beyond the clamor and look at the facts. One fact is that we don't really know the cost-benefit ratio of accommodating disabled and elderly people in public transportation. How much do the cost-per-rider estimates currently being bandied about reflect the start-up problems of a new technology and low ridership associated with a brand new service? How many people would never choose to use mass transit because of their own physical needs, their personal preference or their schedules? How much will it cost in ever-increasing gasoline prices to run transit vehicles in perpetuity for all of the disabled and elderly people if they choose to use this form of transportation the way the able-bodied use mass transit for shopping, leisure and other activities as well as work or emergency trips?

We are being asked to deny disabled people rights to public transportation forever simply because we cannot afford to fulfill them today.

The fact is that denial of transportation rights *can* lead to denial of other rights.

Why should educators, health providers and other institutions beleaguered with unbalanced budgets not seek the same route that the public transit lobbyists took, and find a friend in Congress to introduce an exemption for them from all that Section 504 requires? If this transportation effort succeeds, others will follow.

The current controversy has taught us that the age of advocacy is not over. What is past is the age when demands raised by disabled people were automatically labeled "good" and the opponents were automatically labeled "bad." The backlash symbolizes a coming of age for the handicapped rights movement, a recognition that we cannot merely flaunt our disability, but must also have reason and right on our side if we are to win the political battles ahead. In that sense, the backlash is an indication that we are moving forward.

NOTE

In proceeding through the materials in the remainder of this volume, consider whether the rather pessimistic forecasts for the civil rights movement of handicapped persons in the 1980s presented in these articles have been borne out by subsequent developments.

# 2

# EQUAL EDUCATIONAL OPPORTUNITY

Patrick P. Spicer

## SUMMARY OF DOCTRINAL DEVELOPMENTS

NO ASPECT OF THE LEGAL RIGHTS OF HANDICAPPED PERSONS has seen more frequent and significant developments than that pertaining to education, both at the elementary/ secondary level and in higher education.

Since 1979, judicial interpretation of Sec. 504 and PL 94-142 has been to a great extent groundbreaking in nature, particularly with respect to the latter statute which has been in effect since 1977. Both federal and state courts have been called on to rule on issues regarding, for example, the provision of related services to handicapped children, payment for residential placements, and the validity of expulsions of handicapped children. The results reached on these and other issues, while uniform on certain issues, have varied, both in impact and substance, on others, particularly with respect to judicial decisions reached in 1981 and 1982.

Two of the most significant decisions relative to the rights of handicapped persons have come in the area of education. In *Davis v. Southeastern Community College,* the Supreme Court had occasion to interpret Sec. 504 as it applied to higher education, and in *Rowley v. Board of Education of Hendrick Hudson Central School District,* the Court handed down a decision interpreting the educational standard required by PL 94-142. This latter decision promises to have a momentous impact on the determination of the nature and extent of the public school systems' legal obligations to handicapped children, an impact that in 1983 is only beginning to be realized.

## G.  FEDERAL LEGISLATION

### 1.  Content and Enforcement in General

p. 200—REPLACE the second sentence of the first paragraph of Note 2 with the following:

The ruling that Sec. 504 creates a private cause of action has subsequently been adopted by numerous courts, e.g., *Lloyd v. Regional Transportation Authority,* 548 F.2d 1277 (7th Cir. 1977); *Leary v. Crapsey,* 566 F.2d 863 (2d Cir.); *United Handicapped Federation v. Andre,* 558 F.2d 413 (8th Cir. 1977); *National Association for*

the Advancement of Colored People v. Wilmington Medical Center, 599 F.2d 1247
(3rd Cir. 1979); Kling v. County of Los Angeles, 633 F.2d 876 (9th Cir. 1980), but
Hairston was one of the first decisions to so hold.

p. 201—REPLACE Mattie T. v. Holladay and the notes that follow with the following:

## Tatro v. State of Texas
United States Court of Appeals for the Fifth Circuit, 1980
625 F.2d 557

Before Goldberg, Tate, and Sam D. Johnson, Circuit Judges.
Goldberg, Circuit Judge.

Amber Tatro is a four-years-old child who suffers from myelomeningocele, a
birth defect commonly known as spina bifida. As a result of this congenital defect,
Amber suffers from orthopedic and speech handicaps and from a neurogenic bladder.
This latter condition prevents Amber from being able to empty her bladder voluntarily.
As a result, Amber must be catheterized every three to four hours in order to function
normally without the danger of developing chronic kidney infection. . . . Amber's
parents, plaintiffs, sued in district court in accordance with 20 U.S.C. § 1415(e)(2).
They contend that because the IEP contains no provision for CIC, the school district
has violated the EAHCA, 20 U.S.C. § 1412(1), by failing to provide a free appropriate
public education to Amber. They also contend that the school district has violated
section 504 of the Rehabilitation Act of 1973, ("section 504"), as amended, 29
U.S.C. § 794. The case reaches us from the district court's denial of plaintiffs' motion
for a preliminary injunction to require the school district to provide CIC. For the
reasons detailed below, we vacate and remand.

\* \* \*

II. Section 504

The district court gave plaintiff's claim under section 504 of the Rehabilitation
Act of 1973 rather short shrift. The gravamen of its holding is that section 504 does not
require the school district to provide CIC to Amber because "[p]laintiffs cannot
convert a statute prohibiting discrimination in certain governmental programs to a
statute requiring, in essence, the setting up of governmental health care for people
seeking to participate in such programs." This conclusion is incorrect.

In Camenisch v. University of Texas, 616 F.2d 127 (5th Cir. 1980), plaintiff, a
deaf graduate student at the University of Texas, brought suit against the University
because of its refusal to provide him with sign language interpreter services, an aid
which he claimed was necessary for his participation in the University's programs. We
affirmed the district court's grant of a preliminary injunction requiring the University
to provide interpreter services. We held that the failure to provide interpreter services
amounted to the exclusion of plaintiff from the University's programs and hence
violated section 504. See id. at 133.

Analogously, Amber has been excluded from the school district's programs by
the district's refusal to provide CIC. Without the provision of CIC to Amber, she will

be unable to participate in the preschool programs of the school district. Such exclusion is expressly condemned by section 504.

Defendants contend that *Southeastern Community College* v. *Davis*, 442 U.S. 397, 99 S.Ct. 2361, 60 L.Ed.2d 980 (1979), dictates the contrary result. This assertion is incorrect. As we observed in *Camenisch, supra*, ''the Supreme Court's decision in *Southeastern Community College* says only that Section 504 does not require a school to provide services to a handicapped individual for a program for which the individual's handicap precludes him from ever realizing the principal benefits of the training.'' *Id.* at 133. Thus, like *Camenisch*, this case is distinguishable from *Southeastern Community College* because, with the provision of CIC, Amber will be able to perform well in school and thus realize the principal benefits of the school district's program. The school district's failure to provide CIC therefore violates section 504.

VACATED and REMANDED for proceedings not inconsistent with this opinion.

NOTES

1.  The court in interpreting Sec. 504 in *Tatro*, distinguishes the Supreme Court's decision in *Southeastern Community College* v. *Davis*, 442 U.S. 397 (1979) (presented below at p. 24) by pointing out that ''. . . with the provision of CIC, Amber will be able to perform well in school and thus realize the principal benefits of the school district's program.'' Is this analysis correct or even necessary in light of the Department of Education regulation set out below?

> **Reg. 104.3.  Definitions.**
> As used in this part, the term:
> (k) ''Qualified handicapped person'' means:
> (2) With respect to public preschool elementary, secondary, or adult educational services, a handicapped person (i) of an age during which nonhandicapped persons are provided such services, (ii) of any age during which it is mandatory under state law to provide such services to handicapped persons, or (iii) to whom a state is required to provide a free appropriate public education under § 612 of the Education of the Handicapped Act;

2.  On remand, the federal district court, which had originally held that catheterization was not required under Sec. 504 grudgingly reversed its ruling in light of the Circuit Court's decision. See *Tatro* v. *Texas*, 516 F. Supp. 968 (N.D. Tex. 1981).

p. 202—INSERT, as an addition to bracketed material at the bottom of the page, the following:

After the creation of a separate Department of Education, that Department established its own Sec. 504 regulations which were published in 45 Federal Register 30936 (1980) and codified at 34 Code of Federal Regulations Part 104.

p. 212—REPLACE sections (a) through (f) of Note 1 with the following:

a.  *New York Association for Retarded Citizens* v. *Carey*, 612 F.2d 644 (2d Cir. 1979)—school system's plan to isolate mentally retarded children who were carriers of the virus hepatitus B from being educated with nonhandicapped children held violative of Sec. 504.

b. *S-1* v. *Turlington,* 635 F.2d 342 (5th Cir.)—handicapped child's expulsion prior to the invocation of Sec. 504's procedural protections violated Sec. 504; see p. 73 below.

c. *Helms* v. *McDaniel,* 657 F.2d 800 (5th Cir. 1981)—Georgia system of educational placement hearings which allowed the findings of the state hearing officer to be rejected by the state board of education violated Sec. 504.

d. *New Mexico Association of Retarded Citizens* v. *New Mexico,* 495 F. Supp. 391 (D.N.M. 1980)—failure of state to provide free, appropriate education to its handicapped children violated Sec. 504.

e. *Ross* v. *Allen,* 515 F. Supp. 972 (S.D.N.Y. 1981)—school psychologist who was dismissed from her position for allegedly informing a parent that her child's school had violated Sec. 504 when it suspended the child, had standing under Sec. 504 to challenge her dismissal.

f. *Gladys J.* v. *Pearland Independent School District* 520 F. Supp. 869 (S.D. Tex. 1981)—handicapped child's educational placement found not to comply with the requirements of Sec. 504.

p. 213—REPLACE Note 2 in its entirety with the following:

### SOUTHEASTERN COMMUNITY COLLEGE v. DAVIS

*Supreme Court of the United States, 1979*
*442 U.S. 397*

MR. JUSTICE POWELL delivered the opinion of the Court.

This case presents a matter of first impression for this Court: Whether § 504 of the Rehabilitation Act of 1973, which prohibits discrimination against an "otherwise qualified handicapped individual" in federally funded programs "solely by reason of his handicap," forbids professional schools from imposing physical qualifications for admission to their clinical training programs.

I

Respondent, who suffers from a serious hearing disability, seeks to be trained as a registered nurse. During the 1973–1974 academic year she was enrolled in the College Parallel program of Southeastern Community College, a state institution that receives federal funds. Respondent hoped to progress to Southeastern's Associate Degree Nursing program, completion of which would make her eligible for state certification as a registered nurse. In the course of her application to the nursing program, she was interviewed by a member of the nursing faculty. It became apparent that respondent had difficulty understanding questions asked, and on inquiry she acknowledged a history of hearing problems and dependence on a hearing aid. She was advised to consult an audiologist.

On the basis of an examination at Duke University Medical Center, respondent was diagnosed as having a "bilateral, sensori-neural hearing loss." App. 127a. A change in her hearing aid was recommended, as a result of which it was expected that she would be able to detect sounds "almost as well as a person would who has normal hearing." *Id.,* at 127a–128a. But this improvement would not mean that she could discriminate among sounds sufficiently to understand normal spoken speech. Her lipreading skills would remain necessary for effective communication: "While wearing the hearing aid, she is well aware of gross sounds occurring in the listening environment. However, she can only be responsible for speech spoken to her, when the talker gets her attention and allows her to look directly at the talker." *Id.*, at 128a.

Southeastern next consulted Mary McRee, Executive Director of the North Carolina Board of Nursing. On the basis of the audiologist's report, McRee recommended that respondent not be admitted to the nursing program. In McRee's view, respondent's hearing disability made it unsafe for her to practice as a nurse. In addition, it would be impossible for respondent to participate safely in the normal clinical training program, and those modifications that would be necessary to enable safe participation would prevent her from realizing the benefits of the program: "To adjust patient learning experiences in keeping with [respondent's] hearing limitations could, in fact, be the same as denying her full learning to meet the objectives of your nursing programs." *Id.*, at 132a–133a.

After respondent was notified that she was not qualified for nursing study because of her hearing disability, she requested reconsideration of the decision. The entire nursing staff of Southeastern was assembled, and McRee again was consulted. McRee repeated her conclusion that on the basis of the available evidence, respondent "has hearing limitations which could interfere with her safely caring for patients." *Id.*, at 139a. Upon further deliberation, the staff voted to deny respondent admission.

Respondent then filed suit in the United States District Court for the Eastern District of North Carolina, alleging both a violation of § 504 of the Rehabilitation Act of 1973, 87 Stat. 394, as amended, 29 U. S. C. A. § 794 (Supp. 1979), and a denial of equal protection and due process. After a bench trial, the District Court entered judgment in favor of Southeastern. 424 F. Supp. 1341 (1976). It confirmed the findings of the audiologist that even with a hearing aid respondent cannot understand speech directed to her except through lipreading, and further found:

> [I]n many situations such as an operation room intensive care unit, or post-natal care unit, all doctors and nurses wear surgical masks which would make lipreading impossible. Additionally, in many situations a Registered Nurse would be required to instantly follow the physician's instructions concerning procurement of various types of instruments and drugs where the physician would be unable to get the nurse's attention by other than vocal means. *Id.*, at 1343.

Accordingly, the court concluded:

> [Respondent's] handicap actually prevents her from safely performing in both her training program and her proposed profession. The trial testimony indicated numerous situations where [respondent's] particular disability would render her unable to function properly. Of particular concern to the court in this case is the potential of danger to future patients in such situations. *Id.*, at 1345.

Based on these findings, the District Court concluded that respondent was not an "otherwise qualified handicapped individual" protected against discrimination by § 504. In its view, "[o]therwise qualified, can only be read to mean otherwise able to function sufficiently in the position sought in spite of the handicap, if proper training and facilities are suitable and available." 424 F. Supp., at 1345. Because respondent's disability would prevent her from functioning "sufficiently" in Southeastern's nursing program, the court held that the decision to exclude her was not discriminatory within the meaning of § 504.

On appeal, the Court of Appeals for the Fourth Circuit reversed. 574 F.2d 1158 (1978). It did not dispute the District Court's findings of fact, but held that the court had misconstrued § 504. In light of administrative regulations that had been promulgated while the appeal was pending, see 42 Fed. Reg. 22676 (1977), the appellate court believed that § 504 required Southeastern to "reconsider plaintiff's application for admission to the nursing program without regard to her hearing ability." 574 F.2d, at 1160. It concluded that the District Court had erred in taking respondent's handicap into account in determining whether she was "otherwise qualified" for the program, rather than confining its inquiry to her "academic and technical qualifications." *Id.*, at 1161. The Court of Appeals also suggested that § 504 required "affirmative conduct" on the part of Southeastern to modify its program to accommodate the disabilities of applicants, "even when such modifications become expensive." 574 F.2d, at 1162.

Because of the importance of this issue to the many institutions covered by § 504, we granted certiorari. 439 U.S. 1065 (1979). We now reverse.

## II

As previously noted, this is the first case in which this Court has been called upon to interpret § 504. It is elementary that "[t]he starting point in every case involving construction of a statute is the language itself." *Blue Chip Stamps* v. *Manor Drug Stores*, 421 U.S. 723, 756 (1975) (Powell, J., concurring); see *Greyhound Corp.* v. *Mt. Hood Stages, Inc.*, 437 U.S. 322, 330 (1978); *Santa Fe Industries, Inc.* v. *Green*, 430 U.S. 462, 472 (1977). Section 504 by its terms does not compel educational institutions to disregard the disabilities of handicapped individuals or to make substantial modifications in their programs to allow disabled persons to participate. Instead, it requires only that an "otherwise qualified handicapped individual" not be excluded from participation in a federally funded program "solely by reason of his handicap," indicating only that mere possession of a handicap is not a permissible ground for assuming an inability to function in a particular context.

The Act defines "handicapped individual" as follows:

The term "handicapped individual" means any individual who (A) has a physical or mental disability which for such individual constitutes or results in a substantial handicap to employment and (B) can reasonably be expected to benefit in terms of employability from vocational rehabilitation services provided pursuant to subchapters I and III of this chapter. For the purposes of subchapters IV and V of this chapter, such term means any person who (A) has a physical or mental impairment which substantially limits one or more of such person's major life activities, (B) has a record of such an impairment, or (C) is regarded as having such an impairment. § 7 (7) of the Rehabilitation Act of 1973, 87 Stat. 361, as amended, 88 Stat. 1619, 89 Stat. 2, 29 U.S.C.A. § 706 (7) (Supp. 1979).

This definition comports with our understanding of § 504. A person who has a record of, or is regarded as having, an impairment may at present have no actual incapacity at all. Such a person would be exactly the kind of individual who could be "otherwise qualified" to participate in covered programs. And a person who suffers from a limiting physical or mental impairment still may possess other abilities that permit him to meet the requirements of various programs. Thus, it is clear that Congress included among the class of "handicapped" persons covered by § 504 a range of individuals who could be "otherwise qualified." See S. Rep. No. 93-1297, pp. 38–39 (1974).

The court below, however, believed that the "otherwise qualified" persons protected by § 504 include those who would be able to meet the requirements of a particular program in every respect except as to limitations imposed by their handicap. See 574 F.2d, at 1160. Taken literally, this holding would prevent an institution from taking into account any limitation resulting from the handicap, however disabling. It assumes, in effect, that a person need not meet legitimate physical requirements in order to be "otherwise qualified." We think the understanding of the District Court is closer to the plain meaning of the statutory language. An otherwise qualified person is one who is able to meet all of a program's requirements in spite of his handicap.

The regulations promulgated by the Department of HEW to interpret § 504 reinforce, rather than contradict, this conclusion. According to these regulations, a "[q]ualified handicapped person" is, "[w]ith respect to postsecondary and vocational education services, a handicapped person who meets the academic and technical standards requisite to admission or participation in the [school's] education program or activity . . . ." 45 CFR § 84.3 (k) (3) (1978). An explanatory note states:

> The term "technical standards" refers to all nonacademic admissions criteria that are essential to participation in the program in question. 45 CFR pt. 84, App. A, p. 405 (1978) (emphasis supplied).

A further note emphasizes that legitimate physical qualifications may be essential to participation in particular programs. We think it clear, therefore, that HEW interprets the "other" qualifications which a handicapped person may be required to meet as including necessary physical qualifications.

### III

The remaining question is whether the physical qualifications Southeastern demanded of respondent might not be necessary for participation in its nursing program. It is not open to dispute that, as Southeastern's Associate Degree Nursing program currently is constituted, the ability to understand speech without reliance on lipreading is necessary for patient safety during the clinical phase of the program. As the District Court found, this ability also is indispensable for many of the functions that a registered nurse performs.

Respondent contends nevertheless that § 504, properly interpreted, compels Southeastern to undertake affirmative action that would dispense with the need for effective oral communication. First, it is suggested that respondent can be given individual supervision by faculty members whenever she attends patients directly. Moreover, certain required courses might be dispensed with altogether for respondent. It is not necessary, she argues, that Southeastern train her to undertake all the tasks a registered nurse is licensed to perform. Rather, it is sufficient to make § 504 applicable if respondent might be able to perform satisfactorily some of the duties of a registered nurse or to hold some of the positions available to a registered nurse.

Respondent finds support for this argument in portions of the HEW regulations discussed above. In particular, a provision applicable to postsecondary educational programs requires covered institutions to make "modifications" in their programs to accommodate handicapped persons, and to provide "auxiliary aids" such as sign-language interpreters. Respondent argues that this regulation imposes an obligation to ensure full participation in covered programs by handicapped individuals and, in particular, requires Southeastern to make the kind of adjustments that would be necessary to permit her safe participation in the nursing program.

We note first that on the present record it appears unlikely respondent could benefit from any affirmative action that the regulation reasonably could be interpreted as requiring. Section 84.44 (d) (2), for example, explicitly excludes "devices or services of a personal nature" from the kinds of auxiliary aids a school must provide a handicapped individual. Yet the only evidence in the record indicates that nothing less than close, individual attention by a nursing instructor would be sufficient to ensure patient safety if respondent took part in the clinical phase of the nursing program. See 424 F. Supp., at 1346. Furthermore, it also is reasonably clear that § 84.44 (a) does not encompass the kind of curricular changes that would be necessary to accommodate respondent in the nursing program. In light of respondent's inability to function in clinical courses without close supervision, Southeastern, with prudence, could allow her to take only academic classes. Whatever benefits respondent might realize from such a course of study, she would not receive even a rough equivalent of the training a nursing program normally gives. Such a fundamental alteration in the nature of a program is far more than the "modification" the regulation requires.

Moreover, an interpretation of the regulations that required the extensive modifications necessary to include respondent in the nursing program would raise grave doubts about their validity. If these regulations were to require substantial adjustments in existing programs beyond those necessary to eliminate discrimination against otherwise qualified individuals, they would do more than clarify the meaning of § 504. Instead, they would constitute an unauthorized extension of the obligations imposed by that statute.

The language and structure of the Rehabilitation Act of 1973 reflect a recognition by Congress of the distinction between the evenhanded treatment of qualified handicapped persons and affirmative efforts to overcome the disabilities caused by handicaps. Section 501 (b), governing the employment of handicapped individuals by the Federal Government, requires each federal agency to submit "an affirmative action program plan for the hiring, placement, and advancement of handicapped individuals . . . ." These plans "shall include a description of the extent to which and methods whereby the special needs of handicapped employees are being met." Similarly, § 503 (a), governing hiring by federal contractors, requires employers to "take affirmative action to employ and advance in employment qualified handicapped individuals . . . ." The President is required to promulgate regulations to enforce this section.

Under § 501 (c) of the Act, by contrast, state agencies such as Southeastern are only "encourage[d] . . . to adopt and implement such policies and procedures." Section 504 does not refer at all to affirmative action, and except as it applies to federal employers it does not provide for implementation by administrative action. A comparison of these provisions demonstrates that Congress understood accommodation of the needs of handicapped individuals may require affirmative action and knew how to provide for it in those instances where it wished to do so.

Although an agency's interpretation of the statute under which it operates is entitled to some deference, "this deference is constrained by our obligation to honor the clear meaning of a statute, as revealed by its language, purpose and history." *Teamsters* v. *Daniel*, 439 U.S. 551, 566 n. 20 (1979). Here, neither the language, purpose, nor history of § 504 reveals an intent to impose an affirmative action obligation on all recipients of federal funds. Accordingly, we hold that even if HEW has attempted to create such an obligation itself, it lacks the authority to do so.

## IV

We do not suggest that the line between a lawful refusal to extend affirmative action and illegal discrimination against handicapped persons always will be clear. It is possible to envision situations where an insistence on continuing past requirements and practices might arbitrarily deprive genuinely qualified handicapped persons of the opportunity to participate in a covered program. Technological advances can be expected to enhance opportunities to rehabilitate the handicapped or otherwise to qualify them for some useful employment. Such advances also may enable attainment of these goals without imposing undue financial and administrative burdens upon a State. Thus, situations may arise where a refusal to modify an existing program might become unreasonable and discriminatory. Identification of those instances where a refusal to accommodate the needs of a disabled person amounts to discrimination against the handicapped continues to be an important responsibility of HEW.

In this case, however, it is clear that Southeastern's unwillingness to make major adjustments in its nursing program does not constitute such discrimination. The uncontroverted testimony of several members of Southeastern's staff and faculty established that the purpose of its program was to train persons who could serve the nursing profession in all customary ways. See, e.g., App. 35a, 52a, 53a, 71a, 74a. This type of purpose, far from reflecting any animus against handicapped individuals, is shared by many if not most of the institutions that train persons to render professional service. It is undisputed that respondent could not participate in Southeastern's nursing program unless the standards were substantially lowered. Section 504 imposes no requirement upon an educational institution to lower or to effect substantial modifications of standards to accommodate a handicapped person.

One may admire respondent's desire and determination to overcome her handicap, and there well may be various other types of service for which she can qualify. In this case, however, we hold that there was no violation of § 504 when Southeastern concluded that respondent did not quality for admission to its program. Nothing in the language or history of § 504 reflects an intention to limit the freedom of an educational institution to require reasonable physical qualifications for admission to a clinical training program. Nor has there been any showing in this case that any action short of a substantial change in Southeastern's program would render unreasonable the qualifications it imposed.

V

Accordingly, we reverse the judgment of the court below, and remand for proceedings consistent with this opinion.

*So ordered.*

NOTES

1. The *Davis* case represents the first, and at this writing, the only occasion the Supreme Court has decided a Sec. 504 claim on its merits. As the leading precedent in the interpretation of Sec. 504, *Davis* is relied upon heavily by lower courts when ruling on Sec. 504 issues.

2. The Supreme Court ruled in *Davis* that a recipient need not make "substantial modifications" to its programs to allow a handicapped person to participate in it, if the person could not reasonably be expected to perform the tasks that a typical graduate of its program would be required to perform. In so ruling the Court precludes particular handicapped persons, who after graduating from a certain program could find a position within the profession or specialty that would not create the "public safety" problem the Court finds so troublesome in *Davis*, from gaining access to the program. Is this result consistent with the intent of Sec. 504?

3. The analysis utilized in *Davis* is comparable to the analysis developed by many federal courts in Sec. 504 employment decisions: if a handicapped person can substantially perform the tasks required by a certain job, then the employer is required to make "reasonable accommodations" in order to allow the handicapped person to work in that position. Analogously, it appears under *Davis,* that if a handicapped person could substantially perform the usual tasks that a graduate of a certain program would be expected to perform, then the recipient is under a duty to make "reasonable accommodations" to allow the handicapped person to participate in its program.

4. Sec. 504 and the regulations issued thereafter pertaining to education have been relied upon in several other cases brought by handicapped college and postgraduate students:

a. *Camenisch* v. *University of Texas,* 616 F.2d 127 (5th Cir. 1980); REMANDED ON OTHER GROUNDS, *University of Texas* v. *Camenisch,* ____ U.S. ____, 101 S.Ct. 1830 (1981)—preliminary injunction issued under Sec. 504 requiring higher education recipient to provide an interpreter for deaf student free of charge.

b. *Kling* v. *County of Los Angeles,* 633 F.2d 876 (9th Cir. 1980)—preliminary injunction issued under Sec. 504 ordering handicapped plaintiff admitted to the defendant's nursing school program.

c. *Pushkin* v. *Regents of the University of Colorado,* 504 F. Supp. 1292 (D. Colo. 1981)—defendants violated Sec. 504 by basing their denial of admission of handicapped doctor on preconceptions they had concerning the doctor's handicap.

d. *Jones* v. *Illinois Department of Rehabilitation Services,* 504 F. Supp. 1244 (N.D. Ill. 1981)—deaf college student entitled to the services of an interpreter without charge under Sec. 504.

e. *Wright* v. *Columbia University,* 520 F. Supp. 789 (E.D. Pa. 1981)—preliminary injunction issued under Sec. 504 ordering defendant to allow monocular student to participate in intercollegiate athletics.

f. *Doe* v. *New York University,* 511 F. Supp. 606 (S.D.N.Y. 1981)—medical student challenged school's refusal to readmit her after she took a leave of absence because of psychological problems as a violation of Sec. 504; court granted student's motion to restore the case to the court's active calendar as no administrative resolution of the case seemed imminent.

g. *Crawford* v. *University of North Carolina,* 440 F. Supp. 1047 (M.D.N.C., 1977)—preliminary injunction issued under Sec. 504 ordering university to provide interpreter for deaf student, conditioned upon plaintiff initiating complaint with HEW.

p. 236—INSERT the following after the regulation and before *Lora:*

The regulations implementing P.L. 94-142 were recodified at Title 34, Code of Federal Regulations, Part 300 after the establishment of the Department of Education.

### BOARD OF EDUCATION OF THE HENDRICK HUDSON CENTRAL SCHOOL DISTRICT V. ROWLEY

*Supreme Court of the United States, 1982*
___*U.S.*___, *102 S.Ct. 3034*

JUSTICE REHNQUIST delivered the opinion of the Court.

This case presents a question of statutory interpretation. Petitioners contend that the Court of Appeals and the District Court misconstrued the requirements imposed by Congress upon States which receive federal funds under the Education for All Handicapped Children Act. We agree and reverse the judgment of the Court of Appeals.

I

The Education for All Handicapped Children Act of 1975 (Act), 20 U. S. C. § 1401 *et seq.,* provides federal money to assist state and local agencies in educating handicapped children, and conditions such funding upon a State's compliance with extensive goals and procedures. The Act represents an ambitious federal effort to promote the education of handicapped children, and was passed in response to Congress' perception that a majority of handicapped children in the United States "were either totally excluded from schools or [were] sitting idly in regular classrooms awaiting the time when they were old enough to 'drop out.'" H.R. Rep. No. 94-332, p. 2 (1975). The Act's evolution and major provisions shed light on the question of statutory interpretation which is at the heart of this case.

Congress first addressed the problem of educating the handicapped in 1966 when it amended the Elementary and Secondary Education Act of 1965 to establish a grant program "for the purpose of assisting the States in the initiation, expansion, and improvement of programs and projects . . . for the education of handicapped children." Pub. L. No. 89-750, § 161, 80 Stat. 1204 (1966). That program was repealed in 1970 by the Education for the Handicapped Act, Pub. L. No. 91-230, 84 Stat. 175,

Part B of which established a grant program similar in purpose to the repealed legislation. Neither the 1966 nor the 1970 legislation contained specific guidelines for state use of the grant money; both were aimed primarily at stimulating the States to develop educational resources and to train personnel for educating the handicapped.

Dissatisfied with the progress being made under these earlier enactments, and spurred by two district court decisions holding that handicapped children should be given access to a public education, Congress in 1974 greatly increased federal funding for education of the handicapped and for the first time required recipient States to adopt "a goal of providing full educational opportunities to all handicapped children." Pub. L. 93-380, 88 Stat. 579, 583 (1974) (the 1974 statute). The 1974 statute was recognized as an interim measure only, adopted "in order to give the Congress an additional year in which to study what if any additional Federal assistance [was] required to enable the States to meet the needs of handicapped children." H.R. Rep. No. 94-332, *supra,* p. 4. The ensuing year of study produced the Education for All Handicapped Children Act of 1975.

In order to qualify for federal financial assistance under the Act, a State must demonstrate that it "has in effect a policy that assures all handicapped children the right to a free appropriate public education." 20 U. S. C. § 1412(1). That policy must be reflected in a state plan submitted to and approved by the Commissioner of Education, § 1413, which describes in detail the goals, programs, and timetables under which the State intends to educate handicapped children within its borders. §§ 1412, 1413. States receiving money under the Act must provide education to the handicapped by priority, first "to handicapped children who are not receiving an education" and second "to handicapped children . . . with the most severe handicaps who are receiving an inadequate education," § 1412(3), and "to the maximum extent appropriate" must educate handicapped children "with children who are not handicapped." § 1412(5). The Act broadly defines "handicapped children" to include "mentally retarded, hard of hearing, deaf, speech impaired, visually handicapped, seriously emotionally disturbed, orthopedically impaired, [and] other health impaired children, [and] children with specific learning disabilities." § 1401(1).

The "free appropriate public education" required by the Act is tailored to the unique needs of the handicapped child by means of an "individualized educational program" (IEP). § 1401(18). The IEP, which is prepared at a meeting between a qualified representative of the local educational agency, the child's teacher, the child's parents or guardian, and, where appropriate, the child, consists of a written document containing

> (A) a statement of the present levels of educational performance of the child, (B) a statement of annual goals, including short-term instructional objectives, (C) a statement of the specific educational services to be provided to such child, and the extent to which such child will be able to participate in regular educational programs, (D) the projected date for initiation and anticipated duration of such service, and (E) appropriate objective criteria and evaluation procedures and schedules for determining, on at least an annual basis, whether instructional objectives are being achieved. § 1401(19).

Local or regional educational agencies must review, and where appropriate revise, each child's IEP at least annually. § 1404(a)(5). See also §§ 1413(a)(11), 1414(a)(5).

In addition to the state plan and the IEP already described, the Act imposes extensive procedural requirements upon States receiving federal funds under its provisions. Parents or guardians of handicapped children must be notified of any proposed change in "the identification, evaluation, or educational placement of the child or the provision of a free appropriate public education to the child," and must be permitted to bring a complaint about "any matter relating to" such evaluation and education. § 1415(b)(1)(D) and (E). Complaints brought by parents or guardians must be resolved at "an impartial due process hearing," and appeal to the State educational agency must be provided if the initial hearing is held at the local or regional level. § 1415(b)(2) and (c). Thereafter, "[a]ny party aggrieved by the findings and decisions" of the state administrative hearing has "the right to bring a civil action with respect to the complaint . . . in any State court of competent jurisdiction or in a district court of the United States without regard to the amount in controversy." § 1415(e)(2).

Thus, although the Act leaves to the States the primary responsibility for developing and executing educational programs for handicapped children, it imposes significant requirements to be followed in the discharge of that responsibility. Compliance is assured by provisions permitting the withholding of federal funds upon determination that a participating state or local agency has failed to satisfy the requirements of the Act, §§ 1414(b)(2)(A), 1416, and by the provision for judicial review. At present, all States except New Mexico receive federal funds under the portions of the Act at issue today. Brief for the United States as *Amicus Curiae* 2, n. 2.

## II

This case arose in connection with the education of Amy Rowley, a deaf student at the Furnace Woods School in the Hendrick Hudson Central School District, Peekskill, New York. Amy has minimal residual hearing and is an excellent lipreader. During the year before she began attending Furnace Woods, a meeting between her parents and school administrators resulted in a decision to place her in a regular kindergarten class in order to determine what supplemental services would be necessary to her education. Several members of the school administration prepared for Amy's arrival by attending a course in sign-language interpretation, and a teletype machine was installed in the principal's office to facilitate communication with her parents who are also deaf. At the end of the trial period it was determined that Amy should remain in the kindergarten class, but that she should be provided with an FM hearing aid which would amplify words spoken into a wireless receiver by the teacher or fellow students during certain classroom activities. Amy successfully completed her kindergarten year.

As required by the Act, an IEP was prepared for Amy during the fall of her first-grade year. The IEP provided that Amy should be educated in a regular classroom at Furnace Woods, should continue to use the FM hearing aid, and should receive instruction from a tutor for the deaf for one hour each day and from a speech therapist for three hours each week. The Rowleys agreed with the IEP but insisted that Amy also be provided a qualified sign-language interpreter in all of her academic classes. Such an interpreter had been placed in Amy's kindergarten class for a two-week experimental period, but the interpreter had reported that Amy did not need his services at that time. The school administrators likewise concluded that Amy did not need such an interpreter in her first-grade classroom. They reached this conclusion after consulting the school district's Committee on the Handicapped, which had received expert evidence from Amy's parents on the importance of a sign-language interpreter, received testimony from Amy's teacher and other persons familiar with her academic and social progress, and visited a class for the deaf.

When their request for an interpreter was denied, the Rowleys demanded and received a hearing before an independent examiner. After receiving evidence from both sides, the examiner agreed with the administrators' determination that an interpreter was not necessary because "Amy was achieving educationally, academically, and socially" without such assistance. App. to Pet. for Cert. F-22. The examiner's decision was affirmed on appeal by the New York Commissioner of Education on the basis of substantial evidence in the record. *Id.*, at E-4. Pursuant to the Act's provision for judicial review, the Rowleys then brought an action in the United States District Court for the Southern District of New York, claiming that the administrators' denial of the sign-language interpreter constituted a denial of the "free appropriate public education" guaranteed by the Act.

The District Court found that Amy "is a remarkably well-adjusted child" who interacts and communicates well with her classmates and has "developed an extraordinary rapport" with her teachers. 483 F. Supp. 528, 531. It also found that "she performs better than the average child in her class and is advancing easily from grade to grade," *id.*, at 534, but "that she understands considerably less of what goes on in class than she would if she were not deaf" and thus "is not learning as much, or performing as well academically, as she would without her handicap," *id.*, at 532. This disparity between Amy's achievement and her potential led the court to decide that she was not receiving a "free appropriate public education," which the court defined as "an opportunity to achieve [her] full potential commensurate with the opportunity provided to other children." *Id.*, at 534. According to the District Court, such a standard "requires that the potential of the handicapped child be measured and compared to his or her performance, and that the remaining differential or 'shortfall' be compared to the shortfall experienced by nonhandicapped children." *Ibid.* The District Court's definition arose from its assumption that the responsibility for "giv[ing] content to the requirement of an 'appropriate education' " had "been left entirely to the federal courts and the hearing officers." *Id.*, at 533.

A divided panel of the United States Court of Appeals for the Second Circuit affirmed. The Court of Appeals "agree[d] with the [D]istrict [C]ourt's conclusions of law," and held that its "findings of fact [were] not clearly erroneous." 632 F.2d 945, 947 (1980).

We granted certiorari to review the lower courts' interpretation of the Act. 454 U.S. ____ (1981). Such review requires us to consider two questions: What is meant by the Act's requirement of a "free appropriate public education"? And what is the role of state and federal courts in exercising the review granted by § 1415 of the Act? We consider these questions separately.

## III

### A

This is the first case in which this Court has been called upon to interpret any provision of the Act. As noted previously, the District Court and the Court of Appeals concluded that "[t]he Act itself does not define 'appropriate education,'" 483 F. Supp., at 533, but leaves "to the courts and the hearing officers" the responsibility of "giv[ing] content to the requirement of an appropriate education." *Ibid.* See also 632 F.2d, at 947. Petitioners contend that the definition of the phrase "free appropriate public education" used by the courts below overlooks the definition of that phrase actually found in the Act. Respondents agree that the Act defines "free appropriate public education," but contend that the statutory definition is not "functional" and thus "offers judges no guidance in their consideration of controversies involving the 'identification, evaluation, or educational placement of the child or the provision of a free appropriate public education.'" Brief for Respondents 28. The United States, appearing as *amicus curiae* on behalf of respondents, states that "[a]lthough the Act includes definitions of "free appropriate public education' and other related terms, the statutory definitions do not adequately explain what is meant by 'appropriate.'" Brief for United States as *Amicus Curiae* 13.

We are loath to conclude that Congress failed to offer any assistance in defining the meaning of the principal substantive phrase used in the Act. It is beyond dispute that, contrary to the conclusions of the courts below, the Act does expressly define "free appropriate public education":

> The term "free appropriate public education" means *special education* and *related services* which (A) have been provided at public expense, under public supervision and direction, and without charge, (B) meet the standards of the State educational agency, (C) include an appropriate preschool, elementary, or secondary school education in the State involved, and (D) are provided in conformity with the individualized education program required under section 1414(a)(5) of this title. § 1401(18) (emphasis added).

"Special education," as referred to in this definition, means "specially designed instruction, at no cost to parents or guardians, to meet the unique needs of a handicapped child, including classroom instruction, instruction in physical education, home instruction, and instruction in hospitals and institutions." § 1401(16). "Related services" are defined as "transportation, and such developmental, corrective, and other supportive services . . . as may be required to assist a handicapped child to benefit from special education." § 1401(17).

Like many statutory definitions, this one tends toward the cryptic rather than the comprehensive, but that is scarcely a reason for abandoning the quest for legislative intent. Whether or not the definition is a "functional" one, as respondents contend it is not, it is the principal tool which Congress has given us for parsing the critical phrase of the Act. We think more must be made of it than either respondents or the United States seems willing to admit.

According to the definitions contained in the Act, a "free appropriate public education" consists of educational instruction specially designed to meet the unique needs of the handicapped child, supported by such services as are necessary to permit the child "to benefit" from the instruction. Almost as a checklist for adequacy under the Act, the definition also requires that such instruction and services be provided at public expense and under public supervision, meet the State's educational standards, approximate the grade levels used in the State's regular education, and comport with the child's IEP. Thus, if personalized instruction is being provided with sufficient supportive services to permit the child to benefit from the instruction, and the other items on the definitional checklist are satisfied, the child is receiving a "free appropriate public education" as defined by the Act.

Other portions of the statute also shed light upon congressional intent. Congress found that of the roughly eight million handicapped children in the United States at the time of enactment, one million were "excluded entirely from the public school system" and more than half were receiving an inappropriate education. Note to § 1401. In addition, as mentioned in Part I, the Act requires States to extend educational services first to those children who are receiving no education and second to those children who are receiving an "inadequate education." § 1412(3). When these express statutory findings and priorities are read together with the Act's extensive procedural requirements and its definition of "free appropriate public education," the face of the statute evinces a congressional intent to bring previously excluded handicapped children into the public education systems of the States and to require the States to adopt *procedures* which would result in individualized consideration of and instruction for each child.

Noticeably absent from the language of the statute is any substantive standard prescribing the level of education to be accorded handicapped children. Certainly the language of the statute contains no requirement like the one imposed by the lower courts—that States maximize the potential of handicapped children "commensurate with the opportunity provided to other children." 483 F. Supp., at 534. That standard was expounded by the District Court without reference to the statutory definitions or even to the legislative history of the Act. Although we find the statutory definition of "free appropriate public education" to be helpful in our interpretation of the Act, there remains the question of whether the legislative history indicates a congressional intent that such education meet some additional substantive standard. For an answer, we turn to that history.

B

(i)

As suggested in Part I, federal support for education of the handicapped is a fairly recent development. Before passage of the Act some States had passed laws to improve the educational services afforded handicapped children, but many of these children were excluded completely from any form of public education or were left to fend for themselves in classrooms designed for education of their nonhandicapped peers. The House Report begins by emphasizing this exclusion and misplacement, noting that millions of handicapped children "were either totally excluded from schools or [were] sitting idly in regular classrooms awaiting the time when they were old enough to 'drop out.' " H.R. Rep. No. 94-332, *supra,* at 2. See also S. Rep. No.

94-168, p. 8 (1975). One of the Act's two principal sponsors in the Senate urged its passage in similar terms:

> While much progress has been made in the last few years, we can take no solace in that progress until all handicapped children are, in fact, receiving an education. The most recent statistics provided by the Bureau of Education for the Handicapped estimate that . . . 1.75 million handicapped children do not receive any educational services, and 2.5 million handicapped children are not receiving an appropriate education. 121 Cong. Rec. 19486 (1975) (remarks of Sen. Williams).

This concern, stressed repeatedly throughout the legislative history, confirms the impression conveyed by the language of the statute: By passing the Act, Congress sought primarily to make public education available to handicapped children. But in seeking to provide such access to public education, Congress did not impose upon the States any greater substantive educational standard than would be necessary to make such access meaningful. Indeed, Congress expressly "recognize[d] that in many instances the process of providing special education and related services to handicapped children is not guaranteed to produce any particular outcome." S. Rep. No. 94-168, *supra,* at 11. Thus, the intent of the Act was more to open the door of public education to handicapped children on appropriate terms than to guarantee any particular level of education once inside.

Both the House and the Senate reports attribute the impetus for the Act and its predecessors to two federal court judgments rendered in 1971 and 1972. As the Senate Report states, passage of the Act "followed a series of landmark court cases establishing in law the right to education for all handicapped children." S. Rep. No. 94-168, *supra,* at 6. The first case, *Pennsylvania Association for Retarded Children* v. *Commonwealth of Pennsylvania (PARC),* 334 F. Supp. 1257 (1971), 343 F. Supp. 279 (E.D. Pa. 1972), was a suit on behalf of retarded children challenging the constitutionality of a Pennsylvania statute which acted to exclude them from public education and training. The case ended in a consent decree which enjoined the State from "deny[ing] to any mentally retarded child *access* to a free public program of education and training." 334 F. Supp., at 1258 (emphasis added).

*PARC* was followed by *Mills* v. *Board of Education of the District of Columbia,* 348 F. Supp. 866 (DC 1972), a case in which the plaintiff handicapped children had been excluded from the District of Columbia public schools. The court's judgment, quoted at page 6 of the Senate Report on the Act, provided

> [t]hat no [handicapped] child eligible for a publicly supported education in the District of Columbia public schools shall be *excluded* from a regular school assignment by a Rule, policy, or practice of the Board of Education of the District of Columbia or its agents unless such child is provided (a) *adequate* alternative educational services suited to the child's needs, which may include special education or tuition grants, and (b) a constitutionally adequate prior hearing and periodic review of the child's status, progress, and the *adequacy* of any educational alternative. 348 F. Supp., at 878 (emphasis added).

*Mills* and *PARC* both held that handicapped children must be given *access* to an adequate, publicly supported education. Neither case purports to require any particular substantive level of education. Rather, like the language of the Act, the cases set forth extensive procedures to be followed in formulating personalized educational programs for handicapped children. See 348 F. Supp., at 878–883; 334 F. Supp., at 1258–1267. The fact that both *PARC* and *Mills* are discussed at length in the legislative reports suggests that the principles which they established are the principles which, to a significant extent, guided the drafters of the Act. Indeed, immediately after discussing these cases the Senate Report describes the 1974 statute as having "incorporated the major principles of the right to education cases." S. Rep. No. 94-168, *supra,* at 8. Those principles in turn became the basis of the Act, which itself was designed to effectuate the purposes of the 1974 statute. H.R. Rep. No. 94-332, *supra,* at 5.

That the Act imposes no clear obligation upon recipient States beyond the requirement that handicapped children receive some form of specialized education is perhaps best demonstrated by the fact that Congress, in explaining the need for the Act, equated an "appropriate education" to the receipt of some specialized educational services. The Senate Report states: "[T]he most recent statistics provided by the Bureau of Education for the Handicapped estimate that of the more than 8 million children . . . with handicapping conditions requiring special education and related services, only 3.9 million such children are receiving an appropriate education." S. Rep. No. 94-168, *supra,* at 8. This statement, which reveals Congress' view that 3.9 million handicapped children were "receiving an appropriate education" in 1975, is followed immediately in the Senate Report by a table showing that 3.9 million handicapped children were "served" in 1975 and a slightly larger number were "unserved." A similar statement and table appear in the House Report. H.R. Rep. No. 94-332, *supra,* at 11–12.

It is evident from the legislative history that the characterization of handicapped children as "served" referred to children who were receiving some form of specialized educational services from the States, and that the characterization of children as "unserved" referred to those who were receiving no specialized educational services. For example, a letter sent to the United States Commissioner of Education by the House Committee on Education and Labor, signed by two key sponsors of the Act in the House, asked the Commissioner to identify the number of handicapped "children served" in each State. The letter asked for statistics on the number of children "being served" in various types of "special education program[s]" and the number of children who were not "receiving educational services." Hearings on S. 6 before the Subcommittee on the Handicapped of the Senate Committee on Labor and Public Welfare, 94th Cong., 1st Sess., 205–207 (1975). Similarly, Senator Randolph, one of the Act's principal sponsors in the Senate, noted that roughly one-half of the handicapped children in the United States "are receiving special educational services." *Id.,* at 1. By characterizing the 3.9 million handicapped children who were "served" as children who were "receiving an appropriate education," the Senate and House reports unmistakably disclose Congress' perception of the type of education required by the Act: an "appropriate education" is provided when personalized educational services are provided.

(ii)

Respondents contend that "the goal of the Act is to provide each handicapped child with an equal educational opportunity." Brief for Respondents 35. We think, however, that the requirement that a State provide specialized educational services to handicapped children generates no additional requirement that the services so provided be sufficient to maximize each child's potential "commensurate with the opportunity provided other children." Respondents and the United States correctly note that Congress sought "to provide assistance to the States in carrying out their responsibilities under . . . the Constitution of the United States to provide equal protection of the laws." S. Rep. No. 94-168, *supra*, at 13. But we do not think that such statements imply a congressional intent to achieve strict equality of opportunity or services.

The educational opportunities provided by our public school systems undoubtedly differ from student to student, depending upon a myriad of factors that might affect a particular student's ability to assimilate information presented in the classroom. The requirement that States provide "equal" educational opportunities would thus seem to present an entirely unworkable standard requiring impossible measurements and comparisons. Similarly, furnishing handicapped children with only such services as are available to nonhandicapped children would in all probability fall short of the statutory requirement of "free appropriate public education"; to require, on the other hand, the furnishing of every special service necessary to maximize each handicapped child's potential is, we think, further than Congress intended to go. Thus to speak in terms of "equal" services in one instance gives less than what is required by the Act and in another instance more. The theme of the Act is "free appropriate public education," a phrase which is too complex to be captured by the word "equal" whether one is speaking of opportunities or services.

The legislative conception of the requirements of equal protection was undoubtedly informed by the two district court decisions referred to above. But cases such as *Mills* and *PARC* held simply that handicapped children may not be excluded entirely from public education. In *Mills,* the District Court said:

> If sufficient funds are not available to finance all of the services and programs that are needed and desirable in the system then the available funds must be expended equitably in such a manner that no child is entirely excluded from a publicly supported education consistent with his needs and ability to benefit therefrom. 348 F. Supp., at 876.

The *PARC* Court used similar language, saying "[i]t is the commonwealth's obligation to place each mentally retarded child in a free, public program of education and training appropriate to the child's capacity. . . ." 334 F. Supp., at 1260. The right of access to free public education enunciated by these cases is significantly different from any notion of absolute equality of opportunity regardless of capacity. To the extent that Congress might have looked further than these cases which are mentioned in the legislative history, at the time of enactment of the Act this Court had held at least twice that the Equal Protection Clause of the Fourteenth Amendment does not require States to expend equal financial resources on the education of each child. *San Antonio School District* v. *Rodriguez,* 411 U.S. 1 (1975); *McInnis* v. *Shapiro,* 293 F. Supp. 327 (N.D. Ill. 1968), *aff'd sub nom, McInnis* v. *Ogilvie,* 394 U.S. 322 (1969).

In explaining the need for federal legislation, the House Report noted that "no congressional legislation has required a precise guarantee for handicapped children, i.e. a basic floor of opportunity that would bring into compliance all school districts with the constitutional right of equal protection with respect to handicapped children."

H.R. Rep. No. 94-332, *supra*, at 14. Assuming that the Act was designed to fill the need identified in the House Report—that is, to provide a "basic floor of opportunity" consistent with equal protection—neither the Act nor its history persuasively demonstrate that Congress thought that equal protection required anything more than equal access. Therefore, Congress' desire to provide specialized educational services, even in furtherance of "equality," cannot be read as imposing any particular substantive educational standard upon the States.

The District Court and the Court of Appeals thus erred when they held that the Act requires New York to maximize the potential of each handicapped child commensurate with the opportunity provided nonhandicapped children. Desirable though that goal might be, it is not the standard that Congress imposed upon States which receive funding under the Act. Rather, Congress sought primarily to identify and evaluate handicapped children, and to provide them with access to a free public education.

(iii)

Implicit in the congressional purpose of providing access to a "free appropriate public education" is the requirement that the education to which access is provided be sufficient to confer some educational benefit upon the handicapped child. It would do little good for Congress to spend millions of dollars in providing access to a public education only to have the handicapped child receive no benefit from that education. The statutory definition of "free appropriate public education," in addition to requiring that States provide each child with "specially designed instruction," expressly requires the provision of "such . . . supportive services . . . as may be required to assist a handicapped child *to benefit* from special education." § 1401(17) (emphasis added). We therefore conclude that the "basic floor of opportunity" provided by the Act consists of access to specialized instruction and related services which are individually designed to provide educational benefit to the handicapped child.

The determination of when handicapped children are receiving sufficient educational benefits to satisfy the requirements of the Act presents a more difficult problem. The Act requires participating States to educate a wide spectrum of handicapped children, from the marginally hearing-impaired to the profoundly retarded and palsied. It is clear that the benefits obtainable by children at one end of the spectrum will differ dramatically from those obtainable by children at the other end, with infinite variations in between. One child may have little difficulty competing successfully in an academic setting with nonhandicapped children while another child may encounter great difficulty in acquiring even the most basic of self-maintenance skills. We do not attempt today to establish any one test for determining the adequacy of educational benefits conferred upon all children covered by the Act. Because in this case we are presented with a handicapped child who is receiving substantial specialized instruction and related services, and who is performing above average in the regular classrooms of a public school system, we confine our analysis to that situation.

The Act requires participating States to educate handicapped children with nonhandicapped children whenever possible. When that "mainstreaming" preference of the Act has been met and a child is being educated in the regular classrooms of a public school system, the system itself monitors the educational progress of the child.

Regular examinations are administered, grades are awarded, and yearly advancement to higher grade levels is permitted for those children who attain an adequate knowledge of the course material. The grading and advancement system thus constitutes an important factor in determining educational benefit. Children who graduate from our public school systems are considered by our society to have been "educated" at least to the grade level they have completed, and access to an "education" for handicapped children is precisely what Congress sought to provide in the Act.

## C

When the language of the Act and its legislative history are considered together, the requirements imposed by Congress become tolerably clear. Insofar as a State is required to provide a handicapped child with a "free appropriate public education," we hold that it satisfies this requirement by providing personalized instruction with sufficient support services to permit the child to benefit educationally from that instruction. Such instruction and services must be provided at public expense, must meet the State's educational standards, must approximate the grade levels used in the State's regular education, and must comport with the child's IEP. In addition, the IEP, and therefore the personalized instruction, should be formulated in accordance with the requirements of the Act and, if the child is being educated in the regular classrooms of the public education system, should be reasonably calculated to enable the child to achieve passing marks and advance from grade to grade.

## IV

## A

As mentioned in Part I, the Act permits "[a]ny party aggrieved by the findings and decision" of the state administrative hearings "to bring a civil action" in "any State court of competent jurisdiction or in a district court of the United States without regard to the amount in controversy." § 1415(e)(2). The complaint, and therefore the civil action, may concern "any matter relating to the identification, evaluation, or educational placement of the child, or the provision of a free appropriate public education to such child." § 1415(b)(1)(E). In reviewing the complaint, the Act provides that a court "shall receive the record of the [state] administrative proceeding, shall hear additional evidence at the request of a party, and, basing its decision on the preponderance of the evidence, shall grant such relief as the court determines is appropriate." § 1415(e)(2).

The parties disagree sharply over the meaning of these provisions, petitioners contending that courts are given only limited authority to review for state compliance with the Act's procedural requirements and no power to review the substance of the state program, and respondents contending that the Act requires courts to exercise *de novo* review over state educational decisions and policies. We find petitioners' contention unpersuasive, for Congress expressly rejected provisions that would have so severely restricted the role of reviewing courts. In substituting the current language of the statute for language that would have made state administrative findings conclusive if supported by substantial evidence, the Conference Committee explained that courts were to make "independent decision[s] based on a preponderance of the evidence." S. Conf. Rep. No. 94-455, *supra*, at 50. See also 121 Cong. Rec. 37416 (1975) (remarks of Sen. Williams).

But although we find that this grant of authority is broader than claimed by petitioners, we think the fact that it is found in § 1415 of the Act, which is entitled "Procedural Safeguards," is not without significance. When the elaborate and highly specific procedural safeguards embodied in § 1415 are contrasted with the general and somewhat imprecise substantive admonitions contained in the Act, we think that the importance Congress attached to these procedural safeguards cannot be gainsaid. It seems to us no exaggeration to say that Congress placed every bit as much emphasis upon compliance with procedures giving parents and guardians a large measure of participation at every stage of the administrative process, see, e.g. § 1415(a)–(d), as it did upon the measurement of the resulting IEP against a substantive standard. We think that the Congressional emphasis upon full participation of concerned parties throughout the development of the IEP, as well as the requirements that state and local plans be submitted to the Commissioner for approval, demonstrate the legislative conviction that adequate compliance with the procedures prescribed would in most cases assure much if not all of what Congress wished in the way of substantive content in an IEP.

Thus the provision that a reviewing court base its decision on the "preponderance of the evidence" is by no means an invitation to the courts to substitute their own notions of sound educational policy for those of the school authorities which they review. The very importance which Congress has attached to compliance with certain procedures in the preparation of an IEP would be frustrated if a court were permitted simply to set state decisions at nought. The fact that § 1415(e) requires that the reviewing court "receive the records of the [state] administrative proceedings" carries with it the implied requirement that due weight shall be given to these proceedings. And we find nothing in the Act to suggest that merely because Congress was rather sketchy in establishing substantive requirements, as opposed to procedural requirements for the preparation of an IEP, it intended that reviewing courts should have a free hand to impose substantive standards of review which cannot be derived from the Act itself. In short, the statutory authorization to grant "such relief as the court determines is appropriate" cannot be read without reference to the obligations, largely procedural in nature, which are imposed upon recipient States by Congress.

Therefore, a court's inquiry in suits brought under § 1415(e)(2) is twofold. First, has the State complied with the procedures set forth in the Act? And second, is the individualized educational program developed through the Act's procedures reasonably calculated to enable the child to receive educational benefits? If these requirements are met, the State has complied with the obligations imposed by Congress and the courts can require no more.

## B

In assuring that the requirements of the Act have been met, courts must be careful to avoid imposing their view of preferable educational methods upon the States. The primary responsibility for formulating the education to be accorded a handicapped child, and for choosing the educational method most suitable to the child's needs, was left by the Act to state and local educational agencies in cooperation with the parents or guardian of the child. The Act expressly charges States with the responsibility of "acquiring and disseminating to teachers and administrators of programs for handicapped children significant information derived from educational research, demonstration, and similar projects, and [of] adopting, where appropriate, promising educational practices and materials." § 1413(a)(3). In the face of such a clear statutory directive, it seems highly unlikely that Congress intended courts to overturn a State's choice of appropriate educational theories in a proceeding conducted pursuant to § 1415(e)(2).

We previously have cautioned that courts lack the "specialized knowledge and experience" necessary to resolve "persistent and difficult questions of educational policy." *San Antonio School District* v. *Rodriguez*, 411 U.S. 1, 42 (1973). We think that Congress shared that view when it passed the Act. As already demonstrated, Congress' intention was not that the Act displace the primacy of States in the field of education, but that States receive funds to assist them in extending their educational systems to the handicapped. Therefore, once a court determines that the requirements of the Act have been met, questions of methodology are for resolution by the States.

## V

Entrusting a child's education to state and local agencies does not leave the child without protection. Congress sought to protect individual children by providing for parental involvement in the development of State plans and policies, *supra*, at 4–5 and n. 6, and in the formulation of the child's individual educational program. As the Senate Report states:

> The Committee recognizes that in many instances the process of providing special education and related services to handicapped children is not guaranteed to produce any particular outcome. By changing the language [of the provision relating to individualized educational programs] to emphasize the process of parent and child involvement and to provide a written record of reasonable expectations, the Committee intends to clarify that such individualized planning conferences are a way to provide parent involvement and protection to assure that appropriate services are provided to a handicapped child. S. Rep. No. 94-168, *supra*, at 11–12. See also S. Conf. Rep. No. 94-445, p. 30 (1975); 45 CFR § 121a.345 (1980).

As this very case demonstrates, parents and guardians will not lack ardor in seeking to ensure that handicapped children receive all of the benefits to which they are entitled by the Act.

## VI

Applying these principles to the facts of this case, we conclude that the Court of Appeals erred in affirming the decision of the District Court. Neither the District Court nor the Court of Appeals found that petitioners had failed to comply with the procedures of the Act, and the findings of neither court would support a conclusion that Amy's educational program failed to comply with the substantive requirements of the Act. On the contrary, the District Court found that the "evidence firmly establishes that Amy is receiving an 'adequate' education, since she performs better than the average child in her class and is advancing easily from grade to grade." 483 F. Supp., at 534. In light of this finding, and of the fact that Amy was receiving personalized instruction and related services calculated by the Furnace Woods school administrators to meet her educational needs, the lower courts should not have concluded that the Act requires the provision of a sign-language interpreter. Accordingly, the decision of the Court of Appeals is reversed and the case is remanded for further proceedings consistent with this opinion.

*So ordered.*

[The concurring opinion of Justice Blackmun is omitted.]

Justice White, with whom Justice Brennan and Justice Marshall join, dissenting.

In order to reach its result in this case, the majority opinion contradicts itself, the language of the statute, and the legislative history. Both the majority's standard for a "free appropriate education" and its standard for judicial review disregard congressional intent.

I

The majority first turns its attention to the meaning of a "free appropriate public education." The Act provides:

> The term "free appropriate public education" means special education and related services which (A) have been provided at public expense, under public supervision and direction, and without charge, (B) meet the standards of the State educational agency, (C) include an appropriate preschool, elementary, or secondary school education in the State involved, and (D) are provided in conformity with the individualized education program required under section 1414(a)(5) of this title. 20 U.S.C. 1401 (18).

The majority reads this statutory language as establishing a congressional intent limited to bringing "previously excluded handicapped children into the public education systems of the States and requiring the States to adopt *procedures* which would result in individualized consideration of and instruction for each child." *Ante,* at 12. In its attempt to constrict the definition of "appropriate" and the thrust of the Act, the majority opinion states, "Noticeably absent from the language of the statute is any substantive standard prescribing the level of education to be accorded handicapped children. Certainly the language of the statute contains no requirement like the one imposed by the lower courts—that States maximize the potential of handicapped children commensurate with the opportunity provided to other children." *Ante,* at 12, quoting 483 F. Supp. at 534.

I agree that the language of the Act does not contain a substantive standard beyond requiring that the education offered must be "appropriate." However, if there are limits not evident from the face of the statute on what may be considered an "appropriate education," they must be found in the purpose of the statute or its legislative history. The Act itself announces it will provide a "*full* educational opportunity to all handicapped children." 20 U.S.C. § 1412(2)(A) (emphasis added). This goal is repeated throughout the legislative history, in statements too frequent to be "passing references and isolated phrases." *Ante,* at 27, n. 26, quoting *Department of State* v. *Washington Post Co.,* ____ U.S. ____ (1982). These statements elucidate the meaning of "appropriate." According to the Senate Report, for example, the Act does "guarantee that handicapped children are provided *equal* educational opportunity." S. Rep. No. 94-168, at 9 (1975) (emphasis added). This promise appears throughout the legislative history. See 121 Cong. Rec. 19482–19483 (1975) (remarks of Sen. Randolph); *id.*, at 19504 (Sen. Humphrey); *id.*, at 19505 (Sen. Beall); *id.*, at 23704 (Rep. Brademas); *id.*, at 25538 (Rep. Cornell); *id.*, at 25540 (Rep. Grassley); *id.*, at 37025 (Rep. Perkins); *id.*, at 37030 (Rep. Mink); *id.*, at 37412 (Sen. Taft); *id.*, at 37413 (Sen. Williams); *id.*, at 37418–37419 (Sen. Cranston); *id.*, at 37419–37420 (Sen. Beall). Indeed, at times the purpose of the Act was described as tailoring each handicapped child's educational plan to enable the child "to achieve his or her maximum potential." H.R. Rep. No. 94-332, 94th Cong., 1st Sess. 13, 19 (1975), see 121 Cong. Rec. 23709 (1975). Sen. Stafford, one of the sponsors of the Act, declared, "We can all agree that the education [given a handicapped child] should be equivalent, at least, to the one those children who are not handicapped receive." 121 Cong. Rec. 19483 (1975). The legislative history thus directly supports the conclusion that the Act intends to give handicapped children an educational opportunity commensurate with that given other children.

The majority opinion announces a different substantive standard, that "Congress did not impose upon the States any greater substantive standard than would be necessary to make such access meaningful." *Ante,* at 13. While "meaningful" is no more enlightening than "appropriate," the Court purports to clarify itself. Because Amy was provided with *some* specialized instruction from which she obtained *some* benefit and because she passed from grade to grade, she was receiving a meaningful and therefore appropriate education.

This falls far short of what the Act intended. The Act details as specifically as possible the kind of specialized education each handicapped child must receive. It would apparently satisfy the Court's standard of "access to specialized instruction and related services which are individually designed to provide educational benefit to the handicapped child," *ante,* at 24, for a deaf child such as Amy to be given a teacher with a loud voice, for she would benefit from that service. The Act requires more. It defines "special education" to mean "specifically designed instruction, at no cost to parents or guardians, to *meet the unique needs* of a handicapped child. . . ." § 1401(16) (emphasis added). Providing a teacher with a loud voice would not meet Amy's needs and would not satisfy the Act. The basic floor of opportunity is instead, as the courts below recognized, intended to eliminate the effects of the handicap, at least to the extent that the child will be given an equal opportunity to learn if that is reasonably possible. Amy Rowley, without a sign language interpreter, comprehends less than half of what is said in the classroom—less than half of what normal children comprehend. This is hardly an equal opportunity to learn, even if Amy makes passing grades.

Despite its reliance on the use of "appropriate" in the definition of the Act, the majority opinion speculates that "Congress used the word as much to describe the settings in which the children should be educated as to prescribe the substantive content or supportive services of their education." *Ante,* at 20, n. 21. Of course, the word "appropriate" can be applied in many ways; at times in the Act, Congress used it to recommend mainstreaming handicapped children; at other points, it used the word to refer to the content of the individualized education. The issue before us is what standard the word "appropriate" incorporates when it is used to modify "education." The answer given by the Court is not a satisfactory one.

## II

The Court's discussion of the standard for judicial review is as flawed as its discussion of a "free appropriate public education." According to the Court, a court can ask only whether the State has "complied with the procedures set forth in the Act" and whether the individualized education program is "reasonably calculated to enable the child to receive educational benefit." *Ante,* at 30. Both the language of the Act and the legislative history, however, demonstrate that Congress intended the courts to conduct a far more searching inquiry.

The majority assigns major significance to the review provision's being found in a section entitled "Procedural Safeguards." But where else would a provision for judicial review belong? The majority does acknowledge that the current language, specifying that a court "shall receive the record of the administrative proceeding, shall hear additional evidence at the request of a party, and basing its decision on the preponderance of the evidence, shall grant such relief as the court determines is appropriate," § 1415(e)(2), was substituted at Conference for language that would have restricted the role of the reviewing court much more sharply. It is clear enough to me that Congress decided to reduce substantially judicial deference to state administrative decisions.

The legislative history shows the judicial review is not limited to procedural matters and that the state educational agencies are given first, but not final, responsibility for the content of a handicapped child's education. The Conference Committee directs courts to make an "independent decision." S. Conf. Rep. No. 94-455, at 50. The deliberate change in the review provision is an unusually clear indication that Congress intended courts to undertake substantive review instead of relying on the conclusions of the state agency.

On the floor of the Senate, Senator Williams, the chief sponsor of the bill, committee chairman, and floor manager responsible for the legislation in the Senate, emphasized the breadth of the review provisions at both the administrative and judicial levels:

> Any parent or guardian may present a complaint concerning *any matter* regarding the identification, evaluation, or educational placement of the child or the provision of a free appropriate public education to such a child. In this regard, Mr. President, I would like to stress that the language referring to "free appropriate education" has been adopted to make clear that a complaint may involve matters such as questions respecting a child's individualized education program, questions of whether special education and related services are being provided without charge to the parents or guardians, questions relating to whether to the services provided a child meet the standards of the State education agency, or *any other question* within the scope of the definition of "free appropriate public education." In addition, it should be clear that a parent or guardian may present a complaint alleging that a State or local education agency has refused to provide services

to which a child may be entitled or alleging that the State or local educational agency has erroneously classified a child as a handicapped child when, in fact, that child is not a handicapped child. 121 Cong. Rec. 37415 (emphasis added).

There is no doubt that the state agency itself must make substantive decisions. The legislative history reveals that the courts are to consider, *de novo*, the same issues. Senator Williams explicitly stated that the civil action permitted under the Act encompasses all matters related to the original complaint. *Id.*, at 37416.

Thus, the Court's limitations on judicial review have no support in either the language of the Act or the legislative history. Congress did not envision that inquiry would end if a showing is made that the child is receiving passing marks and is advancing from grade to grade. Instead, it intended to permit a full and searching inquiry into any aspect of a handicapped child's education. The Court's standard, for example, would not permit a challenge to part of the IEP; the legislative history demonstrates beyond doubt that Congress intended such challenges to be possible, even if the plan as developed is reasonably calculated to give the child some benefits.

Parents can challenge the IEP for failing to supply the special education and related services needed by the individual handicapped child. That is what Rowleys did. As the Government observes, "courts called upon to review the content of an IEP, in accordance with 20 U.S.C. § 1415(e) inevitably are required to make a judgment on the basis of the evidence presented, concerning whether the educational methods proposed by the local school district are 'appropriate' for the handicapped child involved." Brief for United States as *Amicus Curiae* 13. The courts below, as they were required by the Act, did precisely that.

Under the judicial review provisions of the Act, neither the District Court nor the Court of Appeals was bound by the state's construction of what an "appropriate" education means in general or by what the state authorities considered to be an appropriate education for Amy Rowley. Because the standard of the courts below seems to me to reflect the congressional purpose and because their factual findings are not clearly erroneous, I respectfully dissent.

NOTES

1. The Supreme Court's decision in *Rowley* represents the first, and at this writing, the only occasion the Court has interpreted the Education for All Handicapped Children Act (EAHCA). As such, *Rowley* is the leading precedent for courts to follow in deciding EAHCA issues.

The majority opinion, while clearly lending a limited interpretation to the educational standard required by the EAHCA, nonetheless provides a good overview of the fundamental provisions of the law, such as the procedural safeguards, the Individualized Education Programs, least restrictive environment, and access to records.

2. The Court in making its ruling in *Rowley* seems to have reached a policy decision and then found the appropriate legislative history to substantiate it. The problem with this approach is that, as the dissent points out, there existed a substantial amount of

legislative history to support the notion rejected by the majority—that handicapped children are entitled under the EAHCA to an educational opportunity commensurate with that offered nonhandicapped children.

3.  Does the Court's limited interpretation of the educational standard required by the EAHCA in some respects have the effect of punishing Amy Rowley for her above average intelligence? Another child similarly handicapped, but having less intelligence, might well qualify for an interpreter under the Court's analysis.

Is there a possibility that a certain handicapped child could, in effect, become nonhandicapped because the child had enough raw ability to compensate for the lack of a related service seemingly needed to neutralize the effect of the child's handicap? Does the definitional section of the EAHCA or its regulations pertaining to definitions accommodate such a result?

4.  One of the more problematic aspects to the Court's ruling in *Rowley* is the limitation of the federal or state court review authorized by the EAHCA. The statutory language and the legislative history, as the dissent points out, seem to leave little doubt that courts were to make *de novo* reviews of the State administrative decisions and, if necessary, make independent decisions about what constituted an appropriate education for a particular child.

Thus, the more likely conclusion is that Congress intended the courts to act as final arbiters, when necessary, in the process of developing educational programs for handicapped children. The Court's admonition that ". . . courts must be careful to avoid imposing their view of preferable educational methods upon the States" clouds the issue. The Court's language implies that where States have offered an appropriate educational program courts might still tinker with it. In such instances, however, if a court determines that an appropriate educational program is being offered, then the Congress did not intend nor does the EAHCA authorize any further judicial involvement on that particular matter. Where, however, an inappropriate program is being offered, limiting courts to simply making that determination and remanding without authority, at the least, to provide instructions or guidelines as to what an appropriate educational program might be, means that handicapped children will be subject to the historical problem of footdragging at the State and local level. Such footdragging and corresponding administrative delay if the new program is appealed were precisely the type of problems the EAHCA was designed to eliminate.

p. 241—REPLACE text of Note 2 with the following:

Two cases which provide excellent illustrations of the scope and reach of P.L. 94-142 are *Green* v. *Johnson,* 513 F. Supp. 965 (D. Mass. 1981) and *Garrity* v. *Gallen,* 522 F. Supp. 171 (D. N.H. 1981). In *Green* the court held that handicapped inmates of county correctional facilities in Massachusetts who were under the age of 22 and had not graduated from high school were entitled to a free, appropriate education under P.L. 94-142. The court in *Garrity* held that residents of a state school for the mentally retarded were entitled to a free, appropriate education under P.L. 94-142.

p. 245—INSERT the following after the last paragraph of the note:

*Stemple* v. *Board of Education of Prince George's County* is now reported at 464 F. Supp. 258 (D. Md. 1979); AFF'D ON OTHER GROUNDS, 623 F.2d 893 (4th Cir. 1980), petition for certiori denied 450 U.S. 911 (1981).

For a case that discussed the effect P.L. 94-142 had in determining the appropriate placement for a deaf child see *Springdale School District # 50* v. *Grace,* 656 F.2d 300 (8th Cir. 1981) (reprinted below at pp. 79–82).

## BATTLE v. COMMONWEALTH OF PENNSYLVANIA

*United States Court of Appeals for the Third Circuit, 1980*
*629 F.2d 269, petition for certiori denied, 452 U.S. 968 (1981)*

Before HUNTER, VAN DUSEN, and SLOVITER, Circuit Judges.

Opinion of the Court

JAMES HUNTER, III, Circuit Judge.

The Education for All Handicapped Children Act, 20 U.S.C. §§ 1401–1420 (1976), requires that every state which elects to receive federal assistance under the Act provide all handicapped children with the right to a "free appropriate public education," *id.* § 1412, and establishes detailed procedures for implementing that right. *Id.* § 1415. The Commonwealth of Pennsylvania, a recipient of aid under the Act, has established an administrative policy which sets a limit of 180 days of instruction per year for all children, handicapped or not. We are called upon, in this case of first impression, to examine the scope and purpose of this recent act and to decide whether Pennsylvania's policy and the statute may coexist. We conclude that they may not.

I

This case is before us on interlocutory appeal from the grant of declaratory and injunctive relief ordered pursuant to a finding by the district court that the 180 day rule deprives the members of the plaintiff class of a free appropriate public education and violates their right to procedural safeguards under the Act. We have jurisdiction under 28 U.S.C. § 1292(a)(1) (1976).

The case began as three class actions which were filed in January of 1978 by five handicapped children and their parents. The actions were consolidated for trial on their common injunctive and declaratory issues and the class of "[a]ll handicapped school aged persons in the Commonwealth of Pennsylvania who require or who may require a program of special education and related services in excess of 180 days per year and the parents or guardians of such persons" was certified. *Armstrong* v. *Kline,* 476 F. Supp. 583, 586 (E.D.Pa. 1979).

\* \* \*

### B. The Plaintiff Class

Although the plaintiff class has been broadly defined, the district court classified the handicapped children involved into two general groups: the severely and profoundly impaired by mental retardation alone or, as is frequently the case, combined with other impediments; and the severely emotionally disturbed. These conditions vary greatly from child to child and generalization is difficult and may suggest seductively simple solutions. However, it is necessary briefly to attempt to describe the salient characteristics of these children.

The Severely and Profoundly Impaired (SPI) are generally regarded as children whose I.Q. is below 30.

\* \* \*

Severely Emotionally Disturbed (SED) children suffer from a wide variety of disturbances including autism, characterized by an inability to relate to and communicate with others, symbiosis, marked by an inseparable relationship with one other person, and schizophrenia which is characterized by strange relationships with other individuals and an inability to cope with reality. *Id.* at 589–90.

\* \* \*

The district court found that "as a result of programming interruptions some SPI children lose a large amount of skills and development . . . ." *Id.* at 593. A similar regression of skill development is found among SED children who also experience a decline in emotional development. Although this regression also occurs in nonhandicapped children, the effect is significantly greater among many SPI and SED children.

\* \* \*

IV

The core of this case is the conflict between the 180 day rule and the statutory mandate of "free appropriate public education." The district court concluded that the Act provides a specific educational goal for members of the plaintiff class. We believe that by focusing on the Act as providing a particular educational goal, the district court erred. Rather, the Act contemplates that in the first instance each state shall have the responsibility of setting individual educational goals and reasonable means to attain those goals. The Act, however, imposes strict procedural requirements to insure the proper formulation of a free appropriate public education. We conclude that the 180 day rule precludes the proper determination of the content of a free appropriate public education and, accordingly, that it violates the Act.

\* \* \*

V

At the core of the Act is a detailed procedure for determining the contours of the free appropriate public education to be delivered to each child. 20 U.S.C. § 1415 (1976); *see Lora* v. *Board of Educ.*, 456 F. Supp. 1211, 1227 (E.D.N.Y. 1978). *See generally* Harvard Note, *supra,* at 1108–13; Michigan Note, *supra,* at 137–51. We believe that these procedural safeguards require individual attention to the needs of each handicapped child. *See Lora* v. *Board of Educ.*, 456 F. Supp. at 1226 (clear national commitment to meet each child's special needs in a complete and integrated way); Michigan Note, *supra,* 123. The strongest statement of this requirement is the statutory mandate of individualized educational programs. The IEP is the statutory vehicle for formulating the educational objectives and the educational program for each child. We consider it most persuasive that at this fundamental point in the educational decisionmaking process, the statute requires consideration of each individual child. Nor do the later procedures required by the Act depart from this emphasis. The appeal prescribed by the Act is an appeal from the decisions reflected in IEP. *See* 20 U.S.C. § 1415(b)(2) (1976). Moreover, as difficult as it is to define the scope of the "unique needs" which must be met by special education, *see id.* § 1401(16), there can be little doubt that by requiring attention to "unique needs," the Act demands that special education be tailored to the individual.

This emphasis on the individual is necessary in light of the wide variety of the handicapping conditions covered by the Act. The Act explicitly includes the following children within the meaning of "handicapped children"

> mentally retarded, hard of hearing, deaf, speech impaired, visually handicapped, seriously emotionally disturbed, orthopedically impaired, or other health impaired children, or children with specific learning disabilities, who by reason thereof require special education and related services.

*Id.* § 1401(1).    Indeed, even within the limited conditions which characterize the plaintiff class there is a wide divergence of educational characteristics. This divergence is reflected in the findings of the district court which note the variance among members of the plaintiff class in their degree of impairment, 476 F. Supp. at 588–90, their recovery time from regression, *id.* at 596–97, and the ability of their parents to provide programming, *id.* at 594–95.

We believe the inflexibility of the defendants' policy of refusing to provide more than 180 days of education to be incompatible with the Act's emphasis on the individual. Rather than ascertaining the reasonable educational needs of each child in light of reasonable educational goals, and establishing a reasonable program to attain those goals, the 180 day rule imposes with rigid certainty a program restriction which may be wholly inappropriate to the child's educational objectives. This, the Act will not permit.

To be sure, the Act contemplates that reasonable educational standards may be set by the states. *See* 20 U.S.C. § 1401(18)(B) (1976) (definition of "free appropriate public education"); *id.* § 1412(2)(B) (development of state plan detailing policies and procedures). We believe, however, that these standards must allow for individual consideration of each handicapped child.

Moreover, in promulgating these standards, the Act contemplates review and approval by the Commissioner of Education, *id.* § 1413(c), as well as procedural safeguards including public notice and comment, *id.* § 1412(7)(B). In this way the Act assures that any state standard will be filtered through both the state educational agency, with its expertise and sensitivity to both educational and fiscal matters, the Commissioner of Education, with his expertise, and the general public. Where an inflexible rule has not been afforded this consideration it certainly must fall.

* * *

We therefore conclude that inflexible application of a 180 day maximum prevents the proper formulation of appropriate educational goals for individual members of the plaintiff class.

* * *

NOTE

The decision in *Battle* is based on one of the core concepts underpinning P.L. 94-142—educational services should be provided to handicapped children on an individualized basis.

**2. Specific Issues**

    **a. Due Process Procedural Rights**

p. 255—INSERT after the Notes, the following:

CONCERNED PARENTS AND CITIZENS FOR THE CONTINUING EDUCATION AT
MALCOLM X
v. NEW YORK CITY BOARD OF EDUCATION

*United States Court of Appeals for the Second Circuit, 1980*
*629 F.2d 751*

Before FEINBERG, Chief Judge, and NEWMAN and KEARSE, Circuit Judges.

FEINBERG, Chief Judge:

This case involves the interpretation of the Education for All Handicapped Children Act of 1975, one of the many recent congressional enactments that bring new and complex questions into the federal courts. The New York City Board of Education and various Board officials and trustees (hereafter collectively referred to as the Board) appeal from an order entered in the United States District Court for the Southern District of New York, Robert L. Carter, J., holding that the Board had violated the Act by transferring approximately 185 handicapped children from Public School 79 to other schools in Manhattan School District 5 without providing adequate prior notice and a hearing to the parents or guardians of such children. The court's order compelled the Board to provide the transferred students with "those curricular and extra-curricular programs and related services which were available to plaintiff children at P.S. 79." For reasons stated below, we hold that the transfer did not violate the Act and we reverse the order of the district court.

* * *

II

On the record before us, it is clear that the transfer of students from P.S. 79 was poorly planned, and that the move was disconcerting to many of the handicapped children that had attended the school. Moreover, as the district court found, the schools to which the students were transferred do not in all respects duplicate the "extremely innovative educational program" formerly provided to handicapped children at P.S. 79. However, the issue before us is not whether the Board acted wisely or carried out its decision properly. Instead, the narrow question on this appeal is whether the transfer of handicapped children in special classes at one school to substantially similar classes at other schools within the same school district constitutes a change in "placement" sufficient to trigger the Act's prior notice and hearing requirements.

The primary purpose of the Act is to encourage states, through the use of fiscal incentives, to provide a "free appropriate public education" for all handicapped children. See, e.g., 20 U.S.C. § 1412(1). In furtherance of this goal, the Act also embodies a range of procedures designed to ensure that fundamental decisions concerning the education of handicapped children are made correctly and with appropriate input from the parents or guardians of such children. See generally Note, Enforcing the Right to an "Appropriate" Education: The Education for All Handicapped Children Act of 1975, 92 Harv.L.Rev. 1103 (1979). The interpretation of one such procedural mechanism is at issue here. Pursuant to 20 U.S.C. § 1415(b)(1)(C), whenever an educational agency covered by the Act

> (i) proposes to initiate or *change* or
> (ii) refuses to initiate or *change* the identification, evaluation, or *educational placement* of the child or the provision of a free appropriate education to the child, (emphasis supplied)

it must provide the parents or guardian of the child with prior written notice. Other subsections of § 1415(b) require the agency to provide parents or guardians in such cases with an opportunity for "an impartial due process hearing." See §§ 1415(b)(1)(D), 1415(b)(2). The statute fails to define "change . . . [in] educational placement." The district court, in concluding that the Board's action violated these procedural requirements, construed the term to encompass the transfer of handicapped students between schools in the same district, as well as any other significant alteration in the curriculum, extra-curricular offerings, support services, class composition, or teacher assignments provided to handicapped children. Although this is a possible reading of the section, we nonetheless believe that the term "educational placement" refers only to the general type of educational program in which the child is placed. So construed, the prior notice and hearing requirements of § 1415(b) would not be triggered by a decision, such as that made by the Board in this case, to transfer the special education classes at one regular school to other regular schools in the same district.

Several factors support this conclusion. First, in § 1415(b)(1)(C) the term "educational placement" is used in the context of changes in the "identification, evaluation, or educational placement" of the handicapped child. This language suggests that the full notice and hearing requirements of § 1415(b) were limited to certain fundamental decisions regarding the existence and classification of a handicap, and the most appropriate type of educational program for assisting a child with such a handicap. The legislative history of the Act supports this interpretation, for it indicates that a primary concern of Congress in enacting these procedural protections of § 1415(b) was to prevent the erroneous identification or classification of children as handicapped and the impairment of their subsequent education by ensuring that parents would be afforded prior notice and an opportunity to participate in such fundamental determinations. The Senate Report, for example, notes that the Committee on Labor and Public Welfare was "deeply concerned about practices and procedures which result in classifying children as having handicapping conditions when, in fact, they do not have such conditions." S.Rep. No. 94-168, 94th Cong., 1st Sess. 26 (1975), reprinted in [1975]

U.S. Code Cong. & Admin. News, pp. 1425, 1450–51. Thus the reference to "educational placement" in § 1415(b)(1)(C) would appear to refer to the general educational program in which a child who is correctly identified as handicapped is enrolled, rather than mere variations in the program itself, which the district court apparently believed could constitute a change in placement.

The regulations implementing the Act also interpret the term "placement" to mean only the general program of education. The Act embodies a statutory preference for "mainstreaming," or the maximum possible integration of handicapped children with nonhandicapped children, 20 U.S.C. § 1412(5)(B), and the regulations implementing this preference provide in pertinent part:

> § 121a.551 Continuum of alternative placements
> (a) Each public agency shall insure that a continuum of alternative placements is available to meet the needs of handicapped children for special education and related services.
> (b) The continuum required under paragraph (a) of this section must:
> (1) Include the alternative placements listed in the definition of special education under § 121a.13 of Subpart A (instruction in regular classes, special schools, home instruction, and instruction in hospitals and institutions). . . .

45 C.F.R. § 121a.551. Thus, the regulations use the term "placement" to refer only to the general educational programs provided for handicapped children, and the reference to a "change" in "educational placement" in § 1415(b)(1)(C) would therefore apparently encompass only decisions to transfer a child from one type of program to another. For example, a decision to transfer a handicapped child from a special class in a regular school to a special school would involve the sort of fundamental alteration in the child's education requiring prior parental notification under § 1415(b).

Finally, strong policy considerations support a restrictive interpretation of the meaning of "educational placement" in § 1415(b)(1)(C). As previously noted, in concluding that the transfer of students from P.S. 79 had violated that section, the district court ordered the Board to make numerous minor alterations and additions in the educational programs of the handicapped children at their new locations.

* * *

While not explicitly stated, it appears that the district court considered the removal of any of the [above] programs, some of which were privately sponsored rather than provided by the Board, to constitute a change in "educational placement" requiring prior notice and a hearing under § 1415(b). Such an interpretation of the Act would virtually cripple the Board's ability to implement even minor discretionary changes within the educational programs provided for its students; that interpretation would also tend to discourage the Board from introducing new activities or programs or from accepting privately sponsored programs. Further, the educational agency would lack any workable standard for assessing whether a particular contemplated decision might constitute a change in "educational placement." Moreover, given the full hearing required by the section and the right to obtain judicial review of adverse decisions, see § 1415(e)(1), the implementation of such changes could be forestalled indefinitely. More explicit statutory language is required to justify an interpretation that would so constrain the discretion of educational agencies as to when such determinations should be put into effect.

[2] Thus, we conclude that the term "educational placement" refers only to the general educational program in which the handicapped child is placed and not to all the various adjustments in that program that the educational agency, in the traditional exercise of its discretion, may determine to be necessary. Given this interpretation, we do not believe on the record before us that the transfer of students from P.S. 79 constituted a change in placement sufficient to trigger the prior notice and hearing provisions of § 1415(b). The transferred handicapped students remain in the same classification, the same school district, and the same type of educational program—special classes in regular schools.

\* \* \*

Accordingly, we conclude that the Board was not required under the Act to give parents of handicapped children at P.S. 79 prior notice and a full due process hearing before the transfer of such students to other regular schools within the district.

NOTE

The decision in *Malcolm X* represents the major precedent in the interpretation of what constitutes a "change in placement" for the purposes of P.L. 94-142 and its regulations. The court's opinion is a good example of the traditional deference the federal judiciary pays local school authorities.

### ROBERT M. v. BENTON

*United States Court of Appeals for the Eighth Circuit, 1980*
*634 F.2d 1139*

Before BRIGHT, ROSS, and ARNOLD, Circuit Judges.

BRIGHT, Circuit Judge.

Robert M., as next friend of Renee K., brought this complaint against Iowa school officials after the latter decided to place Renee K. in special education classes. Dr. Robert D. Benton, Iowa Superintendent of Public Instruction, now appeals from the district court judgment declaring that he violated a provision of the Education for All Handicapped Children Act of 1975 (the Act) by presiding over the due process hearing to which Renee K. was entitled under the Act. Dr. Benton contends on appeal that the district court misinterpreted this statutory provision.

We previously remanded this case to the district court for a clarification of jurisdictional issues not raised by the parties. *Robert M.* v. *Benton*, 622 F.2d 370 (8th Cir. 1980). We now reach the merits and affirm the district court judgment.

\* \* \*

After exhausting his administrative remedies Robert M. commenced this suit against Iowa school officials for declaratory and injunctive relief. In part, Robert M. alleged that Dr. Benton had violated that provision of the Act which bars a state educational agency's employee from conducting a due process hearing required by the Act. 20 U.S.C. § 1415(b)(2) (1976). He also alleged other statutory and constitutional violations. Robert M. moved for partial summary judgment on his claim that Dr.

Benton had violated the Act by serving as the hearing officer in Renee K.'s case. The district court ordered that the motion be sustained and remanded the case for a new hearing presided over by an outside hearing officer. Dr. Benton appealed.

* * *

*II. Analysis*

This case presents us with a single, narrow issue of statutory construction: whether Dr. Benton is an "employee of such agency * * * involved in the education" of Renee K. within the meaning of section 1415(b)(2) and thus prohibited from conducting any due process hearing to which she is entitled under the Act. The district court found that Dr. Benton, Iowa's Superintendent of Public Instruction, was not technically an employee of the State Department of Public Instruction but rather its director in conjunction with the State Board of Public Instruction. The court concluded that Dr. Benton must be considered an employee of Iowa's state educational agency, and held accordingly that the hearing over which he presided violated the Act's provision requiring an impartial hearing officer.

On appeal Dr. Benton argues, in effect, that the statutory provision applies only to employees of *direct* providers of educational services. As Superintendent of Public Instruction and an employee of the State Board of Public Instruction, Dr. Benton is not employed by a direct provider of educational services (*i.e.*, the local school board), but rather merely exercises supervisory authority over such a provider. Dr. Benton contends, therefore, that he is not employed by an agency "involved in the education" of Renee K. and that the district court erroneously prohibited him from conducting due process hearings under the Act. Although the argument is a plausible one under the imprecise statutory language, we reject that contention in light of the Act's unusually clear and relevant legislative history.

The Act emerged in its present form from a congressional conference committee which settled differences in the House and Senate versions of the bill. *See generally* S.Conf.Rep. No. 94-455, 94th Cong., 1st Sess. 27–55 (1975), *reprinted in* [1975] U.S. Code Cong. & Admin. News, pp. 1425, 1480–1508. The bill passed by the Senate originally provided that "the impartial due process hearing [mandated by the Act] will not be conducted by an employee of the State or local educational agency directly involved in the education or care of the child[.]" *Id.* at 47, [1975] U.S. Code Cong. & Admin. News at 1500. Expressly to clarify the minimum standard of impartiality applicable to individuals conducting due process hearings, however, the conference substituted language providing that "no hearing may be conducted by an employee of the State or local educational agency involved in the education or care of the child." *Id.* at 49, [1975] U.S. Code Cong. & Admin. News at 1502. The Senate Conference Report therefore indicates that the Act, promulgated as the conference substitute for differing House and Senate versions of the bill and passed in November 1975 by both Houses, intentionally expanded its prohibition to include employees of state educational agencies not directly involved in the education of the child and so to disqualify them from serving as hearing officers under section 1415(b)(2). As Iowa's Superintendent of Public Instruction, Dr. Benton is employed by the State Board of Public Instruction, which clearly is involved, although indirectly, in the education of

Renee K. We therefore conclude that the Act forbids him from serving as her due process hearing officer.

\* \* \*

## MONAHAN v. STATE OF NEBRASKA

*United States District Court for the District of Nebraska, 1980*
*491 F. Supp. 1074, Aff'd in Part, Vacated in Part, 645 F.2d 592 (8th Cir. 1981)*

Memorandum

DENNEY, District Judge.

Under the Education of All Handicapped Children Act of 1975, states which accept federal assistance for the education of the handicapped are required to provide the parents of handicapped children with certain procedural safeguards. Included among these safeguards is the requirement that a person aggrieved by the educational placement of a handicapped child "shall have an opportunity for an impartial due process hearing" to determine the propriety of the school district's placement of the child. 20 U.S.C. § 1415(b)(2).

The primary issue raised by the plaintiffs' complaint is whether Nebraska statutory law conforms with the procedural requirements of the federal act. This issue focuses on L.B. 871, which was enacted by the Nebraska Unicameral in an effort to comply with the procedures outlined in the Act. *See* L.B. 871, §§ 4–11, 1978 Neb. Laws 887–89 (codified in Neb. Rev. Stat. §§ 43-661 *et seq.*). The plaintiffs contend that L.B. 871 is not consistent with federal law because the Nebraska statute fails to provide parents with an impartial due process hearing. Specifically, the plaintiffs allege that the power of the State Commissioner of Education under L.B. 871 to review the decision made in a due process hearing prevents such hearings from being impartial under federal law.

The matter presently before the Court is the plaintiffs' request for a preliminary injunction.

\* \* \*

The Education of All Handicapped Children Act provides specific procedural safeguards which must be adopted by states receiving funds under the Act. These safeguards govern educational proceedings in Nebraska, since it is a recipient of funds under the Act. Thus, any Nebraska law which is inconsistent with these federally mandated procedures is superseded by the federal law. *See Robert M.* v. *Benton*, No. 79-4007 (N.D. Iowa August 13, 1979); *Compochiaro* v. *Califano*, No. H-78-64 (D. Conn. May 18, 1978).

Under the Act, any parent who complains about the educational placement of a handicapped child shall be given an opportunity for an impartial due process hearing. 20 U.S.C. § 1415(b)(2). These due process hearings may be held at either the state or local level, whichever is designated by state law. 20 U.S.C. § 1415(b)(2). Under Nebraska law, the due process hearings are held at the state level. Neb. Rev. Stat. § 43-662. When the due process hearings are held at the state level, the Act provides that any decision made in that hearing shall be final, subject only to judicial review. 20 U.S.C. § 1415(e)(1).

Comparing the federal procedural scheme to that of Nebraska, the Court finds an important inconsistency between the state and federal procedures. The Nebraska law provides that the due process hearings shall be conducted by the State Department of Education using impartial hearing officers. Neb. Rev. Stat. §§ 43-662, 43-663. However, in contrast to the federal guidelines, a final decision is not made in the due process hearing. Rather, the hearing officer merely prepares a report which is then delivered to the Commissioner of Education. This report contains the hearing officer's "findings of facts based on the evidence presented and decisions based on such findings." Neb. Rev. Stat. § 43-662. Once the Commissioner receives the report, the Nebraska statute provides:

> After reviewing such findings and decisions the Commissioner of Education shall then recommend or direct such action as may be necessary.
> Neb. Rev. Stat. § 43-662.

Based on this statutory language, it appears that the Commissioner of Education has the discretionary authority to accept, reject or modify the decision made in the due process hearing. Such discretion conflicts with the federal requirement that the decision made in the due process hearing shall be final except for judicial review. 20 U.S.C. § 1415(e)(1). *See Matter of "A" Family*, Mont., 602 P.2d 157, 166–67 (1979).

\* \* \*

The plain language of § 43-662 clearly indicates that the Commissioner was intended to do more than merely rubber stamp the hearing officer's decision. In pertinent part, the statute provides:

> After *reviewing* [the hearing officer's] findings and decisions, the Commissioner of Education shall then recommend or direct such action as may be *necessary*. (emphasis supplied)
> Neb. Rev. Stat. § 43-662.

This language clearly gives the Commissioner the authority to *review* the hearing officer's decision and to direct such action as may be *necessary*.

\* \* \*

The only interpretation which gives meaning to all the language of Neb. Rev. Stat. § 43-662 is one which gives the Commissioner some discretionary authority over the hearing officer's decision. The statute plainly states that the Commissioner is to review the hearing officer's decision and is to direct any necessary action. At a minimum, this language should be read as giving the Commissioner authority to review the hearing officer's decision, and then to determine what action is necessary.

This interpretation of the Nebraska statute is further supported by Nebraska Department of Education Rule 55. This rule governs special education appeals and provides:

> After the completion of a hearing, the hearing officer shall prepare a report setting forth the petition, the answer, the substance of the evidence presented at the hearing, his findings of fact, and his decision and *recommendation for action*. Rule 55(8)(a) of the Nebraska Department of Education.

This rule clearly indicates that the hearing officer does not have the authority to make a final decision on the issue of what action should be taken in a particular case. Rather, he is limited to making a "recommendation for action." This recommendation is then conveyed to the Commissioner, who then directs such action as may be "necessary and proper." Rule 55(8)(b). These rules read in combination show that the Commissioner, not the hearing officer, makes the final decision on what action should be taken following a due process hearing. *Compare Matter of "A" Family, supra,* 602 P.2d at 166–67 (where an overbroad statute was corrected by education department rules which made clear that the hearing officer's decision was final).

Any interpretation of Neb. Rev. Stat. § 43-662 which gives the Commissioner authority to modify the hearing officer's decision creates a conflict between the Nebraska statute and the federal requirement that the hearing officer's decision shall be final. This, however, is the only reasonable interpretation of the statute's plain language and of the rules of the Department of Education. This Court, therefore, finds that the plaintiffs have raised sufficiently serious questions as to the validity of the Nebraska procedure to make them fair grounds for litigation.

* * *

NOTE

The *Robert M.* and *Monahan* cases are judicial ratifications of two important principles embodied in the P.L. 94-142 provisions pertaining to due process procedural rights. In *Robert M.*, the court expostulated the impartiality requirement—due process hearing officers could not be employed in any other aspect by the school agency concerned. In *Monahan,* the court held that the decision by the hearing officer must be final unless appealed pursuant to the P.L. 94-142 scheme—no state or local education official can modify the hearing officer's decision. These two principles are crucial to the P.L. 94-142 due process scheme because they help to assure that decisions are made objectively. Prior to the passage of P.L. 94-142, school agency officials often made placement decisions about handicapped children while at the same time having responsibility for potentially conflicting matters such as adhering to the school system's budget.

### Doe v. Anrig

*United States District Court for the District of Massachusetts, 1980*
*500 F. Supp. 802*

Memorandum and Orders

Garrity, District Judge.

This action is an appeal from an adverse ruling rendered by the Massachusetts Department of Education's Bureau of Special Education Appeals (Bureau) under the Education of the Handicapped Act, 20 U.S.C. § 1401 et seq. Plaintiffs, a child Joseph Doe with special educational needs and his parents, seek judicial review of a Bureau decision holding that the individual educational plans proposed by the Franklin Public Schools for the school years 1978–1979 and 1979–1980 were adequate and appropriate to meet Joseph's needs. In addition, plaintiffs seek judicial review of a 1977–1978 educational plan which they initially accepted, but later rejected. Plaintiffs have not sought administrative review by the Bureau of the 1977–1978 plan.

\* \* \*

The governing federal statute is the Education of the Handicapped Act. The principal provisions applicable here were added in 1975 by the passage of an amendment to that Act providing for Assistance for Education of All Handicapped Children, codified in 20 U.S.C. §§ 1411–1420. These provisions became effective October 1, 1977. Comprehensive regulations, which were promulgated on August 23, 1977, appear at 45 C.F.R. § 121a. Both the statute and the regulations delineate certain procedural safeguards which the state must afford parents and guardians of handicapped children, in order to obtain federal funds under the Act. 20 U.S.C. § 1415; 45 C.F.R. § 121a.500 et seq. The federal scheme also specifies the circumstances under which a party aggrieved by a state agency's decision may appeal to state or federal court. 20 U.S.C. § 1415(e); 45 C.F.R. § 121a.509–512.

The Massachusetts statutory framework likewise prescribes the procedural rights and judicial remedies of parties aggrieved by the Bureau's decision on a child's individual education plan. The principal statute involved is entitled Education of Children with Special Needs. This statute was added by chapter 766 of the Acts of 1972, which became effective September 1, 1974 and was codified in Mass. G.L. c. 71B. The crucial provisions, including those governing appeal procedures, appear in section 3. State regulations promulgated under c. 766 are codified in 603 C.M.R. § 28.00, and are dated September 1, 1978, which is approximately one year after the date of the federal regulations and the effective date of the federal statute. Chapter 4 of the state regulations at volume 16, pp. 322–329, deals with appeal procedures.

A difficulty in ruling upon the defendants' motions to dismiss for the 1978–79 and 1979–80 years arises from the federal law's apparent assumption of a state procedural scheme different from that enacted in Massachusetts and, to a lesser extent, from the failure of the Massachusetts statute and regulations to include any reference to the availability of an appeal to the federal court system. Specifically, the federal statute mandating various procedural safeguards, 20 U.S.C. § 1415, permits judicial review after either (1) an impartial due process hearing by the state educational agency of parents' complaints about school committee decisions or (2) an impartial review by the state educational agency of a due process hearing conducted at the local level. 20 U.S.C. § 1415(e). But the federal law does not contemplate review by a state educational agency of a due process hearing conducted by a state educational agency, which is the structure provided by the Massachusetts law.

The administrative review mechanism in Massachusetts is set forth both in the statute and in the implementing regulations. Chapter 766, Mass. G.L. c. 71B, § 3, provides that where an individual education plan for a special needs child is in dispute, a due process hearing must be conducted by the Bureau of Special Education Appeals, i.e., the state educational agency. If the parents, guardians or custodians of the child do not accept the Bureau determination, the matter is referred automatically to the State Advisory Commission (SAC), a second agency at the state level. The provision conferring appellate responsibilities on the SAC appears in the 13th unnumbered paragraph of Mass. G.L. c. 71B, § 3, as follows:

> If the parents, guardians or persons with custody reject the educational placements recommended by the department and desire a program other than a regular education

program, the matter *shall be referred* to the state advisory commission on special education to be heard at its next meeting. The commission shall make a determination within thirty days of said meeting regarding the placement of the child. If the parents, guardians or persons with custody reject this determination, they may proceed to the superior court with jurisdiction over the residence of the child and said court shall be authorized to order the placement of the child in an appropriate education program. (Emphasis added.)

Ancillary provisions in the state regulations are at 603 C.M.R. ¶ 610.0, which states:

> *SAC: Appeals.*
> In addition to the duties specified in ¶¶ 608.0 and 609.0, the SAC shall decide appeals in accordance with Chapter 4 and G.L. c. 71B, § 3. The SAC shall establish any procedures which are necessary or desirable to enable it to determine such appeals.

and ¶ 405.2, which provides that a parent's "rejection of the decision of the Bureau shall automatically constitute an appeal to the SAC without the necessity of the parent's separately requesting such an appeal."

It would seem, therefore, that under the Massachusetts statute and regulations, SAC review of a Bureau decision adverse to the wishes of the parents is mandatory and that in bypassing the SAC, the plaintiffs in the instant case have evaded the provisions of Massachusetts law.

On the other hand, where the initial due process hearing is conducted by a state agency in the first instance, as in Massachusetts, further administrative review is not authorized—at least not explicitly—by the federal statute and implementing regulations. Federal law permits an appeal to a district or state court of competent jurisdiction after the initial due process hearing if the hearing is held by the state agency, i.e., the Bureau, or after review by the state agency if the initial hearing is held at the local level. In 20 U.S.C. § 1415(e)(2) the Act provides specifically as follows:

> Any party aggrieved by the findings and decision made under subsection (b) of this section who does not have the right to an appeal under subsection (c) of this section, and any party aggrieved by the findings and decision under subsection (c) of this section, *shall have the right to bring a civil action with respect to the complaint presented pursuant to this section, which action may be brought in any State court of competent jurisdiction or in a district court of the United States* without regard to the amount in controversy. In any action brought under this paragraph the court shall receive the records of the administrative proceedings, shall hear additional evidence at the request of a party, and, basing its decision on the preponderance of the evidence, shall grant such relief as the court determines is appropriate. (Emphasis added.)

In providing for judicial review of "the findings and decisions made under subsection (b)," the federal statute must be referring, insofar as it deals with Massachusetts procedures, to the impartial due process hearing conducted by the Bureau. Hence what appears to be a *prima facie* conflict between the state and federal laws: state law requires administrative review by the SAC and federal law permits judicial review of a Bureau decision without resort to the SAC.

A similar inconsistency between the state and federal laws may be found in the provisions relating to the administrative finality of the Bureau's decision. Plainly, under the Massachusetts scheme the decision of the Bureau is not final and may be reversed or modified by the SAC. On the other hand, 20 U.S.C. § 1415(e)(1) provides,

"A decision made in a hearing conducted pursuant to paragraph (2) of subsection (b) of this section shall be final, . . ." (with exceptions not here applicable).

Defendants contend that § 1415(e)(2) does not confer any right to immediate judicial review. They point out that the Act, read as a whole, affords the states much flexibility in formulating and implementing the procedural safeguards mandated by § 1415 and rely on subsection (b)(1) of that section, which states that the procedures required by that section "shall include, but shall not be limited to" the particular safeguards enumerated in subsections (b) and (c). See also 115 C.F.R. § 121a.506. True, the case law underscores the states' need for leeway in establishing procedural safeguards. As stated in *Eberle* v. *Board of Public Education*, D. Pa., 1977, 444 F. Supp. 41, 43:

> These subsections provide the basic structure for the establishment of a review procedure by the states. *More elaborate due process guarantees may be instituted by individual states.* (Emphasis added.)

> * * *

On the other hand, it is clear that Congress intended swift, meaningful review of due process hearing decisions. The legislative history of the federal Act expresses a strong interest in resolving disputes over individual education plans without delay.

> * * *

This concern is reflected in a comment to federal regulation 45 C.F.R. § 121a.506, which permits states to use mediation as an intervening step prior to conducting a formal due process hearing, but concludes at p. 352, "However, mediation may not be used to deny or delay parents' rights under this subpart." Significantly, under the Massachusetts scheme, intervals of more than two months could be consumed by SAC reviews.

In addition to the federal interest in avoiding delay, there is also a strong federal interest in assuring that any appellate review of the initial due process decision is full, fair, and independent. Subsection (e)(2) of § 1415 contains strong provisions for judicial review. The reviewing court is not limited to the administrative record, but is authorized to receive new evidence, and the decision is to be made *de novo,* based upon the preponderance of the evidence. Thus, there is a strong federal concern that any review be meaningful as well as speedy.

Yet the composition of the SAC, the procedures governing its review of individual education plans, and the nature and extent of its other administrative duties dilute its capacity for quick and meaningful review. First, SAC's membership must include handicapped individuals, secondary school teachers, parents and teachers, as well as experts in special needs programs. 20 U.S.C. § 1413(a)(12). See also 45 C.F.R. § 121a.650–653. State law also mandates participation by many divergent groups. Mass. G.L. c. 15, § 1Q; 603 C.M.R. § 28.607–611. There are presently 14 members of the SAC and they meet only monthly. Second, the procedures applicable to SAC's consideration of individual education plans do not assure impartial or independent review. Under 603 C.M.R. ¶ 406.0, SAC must comply with paragraphs (7) and (8) of Mass. G.L. c. 30A, § 11, the Massachusetts Administrative Procedure Act. Under paragraph 7 of Mass. G.L. c. 30A, § 11, it is permissible for the SAC to make a decision without having heard or read any evidence, and to handle appeals on an ad hoc basis. Furthermore, it is the policy of the SAC to accept written argument only. Third, reviewing individual education plans is essentially peripheral to SAC's primary functions under state and federal law. Under Mass. G.L. c. 15, § 1Q, which establishes the commission, SAC's principal responsibility is the annual submission of a report to the State Department of Education. These annual reports evaluate the quality and adequacy of special education programs in the commonwealth and recommend improvements. The SAC reports are accorded great weight in the formulation of the state's programs for educating the handicapped. In fact, if the State Department of Education decides not to implement the SAC recommendations and agreement cannot be reached informally, public hearings must be held to resolve any dispute between the commission and the department. In addition, 20 U.S.C. § 1413(a)(12) requires that, to fulfill its responsibilities as a state advisory panel under the federal Act, SAC must advise the state educational agency of unmet needs within the state in the education of handicapped children; comment publicly on any proposed state rules or regulations regarding the education of handicapped children and the procedures for distributing the federal funds available under the Act; and assist the state in developing and reporting such data and evaluations as may assist the federal Department of Education in evaluating the state's programs for education of the handicapped. Significantly, the federal regulation, 45 C.F.R. § 121a.652, which implements 20 U.S.C. § 1413(a)(12), does not include review of individual education plans among the functions to be performed by advisory panels.

 Since the interests involved—both state and federal—are important, we hesitate to proceed without some representation from the Department of Education, the agency that is primarily responsible for reconciling them. The Department's participation in some form is particularly appropriate in this case since it has primary responsibility for the approval of state plans under the Act. 20 U.S.C. § 1416. The major purpose of the Act is to provide funding for special needs programs: a state's compliance with the procedural safeguards mandated by § 1415 is a precondition of such federal funding.

* * *

Procedural Order

 Accordingly it is ordered that counsel confer with a view to soliciting the participation of the Department of Education in these proceedings either as a party or an *amicus curiae* and to stipulating a reference to the Department of the following questions:

1. May a parent bring a civil action in this court under 20 U.S.C. § 1415(e)(2) without presenting his complaint to the Massachusetts State Advisory Commission for Special Education?
2. Does the Massachusetts Annual Program Plan for fiscal year 1980 have the approval of the Department of Education in the light of the absence of any reference in the Massachusetts statutes and regulations to the availability of review in a district court of the United States?
3. Is the appellate function of the Massachusetts SAC, in the light of its organization and procedures as described in this memorandum, consistent with federal law?

* * *

## TOWN OF BURLINGTON v. DEPARTMENT OF EDUCATION OF THE COMMONWEALTH OF MASSACHUSETTS

*United States Court of Appeals for the First Circuit, 1981*
*655 F.2d 428*

Before COFFIN, Chief Judge, BOWNES, Circuit Judge, WYZANSKI, Senior District Judge.

COFFIN, Chief Judge.

The ultimate question to be decided in this case is whether the Town of Burlington, Massachusetts must pay for the special education of John Doe, Jr. The district court held that the Massachusetts Department of Education's decision that the Town must reimburse Doe, Jr.'s father was supported by substantial evidence as a matter of state law. It also denied the Town's motion for stay of the Department's decision and granted Mr. Doe's and the Department's motions that the Department's decision be enforced during the pendency of the action. The Town appeals all three judgments. We vacate the first and third judgments and affirm the second judgment.

\* \* \*

We hold that the district court erred in granting summary judgment for the defendants under state law because we conclude that state law cannot be applied when review under federal law is sought. By its terms 20 U.S.C. § 1415(e)(1) provide that decisions by the state educational agency "shall be final, except that any party" has judicial appeal rights under 20 U.S.C. § 1415(e)(2). That subsection provides for review *in state or federal court*. It also sets forth the procedure and standards for this review: "In any action brought under this paragraph the court shall receive the records of the administrative proceedings, shall hear additional evidence at the request of a party, and, basing its decision on the preponderance of the evidence, shall grant such relief as the court determines is appropriate." *Id.*

This federal specification for review, when invoked, seems to us designed to occupy the field over an inconsistent state provision. Here the arguably applicable state review provision—part of the state's general administrative procedure legislation—calls for, *inter alia,* judicial review governed by the substantial evidence standard. Mass. Gen. Laws Ann. ch. 30A, § 14. This standard does conflict with the federal standard; we can imagine many judicial reviews that would uphold an agency decision as based on substantial evidence but that would reach a different result were new evidence to be taken and judged under the more rigorous "preponderance of the evidence" standard.

This conflict could lead to results that should be avoided. For instance, the Department might have ruled in this suit that the Town's proposed plan was faulty but that appropriate relief was something other than what Mr. Doe sought. One aggrieved party might have selected a state forum for review under state law while the other filed in federal court claiming review under the federal standard. If both review provisions legitimately coexisted, the resolution of the controversy could inspire an unseemly race to judgment. Even this would not dependably produce consistency. A decision based simply on substantial evidence would not be res judicata for an issue to be decided by the more probing preponderance of the evidence standard. The converse situation would often be more settled, since a finding under the preponderance standard would generally control the substantial evidence question. But inconsistencies could appear here as well. The federal provision directs that the reviewing court "shall hear additional evidence at the request of a party," while the state provision normally confines its review to the record developed by the agency. *See* Mass. Gen. Laws Ann. ch. 30A, § 14(6) (West 1979). A preponderance-of-the-evidence holding based on an expanded record could present a different legal issue than that faced on a substantial evidence review of a limited record, thus again presenting the specter of inconsistent federal and state judgments, one which might attempt to affirm and enforce the Department's ruling while the other sought to overturn it.

We therefore vacate the district court's decision concerning state law that does not apply in this case. This will leave the scheduled trial on the federal count as the sole mechanism of judicial review in this case.

* * *

NOTE

The issues discussed in the *Anrig* and *Town of Burlington* decisions highlight the significant and frequently difficult interplay between the federal and state systems intrinsic to P.L. 94-142.

### STEMPLE v. BOARD OF EDUCATION OF PRINCE GEORGE'S COUNTY

*United States Court of Appeals for the Fourth Circuit, 1980*
*623 F.2d 893, petition for certiori denied, 450 U.S. 911 (1981)*

Before WINTER, BUTZNER and PHILLIPS, Circuit Judges.

WINTER, Circuit Judge:

Plaintiff, by her father, sued the Board of Education of Prince George's County, Maryland (the County), the Maryland State Board of Education (the State) and, in their individual and official capacities, the persons comprising both bodies to obtain a reimbursement for the tuition cost of her private education. Deeming the proffered educational program in the public schools inadequate for her needs, her parents withdrew her from the public schools and enrolled her in a private school for handicapped children. Plaintiff also challenged the state regulation assigning the burden of proof in state administrative proceedings, in which she contested the adequacy of the public program and the appropriateness of her school assignment. The district court dismissed the complaint, *Stemple* v. *Board of Ed. of Prince George's County*, 464 F. Supp. 258 (D. Md. 1979), and plaintiff appealed. We affirm, albeit for reasons different from those assigned by the district court.

* * *

II

In plaintiff's appeal, her principal contention is that the district court was in error in ruling that § 615 of EHCA was unavailable to permit substantive and procedural review of the state administrative proceedings. She argues that she sought review to vindicate rights theretofore granted in federal and state statutes, not the creation of those rights; and therefore she seeks no retrospective application of § 615. In any event, she contends further, retroactive application of § 615 would be proper under *Bradley* v. *School Bd. of City of Richmond,* 416 U.S. 696, 94 S.Ct. 2006, 40 L.Ed.2d 476 (1974). Her remaining contentions are that, in the administrative proceedings, the burden of proof was improperly placed on her, and the Maryland bylaw with respect to burden of proof violates federal law. She also asserts that her claim for tuition reimbursement is not barred by the eleventh amendment.

As we view plaintiff's appeal, we need not decide any of the issues that she seeks to raise. Her case reaches us in the posture that the sole ultimate issue to be decided is her claim to tuition reimbursement either for the school year 1976–77 or for the entire period that she attended the private school. She has voluntarily returned to public school; thus any contentions about the burden of proof in administrative proceedings or the effect of the eleventh amendment in the context of this case are real issues only to the extent that they affect her right to reimbursement. By the language of § 615, if it is assumed to be applicable here, we think that plaintiff has no right to reimbursement, and that there is thus no need to decide the various issues that she seeks to raise. We elaborate on our conclusion that plaintiff cannot obtain tuition reimbursement under § 615 in what follows.

\* \* \*

Section 615, a totally new enactment, was adopted to achieve the last objective. It accomplishes a number of things. It requires any state, local or intermediate educational agency receiving federal funds to establish and maintain certain minimum procedures. § 615(a). These include: a parent's right of inspection of relevant records, designation of a surrogate for a child's parents or guardian if they are not known, written notice and an opportunity to be heard whenever an agency proposes to initiate or refuses to initiate a change in a child's placement, and a right to an "impartial due process hearing." § 615(b)(1)–(2). The section provides further that, if the required hearing is conducted by a local or intermediate educational agency or unit, a person aggrieved by the decision shall have a right to appeal to the state educational agency, § 615(c), where he shall have the right to be represented by counsel, to present evidence and confront, cross-examine and compel the attendance of witnesses, to receive a record of the hearing, and to receive written findings of fact and decisions. § 615(d). The decision made in a hearing conducted in accordance with the provisions of § 615 is final subject to the right of appeal, and the decision of a local or intermediate unit (where there is no right of appeal) or the decision of a state educational agency may be reviewed in an action instituted in a state court of competent jurisdiction or a district court of the United States without regard to the amount in controversy. § 615(e)(1) and (2).

Significant for our purposes is the further provision of that section, § 615(e)(3):

> During the pendency of any proceedings conducted pursuant to this section, unless the State or local educational agency and the parents or guardian otherwise agree, the child shall remain in the then current educational placement of such child, or, if applying for initial admission to a public school, shall, with the consent of the parents or guardian, be placed in the public school program until all such proceedings have been completed.

Section 615(e)(3) has little specific legislative history of its own. It is mentioned only in the Joint Explanatory Statement of the Conference Committee (Sen. Conf. R. No. 94-455; Home Conf. R. No. 94-664, both of the 94th Cong. 1st Sess.), where it is said:

> The provisions of existing law with respect to the binding effect of due process hearings and appropriate administrative and judicial review of such hearings are clarified and language is also adopted to require that during the pendency of any administrative or judicial proceedings regarding a complaint, unless the State or local educational agency and the parents or guardian of the child otherwise agree, the child involved in the complaint shall remain in his or her present educational placement, or, if the complaint involves an application for initial admission to public school the child shall, with the consent of the parents or guardian be placed in the public school program until the completion of all such proceedings.

U.S. Code Cong. and Admin. News, 1503 (1975).

Taken literally, the language of § 615(e)(3) creates a duty on the part of parents who avail themselves of the hearing and review provisions of § 615 to keep their child in his current educational assignment while the hearing and review provisions are pending, absent agreement between them and the education authorities that some different arrangement be made. Of course, that duty may not be totally enforceable by the state, but it certainly negates any right on the part of parents, in violation of the duty and in the absence of agreement, to elect unilaterally to place their child in private school and recover the tuition costs thus incurred.

To the extent that we can discern legislative intent from overall consideration of the 1975 act and its forebears and the brief, specific reference to § 615(e)(3) in the legislative history, we think that the statute should be given the literal effect we have described. By enactment of the 1975 legislation, Congress was assuming major control and major financing of the national program of education of handicapped children. As part of that effort, Congress was providing for the strengthening and upgrading of evaluation procedures and it enacted a generous bill of rights for parents, guardians, and surrogates of handicapped children who might wish to contest the evaluation and placement policies of educational authorities. There would be reason and design in saying that while the procedures for administrative hearing, administrative review and judicial review mandated by Congress were being employed, the status quo should be preserved unless it was altered by consent. The concept of preserving the status quo even including the payment of benefits (*see, e.g.,* Longshoremen's and Harbor Workers' Compensation Act § 21(b), 33 U.S.C. § 921(b), pending litigation at the administrative and judicial level until an ultimate resolution is reached is a familiar one in American law. For example, under Rule 65, F.R.Civ.P., courts will ordinarily refrain from issuing preliminary injunctions which threaten to disturb the status quo and they will frame any equitable relief to preserve the last uncontested status between the parties which preceded the controversy until the outcome of the final hearing. 11 Wright and Miller, Federal Practice and Procedure § 2948, at 464–66. Thus we think that the statute means just what it says; and since there was a duty not to move plaintiff until a final decision, plaintiff is lacking in any right to recover tuition payments for her parents' unilateral decision to send her to a private school while she was seeking redress for the claimed violation of her rights.

Plaintiff contends that § 615(e)(3) is inapplicable to her, because her parents' decision to send her to a private school was made before the administrative and appeal provisions of § 615 were initially invoked. We reject this contention. It places too restricted a reading on § 615(e)(3). We do not think that the application of § 615(e)(3) depends upon the fine distinction between whether proceedings under § 615 are initiated before or after the duty to preserve the status quo is breached. The duty, it seems to us, arises as soon as school authorities make a decision as to identification, evaluation and placement of a handicapped child and continues until a decision not to contest it is reached or, if a contest ensues, until that contest is finally determined.

In summary, we do not decide plaintiff's several contentions. We decide only that *if* plaintiff is entitled to avail herself of the remedies in § 615 (a question we also do not decide), they will avail her nothing with regard to reimbursement of tuition expense. Her subsidiary contentions have become moot since she voluntarily returned to public school.

AFFIRMED.

### MONAHAN v. STATE OF NEBRASKA

*United States District Court for the District of Nebraska, 1980*
*491 F. Supp. 1974, 1088–1090, Aff'd in Part,*
*Vacated in Part, 645 F.2d 592 (8th Cir. 1981)*

[See pp. 57–59, above.]

### IV

Part of the preliminary relief sought by the plaintiffs is an order requiring the defendants to provide Marla and Daniel with an educational placement pending resolution of this suit. The provisional placement of these children during this litigation is governed by the Education of All Handicapped Children Act:

> During the pendency of any proceedings conducted pursuant to this section, unless the State or local educational agency and the parents or guardian otherwise agree, the child *shall* remain in the *then current educational placement* of such child . . . until all such proceedings have been completed. (emphasis supplied).
> 20 U.S.C. § 1415(e)(3).

This provision is designed to preserve the status quo pending resolution of judicial or administrative proceedings held under the Act. 45 C.F.R. § 121a.513 (1979). *See New York State Ass'n for Retarded Children, supra,* 466 F. Supp. at 486. In essence, it is like an automatic preliminary injunction which maintains the child's then current educational placement. However, unlike a preliminary injunction, the statute replaces "the Court's discretionary consideration of irreparable harm and likelihood of success on the merits with an absolute rule in favor of the status quo." *Gargani* v. *The School Committee of Cranston,* No. 77-0612, slip op. at 6 (D.R.I. May 4, 1978). The Court is therefore without the power to place a child in any provisional placement except for his then current educational placement. *Campochiaro* v. *Califano,* No. H-78-64, slip op. at 10 (D. Conn. May 18, 1978). Thus, to the extent that plaintiffs seek an interim placement other than Marla's and Daniel's then current educational placement, the request must be denied.

Although the Act simplifies the determination of where to place a child during litigation, two issues remain to be resolved in the instant case. First, the Court must ascertain what is Marla's and Daniel's "then current educational placement." Unfortunately, this determination is somewhat unguided since this term is not defined in the Act. Having determined the child's then current placement, the Court must next decide who is to pay the costs of this placement during the proceedings. The resolution of these issues depends on facts unique to each plaintiff. The Court will therefore discuss each plaintiff's claim separately.

### Plaintiff Monahan

The factual setting of the Monahan claim is unique. During the 1978–1979 school year, Daniel was attending the Madonna School, a private school for the mentally retarded. This placement was apparently acceptable to both the school district and Daniel's parents. The cost of tuition at Madonna was paid by the Omaha School District.

By June of 1979, Daniel's physical condition had deteriorated to the point that he had become confined to a wheelchair. Since Madonna was not equipped to educate wheelchair bound students, Daniel was forced to leave the school at the end of the 1978–1979 school year. It should be emphasized that this change of placement was necessitated by factors beyond the control of either the Omaha School District or the Monahans. In any event, it would appear that at this point, Daniel was without an educational placement since he could not return to Madonna, his former educational placement.

Upon learning of Daniel's termination at Madonna, Monahan obtained a new educational evaluation of Daniel from the Millard School District. This evaluation recommended George Norris Elementary School as an appropriate educational placement for Daniel. Monahan then took this recommendation to Dr. Samuelson and requested that the Omaha School District pay for Daniel's education at Millard. Until this request was made in July of 1979, it does not appear that the Omaha School District had been informed that Daniel could not return to the Madonna School. In any event, the school district refused to pay for the Millard placement.

This factual setting presents a difficult question of the proper interpretation of the term "then current educational placement." Normally, the then current placement is determined at the time a complaint is submitted to the local school district, since such a complaint would be the beginning of an administrative proceeding provided by the Act. *Stuart* v. *Nappi,* 443 F. Supp. 1235, 1241 (D. Conn. 1978). See 20 U.S.C. § 1415(b)(1)(E). However the factual setting of the Monahan claim does not fit this normal situation. When Monahan in July of 1979 requested the Omaha School District to pay for the Millard placement, Daniel had no educational placement. At that time, Daniel could not return to his former placement at Madonna because of his physical condition. In addition, the proposed placement at George Norris was merely a recommendation which had never been implemented.

The Court, however, need not resolve the issue of what is Daniel's then current educational placement because neither party objects to Daniel's continued placement at George Norris. Monahan has requested that this Court permit Daniel to remain in the Millard School and has argued that 20 U.S.C. § 1415(e)(3) requires such a placement. For their part, the defendants have raised no objections to the George Norris placement pending resolution of this suit. Since the parties do not object to Daniel's placement at George Norris during the pendency of this suit, the Court will treat this placement as Daniel's then current educational placement under 20 U.S.C. § 1415(e)(3).

The designation of George Norris as Daniel's then current educational placement does not resolve the issue of who should pay for this placement during the instant litigation. For the reasons discussed below, this Court is of the opinion that Monahan should continue to pay the costs of this placement.

The Act prohibits any change in a child's then current educational placement once a proceeding under the Act has been initiated. The purpose of this requirement is to ensure that the status quo is maintained during pendency of a proceeding. Thus, neither party is permitted to make a unilateral change in the education of the child. Moreover, the maintenance of the status quo requires that the school district *continue* to finance an educational placement which it had financed prior to the commencement of the proceeding. The operation of this requirement is illustrated by the following hypothetical situation.

Assume that prior to any proceedings under the Act, a child is being educated in educational placement "A" at school district expense. The school district then gives the parents notice of a proposed change in placement, and the parents file a complaint under the Act. In such a situation, the Act requires that this child remain in placement "A" and that the school district continue to pay for a child's education in placement "A" as it had done previously. Any refusal by the school district to continue payment would amount to a change in placement prohibited by the Act. *See Gargani* v. *The School Committee of the City of Cranston,* No. 77-0612, slip op. at 7 (D.R.I. May 4, 1978). Thus, the maintenance of the status quo under the Act requires not only that a child be educated in the same placement during any proceeding under the Act, but also that no change in the financing of that placement occur.

Unlike the hypothetical situation, the maintenance of the status quo in the Monahan case does not require that the defendants pay for Daniel's education pending resolution of this litigation. The status quo in the instant case is Daniel's placement at George Norris paid for by Daniel's father. In contrast to the hypothetical situation, the Omaha School District had at no time paid the costs of the George Norris placement. Thus, the case does not present a situation where the school district has refused to continue to provide financial assistance which it had given prior to the filing of the complaint. To maintain the status quo in the instant case, Daniel should remain in his then current placement at George Norris and his father should continue to pay the costs of the placement as he has done in the past. Requiring the Omaha School District to finance the George Norris placement would be a change in the status quo, since such payments had never been provided in the past.

*Plaintiff Rose*

The factual setting of the Rose claim is similar to the hypothetical situation set out above. Prior to the 1978–79 school year, Marla was attending Beveridge Junior High School. In June of 1978, Marla's parents received notice of a proposed change of placement. The Roses were not satisfied with this proposed change and filed a complaint with the local school authorities in the summer of 1978. Although various administrative and judicial proceedings followed the filing of this complaint, the facts presented here are sufficient to determine Marla's then current educational placement under 20 U.S.C. § 1415(e)(3).

Under § 1415(e)(3), Marla is entitled to remain in her then current educational placement throughout any of the proceedings which are held pursuant to the Act. The then current educational placement is determined at the time that a complaint is filed under the Act. *Stuart* v. *Nappi, supra,* 443 F. Supp. at 1241. In the instant case, Marla's educational placement at the time her father filed a complaint with the Omaha School District was at the Beveridge Junior High School, where she attended both regular and special education classes. The cost of this placement was borne by the Omaha School District. Thus, this placement is her then current educational placement under § 1415(e)(3) and she is entitled to remain in this placement throughout all the proceedings held under the Act. In addition, the cost of this placement shall be borne by the Omaha School District.

This holding which requires Marla to be readmitted to the Omaha public schools does not mean that Marla must be placed in Beveridge Junior High. If other schools can provide the same type of education that she received at Beveridge, then placement in those schools would satisfy 20 U.S.C. § 1415(e)(3). See Stipulation of the Parties in CV 79-0-300 [Exhibit # 6].

* * *

NOTES

1.  The *Stemple* and *Monahan* decisions have serious negative ramifications for parents of children with handicaps that make time spent without appropriate education virtually unrecoverable. Such children could spend months and even years without appropriate education while their cases go through the due process continuum and the judicial process if their parents lacked the necessary funds to pay for the type of placement that was required.

Such a result, seemingly inconsistent with the intent of P.L. 94-142, could have been avoided had the courts in *Stemple* and *Monahan* allowed the parents to place their child, at public expense, in what they considered to be an appropriate placement. If a final determination is made that the placement chosen was inappropriate, then they could be ordered to repay the school agency all amounts expended for the inappropriate placement.

While there is obvious potential for abuse of such an approach, it would seem to be outweighed by the damage done certain handicapped children under the *Stemple* and *Monahan* approach. Additionally, there is potential for abuse by school agencies of the latter approach since they have a duty to provide a free, appropriate education to handicapped children only up to a certain age, generally 21. Thus handicapped children have only a certain period of time in which to "collect" their free, appropriate education. By denying the child the appropriate placement, the school agency could save itself the expense of its provision for whatever period of time was necessary for the administrative and/or judicial process to make a final determination, a period of time that can often be quite lengthy. There is little to deter school agencies from taking advantage of this maneuver as few courts have been willing to allow a handicapped child to receive free, appropriate education past the age of 21 designed to compensate the child for previous inappropriate education. See Note 2 below.

2.   The issue of the availability of monetary damages under P.L. 94-142 has been a contentious one. Some courts have held that the statute allows for a damage remedy, e.g., *Boxall* v. *Sequoia Union School District*, 464 F. Supp. 1104 (N.D. Cal. 1979); or that damages can be recovered under special circumstances, e.g., *Anderson* v. *Thompson*, 658 F.2d 1205 (7th Cir. 1981) (damages available in exceptional circumstances); *Tatro* v. *State of Texas*, 516 F. Supp. 968 (N.D. Tx. 1981) (damages available where parents must pay for costs of alternative sources of education due to school's failure to provide a required related service which would allow child to be educated without risk of harm); *Campbell* v. *Talladega County Board of Education*, 518 F. Supp. 47 (N.D. Ala. 1981) (school agency ordered to provide educational services to retarded child for 2 years past the age of 21, in order to compensate for past educational deprivations).

However, the majority of courts have held that no damage remedy is available under P.L. 94-142, e.g., *Hines* v. *Pitt County Board of Education*, 497 F. Supp. 403 (E.D.N.C. 1980); *Meiner* v. *Missouri*, 498 F. Supp. 944 (E.D. Mo. 1980). Other courts have held that even if there is a damage remedy available under P.L. 94-142, such a remedy cannot be applied against a State defendant, because of 11th Amendment immunity. See *Hark* v. *School District of Philadelphia*, 505 F. Supp. 727 (E.D. Pa. 1980).

3.   Another issue frequently litigated with regard to P.L. 94-142 is the availability of attorney's fees under the statute. Courts generally have awarded attorney's fees to the prevailing party in special education cases filed under Sec. 504. See, for example, *Fells* v. *Brooks*, 522 F. Supp. 30 (D.D.C. 1981). However, most courts have shown a reluctance to award attorney's fees in cases filed under P.L. 94-142, since that statute, unlike Sec. 504, does not have a specific section authorizing awards of attorney's fees. See, for example, *Hines* v. *Pitt County Board of Education*, 497 F. Supp. 403 (E.D.N.C. 1980).

The *Hines* court also ruled that although the case was filed under both P.L. 94-142 and Sec. 504, attorney's fees were not available under Sec. 504 because the P.L. 94-142 claim was the focal point of the litigation, with little reliance placed on the Sec. 504 claim by the plaintiffs. Other courts have granted attorney's fees in such cases without considering the extent of the role played by either statute.

Most courts have ruled that where a Sec. 1983 claim is appended to a P.L. 94-142 claim, no attorney's fees can be awarded pursuant to the Sec. 1983 claim because the Sec. 1983 claim added nothing to the P.L. 94-142 claim. See, for example, *Tatro* v. *Texas*, 516 F. Supp. 968 (N.D. Tex. 1981). However, where effective relief was available only under Sec. 1983, in a case filed under both P.L. 94-142 and

Sec. 1983 one court awarded attorney's fees but only for the work performed while Sec. 1983 provided the only effective remedy.

### b.  Dealing with Handicaps as Disciplinary Problems

p. 273—INSERT, after Note 2, the following:

### S-1 v. TURLINGTON

*United States Court of Appeals for the Fifth Circuit, 1981*
*635 F.2d 342*

Before VANCE, HATCHETT and ANDERSON, Circuit Judges.

HATCHETT, Circuit Judge.

In this appeal, we are called upon to decide whether nine handicapped students were denied their rights under the provisions of the Education for All Handicapped Children Act, 20 U.S.C. §§ 1401–1415, or section 504 of the Rehabilitation Act of 1973, codified at 29 U.S.C. § 794, and their implementing regulations. The trial court found a denial of rights and entered a preliminary injunction against the state and local officials. Defendants attack the trial court's entry of a preliminary injunction as an abuse of discretion. Because we find that the trial court did not abuse its discretion in entering the preliminary injunction, we affirm.

Facts

Plaintiffs, S-1, S-2, S-3, S-4, S-5, S-6, and S-8, were expelled from Clewiston High School, Hendry County, Florida, in the early part of the 1977–78 school year for alleged misconduct. Each was expelled for the remainder of the 1977–78 school year and for the entire 1978–79 school year, the maximum time permitted by state law. All of the plaintiffs were classified as either educable mentally retarded (EMR), mildly mentally retarded, or EMR/dull normal. It is undisputed that the expelled plaintiffs were accorded the procedural protections required by *Goss* v. *Lopez,* 419 U.S. 565, 95 S.Ct. 729, 42 L.Ed.2d 725 (1975). Except for S-1, they were not given, nor did they request, hearings to determine whether their misconduct was a manifestation of their handicap. Regarding S-1, the superintendent of Hendry County Schools determined that because S-1 was not classified as seriously emotionally disturbed, his misconduct, as a matter of law, could not be a manifestation of his handicap.

At all material times, plaintiffs S-7 and S-9 were not under expulsion orders. S-7 was not enrolled in high school by his own choice. In October, 1978, he requested a due process hearing to determine if he had been evaluated or if he had an individualized educational program. S-9 made a similar request in October, 1978. Shortly before her request, S-9's guardian had consented to the individualized educational program being offered her during that school year. The superintendent denied both student's requests, but offered to hold conferences in order to discuss the appropriateness of their individualized educational programs.

Plaintiffs initiated this case alleging violations of their rights under the Education for all Handicapped Children Act, (EHA) 20 U.S.C. §§ 1401–1415, and section 504 of the Rehabilitation Act of 1973, 29 U.S.C. § 794. Plaintiffs sought preliminary and permanent injunctive relief compelling state and local officials to provide them with the educational services and procedural rights required by the EHA, section 504, and their implementing regulations.

\* \* \*

## Statement of Issues

In an appeal from an order granting preliminary relief, the applicable standard of review is whether the issuance of the injunction, in light of the applicable standard, constitutes an abuse of discretion. *Doran* v. *Salem Inn, Inc.,* 422 U.S. 922, 95 S.Ct. 2561, 45 L.Ed.2d 648 (1975); *Canal Authority of State of Florida* v. *Callaway,* 489 F.2d 567 (5th Cir. 1974). Therefore, in order to decide whether the trial court abused its discretion in entering the preliminary injunction, we must resolve the following issues: (1) whether an expulsion is a change in educational placement thereby invoking the procedural protections of the EHA and section 504; (2) whether the EHA, section 504, and their implementing regulations contemplate a dual system of discipline for handicapped and non-handicapped students; (3) whether the burden of raising the question, whether a student's misconduct is a manifestation of the student's handicap, is on the state and local officials or on the student; (4) whether the EHA and its implementing regulations required the local defendants to grant S-7 and S-9 due process hearings; and, (5) whether the trial judge properly entered the preliminary injunction against the state defendants.

\* \* \*

## First Issue

With regard to plaintiff S-1, the trial court found that the school officials entrusted with the expulsion decision determined at the disciplinary proceedings that S-1's misconduct was unrelated to his handicap. The trial court, however, held that this determination was made by school board officials who lacked the necessary expertise to make such a determination. The trial court arrived at this conclusion by holding that an expulsion is a change in educational placement. Under 45 CFR § 121a.533(a)(3) and 45 CFR § 84.35(c)(3), evaluations and placement decisions must be made by a specialized and knowledgeable group of persons.

The trial court's finding presents the novel issue in this circuit whether an expulsion is a change in educational placement, thereby invoking the procedural pro-tections of both the EHA and section 504 of the Rehabilitation Act. In deciding this issue, the EHA and section 504, as remedial statutes, should be broadly applied and liberally construed in favor of providing a free and appropriate education to handi-capped students.

The EHA, section 504, and their implementing regulations do not provide this court any direction on this issue. We find the reasoning of the district court in *Stuart* v. *Nappi,* 443 F.Supp. 1235 (D. Conn. 1978), persuasive. In *Stuart,* a child was diag-nosed as having a major learning disability caused by either a brain disfunction or a perceptual disorder. She challenged the use of disciplinary proceedings which, if completed, would have resulted in her expulsion for participating in a schoolwide disturbance. The trial court held that the proposed expulsion constituted a change in educational placement, thus requiring the school officials to adhere to the procedural protections of the EHA. In so holding, the court stated:

> The right to an education in the least restrictive environment may be circumvented if schools are permitted to expel handicapped children [without following the procedures prescribed by the EHA]. . . . An expulsion has the effect not only of changing a student's placement, but also of restricting the availability of alternative placements. For example, plaintiff's expulsion may well exclude her from a placement that is appropriate for her academic and social development. This result flies in the face of the explicit mandate of the handicapped act which requires that all placement decisions be made in conformity with a child's right to an education in the least restrictive environment. [Citation omitted.]

443 F.Supp. at 1242–43.

We agree with the district court in *Stuart,* and therefore hold that a termination of educational services, occasioned by an expulsion, is a change in educational placement, thereby invoking the procedural protections of the EHA.

The proposition that an expulsion is a change in educational placement has been cited with approval in *Sherry* v. *New York State Education Department,* 479 F.Supp 1328 (W.D.N.Y. 1979) (legally blind and deaf student that suffered from brain damage and emotional disorder which made her self abusive suspended because of insufficient staff to care for her), and *Doe* v. *Koger,* 480 F.Supp. 225 (N.D.Ind. 1979) (EHA case in which mildly mentally handicapped student was expelled for the remainder of the school term for disciplinary reasons pursuant to the procedures provided for all Indiana public school disciplinary expulsions). As stated by the district court in *Doe* v. *Koger,* our holding that expulsion of a handicapped student constitutes a change in educational placement distinguishes the handicapped student in that, "unlike any other disruptive child, before a disruptive handicapped child can be expelled, it must be determined whether the handicap is the cause of the child's propensity to disrupt. This issue must be determined through the change of placement procedures required by the handicapped act." *Doe* v. *Koger,* 480 F.Supp. at 229.[9]

Second Issue

The school officials point out that a group of persons entrusted with the educational placement decision could never decide that expulsion is the correct placement for a handicapped student, thus insulating a handicapped student from expulsion as a disciplinary tool. They further state that Florida law does not contemplate this result because expulsion is specifically provided for under Florida law as a disciplinary tool

---

[9]This opinion does not infringe upon the traditional authority and responsibility of the local school board to ensure a safe school environment. A comment to the regulations provides: "While the placement may not be changed, this does not preclude dealing with children who are endangering themselves or others." 45 C.F.R. § 121(a)513 (comment). Thus the local school board retains the authority to remove a handicapped child from a particular setting upon a proper finding that the child is endangering himself or others. In such case, the child would of course be remanded to the special change of placement procedures for reassignment to an appropriate placement. It is appropriate to superimpose this very limited authority, as contemplated by the above quoted comment, because nothing in the statute, the regulations, or the legislative history suggests that Congress intended to remove from local school boards who alone are accountable to the entire school community their long-recognized authority and responsibility to ensure a safe school environment.

for all students. While the trial court declined to decide the issue whether a handicapped student can ever be expelled, we cannot ignore the gray areas that may result if we do not decide this question. We therefore find that expulsion is still a proper disciplinary tool under the EHA and section 504 when proper procedures are utilized and under proper circumstances. We cannot, however, authorize the complete cessation of educational services during an expulsion period.

## Third Issue

State defendants focus their attention on the fact that, with the exception of S-1, none of the expelled plaintiffs raised the argument, until eleven months after expulsion, that they could not be expelled unless the proper persons determined that their handicap did not bear a causal connection to their misconduct. By this assertion, we assume that state defendants contend that the handicapped students waived their right to this determination. The issue is therefore squarely presented whether the burden of raising the question whether a student's misconduct is a manifestation of the student's handicap is on the state and local officials or on the student. The EHA, section 504, and their implementing regulations do not prescribe who must raise this issue. In light of the remedial purposes of these statutes, we find that the burden is on the local and state defendants to make this determination. Our conclusion is buttressed by the fact that in most cases, the handicapped students and their parents lack the wherewithal either to know or to assert their rights under the EHA and section 504.

## Fourth Issue

The next issue is whether the EHA and its implementing regulations required the local defendants to grant S-7 and S-9 due process hearings. The school officials suggest that because S-7 had voluntarily withdrawn from school, he was not entitled to a due process hearing. With regard to S-9, the school officials assert that because she had previously agreed to the educational program being offered her during the school year, she was not entitled to a due process hearing. They also suggest that the conference offered by the superintendent was an adequate substitute for the due process hearings. They cite 45 CFR 121a.506 as support for their argument. Under this regulation, the Department of Health, Education and Welfare (HEW) (now Health and Human Services), states in a comment that mediation can be used to resolve differences between parents and agencies without the development of an adversarial relationship.

The Justice Department, as amicus curiae, and the trial court, point out that under 20 U.S.C. § 1415(b)(1), parents and guardians of handicapped children must have "an opportunity to present complaints with respect to *any* matter relating to the identification, evaluation, or educational placement of the child, or the provision of a free appropriate public education to such child." (Emphasis added.) The statute also states, in section 1415(b), that "whenever a complaint has been received under paragraph (1) of this subsection, the parents or guardian shall have an opportunity for an impartial due process hearing. . . ." No exception is made for handicapped students who voluntarily withdraw from school or previously agree to an educational placement. With regard to defendants' argument under 45 CFR § 121a.506, HEW states in the same comment that mediation may not be used to deny or delay a parent's rights under this subpart. In the circumstances, the trial judge correctly found that plaintiffs S-7 and S-9 were entitled to due process hearings.

### Fifth Issue

State defendants advance three arguments that deserve comment. First, they assert that the trial judge erred in analyzing section 504 in light of the Supreme Court's decision in *Southeastern Community College* v. *Davis,* 442 U.S. 397, 99 S.Ct. 2361, 60 L.Ed.2d 980 (1979). In that case, the issue was whether section 504, which prohibits discrimination against an otherwise qualified handicapped individual enrolled in a federally funded program, solely by reason of his handicap, forbids professional schools from imposing physical qualifications for admission to their clinical training program. The Supreme Court held that section 504 did not forbid professional schools from imposing physical qualifications for admission. Without discussing *Southeastern* any further, it is clear that it does not apply to this case. Physical qualifications are not at issue in this case. Furthermore, we do not deal here with a professional school.

Secondly, state defendants argue that the trial court erred in imposing the EHA as a requirement at the time of the expulsions because the EHA was not effective in Florida until September 1, 1978. The trial court did not impose the EHA as a requirement at the time of the expulsion. The court found that the expelled plaintiffs became entitled to the protections of the EHA on September 1, 1978. As such, the expelled plaintiffs became entitled to a free and appropriate education in the least restrictive environment. In fact, under 20 U.S.C. § 1412(3), because plaintiffs were not receiving educational services on September 1, 1978, they fell within a special class of handicapped students entitled to priority regarding the provision of a free and appropriate education. The only way in which the expulsions could have continued as of September 1, 1978, is if a qualified group of individuals determined that no relationship existed between the plaintiffs' handicap and their misconduct. Furthermore, section 504, effective at the time of the expulsions, provides protections and procedures similar to those of the EHA. *See North* v. *District of Columbia Board of Education,* 471 F.Supp. 136 (D.D.C. 1979).

Finally, the state officials argue that the trial court improperly entered the injunction against them. They assert that they lack the authority to intervene in the expulsion proceedings because disciplinary matters are exclusively local. While this argument may be true regarding nonhandicapped students, it is inapplicable to handicapped students. Expulsion proceedings are of the type that may serve to deny an education to those entitled to it under the EHA. Under 20 U.S.C. § 1412(6), the state educational agency is:

> Responsible for assuring that the requirements of this sub-chapter be carried out and that all educational programs for handicapped children within the state, including all such programs administered by any other state or local agency, will be under the general supervision of the persons responsible for educational programs for handicapped children in the state educational agency and shall meet educational standards of the state educational agency.

Clearly, the state officials were empowered to intervene in the expulsion proceedings under 20 U.S.C. § 1412(6).

## Conclusion

Accordingly, we hold that under the EHA, section 504, and their implementing regulations: (1) before a handicapped student can be expelled, a trained and knowledgeable group of persons must determine whether the student's misconduct bears a relationship to his handicapping condition; (2) an expulsion is a change in educational placement thereby invoking the procedural protections of the EHA and section 504; (3) expulsion is a proper disciplinary tool under the EHA and section 504, but a complete cessation of educational services is not; (4) S-7 and S-9 were entitled to due process hearings; and, (5) the trial judge properly entered the preliminary injunction against the state defendants. In the circumstances, the trial judge did not abuse his discretion in entering the injunction.

AFFIRMED.

## NOTES

1.  Prior to *Turlington,* most courts that had touched on the issue ruled that a handicapped child could be expelled, i.e., have all educational services terminated, if the child's disruptive behavior was shown to be unrelated to his or her handicap. See, for example, *Doe* v. *Koger,* 480 F. Supp. 225 (N.D. Ind. 1979). The *Turlington* court, by way of dicta, indicates that a complete cessation of educational services would violate Sec. 504 and P.L. 94-142. For the *Turlington* court, an expulsion means the child's permanent removal from his or her current educational placement only.

2.  The *Turlington* court notes that the P.L. 94-142 regulations allow schools to immediately, i.e., prior to the due process hearings, change a handicapped child's placement in an emergency situation. The regulations do not specifically allow parents an analogous privilege. Under the "then current placement" provision discussed in the *Stemple* and *Monahan* cases, above at p. 65 and p. 68, parents cannot remove their handicapped child from his or her current placement. Any unilateral change in placement initiated by the parents would have to be funded by the parents under the *Stemple* and *Monahan* rationales.

However, in *Tatro* v. *Texas,* 516 F. Supp. 968 (N.D. Tex. 1981), the court allowed parents to be reimbursed for expenses incurred in placing their handicapped child in a placement different from that offered by the school. The *Tatro* court distinguished its ruling from that in *Stemple* and *Monahan* on the basis that it was dealing with a situation where the child was applying for initial admission and where the placement offered by the school could have possibly endangered the child. The *Tatro* ruling can thus be viewed to some extent as a judicial creation of a limited emergency privilege for parents.

### c.  Placement Alternatives

p. 293—INSERT after the Note the following:

## SPRINGDALE SCHOOL DISTRICT v. GRACE
*United States Court of Appeals for the Eighth Circuit, 1981*
*656 F.2d 300*

Before HEANEY and HENLEY, Circuit Judges, and NICHOL, Senior District Judge.

NICHOL, Senior District Judge.

This is an appeal by the plaintiff-appellant, Springdale School District # 50 of Washington County (Springdale School), from the judgment of the district court in favor of the defendant-appellees, Sherry Grace and her parents, the Arkansas State Department of Education and its director, and the State Board of Education and its members. The district court found that under the provisions of the Education for All Handicapped Children Act, 20 U.S.C. sections 1401–1461 (1970) (Act), the Springdale School could provide Sherry Grace with a free appropriate education. Based upon this finding the district court affirmed the decision of the Arkansas Department of Education with respect to the Individualized Education Program (IEP) developed for the 1979–80 school year for Sherry Grace. We affirm.

The facts giving rise to the present controversy are well set out by the district court opinion. *Springdale School Dist. v. Grace,* 494 F.Supp. 266 (W.D. Ark. 1980). Sherry Grace is an eleven year old girl who is profoundly and prelingually deaf, having either been born deaf or lost her hearing before she developed speech. She has a 95% loss of hearing which renders her completely deaf for all purposes.

Sherry received no formal education or training in communication until, at the age of four, she was enrolled in a special program for children with hearing impairments at Bates Elementary School in Fayetteville, Arkansas. Since the children in this program retain some hearing they are orally instructed. A person like Sherry who is profoundly deaf can only visually receive instructions. As the district court found, "(I)f one is profoundly and prelingually deaf, he lacks the concept of language and must not only receive visual instruction, but also must be taught the most rudimentary matters concerning language." *Springdale School Dist. v. Grace, supra* at 267. The Bates program for hearing impaired children proved inadequate to meet Sherry's needs, and although in the program for two years Sherry made little or no progress. When she left the Bates program Sherry's language level was that of a child of two years and two months.

When Sherry was six years old her parents moved to Little Rock, Arkansas, and there enrolled Sherry in the Arkansas School for the Deaf as a day student. Sherry attended the School for the Deaf for three years. The school employs the total communication system. While there she progressed from having a language level of a two year old to being able to read at the second grade level. Since she was able to communicate with others and participate in the life of the school, her confidence and social ability also developed.

After three years in Little Rock, Sherry's parents, over the protests of Sherry's teacher, took Sherry out of the School for the Deaf and moved back to Springdale, Arkansas. There they enrolled Sherry in the fourth grade at the Springdale School.

After testing Sherry and consulting with her parents the Springdale School formulated an IEP for Sherry. The IEP noted that Sherry should be taught by a certified teacher of the deaf who employs total communication. Sherry's lack of the skills of the average fourth grader in reading, spelling and arithmetic, and her below level general knowledge prompted the Springdale School in the IEP to state that the Arkansas School for the Deaf was the proper school to meet Sherry's unique needs.

Although the Graces otherwise agreed with the Springdale School's assessment of Sherry's needs, they disagreed with that portion of the IEP which stated that the School for the Deaf was the proper school for Sherry. Under the provisions of the Act a temporary IEP was formulated allowing for Sherry to remain at the Springdale School while her parents sought review of the disputed portion of the IEP. See 20 U.S.C. section 1415 for procedural safeguards. After proper notice and pre-hearing conferences a due process hearing was held on November 7, 1979. The hearing officer reversed the disputed portion of the IEP holding that the Springdale School was wrong and that Sherry could receive an appropriate education at the Springdale School. The Springdale School appealed to the Coordinator, Department of Education Special Education Section, who affirmed the decision of the hearing officer. Upon affirmance, in January, 1980, a full-time certified teacher of the deaf was provided for Sherry.

In February, 1980, the Springdale School initiated this action in district court pursuant to section 1415(e)(2) of the Act seeking review of the appeals officer's decision that Sherry be educated at the Springdale School and not sent to the School for the Deaf. The district court initially found that the Arkansas School for the Deaf could provide Sherry with the *best free education. Springdale School Dist.* v. *Grace, supra* at 271. The court, however, went on to hold that the Act requires simply that the State, through its local educational district, provide each handicapped child with a *free, appropriate education. Id.* at 272. The court then held that, under the standard set forth in the Act, a preponderance of the evidence proved that the Springdale School could provide Sherry with an appropriate education. The court also found that the Springdale School satisfies the requirements of mainstreaming found in the Act. 20 U.S.C. sections 1412(5)(B) and 1414(a)(1)(C)(iv). *Id.* at 273. Finally, the district court granted the Grace's motion for an injunction forcing the Springdale School to provide Sherry with a certified teacher of the deaf for the 1980–81 term only. The court denied the Grace's request for attorney fees.

The Springdale School filed this timely appeal. Three issues are raised for consideration by the Court:

1. Whether the district court's ruling that Sherry could be appropriately educated at the Springdale School as opposed to the School for the Deaf is an erroneous interpretation of the law and contrary to the Act and/or Arkansas law?
2. Whether the district court's finding that the Springdale School could provide Sherry an appropriate education is clearly erroneous?
3. Whether the district court erred in holding that it had no jurisdiction to consider the Arkansas law?

The Act requires that Sherry be provided with a free appropriate education. 20 U.S.C. section 1412. In order to determine what is appropriate to meet the handicapped child's needs the Act requires that an IEP be developed at least annually for the child. 20 U.S.C. section 1414(a)(5). It is the 1979–80 IEP that is at issue here.

It is evident from the well reasoned opinion of the district court that the question of what educational facility is appropriate for Sherry was carefully considered and analyzed. The district court found that the School for the Deaf would provide Sherry with the *best* education. In reaching this conclusion the court noted that the most important thing for Sherry at this stage of life was to learn language skills and that the School for the Deaf is the best place for that purpose. The School for the Deaf would also provide Sherry with proper role models since many of the people employed there are themselves profoundly deaf. Further, Sherry would be able to practice total communication in school as well as in many extra-curricular activities such as Girl Scouts.

The district court, although convinced that the best place for Sherry is the School for the Deaf, correctly followed the Act's requirements when it determined that it was not the State's duty to provide the *best* education, but instead states are required to provide an *appropriate* education.

A definitive answer to what constitutes an appropriate education is lacking in the Act and the regulations promulgated thereunder. Therefore, the courts, in reviewing claims brought under the Act have attempted to establish standards for determining what is an appropriate education. The results are far short of uniform. They run a broad spectrum. *Kruelle* v. *Biggs,* 489 F.Supp. 169 (D. Del. 1980) (Maximization of learning potential); *Rowley* v. *Bd. of Ed. of Hendrick Hudson Cent. S.D.,* 483 F.Supp. 528 (S.D.N.Y. 1980) (full potential commensurate with opportunity provided to nonhandicapped children); *DeWalt* v. *Burkholder,* 3 E.H.L.R. 551:550 (E.D.Va. 1980) (most appropriate); *Armstrong* v. *Kline,* 476 F.Supp. 583 (E.D.Pa. 1979) (sufficient to make handicapped person independent and self-sufficient).

The district court adopted, and we affirm the standard set forth in *Rowley* v. *Bd. of Ed. of Hendrick Hudson Cent. S.D., supra* at 534:

> An ''appropriate education'' could mean an ''adequate'' education—that is, an education substantial enough to facilitate a child's progress from one grade to another and to enable him or her to earn a high school diploma. An ''appropriate education'' could also mean one which enables the handicapped child to achieve his or her full potential. Between those two extremes, however, is a standard which I conclude is more in keeping with the regulations, with the Equal Protection decisions which motivated the passage of the Act, and with common sense. This standard would require that each handicapped child be given the opportunity to achieve his full potential commensurate with the opportunity provided to other children.

The *Rowley* standard provides the handicapped child with the opportunity to achieve her full potential but takes into account that such a task is equally fair and feasible only to the extent that such opportunity must be commensurate with the opportunity granted to nonhandicapped in the same system. The district court noted, as did the court in *Rowley, supra* at 534, and we are greatly swayed by it, that:

> The school provides the nonhandicapped child an opportunity to learn the basics and to learn them well enough so that he might excel in his secondary courses. But the Springdale school does not turn every one of its students into academicians or profes-

sionals, or even successful secondary students. The home life of the child, his parents' interests and the child's cultural and sociological environment often determine the child's academic success and attainment or lack of such.

*Springdale School Dist.* v. *Grace, supra* at 272. Sherry will be receiving instruction in reading, arithmetic, spelling, telling of time, health, social sciences and art by a certified teacher of the deaf along with instruction in manual communication, lip reading, writing and speaking. As the district court observed, although it is likely that Sherry could learn more quickly at the School for the Deaf, both schools would be teaching her through certified teachers of the deaf. The fact that Sherry may not, like many nonhandicapped children, reach her full potential is not due to any error in the district court's interpretation of the Act or its finding that the Springdale School could appropriately educate Sherry, but instead may well result from forces outside the school environment. The Act cannot remedy a child's cultural and sociological environment nor force parents, by threatening to remove the child from the home, to become partners with the state in insuring that a child reach her full potential. We therefore agree with the district court that Sherry will be offered, through the extra services provided, an opportunity to achieve her full potential commensurate with the opportunity offered to all the Springdale School students and thus will receive an appropriate education at the Springdale School.

Our holding today is further supported by the mainstreaming requirements of the Act. Sections 1412(5)(B) and 1414(a)(1)(C)(iv) of the Act require that "to the maximum extent" possible, without sacrificing the child's right to an appropriate education, the handicapped must be educated with the nonhandicapped. The regulations required that the handicapped child not only be educated as close to home as possible, but also that when possible the child should be educated in the school which he or she would attend if not handicapped. At the Springdale School Sherry would be with nonhandicapped children for physical education, library, and possibly penmanship, science, health, social studies, music and art. At the School for the Deaf, however, Sherry would have virtually no contact with nonhandicapped children. Although Sherry's case does appear to be one in which an institution would better serve her needs, the Act's requirements are clear. The district court properly found that Sherry can receive an appropriate education at the Springdale School which also allows her to be educated with nonhandicapped students.

The Springdale School's final allegation of error on the part of the district court involves the district court's refusal to consider Arkansas law as it applies to this controversy. We find this argument to be without merit. The complaint filed by the Springdale School sought review, under section 1415(e) of the Act, of the administrative proceedings provided for under the Act. The applicable law and standards set forth thereunder are federal, and the district court was not required to apply state law. If every state had a different standard for determining "appropriate," the needs of some handicapped children "may not be adequately met if the local programs are measured against a statutory goal which is permitted to vary with the happenstance of the state in which the child lives." *Battle* v. *Com. of Pa.*, 629 F.2d 269, 284 (3d Cir. 1980) (Sloviter, Circuit Judge, dissenting). The district court was not incorrect in limiting its review to the applicable federal law.

AFFIRMED.

NOTE

The decision in *Springdale* provides a good illustration of the full scope of the concept of an appropriate education as it has been defined by P.L. 94-142. The concept, as the court points out, includes not only strictly educational components, but also the least restrictive environment provision, which must be taken into account by educators before developing an educational program for a handicapped child.

## ESPINO V. BESTEIRO
*United States District Court for the Southern District of Texas, 1981*
*520 F. Supp. 905*

Memorandum and Order

VELA, District Judge.

This action was brought by Raul Espino, Jr., a seven year old multi-handicapped child who cannot adequately regulate his body temperature, by and through his parents, seeking declaratory and injunctive relief and damages for the alleged failure of Defendants to provide him with an education in the "least restrictive environment appropriate to his individuals needs." It is alleged that the failure of Defendants to provide Raul with a fully air-conditioned classroom wherein he can interact fully with his peers, and their decision instead to provide him with an air-conditioned plexiglass cubicle within a regular non air-conditioned classroom, violate the Education for All Handicapped Children Act of 1975 (EAHCA), 20 U.S.C. §§ 1401–1420, and the regulations promulgated thereunder; the Rehabilitation Act of 1973, § 504, 29 U.S.C. § 794; and the Civil Rights Act of 1871, 42 U.S.C. § 1983. Pendent claims based on Texas statutory law are also made.

An evidentiary hearing was held on Plaintiffs' Motion for Preliminary Injunction on August 3, 1981. Based on a preponderance of the evidence, this Court is of the opinion that Plaintiffs' Motion is meritorious in that plaintiffs have demonstrated a likelihood of success on the merits of their claim under the EAHCA and its implementing regulations and have met the other requisites for equitable relief. Plaintiffs' Motion for Preliminary Injunction is therefore GRANTED in accordance with the terms of this Memorandum and Order.

\* \* \*

*II. Likelihood of Success on the Merits*

The EAHCA is a remedial statute and should be broadly applied and liberally construed in favor of providing an appropriate education to handicapped students. *S-1 v. Turlington*, 635 F.2d 342, 347 (5th Cir. 1981). The problem before this court can thus be stated in relatively simple terms—is Raul Espino, Jr. being provided with an "appropriate education" under the EAHCA? For the reasons set forth below, this court feels that Plaintiffs have demonstrated that they are likely to prevail on their contention that Raul is not being provided with an appropriate education.

The "mainstreaming" provisions of the EAHCA, as set out previously, require that a handicapped child be educated with his non-handicapped peers "to the maximum extent appropriate" and that any removal from the regular educational environment occurs only when the nature of the handicap is such that education in regular classes with the use of supplementary aids "cannot be achieved satisfactorily." 20 U.S.C. § 1412(5)(B). *See Tatro* v. *Texas*, 625 F.2d 557, 561 (5th Cir. 1980). In the case at bar, it is undisputed that air-conditioning is a supplementary aid or "related service" which Raul Espino, Jr. needs in order to be able to attend school during the hotter months of the year. There is no evidence to suggest that a fully air-conditioned environment would be inappropriate for Raul's educational needs. There is also no evidence which suggests that a regular classroom at Egly Elementary cannot be satisfactorily modified to provide such an environment. In this set of circumstances it seems self evident that the decision to provide air-conditioning for Raul in a plexiglass cubicle, and therefore at times segregate him from his non-handicapped classmates, is prima facie a violation of the mainstreaming provisions of the EAHCA.

Assuming that Raul's placement in the cubicle is not to the "maximum extent appropriate," the analysis then must focus on whether it is a reasonably appropriate accommodation in that it provides for Raul's special needs "to the maximum extent practicable" and consistent with the mainstreaming provisions of the Act. 20 U.S.C. § 1414(a)(1)(C)(iv). One court has suggested that the important personal needs of an individual handicapped child must be balanced against the realities of limited funding in reaching a reasonable accommodation. *Pinkerton* v. *Moye*, 509 F.Supp. 107, 112–13 (W.D.Va.1981). At least one commentator has recognized that "appropriate" cannot mean the best possible education a school can provide if given access to unlimited funds, but that the EAHCA contemplates a standard between the best education and merely opening the doors of a regular classroom to those capable of learning without special assistance. Note, *Enforcing the Right to An "Appropriate" Education: The Education for All Handicapped Children Act of 1975*, 92 Harv.L.Rev. 1103, 1125 (1979). *See also, Pinkerton, supra*, at 113. Defendants in this case have not made a serious contention that maintaining a fully air-conditioned environment for Raul is prohibited by the financial condition of the BISD. The evidence presented suggests that the cost of air-conditioning a classroom would be minimal in relation to the amount of federal funds received by BISD and BISD's total budget. Balancing the important needs of Raul Espino, Jr. for an air-conditioned environment within which he can be effectively mainstreamed and interact fully with non-handicapped students, against the cost to BISD of providing him with such an environment, it cannot be said that the provision of an air-conditioned cubicle, with its concomitant isolative effect on Raul when it is being used, represents a reasonable accommodation resulting from the fiscal impracticability of providing air-conditioning for him to the maximum extent appropriate.

Realizing that the concept of "practicability" is not necessarily limited to monetary considerations, this court must analyze the other reasons advanced for the existence of the cubicle to determine whether it presents a reasonably appropriate accommodation. Superintendent Besteiro felt that a fully air-conditioned classroom for Raul's class might open "Pandora's box" in that parents of children in non-air-conditioned classrooms and the children's teachers would complain of unequal treatment in that one teacher and Raul's classmates would receive the benefits of air-conditioning during the hot months of the school year. Yet, Mr. Besteiro testified that he had received no official requests seeking air-conditioning for students other than

Raul. A purely theoretical risk of parental or teacher complaints is probably insufficient to offset the countervailing needs of Raul Espino, Jr. for an education with his peers "to the maximum extent appropriate" and does not substantially justify segregation from his classmates in the cubicle. *See New York State Ass'n for Retarded Children, Inc.* v. *Carey,* 466 F.Supp. 487, 503 (E.D.N.Y.1979). The same rationale applies to Dr. Schraer's reasoning that he thought it would be difficult to maintain a stable temperature for Raul in an air-conditioned classroom full of children. (This argument is further weakened by the fact that Raul has experienced no difficulty in the school's air-conditioned cafeteria while attending lunch with other students and by the fact that Raul is now able to tolerate a higher range of temperature variance.)

Dr. Schraer additionally felt that provision of an air-conditioned classroom for Raul and its derivative benefits to his nonhandicapped classmates would violate Bulletin 871 of the state's Special Education Program, since it allows the use of funds for a specific handicapped child but does not refer to expenditures of funds on nonhandicapped children. The evidence indicates that at institutions like the Lincoln Park School, the state allows handicapped children who do not medically need air-conditioning (e.g.—the mentally retarded) to derive its benefits from classmates who do need it. The evidence also indicated that Bulletin 871 does not allow for the expenditure of special education funds on air-conditioning for visually handicapped students who do not need it for medical reasons. Yet, the Regional School for the Deaf, who students presumably have no medical need for air-conditioning, is provided with an air-conditioned classroom. In this state of affairs it is by no means clear that it would necessarily violate the Bulletin if Raul's non-handicapped classmates would derive benefits from funds expended for Raul's legitimate medical needs, and such a rationale is probably insufficient to justify placement of Raul in a cubicle. (It must be noted that the EAHCA gives courts broad authority to prescribe details of educational policy in individual cases, and a Judge can presumably order implementation of whatever program he or she deems appropriate. 20 U.S.C. § 1415(e)(2). A state's autonomy in regulating the education of its handicapped children is thus to a great extent fettered by the conditions imposed upon it due to the receipt of EAHCA funds.)

Finally, in retrospective, Dr. Schraer feels that Raul's sterling performance in the first grade proves that he is being provided with an appropriate education. While there is no question that Raul's grades establish that he is receiving an "adequate" education, this does not necessarily mean that he is receiving an "appropriate" education. One court has held that an "appropriate" education is one which lies between the extremes of a merely adequate education (*i.e.,* one that is substantial enough to facilitate a child's progress from grade to grade) and one which enables a handicapped child to achieve his or her full potential. *Rowley* v. *Board of Education (Rowley I),* 483 F.Supp. 528, 534 (S.D.N.Y.1980). The *Rowley I* Court found that the appropriate standard would require that each handicapped child be given an opportunity to achieve his or her full potential commensurate with the opportunity provided to other children. *Id. See also Springdale School Dist.* v. *Grace,* 494 F.Supp. 266, 272 (W.D.Ark.1980). It is apparent that Raul misses out on a great deal of class interaction and group participation while he is confined to the cubicle. This is of particular significance in Raul's case since the ARD committee which decided to mainstream

Raul felt that the Moody facility was "too restrictive" to meet his "intellectual and social needs." Full social interaction is an important part of today's educational curriculum and is even more vital to a child like Raul who necessarily suffers a certain degree of isolation as a result of his handicap. While it is true that Raul's scholarship is superb and he displays no psychological damage as a result of his semi-isolation in the cubicle, he derives no educational benefits from it. Under the circumstances it is doubtful that Raul is being provided an opportunity for maximization of his social interaction skills commensurate with that provided to other students in his class. Raul's excellent academic performance and his ability to get along with his classmates attest to his courage and tenacity, and he should not be penalized for the fruits of his own efforts. For these reasons this Court feels that the placement of Raul in the cubicle may deprive him of a full educational opportunity and may not be in conformity with his IEP as originally espoused in the ARD committee's original report. If this indeed is the case, Raul is not being provided with an "appropriate" education under the EAHCA.

\* \* \*

ORDERED that pending further order of this Court Defendants are hereby enjoined from further denying Plaintiff, Raul Espino, Jr. a free appropriate education in violation of 20 U.S.C. § 1401 *et seq.* by refusing to provide him with an air-conditioned environment wherein he can fully interact with his non-handicapped peers and obtain social and educational benefits commensurate with that provided to non-handicapped students; . . .

NOTE

The *Espino* case is an excellent example of how the least restrictive environment provision may affect the school environment in which the child is ultimately placed. The issue in *Espino* goes beyond what type of general educational placement would comply with the least restrictive environment provision. Instead, the case deals with the issue of how, once a general placement is chosen, the specifics of its physical make-up may have to be altered in order to allow a child to be integrated with nonhandicapped children to the maximum extent appropriate.

### d. Payment for Private School Programs

p. 295—INSERT, after Note 3, the following:

KRUELLE v. NEW CASTLE COUNTY SCHOOL DISTRICT
United States Court of Appeals for the Third Circuit, 1981
642 F.2d 687

Before ADAMS, VAN DUSEN and GIBBONS, Circuit Judges.

Opinion of the Court

ADAMS, Circuit Judge.

This case presents two issues arising under the Education for All Handicapped Children Act of 1975, P.L. 94-142, 20 U.S.C. §§ 1401 *et seq.* (Education Act), that are of first impression for this Court. First, did the district court err in determining that Paul Kruelle is entitled to residential placement under the Education Act? Second, did the district court err in holding the Delaware State Board of Education responsible for providing Paul with an appropriate education in conformity with the Act?

## I

Appellee is profoundly retarded and is also afflicted with cerebral palsy. At age thirteen he has the social skills of a six month old child and his I.Q. is well below thirty. As found by the district court, "he cannot walk, dress himself, or eat unaided. He is not toilet trained. He does not speak, and his receptive communication level is extremely low. In addition to his physical problems, he has had a history of emotional problems which result in choking and self-induced vomiting when experiencing stress." *Kruelle* v. *Biggs,* 489 F.Supp. 169, 172 (D.Del.1980).

\* \* \*

## IV

Significantly, all parties concede that Paul needs full-time assistance from the state of Delaware beyond that available in any day school program. It is also uncontroverted that the Education Act specifically provides for residential placement in certain instances. *See* 20 U.S.C. §§ 1401(16), 1413(a)(4)(B); 45 C.F.R. § 1212.302. The question, then, is whether the trial judge correctly construed the Education Act as requiring more continuous supervision for Paul than he was receiving under the Meadowood Program in order to meet the standard of a free appropriate education.

Based on our careful review of the record, we cannot find that the district court erred in holding that the six-hour day provided by the Meadowood program was an inappropriate education given the terms of the Act. The trial judge's conclusion that Paul required more continuous care is supported generally by the logic of the decision in *Battle* v. *Commonwealth of Pennsylvania,* 629 F.2d 269 (3d Cir. 1980), and more specifically by analogous case law emerging in other federal courts. Just as in *Battle* we held that the *per se* application of the 180 school-day rule accepted as appropriate for the nonhandicapped cannot be presumed to satisfy the unique needs of handicapped children, here the school authorities are incorrect to assume that conforming to the six-hour day that suffices for nonhandicapped children will similarly fulfill their obligations with respect to Paul.

The school district seeks to avoid the thrust of *Battle* by centering its challenge on the proposition that here the residential placement is required only for reasons of medical and domiciliary care, not for educational purposes. But as the *Battle* opinion explained, the concept of education is necessarily broad with respect to persons such as Paul. "Where basic self-help and social skills such as toilet training, dressing, feeding and communication are lacking, formal education begins at that point." 629 F.2d 269, 275. And Congress was clearly aware of children with needs similar to those of Paul, and was quite conscious of the foundational nature of their education. The Education Act unqualifiedly provides for a free appropriate education for all handicapped children, "regardless of the severity of their handicap," 20 U.S.C. § 1412(2)(C). It explicitly directs that all children not presently receiving an education and those "with the most severe handicaps who are receiving an inadequate education," 20 U.S.C. § 1412(3), be given priority.

Analysis must focus, then, on whether full-time placement may be considered necessary for educational purposes, or whether the residential placement is a response to medical, social or emotional problems that are segregable from the learning process. This Court is not the first to attempt to distinguish between residential placement that is a necessary predicate for learning and the provision of services that are unrelated to learning skills. One of the early cases to grapple with this issue, *North v. Dist. of Columbia Board of Education*, 471 F.Supp. 136 (D.D.C.1979), actually collapsed the distinction by declaring the impossibility of separating emotional and educational needs in complex cases. *North* is almost indistinguishable on the facts from the present case. It also involved the same issue: whether placement was required for emotional problems and was therefore the responsibility of the parents or social service agencies or whether full-time placement was a necessary ingredient for learning. The *North* court enjoined the school board from denying a sixteen-year old multiply-handicapped epileptic free placement in a residential academic program because it found the social, emotional, medical and educational problems to be so intertwined "that realistically it is not possible for the court to perform the Solomon-like task of separating them." 471 F.Supp. at 141. However, as later cases demonstrate, the claimed inextricability of medical and educational grounds for certain services does not signal court abdication from decision-making in difficult matters. Rather, the unseverability of such needs is the very basis for holding that the services are an essential prerequisite for learning.

\* \* \*

Having determined that the district court did not err in holding that Paul's existing IEP was inadequate and in approving, at least temporarily, residential placement for Paul, we cannot say that the trial judge erred in assigning responsibility to the State Board of Education. The Education Act unambiguously provides that:

> The state educational agency shall be responsible for assuring that the requirements of this subchapter are carried out and that all educational programs for handicapped children within the State, including all such programs administered by any other State or local agency, will be under the general supervision of the persons responsible for educational programs for handicapped children in the State educational agency and shall meet education standards of the State educational agency.

20 U.S.C. § 1412(6).

Both a general, congressional perception of the state's primary responsibility to provide a publicly-supported education for all children and a specific intent to centralize this responsibility underlie this explicit statutory mandate.

The legislative history indicates that the full committee considered the establishment of a single agency on which to focus responsibility for assuring the right to education of all handicapped children to be of paramount importance:

> Without this requirement, there is an abdication of responsibility for the education of handicapped children. Presently, in many States, responsibility is divided, depending upon the age of the handicapped child, sources of funding, and type of services delivered. While the committee understands that different agencies may, in fact, deliver

services, the responsibility must remain in a central agency overseeing the education of handicapped children, so that failure to deliver services or the violation of the rights of handicapped children is squarely the responsibility of one agency.

See S.Rep.No. 168, 94th Cong., 1st Sess. 24 reprinted in [1975] U.S. Code Cong. & Ad. News 1425, 1448.
The regulations implementing § 1412(6) of the Education Act, which essentially track the statutory language and specifically note the congressional desire for a central point of accountability, further underscore the intent to assure a single line of responsibility. By placing the burden for coordinating efforts and financial arrangements for Paul's education on the State Board of Education, the trial judge was both reflecting legislative intent and appropriately observing the limits of his institutional role. Rather than rigidly prescribe for the state how various local and state agencies should contribute to the provision of a free education for Paul, the federal court left such interactions to the discretion of the state officials involved.

Thus, the state, in contending that it functions solely as a supervisory agency and should not be responsible for coordinating efforts to develop an IEP for Paul or to insure funding, distorts the import of the district court's directive. The argument both mischaracterizes the nature of the accountability that the trial judge ascribed to the State Educational Agency and is contradicted by federal and state statutes and existing Delaware regulations. The district court did not direct, as the state appellants suggest, that the State Board engage in the detailed development of a specific educational program for Paul. Instead, in conformity with both federal and state statutes, the State Board was to insure that a proper evaluation of Paul's needs be undertaken and an appropriate plan be implemented. See 20 U.S.C. § 1412(5), (6), (7); 14 Del.C. § 3120. Resolution of any interagency conflicts or delegation of duties from state to regional and local levels was left, as it should have been, in the hands of the state officials.

* * *

VI

We conclude that the district did not err in ordering residential placement for Paul under the terms of the Education Act. Further, the court was not in error in placing responsibility for providing an appropriate education for Paul on the State Board of Education. Accordingly, the judgment of the district court will be affirmed.

NOTE

The principle expostulated in Kruelle is one of the most significant incorporated in P.L. 94-142 and its regulations—that the education received by a handicapped child should not, and cannot, be broken down into component parts which may under traditional educational approaches be considered noneducational in nature. As the court points out, such traditional analysis had in the time before the passage of P.L. 94-142 been used to allow different state and local agencies to pass responsibility for provision of certain services back and forth, which in turn caused the denial of necessary services to many handicapped children. P.L. 94-142 was designed to place ultimate responsibility on the state education agencies for the delivery of educational services to handicapped children in order to eliminate this problem.

p. 295—ADD a new subsection after Subsection d as follows:

### e.  Related Services

#### TATRO v. STATE OF TEXAS

*United States Court of Appeals for the Fifth Circuit, 1980*
*625 F.2d 557, 560–564*

(See pp. 22–23, above.)

### I.  The EAHCA

The Education for All Handicapped Children Act of 1975, 89 Stat. 773 (1975), was sparked by an "[i]ncreased awareness of the educational needs of handicapped children and landmark court decisions establishing the right to education for handicapped children . . . ."

$$* * *$$

To ensure the provision of proper services, Congress mandated that recipients of federal funds must assure "all handicapped children the right to a free appropriate public education," 20 U.S.C.A. § 1412(1) (West 1978), which consists of special education and related services. *See id.* § 1401(18). The battle lines in this case have been drawn on the issue whether the provision of CIC to Amber, a handicapped child within the meaning of the EAHCA, *see id.* § 1401(1), is a related service.

The district court held that CIC is not. It observed that there are only two categories of related services: (1) transportation required to assist a handicapped child to benefit from special education, and (2) developmental, corrective, and supportive services necessary to assist a handicapped to benefit from special education. It properly concluded that CIC is not transportation and that CIC is neither developmental nor corrective. The district court noted that "CIC is supportive of Amber's education in the sense that it is required at sufficiently frequent intervals that her education and CIC must proceed apace," and that "[o]ne can argue that read literally, every necessary life support system must be furnished." Nevertheless, the district court concluded that there was "no congressional intent to sweep broadly in its usage of the word 'related.'" The court thus held that "to be related in the statutory sense the service requirement must arise from the effort to educate. There is a difference between maintenance of life systems and enhancing a handicapped person's ability to learn. The CIC is essential to Amber's life but once that life maintenance service is provided, it is unrelated to her learning skills."

The district court further observed that the regulations implementing the EAHCA construe related services to include "school health services," which are defined as "services provided by a qualified school nurse or other qualified person." 45 C.F.R. § 121a.13(b)(10) (1979). Despite the fact that CIC comports with this definition of school health services, the district court held that school health services, to be a class of related services, must, like all categories of related services, arise from the effort to educate in order to fit within the statutory definition. Hence, CIC did not fit the bill. We find that the district court erred.

As the district court correctly observed, CIC falls within a literal interpretation of the statutory definition of related services. Quite simply put, without the provision of CIC, Amber cannot benefit from the special education to which she is entitled, for, without CIC, she cannot be present in the classroom at all. Thus, CIC is a supportive service required to assist Amber to benefit from her special education.

Nevertheless, the district court felt compelled to limit the literal words of 20 U.S.C. § 1401(17) because it perceived a need to circumscribe the scope of related services lest "every necessary life support system . . . be furnished." This perception, however, ignored the fact that the EAHCA contains its own limitations on the type of life support services that must be provided as related services. First, in order to be entitled to any related services at all, a child must be handicapped so as to require special education. 45 C.F.R. § 121a.14 (1979) (comment one); *see* 20 U.S.C.A. § 1401(1) (reprinted at note 11 *supra*). Second, the life support service must be necessary to aid a handicapped child to benefit from the special education to be provided. *See id.* § 1401(17). Thus, a life support service would not be a related service if it did not have to be provided during school hours, but instead could be performed at some other time. Third, in order to be a related service, the life support service must be one which a nurse or other qualified person can perform. 45 C.F.R. § 121a.13(b)(10) (1979). Excluded from the term "related services" are those health-related activities which must be performed by a licensed physician that are not provided "to determine a child's medically related handicapping condition which results in the child's need for special education and related services." *Id.* § 121a.13(4). Thus, even under a literal interpretation of the statutory definition, the types of life support services needed by a child which can be related services are limited.

Moreover, the district court's deviation from the literal words of the statute ignored a mandate contained in the EAHCA which is additional to the congressional requirement that states furnish each handicapped child a free appropriate public education consisting of special education and related services. The language of 20 U.S.C.A. § 1412(5) (West 1978) is quite unequivocal:

> In order to qualify for assistance under this subchapter in any fiscal year, a State shall demonstrate to the Commissioner that the following conditions are met:
> (5) The State has established . . . procedures to assure that, to the maximum extent appropriate, handicapped children, including children in public or private institutions or other care facilities, are educated with children who are not handicapped, and that special classes, separate schooling, or other removal of handicapped children from the regular educational environment occurs only when the nature or severity of the handicap is such that education in regular classes with the use of supplementary aids and services cannot be achieved satisfactorily . . . .

Construing the term "related services" to exclude services like CIC, necessary to keep a handicapped child in the classroom, would completely eviscerate this mandate. This we cannot do. In light of this categorical congressional judgment that handicapped children should be educated in the regular classrooms to the maximum extent appropriate, and given the existence of limitations in the statute which circumscribe the types of life support systems which must be provided as related services, we hold that the words "supportive services . . . as may be required to assist a handicapped child to benefit from special education" must be read literally to include the provision of CIC to Amber Tatro.

* * *

NOTE

On remand, the district court went to great lengths to base its decision that catheterization was a required related service on the fact that catheterization was a school health service under Texas law. See *Tatro* v. *Texas,* 516 F. Supp. 968 (N.D. Tex. 1981). If the Texas legislature were to pass legislation that eliminated catheterization as a school health service, would it no longer be a required related service under P.L. 94-142 for handicapped children in Texas?

### KRUELLE v. NEW CASTLE COUNTY SCHOOL DISTRICT

(See pp. 86–89, above.)

NOTE

Responsibility for payment for related services is closely intertwined with the issue of responsibility for payment for a residential program, since a large number of related services are necessarily included in a residential program. The *Kruelle* case provides a good example of how, in deciding a residential program is appropriate, a court also faces the issue of whether, for example, certain domiciliary services should be paid for by the school agency as required related services.

## H.  SCHOOL RECORDS

p. 305—INSERT after Note 2, the following:

3.   The following is excerpted from *Powell* v. *Defore,* No. 81-71-MAC (M.D. Ga., Jan. 11, 1982).

> Finally, there is no basis for this court to order defendants to destroy all records pertaining to plaintiff's placement in self-contained learning disabilities class and special education resource class. These are legitimate and truthful records of plaintiff's past special education needs and background, and may be used to plaintiff's teachers in the future. The regulations at 45 C.F.R. § 121a.573 provide that records maintained pursuant to the EAHCA may be destroyed at the request of the parents when they are no longer needed to provide educational services to the child. That is a decision which must be left to proper officials in the Bibb County school system. The court does not believe that any harmful stigma or label with [*sic*] attach to plaintiff because of his past special education needs.

The preceding paragraph is one of the few judicial analyses of the P.L. 94-142 educational records provisions. Under the regulations, can records ever be destroyed without the prior agreement of the school agency that they should be destroyed? Could parents obtain an order as a result of a hearing to have records destroyed?

## I.  OTHER PROBLEMS

### 2.  Misclassification

p. 314—INSERT after the regulations and before ADDITIONAL READING, the following:

## LARRY P. v. RILES

*United States District Court for the Northern District of California, 1979*
*495 F. Supp. 926*

PECKHAM, Chief Judge.

Plaintiffs, representing the class of black children in California who have been or in the future will be wrongly placed and maintained in special classes for the "educable mentally retarded" ("E.M.R.") challenge the placement process for those classes and particularly certain uses of standardized individual intelligence ("I.Q.") tests in California. They contend that the I.Q. tests in their present form are biased and that defendants have discriminated against black children by using those tests. The tests allegedly result in the misplacement of black children in special classes that doom them to stigma, inadequate education, and failure to develop the skills necessary to productive success in our society. Black children represent only 10 percent of the present general student population in California, but provide some 25 percent of the population enrolled in E.M.R. classes.

These testing and placement problems arise in a setting of educational failure. California's schools have been unable to meet the educational needs of disadvantaged minorities such as the black children who brought this case. As a result, poor minority children tend not only to start out behind their white, middle-class counterparts, but also tend to fall increasingly farther behind after exposure to the public school system. Defendant Wilson Riles stated in 1969, before he became Superintendent of Public Instruction, that disadvantaged black children, on the average, learn only about .7 as much as middle-class white children in any given year. More recent data confirmed that analysis. Black children fall increasingly behind to the point that it is not unusual for high school students to be reading at the third grade level and performing at only the fourth grade level in mathematics. The disproportionate placement of black children into E.M.R. classes is but one aspect of this troublesome situation.

Courts cannot solve our educational problems, but they played a part in the incremental effort to improve those aspects of our educational systems that effectively deny minorities an equal opportunity to succeed. In particular, the phenomenon of special education such as that for the "mentally retarded" has not yet been subjected to much judicial scrutiny. We have been forced in this case to enter that complicated area, and it raises special problems for court intervention.

A principal focus of this litigation is on testing—on the use of individual I.Q. tests—to classify black children and assign them to E.M.R. classes. Much of the more then [*sic*] 10,000-page transcript of the trial represents detailed expert testimony about these tests. The court has necessarily been drawn into the emotionally charged debate about the nature of "intelligence" and its basis in "genes" or the "environment." This debate, which finds reknowned experts disagreeing sharply, obviously cannot be resolved by judicial decree. Despite these problems, however, court intervention has been necessary. The history of this litigation has demonstrated the failure of legislators and administrative agencies to confront problems that clearly had to be faced, and it has revealed an all too typical willingness either to do nothing or to pass on issues to the courts.

Fortunately, the "scientific controversy" surrounding the I.Q. tests has not materialized to the extent that might have been expected. The experts have tended to agree about what I.Q. tests can and cannot do, even if they disagree about the utility of I.Q. testing for E.M.R. placement. Our decision, therefore, rests more on a consensus than on the testimony of any one line of experts. Given that consensus, coupled with the other factors present in this case, there is no choice but to invalidate California's present system of classification of black children for E.M.R. classes. The bases for this ruling, both statutory and constitutional, will be explained in detail below, but it may be helpful to summarize them briefly at the outset before proceeding to the main body of the opinion.

### Summary

This court finds in favor of plaintiffs, the class of black children who have been or in the future will be wrongly placed or maintained in special classes for the educable mentally retarded, on plaintiffs' statutory and state and federal constitutional claims. In violation of Title VI of the Civil Rights Act of 1964, the Rehabilitation Act of 1973, and the Education for All Handicapped Children Act of 1975, defendants have utilized standardized intelligence tests that are racially and culturally biased, have a discriminatory impact against black children, and have not been validated for the purpose of essentially permanent placements of black children into educationally dead-end, isolated, and stigmatizing classes for the so-called educable mentally retarded. Further, these federal laws have been violated by defendants' general use of placement mechanisms that, taken together, have not been validated and result in a large overrepresentation of black children in the special E.M.R. classes.

\* \* \*

*3. The Rehabilitation Act of 1973 and the Education for All Handicapped Children Act of 1975—Another "Effects Test"*

These two federal statutory schemes closely overlap and embrace an educational philosophy contrary to that which has at least until very recently characterized California's treatment of E.M.R.'s. "Mainstreaming" has become the theme of federal law, while California has opted to isolate E.M.R.'s in special day classes.

The first of the two laws, section 504 of the Rehabilitation Act of 1973, 29 U.S.C. § 794, as amended in 1974, prevents discrimination against the handicapped in programs that receive federal funding. It covers persons who are actually handicapped or "who are regarded" as handicapped, such as the plaintiffs in this case. Section 504 extends to these persons the same broad protections against discrimination already provided against discrimination on the basis of race by Title VI of the Civil Rights Act of 1964.

> No otherwise qualified handicapped individual in the United States . . . shall, solely by reason of his handicap, be excluded from the participation in, be denied the benefits of, or be subjected to discrimination under any program or activity receiving Federal financial assistance.

It is clear from the legislative history of the law, as well as the interpretative regulations which have been in effect since June 3, 1977, 45 C.F.R. Pt. 84, that one abuse sought to be corrected was the erroneous denial of admission into regular classes.

The Education for All Handicapped Children Act of 1975, 20 U.S.C. § 1401 *et seq.*, with its emphasis on procedural protection in programs funded under its terms, also addresses classification into special classes. In addition, the act provides that in order to qualify for federal assistance, which California is now receiving and which has led to much of the statutory reform embodied in the Master Plan, a state must, *inter alia,* establish

> (A) procedural safeguards as required by section 1415 of this title, (B) procedures to assure that to the maximum extent appropriate, handicapped children, including children in public or private institutions or other care facilities, are educated with children who are not handicapped, and that special classes, separate schooling, or other removal of handicapped children from the regular educational environment occurs only when the nature or severity of the handicap is such that education in regular classes with the use of supplementary aids and services cannot be achieved satisfactorily, and (C) procedures to assure that *testing and evaluation materials and procedures utilized for the purposes of evaluation and placement of handicapped children will be selected and administered so as not to be racially or culturally discriminatory.* [Emphasis supplied.]

20 U.S.C. § 1412(2)(D)(5). The emphasized language, it should be noted initially, restates the concern with racial impact set out in *Lau,* Title VI, and the August 1975 memorandum. The analysis undertaken in the previous section suggests the same conclusion. Beyond this overlap, however, the E.H.A. and the Rehabilitation Act provide a more specific concern with the validity of evaluation materials used for diagnosis of educational needs and placement into special classes.

The basic aims of the E.H.A. and Rehabilitation Act, as relevant to this litigation, are to ensure the proper classification of children and promote, to the maximum extent possible, the "mainstreaming" of children into regular classes. Accordingly, virtually identical regulations under the two statutes describe allowable practices for decision on proper classroom placement and curriculum design. Both sets of regulations provide, with respect to testing, that state and local educational agencies

> shall establish standards and procedures for the evaluation and placement of persons who, because of handicap, need or are believed to need special education or related services which ensure that:
> (1) Tests and other evaluation materials have been validated for the specific purpose for which they are used and are administered by trained personnel in conformance with the instructions provided by their producer;
> (2) Tests and other evaluation materials include those tailored to assess specific areas of educational need and not merely those which are designed to provide a single general intelligence quotient;

45 C.F.R. § 84.35(b); 45 C.F.R. § 121a.532(a). These regulations therefore require that the tests and other evaluation materials be "validated for the specific purpose for which they are used." We must examine in some detail the meaning of validation in the school placement setting.

* * *

We must inquire whether the tests have been validated for the black children who are members of the plaintiff class, given the disproportionately low test scores of those children and the critical effect of those scores in keeping black children from full participation in regular classes. We are not concerned now with predictions of performance, but rather whether the tests are validated with respect to the characteristics consistent with E.M.R. status and placement in E.M.R. classes. E.M.R. classes exist, it will be recalled, "for people whose mental capabilities make it impossible for them to profit from the regular educational program." "Mental retardation" is the touchstone, and retardation must make it "impossible" to profit from the regular classes, even with remedial instruction. Defendants have the burden of showing validation of intelligence tests with respect to these characteristics.

\* \* \*

The answer . . . is that validation has been assumed, not established, for blacks. The tests were developed and standardized in the United States on white, essentially middle-class groups, and if they were then validated with independent indicia of mental retardation justifying placement in isolated, dead-end classes, it was done on the basis of that population. Although several leading figures in the early testing movement saw no problem with this situation, given their own racial prejudices or at least strong ethnocentrism, others, including Dr. Wechsler, the developer of the Wechsler battery of tests central to this litigation, frankly admitted the problem. Wechsler stated in 1944 that the tests were not valid for "the colored population of the United States." His tests, like the others involved here, had not been made suitable for minority racial and ethnic groups. The tests had been adjusted, for example, to eliminate differences in the average scores between the sexes, but a comparable effort was not made and has never been made for black and white children.

\* \* \*

**Parents in Action on Special Education (PASE) v. Hannon**

*United States District Court for the Northern District of Illinois, 1980*
*506 F. Supp. 831*

Memorandum Decision

Grady, District Judge.

This case presents the question whether standard intelligence tests administered by the Chicago Board of Education are culturally biased against black children. The action is brought on behalf of all black children who have been or will be placed in special classes for the educable mentally handicapped ("EMH") in the Chicago school system. The defendants are the Chicago Board of Education and its officers responsible for administration of the relevant programs. The named plaintiffs are two black children who were placed in EMH classes after achieving low scores on standard intelligence tests.

\* \* \*

I conclude that plaintiffs' have failed to prove their contention that the Wechsler and Stanford-Binet IQ tests are culturally unfair to black children, resulting in discriminatory placement of black children in classes for the educable mentally handicapped. Plaintiffs, however, claim that it is not their burden to show the tests are culturally biased against black children. Rather, they claim that defendants must prove the tests are culturally fair to black children. They base this argument on a provision of the Education of the Handicapped Act, 20 U.S.C. § 1412(5)(C), requiring, as a qualification for federal funding of education for the handicapped, that a state demonstrate it has established

> . . . procedures to assure that testing and evaluation materials and procedures utilized for the purposes of evaluation and placement of handicapped children will be selected and administered so as not to be racially or culturally discriminatory. Such materials or procedures shall be provided and administered in the child's native language or mode of communication, unless it clearly is not feasible to do so, and no single procedure shall be the sole criterion for determining an appropriate educational program for a child.

Federal funds do provide a portion of the financing for defendants' EMH program, and the Department of Health, Education and Welfare has periodically reviewed defendants' assessment policies and procedures. The Department has not taken a position as to whether the standard IQ tests violate the statute or any regulation it has promulgated under the statute.

I do not read the statute as relieving plaintiffs of the burden of proof. The requirement that "materials and procedures" used for assessment be non-discriminatory, and that no single procedure be the sole criterion for assessment, seems to me to contemplate that the process as a whole be non-discriminatory. It does not require that any single procedure, standing alone, be affirmatively shown to be free of bias. The very requirement of multiple procedures implies recognition that one procedure, standing alone, could well result in bias and that a system of cross-checking is necessary.

* * *

*The Larry P. Case*

This is not a case of first impression. The exact issue of racial bias in the WISC, WISC-R and Stanford-Binet tests has been decided by Judge Robert F. Peckham of the United States District Court for the Northern District of California in the case of *Larry P., by his Guardian ad Litem, Lucille P., et al.* v. *Wilson Riles, Superintendent of Public Instruction for the State of California, et al.*, 495 F.Supp. 926 (1979). Plaintiffs rely upon that decision heavily, since Judge Peckham held that the tests are culturally biased against black children. Judge Peckham heard a number of the same witnesses who testified here, including Professors Kamin, Albee and Williams and Dr. Gloria Powell. He found their testimony persuasive. Judge Peckham's lengthy and scholarly opinion is largely devoted to the question of what legal consequences flow from a finding of racial bias in the tests. There is relatively little analysis of the threshold question of whether test bias in fact exists, and Judge Peckham even remarked that the cultural bias of the tests ". . . is hardly disputed in this litigation. . . ." (p. 959; *see also* n. 69). I find reference to specific test items on only one page (p. 958) of the opinion. Judge Peckham mentions the WISC "fight" item, finds that it is culturally biased against blacks and then remarks, "Similarly, it may be that such questions as who wrote Romeo and Juliet, who discovered America, and who invented the lightbulb, are culturally biased." Finally, Judge Peckham noted that ". . . such skills as 'picture arrangement' may be tested in a biased fashion if the pictures, which generally are of caucasian persons, relate to situations more typical of white, middle class, life than the experiences of many black children." (p. 958).

As is by now obvious, the witnesses and the arguments which persuaded Judge Peckham have not persuaded me. Moreover, I believe the issue in the case cannot properly be analyzed without a detailed examination of the items on the tests. It is clear that this was not undertaken in the *Larry P.* case.

## Conclusion

I have found one item on the Stanford-Binet and a total of eight items on the WISC and WISC-R to be culturally biased against black children, or at least sufficiently suspect that their use is in my view inappropriate. These few items do not render the tests unfair and would not significantly affect the score of an individual taking the test. The evidence fails to show that any additional test items are racially or culturally unfair or suspect.

I believe and today hold that the WISC, WISC-R and Stanford-Binet tests, when used in conjunction with the statutorily mandated ["other criteria] for determining an appropriate educational program for a child" (20 U.S.C. § 1412(2)(D)(5), do not discriminate against black children in the Chicago public schools. Defendants are complying with that statutory mandate.

Intelligent administration of the IQ tests by qualified psychologists, followed by the evaluation procedures defendants use, should rarely result in the misassessment of a child of normal intelligence as one who is mentally retarded. There is no evidence in this record that such misassessments as do occur are the result of racial bias in test items or in any other aspect of the assessment process currently in use in the Chicago public school system.

I find the issues in favor of the defendants and against the plaintiffs. The Clerk is directed to enter judgment for the defendants.

NOTES

1. The *Larry P.* case has an extensive procedural history. It was first filed in 1971 and an order granting a preliminary injunction was issued in 1972. See *Larry P.* v. *Riles,* 343 F. Supp. 1306 (N.D. Cal. 1972). After appeals and other procedural maneuvers, the case came to trial on the merits. The opinion printed above is the court's decision in the trial.

2. Both the *Larry P.* and *PASE* opinions have been extensively edited due to their length. Excerpted here is the courts' treatment of the plaintiffs' Sec. 504 and P.L. 94-142 claims.

However, the courts also dealt with several other causes of action brought by the plaintiffs, including federal constitutional and statutory claims. Both opinions provide good analyses of different aspects of the misclassification problem. For example, the *PASE* case provides a detailed analysis of the specific IQ questions at issue, while the *Larry P.* opinion gives an excellent overview of the history of the use of IQ tests and its relationship to the misclassification problem.

3. The ruling in *Larry P.* seems to be based on the provision of the P.L. 94-142 regulations requiring validity of testing materials rather than the provision pertaining directly to racially and culturally discriminating materials. By comparison, the court in *PASE* held that the specific testing items in dispute, while in themselves questionable, were not racially and culturally discriminatory when used in conjunction with the other

evaluation safeguards included in the regulations. The *PASE* court's reasoning seems somewhat strained in light of the fact that the defendant school authorities had a duty to comply with each regulatory provision separately—compliance with certain of the regulatory provisions should not be allowed to negate possible noncompliance with a separate and independent regulatory provision.

# 3

# EMPLOYMENT

**Robert L. Burgdorf Jr.**

## SUMMARY OF DOCTRINAL DEVELOPMENTS

A SIGNIFICANT AMOUNT OF LITIGATIVE ACTIVITY has been initiated regarding the rights of handicapped persons to equal opportunities in employment. A general trend of increasingly sophisticated analysis and standards for examining employment discrimination has developed. This has led to a major reversal of direction in a number of cases that disagree with the *Trageser* decision and take a more positive and expansive view of the rights available to handicapped persons under Section 504 in regard to employment.

## A. THE NATURE AND SOURCES OF THE PROBLEM

### 2. Scope of the Problem

p. 319—INSERT before the beginning of Section B:

NOTE

The E. I. Dupont Company has been something of a leader in employing handicapped workers with a variety of serious disabilities and in documenting the performance of these handicapped employees. The report from DuPont's 1981 survey regarding its handicapped workers summarizes its conclusions: "DuPont studies over a period of 25 years have shown that the performance of handicapped employees is equivalent to that of their nonimpaired co-workers. In safety, job duties and attendance the handicapped hold their own. . . . The results bear out the conclusion that, given the opportunity, handicapped employees are indeed equal to the task." E. I. DuPont de Nemours and Company, *Equal to the Task: 1981 DuPont Survey of Employment of the Handicapped*, at p. 4 (1982).

## D. STATE LAW

### 1. Statutory Provisions

p. 336—INSERT before the *Chicago, Milwaukee, St. Paul & Pacific R.R. Co.* case:

## CONNECTICUT INSTITUTE FOR THE BLIND V.
## CONNECTICUT COMMISSION ON HUMAN RIGHTS AND OPPORTUNITIES
### Supreme Court of Connecticut, 1978
### 176 Conn. 88, 405 A.2d 618

Before COTTER, C. J., and LOISELLE, BOGDANSKI, SPEZIALE and PETERS, J. J. PETERS, Associate Justice.

This is an appeal by the Commission on Human Rights and Opportunities. The commission, acting on the complaint of a person handicapped by virtue of a visual disability, found that the Connecticut Institute for the Blind had unlawfully refused employment to the complainant, in violation of § 31-126 of the General Statutes. The Institute filed a petition to the Court of Common Pleas praying that this determination be modified or set aside. The court disallowed the claim of discrimination. The commission now asks this court to review and to reverse the judgment of the court below.

The facts on which the commission acted are as follows: The complainant in this case is Ellen Steinberg Schuman. The respondent before the commission, and the plaintiff in the trial court, is the Connecticut Institute for the Blind (hereinafter referred to as the Institute) which operates the Oak Hill School for the Blind in Hartford. The defendant in the trial court is the Commission on Human Rights and Opportunities.

The complainant was employed by the Institute in the Oak Hill School's upper school, in the position of teacher's aide, from February to June of 1974. Her employment was terminated in June of 1974 when her position was abolished for budgetary reasons; her work record was satisfactory despite her visual impairment. The complainant then applied for a teacher's aide position in the Oak Hill School's lower school. She was denied employment primarily because the Institute determined that this position required a person with "normal visual acuity" since it entailed supervision of young children with severe multiple disabilities. "Normal visual acuity" was stated by the personnel director of the Oak Hill School to require "20/20 vision." The complainant's vision is impaired because of congenital cataracts in both eyes and by congenital nystagmus; her central acuity with corrective lenses is in the range of 20/45 to 20/50, with blurring caused by the nystagmus.

The complainant filed a complaint with the defendant Commission on Human Rights and Opportunities alleging that the plaintiff's failure to consider her for employment as a teacher's aide in the position specified was discrimination which constituted an unfair employment practice within § 31-126 of the General Statutes. The commission heard testimony that an individual's functional vision, his or her actual perception, is affected by intelligence, attention, mood and other subjective factors. There was testimony that the plaintiff's policy was to place all visually disabled applicants in a class and to deny them employment without examination of individual capabilities. The commission also received testimony from other visually handicapped teachers that they have successfully taught multiply handicapped children of all ages. On the basis of this and other evidence, the commission concluded that the Institute had engaged in an unfair employment practice.

The issue before us is whether the trial court erred when, despite acceptance of the facts found by the commission, the court ruled that the Institute's failure to employ the complainant was justified. The court accepted the commission's conclusion that the complainant had established a prima facie case within § 31-126, which provides, in pertinent part: "It shall be an unfair employment practice (a) For an employer . . . , except in the case of a bona fide occupational qualification or need, because of the . . . physical disability, including, but not limited to, blindness of any individual, to refuse to hire or employ or to bar . . . from employment such individual or to discriminate against him in compensation or in terms, conditions or privileges of employment." The court held, however, contrary to the determination of the commission, that the conduct of the Institute in this case fell within the exception for "a bona fide occupational qualification or need." Specifically, the court ruled that good vision is directly related to, and therefore a valid job qualification for, successful performance in the position of teacher's aide in the plaintiff's lower school classes for multiply disadvantaged children. It therefore concluded that the plaintiff had carried its burden of showing that the complainant's disability prevented her from adequately performing this particular job and was, therefore, within the exception to § 31-126.

* * *

This appeal is now limited to the legal standard, and the factual underpinning, by which the exception in § 31-126(a) for a "bona fide occupational qualification or need" is to be tested. The commission argues that the court below erred in its determination of the criteria by which to judge the relationship between physical disability and bona fide occupational need. The commission also asserts that the court erred in substituting its judgment for that of the hearing tribunal as to the weight of evidence on questions of fact.

The scope of a "bona fide occupational qualification" as a defense to a complaint of discrimination depends in part upon the reason advanced for the allegedly discriminatory conduct. Some job disqualifications arise out of employment criteria, such as intelligence tests, which are neutral on their face but have disproportionate impact on protected classes of workers. Such disqualifications come within the holding of *Griggs* v. *Duke Power Co.*, 401 U.S. 424, 91 S.Ct. 849, 28 L.Ed.2d 158 (1971); *Evening Sentinel* v. *National Organization for Women*, 168 Conn. 26, 36–37, 357 A.2d 498 (1975); *Bridgeport Guardians, Inc.* v. *Members of Bridgeport Civil Service Commission*, 482 F.2d 1333, 1337 (2d Cir., 1973); these disqualifications are valid if, despite their admittedly adverse impact, they bear a significant relationship to successful job performance. Other job disqualifications are not facially neutral but directly disqualify on a basis which is made a suspect classification by the terms of Connecticut's Fair Employment Practices Act, chapter 563 of the General Statutes; such disqualifications are only justified by bona fide occupational need, an exception described in *Evening Sentinel* v. *National Organization for Women, supra*, 168 Conn. 38, 357 A.2d 498, as "stringent and narrow."

In the case before us, the complainant was refused employment because of her visual handicap, and not on the basis of any facially neutral job qualification. Although the hearing tribunal and the trial court differed in their formulation of a test of job-relatedness, both assumed that some version of the *Griggs* test was appropriate. In this they were in error. The plaintiff's requirement that its lower school teachers' aides have normal vision serves as a direct disqualification of anyone with a visual handicap, in the same way that an advertisement of jobs for men only serves automatically to disqualify women. The plaintiff cannot meet the test of a bona fide occupational qualification by creating an irrebuttable presumption that visually handicapped employees, as a class, are unable adequately to perform duties as teachers' aides. As this court said in *Evening Sentinel, supra,* 35, 357 A.2d 504, the purpose of § 31-126 is "to prohibit acts, not status. It is part of a policy to eliminate . . . discrimination in its subtle as well as overt forms. The very act of classifying individuals by means of criteria irrelevant to the ultimate end sought to be accomplished operates in a discriminatory manner. Such discrimination is destructive to society as a whole in that it eliminates a class of individuals who otherwise could have made vital and fresh contributions. [Citation omitted.]"

The standard for a bona fide occupational qualification purposely imposes a heavy burden on an employer whose refusal to hire is prima facie discriminatory within § 31-126. In *Evening Sentinel, supra,* 36, 357 A.2d 505, that standard was stated to require a showing that "no member of the class excluded is physically capable of performing the tasks required by the job." *Evening Sentinel* also held (p. 29, 357 A.2d p. 501) that § 31-126 did not permit "classification based upon sex to be treated differently from classifications based upon race, religion, age, national origin or ancestry," the then-existing suspect classifications in the Fair Employment Practices Act. Although *Evening Sentinel* could not, in terms, apply to discrimination against the physically handicapped, who did not come within the ambit of § 31-126 until 1973, there is no basis to depart from its holdings on the facts of this case. It is unfortunate that the first test of the rights of the handicapped involves a confrontation between a plaintiff long committed to training the handicapped and a defendant long committed to eliminating unlawful discrimination. It is, however, eminently clear that the plaintiff's blanket exclusion of anyone without normal visual acuity, without any effort to define the specifications of the position of teacher's aide or to test the capacities of the complainant for that position, cannot stand. Blanket exclusions, no matter how well motivated, fly in the face of the command to individuate that is central to fair employment practices.

The trial court therefore erred when it sustained the plaintiff's appeal and denied the complainant's claim of discrimination.

* * *

NOTES

1. The distinction drawn by the court between a bona fide occupational qualification (BFOQ) and job-relatedness or "business necessity" is an important conceptual differentiation in equal employment opportunities analysis, although the distinction is sometimes ignored by uninformed legal analysts. As the court points out, the BFOQ exception applies only to employment criteria that directly disqualify members of the protected classes (e.g., only whites, males, or able-bodied persons need apply). Such exclusions of protected classes can be defended only when the employer can demonstrate that they are necessary as a BFOQ, i.e., that the qualifications are a direct and

necessary prerequisite to the job at issue and that no member of the excluded class is capable of performing the job. BFOQ analysis does not apply to employment criteria or actions that do not directly single out the protected class, even if they have an unequal or disproportionate effect on the class. Criteria or conduct that have a disproportionate or relatively adverse impact upon a protected class, but that do not directly single the class out for disparate treatment, are evaluated on a lesser analytic standard under which an employment practice can be defended by demonstrating that its application is a matter of business necessity or that it bears a significant relationship to job performance.

2.   The court's condemnation of "blanket exclusions" and its prescription of "individuation" in job eligibility determinations is underscored by the decision of a Wisconsin court in *Fraser Shipyards, Inc.* v. *Dep't of Indus., Labor & Human Relations,* 13 Fair Empl. Prac. Cas. 1809 (Wis. Cir. Ct. 1976). The *Fraser Shipyards* court ruled that exclusion of two diabetics from jobs as welders was in violation of a state law prohibiting discrimination on the basis of handicap. The court indicated that although the employer had made a showing that *some* diabetics would be unqualified for the position of welder due to a history of blackouts, the employer had made no such showing with regard to the particular diabetics involved in the case. *Id.* at 1810.

3.   In *In re Unlawful Employment Practices Based Upon a Physical Handicap by Montgomery Ward and Company, Inc.,* 280 Or. 163, 570 P.2d 76 (1977), the Supreme Court of Oregon discussed the standard to be applied in cases of employment discrimination under the Handicapped Persons' Civil Rights Act, O.R.S. 659.400 *et seq.* The administrative enforcement officer, Oregon's Commissioner of Labor, had directed that a handicap could justify refusal to employ because of danger of injury to the prospective employee, but only if there was a "high probability" of such injury. The Oregon Court of Appeals had ruled that only a "reasonable possibility" of such an injury needed to be shown. The Supreme Court of Oregon sought to formulate a standard between the two extremes and ruled that an employer is obligated not to reject a prospective employee because of a physical or mental handicap unless there is "a probability either that the employee cannot do the job in a satisfactory manner or that he can do so only at the risk of incapacitating himself." *Id.* at 570 P.2d 79. The court indicated that the employer's good faith or the reasonableness of the employer's belief that the employee cannot do the job "does not control the employee's employment rights under the statute." *Ibid.* How does this standard compare to the "significant relationship to successful job performance" formulation in the Connecticut case?

4.   There may be special deference given to employment criteria for jobs related to public health or safety. For cases upholding the exclusion of certain handicapped applicants from jobs as police officers and firefighters, see *McCrea* v. *Cunningham,* 202 Neb. 638, 277 N.W.2d 52(1979), and *City of Appleton* v. *Labor and Industry Review Commission,* No. 78-CV-2002, 20 E.P.D. 11,742 (Wisc. Cir. Ct., Dane County, July 9, 1979). Cf., *Southeastern Community College* v. *Davis,* pp. 24–30, *supra; Duran* v. *City of Tampa,* pp. 351–356 and 410–411 of the Casebook; *Davis* v. *Bucher,* pp. 416–424 of the Casebook.

## Holland v. The Boeing Co.

*Supreme Court of Washington, 1978*
*90 Wash.2d 384, 583 P.2d 621*

Hamilton Justice.

Appellant Boeing Company seeks review of a judgment in favor of respondent Holland. Appellant was found to have violated RCW 49.60.180 by discriminating against respondent, a handicapped employee. We affirm the trial court's judgment.

Respondent, a 45-year-old man, has suffered from cerebral palsy since birth. His illness manifests itself in spontaneous muscular contractions of various portions of his body. In spite of this handicap, respondent has been gainfully employed with appellant for over 20 years. He progressed in employment from a Grade 5 Storekeeper to a Grade 9 Electronics Technician. As a technician, respondent analyzed electronics systems, performed routine checks on equipment, and made certain repairs. His handicap did not prevent him from adequately performing these tasks.

Sometime in 1974 appellant selectively reassigned respondent to an equal grade position in an area known as Facilities Support. On this new assignment, more manual dexterity was required of respondent than was required in the technician assignment. In addition, the work in the Facilities Support area included certified soldering which respondent was incapable of performing.

After the transfer to the Facilities Support area, respondent's work performance was closely monitored. As it became apparent he was not able to carry out his new assignments with an acceptable degree of competence, letters documenting his lack of ability were written and placed in his personnel file. He was given dexterity tests, the results of which further evidenced his deficiencies. Eventually, he was approached by a supervisor about the possibility of reassignment and reduction in grade.

Respondent, having spent almost 22 years advancing himself, expressed opposition to the downgrade. Appellant, in response to this opposition, made an effort to place him in an equal grade position. It circulated his personnel folder among various supervisors. The folder, however, then contained sufficient negative material to discourage supervisory interest in respondent. When efforts to place him in an equal grade position were unsuccessful, appellant offered him a Grade 5 Storekeeper position. Respondent initially refused this offer, but upon reconsideration accepted. This lawsuit followed.

Respondent's case was tried to the court, sitting without a jury. His theory was that appellant committed an unfair practice by reassigning him to a job it knew, or reasonably should have known, he could not perform. The reassignment led directly to this downgrade, which he claimed was also an unfair practice.

Appellant denied any unfairness and contended it was not required to expend special effort on behalf of respondent or other handicapped employees.

The court, after hearing extensive testimony, determined that appellant was required by the terms of RCW 49.60 to make *reasonable accommodation* for handicapped employees. Using this standard, it concluded appellant's actions with respect to respondent constituted a violation of the law against discrimination, RCW 49.60.

Appellant makes five assignments of error. The first three relate to the reasonable accommodation standard and the sufficiency of evidence in support of the court's findings of fact and conclusions of law in this respect.

\* \* \*

Appellant first argues the trial court erred by interpreting RCW 49.60 to require that employers make reasonable accommodation to the handicapped employee when reassigning personnel. The proper interpretation of RCW 49.60.180 as it relates to handicap discrimination is an issue of first impression.

RCW 49.60.180 is part of a comprehensive law by which the legislature declared it is an individual's *civil right* to be free from various types of discrimination. RCW 49.60.030. The express purpose of the law is the elimination of discrimination. RCW 49.60.010. And the legislature has directed liberal construction of the provisions of RCW 49.60 in order to accomplish its purpose. RCW 49.60.020.

In 1973, the legislature amended the law against discrimination, RCW 49.60, to include a prohibition against discrimination in employment because of physical, mental, or sensory handicaps. It recognized that the disabled, like many minority groups, face serious problems in seeking employment. Laws of 1973, 1st Ex.Sess., ch. 214, § 1, p. 1648. Comment, RCW 49.60: *A Discriminating Look,* 13 Gonzaga L.Rev. 190 (1977). Legislation dealing with equality of sex or race was premised on the belief that there were no inherent differences between the general public and those persons in the suspect class. The guarantee of equal employment opportunities for the physically handicapped is far more complex.[1]

The physically disabled employee is clearly different from the nonhandicapped employee by virtue of the disability. But the difference is a disadvantage only when the work environment *fails* to take into account the unique characteristics of the handicapped person. See *Potluck Protections for Handicapped Discriminatees: The Need to Amend Title VII to Prohibit Discrimination on the Basis of Disability,* 8 Loy.Chi.L.J. 814 (1977). Identical treatment may be a source of discrimination in the case of the handicapped, whereas different treatment may eliminate discrimination against the handicapped and open the door to employment opportunities.

RCW 49.60 contains a strong statement of legislative policy. See RCW 49.60.010 and .030. When, in 1973, the legislature chose to make this policy applicable to discrimination against the handicapped, we believe it is clear it mandated positive steps be taken. An interpretation to the contrary would not work to eliminate discrimination. It would instead maintain the *status quo* wherein work environments and job functions are constructed in such a way that handicaps are often intensified because some employees are not physically identical to the "ideal employee."

Further, the concept of definitive relief, by means of a *reasonable accommodation* to the handicapped employee, is found in an administrative regulation issued

---

[1] It is estimated that there are 22 million physically disabled persons in the United States, yet only 800,000 are employed. In addition, estimates put the number of persons suffering from mental retardation at 5.5 million. The economic cost of unemployment of these persons is obvious. The human cost, in terms of suffering or wasted lives, is distressing. Note, *Abroad in the Land: Legal Strategies to Effectuate the Rights of the Physically Disabled,* 61 Geo.L.Rev. 1501 (1973); *Equal Employment and the Disabled: A Proposal,* 10 Colum.J.Law & Soc.Prob. 457 (1974).

pursuant to RCW 49.60. WAC 162-22-080.[2] The regulation, as the construction of the statute by those whose duty it is to administer its terms, is entitled to be given great weight. *Hama Hama Co.* v. *Shorelines Hearings Bd.*, 85 Wash.2d 441, 536 P.2d 157 (1975).

Thus, we hold the trial court correctly interpreted the meaning of RCW 49.60.180(1), (2), and (3).[3] It is an unfair practice for an employer to fail or refuse to make reasonable accommodations to the physical limitations of handicapped employees.

In adopting this standard, we reject appellant's suggestion that we follow the de minimus effort test set forth in *Trans World Airlines, Inc.* v. *Hardison*, 432 U.S. 63, 97 S.Ct. 2264, 53 L.Ed.2d 113 (1977). *Hardison* did not involve a handicapped individual; rather, it involved religious discrimination. Thus, its test was defined in a case arising under Title VII of the Civil Rights Act of 1964, 42 U.S.C. § 2000e-2(a)(1) (1970). Congress has not chosen to prohibit handicap discrimination under Title VII. Instead, it has enacted the Rehabilitation Act of 1973, 29 U.S.C. §§ 701-794 (Supp. V, 1975), to secure employment opportunities for the handicapped. Congress recognized, as do we, that discrimination on the basis of handicap is different in many respects from other types of employment discrimination. *See* Wright, *Equal Treatment of the Handicapped by Federal Contractors*, 26 Emory L.J. 65 (1977). Accordingly, we are not persuaded by appellant's contention on this score.

Appellant next argues that even if Washington law requires reasonable accommodation to the handicapped, reversal is warranted since there is *no* evidence to support the trial court's findings and conclusions that it failed to accommodate respondent.

\* \* \*

The record in this case reflects appellant was aware of respondent's disability and physical limitations. In fact, some years prior to this litigation respondent had attempted to receive certification in soldering and was unable to do so. Further, the record contains substantial testimony regarding appellant's transfer procedures. Several options were potentially available to appellant which would have accommodated respondent. The appellant, however, chose not to accommodate him. It shifted re-

---

[2]WAC 162-22-080(1), which appears to address physical barriers, states:

"(1) It is an unfair practice for an employer to fail or refuse to make reasonable accommodations to the sensory, mental, or physical limitations of employees, unless the employer can demonstrate that such an accommodation would impose an undue hardship on the conduct of the employer's business."

[3]"It is an unfair practice for any employer:

"(1) To refuse to hire any person because of such person's age, sex, marital status, race, creed, color, national origin, or the presence of any sensory, mental, or physical handicap, unless based upon a bona fide occupational qualification: *Provided,* That the prohibition against discrimination because of such handicap shall not apply if the particular disability prevents the proper performance of the particular worker involved.

"(2) To discharge or bar any person from employment because of such person's age, sex, marital status, race, creed, color, national origin, or the presence of any sensory, mental, or physical handicap.

"(3) To discriminate against any person in compensation or in other terms or conditions of employment because of such person's age, sex, marital status, race, creed, color, national origin, or the presence of any sensory, mental, or physical handicap: *Provided,* That it shall not be an unfair practice for an employer to segregate washrooms or locker facilities on the basis of sex, or to base other terms and conditions of employment on the sex of employees where the board by regulation or ruling in a particular instance has found the employment practice to be appropriate for the practical realization of equality of opportunity between the sexes.

". . ." RCW 49.60.180.

spondent to a position in which the trial court found it should have known he could not succeed. It then downgraded him. The trial court concluded these actions were unfair practices. The challenged findings of fact upon which the court's conclusions rest are supported by the record, and we cannot substitute our judgment for that of the trial court. *Seattle-First Nat'l Bank* v. *Brommers,* 89 Wash.2d 190, 199, 570 P.2d 1035 (1977).

Appellant further contends the evidence presented by respondent does not meet his burden of proof as it fails to prove he was qualified for another available position. *See McDonnell Douglas Corp.* v. *Green,* 411 U.S. 792, 93 S.Ct. 1817, 36 L.Ed.2d 668 (1973).

Appellant's argument ignores the essence of respondent's complaint, which is: Arbitrary removal from an otherwise available position and placement in a position where, because of his handicap, he was destined to fail. *McDonnell Douglas* is a failure-to-employ case; the discrimination here alleged by respondent arose from a discriminatory *transfer.* Respondent met his burden of proof by showing the transfer was not the *necessary* result of a reduced workload, since the appellant could have utilized a procedure such as lateral transfers in order to accommodate him.

* * *

WRIGHT, C. J., and ROSELLINI, STAFFORD, BRACHTENBACH, HOROWITZ, DOLLIVER and HICKS, J. J., concur.

NOTES

1.   The *Holland* court was one of the first judicial tribunals to interpret and apply the requirement of reasonable accommodation to handicapped persons. As the court notes in its discussion of the *Hardison* case, the concept of reasonable accommodation was apparently first developed in the context of religious discrimination. Its application to handicapped people and its incorporation into the federal regulations (see section 84.12 of the regulations on p. 413 of the Casebook) marked an important doctrinal advance. For a discussion of reasonable accommodation analysis under federal law, see *Prewitt* v. *United States Postal Service* at pp. 113–127 below.

2.   The questions of how much accommodation is "reasonable" and what types of burdens constitute an "undue hardship" will obviously provide the grist for litigative mills in the future.

3.   In portions of the opinion not included here, the court awarded the plaintiff attorney's fees under the Washington statute and also upheld an order of the trial court requiring the Boeing Company to reimburse Mr. Holland for vacation time he expended during the trial of the case. 583 P.2d at 625.

p. 336—REPLACE Note 1 with the following:

1.   Does the court's definition of *handicap* mesh well with the requirement of reasonable accommodation as in the *Holland* case? Does the specification of the requirements placed upon the employer have any relationship to the definition that is adopted?

p. 336—after Note 2, insert:

3.  The only United States Supreme Court decision dealing with a state statute prohibiting employment discrimination on the basis of handicap is *Logan* v. *Zimmerman Brush Co.,* _____ U.S. _____, 102 S.Ct. 1148 (1982). The *Logan* case involved a complaint filed with the Illinois Fair Employment Practices Commission by a man who charged that he had been dismissed from his job because of his physical handicap (short left leg). Under the Illinois statute, the Commission had 120 days from the filing of the complaint to convene a factfinding conference. The Commission failed to comply with this 120 day time limit, thereby losing its jurisdiction to pursue the matter, and effectively extinguishing the complainant's cause of action under the statute. The Supreme Court ruled that the Illinois Fair Employment Practices Act created a property interest in a complainant's rights under the Act. In light of this property interest, the Commission's failure to provide the complainant a hearing in regard to his claim constituted a denial of due process, as it involved the taking of property without an opportunity for a hearing. *Id.* at 102 S.Ct. 1153–1159. The Court declared that "Logan is entitled to have the Commission consider the merits of his charge, based upon the substantiality of the available evidence, before deciding whether to terminate his claim." *Ibid.* Does this rationale prohibit the imposition of any procedural prerequisites whatever to claims under states' antidiscrimination and fair employment laws?

## E.  THE UNITED STATES CONSTITUTION

### 1.  The Fourteenth Amendment
### b.  Due Process
p. 356—INSERT before the beginning of Subsection 2:

### BROWN v. SIBLEY
*United States Court of Appeals for the Fifth Circuit, 1981*
*650 F.2d 760*

Before INGRAHAM, POLITZ and WILLIAMS, Circuit Judges.

INGRAHAM, Circuit Judge:

Named plaintiffs, visually impaired employees of Mississippi Industries for the Blind (MIB), brought a class action against that state agency and its officials alleging employment discrimination violative of . . . the fourteenth amendment to the United States Constitution.

\* \* \*

This cause was filed as a class action in December 1978 by named plaintiffs Alfred Brown, William King, and Willie Mallet. Named plaintiffs alleged employment discrimination against visually impaired employees at MIB. They specifically alleged that they had been denied promotion to supervisory and nonmanual labor positions at MIB because of their handicaps. They sought relief in the form of promotions to supervisory positions, back pay, damages, and attorney fees and costs. After discovery the district court certified a plaintiff class in June 1979 and defined it as follows:

> All visually handicapped individuals qualified for supervisory and non-manual labor positions at Mississippi Industries for the Blind, but who solely because of their visual

handicap, have been, are being, or will be prevented by defendants from advancing to such positions.[1]

\* \* \*

Named plaintiffs allege on behalf of themselves and the certified class discriminatory treatment at the hands of MIB violative of the fourteenth amendment and 42 U.S.C. § 1983 (1976). First, they allege the existence of an unwritten policy at MIB to the effect that the visually impaired cannot work in supervisory and nonmanual labor positions. This policy is said to constitute an "irrebuttable presumption" in violation of the due process clause of the fourteenth amendment. *See generally Cleveland Board of Education* v. *LaFleur,* 414 U.S. 632, 94 S.Ct. 791, 39 L.Ed.2d 52 (1974); *Vlandis* v. *Kline,* 412 U.S. 441, 93 S.Ct. 2230, 37 L.Ed.2d 63 (1973).

Whatever the present vitality of the "irrebuttable presumption" doctrine as distinct from traditional equal protection concerns, *see generally Elkins* v. *Moreno,* 435 U.S. 647, 658–61, 98 S.Ct. 1338, 1345–47, 55 L.Ed.2d 614 (1978); J. Nowak, R. Rotunda & N. Young, Handbook on Constitutional Law 497 (1978), we agree with the district court that there is no such presumption operative at MIB. Visually impaired persons have held supervisory and nonmanual labor positions at MIB in the past and continue to do so today. Even *if* there were some "presumption" as to the inability of these people to hold such positions, it obviously is "rebuttable," as demonstrated by the past and present employment of the visually impaired in those positions.

Second, named plaintiffs allege that MIB's treatment of the visually impaired as being unfit for supervisory and nonmanual labor positions creates "an arbitrary, discriminatory, and unreasonable classification" that violates their rights to equal protection of the laws. An examination of the record indicates that in making its promotion decisions for supervisory and nonmanual labor positions MIB is concerned with the safety of its employees and with the workmanlike performance of the contractual relationships from which it earns income to sustain its operations. Named plaintiffs do not appear to contend that MIB's alleged policy bears no rational relationship to those legitimate governmental concerns. Rather, they contend that "the physically handicapped are a suspect classification of our population and any state discrimination against the handicapped must be subjected to the strict scrutiny test under the Equal Protection Clause of the Fourteenth Amendment."

Named plaintiffs' request for strict judicial scrutiny under the equal protection clause is misplaced. No court has ever declared that handicapped persons constitute a suspect class for purposes of equal protection analysis, and we decline to do so today. Since neither can they claim the benefits of a suspect classification nor were they subjected to the deprivation of any fundamental constitutional right, *see San Antonio Independent School District* v. *Rodriguez,* 411 U.S. 1, 93 S.Ct. 1278, 36 L.Ed.2d 16

---

[1]Persons with visual impairment experience varying degrees of disability. For administrative and recordkeeping purposes, including eligibility to qualify for certain federal procurement contracts, MIB uses the following classifications: totally blind; legally blind (eyesight in best eye less than 20/200 corrected); visually handicapped (eyesight in best eye less than 20/70 corrected). It is clear from the record that, in defining the certified class, the district court did not use the term "visually handicapped" in this specialized sense. Rather, the district court included in the class the visually handicapped, the legally blind, and the totally blind.

(1973), the only inquiry is whether MIB's alleged classification scheme is "rationally related to the [state agency's] objective." *Massachusetts Board of Retirement* v. *Murgia,* 427 U.S. 307, 315, 96 S.Ct. 2562, 2568, 49 L.Ed.2d 520 (1976). "The constitutional safeguard is offended only if the classification rests on grounds wholly irrelevant to the achievement of the [state agency's] objective." *McGowan* v. *Maryland,* 366 U.S. 420, 425, 81 S.Ct. 1101, 1104, 6 L.Ed.2d 393 (1961).

Analyzing their claims under the rational relationship test, we find that MIB's conduct does not offend the fourteenth amendment. After noting the various supervisory and nonmanual labor positions formerly or currently held by visually impaired persons, the district court found that certain aspects of the remaining supervisory and nonmanual labor positions involved detailed reading and writing, driving of vehicles, quality control duties, pattern cutting skills, or careful inventorying of materials. These findings were not clearly erroneous. *See* Fed.R.Civ.P. 52(a); *United States* v. *United States Gypsum Co.,* 333 U.S. 364, 395, 68 S.Ct. 525, 541, 92 L.Ed. 746 (1947). MIB's underlying assumption that sight is required for certain of the skills demanded of its supervisory and nonmanual labor employees is certainly not irrational: in terms of likelihood, MIB reasonably could assume that a sighted person could more safely and proficiently perform those skills than could one with a disabling visual impairment. MIB "is not compelled to verify logical assumptions with statistical evidence" in order to pass muster under the rational relationship test. *Hughes* v. *Alexandria Scrap Corp.,* 426 U.S. 794, 812, 96 S.Ct. 2488, 2499, 49 L.Ed.2d 220 (1976).

More fundamentally, named plaintiffs failed to establish that MIB actually classifies visually impaired persons as a group as being unfit for supervisory and nonmanual labor positions. The district court concluded that the failure of these named plaintiffs to secure the supervisory position they sought was not due to discrimination by MIB on the basis of their respective handicaps, and that MIB had not engaged in a pattern or practice of failure to promote the otherwise qualified visually impaired to supervisory and nonmanual labor positions. These conclusions were not erroneous. Like their due process claims, the equal protection claims of named plaintiffs and the class they represent must fail.

\* \* \*

NOTES

1. In portions of the opinion not included here, the court also ruled that the plaintiffs had no cause of action under Section 504 of the Rehabilitation Act because of a lack of a showing of federal financial assistance (650 F.2d at 769–771; see pp. 409–431 of the Casebook and pp. 137–170 below), nor under Section 503 (650 F.2d at 763–765; see pp. 370–409 of the Casebook and pp. 128–137 below).

2. In regard to the court's assertion that "No court has ever declared that handicapped persons constitute a suspect class for purposes of equal protection analysis," see *In re G.H.,* pp. 113–120 of the Casebook and *Fialkowski* v. *Shapp,* pp. 122–125 of the Casebook.

3. *Carmi* v. *Metropolitan St. Louis Sewer District,* 620 F.2d 672 (8th Cir. 1980), involved a plaintiff with Progressive Peroneal Atrophy, a rare, hereditary condition

that results in deterioration of the muscles and nerves of the hands and feet, who had been denied a job as a storekeeper at a city sewage treatment plant. Using a rational basis standard, the court ruled that the decision not to hire the plaintiff was not a violation of equal protection, as it was related to the need for the storekeeper to be able to lift and move heavy objects. In addition, the court held that the plaintiff could claim no denial of due process because, as a mere job applicant, "[h]is interest in employment . . . did not rise to the level of a constitutionally protected property interest." 620 F.2d at 676. Contrast this result with the *Gurmankin* and *Duran* cases. Are these decisions reconcilable?

4.  In *Hutchings* v. *Erie City and County Library Board of Directors*, 516 F.Supp. 1265 (W.D.Pa. 1981), a librarian with multiple sclerosis alleged that she had been demoted, reprimanded, harassed, and otherwise discriminated against because of her handicap. Although the court in *Hutchings* agreed with the *Brown* v. *Sibley* court that the rational relationship test was the applicable standard, it ruled that the plaintiff had stated a cause of action under Section 1983 for a violation of equal protection: "the gravamen of the plaintiff's complaint is that she has been discriminated against and harassed solely on the basis of her handicap. At present the defendants have not provided any explanation for these alleged acts of discrimination." At 516 F.Supp. 1270. Contrast this situation with those in *Brown* v. *Sibley* and in *Carmi*. If a plaintiff is able to prove "harassment" because of a handicap, how can an employer demonstrate a rational relationship to a legitimate governmental objective?

## F.  FEDERAL LEGISLATION AND REGULATIONS

### 1.  Jobs with United States Government Agencies

p. 370—INSERT before the beginning of Subsection 2:

### PREWITT v. UNITED STATES POSTAL SERVICE

*United States Court of Appeals for the Fifth Circuit, 1981*
*662 F.2d 292*

Before RUBIN, RANDALL and TATE, Circuit Judges.

TATE, Circuit Judge:

Claiming that the United States Postal Service unlawfully denied him employment due to his physical handicap, the plaintiff, George Dunbar Prewitt, Jr., brought this action against the postal service. Prewitt contended that he was physically able to perform the job for which he applied despite his handicap, even though the postal service's physical requirements indicate that only persons in "good physical condition" can perform the job because it involves "arduous" work. Prewitt alleged, inter alia, that the postal service thus violated his rights under the Rehabilitation Act of 1973, as amended, 29 U.S.C. § 701 *et seq.* Prewitt filed this suit as a class action, after he was denied employment as a clerk/carrier at the Greenville, Mississippi post office. The district court granted the postal service's motion for summary judgment. On Prewitt's appeal, we find that the plaintiff has raised genuine issues of material fact as to 1) whether the postal service's physical requirements for postal employment are sufficiently "job related" to provide lawful grounds for the refusal to hire Prewitt, and 2) whether the postal service has breached its duty to make "reasonable accommodation" for handicapped persons such as Prewitt. Accordingly, we reverse the summary judgment of the district court, and remand the case for further proceedings in accordance with this opinion.

### The Factual Background

The plaintiff Prewitt is a disabled Vietnam war veteran. Due to gunshot wounds, he must endure limited mobility of his left arm and shoulder. Nevertheless, in May 1970 (prior to his rejection for re-employment in 1978 that gave rise to this lawsuit), Prewitt applied for a position as a distribution clerk in the Jackson, Mississippi post office, a position which, according to the job description, "require[s] arduous physical exertion involving prolonged standing, throwing, reaching, and may involve lifting sacks of mail up to 80 pounds." Prewitt was hired after passing the requisite written and medical examinations, and it is undisputed that, despite his handicap, he performed his duties in a competent, entirely satisfactory manner.

Prewitt resigned his position at the Jackson post office in September 1970 to return to school. He testified in his affidavit, which we must regard as true for summary judgment purposes, that his physical condition did not diminish in any significant way between May 1970 and September 1978, when he applied for the position at the Greenville post office that gave rise to this lawsuit. Prewitt questions the failure of the postal service to re-employ him in 1978, due to a physical handicap, for a position as clerk/carrier, a position with similar physical requirements to those of the job that he had satisfactorily performed in 1970.

After applying for the clerk/carrier position at Greenville in 1978, Prewitt took and passed a standard written examination. He received a final rating of 92.8 (basic rating of 82.8 plus a 10 point compensable veteran's preference), which placed him second on the roster of eligible applicants. Physical suitability for the position, however, remained to be determined.

According to the postal services qualification standards, the duties of a carrier "are arduous and require that the incumbent be in good physical condition." Thus, a medical form which was given to Prewitt indicates that applicants for this position must meet a wide range of physical criteria, including, inter alia, the ability to see, hear, lift heavy weights, carry moderate weights, reach above shoulder, and use fingers and both hands. According to the affidavit of Postmaster Charles Hughes, the duties of a clerk/carrier require stooping, bending, squatting, lifting up to seventy pounds, standing for long periods, stretching arms in all directions, reaching above and below the shoulder, and some twisting of the back.

To determine whether Prewitt could meet these physical standards, the Greenville postal authorities asked Prewitt to authorize the Veteran's Administration (VA) to release his medical records to the postal service for examination, and Prewitt complied with this request. The VA records, which apparently were made in 1970 before Prewitt was awarded disability benefits, indicated that Prewitt had a 30% service-related disability that caused "limitation of motion of left shoulder and atrophy of trapezius," as well as that he had a kidney disease, hypertension, and an eye condition not related to his armed forces service. The VA report was analyzed by Dr. Cenon Baltazar, a postal medical officer, who reported: "Limited records pertaining to [Prewitt] showed limitation of left shoulder and atrophy of trapezius muscle. This is not suitable for full performance as required of postal service positions unless it is a desk job." Prewitt subsequently received from Hughes a terse, two sentence letter informing him that Dr. Baltazar had determined that he was "medically unsuitable for postal employment." The letter did not state any reasons for this finding of unsuitability.

After receiving word of this adverse determination, Prewitt contacted Hughes to dispute the conclusion of the medical officer. Hughes told Prewitt that there was no appeal from the decision, but that the decision would be reconsidered at the local level if Prewitt would undergo an examination, at his own expense, by a private physician. In fact, Prewitt did have the right to appeal to the postal service's regional medical director. After belatedly learning of this right, Prewitt exercised his right to appeal, but he chose not to undergo a new physical examination. The regional medical officer, Dr. Gedney, examined the VA report and concluded that Prewitt was medically unsuitable. Unlike Dr. Baltazar, who relied solely on Prewitt's shoulder injury as the basis for his adverse determination, Dr. Gedney also mentioned the kidney disease (which Dr. Gedney stated is an unpredictably progressive disease that could possibly be aggravated by arduous duty) and hypertension. Based on Dr. Gedney's report, the regional office sustained the adverse determination and told Prewitt that there were no further medical appeal rights. Again, the letter did not inform Prewitt of the medical reasons upon which this conclusion was based.

Although the regional office correctly stated that there were no further *medical* appeal rights, in fact Prewitt had available to him an entirely independent chain of administrative review of the adverse determination through the postal service's equal employment opportunity (EEO) office. Prewitt filed an EEO complaint, alleging that the postal service had discriminated against him on the basis of his handicap by finding him unsuitable for postal employment. The EEO office conducted an investigation and found that the same medical officer who had disqualified Prewitt had ruled three other disabled or physically handicapped applicants suitable for postal employment. The investigation also revealed that the Greenville post office had hired fourteen persons classified as disabled and/or physically handicapped. Relying on these findings, the EEO office found no discrimination and advised Prewitt that he could appeal its decision to the Office of Appeals and Review of the Equal Employment Opportunity Commission (EEOC).

As permitted by statute, 42 U.S.C. § 2000e-16(c), made applicable to the handicapped by 29 U.S.C. § 794a(a)(1), instead of appealing to the EEOC, Prewitt filed this suit in the district court. No contention is made by the postal service that Prewitt did not exhaust administrative remedies. The postal service responded to Prewitt's complaint with a motion for summary judgment, contending that it had rejected Prewitt for valid medical reasons, and that Prewitt's refusal to take a physical examination had precluded it from making a re-evaluation. The plaintiff responded that postal service regulations required that applicants be given a current physical examination before a medical determination is made, and therefore, even though Prewitt was afforded an opportunity to take a physical after his determination was made, the determination of medical unfitness was invalid. Prewitt further argued that the regulations entitled him to a free physical examination, so that he was not required to bear the expense of an examination by a private physician. Finally, Prewitt noted that in view of the undisputed fact that he had been able to perform completely a similar job in 1970, the postal service had failed to articulate any legitimate reason for its finding of medical unsuitability.

The district court reasoned that:

> The key to this case lies in plaintiff's continued refusal to take a current physical examination. This refusal has rendered meaningless the defendant's attempt to reevaluate plaintiff's current physical condition, though the postal service gave plaintiff ample opportunity to supplement the information available to it. The postal service extended plaintiff this opportunity at the initial stage of the procedure, and the opportunity remained open to plaintiff throughout the appellate process. Plaintiff simply cannot base a claim upon a 1970 medical examination when the Veterans Administration records presently available to defendant disclose substantial disability. . . .

Accordingly, the district court granted the postal service's motion for summary judgment, and struck the class action allegations in Prewitt's complaint.

## The Applicable Legal Principles

Our trial brother fell into error of law in his analysis by his implicit assumption that the "substantial disability" disclosed by the Veterans Administration records provided the postal service with legally sufficient grounds for rejecting Prewitt's bid for the clerk/carrier position. For reasons stated below, we find, construing the evidence in the light most favorable to the party resisting summary judgment, that under the Rehabilitation Act of 1973, as amended, a genuine issue of material fact exists as to whether the postal service's physical requirements for postal employment are sufficiently "job related" to provide lawful grounds for the refusal to hire Prewitt.

### 1. The Applicability of the Rehabilitation Act to Federal Government Hiring

Only since 1978 have handicapped individuals been entitled to bring private actions against federal agencies for violations of the Rehabilitation Act. This is apparently the first case in which a federal appellate court has been called upon to determine the nature and extent of this newly-created private right. We shall therefore examine the history of this legislation in some detail.

Congress passed the Rehabilitation Act of 1973 for the express purpose, inter alia, of "promot[ing] and expand[ing] employment opportunities in the public and private sectors for handicapped individuals." 29 U.S.C. § 701(8). In addition to creating a number of wide-ranging federally-funded programs designed to aid handicapped persons in assuming a full role in society, the Act, in its Title V, established the principle that (a) the federal government, (b) federal contractors, and (c) recipients of federal funds cannot discriminate against the handicapped.

The duties of each of these three classes of entities were set forth in separate sections. Section 503 of the Act, 29 U.S.C. § 793, required federal contractors to include in their contracts with the United States a provision mandating that, in employing persons to carry out the contract, "the party contracting with the United States shall take affirmative action to employ and advance in employment qualified handicapped individuals. . . ." Section 504, 29 U.S.C. § 794, which imposed duties on recipients of federal funds, provided: "No otherwise qualified handicapped individual . . . shall, solely by reason of his handicap, be excluded from participation in, be denied the benefits of, or be subjected to discrimination under any program or activity receiving federal financial assistance."

The duties of the federal government itself were set forth in section 501(b), 29 U.S.C. § 791(b) which stated:

> Each department, agency, and instrumentality (including the United States Postal Service and the Postal Rate Commission) in the executive branch shall . . . submit to the Civil Service Commission and to the [Interagency Committee on Handicapped Employees] an affirmative action program plan for the hiring, placement, and advancement of handicapped individuals in such department, agency, or instrumentality. Such plan shall include a description of the extent to which and methods whereby the special needs of handicapped employees are being met.

\* \* \*

A Senate committee report commenting on section 501 emphasized that "the Federal Government must be an equal opportunity employer, and that this equal opportunity must apply fully to handicapped individuals."[9] As Senator Cranston subsequently commented in connection with 1978 amendments strengthening the federal employment rights of the handicapped, "[t]he legislative history of the section 501 illustrates that with respect to the employment of handicapped individuals, Congress expected the Federal Government should be a leader."[10] In the words of Senator Williams, Congress enacted section 501 "to require that the Federal Government itself act as the model employer of the handicapped and take affirmative action to hire and promote the disabled."[11]

Under the original 1973 Rehabilitation Act, a private cause of action founded on handicap discrimination was not recognized upon section 501 as against a federal government employer; the literal statutory wording merely required federal agencies to *submit* affirmative actions plans.[12] However, due to differences in statutory wording, all courts that considered the issue found that section 504 established a private cause of action for handicapped persons subjected to discrimination by recipients of federal funds,[13] while the federal courts split on the question whether the same was true under

---

[9]S.Rep.No.93-318, 93d Cong., 1st Sess., at 49 (1973), U.S.Code Cong. & Admin. News 1973, pp. 2076, 2122.

[10]Cong.Rec. S15591 (Sept. 20, 1978).

[11]Rehabilitation of the Handicapped Programs 1976: Hearings Before the Subcommittee on the Handicapped of the Committee on Labor and Public Welfare, 94th Cong., 2d Sess., at 1502 (1976), *quoted in* Linn, *Uncle Sam Doesn't Want You: Entering the Federal Stronghold of Employment Discrimination Against Handicapped Individuals,* 27 DePaul L.Rev. 1047, 1060 (1978).

[12]*See Counts* v. *United States Postal Service,* 17 F.E.P. Cases 1161, 1165 (N.D.Fla.1978), *reversed due to statutory changes,* 631 F.2d 46 (5th Cir. 1980), *Coleman* v. *Darden,* 15 F.E.P. Cases 272, 273 (D.Colo.1977), *aff'd,* 595 F.2d 533 (10th Cir. 1979); B. Schlei & P. Grossman, Employment Discrimination Law 65 (Supp. 1979). *But see* Linn, *supra* note 11, at 1056–71 (urging recognition of a private right of action under section 501).

[13]*See Camenisch* v. *University of Texas,* 616 F.2d 127, 131 (5th Cir. 1980), *vacated on other grounds,* _____ U.S. _____, 101 S.Ct. 1830, 68 L.Ed.2d 175 (1981), and cases from the Seventh, Second, Eighth, Fourth, and Third Circuits cited therein.

section 503 for individuals subjected to handicap discrimination by federal contractors.[14]

In 1978, the Rehabilitation Act was amended to provide a private cause of action in favor of persons subjected to handicap discrimination by the federal government employing agencies. In the House, an amendment was adopted and ultimately enacted by the Congress that extended section 504's proscription against handicap discrimination to "any program or activity conducted by an Executive agency or by the United States Postal Service;"[15] the legislative history, as well as the judicial interpretations (see note 13), fully recognized that a private right of action had been created by section 504.[16]

The Senate, at the same time, added a new section 505(a)(1) to the Rehabilitation Act, which created a private right of action under section 501. The provision states:

> The remedies, procedures, and rights set forth in section 717 of the Civil Rights Act of 1964 [42 U.S.C. § 2000e-16], including the application of sections 706(f) through 706(k), [42 U.S.C. § 2000e-5], shall be available, with respect to any complaint under section 501 of this Act, to any employee or applicant for employment aggrieved by the final deposition of such complaint, or by the failure to take final action on such complaint.

Section 717 of Title VII of the Civil Rights Act, 42 U.S.C. § 2000e-16, to which section 501 is explicitly tied by the new section 505, mandates that all federal personnel actions be made "free from any discrimination based on race, color, religion, sex, or national origin." The provision further provides for a private right of action in favor of those whose claims of discrimination have not been satisfactorily resolved by administrative procedures. However, before an individual can bring a section 717 action in court, strict procedural requirements with respect to exhaustion of administrative remedies must be fulfilled. *See* 42 U.S.C. § 2000e-16(c). Once administrative remedies have been exhausted, however, an individual is entitled to de novo consideration of his discrimination claims in the district court; however, prior admin-

---

[14]*Compare Brown* v. *Sibley,* 650 F.2d 760, 763–65 (5th Cir. 1981); *Rogers* v. *Frito-Lay, Inc.,* 611 F.2d 1074 (5th Cir. 1980); *Hooper* v. *Equifax, Inc.,* 611 F.2d 134, 135 (8th Cir. 1979); *Anderson* v. *Erie Lackawanna Railway Co.,* 468 F.Supp. 934 (E.D.Ohio 1979); *Wood* v. *Diamond State Telephone Co.,* 440 F.Supp. 1003, 1010 (D.Del.1977); *and Moon* v. *Roadway Express, Inc.,* 439 F.Supp. 1308, 1310 (N.D.Ga. 1977) *with Clarke* v. *FELEC Services, Inc.,* 489 F.Supp. 165, 169 (D.Alaska 1980); *Hart* v. *Alameda County,* 485 F.Supp. 66, 76 (N.D.Cal. 1979); *Chaplin* v. *Consolidated Edison Co.,* 482 F.Supp. 1165, 1173 (S.D.N.Y.1980); *Duran* v. *City of Tampa,* 430 F.Supp. 75, 78 (M.D.Fla. 1977); *Drennon* v. *Philadelphia General Hospital,* 428 F.Supp. 809, 816 (E.D.Pa.1977); and *Rogers* v. *Frito-Lay, Inc., supra,* 611 F.2d at 1085 (Goldberg, J., dissenting).

[15]The amended section 504, 29 U.S.C. § 794, now states in pertinent part:

> No otherwise qualified handicapped individual in the United States, as defined in section 706(7) of this title shall, solely by reason of his handicap, be excluded from the participation in, be denied the benefits of, or be subjected to discrimination under any program or activity receiving Federal financial assistance or any program *or activity conducted by any Executive agency or by the United States Postal Service.* (Emphasis supplied.)

[16]*See, e.g.,* the legislative history cited by Judge Goldberg in his dissenting opinion in *Rogers* v. *Frito-Lay, Inc.,* 611 F.2d 1074, 1096–98 (5th Cir. 1980), a *section 503 case.* Although the *Rogers* majority held that this legislative history does not prove the existence of a private right of action under *section 503* of the Rehabilitation Act, this legislative history at least shows that the 1978 Congress had no quarrel with the near-unanimous judicial interpretation of *section 504.*

istrative findings made with respect to an employment discrimination claim may be admitted into evidence at the trial de novo. *See Chandler* v. *Roudebush,* 425 U.S. 840, 863–64, 96 S.Ct. 1949, 1960–61, 48 L.Ed.2d 416 (1976).

The Senate Committee on Human Resources explained its reasons for granting the rights set forth in section 717 to section 501 plaintiffs:

> In testimony before the Subcommittee on the Handicapped, Deborah Kaplan of the Disability Rights Center noted that she had been examining the implementation of section 501 and recommended that legislative changes be made to "make it stronger and easier to enforce and to provide the same civil rights protection to the disabled that other minorities have in employment with the Federal Government." Ms. Kaplan's group discovered that in the first 2 years after enactment of section 501 "only 12 Federal agencies have increased their rate of hiring disabled employees by more than 3 percent."
>
> The committee believes now as it did in 1973 that the Federal Government must be "an equal opportunity employer." The amendment to section 501 will aid in attaining that goal by providing for individuals aggrieved on the basis of their handicap the same rights, procedures, and remedies provided individuals aggrieved on the basis of race, creed, color, or national origin. . . . Further, application of the title VII provisions makes specific the right to bring a private right of action with respect to section 501, subject, of course, to the provision for exhaustion of administrative remedies and other rules and procedures set forth in title VII.

Sen.Rep.No.95-890, 95th Cong., 2d Sess., at 18–19 (1978). *See also* Cong.Rec. S15591 (Daily ed. Sept. 20, 1978) (remarks of Sen. Cranston).

The scope of the federal government's obligations under section 501 received Senate attention during debate on a proposed amendment to the proposed new section 505(a)(1). An amendment offered by Senator McClure would have added the following clause at the end of section 505(a)(1): "provided, however, that no equitable relief or affirmative action remedy disproportionately exceeding actual damages in the case shall be available under this section." Cong.Rec. S15664 (Daily ed. Sept. 21, 1978). Senator McClure explained that his amendment "would provide that the federally financed affirmative action remedy . . . could not be used to initiate massive construction projects for relatively minor temporal damages." *Id.*

Senators Cranston and Stafford spoke in opposition to the McClure amendment. Senator Cranston remarked:

> I believe that the requirement with respect to Federal Contractors and grantees should be no less stringent than the requirements attached to the Federal Government. The amendment offered by the Senator from Idaho would create an unwise and unrealistic distinction with respect of employment between the obligations of the Federal Government and the obligations of Federal contractors and grantees. Ironically, the Senator's amendment would limit—with a financial test—the Federal Government's obligation of being an equal opportunity employer. Federal contractors and grantees would—appropriately—continue to be required to be equal opportunity employers. Rather than a leader in this field, the Federal Government would become a distant also-ran requiring more of its grantees and contractors than it would be willing to require of itself.

*Id.* at S15665–66.

The dispute was resolved when Senator McClure and the managers of the bill agreed upon the following compromise language: "In fashioning an equitable or affirmative action remedy under such section [section 501], a court may take into account the reasonableness of the cost of any necessary workplace accommodation, and the availability of alternative therefor or other appropriate relief.'' *Id.* at S15667. As thus amended, the new section 505(a)(1) was enacted into law, and is now codified as 29 U.S.C. 794a(a)(1).[17]

In summary, the 1978 amendments to the Rehabilitation Act 1) established a private right of action, subject to the same procedural constraints (administrative exhaustion, etc.) set forth in Title VII of the Civil Rights Act, in favor of section 501 claimants, and 2) extended section 504's proscription against handicap employment discrimination to cover the activities of the federal government itself.

Thus, by its 1978 amendments to the Rehabilitation Act, Congress clearly recognized both in Section 501 and in section 504 that individuals now have a private cause of action to obtain relief for handicap discrimination on the part of the federal government and its agencies. The amendments to section 504 were simply the House's answer to the same problem that the Senate saw fit to resolve by strengthening section 501. The joint House-Senate conference committee could have chosen to eliminate the partial overlap between the two provisions, but instead the conference committee, and subsequently Congress as a whole, chose to pass both provisions, despite the overlap. ''When there are two acts upon the same subject, the rule is to give effect to both if possible.'' *United States* v. *Borden Co.,* 308 U.S. 188, 198, 60 S.Ct. 182, 188, 84 L.Ed. 181 (1939). By this same principle, in order to give effect to *both* the House and the Senate 1978 amendments finally enacted, we must read the exhaustion of administrative remedies requirement of section 501 into the private remedy recognized by both section 501 and section 504 for federal government handicap discrimination.

### 2. *Prewitt's Present Claim(s) of Handicap Discrimination*

In the present suit, Prewitt claims that, despite his handicap, he is physically able to perform the job for which he applied, but that the postal service's physical requirements, neutral on their face, had *disparate impact* upon a person with his particular handicap and that they excluded him from employment that in fact he was physically able to perform. The present case was dismissed on summary judgment, through a failure to take into account the principles applicable to the federal government by the Rehabilitation Act of 1973, as amended in 1978; due to disputed issues of material fact, as will be stated, summary judgment was improvidently granted.

To anticipate issues that will arise on the remand, we will also take judicial notice of further factual developments set forth in the record of a companion suit, which was consolidated with the present one for appeal, an opinion in which is rendered this same date, *Prewitt* v. *United States Postal Service,* 662 F.2d 311 (5th

---

[17]The new section 505(a)(1), 29 U.S.C. § 794a(a)(1), added by the Senate amendment to the Rehabilitation Act provides:

> The remedies, procedures, and rights set forth in section 717 of the Civil Rights Act of 1964, including the application of sections 706(f) through 706(k), shall be available, with respect to any complaint under section 791 of this title, to any employee or applicant for employment aggrieved by the final disposition of such complaint, or by the failure to take final action on such complaint. In fashioning an equitable or affirmative action remedy under such section, a court may take into account the reasonableness of the cost of any necessary work place accommodation, and the availability of alternatives therefor or other appropriate relief in order to achieve an equitable and appropriate remedy.

Cir. 1981), Docket No. 81-4205 (1981). This latter case concerns Prewitt's suit with regard to the 1980 rejection of his new application for employment for a position as a substitute rural carrier at the Greenville post office. At a hearing on Prewitt's motion for a preliminary injunction, after which the district court dismissed Prewitt's complaint (a dismissal we vacate today), testimony was submitted by the postal service that made specific the factual reasons why the postal service believes Prewitt had to be rejected because of his physical condition. The physical requirements for the substitute rural carrier position for which Prewitt applied in 1980, it should be noted, are much the same as those for the clerk-carrier position involved in the present suit.

One of the chief physical factors upon which the postal service bases its refusal to hire Prewitt is that, due to Prewitt's inability to lift his left arm above shoulder level, the employing authority feels that he cannot "case" (sort) the mail that he would be required to deliver on his route. Because a carrier is required to lift above shoulder level with both hands to remove stacks of mail from a six-foot-high top ledge, the postal service contends that Prewitt would not be able to do this part of the job without some workplace modification—however, the postal service witness admitted, for instance, that Prewitt could be accommodated simply by lowering the legs to which the shelves are attached. Only if Prewitt, despite his handicap, can perform the essential duties of the position in question despite his handicap, without the need for any workplace accommodation, can it be said that he was a victim of "disparate impact" discrimination. However, even if Prewitt cannot so perform, he might still be entitled to relief if he was a victim of "surmountable barrier" discrimination, *i.e.*, if he was rejected even though he could have performed the essentials of the job if afforded reasonable accommodation.[19]

Since both issues will arise on the remand, we will therefore note the principles applicable to judicial determination of both cases involving claims of "disparate impact" and also of "surmountable barrier" ("the duty to make reasonable accommodation") discrimination against a handicapped person.

Preliminarily, however, we should observe that section 501 requires affirmative action on the part of federal agencies; unlike section 504 of the Rehabilitation Act and Title VII of the Civil Rights Act which usually require only nondiscrimination. In *Ryan* v. *Federal Deposit Insurance Corp.*, 565 F.2d 762, 763 (D.C.Cir.1977), the court held, and we agree, especially in light of the 1978 amendments, that section 501

---

[19]Commentators have identified four distinct types of discriminatory barriers that handicapped persons must confront when seeking employment: 1. Intentional discrimination for reasons of social bias (racial, sexual, religion, handicap, etc.); 2. neutral standards with disparate impact; 3. surmountable impairment barriers; and 4. insurmountable impairment barriers. *See* Note, *Accommodating the Handicapped: The Meaning of Discrimination Under Section 504 of the Rehabilitation Act*, 55 N.Y.U. L.Rev. 881, 883–84 (1980). *See also* Gittler, *Fair Employment and the Handicapped: A Legal Perspective*, 27 DePaul L.Rev. 953, 958–66 (1978).

The present complaints by Prewitt involve alleged "disparate impact" and a "surmountable barrier" handicap-discrimination.

The Title VII jurisprudence·is, we believe, for the most part applicable to intentional social-bias discrimination against handicapped persons. *See Texas Department of Corrections* v. *Burdine*, 450 U.S. 248, 101 S.Ct. 1089, 67 L.Ed.2d 207 (1981) and *McDonnell Douglas Corp.* v. *Green*, 411 U.S. 792, 93 S.Ct. 1817, 36 L.Ed.2d 668 (1973). Likewise, as will be noted in the text, the Title VII disparate impact decisions are relevant in the determination of disparate impact handicap discrimination. Surmountable and insurmountable barriers raise issues that for the most part are peculiar to handicap discrimination.

requires that federal agencies do more than just *submit* affirmative plans—section 501 "impose[s] a duty upon federal agencies to structure their procedures and programs so as to ensure that handicapped individuals are afforded equal opportunity in both job assignment and promotion." Although *Ryan*, which was decided prior to the 1978 amendments, did not recognize a private right of action under section 501, the court held that the defendant federal agency should amend its procedures to provide an administrative forum through which handicapped individuals could enforce their section 501 rights. *Id.* at 764. Subsequent to *Ryan*, the Civil Service Commission, and its successor enforcement agency, the EEOC, promulgated administrative regulations that define the section 501 duties of federal agencies, *see* 29 C.F.R. §§ 1613.704 *et seq.*, which for instance (see below) include the duty to make reasonable accommodation to employ a handicapped person, *see* 29 C.F.R. § 1613.704. These regulations are the administrative interpretation of the Act by the enforcing agency and are therefore entitled to some deference in our attempt to determine the applications of this statute. *See Southeastern Community College* v. *Davis*, 442 U.S. 397, 99 S.Ct. 2361, 2369, 60 L.Ed.2d 980 (1979); *Albemarle Paper Co.* v. *Moody*, 422 U.S. 405, 431, 95 S.Ct. 2362, 2378, 45 L.Ed.2d 280 (1975); *Griggs* v. *Duke Power Co.*, 401 U.S. 424, 433–34, 91 S.Ct. 849, 854–55, 28 L.Ed.2d 158 (1971).

### 3. *"Disparate Impact" Discrimination*

*Griggs* v. *Duke Power Company*, *supra*, may be considered the seminal decision concerning instances whereby a facially neutral employment policy has a discriminatory impact upon the employment of individuals statutorily protected against discrimination. There the Court held that an employer's use of written tests and a high school degree requirement violated Title VII of the Civil Rights Act of 1964 because the criteria were not shown to be related to job performance. The unanimous Court reasoned: "The Act proscribes not only overt discrimination but also practices that are fair in form, but discriminatory in operation. The touchstone is business necessity. If an employment practice which operates to exclude Negroes cannot be shown to be related to job performance, the practice is prohibited." 401 U.S. at 431, 91 S.Ct. at 853. *See also Albermarle Paper Co.* v. *Moody*, *supra*. In *Dothard* v. *Rawlinson*, 433 U.S. 321, 97 S.Ct. 2720, 53 L.Ed.2d 786 (1977), the Court extended *Griggs* and held that the use of physical requirements (specifically, a 120 pound minimum weight requirement) as employment criteria violates Title VII if the criteria disproportionately exclude women and are not shown by the employer to be job related. *Id.* 433 U.S. at 328–331, 97 S.Ct. at 2726–28.

In the discriminatory impact context, a plaintiff need not prove that the employer acted with discriminatory intent. *Griggs*, *supra*, 401 U.S. at 430–32, 91 S.Ct. at 853–54; *Teamsters* v. *United States*, 431 U.S. 324 n.15, 97 S.Ct. 1843, 1854 n. 15, 52 L.Ed.2d 396 (1977). All a plaintiff need prove to establish a prima facie case is that the challenged standard disparately disadvantages the protected group of which he is a member, and that he is qualified for the position under all but the challenged criteria. The burden of persuasion then shifts to the employer to prove that the challenged criteria are "job related," *i.e.*, that they are required by "business necessity." *Moody*, *supra*, 422 U.S. at 425, 95 S.Ct. at 2375; *Griggs*, *supra*, 401 U.S. at 431, 91 S.Ct. at 853; *Johnson* v. *Uncle Ben's, Inc.*, 657 F.2d 750 (5th Cir. 1981).

The EEOC regulations adopt a *Griggs*-type approach in the disparate impact handicap discrimination context. They require federal agencies not to use any selection criterion that "screens out or tends to screen out qualified handicapped persons or any class of handicapped persons" unless the criterion, as used by the agency, is shown to be "job-related for the position in question." 29 C.F.R. § 1613.705. The test is whether a handicapped individual who meets all employment criteria except for the challenged discriminatory criterion "can perform the essential functions of the position in question without endangering the health and safety of the individuals or others." If the individual can so perform, he must not be subjected to discrimination. 28 C.F.R. §§ 1613.702(f) & .703. Cf. *New York State Association for Retarded Children* v. *Carey,* 612 F.2d 644, 649–50 (2d Cir. 1979) (discriminatory exclusion of handicapped children from regular public school classes unlawful in the absence of "at least some substantial showing" by the school authorities that the exclusion is necessary).

In our opinion, in the disparate impact context, there should be only minor differences in the application of the *Griggs* principles to handicap discrimination claims. One difference, however, is that, when assessing the disparate impact of a facially-neutral criterion, courts must be careful not to group all handicapped persons into one class, or even into broad subclasses. This is because "the fact that an employer employs fifteen epileptics is not necessarily probative of whether he or she has discriminated against a blind person."[20]

In a section 504 handicap discrimination case, the Supreme Court held that the Rehabilitation Act does not require redress of "insurmountable barrier" handicap discrimination—that the statutory language prohibiting discrimination against an "otherwise qualified handicapped individual" means qualified "*in spite*" of his handicap, not qualified in all respects except for being handicapped. *Southeastern Community College* v. *Davis,* 442 U.S. 397, 406, 99 S.Ct. 2361, 2367, 60 L.Ed.2d 980 (1979) (emphasis added).

The *Davis* rationale is equally controlling in the employment discrimination context. Accordingly, employers subject to the Rehabilitation Act need not hire handicapped individuals who cannot fully perform the required work, even with accommodation. However, while *Davis* demonstrates that only individuals who are qualified "in spite of " their handicaps need be hired, *Griggs* and its progeny dictate that the employer must bear the burden of proving that the physical criteria are job related. If the employer does this, then the burden of persuasion to show that he can satisfy these criteria rests on the handicapped applicant.

4. *"Surmountable Barrier" Discrimination, or the Duty to Make Reasonable Accommodation*

Federal employers, including the postal service, are obliged by section 501(b) to provide reasonable accommodation for the handicapped.[21] As the *Davis* Court

---

[20]Gittler, *supra* note 19, at 972. Thus, the postal service's reliance on the fact that the Greenville office has hired numerous handicapped persons is misplaced.

[21]This court has consistently held that section 504 also mandates reasonable accommodation, thus prohibiting surmountable barrier discrimination by federal grantees against the handicapped. *See Majors* v. *Housing Authority of the County of DeKalb Georgia,* 652 F.2d 454, 457–58 (5th Cir. 1981); *Tatro* v. *State of Texas,* 625 F.2d 557, 564 (5th Cir. 1980); *Camenisch* v. *University of Texas,* 616 F.2d 127, 132–33 (5th Cir. 1980), *vacated on other grounds,* _____ U.S. _____, 101 S.Ct. 1830, 68 L.Ed.2d 175 (1981).

pointed out, 442 U.S. at 410, 99 S.Ct at 2369, section 501(b), unlike section 504, explicitly requires federal government employers to undertake "affirmative action" on behalf of the handicapped. And the new section 505, added by Congress in 1978, explicitly permits courts to fashion "an equitable or affirmative action remedy" for violations of section 501, with the caveat that "the reasonableness of the cost of any necessary workplace accommodation" should be taken into account. The legislative intent reflected in the creation of a handicap discrimination private action clearly shows that federal government employers must make reasonable accommodation for handicapped job applicants.

There is a dearth of decisional law on this issue.[22] However, the EEOC administrative regulations, which, as noted above, are entitled to deference, provide some basis for outlining the contours of the surmountable barrier accommodation duty. The relevant EEOC regulation, 29 C.F.R. § 1613.704, provides:

> (a) An agency shall make reasonable accommodation to the known physical or mental limitations of a qualified handicapped applicant or employee unless the agency can demonstrate that the accommodation would impose an undue hardship on the operation of its program.
> (b) Reasonable accommodation may include, but shall not be limited to: (1) Making facilities readily accessible to and usable by handicapped persons, and (2) job restructuring, part-time or modified work schedules, acquisition or modification of equipment or devices, appropriate adjustment or modification of examinations, the provision of readers and interpreters, and other similar actions.
> (c) In determining pursuant to paragraph (a) of this section whether an accommodation would impose an undue hardship on the operation of the agency in question, factors to be considered include: (1) The overall size of the agency's program with respect to the number of employees, number and type of facilities and size of budget; (2) the type of agency operation, including the composition and structure of the agency's work force; and (3) the nature and the cost of the accommodation.

Thus, under subsection (a) of this provision, the burden of proving inability to accommodate is upon the employer. The administrative reasons for so placing the burden likewise justify a similar burden of proof in a private action based upon the Rehabilitation Act. The employer has greater knowledge of the essentials of the job than does the handicapped applicant. The employer can look to its own experience, or, if that is not helpful, to that of other employers who have provided jobs to individuals with handicaps similar to those of the applicant in question. Furthermore, the employer

---

[22]Outside the handicap discrimination context, the "reasonable accommodation" issue has arisen in cases involving persons who claim a right to accommodation of their religious duty to refrain from working on certain days. In *Trans World Airlines* v. *Hardison*, 432 U.S. 63, 84, 97 S.Ct. 2264, 2277, 53 L.Ed.2d 113 (1977), the Supreme Court interpreted § 701(j) of the Civil Rights Act of 1964, 42 U.S.C. § 2000e(j), which requires employers to accommodate such religious practices, unless to do so would impose "undue hardship." The Court held that an employer need not accommodate such persons if the accommodation would require "more than a *de minimis* cost."

The *Hardison* principles are not applicable in the federal-employer handicap discrimination context. Congress clearly intended the federal government to take measures that would involve more than a *de minimis* cost. As the debate over the McClure amendment shows, Congress was even unwilling to approve language that would have limited the government's duty to make reasonable accommodation to instances in which the cost of accommodation does not "disproportionately exceed[] actual damages." *See* text at note 17 *supra*.

may be able to obtain advice concerning possible accommodations from private and government sources. *See* Note, *Accommodating the Handicapped: Rehabilitating Section 504 After* Southeastern, 80 Colum.L.Rev. 171, 187–88 (1980).

Although the burden of persuasion in proving inability to accommodate always remains on the employer, we must add one caveat. Once the employer presents credible evidence that indicates accommodation of the plaintiff would not reasonably be possible, the plaintiff may not remain silent. Once the employer presents such evidence, the plaintiff has the burden of coming forward with evidence concerning his individual capabilities and suggestions for possible accommodations to rebut the employer's evidence. *See* Note, *supra,* 80 Colum.L.Rev. at 189.

In addition, subsections (a) and (c) of 29 C.F.R. § 1613.704, which limit the employer's duty to accommodate to instances where accommodation would not impose "undue hardship" and define the factors to be used in determining whether a particular accommodation would impose "undue hardship," accurately express congressional intent. The second sentence of section 505, which admonishes the courts to "take into account the reasonableness of the cost of any necessary workplace accommodation," was added as compromise language in response to Senator McClure's concern that federal employers might be obliged "to initiate massive construction projects." The EEOC regulations adequately respond to this concern.

### Genuine Disputed Issues of Material Fact Preclude Summary Judgment

The factual showing before the district court was that the postal service rejected Prewitt's application for employment because it felt, on the basis of the medical records supplied to it, that Prewitt could not perform the "arduous" duties of the position. In view of the undisputed fact that Prewitt had satisfactorily performed a similar postal job in 1970 despite his physical handicap, as well as of his *uncontradicted* affidavit that his physical condition was substantially unchanged since then, Prewitt raised a genuine dispute issue of material fact as to whether the postal service's physical standards for employment are sufficiently "job related" to justify the employer's refusal to hire him. Under the applicable legal principles earlier set forth, therefore, the postal service is not shown under the facts thus far educed to have been justified as a matter of law in denying Prewitt's application. The summary judgment must therefore be reversed.[23]

We should note that the postal service contends that the postal service rejected him because he refused its request that he take a current physical examination to establish his medical suitability for employment. This contention is based upon the showing that, *after* Prewitt was found medically unsuitable for employment, he was informally advised by the local postmaster that he would be reconsidered if he secured a new medical examination.

However, the record reveals that Prewitt's application was rejected because he was found to be medically unsuitable (without notifying Prewitt of the specific medical

---

[23]Further, from the factual showing educed at the hearing in the companion appeal, 662 F.2d 311 (1981), we know that on the remand a substantial factual issue will arise as to whether the postal service has complied with its duty to make a reasonable accommodation for Prewitt's handicap, insofar as its refusal to employ him is based upon his inability to use his left arm to lift items off a six-foot-high ledge.

reasons), not because he refused to furnish any further or more current medical information.

Indeed, Prewitt's essential position was that his physical condition and the effect of his disability was unchanged since 1970 and that, even accepting the disability reflected by the VA medical reports upon which the postal service relied, he was physically qualified to perform the duties of the position for which he applied, as instanced by his earlier satisfactory performance of the duties of a similar postal position.

## On the Remand

On the basis of the factual showing thus far made, we reverse the summary judgment dismissing Prewitt's handicap-discrimination claim. We remand for further proceedings in accordance with the views set forth in this opinion. To summarize:

(1) Prewitt, the disabled claimant, may establish a prima facie of unlawful discrimination by proving that: (a) except for his physical handicap, he is qualified to fill the position; (b) he has a handicap that prevents him from meeting the physical criteria for employment; and (c) the challenged physical standards have a disproportionate impact on persons having the same handicap from which he suffers. To sustain this prima facie case, there should also be a facial showing or at least plausible reasons to believe that the handicap can be accommodated or that the physical criteria are not "job related."

(2) Once the prima facie case of handicap discrimination is established, the burden of persuasion shifts to the federal employer to show that the physical criteria offered as justification for refusal to hire the plaintiff are "job related," *i.e.*, that persons who suffer from the handicap plaintiff suffers and who are, therefore, unable to meet the challenged standards, cannot safely and efficiently perform the essentials of the position in question. If the issue of reasonable accommodation is raised, the agency must then be prepared to make a further showing that accommodation cannot reasonably be made that would enable the handicapped applicant to perform the essentials of the job adequately and safely; in this regard, the postal service must "demonstrate that the accommodation would impose an undue hardship on the operation of its program," 29 C.F.R. § 1613.704(a), taking into consideration the factors set forth by 704(c) of the cited regulation.

(3) If the employer proves that the challenged requirements are job related, the plaintiff may then show that other selection criteria without a similar discriminatory effect would also serve the employer's legitimate interest in efficient and trustworthy workmanship. *Dothard* v. *Rawlinson*, 433 U.S. 321, 329, 97 S.Ct. 2720, 2726, 53 L.Ed.2d 786 (1977); *Johnson* v. *Uncle Ben's, Inc.*, 657 F.2d 750, 752 (5th Cir. 1981). When the issue of reasonable accommodation is raised, the burden of persuasion in proving inability to accommodate always remains on the employer; however, once the employer presents credible evidence that reasonable accommodation is not possible or practicable, the plaintiff must bear the burden of coming forward with evidence that suggests that accommodation may in fact be reasonably made.

## Conclusion

We of course express no opinion as to the merits of Prewitt's claim. If he is unable to perform the essentials of the position for which he has applied, with or without reasonable accommodation, the postal service need not hire him. The ultimate test is whether, with or without reasonable accommodation, a handicapped individual who meets all employment criteria except for the challenged discriminatory criterion "can perform the essential functions of the position in question without endangering the health and safety of the individuals *or* others." 28 C.F.R. § 1613.702(f). Since a disputed issue of material fact is shown as to this issue, the summary judgment granted by the district court must be REVERSED.

## NOTES

1. The *Prewitt* decision is perhaps the most comprehensive judicial discussion to date of the analytical standards and concepts applicable to employment discrimination cases under Sections 501, 504, and 505. For an examination of similar standards under state antidiscrimination laws, see pp. 102–110 above. For a thoughtful and thorough discussion of such standards under federal statutes, state statutes, and constitutional provisions, see Lang, "Protecting the Handicapped from Employment Discrimination: The Job-Relatedness and Bona Fide Occupational Qualification Doctrines," 27 *De-Paul L. Rev.* 989 (1978).

2. *Shirey* v. *Devine*, 670 F.2d 1188 (D.C.Cir. 1982), involved a deaf employee of the National Aeronautics and Space Administration who was denied job tenure protection available to other employees because he had been hired under a special program for handicapped workers which was "excepted" from the normal competitive employment process. The court ruled that Section 501's "affirmative action" requirement prohibits any permanent denial of equal status of handicapped workers, at 670 F.2d 1200, and that the government was, therefore, required to afford full job benefits to proven handicapped employees, even though they had been hired through excepted service procedures, at 670 F.2d 1203. The court's opinion contains a thorough discussion of the interrelationship between Section 501 and excepted service hiring programs. For a discussion of certain other processes, including "temporary limited appointment" and "career-conditional status," by which handicapped persons may enter federal government employment, see *Shaposka* v. *United States*, 563 F.2d 1013 (U.S.Ct.Claims 1977) (in circumstances of case, deaf employee of National Archives held entitled to procedural protections available to nonhandicapped persons in competitive service positions).

3. In *Doe* v. *Hampton*, 566 F.2d 265 (D.C.Cir. 1977), a clerk-typist in the Bureau of Engraving and Printing was dismissed from her job due to her mental condition, which had resulted in frequent absences from work, erratic and disruptive behavior, and refusal to perform assigned tasks. In reviewing the decision to terminate her employment, the Court of Appeals for the District of Columbia held that the following standard should be applied: "there must be a clear and direct relationship demonstrated between the articulated grounds for an adverse personnel action and either the employee's ability to accomplish his or her duties satisfactorily or some other legitimate governmental interest promoting the 'efficiency of the service.'" At 566 F.2d 272. In the context of the *Doe* case, the court ruled that the standard had been met. Nonetheless, the case was remanded to the trial court for a determination of the feasibility of reassignment to another job or extension of leave-without-pay opportunities as alternatives to complete termination of employment. *Id.* at 279–284. How do the standards applied in *Doe* compare with those set out in the *Prewitt* case?

## 2. Federal Government Contracts

pp. 371–374—REPLACE the *Rogers* v. *Frito-Lay, Inc.* case in its entirety with the following:

ROGERS v. FRITO-LAY, INC.

and

MOON v. ROADWAY EXPRESS, INC.

*United States Court of Appeals for the Fifth Circuit, 1980*
*611 F.2d 1074, cert. den., 449 U.S. 889*

Appeals from the United States District Courts for the Northern Districts of Texas and Georgia.

Before GOLDBERG, FAY and RUBIN, Circuit Judges.

ALVIN B. RUBIN, Circuit Judge:

The issue before us can be simply stated: section 503 of the Rehabilitation Act of 1973 requires every contract in excess of $2,500 with any federal department to "contain a provision requiring that, in employing persons to carry out" the contract, the contracting parties "shall take affirmative action to employ and advance in employment qualified handicapped individuals." 29 U.S.C. § 793. It also provides that any handicapped individual who believes any contractor has failed to comply with this agreement may file a complaint with the Department of Labor. Does this statute also impliedly authorize such an individual to file a civil action in a United States District Court seeking damages for the contractor's failure?

Because each of these cases comes to us on appeal from a judgment of dismissal for failure to state a claim, we assume that, as alleged in the complaints, each of the plaintiffs is a qualified handicapped person and each was discharged because of handicaps. This merely means our inquiry is warranted; it is not decisive, for the heart of the problem is whether Congress intended to benefit the qualified handicapped by giving them a particular right: the right to sue in federal court for relief from the discriminatory conduct of federal contractors.

The Rehabilitation Act of 1973 was adopted after presidential vetoes had stymied two earlier attempts to enhance federal aid to handicapped persons. Most of the controversy surrounding the bill and its predecessors focused on wide ranging programs, to be federally funded, designed to aid handicapped persons in assuming a full role in society, and on the appropriations that would be required if the measure were adopted. Consequently, Congress devoted little of its discussion to its intentions regarding section 503. *See* Sen.Rep.No. 93-318, 93d Cong., 1st Sess., pp. 12–16 (1973), U.S.Code Cong. & Admin.News, p. 2076. The statute's muteness, therefore, is not given meaning by voices in the legislative background. The plaintiffs ask us to find not only significance in the silence, but also the specific message of intent to bestow a private cause of action.

Federal courts are not common law courts of general jurisdiction. Limited by the express language of the Constitution, and the functional role it allots to the judiciary, we can recognize the cause of action only if it has been created by statute. *See Cannon* v. *University of Chicago*, 1979, 441 U.S. 677, 717, 99 S.Ct. 1946, 1968, 60

L.Ed.2d 560, 587 (Rehnquist, J., concurring). Therefore, our answer to the question in this case depends, the authorities and the parties all agree, on whether Congress intended, when this statute was enacted, to create such a method of enforcing the statutory policy. Because Congress did not speak to us unequivocally, either in the statute or in some other authoritative fashion, we must seek an answer in the history of enactment of the statute and in analogies to what the courts have derived from other statutes.

Having done so, in a manner we describe below, we have concluded that Congress has not authorized a private cause of action.

## I

In two cases decided within the last five years, the Supreme Court, summarizing its reflections in other prior cases, has told us how to seek intimations sufficient to read statutory silence as affirmative or negative. *Cort* v. *Ash,* 1975, 422 U.S. 66, 95 S.Ct. 2080, 45 L.Ed.2d 26; *Cannon* v. *University of Chicago,* 1979, 441 U.S. 677, 99 S.Ct. 1946, 60 L.Ed.2d 560. We are directed to consider four factors; but we are warned, as we should surely already know, that mechanical adherence to any multiple-part test is injurious and negates the very judgmental wisdom that is sought from courts. *See id.* at 717, 99 S.Ct. at 1968, 60 L.Ed.2d at 587 (Rehnquist, J., concurring). Our obligation is to determine, to the best of our abilities, whether Congress intended to create the private right of action plaintiffs seek to bring in federal court; even were we satisfied that some of the *Cort* factors supported implying such a right, we could not do so if unconvinced that Congress intended such a remedy. *See Transamerica Mortgage Advisors, Inc.* v. *Lewis,* 1979, ____ U.S. ____, 100 S.Ct. 242, 62 L.Ed.2d 146; *Touche Ross & Co.* v. *Redington,* 1979, 442 U.S. 560, 99 S.Ct. 2479, 61 L.Ed.2d 82.

A.   *Was the Plaintiff One of the Class for Whose Especial Benefit the Statute was Enacted?*

The statute was intended at the least to direct federal agencies to use their purchasing power so as to improve employment opportunities for "qualified handicapped persons." But it would be facile simply to conclude that, because Congress had handicapped persons in mind when it enacted section 503 and mentioned them in the statute, the first *Cort* factor is satisfied. What *Cort* demands is not that we determine whether Congress intended to aid a particular class of persons, but that we ascertain whether Congress intended to "create a federal right in favor of the plaintiff." *Cort* v. *Ash,* 1975, 422 U.S. 66, 78, 95 S.Ct. 2080, 2088, 45 L.Ed.2d 26, 36. To this end, "the right—or duty-creating language of the statute has generally been the most accurate indicator of the propriety of implication of a cause of action." *Cannon* v. *University of Chicago,* 1979, 441 U.S. 677, 690 N. 13, 99 S.Ct. 1946, 1954 n. 13, 60 L.Ed.2d 560, 571 n. 13.

The words of the statute, which are remarkably plain and jargon-free, do not indicate that it is aimed at overcoming those barriers to the employment of a qualified handicapped person that can be surmounted only by costly action or major programs. What is required of the employer could be as simple as providing a ramp for wheelchairs over a stairway or as complex as installing altered machinery, or it may, of course, be that apparently simple but much more difficult problem of eliminating prejudice, a¹ disease so deep rooted that it caused Clemenceau to say, "a citizen is sometimes called upon to make a greater sacrifice for his country than the sacrifices of his life, namely, to sacrifice his prejudices."

The statutory language does not imply on its face any intention to endow the handicapped with a direct suit after suffering handicap-based discrimination. It merely requires those who give out federal contracts to obligate contractors to take affirmative steps to employ and advance handicapped persons.[5] The duty it directly creates is imposed upon federal departments and agencies, not upon contractors. The statute does not confer a clearly defined right on the benefitted class. There is no intimation that every qualified handicapped person has a right to affirmative action in his particular case; what is apparent is that those who control federal contracts have a duty to make and enforce contracts containing the requisite clause. The handicapped may have simply the right to petition those who administer federal contracts to perform their duty.

The language of the statute is thus unlike those statutes that unequivocally focus on the benefitted class in their right—or duty-creating language. See, e.g., id., 441 U.S. at 681 n. 3, 99 S.Ct. at 1950 n. 3, 60 L.Ed.2d at 567 n. 3 ("No person . . . shall be excluded . . . ." 20 U.S.C. § 1681); Allen v. State Board of Elections, 393 U.S. 544, 554–55, 89 S.Ct. 817, 825–26, 22 L.Ed.2d 1, 11. ("No person shall be denied . . ."). It is, however, not unlike language that the Cannon court indicated would be sterile ground for implying a cause of action: "[t]here would be far less reason to infer a private remedy in favor of individual persons if Congress . . . had written [the statute] simply as a ban on discriminatory conduct by recipients of federal funds or as a prohibition against the disbursement of public funds to . . . institutions engaged in discriminatory practices." Cannon v. University of Chicago, 1979, 441 U.S. 677, 690–93 and n.14, 99 S.Ct. 1946, 1954–55 and n. 14, 60 L.Ed.2d 560, 571–573 and n. 14 (footnote omitted). Here, that is precisely what Congress did.

The duty-creating phrases are not conclusive, but they make inference of a private cause of action more difficult. When a statute is structured as a directive to federal agencies and does not clearly define a right inhering in individual members of a

---

[5]We are aware that the affirmative action clause inserted in federal contracts pursuant to 29 U.S.C. § 793 bans discrimination on the basis of handicaps. See 41 C.F.R. § 60-741.4 (1978). There is also language in the legislative history indicating that the section has an antidiscrimination component. See Rep. No. 93-318, 93d Cong., 2d Sess. (1973). See generally, Note, Private Rights of Action for Handicapped Persons under Section 503 of the Rehabilitation Act, 13 Val. U.L.Rev. 453 (1979). However, its principal thrust is to ensure that federal contractors will take affirmative steps to employ the handicapped, see S.Rep.No. 93-318, 93d Cong., 2d Sess. (1973); S.Conf.Rep.No. 93-1270, 93d Cong., 2d Sess. (1974), and the legislative history does not provide any basis for defining the nature of the antidiscrimination component we are asked to read into the affirmative action language of the statute.

The plaintiffs do not assert a claim based on putative status as third party beneficiaries of a federal contract, and we do not undertake to discuss the issues, neither briefed nor argued on appeal, whether a federal contract containing provisions required by statute creates a third-party beneficiary relationship, see Restatement of Contracts, §§ 133–147 (1932), and what would be the jurisdictional basis for a suit by such a third-party beneficiary in a federal court. If the thesis is plausible, we would also need to consider whether implication of a third-party beneficiary claim turns on the same considerations as implication of a private cause of action.

benefitted class, there must be persuasive evidence in the legislative history that Congress intended to confer such a right before the courts are justified in concluding that one exists. *See Transamerica Mortgage Advisors, Inc.* v. *Lewis,* 1979, \_\_\_\_ U.S. \_\_\_\_, 100 S.Ct. 242, 62 L.Ed.2d 146.

> B.  *Is There Any Indication of Legislative Intent, Explicit or Implicit, Either to Create Such a Remedy or to Deny One?*

In trying to learn Congressional intent by examining the legislative history of a statute, we look to the purpose the original enactment served, the discussion of statutory meaning in committee reports, the effect of amendments—whether accepted or rejected—and the remarks in debate preceding passage.

The scant discussion of section 503 that occurred during the process of enactment of the Rehabilitation Act of 1973 does not indicate that Congress contemplated a private right of action for handicapped persons. The only explicit statements of Congressional intent are found in connection with later legislation, corollary to section 503. We are urged to find meaning in section 503 as a result of later statutes and of remarks by individual Congressmen made at a later time.

The retroactive wisdom provided by the subsequent speech of a member of Congress stating that yesterday we meant something that we did not say is an ephemeral guide to history. Though even God cannot alter the past, historians can, *compare* Samuel Butler, Creation Revisited, c. 14, and other mortals are not free from the temptation to endow yesterday with the wisdom found today. What happened after a statute was enacted may be history and it may come from members of the Congress, but it is not part of the legislative history of the original enactment.

Later statutes may provide guidance. The Supreme Court has on occasion referred to the language of a later statutory amendment, whether independent or amendatory, in interpreting an earlier one. When thus utilized, the role of the later statute is not primarily historical: it repeals, modifies, adds to or subtracts from the earlier one by its own force. Its enactment stems from Congressional legislative power to repeal or alter what it has done. When such a statute has been adopted, the question becomes one of interpreting the two enactments together.

The two amendments to Title V that have been adopted leave the question of individual right to sue almost as murky as did the original text. In 1974 Congress amended the newly enacted Rehabilitation Act. One of the purposes and results of the amendment was to clarify the definition of "handicapped person" under sections 503 and 504 of the Act. Although the adopted amendment did not affect the substance of either section, the legislators utilized the legislative process to express their views on the intended scope of those sections as originally adopted.

The most extensive discussions of the two sections appear in the Senate Conference Committee Report on the amendments. Sen.Conf.Rep.No. 93-1270, 93d Cong., 2d Sess. 25–28 (1974). Even then, little attention was directed to enforcement of section 503, but section 504 enforcement was discussed in detail. The Report equated section 504 to section 601 of the Civil Rights Act of 1964, 42 U.S.C. § 2000d and section 901 of the Education Amendments of 1972, 20 U.S.C. § 1681. Like those sections, the conferees stated. section 504 is to be enforced by administrative and judicial means, including a private judicial remedy for those harmed by violations of the section.

The Committee failed to make similarly explicit any understanding that section 503 would entail a private judicial remedy. It did, however, note the intent that "sections 503 and 504 be administered in such a manner that a consistent, uniform, and effective federal approach to discrimination against handicapped persons would result." Sen.Conf.Rep.No. 93-1270, *supra*, at 27. This might prompt the conclusion that a private judicial remedy was intended under both sections. But the occasional mentions of section 503 contain no direct statement of an intention to create a private cause of action. Even as straws in the wind, these statements indicate cross currents rather than a stout breeze from one direction.

The appellants find their strongest argument in an implication they seek to draw from enactment in 1978 of an amendment to the Rehabilitation Act of 1973 that added a new section providing for attorney's fees in any action "to enforce or charge a violation of a provision of this subchapter." This undoubtedly authorizes an attorney's fee in actions brought to enforce section 503; but it does not necessarily follow that the amendment is intended to authorize private individuals to file civil actions under that section.

We are aware that the Senate report states: "the availability of attorney's fees should assist in vindicating private rights of action in the case of section 502 and 503 cases, as well as those arising under section 501 and 504," S.Rep.No. 95-890, 95th Cong.2d Sess. 19 (1978), and that the House report contains similar language.

It may, therefore, fairly be said that the 1978 committees of both Houses assumed that a private cause of action had somehow been created in the past. The existence of such a postulate is neither logical nor legislative basis to conclude that the 1973 statute did in fact create the action; and, if the 1973 statute did not authorize the cause of action, the 1978 statute evidences no intention to create one. An assumption is not a law.

A statement indicating that section 503 creates a private cause of action was made by a Senate Committee in 1979. "The Committee" in 1978 or 1979 is not the committee that recommended the legislation enacted in 1974. Had this statement been made in the report of the committee that recommended the legislation, it would indeed be part of the statutory history. When uttered five years later it is mere commentary. Moreover, a committee is not the Congress. It cannot create a Congressional intent that did not exist, or amend a statute by a report. *Cf. In re Beef Industry Antitrust Litigation*, 5 Cir. 1979, 589 F.2d 786 (opinion of two Congressmen on applicability of House of Representative's rule is not binding on court; rather, court must evaluate rule with attention to practice of entire Congress).

The legislative history of section 503 is void of explanatory statements contemporaneous with its passage. What happened subsequently is either ambiguous, or an assumption not shown to have been warranted; it is also the product of members of a Congress so distant in time from the enacting Congress that we cannot accept their remarks as an accurate expression of the earlier Congress's intent. We must, therefore, rely on whatever may be implicit in the statute.

The strongest argument for implication of a cause of action is that such a right is created by other provisions of the same law. That analogy is false; it attempts to achieve like conclusions from different premises.

The Rehabilitation Act contains both the provision (section 503) requiring federal contracts to obligate contractors to take affirmative action, 29 U.S.C. § 793, and, in the section immediately following, a provision forbidding discrimination in federal grants. The language of the two sections is different:

> 29 U.S.C. § 793 (§ 503)
>
> Any contract in excess of $2500 entered into by any Federal department . . . for the procurement of personal property and nonpersonal services . . . shall contain a provision requiring that, in employing persons to carry out such contract the party contracting with the United States shall take affirmative action to employ and advance in employment qualified handicapped individuals. . . .
>
> 29 U.S.C. § 794 (§ 504)
>
> No otherwise qualified individual in the United States . . . shall, solely by reason of his handicap, be excluded from participation in, be denied the benefits of, or be subjected to discrimination under any program or activity reviewing Federal financial assistance . . . .

A number of courts have held that section 504 creates a private cause of action in favor of qualified handicapped persons discriminated against in programs that receive federal grants. *See, e.g., United Handicapped Federation* v. *Andre*, 8 Cir. 1977, 558 F.2d 413; *Kampmeier* v. *Nyquist*, 2 Cir. 1977, 553 F.2d 296, 299; *Lloyd* v. *Regional Transportation Authority*, 7 Cir. 1977, 548 F.2d 1277; *Davis* v. *Bucher*, E.D.Pa.1978, 451 F.Supp. 791; *Doe* v. *New York University*, S.D.N.Y.1978, 442 F.Supp. 522 (dictum); *Barnes* v. *Converse College*, D.S.C. 1977, 436 F.Supp. 635; *Gurmankin* v. *Costanzo*, E.D.Pa.1976, 411 F.Supp. 982, *aff'd*, 3 Cir. 1977, 556 F.2d 184. Moreover, in *Cannon* v. *University of Chicago*, 1979, 441 U.S. 677, 99 S.Ct. 1946, 60 L.Ed.2d 560, the Supreme Court found an implied cause of action in Title IX of the Education Amendments of 1972 for violation of § 901(a) which provides, "No person in the United States shall, on the basis of sex, be excluded from participation in, be denied the benefits of, or be subjected to discrimination under any education program or activity receiving Federal financial assistance."

The parallel in construction between Title IX and section 504 is evident. The differences between this common design and the mandate of section 503 are equally clear: section 503 does not outlaw discrimination; it requires affirmative action covenants to be inserted in government contracts.

Section 503 also incorporates a specific method of enforcing the contractual provision; contractors who do not abide by their undertaking may be subjected to sanctions by the Department of Labor. The statute expressly discusses administrative enforcement and the regulations emphasize conciliation and persuasion as methods of dispute resolution. *See* 41 C.F.R. § 60-741.26(g)(2). Section 504, on the other hand, does not expressly provide for administrative enforcement.

Save for their common endeavor to aid the handicapped, the two sections have little in common. The words of section 503 convey no message that the same remedies should be available as those afforded for violation of section 504.

The type of assistance afforded by section 503 to aid persons whom the government wishes to benefit by its contracting power has been afforded in the past. Both Executive Order 11246, promulgated in 1965, and its predecessor 10925, promulgated in 1961, required government contractors to agree to include nondiscrimination and affirmative action provisions in their contracts with the Government. We have declined to infer a private cause of action under such an executive order containing language similar to that of section 503. See *Farkas* v. *Texas Instruments, Inc.*, 5 Cir. 1967, 375 F.2d 629, cert. *denied*, 389 U.S. 977, 88 S.Ct. 480, 19 L.Ed.2d 471 (Exec. Order 10925); *see also Farmer* v. *Philadelphia Electric Co.*, 3 Cir. 1964, 329 F.2d 3 (Exec. Order 10925 and predecessors); *Traylor* v. *Safeway Stores, Inc.*, N.D.Cal.1975, 402 F.Supp. 871 (Exec. Order 11246 as amended by 11375). The rationale of these decisions is that litigation would disrupt the administrative scheme established by the order and the supplementing regulations.

These decisions should have given Congress fair grounds to believe that, when it enacted section 503, federal courts would not infer a private cause of action under it and that, if it intended a different result, it should make its mandate explicit. *Cf. Cannon* v. *University of Chicago*, 1979, 441 U.S. 696, 698, 99 S.Ct. 1946, 1957–58, 60 L.Ed.2d 575, 576 (uses the interpretation of Title VI at the time Title IX was enacted to divine Congressional intent concerning Title IX). Indeed, the Executive Order is referred to in the scant legislative history of section 503.

Moreover, our court, like others, has generally not inferred private causes of action under statutes regulating employee-employer relationships. *See, e.g., Jeter* v. *St. Regis Paper Co.*, 5 Cir. 1975, 507 F.2d 973 (no private right of action under Occupational Health and Safety Act, 29 U.S.C. §§ 651–678); *Martinez* v. *Behring's Bearings Service, Inc.*, 5th Cir. 1974, 501 F.2d 104 (no private right of action for wrongful death under Fair Labor Standards Act, 29 U.S.C. § 215(a)(3)); *Flores* v. *George Braun Packing Co.*, 5 Cir. 1973, 482 F.2d 279 (no implied right against employer for deprivation of job based on illegal employment of foreign nationals under Immigration and Nationality Act, 8 U.S.C. §§ 1101(a)(15)(A)(ii), 1182(9)(14), 1324); *Breitwieser* v. *KMS Industries, Inc.*, 5 Cir. 1972, 467 F.2d 1391, cert. *denied*, 1973, 410 U.S. 969, 93 S.Ct. 1445, 35 L.Ed.2d 705, (no implied right of action to bring a wrongful death action under child labor provisions of Fair Labor Standards Act, 29 U.S.C. § 212); *United States* v. *Lovknit Manufacturing Co.*, 5 Cir. 1951, 189 F.2d 454, cert. *denied*, 342 U.S. 896, 72 S.Ct. 229, 96 L.Ed. 671 (no implied right of action under Walsh-Healey Act, 41 U.S.C. §§ 35–45; dictum).

C. *Is It Consistent With the Underlying Purposes of the Legislative Scheme to Imply Such a Remedy for the Plaintiff?*

As we have already indicated in differentiating section 503 from both section 504 and Title IX, Congress provided a complete administrative scheme to remedy Section 503 violations. The implementing regulations, set forth at length in the footnote, provide explicit details for the operation of that plan.[11] The administrative

---

[11]41 C.F.R. § 60-741-4 provides:

§ 60-741.4 Affirmative action clause.
Each agency and each contractor and subcontractor shall include the following affirmative action clause in

emphasis is on "conciliation and persuasion" and on "informal means" of resolution. The regulations make no provision for a private cause of action, suggesting that a private judicial remedy may be difficult to harmonize with the administrative enforcement framework. In addition, Title IX contained a provision for the award of attorney's fees, passed contemporaneously with the act, which indicated that the very Congress that passed the law believed a private cause of action existed. No corresponding reason exists to buttress the thesis that section 503 was intended to authorize private litigation.

The provision of an express administrative remedy for qualified handicapped persons creates at least some basis to conclude that a private right of action would be inconsistent with the purposes of the legislative scheme. As the Supreme Court has noted, "This principle of statutory construction reflects an ancient maxim—*expressio unius est exclusio alterius.*" *National Railroad Passenger Corp.* v. *National Association of Railroad Passengers,* 1974, 414 U.S. 453, 458, 94 S.Ct. 690, 693, 38 L.Ed.2d 646, 652. "[W]hen legislation expressly provides a particular remedy or remedies, courts should not expand the coverage of the statute to subsume other remedies," the Court reasoned. *Id.* For, " '[w]hen a statute limits a thing to be done in a particular mode, it includes the negative of any other mode.' *Botany Worsted Mills* v. *United States,* 278 U.S. 282, 289, 49 S.Ct. 129, 132, 73 L.Ed. 379 (1929)." *Id. See also Transamerica Mortgage Advisors, Inc.* v. *Lewis,* 1979, ____ U.S. ____, ____, 100 S.Ct. 242, 247, 62 L.Ed.2d 146, 155 ("where a statute expressly provides a particular remedy or remedies, a court must be chary of reading others into it.").

To determine the message to be found in the void of express Congressional statement, we resort neither to our own notions of sound policy nor to our concept of what best suits the public weal.

Where there is silence, as *Cannon* commands, we seek for affirmative evidence of Congressional intent. Silence may indicate only that the question never occurred to Congress at all, or it may reflect mere oversight in failing to deal with a matter intended to be covered, or it may demonstrate deliberate obscurity to avoid controversy that might defeat the passage of legislation, or it may, indeed, be a result merely of an assumption by Congress that the courts would recognize a private cause of action. The issue is not whether, on the merits, balancing on-the-one-hand with on-the-other, advocates of judicial remedies have a better case than opponents, but whether, considering the purpose and function of the statute and its legislative history, we can find a legislative intent to recognize a judicial remedy.

---

each of its covered government contracts or subcontracts (and modifications, renewals, or extensions thereof if not included in the original contract).

AFFIRMATIVE ACTION FOR HANDICAPPED WORKERS

(a) The contractor will not discriminate against any employee or applicant for employment because of physical or mental handicap in regard to any position for which the employee or applicant for employment is qualified. The contractor agrees to take affirmative action to employ, advance in employment and otherwise treat qualified handicapped individuals without discrimination based upon their physical or mental handicap in all employment practices such as the following: employment, upgrading, demotion or transfer, recruitment, advertising, layoff or termination, rates of pay or other forms of compensation, and selection for training, including apprenticeship.

(b) The contractor agrees to comply with the rules, regulations, and relevant orders of the Secretary of Labor issued pursuant to the Act.

(c) In the event of the contractor's noncompliance with the requirements of this clause, actions for noncompliance may be taken in accordance with the rules, regulations and relevant orders of the Secretary of Labor issued pursuant to the Act.

The task does not lend itself to certitude or dogmatism. Yet principle can shed helpful light even if not the clarity necessary for absolute confidence. The standard is that those who contend a statute has endowed them with a cause of action must establish their proposition. The appellants have not shown that section 503 presents the "atypical situation in which *all* of the circumstances that the Court has previously identified as supportive of an implied remedy are present," *Cannon* v. *University of Chicago,* 1979, 441 U.S. 677, 717, 99 S.Ct. 1946, 1968, 60 L.Ed.2d 560, 587, or even that sufficient of them attended its enactment to warrant the implication.

For these reasons, we decline to do judicially what Congress has not done legislatively, and we AFFIRM both judgments.

p. 374—REPLACE Notes 1 and 2 with the following:

1. In a vigorous and lengthy dissenting opinion not included here, Circuit Judge Goldberg applied the four *Cort* v. *Ash* factors and reached quite a different conclusion from the majority:

> In sum, I think this case is a clear one for the finding of an implied remedy. First, the statutory language reveals a definite intent to confer a benefit upon appellants' class and provides a substantial predicate upon which to premise a private remedy. Second, persuasive evidence of legislative purpose indicates that such a private cause of action was intended to inhere in § 503. There exist not only explicit statements of individual members of Congress and committees of both Houses to support this conclusion, but an enactment of positive law premised upon the existence of such a remedy in § 503 as it was originally enacted. And the agency charged with administering the statute construes it to contain an implied remedy. Settled judicial authority requires that these indicia of congressional intent be given great persuasive value. Further, a private remedy is wholly consistent with the underlying statutory goals. The actions of Congress, the position of the agency charged with enforcing the statute, and judicial precedent make this certain beyond the slightest doubt. Finally, this area is not one pre-empted by state authority.
>
> Having considered in great detail the factors identified by the Supreme Court as relevant to determining the congressional intent, I think there is only one reasonable conclusion: Congress intended qualified handicapped individuals to have a private remedy under § 503. The handicapped face two distinct barriers to full participation in our society—one physical or mental and the other attitudinal. For those individuals who have overcome the physical or mental barrier and established their qualifications, Congress has established protections, under the terms of § 503, from the invidious discrimination that results from the attitudinal barrier. Those protections include a private cause of action in the federal courts. The majority, by its niggardly approach to the inference of the private remedy, has denied this valuable right. Recent Supreme Court decisions have made it clear that private remedies are not lightly to be inferred. The majority, I fear, has overreacted to these words of caution and, instead of vindicating the congressional purpose, defeat it. Their approach would, in my opinion, reduce *Cort* to ashes. 611 F.2d at 1107–1108.

2. Dissenting Judge Goldberg was not alone in criticizing the reasoning of the majority in *Rogers;* another federal court judge took issue with the conclusion of the *Rogers* court that even though Section 505 was clearly intended by Congress to authorize attorney's fees in actions brought under Section 503, it did not follow that private rights of action were intended; the court in *Clarke* v. *FELEC Services, Inc.,* 489

F.Supp. 165 (D. Alaska 1980), termed this "an exercise in legal reasoning which is difficult to folow," *id*. at 168.

> The *Rogers* court admitted that "[i]t may, therefore, fairly be said that the 1978 committees of both Houses assumed that a private cause of action had somehow been created in the past," but the court nonetheless concluded that "[a]n assumption is not a law."
>
> While "an assumption is not a law," neither is a law to be construed as a nullity. This court cannot agree that the United States Congress intended by the enactment of § 505 to create a meaningless passage in the United States Code. *Ibid*.

How valid is this criticism of the reasoning in *Rogers?*

3. What are the implications of the third party beneficiary theory mentioned in footnote 5 of the court's opinion in *Rogers?* How viable is this theory and what are its limitations?

p. 388—RENUMBER Note 2 as Note 3, and INSERT the following after Note 1:

2. The split of judicial opinion as to whether or not Section 503 creates a private right of action, evidenced in the *Rogers, Drennon,* and *Wood* decisions, has continued in subsequent decisions, with the greater weight of precedents, especially at the Court of Appeals level, seeming to be against implying a private right of action under Section 503. Cases holding that there is such a cause of action include: *Davis* v. *Modine Mfg. Co.,* 526 F.Supp. 943 (D.Kan. 1981); *Chaplin* v. *Consol. Edison Co. of N.Y., Inc.,* 482 F.Supp. 1165 (S.D.N.Y. 1980); *Clarke* v. *FELEC Services, Inc.,* 489 F.Supp. 165 (D. Alaska 1980) (see Note 2 on page 127 above); *California Paralyzed Veterans Ass'n* v. *F.C.C.,* 496 F.Supp. 125 (C.D.Cal 1980); *Hart* v. *County of Alameda,* 485 F.Supp. 66 (N.D.Cal. 1979). Decisions holding that there is no such private right of action include: *Beam* v. *Sun Shipbuilding and Dry Dock Co.,* 679 F.2d 1077 (3d Cir. 1982); *Davis* v. *United Air Lines, Inc.,* 662 F.2d 120 (2d Cir. 1981); *Fisher* v. *City of Tucson,* 663 F.2d 861 (9th Cir. 1981); *Simon* v. *St. Louis County, Mo.,* 656 F.2d 316 (8th Cir. 1981); *Simpson* v. *Reynolds Metals Co.,* 629 F.2d 1226 (7th Cir. 1980); *Meyerson* v. *State of Arizona,* 507 F.Supp. 859 (D.Ariz. 1981); *Brown* v. *American Home Products Corp.,* 520 F.Supp. 1120 (D.Kan. 1981); *Anderson* v. *Erie Lackawanna Railway Co.,* 468 F.Supp. 934 (N.D. Ohio 1979).

### 3. Programs Receiving Federal Financial Assistance

p. 411—ADD the following to the end of the Note:

> Subsequent decisions have elaborated somewhat on the tracing of federal funds issue. In *Brown* v. *Sibley,* 650 F.2d 760 (5th Cir. 1981), the court held that employees of the Mississippi Industries for the Blind (MIB) had not stated a valid cause of action under Section 504 because the plaintiffs were not employed in programs that were funded by federal money:

> > The use of the terms chosen to denote the recipients of the federal financial assistance— i.e., "programs" and "activities"—connotes some subset or subsets of a greater entity.

The State of Mississippi, for example, receives "federal financial assistance," in the generic sense of those words, but no one would contend that section 504 therefore reaches all proprietary and governmental activities of the State of Mississippi. Similarly, although MIB does receive some federal financial assistance, named plaintiffs' section 504 claims must address themselves to those MIB programs or activities that are so funded. At 650 F.2d 767.

Therefore, the court concluded that "the receipt of federal financial assistance by a multiprogram entity, for specific application to certain programs or activities, does not, without more, bring all of those multiple programs or activities within the reach of section 504." *Id.* at 767.

Likewise, in *Simpson* v. *Reynolds Metals Co., Inc.*, 629 F.2d 1226 (7th Cir. 1980), the court ruled that the plaintiff did not have a cause of action under Section 504 even though the Reynolds company did have federally funded on-the-job training (OJT) and apprenticeship programs at the plant where the plaintiff was employed and also received payments to veterans in some of these programs:

> Simpson has not contended that he ever sought to participate in or was denied admittance to the apprenticeship program. It is undisputed that he is not a veteran and that he, therefore, could not have been a participant in the program which he alleges constituted "federal financial assistance" to his employer. Neither has he demonstrated his allegedly discriminatory discharge denied him the benefits of the federal financial assistance in issue. Finally, he has not shown, as we doubt he could, since there was never any historical connection between his employment and the apprenticeship program, that he was "subjected to discrimination under any program or activity receiving Federal financial assistance." Even assuming that the OJT program qualifies as "federal financial assistance" under the statute, since plaintiff has not demonstrated any nexus between his discharge and the federal assistance, we find the district court's dismissal of his claim under Section 504 should be affirmed.
>
> The statute does not, as plaintiff seems to contend, generally forbid discrimination against the handicapped by recipients of federal assistance. Instead, its terms apparently require that the discrimination must have some direct or indirect effect on the handicapped persons in the program or activity receiving federal financial assistance. At 629 F.2d 1231–1232.

p. 431—ADD the following to the end of Note 2:

The question of the necessity of exhaustion of administrative remedies under Section 504 has been greatly affected by the Supreme Court's decision in *Cannon* v. *University of Chicago*, 441 U.S. 677 (1979). In *Cannon,* after finding an implied right of action under Title IX, the Court expressly rejected the contention that individuals must pursue administrative procedures for the termination of federal funding for violators of Title IX as a condition precedent to a private cause of action. The Court ruled that cutoff of federal funds to an institution does not afford an appropriate remedy for an individual who has been discriminated against. At 441 U.S. 704–706. Since *Cannon,* a number of courts have held that the same reasoning applies to Section 504 and that, therefore, no exhaustion of administrative remedies is required: *N.A.A.C.P.* v. *Medical Center, Inc.*, 599 F.2d 1247 (3d Cir. 1979); *Camenisch* v. *University of Texas,* 616 F.2d 127 (5th Cir. 1980), vacated as moot, 451 U.S. 390 (1981); *Cain* v.

*Archdiocese of Kansas City, Kansas,* 508 F.Supp. 1021 (D.Kan. 1981); *Cruz* v. *Collazo,* 84 F.R.D. 307 (D.P.R. 1979); *Sherry* v. *New York State Education Dept.,* 479 F.Supp. 1328 (W.D.N.Y. 1979); *Medley* v. *Ginsberg,* 492 F.Supp. 1294 (S.D.W.Va. 1980). *Contra, Hart* v. *County of Alameda,* 485 F.Supp. 66 (N.D.Cal. 1979); *Sheeran* v. *M.A. Bruder & Sons, Inc.,* 524 F.Supp. 567 (E.D.Pa. 1981).

p. 431—INSERT the following at the end of the foregoing addition to Note 2:

3. In *Giles* v. *E.E.O.C.,* 520 F.Supp. 1198 (E.D.Mo. 1981), the court held that a jury trial is not available to a plaintiff in an action under Section 504. The court reasoned that the rights, procedures, and remedies available under Section 717 of Title VII are applicable in a Section 504 case: "Since there is no right to a jury trial under Title VII, there is no such right in an action brought under the Rehabilitation Act." *Id.* at 1200 n.1.

## PREWITT v. UNITED STATES POSTAL SERVICE

[See pp. 113–127, above.]

NOTES

1. The *Prewitt* decision is rendered under both Section 501 and Section 504. How much of the court's analysis and conclusions would apply in an action brought solely under Section 504?

2. For a more extensive discussion of the considerations involved in determining whether or not a handicapped person is "otherwise qualified," a matter that is mentioned briefly in the *Prewitt* decision, see *E.E. Black, Ltd.* v. *Marshall,* pp. 2–13 above.

## SIMON v. ST. LOUIS COUNTY, MISSOURI

*United States Court of Appeals for the Eighth Circuit, 1981*
*656 F.2d 316*

Before HEANEY, STEPHENSON and McMILLIAN, Circuit Judges.

STEPHENSON, Circuit Judge.

Plaintiff-appellant Gary Simon brought an action in the district court alleging that defendants-appellees had illegally discriminated against him because of his physical handicap in refusing to rehire or reinstate him as a commissioned police officer for St. Louis County. Simon appeals from a judgment in favor of appellees on all issues.

\* \* \*

Simon was a commissioned police officer in St. Louis County, Missouri. On November 24, 1971, Simon was shot and wounded, and was diagnosed as having a condition of paraplegia. On July 5, 1972, he was terminated as a St. Louis County commissioned police officer for the stated reason that because of his injury, he was unable to fulfill the duties of a St. Louis County police officer.

Simon was still diagnosed as a paraplegic at the time of trial, in August of 1978 and September of 1979, although his condition had improved somewhat through surgery and rehabilitative treatment. He required the use of leg braces and crutches to walk and could not support the weight of his body on either leg without the aid of crutches. It was further stipulated, and the district court found:

> He cannot run, jump, hop, stoop, turn, pivot or perform similar movements without the aid of a supporting device or the aid of another person. Plaintiff requires the use of braces and crutches to gain ingress and egress from an automobile or other motor vehicle. He cannot drive an automobile without the aid of specially fitted hand controls and automatic transmission.

*Simon* v. *St. Louis County,* 497 F.Supp. 141, 144 (E.D.Mo.1980).

In March of 1976, Simon met with defendant Colonel G. H. Kleinknecht, Superintendent of the St. Louis County Police Department, and requested that he be reinstated as a commissioned police officer. Colonel Kleinknecht refused to consider Simon because he considered Simon to be physically unable to assume the job. Simon made a formal application for a job as a commissioned police officer on August 16, 1976. He has not been reinstated.

The police department is run on a daily basis by the superintendent, who serves under a Board of Police Commissioners. The superintendent is responsible to the Board for the supervision, management, and control of the police department and all its personnel.

* * *

In *Carmi* v. *Metropolitan St. Louis Sewer District,* 620 F.2d 672 (8th Cir. 1980), *cert. denied,* 449 U.S. 892, 101 S.Ct. 249, 66 L.Ed.2d 117 (1981), this court held that an individual plaintiff had a private right of action under section 504 of the Act if a primary objective of the defendant's federal funding was to provide for employment.

We have examined the record in the instant case and agree with the district court that a primary objective for the federal funds going to the St. Louis County Police Department is to provide for the employment of commissioned police officers. Thus, the district court properly concluded that Simon had standing to bring a suit under section 504.

* * *

The district court first addressed the issue of whether Simon was an "otherwise qualified handicapped individual." Relying on *Southeastern Community College* v. *Davis,* 442 U.S. 397, 99 S.Ct. 2361, 60 L.Ed.2d 980 (1979), the district court determined that Simon was not an otherwise qualified person.

*Davis* involved a plaintiff with a serious hearing disability who sought to be trained as a registered nurse. Upon the basis of a medical examination, defendant Southeastern Community College determined that plaintiff's hearing disability made it unsafe for her to practice as a nurse. She could not understand speech without reliance upon lip reading. It was also determined that it would be impossible for plaintiff to participate safely in the normal clinical program without substantial modifications, and that those modifications would in fact keep her from realizing the benefits of the program. She was denied admission into the program and as a result brought suit under section 504. The Supreme Court found that plaintiff could not recover because she had not shown herself to be an otherwise qualified person.

The district court, in the instant case, concluded that Simon could not perform all of the department's physical requirements, and that *Davis* states that "[a]n otherwise qualified person is one who is able to meet all of a program's requirements in spite of his handicap." *Southeastern Community College* v. *Davis, supra,* 442 U.S. at 406, 99 S.Ct. at 2367. The district court therefore held that Simon was not an otherwise qualified applicant. Furthermore, the court found the modifications the police department would have to make would be substantial.

It is our view that the district court's reading of *Davis* is too rigid. The Supreme Court in *Davis* referred to those handicapped persons who could satisfy all of the *"legitimate* physical requirements" of the defendant's program. *Id.* at 406, 99 S.Ct. at 2367. Part III of the *Davis* opinion discusses whether the physical qualifications Southeastern demanded of the applicant were necessary for participation in its nursing programs. It concluded that the ability to understand speech without lip reading was necessary during the clinical phase of the program and indispensible for many functions that a registered nurse performs. *Id.* at 407, 99 S.Ct. at 2367. The Supreme Court noted that the *only evidence in the record* indicated that nothing less than close, individual attention by a nursing instructor would be sufficient to insure patient safety if respondent took part in the clinical phase of the nursing program. *Id.* at 409, 99 S.Ct. at 2368.

The proper focus in this case is therefore whether the requirements set forth by defendants—(1) the ability to be able to effect a forcible arrest and render emergency aid; and (2) the capacity to be freely transferred to all positions in the police department—are necessary and legitimate requirements of the job. The district court implicitly concluded they were, but also found that "plaintiff has shown that he is able to perform many of the tasks of the job of a commissioned police officer with the Department, and, indeed, nearly all of the tasks of some of its very small bureaus without much accommodation at all." *Simon* v. *St. Louis County, supra,* 497 F.Supp. at 151.

Our situation is different from that in *Davis.* There is substantial evidence in the record indicating that the physical requirements of the St. Louis County Police Department were not in fact necessary,[7] or were not required of all officers.[8] There was further evidence indicating that the ability of an officer to be completely transferable among all positions was sometimes not required in fact.[9] Nearly all of the evidence that the requirements (*i.e.* the physical ability to effect a forceful arrest, render aid, and to

---

[7]Depositions indicated that the police departments for Memphis and Kansas City both allowed police officers who became severely handicapped during their employment to remain with the department as commissioned police officers. The depositions indicated those cities' police departments were of the view that there were several useful jobs these individuals could perform.

[8]There were at least three persons testifying for Simon who had been injured during their employment but remained on the force as commissioned police officers. An examination of the record indicates these individuals did not satisfy all of the physical requirements established in the Department Regulations.

[9]The evidence from appellees' records indicated several officers had remained in one department for from four to ten years. These departments included Communications, Criminal Investigation, and Juvenile Affairs. We note that Communications is an area where the district court determined Simon's handicap would not prevent him from performing the great majority of the tasks.

We also note that the fact Simon already has served in different divisions prior to his injury may satisfy much of the purpose behind the department's alleged transferability requirements.

be able to perform all functions of all the departments' positions) are necessary consisted of the testimony of Colonel Kleinknecht.

The Supreme Court in *Davis* stated:

> We do not suggest that the line between a lawful refusal to extend affirmative action
> and legal discrimination against handicapped persons always will be clear. It is possible
> to envision situations where an insistence on continuing past requirements and practices
> might arbitrarily deprive genuinely qualified handicapped persons of the opportunity to
> participate in a covered program. Technological advances can be expected to enhance
> opportunities to rehabilitate the handicapped or otherwise to qualify them for some
> useful employment. Such advances also may enable attainment of these goals without
> imposing undue financial and administrative burdens upon a State. *Thus, situations may
> arise where a refusal to modify an existing program might become unreasonable and
> discriminatory.*

*Southeastern Community College* v. *Davis, supra,* 442 U.S. at 412–13, 99 S.Ct. at
2370 (emphasis added).

Although based upon the record before us we are not prepared to state that this
is a case where the department's refusal to modify its requirements is unreasonable; it
is our view that this case must be remanded to the district court for further consideration of this issue.

On remand, the district court should consider whether the requirements for
police officers of St. Louis County, as testified to at trial by Colonel Kleinknecht, are
reasonable, legitimate, and necessary requirements for all positions within the department. The district court should determine whether the ability to make a forceful arrest
and the ability to perform all of the duties of all of the positions within the department
are in fact uniformly required of all officers. If not uniformly required, they should not
be considered actual requirements for all positions. Also, consideration should be
given to Simon's actual physical condition in combination with Simon's police experience, and further determinations made as to exactly what functions within the department he has the physical abilities to perform. Finally, the court should determine
whether the accommodations necessary in order to employ Simon as a commissioned
police officer are unreasonable.[10]

NOTES

1.   If the ability to make a forceful arrest and the ability to perform all of the duties of
all of the positions in the department are found, in fact, to be uniformly required of all
officers, could the court order such standards to be changed as a matter of "reasonable
accommodation"? Is this implicit in the court's direction that the district court must
consider whether the department's standards are "reasonable, legitimate, and necessary"? Should this be the measure applied to all employment criteria under Section
504?

---

[10]It is clear that there is no requirement upon appellee to "effect substantial modifications of
standards to accommodate a handicapped person." *Southeastern Community College* v. *Davis,* 442 U.S.
397, 413, 99 S.Ct. 2361, 2370, 60 L.Ed.2d 980 (1979). While the district court below held that substantial
accommodations would be required, it is our view that this was based on the yet to be established assumption
that the requirements were in fact necessary to the job.

2.   In portions of the opinion not included here, the court ruled that there is no private right of action under Section 503 and that the plaintiff had not stated valid equal protection and due process claims.

### COLEMAN V. CASEY CTY. BD. OF ED.

*United States District Court for the Western District of Kentucky, 1980*
*510 F.Supp. 301*

Memorandum Opinion

JOHNSTONE, District Judge.

The plaintiff, Marvin Coleman, drove a school bus for the Casey County Board of Education for four years. In 1978, plaintiff's left leg was amputated; he has not worked as a bus driver since that time, although he has undergone rehabilitative training to relearn driving skills. After he learned to drive again, Coleman applied for his former position. The Board of Education refused to rehire him.

Coleman brought his action against the Casey County Board of Education, its members in both their official and individual capacities, the Kentucky Superintendent of Public Instruction, and the Kentucky State Board for Elementary and Secondary Education. He alleges defendants violated his Fourteenth Amendment due process and equal protection rights, together with certain rights created by Section 504 of the federal Rehabilitation Act of 1973, 29 U.S.C. § 794. The matter is before the Court on plaintiff's motion for partial summary judgment, to which defendants have not responded. After reviewing the entire record, the Court believes plaintiff's motion must be granted in part.

Section 504 of the Rehabilitation Act of 1973 (as amended 1978) provides in pertinent part:

> No otherwise qualified handicapped individual . . . shall, solely by reason of his handicap be excluded from the participation in, be denied the benefits of, or be subjected to discrimination under any program or activity receiving Federal financial assistance. . . .

Plaintiff contends he is an "otherwise qualified handicapped individual" entitled to the protection of Section 504. Defendants, in their answers, state they do not have sufficient information upon which to form a belief as to Coleman's contention. However, as previously noted, defendants made no response to plaintiff's summary judgment motion. None of the defendants has offered any evidence or any serious argument that plaintiff is not qualified to operate a school bus safely. Instead, defendants explain they had no alternative but to deny Coleman a bus driving job, because a Kentucky administrative regulation so mandates. That regulation, 702 KAR 5:080(1), promulgated by the State Board for Elementary and Secondary Education, provides:

> No person shall drive a school bus who does not possess both of these natural body parts: feet, legs, hands, arms, eyes, and ears. The driver shall have normal use of the above named body parts. Eyes may be corrected to normal by the use of eyeglasses. The driver shall not have any physical or mental handicap that would affect the driver's ability to operate the school bus in a safe manner.

As far as the record shows, the only reason for the Board of Education's failure to rehire Coleman is that 702 KAR 5:080(1) clearly prohibits the employment as a bus driver of anyone who does not have two natural legs. Thus, this case presents a clear conflict between the federal statute and a state regulation.

I

Before we can address the merits of plaintiff's Section 504 claim, we must consider whether that statute grants plaintiff a right of action. This issue has been very ably addressed by the Commonwealth of Kentucky Office for Public Advocacy as *amicus curiae*.

Section 504 does not expressly provide for private enforcement actions. In such a case, the Court must determine whether the four criteria set out in *Cort* v. *Ash*, 422 U.S. 66, 95 S.Ct. 2080, 45 L.Ed.2d 26 (1975), have been met in order to find an implied private cause of action. The plaintiff must be a member of the class "for whose special benefit" the statute was enacted; there must be evidence of legislative intent to create such a right; implying a private cause of action must be consistent with the underlying purposes of the statute; and the cause of action must be in an area not traditionally reserved to the states and precluded by comity from federal action.

Section 504 was patterned after Title VI of the Civil Rights Act of 1964. All of the remedies and procedures available under the latter statute are available to one protected by Section 504. The Supreme Court ruled in *Cannon* v. *University of Chicago*, 441 U.S. 677, 99 S.Ct. 1946, 60 L.Ed.2d 560 (1979), that Title VI is enforceable by private actions. Further evidence that Congress intended to permit private actions is found in the availability of attorneys' fees under the Rehabilitation Act. 29 U.S.C. § 794a.

The Supreme Court has reserved judgment on whether a private right of action is implied by Section 504, *Southeastern Community College* v. *Davis*, 442 U.S. 397, 99 S.Ct. 2361, 60 L.Ed.2d 980 (1979) ([plaintiffs] are the people in the best position to enforce Section 504, which is designed specifically for their protection).

We find the reasoning of the aforementioned cases persuasive. We have not been referred to, nor have we found, any authority to the contrary. The tests of *Cort.* v. *Ash* are satisfied by the statute in the instant case. Therefore, plaintiff may proceed in this effort to enforce Section 504.

II

Plaintiff has submitted numerous affidavits indicating his ability to operate a school bus despite his loss of limb. He has undergone a substantial amount of rehabilitative driver training and has been evaluated by several driving instructors, each of whom stated without reservation that he is a highly competent bus driver who is not hindered at all by his prosthesis.

In order for plaintiff to operate a bus, it must be equipped with either an automatic transmission or a hand clutch. The Bureau of Rehabilitation Services of the Kentucky Department of Education has offered to provide the Casey County school system with the equipment necessary to accommodate Coleman's special needs, so that the school board would not have to expend any money to employ him.

To the extent the state administrative regulation is in conflict with the federal statute, the Supremacy Clause requires that the regulation yield. Article IV, § 2, Constitution of the United States. *See United States* v. *Georgia Public Service Commission*, 371 U.S. 285, 83 S.Ct. 397, 9 L.Ed.2d 317 (1963); *McDermott* v. *Wisconsin*, 228 U.S. 115, 33 S.Ct. 431, 57 L.Ed. 754 (1912). Under the circumstances present in the case at bar, where it is uncontroverted that plaintiff is well-qualified for the position he seeks, and where no expenditures by defendants would be needed in order to provide the required equipment, Section 504 mandates that Coleman be re-employed as a bus driver.

Our interpretation of Section 504 obviates the necessity of considering plaintiff's equal protection and due process claims.

Plaintiff's motion for partial summary judgment is granted to the extent it seeks to prohibit application of 702 KAR 5:080(1) to plaintiff, and to require plaintiff's re-employment as a school bus driver. We reserve judgment on plaintiff's request for an award of back pay, as well as on all other issues raised by the pleadings. A judgment in conformity with this opinion has this day been entered.

NOTE

The Kentucky regulation at issue in *Coleman* is an almost archetypic example of *de jure* discrimination against handicapped persons. How would the provision have fared under due process and equal protection analysis?

### DOE v. SYRACUSE SCHOOL DISTRICT

*United States District Court for the Northern District of New York, 1981*
*508 F.Supp. 333*
MUNSON, Chief Judge.

Memorandum-Decision and Order

This action was brought by plaintiff John Doe[1] under section 504 of the Rehabilitation Act of 1973, as amended (Act), 29 U.S.C. § 794 (Supp.III 1979), which prohibits discrimination against handicapped individuals in any program or activity receiving federal financial assistance. Defendant Syracuse School District is a recipient of federal funds and is therefore bound under the provisions of the Act. Defendants Lionel Meno, Robert Cecile, and Robert DiFlorio are the District Superintendent, School Board President, and District Personnel Director, respectively. Jurisdiction is predicated upon 28 U.S.C. § 1343(3)(4).

Plaintiff claims that the School District failed to hire him as a teacher's assistant and substitute teacher solely because of his prior mental illness, thereby violating the provisions of the Act. Specifically, plaintiff's second cause of action asserts that the defendant School District made impermissible pre-employment inquiries and refused to hire plaintiff because of his answers to those questions. In response, the defendants argue that plaintiff was not hired because they were overstaffed in plaintiff's area of expertise.

---

[1]In order to protect his privacy, and with regard for the personal nature of this case, plaintiff is proceeding under the pseudonym "John Doe" pursuant to an Order of this Court dated February 26, 1980.

This cause is presently before the Court upon plaintiff's motion for reconsideraton. Plaintiff claims that the Court was mistaken in its Memorandum-Decision and Order dated September 30, 1980, when it denied plaintiff's motion for partial summary judgment as to his second cause of action, which alleged violation of the Rehabilitation Act, 29 U.S.C. § 794, and 45 C.F.R. § 84.14. Defendants have cross-moved to dismiss plaintiff's second cause on the pleadings pursuant to Rule 12(c) of the Federal Rules of Civil Procedure insofar as it alleges that an impermissible pre-employment inquiry violates the Act. Upon careful reconsideration, the Court has determined that there are no material issues of fact in dispute with regard to plaintiff's regulatory claim in his second cause of action and that he is entitled to judgment on this issue as a matter of law. Therefore, plaintiff's motion for reconsideration, and with it, plaintiff's original motion for partial summary judgment, must be granted in part. The denial of the plaintiff's summary judgment motion regarding his statutory claim remains unchanged at this time, given the existence of disputed, triable issues of material facts.

## Facts

In January of 1980, plaintiff discussed employment opportunities with a Ms. Spellman, the Social Studies Supervisor of the Syracuse School District. Plaintiff is apparently certified by the State of New York as a social studies teacher. Consequently, after this conversation, plaintiff submitted his application for the position of teacher's assistant and substitute teacher.

During the course of plaintiff's application procedures, he was asked to complete a vital statistics form. The 31st question on that form inquired whether he had experienced, or had ever been treated for any "migraine, neuralgia, nervous breakdown, or psychiatric treatment." Plaintiff responded affirmatively and it was then disclosed that he had suffered a nervous breakdown during his service with the United States Air Force. In addition, plaintiff also disclosed that as a result of this event and based upon a diagnosis of schizophrenic reaction, he was receiving one hundred percent disability benefits from the Veterans Administration. Following these disclosures, plaintiff was examined by Dr. Paul P. Stobnicke, the School District Physician, and Dr. Alden Starr, the School District Psychiatrist. Dr. Stobnicke found plaintiff to be physically and mentally qualified for the teaching position, subject only to a review after six months. Plaintiff's application for employment was then rejected by the School District, and he commenced this lawsuit on February 26, 1980.

## Rehabilitation Act of 1973

Section 504 of the Rehabilitation Act of 1973 reflects a Congressional determination that programs receiving federal financial assistance are to be operated without discrimination based upon an individual's physical and/or mental handicap. In pertinent part, the statute provides that:

> [n]o otherwise qualified handicapped individual in the United States, as defined in section 706(7) of this title, shall, solely by reason of his handicap, be excluded from the participation in, be denied the benefits of, or be subjected to discrimination under any program or activity receiving Federal financial assistance. . . .

29 U.S.C. § 794. A handicapped individual is defined as:

> any person who (i) has a physical or mental impairment which limits one or more of such person's major life activities; (ii) has a record of such impairment; or (iii) is regarded as having such an impairment.

29 U.S.C. § 706(7)(B).[3]

Section 504 of the Act clearly requires all recipients of federal funds to avoid discrimination against handicapped individuals. *Lloyd* v. *Regional Transp. Auth.*, 548 F.2d 1277, 1280–86 (7th Cir. 1977); S.Rep.No.1297, 93d Cong., 2d Sess., *reprinted in* (1974) U.S.Code Cong. & Ad. News 6373, 6390–91. The section also confers a private right of action upon aggrieved handicapped individuals. *Davis* v. *Southeastern Community College*, 574 F.2d 1158, 1159 (4th Cir. 1978), *rev'd on other grounds*, 442 U.S. 397, 99 S.Ct. 2361, 60 L.Ed.2d 980 (1979); *Leary* v. *Crapsey*, 566 F.2d 863, 865 (2d Cir. 1977); *United Handicapped Fed'n.* v. *Andre*, 558 F.2d 413, 415 (8th Cir. 1977); *Lloyd* v. *Regional Transp. Auth.*, *supra; see also Cort* v. *Ash*, 422 U.S. 66, 95 S.Ct. 2080, 45 L.Ed.2d 26 (1975) (opinion setting out the four factors relevant to a determination of whether a private remedy is implicit in a statute which does not explicitly provide for one).

In order to effectuate this sweeping policy, President Gerald R. Ford directed that the Secretary of Health, Education and Welfare establish rules and regulations necessary to carry out the provisions of section 504; Exec.Order No. ʹ11914, 41 Fed.Reg. 17,871 (1976); these regulations were established in 1977 and are now promulgated in 45 C.F.R. Part 84 (1979).

One basis for plaintiff's second cause of action lies in an alleged violation of 45 C.F.R. § 84.14. This provision limits the scope of pre-employment inquiries. Specifically, it provides that:

> a recipient (of federal funds) may not conduct a pre-employment medical examination or may not make pre-employment inquiries of an applicant as to whether the applicant is a handicapped person or as to the nature or severity of a handicap. A recipient may, however, make pre-employment inquiry into an applicant's ability to perform job-related functions.

45 C.F.R. § 84.14(a).

Plaintiff contends that by asking him whether he had ever experienced a nervous breakdown or had undergone psychiatric treatment, the defendant violated 45 C.F.R. § 84.14 thereby entitling plaintiff to judgment as a matter of law. The defendant argues, however, that its inquiries were made solely to determine plaintiff's present ability to teach, rather than to discriminate against plaintiff based on his pre-

---

[3]Plaintiff's ability to meet the definition of a handicapped individual under 45 C.F.R. § 84.3(j) is unchallenged. Plaintiff has a record of a physical or mental impairment as defined in 45 C.F.R. § 84.3(j)(2)(i), and is likely to be regarded as having such an impairment by the School District. 45 C.F.R. § 84.3(j)(2)(iv). The regulations specifically recognize that persons with histories of mental or emotional illness are beneficiaries of the Act. 45 C.F.R., Part 84, Appendix A, subpart A(3), p. 378, 42 Fed.Reg. 22,686 (1977). In addition, the courts have similarly acknowledged that persons with mental or emotional illnesses or histories of the same are handicapped within the meaning of the Act. *E.G., Doe* v. *Colautti*, 592 F.2d 704 (3d Cir. 1979); *Doe* v. *Marshall*, 459 F.Supp. 1190 (N.D.W.Va.1976). Therefore, the Court finds that plaintiff has proper standing as a handicapped person to sue under the provisions of section 504.

existing condition. In the alternative, the defendant argues that even if its inquiries were impermissive, the plaintiff must still prove that he is "otherwise qualified" for the position, and that his handicap was the sole reason for his nonhiring. The Court must, therefore, determine whether the administrative regulation was violated, and if it was, whether that violation will give rise to strict liability.

## 45 C.F.R. § 84.14

Section 84.14 was promulgated to limit the scope of pre-employment inquiries relating to a potential employee's handicap. In this fashion, an employer is required to base the hiring decision on a person's actual job qualifications, rather than on any perceived limitations. As the regulation expressly provides, a recipient of federal funds "may not make pre-employment inquiry of an applicant as to whether the applicant is a handicapped person or as to the nature or severity of a handicap." 45 C.F.R. § 84.14(a). Therefore, any inquiry relating to a handicap ordinarily would not be permitted, unless such inquiry relates to an applicant's ability to perform job related functions. *Id.* For example, an employer may not ask whether the applicant is an epileptic, but may ask whether the person can perform a particular job without endangering other employees. 45 C.F.R. Part 84, Appendix A, subpart B(18), p. 384, 42 Fed.Reg. 22,689 (1977).

Defendant does not deny that it asked plaintiff whether he was mentally ill or had even been treated for a mental illness; thus, the Court must resolve the question whether such inquiry violated the import of section 84.14. By asking plaintiff about his prior medical and/or emotional condition, defendant claims that it was preparing a complete history of the applicant to determine his present ability to perform the tasks to which he might be assigned. This claim is supported by the testimony of Dr. Stobnicke, the School District Physician, who in an examination before trial, indicated that the District needed to be apprised of all relevant information pertaining to an applicant. As one example, Dr. Stobnicke stated that if an applicant told him that he was a child molester, the doctor would say, "[h]ey, you won't be in the school system with kids. Let's see if we can't find something else for you." E.B.T. at p. 23.

Although the defendants contend that the School District's inquiry was job-related, this assertion is inconsistent with defendants' prior admissions. In its answer, the defendants not only admitted that a history of treatment for mental or emotional problems is no indication of present mental or emotional problems, but they also admitted that a history of treatment for mental or emotional problems is not an indication of plaintiff's present fitness for a position as a teacher's assistant or substitute teacher. Defendant's Answer ¶ 6. At the very minimum, this Court finds that defendant's inquiry was impermissibly phrased. If defendant sincerely wanted to employ persons that were capable of performing their jobs, all it had to ask was whether the applicant was capable of dealing with various emotionally demanding situations. In its present form, however, defendant's question violates both the letter and spirit of section 84.14.

The Secretary of Health, Education and Welfare concluded that a general prohibition of pre-employment inquiries was the most appropriate method for effectuating Section 504 of the Act. 45 C.F.R. Part 84, Appendix A, subpart B(18),

p. 384, 42 Fed. Reg. 22,689 (1977). The Court agrees with the Secretary's conclusion and finds that the defendant's pre-employment inquiry was precisely what the regulation sought to eliminate. In view of the above, the Court finds that the defendant violated 45 C.F.R. § 84.14. Therefore, the only remaining question is whether such a violation entitles plaintiff to judgment as a matter of law.

### Motion for Summary Judgment

It is well established, that on a motion for summary judgment, the moving party has the burden of showing that there is no genuine issue of material fact and that he is entitled to judgment as a matter of law. *Quinn* v. *Syracuse Model Neighborhood Corp.*, 613 F.2d 438, 444–45 (2d Cir. 1980); *Robertson* v. *Seidman & Seidman*, 609 F.2d 583, 591 (2d Cir. 1979); *Heyman* v. *Commerce & Indus. Ins. Co.*, 524 F.2d 1317, 1319 (2d Cir. 1975). Inasmuch as the Court has found that the defendant's pre-employment inquiry violated 45 C.F.R. § 84.14, no genuine issue of material fact remains with respect to plaintiff's second cause of action. Moreover, it has been generally accepted, that properly promulgated, substantive agency regulations have the "force and effect of law." *Chrysler Corp.* v. *Brown*, 441 U.S. 281, 295, 99 S.Ct. 1705, 1714, 60 L.Ed.2d 208 (1979); 3 Mezines, Stein, Gruff, *Administrative Law* § 14.01 (1979). For these reasons it is hereby

ORDERED, that plaintiff's motion for reconsideration, and with it, plaintiff's original motion for partial summary judgment as to the asserted violation of 45 C.F.R. § 84.14, set forth in his second cause of action, be, and the same is hereby granted to the extent specified above; and it is further

ORDERED, that the defendants are hereby enjoined from inquiring, during the nonmedical application process, of prospective job applicants whether they have ever experienced, or have ever received treatment for any mental illnesses; and it is further

ORDERED, that the defendants' motion for judgment on the pleadings be, and the same is hereby denied at this time.

A hearing will be held at a later time to determine the issue of damages.

It is SO ORDERED.

### NOTES

1.   The problems of pre-employment inquiries and medical histories have long been troublesome issues for job applicants having handicaps that are not visible. The handicapped individual is faced with the quandary of concealing the handicap by giving false answers to the questions posed or answering honestly with the very real possibility that the response will result in exclusion from the job being sought. In such circumstances, a refusal to answer or to give the information requested may be interpreted negatively or as an indication of a bad attitude, thus jeopardizing the employment opportunity anyway. The result in the *Doe* case obviates the dilemma by prohibiting the asking of the question in the first place.

2.   In addition to persons with histories of mental illness, the pre-employment inquiry issue has been of particular concern to persons with epilepsy whose seizures are controlled. See *Duran* v. *City of Tampa*, pp. 351–356 and 410–411 of the *Casebook*.

p. 435—INSERT after the Notes:

## JONES v. METROPOLITAN ATLANTA RAPID TRANSIT AUTHORITY
*United States Court of Appeals for the Eleventh Circuit, 1982*
*681 F.2d 1376*

Before VANCE, JOHNSON and HENDERSON, Circuit Judges.

JOHNSON, Circuit Judge:

Plaintiff William E. Jones filed suit alleging that defendant Metropolitan Atlanta Rapid Transit Authority (MARTA) violated Section 504 of the Rehabilitation Act, 29 U.S.C.A. § 794, and various federal regulations by denying him a position as bus driver because of his handicap. The district court, 522 F.Supp. 370, determined that plaintiff lacked standing and dismissed the suit. Plaintiff appeals. We reverse.

### I. Facts

MARTA provides rapid transit for the metropolitan area of Atlanta. The transit authority receives federal financial assistance in the form of engineering and construction grants and operating subsidies from the United States Department of Transportation (DOT). MARTA apparently utilizes a portion of the DOT funds to subsidize wages of certain employment positions, including traffic checkers and bus drivers.

Plaintiff worked for MARTA as a bus driver for 15 years. In March 1976 plaintiff suffered an injury that necessitated the amputation of his right leg. Plaintiff recovered from the injury and was rehired by MARTA as a traffic checker. Plaintiff, however, became dissatisfied with his position and sought reinstatement as a bus driver. Plaintiff asserted that despite his injury he was capable of performing the required functions of a bus driver. MARTA officials concluded that plaintiff's injury prevented him from performing the duties of a bus driver and denied his request for reinstatement.

After exhausting administrative remedies, plaintiff brought an action under Section 504 of the Rehabilitation Act, 29 U.S.C.A. § 794, contending that MARTA discriminated against him on the basis of his handicap. The district court dismissed the suit. The court determined that Section 504 only provided a cause of action against employers that received federal financial assistance for the primary purpose of providing employment. Although MARTA received federal financial assistance, the funding was not primarily intended to provide employment.

The district court did note that plaintiff had standing under regulations promulgated by the DOT. 49 C.F.R. § 27.31. The regulations prohibited discrimination against qualified handicapped people in programs or activities that received federal financial assistance of any kind, not just those receiving funds for purposes of providing employment. The district court determined, however, that the regulations exceeded the scope of Section 504 of the Rehabilitation Act and were therefore invalid. Accordingly, MARTA was not amenable to suit under either the Rehabilitation Act or the DOT regulations.

### II. Statutory Framework

Section 504 of the Rehabilitation Act prohibits discrimination against otherwise handicapped individuals in "any program or activity receiving Federal financial assistance . . . ." 29 U.S.C.A. § 794. The Rehabilitation Act does not, however, specify the remedies, procedures and rights of an aggrieved party. Instead, Section 505 provides that the "remedies, procedures, and rights" of a handicapped individual injured under the Act are found in Title VI of the Civil Rights Act of 1964. 29 U.S.C.A. § 794a.

Section 601 of the Civil Rights Act of 1964 (Title VI) contains sweeping prohibitions against race discrimination by employers.[4] Congress, however, placed significant restrictions upon the breadth of Section 601. Section 604 authorizes a federal department or agency to maintain an action against employers to enforce Title VI *only* if the employer receives federal financial assistance and "a primary purpose of the Federal financial assistance is to provide employment." 42 U.S.C.A. § 2000d–3. Thus in order to bring suit under Title VI, an employer must receive federal funds for purposes of providing employment.

A number of circuits have concluded that Congress intended to incorporate the restrictions found in Section 604 of Title VI into the Rehabilitation Act. *United States* v. *Cabrini Medical Center,* 639 F.2d 908 (2d Cir. 1981); *Carmi* v. *Metropolitan St. Louis Sewer District,* 620 F.2d 672 (8th Cir. 1980), *cert. denied,* 449 U.S. 892, 101 S.Ct. 249, 66 L.Ed.2d 117 (1981); *Trageser* v. *Libbie Rehabilitation Center, Inc.,* 590 F.2d 87 (4th Cir. 1978), *cert. denied,* 442 U.S. 947, 99 S.Ct. 2895, 61 L.Ed.2d 318 (1979). Thus, a plaintiff will not have standing to maintain a suit under Section 504 of the Rehabilitation Act unless the employer receives federal financial assistance and the primary purpose of the assistance is to provide employment. The courts have employed a variety of rationale to justify the incorporation of Section 604 into the Rehabilitation Act. In *Carmi, supra,* the Eighth Circuit essentially concluded that Congress intended the Rehabilitation Act and Title VI to be read *in pari materia.* The Fourth Circuit in *Trageser, supra,* determined that Congress intended to incorporate Section 604 into the Rehabilitation Act when it amended the Act by adding Section 505.

In the absence of controlling precedent in this Circuit[6] and in order to ascertain the correctness of these holdings, we must examine both the language of the relevant statutes and their legislative history.

*III. Section 504 of the Rehabilitation Act*

The starting point for the interpretation of a statute is the language of the act itself. *Perrin* v. *United States,* 444 U.S. 37, 42, 100 S.Ct. 311, 314, 62 L.Ed.2d 199 (1979); *United States* v. *Anderez,* 661 F.2d 404, 406 (5th Cir. 1981). Normally, a

---

[4]Section 601 of the Civil Rights Act of 1964, 42 U.S.C.A. § 2000d, provides:

> No person in the United States shall, on the ground of race, color, or national origin, be excluded from participation in, be denied the benefits of, or be subjected to discrimination under any program or activity receiving Federal financial assistance.

[6]Standing under Section 504 of the Rehabilitation Act was considered by the Court in *Brown* v. *Sibley,* 650 F.2d 760 (5th Cir. 1981). In *Sibley,* the Court determined that a plaintiff did not necessarily have standing simply because the employer received some financial assistance from the federal government. Instead, the plaintiff had to establish that "the program or activity with which he or she was involved, or from which he or she was excluded, itself received or was directly benefited by federal financial assistance." *Id.* at 769. The opinion further stressed that the burden of establishing that the particular program/activity received federal financial assistance "should be slight." *Id.* at 769 n. 14. *Accord, Doyle* v. *Univ. of Ala— Birm.,* 680 F.2d 1323 (11th Cir. 1982); *Simpson* v. *Reynolds Metals Co., Inc.,* 629 F.2d 1226, 1232 (7th Cir. 1980). [*continued next page*]

court will interpret a statute in a manner consistent with the plain meaning of the statutory language. *Fitzpatrick v. Internal Revenue Service,* 665 F.2d 327, 329 (11th Cir. 1982). Where, however, the language of a statute is ambiguous, or leads to absurd results, a court is free to consult the legislative history and discern the true intent of Congress. *American Trucking Assn. Inc. v. I.C.C.,* 659 F.2d 452, 459 (5th Cir. 1981); *Glenn v. United States,* 571 F.2d 270, 271 (5th Cir. 1978).

Section 504 of the Rehabilitation Act specifically prohibits discrimination against qualified handicapped people in "any program or activity receiving Federal assistance . . . . 29 U.S.C.A. § 794. On its face, therefore, the Section applies to programs receiving federal financial aid of any kind. Moreover, nothing in the language of the statute indicates that it was intended to reach only those programs receiving federal financial assistance for the primary purpose of providing employment.[7] Because the statute is unambiguous and does not lead to absurd results, we would normally pretermit our analysis here. Nonetheless, for purposes of clarification and in light of authority to the contrary, *United States v. Cabrini Medical Center, supra; Carmi v. Metropolitan St. Louis Sewer District, supra,* we turn to the legislative history to determine whether Congress intended to restrict application of the Rehabilitation Act to those programs receiving federal financial assistance for the primary purpose of employment. See *Watt v. Alaska,* 451 U.S. 259, 266, 101 S.Ct. 1673, 1677, 68 L.Ed.2d 80 (1981).

Congress enacted the Rehabilitation Act in 1973. Pub.L.No. 93-112, 87 Stat. 355 (1973). Neither the House nor the Senate reports contain even a scintilla of evidence indicating that Congress intended to incorporate Section 604 of Title VI into the Rehabilitation Act and limit the applicability of Section 504 to programs receiving federal financial assistance for the primary purpose of providing employment. The legislative history to Section 504 does not even mention Title VI of the Civil Rights Act. Instead, the reports merely reiterate that Section 504 applies to any program receiving federal financial assistance.[8]

The Rehabilitation Act was amended in 1974. Pub.L.No. 93-516, 88 Stat. 1619 (1974). Congress noted obliquely in the legislative history to the amendments

---

Although holding that the plaintiff had to be involved in a program or activity that directly benefited from federal financial assistance, the Court did not determine whether the financial assistance had to be for the purpose of providing employment. Such a determination was unnecessary to the opinion.

[7]Similarly, a plain reading of Section 604 of the Civil Rights Act of 1964 would appear to render it inapplicable to private suits under the Rehabilitation Act. Section 604 expressly applies only to federal agencies and departments. Thus a federal agency or department must establish that the employer received federal financial assistance for the purpose of employment in order to maintain an action under Title VI. Section 604 does not, on its face, apply to private individuals. Accordingly, even were Section 604 deemed applicable to suits under the Rehabilitation Act, it would seemingly apply only to suits brought by federal agencies or departments and not suits brought by private individuals. *Carmi v. Metropolitan St. Louis Sewer District, supra,* 620 F.2d at 678 (McMillian, J., concurring). *Hart v. County of Alameda,* 485 F.Supp. 66, 72 (N.D.Cal.1979).

[8]For example, the House Report explained the significance of Section 504 by stating that:

> Section [504] provides that no otherwise qualified handicapped individual will be discriminated against or excluded from participation in or benefits from any program or activity receiving Federal assistance.

H.R.No. 244, 93rd Cong. 1st Sess. 35 (1973). U.S.Code Cong. & Ad.News, 1973, p. 2076. The Senate Report contained substantially identical language. S.Rep.No. 318, 93rd Cong., 1st Sess. 50, 70 (1973). U.S.Code Cong. & Ad. News 1973, 2076, 2143.

that Section 504 was "patterned" after Section 601 of Title VI. S.Rep.No. 1297, 93rd Cong., 2d Sess. (1974), *reprinted in* U.S.Code Cong. & Ad.News 6373, 6390. At least one circuit has relied upon this lone reference as indicia that Congress intended to incorporate wholesale the provisions of Title VI, including Section 604, into the Rehabilitation Act. *Carmi v. Metropolitan St. Louis Sewer District, supra,* 620 F.2d 675. We find such an interpretation reads far too much into an isolated reference in the legislative history.

The reference does not indicate an intent to incorporate the strictures of Title VI into the Rehabilitation Act. Viewed in context, the reference constitutes nothing more than acknowledgement that Section 504 was written with the same sweeping language found in Section 601 of Title VI. In fact, the legislative history to the 1974 amendments is replete with notations indicating that Section 504 was intended to encompass programs receiving federal financial assistance of any kind, not just those programs receiving federal financial assistance for the purpose of providing employment.[9] Furthermore, had Congress intended to incorporate wholesale the provisions of Title VI into the Rehabilitation Act, the legislative body would have had no reason to amend the Act in 1978 and provide that the "remedies, procedures, and rights" found in Title VI were applicable to suits under Section 504 of the Rehabilitation Act.[10]

Finally, we note that the Rehabilitation Act is remedial in nature. *Carmi v. Metropolitan St. Louis Sewer District, supra,* 620 F.2d at 677 (McMillian, J., concurring). As a general matter, courts eschew narrow interpretations of remedial statutes. Instead, remedial statutes are normally accorded broad construction in order to effectuate their purpose. *Peyton v. Rowe,* 391 U.S. 54, 65, 88 S.Ct. 1549, 1555, 20 L.Ed.2d 426 (1968); *Ayers v. Wolfinbarger,* 491 F.2d 8, 16 (5th Cir. 1974). Because the legislative history is devoid of language demonstrating that Congress intended Section 604 of Title VI to apply to suits under the Rehabilitation Act, the remedial nature of the Rehabilitation Act mandates that we reject such an interpretation.

---

[9]The Senate Report made clear the broad reach of Section 504. "Section 504 was enacted to prevent discrimination against all handicapped individuals, regardless of their need for, or ability to benefit from, vocational rehabilitation services, *in relation to Federal assistance in employment, housing, transportation, education, health services, or any other Federally aided program.*" (Emphasis added.) S.Rep.No. 1297, 93rd Cong., 2d Sess. 38 (1974), *reprinted in* U.S.Code Cong. & Ad.News 6373, 6388. Similarly, the Report noted that:

> The language of section 504, in following the above-cited Acts, further envisions the implementation of a compliance program which is similar to those Acts, including promulgation of regulations providing for investigation and review of *recipients of Federal financial assistance,* attempts to bring noncomplying recipients into voluntary compliance through informal efforts such as negotiation, and the imposition of sanctions against recipients who continue to discriminate against otherwise qualified handicapped persons on the basis of handicap. Such sanctions would include, where appropriate, the termination of *Federal financial assistance* to the recipient or other means otherwise authorized by law. Implementation of section 504 would also include pregrant analysis of recipients to ensure that *Federal funds* are not initially provided to those who discriminate against handicapped individuals. (Emphasis added.)

S.Rep.No. 1297, *supra,* at 40, *reprinted in* U.S. Code Cong. & Ad.News, *supra,* at 6390.

[10]In any event, the precise import of the statement in the legislative history that Section 504 was "patterned" after Section 601 of the Civil Rights Act of 1964 is at best unclear. Ambiguous and unclear legislative history may not be used to alter the ordinary meaning of statutory language. *Ford Motor Credit Co. v. Cenance,* 452 U.S. 155, 158 n.3, 101 S.Ct. 2239, 2241 n.3, 68 L.Ed.2d 744 (1981); *Dent v. St. Louis-San Francisco Ry. Co.,* 406 F.2d 399, 403 (5th Cir. 1969), *cert. denied,* 403 U.S. 912, 91 S.Ct. 2219, 29 L.Ed.2d 689 (1971); *League to Save Lake Tahoe, Inc. v. Trounday,* 598 F.2d 1164, 1172 (9th Cir.), *cert. denied,* 444 U.S. 943, 100 S.Ct. 299, 62 L.Ed.2d 310 (1979).

*IV. Section 505 of the Rehabilitation Act*

In 1978, Congress again amended the Rehabilitation Act and added Section 505. Pub.L.No. 95–602, 92 Stat. 2955 (1978).[11] The section provides that the "remedies, procedures, and rights" of an aggrieved party are found in Title VI of the Civil Rights Act of 1964. Significantly, Congress did not simply state that suits under Section 504 of the Rehabilitation Act were controlled by Title VI. Instead, Congress made clear that only the "remedies, procedures, and rights" of Title VI were incorporated into the Rehabilitation Act. Section 604, as a substantive restriction on standing, does not constitute a right, remedy or procedure.[12] Thus, under the plain meaning of the language in Section 505, Section 604 of the Civil Rights Act was not incorporated into the Rehabilitation Act.

Any lingering doubt concerning the correct interpretation of Section 505 is dispelled by reference to the legislative history. The legislative history makes clear that Congress intended the amendments to *expand* the remedies of handicapped individuals. *See, e.g.,* 124 Cong.Rec. S-30311 (daily ed., Sept. 20, 1978) (statement by Senator Stafford) ("The bill allows the rehabilitation program to grow and *serve more handicapped individuals and provide these individuals with greater opportunities to maximize their potential.*") (emphasis added); *id.* at S-155591 (daily ed., Sept. 20, 1978) (statement by Senator Cranston); *id.* at S-30303 (statements by Senator Randolph); *id.* at H-13901 (daily ed., May 16, 1978) (statements by Congressman Jeffords). We find it disingenuous to suggest that we read into an amendment intended to broaden remedies under the Act a restriction on standing.[13]

More specifically, the Conference Report to the 1978 Amendments acknowledges that the Rehabilitation Act extends to *any* recipient of federal financial as-

---

[11]The language of Section 505 did not appear in the original House bill. The origin of the language was in the Senate and was added to the final bill at the joint conference. H.Con. R.No. 1780, 95th Cong., 2d Sess. (1978), *reprinted in* U.S.Code Cong. & Ad.News at 7404.

[12]A "remedy" is the means employed to enforce a right or redress an injury. Black's Law Dictionary 1163 (rev. 5th ed. 1979). The term "rights" generally connotes "a power, privilege, faculty, or demand, inherent in one person and incident upon another." Black's Law Dictionary, *supra,* at 1189. Clearly the restrictions found in Section 604 of the Civil Rights Act of 1964 constitute neither a right nor a remedy under the aforementioned definitions.

Procedures prescribe methods of "enforcing rights or obtaining redress for their invasion; machinery for carrying on procedural aspects of a civil or criminal action . . . . As a general rule, laws which fix duties, establish rights and responsibilities among and for persons . . . are 'substantive laws' . . ." Black's Law Dictionary, *supra,* at 1083. By severely restricting the category of people that can maintain an action under the Rehabilitation Act, Section 604 of the Civil Rights Act of 1964 can only be viewed as a substantive limitation on the rights created by Section 504 of the Rehabilitation Act. As such, the restriction cannot be viewed as procedural.

[13]Other evidence demonstrates that the 1978 amendments were intended to *expand* rather than contract the applicability of the Rehabilitation Act. As originally enacted, Section 504 did not make clear that it applied to the federal government as well as state and local governments. In fact, the Justice Department issued an opinion at the request of the Department of Health, Education and Welfare concluding that the Federal Government was exempt from the statute. The 1978 amendments specifically negated the Justice Department's interpretation by extending the Act to execute agencies and the United States Postal Service. *Prewitt* v. *United States Postal Service, supra,* 662 F.2d at 302. As noted by Congressman Jeffords, "[t]his amendment removes [the exemption for the federal government] and applies 504 to the Federal Government as well as State and local recipients of Federal dollars . . . . I think this is fair and appropriate and should go a long way toward developing a uniform and equitable national policy for elimination of discrimination." 124 Cong.Rec. H-13901 (daily ed., May 16, 1978).

sistance. H.Con.R. No. 1780, 95th Cong., 2d Sess. (1978), *reprinted in* U.S.Code Cong. & Ad.News 7375, 7404 (Section 505 insures that the "remedies, procedures, and rights set forth in title VI of the Civil Rights Act of 1964 would be available to any person aggrieved by any act or failure to act by *any recipient of Federal assistance . . . .*") (emphasis added). Furthermore, the discussion of Section 505 in the Conference Report was located in a subsection titled "Attorneys' Fees and Remedies." The title of an act or subsection can be used to help interpret an ambiguous statute. *Russ* v. *Wilkins,* 624 F.2d 914, 922 (9th Cir. 1980). It is reasonable to conclude that the title of this subsection indicates that Congress was adopting the section to provide benefits and remedies for an aggrieved party. On the other hand the restrictions found in Section 604 cannot be construed as either a benefit or a remedy. The explanation of the statute and the title of the subsection therefore establish that Congress did not intend to incorporate Section 604 of the Civil Rights Act into Section 504 of the Rehabilitation Act.

Finally, we note that four years after the adoption of the Rehabilitation Act in 1973, the Department of Health, Education and Welfare enacted regulations that attempted to implement the Act. *See* 45 C.F.R. Part 84. The regulations did not restrict the applicability of the Rehabilitation Act to those programs receiving federal funds for the purpose of providing employment. Instead, the regulations prohibited discrimination against qualified handicapped individuals in programs and activities receiving or benefiting from *any* federal financial assistance. 45 C.F.R. § 84.2(f) & (h); § 84.4.

In enacting Section 505, the Senate report specifically noted the existence of the HEW regulations. Moreover, the report noted that Section 505 did nothing more than codify the rights, remedies and procedures found in the HEW regulations.

> *It is the committee's understanding that the regulations promulgated by the Department of Health, Education, and Welfare with respect to procedures, remedies, and rights under Section 504 conform with those promulgated under Title VI. Thus, [Section 505] codifies existing practice as a specific statutory requirement.* (Emphasis added.)

S.Rep.No. 890, 95th Cong., 2d Sess. 19 (1978), U.S.Code Cong. & Ad.News, 1978 p. 7312. Thus Section 505 was intended to encompass only those remedies, procedures and rights of Title VI found in the HEW regulations. Since the HEW regulations did not utilize or mention the restrictions found in Section 604 of Title VI, Congress obviously did not intend Section 505 to incorporate such a restriction into the Rehabilitation Act.[14]

---

[14]In *Trageser* v. *Libbie Rehab. Cntr. Inc., supra,* 590 F.2d 87, the Fourth Circuit relied upon the language of Section 505 to conclude that Congress intended to incorporate the restrictions of Section 604 into the Rehabilitation Act. We note, however, that the opinion suffers from a number of deficiencies that render its analysis suspect. The *Trageser* court made no attempt to determine whether the restrictions found in Section 604 constituted a right, remedy or procedure within the meaning of Section 505. Moreover, the opinion failed to examine the legislative history of Section 505. As a result, the opinion did not provide any support from the legislative history for its interpretation. In fact, as we have shown, the legislative history indicates a contrary intent. Finally, without providing any supporting authority, the *Trageser* court concluded that Section 604 was intended to apply to actions by private parties. As noted, however, Section 604 states on its face that it applies only to actions brought by federal departments and agencies. *See* note 7, *supra.* Accordingly, we find the reasoning of the opinion decidedly unpersuasive and decline to follow it.

## V. Conclusion

Upon consideration of the issue, we have uncovered no evidence demonstrating that Congress intended to incorporate the limitations of Section 601 of Title VI into the Rehabilitation Act. We therefore effectuate the plain meaning of the language in Sections 504 and 505 and conclude that a plaintiff need not establish that the employer received federal financial assistance for the primary purpose of providing employment in order to have standing. Instead, a plaintiff need only show that the employer received federal financial assistance and that he/she was an intended beneficiary of the assistance. *Doyle* v. *Univ. of Ala.-Birm.*, *supra; Brown* v. *Sibley, supra*. Moreover, our determination leads to the ineluctable conclusion that the DOT regulations were written in a manner consistent with the Rehabilitation Act and were therefore valid.[15]

We of course intimate no position on the merits of plaintiff's claim. Instead, we simply hold that the district court applied the incorrect standard in determining plaintiff's standing to maintain the suit. Accordingly, the decision of the district court is REVERSED and REMANDED for proceedings not inconsistent with this opinion.

NOTE

Until the *Jones* court took another look at the issues, the decision in *Trageser* had had a strong impact upon other courts. Among the decisions that followed the *Trageser* analysis were: *Scanlon* v. *Atascadero State Hospital*, 677 F.2d 1271 (9th Cir. 1982); *United States* v. *Cabrini Medical Center*, 639 F.2d 908 (2d Cir. 1981); *Carmi* v. *Metropolitan St. Louis Sewer District*, 620 F.2d 672 (8th Cir. 1980); *Meyerson* v. *State of Arizona*, 526 F.Supp. 129 (D.Ariz. 1981); *Miller* v. *Abilene Christian University of Dallas*, 517 F.Supp. 437 (N.D.Tex. 1981); *Hall* v. *Board of County Commissioners of Frederick County*, 509 F.Supp. 841 (D.Md. 1981); *Cain* v. *Archdiocese of Kansas City, Kan.*, 508 F.Supp. 1021 (D.Kan. 1981). *Scanlon* v. *Atascadero State Hospital, supra*, contains a very strong dissenting opinion by Circuit Judge Ferguson. Among other things, Judge Ferguson pointed out that the United States Attorney General, the Senate Committee on Labor and Human Resources, the Department of (then) Health, Education and Welfare, and legal commentators were unanimous in agreeing that the *Trageser* court was incorrect in inferring a Congressional intent to limit private rights of action for employment discrimination under Section 504. At 677

---

[15]The DOT regulations prohibit discrimination against qualified handicapped individuals in any program or activity receiving or benefiting from federal financial assistance. 49 C.F.R. § 27.7. The regulations define federal financial assistance as:

> . . . any grant, loan, contract (other than a procurement contract or a contract of insurance or guaranty), or any other arrangement by which the Department provides or otherwise makes available assistance in the form of:
> (a) Funds;
> (b) Services of Federal personnel; or
> (c) Real or personal property or any interest in, or use of such property, including:
> (1) Transfers or leases of such property for less than fair market value or for reduced consideration; and
> (2) Proceeds from a subsequent transfer or lease of such property if the Federal share of its fair market value is not returned to the Federal Government.

49 C.F.R. § 27.5. Thus, the regulations are not limited to employers receiving federal aid for purposes of employment. Instead, they extend to employers receiving or benefiting from any kind of federal financial assistance.

Other federal agencies have adopted similar or identical regulations. *See* 45 C.F.R. Part 85 (Department of Health & Human Services); 13 C.F.R. Part 113 (Small Business Administration); 31 C.F.R. Part 51 (Department of the Treasury).

F.2d 1273–1274. Prior to the *Jones* decision, one of the few opinions expressly disapproving of the *Trageser* line of reasoning was *Hart* v. *County of Alameda*, 485 F.Supp. 66 (N.D.Cal. 1979).

## LE STRANGE V. CONSOLIDATED RAIL CORPORATION

*United States Court of Appeals for the Third Circuit, 1982*
*687 F.2d 767*

Before: ADAMS and WEIS, *Circuit Judges* and BLOCH,* *District Judge.*

BLOCH, *District Judge.*

Plaintiff brought suit, pursuant to §504 of the Rehabilitation Act of 1973, claiming he was denied employment by the defendant because he is handicapped. Section 504, 29 U.S.C. § 794, provides: "No otherwise qualified handicapped individual . . . shall . . . be excluded from the participation in, be denied the benefits of, or be subjected to discrimination under any program or activity receiving Federal financial assistance. . . ." Although the lower court dismissed plaintiff's action because he lacked standing to bring his suit, we think the question posed by this appeal is, in fact, whether § 504's prohibition against discrimination by federal grantees encompasses a ban against employment discrimination.

I

The lower court concluded plaintiff did not have standing to sue defendant for employment discrimination "unless 1) providing employment is a primary objective of the federal aid received by the defendant, or 2) discrimination in employment necessarily causes discrimination against primary beneficiaries of the federal aid." *LeStrange* v. *Consolidated Rail Corp.*, No. 78-0944 (M.D. Pa. Oct. 20, 1981). The court further refined the first prong of its standing test to require the plaintiff to show he is a primary beneficiary of the federal aid received by the defendant, and that the primary objective of the federal aid be to create new jobs, and not merely to maintain employment or to compensate for lost jobs. Plaintiff could not meet either of the two prongs of the lower court's standing test.

This standing test had its genesis in the case of *Trageser* v. *Libbie Rehabilitation Center, Inc.*, 590 F.2d 87 (4th Cir. 1978). The *Trageser* analysis has since been adopted by the Eighth Circuit in *Carmi* v. *Metropolitan St. Louis Sewer District*, 620 F.2d 672 (1980), the Second Circuit in *United States* v. *Cabrini Medical Center*, 639 F.2d 908 (1981), and the Ninth Circuit in *Scanlon* v. *Atascadero State Hospital*, No. 80-5201 (May 24, 1982). *Trageser* and its progeny rely on § 505(a)(2) of the Rehabilitation, Comprehensive Services, and Developmental Disabilities Act of 1978, amending the Rehabilitation Act of 1973, which provides:

> The remedies, procedures, and rights set forth in title VI of the Civil Rights Act of 1964 shall be available to any person aggrieved by any act or failure to act by any recipient of Federal assistance or Federal provider of such . . .

29 U.S.C. § 794a(a)(2).

---

*The Honorable Alan Bloch, United States District Judge for the Western District of Pennsylvania, sitting by designation.

Title VI served as the model for § 504 of the Rehabilitation Act. Section 601 of Title VI provides:

> No person . . . shall, on the ground of race, color, or national origin, be excluded from participation in, be denied the benefits of, or be subjected to discrimination under any program or activity receiving Federal financial assistance.

42 U.S.C. § 2000d.

Section 602 of Title VI authorizes federal departments and agencies to promulgate regulations to enforce §601's prohibition against discrimination, including regulations providing for the termination of federal funding in the event of non-compliance, *id.*, §2000d-1. However, §604 provides:

> Nothing contained in this subchapter shall be construed to authorize action under this subchapter by any department or agency with respect to any employment practice of any employer . . . except where a primary objective of the Federal financial assistance is to provide employment.

*Id.*, §2000d-3.

*Trageser* concludes, first, that §604 limits not only agency action, but also the actions of private litigants. It then concludes that the remedies, procedures and rights of Title VI extended to the victims of handicap discrimination by the 1978 amendments to the Rehabilitation Act includes §604's limitation on the right to bring an action for employment discrimination.

The lower court reformulated the *Trageser* holding into a test for standing, peculiar to §504 actions. We see no reason to formulate any test for standing for §504 actions other than that promulgated by the Supreme Court for general application, that is (a) does the plaintiff allege "that the challenged action has caused him injury in fact, economic or otherwise;" and (b) "[is] the interest sought to be protected by the complainant . . . arguably within the zone of interests [sought] to be protected or regulated by the statute or constitutional guarantee in question." *Association of Data Processing Service Organizations* v. *Camp,* 397 U.S. 150, 152–53 (1970). The relevant question on this appeal would then be whether plaintiff's interest in being free from employment discrimination falls within the zone of interests sought to be protected by §504. However, the correct formulation of the test for standing for §504 actions is not the crucial issue presented by this appeal. For however the test is formulated, the crucial issue is whether §504, as amended in 1978, covers employment discrimination against the handicapped by federal grantees.

## II

The Supreme Court recently confronted this same issue within the context of Title IX of the Education Amendments of 1972, and we believe its approach in *North Haven Board of Education* v. *Bell,* 50 U.S.L.W. 4501 (May 17, 1982), dictates our approach in this case.

Section 901(a) of Title IX, like §504 of the Rehabilitation Act, is modeled after §601 of Title VI of the Civil Rights Act. It provides:

No person . . . shall, on the basis of sex, be excluded from participation in, be denied the benefits of, or be subjected to discrimination under any education program or activity receiving Federal financial assistance. . . .

The Department of Education promulgated regulations pursuant to Title IX, prohibiting federally funded education programs from discriminating in employment on the basis of gender. Two Connecticut public school boards brought separate suits challenging its authority to issue the regulations, arguing Title IX was not meant to reach the employment practices of educational institutions.

The Supreme Court began its analysis by focusing on the statutory language, concluding first that "[A] female employee who works in a federally funded education program is 'subjected to discrimination under' that program if she is paid a lower salary for like work, given less opportunity for promotion, or forced to work under more adverse conditions than are her male colleagues," *id.* at 4503, and, therefore, that, "Because §901(a) neither expressly nor impliedly excludes employees from its reach, we should interpret the provision as covering and protecting these 'persons' unless other considerations counsel to the contrary," *id.* To determine whether "other considerations counsel to the contrary," the Supreme Court looked to the legislative history "for evidence as to whether Congress meant somehow to limit the expansive language of §901," *id.* The Court found no such evidence and held, "Title IX proscribes employment discrimination in federally funded education programs," *id.* at 4507.

## III

The statutory language of §504 of the Rehabilitation Act and §901 of Title IX being virtually identical, we are bound to conclude, like the Supreme Court in *North Haven,* that because §504 "neither expressly nor impliedly excludes employees from its reach, we should interpret the provision as covering and protecting these 'persons' unless other considerations counsel to the contrary." For like female employees, handicapped employees are "subjected to discrimination under" a federally funded program if they are paid lower salaries, given less opportunity for promotion, or forced to work under more adverse conditions than are their non-handicapped colleagues. Similarly, a handicapped individual is certainly "subjected to discrimination under" a federally funded program if, as alleged in our case, he is not hired at all, solely because of his handicap.

Of course, *Trageser* and the courts which have followed it, including the lower court in this case, find counsel to the contrary in §505(a)(2) of the 1978 amendments to the Rehabilitation Act, extending the remedies, procedures and rights of Title VI to victims of handicap discrimination. Title IX contains no provision similar to §505(a)(2). *Trageser* would also argue that §505(a)(2) should be read together with §505(a)(1), 29 U.S.C. §794a(a)(1), extending the remedies, procedures and rights of Title VII to victims of handicap discrimination by the federal government. The failure of Congress to extend Title VII to victims of discrimination by federal grantees indicates to the *Trageser* court its intention to limit the scope of §504 to discrimination other than employment discrimination. We do not believe that the statutory language of

§505(a)(2), even when read in the context of §505(a)(1), indicates a desire to narrow the scope of §504. For this reason, we would nonetheless find §504 prohibits employment discrimination by federal grantees unless anything in the legislative history of either §504 or §505(a)(2) counsels to the contrary.

Section 505(a)(2) extends the remedies, rights and procedures of Title VI to (1) persons; (2) aggrieved by any act or failure to act by either a recipient or a provider of federal funds. Title VI consists of six provisions,[1] and the only one which extends to *persons* any rights or remedies is §603, 42 U.S.C. §2000d-2, providing for judicial review of agency action.

The plain words of §604 limit its application to departments or agencies. Given the statutory scheme of which Title VI is a part, it is not illogical to assume Congress intended precisely what it said and no more. Title VI is, of course, a part of the 1964 Civil Rights Act. The 1964 Civil Rights Act also has a Title VII, which deals exclusively with employment discrimination. In 1964, it prohibited employment discrimination on the basis of race, color or national origin by *any* employer with 15 or more employees working each working day for at least 20 weeks. Obviously, the sweep of Title VII is far broader than Title VI. Clearly, Title VI was never meant to be a prime tool for the enforcement of employment rights.

Title VII created a new federal agency, the Equal Employment Opportunity Commission, to battle employment discrimination. Without the limiting language of §604, Title VI threatened to engage every other department and agency in the same battle, with the potential danger of varying rules, regulations and strategies.

The question of whether §604 also limited the rights of private litigants was unlikely to even occur to the Congress. The only reason for a private litigant to sue for employment discrimination under Title VI is that he failed to meet the administrative requirements to bringing suit under Title VII. Even then, an action brought pursuant to 42 U.S.C. §1983 may provide a wider range of remedies than a Title VI action.[2]

As to the implications raised by §505(a)(1), extending the remedies, procedures and rights of Title VII to victims of discrimination by the federal government, closer analysis undermines the *Trageser* argument that this too indicates Congressional intent to limit §504 to discrimination other than employment discrimination.

Section 505(a)(1) extends particular provisions of Title VII to individuals aggrieved by the final disposition of a complaint brought pursuant to §501 of the Rehabilitation Act. Section 501 requires federal departments, agencies and instrumen-

---

[1]The first provision of Title VI, §601, 42 U.S.C. §2000-d, is the declaration prohibiting discrimination on the basis of race, color, or national origin by federal grantees. The second provision, §602, *id.* §2000d-1, authorizes federal departments and agencies to issue rules, regulations and orders to effectuate the initial prohibition against discrimination. Section 602 also provides that compliance with the regulations may be effected by the termination of federal funding. It further provides for a number of procedures clearly designed, not to protect the victim of discrimination, but the federal grantee. Section 603, *id.* §2000d-2, provides for judicial review of agency action. Section 604, *id.* §2000d-3, prohibits any department or agency from terminating funds for employment discrimination unless a primary goal of the federal program involved is to provide employment. Section 605, *id.* § 2000d-4, exempts from the scope of Title VI programs which receive federal financial assistance by way of a contract of insurance or guaranty.

[2]Some courts have decided that a Title VI litigant is entitled to declaratory and injunctive relief only, and not monetary damages. Drayden v. Needville Independent School Dist., 642 F.2d 129 (5th Cir. 1981); Concerned Tenants Ass'n. v. Indian Trails Apartments, 496 F.Supp. 522 (N.D. Ill. 1980).

talities, including the Postal Service, to develop an affirmative action plan for the hiring, placement and advancement of handicapped individuals. Handicapped employees or prospective employees aggrieved by agency action or inaction may file a complaint with the agency. The particular provisions of Title VII referred to in §505(a)(1) extend to complaining individuals the right to appeal an adverse agency decision to the EEOC and then to bring a civil action in court. The various provisions prescribe various time limitations on agency action and the filing of appeals and civil suits. They further proscribe various court procedures.

Section 505(a)(1) refers alleged victims of employment discrimination on the basis of handicap in the federal government to the very sections of Title VII dealing with employment discrimination on the basis of race, color, religion, sex or national origin in the federal government. Section 505(a)(1) asks the EEOC to do what it is already doing for victims of employment discrimination on one basis for victims of employment discrimination on another basis. The question before the EEOC in either case is the same: was this person discriminated against in the making of some employment decision? Once the EEOC has made its determination, the alleged discriminatee, if dissatisfied, may go to court.

In contrast, extending Title VII rights, remedies and procedures to victims of discrimination by federal grantees would present a host of new issues to the EEOC. First, it would take it beyond the realm of employment discrimination for the first time, to discrimination in housing, access, education, etc. Second, it would ask it to resolve the issue of what is a federally-funded program or activity, a question with which it has no familiarity.

The failure of Congress to extend Title VII to victims of §504 discrimination was obviously intended simply to short-circuit the EEOC, and for obvious reasons. Reading into the statutory framework of §505 an intention to drastically narrow the scope of §504 is a strained interpretation of an otherwise reasonably constructed provision. Support should be found in the legislative history before we should stretch so far.

## IV

In order to be certain that Congress intended what the broad sweep of its language in §504 indicates, we must undertake a two-step analysis of legislative history. Section 504 should be read to prohibit employment discrimination "unless other considerations counsel to the contrary." Considerations counselling to the contrary may be found in the legislative history of §504 of the Rehabilitation Act of 1973 or the legislative history of the 1978 amendments, which introduced §505(a)(2) to the Act. We begin with the 1973 legislative history. Because we believe nothing in that history indicates Congress intended anything less than it said, we then turn to the history of the 1978 amendments to determine if Congress, at that point, intended to narrow the scope of its prior enactment.

## A

The legislation which would eventually become the Rehabilitation Act of 1973 was considered and passed by the Congress three times before it was finally signed into law by President Nixon on September 26, 1973. Sen. Rep. No. 93-318, 93d Cong., 1st Sess., *reprinted* in 1973 U.S. Code Cong. & Ad. News 2076, 2086–2090 [hereinafter cited at Sen. Rep. No. 93-318]. A provision prohibiting discrimination against the handicapped by federal grantees was part of all three measures, *id.* at 2078–2082, although it was not part of the original resolution passed in 1972 by the House. Comm. of Conf. Rep. H.R. 8395, 92d Cong., 2d Sess., *reprinted in* 118 Cong. Rec. 35141, 35163.

All versions of the legislation were lengthy, the first two even lengthier than the third. Certainly, the primary purpose of the legislation was to extend the 53-year-old vocational rehabilitation program, for another period of years, with a new mandate, in the original two bills, to give priority to the severely handicapped. In addition, the bills as originally submitted to the President authorized a program which, for the first time, would have provided rehabilitation services to severely handicapped individuals with no feasible vocational goals. In addition, the original two bills would have created a series of other new programs concentrating on particular sub-groups of the handicapped, such as older deaf and blind individuals, individuals with spinal cord injuries and individuals with end-stage renal disease. Finally, the bills would have mandated certain research and created a number of federal bodies to deal with particular problems of the handicapped. Sen. Rep. No. 93-318, 1973 U.S. Code Cong. & Ad. News at 2078–2079.

The first bill was pocket vetoed by the President on October 27, 1972. 118 Cong. Rec. 37203. The second bill was vetoed on March 27, 1973, 119 Cong. Rec. 9307, and the Senate failed to override the veto a week later, *id.* at 10794. Serious negotiations between the Administration and, primarily, the Senate then began. Sen. Rep. No. 93-318, 1973 U.S. Code & Ad. News, at 2082.

The President's primary objection to the original two bills was that they authorized what he considered to be an excessive and inflationary amount of money to fund the proposed programs. He also objected to what he saw as a change of focus in the highly successful vocational rehabilitation program by requiring priority be given to the severely handicapped. He also opposed the proliferation of categorical grants to fund the new programs and the proliferation of federal commissions, councils and divisions. 118 Cong. Rec. 5880 (first veto memorandum); 119 Cong. Rec. 24570 (second veto memorandum). The final bill that was to become law was trimmed from seven titles to five. It required only that vocational rehabilitation programs give equal, not priority, treatment to the severely handicapped, eliminated all the proposed new programs, including the non-vocational rehabilitation program, eliminated most of the new federal bodies which would have dealt with the problems of the handicapped, and, of course, significantly lowered the amount of money authorized to fund the remaining legislation. Sen. Rep. No. 93-318, 1973 U.S. Code Cong. & Ad. News at 2079–2082.

At no time was there any dispute between the Administration and the Congress over the wisdom of the non-discrimination provision which would eventually be codified in §504. Neither was it ever a matter of controversy between the Senate and the House. Although it was not part of the first House resolution, the Senate version was accepted in conference with no more than the notation, "The House recedes." 118 Cong. Rec. 35163.

It is not surprising, therefore, that despite the pages of legislative history generated by an act debated and passed three times by Congress, that there is little reference to §504. There is *no* direct reference indicating that §504 was not meant to cover employment discrimination. However, there are several both direct and indirect references indicating the contrary.

The Rehabilitation Act was born in the Senate in the newly constituted Subcommittee on the Handicapped of the Committee on Labor and Public Welfare. The subcommittee was charged with examining *all* issues related to the handicapped, not just those raised by the vocational rehabilitation program. 119 Cong. Rec. 5882. The expanded focus of the bill which was reported by the subcommittee was certainly due, in part, to the wide focus of the subcommittee's mandate. The legislative history indicates one of the problems of the handicapped addressed by the subcommittee was the problem of employment discrimination.

Senator Cranston, who chaired the subcommittee for the purpose of considering the legislation extending the vocational rehabilitation program, commented during debate on various criticisms of the program which he felt could not be handled simply by amending the Vocational Rehabilitation Act itself. "Such problems as *unfounded discrimination in employment* and in housing, difficulties of access to places of work and treatment centers, and duplication and fragmentation of services across program lines were voiced repeatedly to the committee," he noted (emphasis added). *Id.*[3]

Discrimination in employment has a particularly detrimental impact on the vocational rehabilitation program, Senator Cranston noted:

> [D]iscrimination in placement, hiring and advancement continue to limit the vocational rehabilitation program's ability to effect successful rehabilitations . . . The expenditure of money on vocational rehabilitation programs is not well spent if we do not at the same time take meaningful steps to eliminate architectural barriers and provide substantial accomplishments in employment for handicapped individuals.

*Id.*

These sentiments of Senator Cranston expressed during debate on the second incarnation of the act were echoed by Senator Taft during debate on the third incarnation of the act:

> The basic purpose of vocational rehabilitation continues to be to help physically and mentally handicapped individuals achieve the ability to work, earn, and live independently in their communities. Yet in spite of the relatively high success of this program, we still have a long way to go . . . Too many handicapped Americans are not served at all, too many lack jobs, and too many are underemployed—utilized in capacities well below the levels of their training, education, and ability.
>
> However, if we are to assure that all handicapped persons may participate fully in the rewards made possible by the vocational rehabilitation program, we must devote more of our energy toward the elimination of the most disgraceful barrier of all— discrimination.

*Id.* at 24587.

And, clearly, the Rehabilitation Act addressed the problem of employment discrimination. As described by Senator Javits, co-sponsor of the act, a member of the

---

[3]*See also,* the remarks of Senator Stafford, the ranking minority member of the subcommittee, 119 Cong. Rec. 5893; and Sen. Rep. No. 93-318, 93d Cong. 1st Sess., *reprinted in* 1973 U.S. Code Cong. & Ad. News 2076, 2078.

subcommittee and ranking minority member of the parent Committee on Labor and Public Welfare. ''This measure draws upon the experience of the past half century and provides new emphasis on the severely handicapped, the homebound, client services and participation, *opportunities for employment of the handicapped* and administration improvements'' (emphasis added). *Id.* at 5887. The bill as originally reported and ultimately enacted into law provided, in sections immediately preceding §504, for affirmative action programs to encourage the hiring of the handicapped by the federal government, 29 U.S.C. §791(b) and federal contractors, 29 U.S.C. §793. It is hard to imagine, in an Act whose primary goal is to enhance the vocational capabilities of the handicapped, that if the legislature had intended to limit the reach of a provision which immediately follows two sections whose express purpose is to encourage the hiring of the handicapped, that someone somewhere in the legislative history would not have said so. On the contrary, several members indicated the opposite.

During debate on the original bill, Senator Javits highlighted several new areas of federal responsibility recognized by the legislation: ''I refer, for example, to . . . provisions for encouraging hiring of the handicapped under Federal contracts and Federal grants.'' 118 Cong. Rec. 32305. Senator Humphrey reviewed those provisions requiring affirmative action by federal contractors and prohibiting discrimination by federal grantees and found they embodied the intent of bills he had introduced earlier which would have amended both Titles VI and VII of the 1964 Civil Rights Act to include the handicapped. *Id.* at 32310. Finally, Senator Williams, chairman of the full Committee on Labor and Public Welfare, during debate on the third version of the bill, reviewed provisions retained from the first two versions, including, ''prohibitions against discrimination in employment in programs assisted with Federal funds.'' 119 Cong. Rec. 24588.

These few direct references to §504 support the conclusion that the intent of Congress matched the broad sweep of its language. We turn now to the question of whether Congress intended to narrow the scope of §504 by the 1978 amendments, specifically §505(a)(2).

### B

Section 505(a)(2) originated in the Senate and was adopted by the Committee of Conference assigned to reconcile the Senate and House versions of the 1978 amendments to the Rehabilitation Act. House Conf. Rep. No. 95-1780, 95th Cong. 2d Sess., *reprinted in* 1978 U.S. Code Cong. & Ad. News 7375, 7404. Although the Joint Explanatory Statement of the Committee of Conference offers no assistance in interpreting the provision, noting only that the House receded in its opposition to §505(a)(2), *id.*, the report of the Senate Committee on Human Resources accompanying the original Senate bill discusses the purpose of the provision.

The Senate Committee notes that the then Department of Health, Education and Welfare had recently issued regulations enforcing the prohibition against handicap discrimination by federal grantees embodied in §504. These regulations are particularly noteworthy because HEW was assigned the task, by executive order, of coordinating the issuance of regulations enforcing §504 by all federal departments and agencies. These regulations, subsequently codified at 45 C.F.R. §84.1 *et seq.*, prohibited discrimination in employment practices, *id*. at §84.11. Nonetheless, the Committee stated:

> It is the committee's understanding that the regulations promulgated by the Department of Health, Education, and Welfare with respect to procedures, remedies, and rights under section 504 conform with those promulgated under title VI. *Thus, this amendment codifies existing practice as a specific statutory requirement.*

Sen. Rep. No. 95-890, 95th Cong. 2d Sess., p. 19 (emphasis added).

The committee further stated that applying the provisions of Title VI to §504 of the Rehabilitation Act would assure "administrative due process, and provide for administrative consistency within the Federal Government." *Id*.

The committee report contains nothing that would indicate it felt HEW exceeded its statutory authority by prohibiting employment discrimination in its recently promulgated regulations. Similarly, no one during the debate in the Senate or House suggested HEW had gone too far. In fact, the only Congressman who directly mentioned the regulations during debate, Representative Dodd, "strongly supported the long-delayed issuance of the section 504 regulations believing then, as now, that the protections they establish for the handicapped are very much needed." 124 Cong. Rec. 13905.

Several proposed amendments to the act, and the debate on them, further indicate that Congress understood §504 to reach employment discrimination, when enacted and as amended. For example, Senator Cannon proposed during debate an amendment which, for the purpose of §503 and §504 of the Rehabilitation Act, would exclude from the definition of handicapped individual an alcoholic or drug abuser "whose condition of alcoholism or drug abuse renders that individual not qualified for employment . . ." The purpose of Senator Cannon's amendment, which was eventually passed and codified at 29 U.S.C. § 707(7)(A), was: "To exclude alcoholics and drug abusers from certain employment provisions of the Rehabilitation Act . . ." 124 Cong. Rec. 30322. Its scope was considerably narrower than a similar measure proposed in the House which would have excluded alcoholics and drug abusers from the definition of handicapped individuals altogether, regardless of whether their condition impacted on their employability or not.

Clearly, Senator Cannon believed §504 reached employment discrimination, and nobody during the debate on his argument suggested otherwise. More specifically, nobody suggested that if §504 had at one time reached employment discrimination, the proposed §505(a)(2) would have the effect of eliminating it from its scope. Senator Williams, chairman of the Committee on Human Resources, spoke in support of Senator Cannon's amendment, which he felt necessary "because of misunderstandings and distortions concerning employment rights of alcoholics and drug dependent persons." *Id*. at 30323. Senator Williams felt the amendment "would reassure employers that it is not the intent of Congress to require any employer to hire a person who is not qualified for the position or who cannot perform competently in his or her job." *Id*.

Senator Hathaway also spoke in support of the amendment because he felt it would protect those many alcoholics and drug addicts who hold jobs and perform them satisfactorily. "Sections 503 and 504 of the Rehabilitation Act protect such persons employed by agencies which receive Federal funds or employers which have Federal contracts from being fired solely because of their alcoholism or drug addiction." *Id.* at 30324.

Another amendment proposed during debate would have amended §505(a)(1) to limit a court in an action brought against the federal government to equitable and affirmative action remedies proportionate to actual damages.[4] 124 Cong. Rec. 30576. Its sponsor, Senator McClure, described the amendment's function as insuring "that mammoth affirmative action remedies involving substantial construction could not be compelled in instances in which actual damages were comparatively small." *Id.*

Senator McClure's amendment was vehemently opposed by Senator Cranston, a sponsor of the 1978 act, on the basis that the federal government should be required to do no less than private employers. Senator Cranston argued:

> The amendment offered by the Senator from Idaho would create an unwise and unrealistic distinction with respect to employment between the obligations of the Federal Government and the obligations of Federal contractors and grantees. Ironically, the Senator's amendment would limit—with a financial test—the Federal Government's obligation of being an equal opportunity employer. Federal contractors and grantees would—appropriately—continue to be required to be equal opportunity employers.

*Id.* at 30577–30578.

Finally, we would note the remarks of Representative Jefford, a member of the Subcommittee on Select Education, which reported the House version of the act, commenting on the creation of the Architectual and Transportation Barriers Compliance Board in § 118 of the amendments:

> [W]e gave this board new and expanded responsibilities *for this one aspect of 504.* It is our thought that by separating only the "physical" barriers . . . from actual discrimination in *jobs*, education, housing, and health, we have taken a significant step forward.

*Id.* at 13901 (emphasis added).

None of the above-quoted references to employment discrimination brought forth any objections from the speakers' colleagues in the House and Senate. Indeed, they did not bring forth so much as a question or request for clarification.

Combining the legislative history looking for the intent of Congress is often a frustrating chore. Often the intent of Congress hinges on the remarks of one or two individuals. *See North Haven, supra* at 4504. Here our task has not been so difficult. Clearly, the legislative history to the 1978 amendments demonstrates a widespread understanding on the part of Congress that §504, even as amended, proscribed employment discrimination against the handicapped.

### C

Post-enactment pronouncements provide confirmation of Congressional intent to cover employment discrimination in §504. The Senate Committee on Labor and

---

[4]A compromise was reached later in debate, which resulted in the following language being inserted in § 505(a)(1): "In fashioning an equitable or affirmative action remedy . . . a court may take into account the reasonableness of the cost of any necessary work place accommodation, and the availability of alternatives therefor or other appropriate relief in order to achieve an equitable and appropriate remedy." 29 U.S.C. § 794a(a)(1).

Human Resources, whose predecessors reported both the 1973 Rehabilitation Act and its 1978 amendments, stated unequivocally one year after *Trageser, supra:*

> [*Trageser*] is not consistent with Congress' original and continuing intent that handicapped individuals be empowered to bring suit in Federal District Court for alleged employment discrimination in violation of [section 504], regardless of the designated use of the Federal funds received by the employer in question.

In 1980, responsibility for coordinating enforcement of §504 by federal departments and agencies was transferred to the Attorney General. In his analysis of rules promulgated pursuant to this authority, the Attorney General took note of HEW's earlier regulations prohibiting employment discrimination, *Trageser* and *Carmi*, the legislative history of both the 1973 Act and the 1978 amendments, and concluded, "[T]he Department believes that the employment practices of recipients of Federal financial assistance are covered by section 504 regardless of the purpose of the assistance . . ." Nondiscrimination Based on Handicap in Federally Assisted Programs—Implementation of Section 504 of the Rehabilitation Act of 1973 and Executive Order 11914, 45 Fed. Reg. 37620, 37628 (1980).

V

Under the holding of the district court, Conrail is prohibited from discriminating against handicapped passengers, but is free to discriminate against the handicapped in employment. Such an analysis of §504, unless supported by the words of the relevant statutes or their legislative history, is absurd.

Thus far, the handicapped have not been extended the broad protections against discrimination extended women and members of other minority groups. Federal law protects the handicapped only if employed by the federal government, or federal contractors or grantees. To eliminate protection against discrimination in employment by federal grantees would eliminate a substantial portion of the small amount of protection afforded the handicapped. What is a commonsensicle approach to Title VI, thus, becomes a devastating blow within the context of the Rehabilitation Act. "In the context of §504 of the Rehabilitation Act, applied *Trageser*-style, §604 operates as a blunder buss." *Scanlon, supra* at 2163 (Ferguson, J., dissenting). *See also, Carmi, supra* at 679 (McMillian, J., concurring). Neither the words of the statutes, nor legislative histories, dictate such a result.

For this reason, the order of the district court is reversed, and the case remanded for further consideration and ultimate disposition on the merits.

————

ADAMS, *Circuit Judge,* concurring in the judgment.

Had this appeal been presented for resolution several months ago, I might well have joined the other four courts of appeals in concluding that the Act was not intended to cover discrimination against the handicapped by private employers. After all, the statute makes no direct reference to private employment, and it certainly is not unreasonable to read the restrictions contained in section 604 of Title VI into the Rehabilitation Act.

Nonetheless, I have concluded that the result reached by the Court in this case is consonant with, and perhaps even compelled by, two recent decisions, one by the Supreme Court, *North Haven Bd. of Educ.* v. *Bell*, 50 U.S.L.W. 4501 (U.S. May 17, 1982), and the second by this Court, *Grove City College* v. *Bell*, No. 80-2383, slip op., (ed Cir. Aug. 12, 1982). And whatever I might think of the wisdom of these two decisions, I am bound to apply them unless they are overruled.

In *North Haven,*[1] *supra,* the Supreme Court concluded that the Department of Education had statutory authority to regulate employment discrimination in education—even though Title IX of the Education Act makes no direct reference to employment, and even though Title IX, which was patterned after Title VI, might be thought to incorporate the employment-regulation restrictions of section 604 of Title VI. Nevertheless, the Justices reasoned that the broad-sweeping language of Title IX, which did not explicitly rule out the regulation of employment discrimination, when coupled with a strong legislative and postenactment history, constituted a sufficient basis from which to infer a congressional intent to bring employees within the protection of Title IX. The *North Haven* analysis, when applied to the words of the Rehabilitation Act—which for all relevant purposes are identical to the words of Title IX—and when considered in connection within the strong legislative history of section 504, would appear to compel a similar conclusion. The theory and analysis underlying *North Haven,* then, would suggest that LeStrange prevail on this appeal.

In addition to *North Haven,* I am persuaded that it would be difficult to arrive at a contrary result in this matter after the recent opinion in *Grove City, supra.* In *Grove City,* also decided under Title IX of the Education Act, a panel of this Court concluded that an entire educational institution is brought within the definition of "program," and therefore subject to regulation under Title IX, if it receives any federal aid, and that aid is general or indirect and not specifically earmarked for a particular educational function within the institution. The logic of *Grove City* would appear to be irreconcilable with the analysis employed in *Trageser* v. *Libbie Rehabilitation Center, Inc.,* 590 F.2d 87 (4th Cir. 1978), *cert. denied,* 442 U.S. 947 (1979), where an employer was deemed to fall within the purview of the Rehabilitation Act only if federal funds were received specifically for employment purposes.

For these reasons I join the judgment of the Court in returning this matter to the district court for further proceedings.

WEIS, *Circuit Judge,* concurring.

I join in the judgment of the court because I believe the case on which the district court relied, *Trageser* v. *Libbie Rehabilitation Center, Inc.,* 590 F.2d 87 (4th Cir. 1978), *cert. denied,* 442 U.S. 947 (1979), 442 U.S. 947 (1979), was erroneously decided. I agree that the issue in this case is not one of standing, as that term is ordinarily used, *see, e.g., Valley Forge Christian College* v. *Americans United for Separation of Church and State,* 50 U.S.L.W. 4103, 4105–06 (Jan. 12, 1982), but is the more direct question of the scope of §504.

*Trageser* held that the prohibition against handicap discrimination in §504 of the Rehabilitation Act is limited by the reference in §505(a)(2) to the provisions of

---

[1]*North Haven* involved claims of gender discrimination committed by two public school districts in Connecticut. The Supreme Court noted that one of those districts, North Haven, "devoted between 46.8% and 66.9% of its federal assistance to the salaries of its employees." 50 U.S.L.W. at 4502.

Title VI of the Civil Rights Act of 1964. That is, a claim of employment discrimination against the handicapped is subject to §604 of Title VI: "Nothing contained in this subchapter shall be construed to authorize action . . . by any department or agency with respect to any employment practice of any employer . . . except where a primary objective of the Federal financial assistance is to provide employment." 42 U.S.C. §2000d-3.

Although it recognized that "§604 expressly curtails the authority of federal departments and agencies," the *Trageser* court concluded that "it also restricts private suits." 590 F.2d at 89. The court cited no authority for its conclusion and I am persuaded that it erred in applying §604 to private suits. The language of §604 confines its application to "action . . . by any department or agency" and does not refer at any point to suits brought by a private individual or entity.

The Rehabilitation Act's reference to Title VI was not intended to restrict the remedies of handicapped individuals but rather to limit the sanctions which government agencies could take against an offending recipient of federal financial assistance. Congress enacted §604 because it feared that when an employment violation occurred, an overzealous federal agency might threaten the very existence of important programs by invoking the remedy of withholding funds.[1] The reference to Title VI in §505(a)(2) of the Rehabilitation Act must therefore be interpreted with the understanding that §604 was drafted to prevent administrative overkill. Viewed in this light, it is clear that the incorporation of §604 narrows not the rights of victims, but only the coercive measures which a "department or agency" can apply against an offender.

The dissenting opinion of Judge Ferguson in *Scanlon* v. *Atascadero State Hospital*, No. 80-5201 (9th Cir. May 24, 1982), analyzes the errors of the *Trageser* opinion at length. I agree with Judge Ferguson and see no need to repeat here the reasoning which underlies the conclusions we both reach. *See also, Carmi* v. *Metropolitan St. Louis Sewer District*, 620 F.2d 672, 676 (8th Cir.), *cert. denied*, 449 U.S. 892 (1980), McMillian, J. (conc.).

It is worth noting that in *NAACP* v. *Wilmington Medical Center, Inc.*, 599 F.2d 1247, 1258 (3d Cir. 1979), this court concluded that there is a private right of action under §504. Our holding today is wholly consistent with that case.

Of course, I intimate no views on the merits of this case and concur in the remand to the district court.

NOTES

1. *North Haven Board of Education* v. *Bell* is reported at 102 S.Ct. 1912. Does the interpretation of the *North Haven* decision in *Le Strange* herald the end of the *Trageser* line of cases?

2. In *Sabol* v. *Board of Education of the Township of Willingboro*, 510 F.Supp. 892 (D.N.J. 1981), a discharged school teacher brought a Section 504 action claiming that he was discharged because of physical handicap. The court ruled that he did not have a cause of action under Section 504, because he had failed to show that the primary

---

[1]During congressional debates, Title VI was commonly referred to as the "cut-off-the-funds title." *See* Comment, *Employment Discrimination Against the Handicapped: Can Trageser Repeal the Private Right of Action*, 54 N.Y.U.L. Rev. 1173, 1186 n. 69.

purpose of the federal financial assistance received by the defendant was to provide employment, and that a showing that the defendant engaged in discrimination against the primary beneficiaries of the federal assistance, handicapped students, was not enough to bring the plaintiff within the purview of Section 504's coverage. *Ross v. Allen*, 515 F.Supp. 972 (S.D.N.Y. 1981) involved a teacher who allegedly had been fired in retaliation for her actions on behalf of a student who had been told to stay home indefinitely because of behavior problems. On a motion to dismiss, the court held that the teacher had stated a cause of action under Section 504, since she was within the "zone of interests" protected by the statute and had allegedly suffered an injury in fact. Can these two holdings be reconciled?

p. 438—ADD a new subsection at the bottom of the page:

## 6. Sheltered Workshops and the National Labor Relations Act

### N.L.R.B. v. LIGHTHOUSE FOR BLIND OF HOUSTON
*United States Court of Appeals for the Fifth Circuit, 1981*
*653 F.2d 206*

Application for Enforcement of an Order of the National Labor Relations Board.

Before BROWN and GARZA, Circuit Judges, and BEER, District Judge.

BEER, District Judge:

The National Labor Relations Board seeks to enforce its order of April 24, 1980, against the Lighthouse for the Blind of Houston ("Lighthouse," hereinafter). The Board's decision and order is reported at 248 NLRB 1366. Our jurisdiction arises by virtue of § 10(e) of the National Labor Relations Act (NLRA), 29 U.S.C. § 151, et seq.

The Board concluded that the Lighthouse violated § 8(a)(5) and (1) of the NLRA by refusing to bargain with the General Drivers, Warehousemen and Helpers Local Union 968 affiliated with the International Brotherhood of Teamsters, Chauffeurs, Warehousemen and Helpers of America ("Union," hereinafter), which had been certified as the exclusive bargaining representative of a production and maintenance unit of employees in the Lighthouse's Workshop A, and by refusing to furnish to the Union relevant wage and employment information concerning such employees. In so doing, the Board rejected the Lighthouse's contentions that the Board did not have statutory jurisdiction over it; that, even if the Board had statutory jurisdiction, it would not effectuate the purposes of the Act to assert jurisdiction over the Lighthouse; and that the blind employees in Workshop A were not "employees" within the meaning of the NLRA. We find that the Board's order is not supported by substantial evidence and that the Lighthouse has not unlawfully refused to bargain with the Union.

Lighthouse for the Blind of Houston is a nonprofit, charitable corporation with a principal office and place of business in Houston, Texas. A 35-member board of directors presides over and directs its operation. No member of the board of directors receives compensation for his services. The largest single group of board members are ladies who have served as volunteers at the Lighthouse in the past 20 years. The rest of the board members come from a cross section of the business and civic community of Houston. In providing social and technical services to blind people in the Houston area, the Lighthouse divides its operation into five departments: social services, volunteer services, library and special services, rehabilitation and industrial. The social services division provides social work and recreational services both at the facility and at the individual's residence to assist blind persons. The volunteer services division provides volunteers to support the various operations of the Lighthouse. The Lighthouse has a library and special services division, which makes braille, large print and talking books available for the unsighted community. The rehabilitation division offers vocational training which is geared toward helping visually impaired persons adapt to their surrounding environment. The fifth department, referred to by the parties as the Industrial Division, employs blind people to manufacture a product for sale, e.g. felt-tipped pens, mops, commercial scrub brushes, disinfectants and detergents. Pursuant to contracts with the U.S. General Services Administration (GSA), many of the felt-tipped pens, as well as the detergent and the disinfectant, are supplied to federal government agencies pursuant to the Wagner O'Day Act, 41 U.S.C. § 46, et seq. (1970).

In 1977, the Industrial Division generated $4,620,000 in revenue from sales of the merchandise mentioned above. This resulted in a so-called profit of $237,000 which was then fed back into the Lighthouse's overall operation. Designation of this amount as "profit" depends, of course, on the bookkeeping methods applied. While there is serious doubt that an actual business-based "profit" was, in fact, earned, there is no doubt that the accounting methods here applied did, in fact, result in a profit figure.

The Industrial Division is divided into Workshop A and Workshop B. Workshop B employees are blind persons who, in many instances, have multiple handicaps and are, thus, unable to be fully productive. Some of these individuals have, after training and rehabilitation in Workshop B, "graduated" to Workshop A.

Workshop A employs approximately 70 individuals, 62 of whom are blind or have severe visual impairments. They perform a variety of packaging and assembling jobs; produce felt-tipped pens, mops and commercial scrub brushes; and bottle disinfectants and detergents. They also perform subcontracting work for various private companies, e.g. assembling fishing rod holders, doing grease check assembly jobs and filling notebook binders with inserts.

Workshop A employees are all paid at least the federal minimum wage for their work. At the time of the representative hearing below, wages in Workshop A ranged from $2.89 per hour to $3.25 or $3.40 per hour, the variations depending on differing levels of productivity. All the Workshop A employees are covered for workmen's compensation, unemployment insurance, hospitalization insurance, certain pension rights, and receive nine paid holidays per year. These workers also receive certain other benefits which vary according to their tenure, including vacation and sick leave.

Workshop A employees are eligible to receive merit raises based on productivity; however, merit raises are subject to recision if production subsequently drops. The progress of each of the workers in Workshop A is evaluated twice a year.

The supervisors in Workshop A are, generally, former workers in Workshop A.

Most of them are blind. They have limited authority to check time cards to make sure that all workers are present, dock workers who are late, approve requests to leave work early or to not come in on a particular day. With regard to discipline, the Lighthouse attempts to resolve problems with its workers by counseling. If a problem can be corrected by counseling and discussion, it is. If a problem persists, it is usually referred to the general manager of the Lighthouse, who then attempts to personally resolve the problem. Failing this, the matter is referred to a workers' committee made up of workers in all departments who are elected each year by the workers themselves. This committee can make final decisions with respect to suspension or termination. In the last four years (prior to 1977), there have been three terminations authorized by this committee. This committee also meets to consider problems of the Lighthouse in general. They are kept informed as to what is projected for the future, the schedule for production, new items being worked on, the holiday situation, vacation schedules and general administration. The Lighthouse has no formal program for placement of blind workers but does attempt to place individuals in private industry on an ad hoc basis, particularly with certain employers. Over the years, there has been an average of four persons a year placed in private employment through Lighthouse-sponsored efforts. Unfortunately, experience indicates that the private sector is not very anxious to hire blind and multi-handicapped workers.

The issues presented here are whether the Board properly asserted jurisdiction over the Lighthouse and whether the Board properly determined that the blind and multi-handicapped workers in the Lighthouse's Workshop A facility are employees covered by the National Labor Relations Act.

A review of the National Labor Relations Act of 1935, 29 U.S.C. § 151, et seq., and its legislative history leads to the conclusion that Congress did not intend or expect the exercise of jurisdiction by the Board over nonprofit institutions in general that do not affect commerce. *NLRB* v. *Catholic Bishop of Chicago,* 440 U.S. 490, 99 S.Ct. 1313, 59 L.Ed.2d 533 (1979).

It is clear from the facts cited above that the individuals who comprise Workshop A and whom the Union now seeks to represent are employees in the generic sense of the word. Those individuals work for a set number of hours a day, perform functions which are of recognized economic value and are paid for the performance of those functions. However, the fundamental relation between those individuals and the Lighthouse is different in many significant aspects from a normal employment relationship.

The focus of the Lighthouse's employment concern is upon rehabilitating its clients and providing the maximum service possible to sheltered workshop clients. For example, regular employees in a typical industrial environment are hired because they have the skill and ability to perform the work involved. Workshop clients, on the other hand, are referred to the workshop by a counselor or social worker precisely because of their inability to perform work in the competitive job market.

The disciplinary structure is not handled in the same manner as in the private industry. When infractions occur, supervisory personnel sit down with the client, talk to him, and try to find out if there was a reason for his problem. If the client cannot be helped in the area where he is working, he is moved to another area. Only if the problem is critical and cannot be handled with counseling, are harsher measures used.

Disciplinary discharges are extremely rare. Furthermore, wage payments based on productivity are completely consistent with the rehabilitative purposes of the sheltered workshop. 29 U.S.C. § 214(c) specifically authorizes sheltered workshops' payment to workers to be based upon severity of handicap and productivity. Such payments do not transform a sheltered workshop into an enterprise in which decisions are governed by economic considerations, rather payments relating to productivity are an integral part of the service provided by the workshop. They foster the goal of rehabilitation by providing an incentive to employees to learn the skills and, thus, become sufficiently acclimated to a work environment to move eventually from the sheltered workshop into the competitive job market.

It is certainly true that the Lighthouse's activities are governed, to some extent, by economic considerations. They must pay sufficient attention to economics to maintain a viable entity capable of rendering necessary rehabilitation services. However, the so-called $237,000 profit made by the Lighthouse in 1977 represents only a negligible impact on commerce, in light of all the circumstances here. If it were not for the moneys received from the federal government, as well as other charitable agencies, the Lighthouse would have lost money in fiscal 1977. Further, the vast majority of the products produced at the Lighthouse go to the General Services Administration of the United States government pursuant to the Wagner O'Day Act. Under this statute, the GSA must purchase the Lighthouse products at a price fixed by a presidential committee. 41 U.S.C. §§ 46–48.

Moreover, it is undisputed in the record that the main purpose of the Lighthouse is to provide a wide range of services to blind and disabled persons in order to enhance the quality of their lives including a serious effort to provide its clients with experience which may lead to employment in the competitive job market. When the Lighthouse receives word of a job that is available in private industry, Lighthouse staff personnel are sent to the job site to assist in fully developing that job for a blind worker. Though approximately 50% of those placed in outside private industry find it necessary to return to the Lighthouse, those who return are never refused.

This unusual "employer-client" relationship centers around a concern for the welfare of the clients. To require collective bargaining in this context is to risk intrusion into the rehabilitative process by bargaining demands which could prejudice the Lighthouse's many faceted efforts at rehabilitation.

Although the Lighthouse clients who are employed in Workshop A are arguably employees within the meaning of the Act, it will not effectuate the purposes of the Act to assert jurisdiction over them. *Goodwill Industries of Southern California,* 231 NLRB 536 (1977).

The Board's contended differentiations between *Goodwill Industries,* supra, and the case at bar are not, in our view, significant. The Board contends that the Lighthouse workers are paid variable wages based upon performance and productivity, and are disciplined using "normal economic and business considerations." As previously noted, the variable wage policy is designed to foster rehabilitation, and discipline procedures certainly vary from those in effect in private industry. On the whole, clients are counseled rather than disciplined, and they are rarely, if ever, discharged. In fact, the record reflects that the Lighthouse's employment policies are commensurate with its rehabilitative objective. Thus, we conclude that the Board's order is not supported by substantial evidence; that the Lighthouse has not unlawfully refused to bargain with the Union.

The Board's application for enforcement of its order is denied.

Enforcement denied.

## Cincinnati Ass'n for the Blind v. N.L.R.B.

*United States Court of Appeals for the Sixth Circuit, 1982*
*672 F.2d 567*

Before Merritt, Martin and Jones, Circuit Judges.

Boyce F. Martin, Jr., Circuit Judge.

This case comes before us on the petition of the Cincinnati Association for the Blind for review of cease and desist and bargaining orders issued by the National Labor Relations Board. The Board has cross-applied for enforcement of its orders. We must determine whether the Board abused its discretion in deciding that visually handicapped workers at the Association's Sheltered Workshop for the Blind are entitled to the protection of the National Labor Relations Act.

In May, 1977, the Communications Workers of America, Local 440, filed a representation petition seeking certification as the collective bargaining representative of the Workshop employees. At a hearing held in August, 1977, the Communications Workers disclaimed further interest in the proceedings; however, Local Union 100, a Teamsters affiliate, came forward and asked to be substituted for the Communications Workers as the petitioner. The Board agreed to the substitution. Local 100 sought to represent "all production and maintenance employees" at the Workshop, a group which included both sighted and visually handicapped workers.

Over the Association's objections, the Board decided that the handicapped workers were "employees" covered by the National Labor Relations Act, asserted jurisdiction, and issued a Direction of Election. 235 N.L.R.B. 1448. An election was duly held in June, 1978 and produced a clear union majority. The Association refused to bargain with the Union, whereupon the Union brought unfair labor practice charges. On September 19, 1979, the Board issued the orders presently on appeal. 233 N.L.R.B. 1140.

The Association asks us to hold that its visually handicapped workers fall outside the purview of the Act. In support of this position, it characterizes those workers not as "employees," but as "clients," whose relationship with the Workshop is rehabilitative or therapeutic rather than typically industrial. The Association raises a second issue by objecting to the Board's certification of a bargaining unit which includes both sighted and handicapped workers.

The Board, on the other hand, contends that its application of the Act to visually handicapped workers is entirely consistent with the statutory purpose. It also defends its approval of a single bargaining unit as a proper exercise of discretion.

Before addressing the merits of this case, we believe a brief description of the Cincinnati Workshop is appropriate as background for the legal arguments.

The Cincinnati Association for the Blind is a non-profit corporation dedicated to the interests of visually handicapped persons in the Cincinnati area. It is organized into five operationally distinct departments: Finance, Office, Casework, Rehabilitation, and Workshop. The Casework and Rehabilitation departments offer training, counseling, technical and social services to all blind members of the community.

Some of the individuals who make use of the Association's social services are referred by caseworkers to the Workshop for possible employment; final employment decisions, however, are the province of the Workshop Manager. At present, about seventy blind persons and four sighted persons perform jobs at the Workshop under the supervision of a managerial staff which includes, in addition to the Manager, four supervisors, a contract sales representative, and an industrial engineer.

The Workshop produces goods under contract with the federal government and a number of private industries. Some of these contracts are secured pursuant to the Wagner-O'Day Act, some through competitive bidding. The Workshop is involved in several types of production, including a paper conversion manufacturing operation, which supplies over half the adding machine tape and teletype paper used by the federal government, and a sizeable assembly and packaging operation which serves several private corporations. In 1976, the Workshop generated revenues in excess of $2,000,000, $144,000 of which represented profit. The Association used this profit to defray unrelated expenses.

With very few exceptions, the blind workers are paid on a piece-rate basis, whereas the sighted employees are paid by the hour. The Fair Labor Standards Act permits sheltered workshops to pay certain handicapped workers less than the current minimum wage; the Cincinnati Workshop holds a certificate of exemption, issued by the Department of Labor, which authorizes a special minimum wage of $1.49 per hour. The Association's blind workers receive holiday pay, vacation pay, workers compensation insurance, and life insurance. Sighted employees receive the same benefits plus a pension plan. Blind and sighted workers alike have a five-day, 8:30 a.m. to 4:30 p.m. work week.

The Workshop does not suspend or terminate blind workers for production errors; those forms of discipline are reserved for serious cases of misconduct such as violence or theft. However, the workers are expected to produce goods which conform to the quality standards of the marketplace. If a handicapped worker receives two reprimands for production errors, he is referred to the Work Evaluation Unit for "retraining." During assignments to this Unit, workers are either not paid at all or paid at a lower rate than they customarily receive.

The Workshop operation is not designed primarily to provide temporary, on-the-job training which would enable blind workers to secure employment elsewhere. On the contrary, the program contemplates long-term employment at the Workshop. Very few handicapped workers ever leave to enter the competitive job market.

We turn now to the principal substantive issue before us—the Board's application of the National Labor Relations Act to the Association's visually handicapped workers. The Association challenges the decision below on two grounds: first, it contends, the workers in question are not "employees" within the meaning of the Act;

and second, even if these workers are statutory "employees," the Board abused its discretion in exercising jurisdiction over them.

We have given both arguments careful consideration and have at length concluded that endorsement of either would exceed the proper bounds of judicial action.

The National Labor Relations Act does not attempt a precise definition of an "employee." Section 2(3) merely states that the "term 'employee' shall include any employee . . . unless this subsection explicitly states otherwise." 29 U.S.C. § 152(3). None of the statutory exceptions bear on this case.

The Association's most serious legal argument that handicapped workers in sheltered workshops fall outside the purview of the Act rests on the premise that Congress intended to exclude them from coverage. If this contention is valid, then the Board exceeded its statutory jurisdiction here.

We have found nothing in the Act's legislative history to indicate that Congress considered the status of the handicapped workers at the time it enacted the statute. The Association points out that between 1967 and 1976 several bills were introduced in the House of Representatives with the following preamble: "A bill to amend the National Labor Relations Act to secure to physically handicapped workers employed in sheltered workshops the right to organize and bargain collectively. . . ." 113 Cong. Rec. 12754 (1967); 113 Cong.Rec. 18355 (1967); 115 Cong.Rec. 7575 (1969); 115 Cong.Rec. 6561 (1969); 117 Cong.Rec. 179 (1971); 119 Cong.Rec. 59 (1973); 122 Cong.Rec. 9176 (1976). At each introduction, this bill was referred to the House Committee on Education and Labor, where it apparently remained. This information, standing alone, is inconclusive of the issue. It reflects only the opinion of the bill's sponsor that the Act in its present form does not protect handicapped workers. We have no indication that a consensus of Congress shares this belief.

In the absence of direct evidence of Congressional intent, the Association asks us to infer from other legislation that the Act does not apply to sheltered workshop workers. It directs our attention to the legislative histories of the Fair Labor Standards Act, 29 U.S.C. § 214(c), the Wagner-O'Day Act, 41 U.S.C. §§ 46–48, and the Rehabilitation Act of 1973, 29 U.S.C. § 701 et seq.[1]

According to the Association, these histories demonstrate that Congress has recognized and approved the "rehabilitative" and "therapeutic" function of sheltered workshops. To some extent, at least, this observation is correct. We do not doubt that Congress has indeed sought to benefit the handicapped through legislation favoring sheltered workshops; we are not persuaded, however, that this policy necessarily implies a Congressional intent to exclude handicapped workers from the National Labor Relations Act.

It is the Association's position that the introduction of collective bargaining into the sheltered workshop milieu will inevitably destroy the "therapeutic" effect of the

---

[1]The Fair Labor Standards Act provides employment opportunities for handicapped workers by permitting workshops to pay wages lower than the prevailing minimum wage. The Wagner-O'Day Act permits the federal government to purchase goods produced at workshops on a non-competitive basis. The Rehabilitation Act of 1973 entitles sheltered workshops to financial assistance for certain programs which offer vocational rehabilitation services to handicapped persons.

workshop experience on the individual worker. Thus, argues the Association, if Congress was disposed to permit collective bargaining in sheltered workshops, it would not, in other legislation, address the sheltered workshop concept in the language of "rehabilitation" and "therapy."

We perceive two flaws in this argument. First, Congress has not indicated that it shares the Association's belief in the fundamental incompatibility of collective bargaining and any form of "therapy." Neither has it expressed a contrary policy. We simply lack a basis on which to make an informed judgment about "Congressional intent" in this area.

Thus, we confront a choice between attempting to "second guess" Congress on a political and philosophical issue and relying on the broad, unequivocal language of the statute. Inasmuch as we cannot adopt the first course without impinging on the legislative function, we feel constrained to pursue the latter. Accordingly, we decline to carve out an exception to the plain language of Section 2(3) of the Act.

In this context, we note that the present case differs significantly from *NLRB* v. *Bell Aerospace*, 416 U.S. 267, 94 S.Ct. 1757, 40 L.Ed.2d 134 (1974). There, after a detailed examination of the Act's pre- and post-enactment history, the Supreme Court held that "managerial employees" belong to a class "so clearly outside the Act that no specific exclusionary provision was thought necessary." *Id*. at 283, 94 S.Ct. at 1766. The *Bell Aerospace* Court had the benefit of an extensive legislative history which permitted it to assess Congress' intent with some confidence. No such insight into Congress' position on the present issue is available to us.

Our second objection to the Association's argument lies in its apparent assumption that the primary, overriding concern of all sheltered workshops is to provide the handicapped with "therapy" and "rehabilitation." Even if we were willing to impute to Congress the Association's theory that collective bargaining has no place in a therapeutic environment, we would have reservations about inferring a blanket exemption from the Act for all sheltered workshops. Although all sheltered workshops presumably have some connection with programs geared to providing social services, the evidence in this and other cases strongly suggests that this "rehabilitative" and "therapeutic" nexus is, in some instances, subordinated to routine business considerations. Thus, even if Congress intended to exempt all *primarily* therapeutic institutions from the Act, some sheltered workshops would fail to qualify.

In practice, the Board has apparently adopted a policy based on this very distinction. It examines workshop operations on a case by case basis and determines whether the guiding principle of each is "rehabilitative" or typically industrial. In its discretion, it then exempts those which fit the former description and asserts jurisdiction over those which display significant economic purposes. *Compare, Goodwill Industries of Southern California*, 231 N.L.R.B. 536 (1977), and *Goodwill Industries of Philadelphia*, N.L.R.B. (1978); with *Chicago Lighthouse For the Blind*, 225 N.L.R.B. 249 (1976), *Lighthouse for the Blind of Houston*, 244 N.L.R.B. 1144 (1979), *enforcement denied*, 653 F.2d 206 (5th Cir. 1981), and the present case. Thus, under present Board practice, workshops which are truly primarily oriented toward providing social services need not fear any potential adverse impact collective bargaining might have on their programs. On the other hand, workers at workshops which closely resemble traditional, for-profit business enterprises enjoy the same legal protections as their counterparts in private industry.

Congress, of course, is free to alter this system of case by case adjudication at any time, and in any manner it sees fit. That it has not yet done so suggests that it is satisfied with the present state of affairs.

Having determined that sheltered workshop workers are not, as a matter of law, excluded from the Act, we must decide if the Board had an adequate factual basis for characterizing these particular workers as "employees."

*NLRB* v. *Hearst Publications, Inc.*, 322 U.S. 111, 64 S.Ct. 851, 88 L.Ed. 1170 (1944), established that the Board enjoys wide discretion in determining an individual or group's "employee" status. As a corollary to this discretion, Board decisions in this area are subject to limited judicial review. "[I]n reviewing the Board's ultimate conclusions, it is not the court's function to substitute its own inferences of fact for the Board's . . . [T]he Board's determination that specified persons are 'employees' under the Act is to be accepted if it has 'warrant in the record' and a reasonable basis in law." *Id.* at 131, 64 S.Ct. at 860, *see also Bayside Enterprises* v. *NLRB*, 429 U.S. 298, 304, 97 S.Ct. 576, 581, 50 L.Ed.2d 494 (1977); *Physicians National House Staff Assn.* v. *Fanning*, 642 F.2d 492 (D.C.Cir.1980), *cert. denied*, 450 U.S. 917, 101 S.Ct. 1360, 67 L.Ed.2d 342 (1981).

Given this standard of judicial review, we have no difficulty upholding the factual inferences which led to the Board's conclusion that these handicapped workers are "employees" under the Act. The Appellant's arguments on this question are variations on a single theme—that the relationship between Workshop and workers differs in certain respects from the norm associated with private industry and that the blind workers are therefore not "true" employees. Our review of the record, however, indicates that the Board took into account the special characteristics of sheltered workshops but remained unpersuaded that these particular handicapped workers were thereby transformed into something other than statutory "employees." The Charging Parties below documented in detail the extent to which the blind workers operate under terms and conditions typical of "employment." The Board, in its discretion, apparently concluded that the similarities between these workers and their counterparts in private industry outweighed the differences. On the present record, we are unprepared to require the Board to shift its emphasis and reach a contrary result.

We now consider the Association's alternative contention that even if its workers are statutory "employees", the Board should have declined to assert jurisdiction in this matter. In support of its argument that the exercise of jurisdiction here "would not effectuate the purposes of the Act", the Association again advances the theory that "rehabilitation" and collective bargaining are antagonistic concepts. In particular, it directs our attention to the Board's decision in *Goodwill Industries of Southern California, supra*. There, the Board did in fact decline jurisdiction over disabled workers on the premise that collective bargaining would disrupt the rehabilitative relationship between employer and employee. The Association contends that *Southern California* and the present case are indistinguishable on their facts and asks us to reverse the Board for failure to treat similarly situated persons in the same manner.

Once again, the Association has entered an area of Board discretion which is subject to limited judicial review, *Glen Manor Home for the Jewish Aged* v. *NLRB*, 474 F.2d 1145 (6th Cir. 1973); *NLRB* v. *Austin Developmental Center*, 606 F.2d 785 (7th Cir. 1979). The Board's decision at the representation stage of these proceedings reveals that the result in this case was based on a finding of fact that economic motives prevail at the Cincinnati Workshop despite the Association's professed "therapeutic" orientation. "The Employer's direction of the workshop is significantly based on economic considerations . . . Normal economic considerations are a significant factor in the Employer-"client" relationship. The Employer's relations with workshop "clients" and the employment conditions existing at the workshop are guided to a great extent by business considerations." 235 N.L.R.B. at 1449. On the present record, we cannot say that the Board's conclusion was an abuse of discretion.

Furthermore, although the Board's decision below is not as detailed as we might like, we believe it does adequately distinguish the facts of the present case from those of *Southern California, supra*. In the first place, the Board emphasized in *Southern California* that its decision did not stand for the proposition that it would decline jurisdiction in all cases involving sheltered workshops. It referred to that case as the "rare, possibly nonrecurring instance where an employer's concern for the welfare of his employees competes with, and in some sense displaces, the union's ordinary concern for employee well-being." 231 N.L.R.B. at 537.

Second, in *Southern California*, Goodwill Industries reserved fifty percent of its job openings for the short-term training of workers who soon moved on to find employment in the competitive market. Thus, in a very real sense, Goodwill operated a rehabilitative vocational clinic; it had on its staff a full-time job placement specialist to help trainees find permanent employment elsewhere. By contrast, the Association's workshop offers long-term employment with little emphasis on the acquisition of skills other than those required for Workshop production.

At Goodwill, counseling and other social services were an integral part of a worker's relationship with the employer. As the Board observed, "Goodwill's work program, and the production associated with it, was one element of the rehabilitation plan, not an enterprise in itself." 335 N.L.R.B. at 1448. On the other hand, workers at the Cincinnati workshop who wish to obtain social services must seek them in the same manner as other blind members of the community.

In short, we agree with the Board that the circumstances of the *Southern California* case differ materially from the situation at the Cincinnati workshop. We therefore reject the Association's contention that the Board's action constituted an abuse of discretion.

Finally, in a separate issue, the Association challenges the Board's certification of a bargaining unit which includes both sighted and handicapped employees. It cites as the basis for its objection certain differences in the Workshop's disciplinary policy toward blind and sighted workers, the piecework versus hourly rate wage structure of the two groups, and the sighted workers' participation in the Association's pension plan. The Board, however, found these minor differences insufficient to affect the "appropriateness" of a bargaining unit in which all employees work closely together and serve interdependent functions. We agree, and decline to disturb this exercise of the Board's discretion. *See Michigan Hospital Service Corp.* v. *NLRB,* 472 F.2d 293 (6th Cir. 1972); *NLRB* v. *Southern Metal Service,* 606 F.2d 512 (5th Cir. 1979).

In concluding our discussion of this case, we note that we are aware of the Fifth Circuit's recent refusal to grant enforcement of the Board's orders in *NLRB* v. *Lighthouse for the Blind of Houston,* 653 F.2d 206 (5th Cir. 1981). Although our information about the facts underlying that case is incomplete, our decision today appears to create a conflict in the law between the Fifth and Sixth Circuits. In this context, suffice it to say that we do not depart lightly from the principle of uniformity in the federal court system; on the contrary, we have reached our present conclusion only after lengthy deliberation on the respective functions of Congress, the Board, and federal Courts of Appeal.

Enforcement granted.

NOTES

1.   Is the Sixth Circuit opinion correct when it states that its decision creates a conflict in the law with the Fifth Circuit, or can the two decisions be reconciled based upon their facts?

2.   As the financial figures in the two cases illustrate, sheltered workshops can be a very big business. In addition to blind persons, there are also sheltered workshops serving orthopedically handicapped, mentally retarded, and other handicapped persons.

3.   The court in the *Lighthouse for Blind of Houston* case notes the unusual nature of the employer-client relationship in the sheltered workshop, centered around a concern for the welfare of the clients. Aside from the paternalistic implications of this view, is the court necessarily correct when it concludes that "[t]o require collective bargaining in this context is to risk intrusion into the rehabilitative process by bargaining demands which could prejudice the Lighthouse's many faceted efforts at rehabilitation"? Are collective bargaining and rehabilitation inherently inconsistent? Does the court's ruling better serve the interests of the clients or of the Lighthouse corporation?

# 4

# ACCESS TO BUILDINGS AND TRANSPORTATION SYSTEMS

Patrick P. Spicer

## SUMMARY OF DOCTRINAL DEVELOPMENTS

THERE HAVE BEEN FEW IF ANY JUDICIAL DEVELOPMENTS in the area of access to buildings. At the same time access to transportation is an area that has seen relatively few, but nonetheless, quite significant judicial decisions. These decisions, interpreting Sec. 504 and its regulations, have had great impact on accessibility of transportation and could also have great bearing on other aspects of the rights of handicapped persons.

## B.   ACCESS TO TRANSPORTATION: UNDERLYING LEGAL PRINCIPLES

### 2.   Common Law Principles
####       b.   Special Rules Regarding Air Travel
p. 460—INSERT the following after Note 2:

ANGEL v. PAN AMERICAN WORLD AIRWAYS, INC.
*United States District Court for the District of Columbia, 1981*
*519 F.Supp. 1173*

Memorandum Opinion and Order

JOYCE HENS GREEN, District Judge.

This matter is before the Court on the motion of the defendant, Pan American World Airways, Inc. (''Pan American''), for summary judgment, the plaintiffs' opposition, and the numerous subsequent filings both pre- and post-oral argument on the motion. Plaintiffs, Michael Angel and his mother, Carolyn Angel, brought this action for injunctive and declaratory relief, seeking also $15,000 compensatory and $10,000 punitive damages for defendant's refusal to transport Michael Angel from Germany to the United States aboard its carrier in the summer of 1977, solely because he has cerebral palsy and was not accompanied by an attendant. A jury trial has been demanded as to those issues raised by their complaint for compensatory and punitive damages.

Jurisdiction is asserted on several bases: 28 U.S.C. § 1331 (federal question), 28 U.S.C. § 1332 (diversity), 28 U.S.C. § 1337 (commerce), 28 U.S.C. §§ 2201–02 (declaratory judgment) and the doctrine of pendant jurisdiction. Venue is alleged under 28 U.S.C. § 1391(a), (b) and (c).

Solely for purposes of this summary judgment motion, plaintiffs' factual allegations are accepted as true and are as follows:

Both plaintiffs are residents of the State of Maryland. The defendant is a New York corporation, having there its principal place of business; it also transacts business in the District of Columbia. Pan American is an air carrier engaged in interstate and foreign air transportation pursuant to a certificate of public convenience and necessity issued by the Civil Aeronautics Board, is regulated by the laws of the United States relating to such interstate and foreign commerce, including the Federal Aviation Act (49 U.S.C. § 1301 *et seq.*) and applicable regulations, and, in connection with such business, has published and filed tariffs with the Civil Aeronautics Board covering carriage of passengers in international transportation, *inter alia,* between Frankfurt, West Germany and the United States, as required by 49 U.S.C. § 1373(a).

Pan American originally moved for partial summary judgment on the theory that it could not establish as a matter of law that plaintiffs were not entitled to the refund value of the passenger ticket at issue. When plaintiffs' pleadings acknowledged that the ticket was without refund value because it was used on the Lufthansa flight taken by plaintiff Michael Angel subsequent to the incident complained of herein, defendant sought summary judgment as to *all* claims. Plaintiffs oppose the motions for partial and complete summary judgment. The matter has been fully explicated by written and oral argument.

Plaintiff, then a student at the University of Maryland, has cerebral palsy, is confined to an electric wheelchair, is unable to walk, to feed himself, or to perform some personal functions without assistance. He can, however, crawl rapidly and take care of many other personal needs, including getting undressed, taking a bath, brushing his teeth, washing his hair, laying out his clothes, setting the alarm clock and getting into bed. He has no difficulty in descending a flight of stairs. His ordinary means of movement is crawling, at which he is quite adept and by which he maneuvers himself. Plaintiff is able to get into and out of an automobile unassisted, has taken trips on the District of Columbia subway system and has flown across the Atlantic Ocean without an attendant and without difficulty. He has repeatedly flown by himself between Washington, D.C. and Florida. He can, and has, seated himself inside an airplane. He can go without food for the duration of a flight and is able, when necessary, (and has so done on four occasions) to get out of his seat, crawl to the lavatory, use the facilities and return to his seat without assistance. In June of 1977, he made arrangements to travel on a charter flight to Europe, a trip he had made twice before without any inconvenience or discomfort. Prior to his departure, Carolyn Angel called Pan American's local reservation agent to ascertain whether her son would be permitted to return on Pan American in the event he curtailed his trip for any reason. The agent assured her, after being fully advised of his physical condition, that he would be able to return via Pan American. Mr. Angel did, in fact, subsequently decide to return earlier and, accompanied to the Frankfurt airport by a friend, attempted to purchase a return ticket from Pan American in late June, 1977. There, a Pan American ticket agent advised him that he could not fly via Pan American unless accompanied by an attendant. Learning of these events, Ms. Angel again telephoned a local Pan American ticket agent to resolve the problem. She was advised to cable her son a prepaid ticket and have him appear at the airport on the date of the flight to assure transport. Plaintiffs followed these instructions but a Pan American agent in Frankfurt on July 11, 1977 again refused Michael Angel permission to board, unless accompanied by an attendant, even though he appeared with both a prepaid ticket and a letter stating that Mr. Angel was physically capable of flying without an attendant. He was told at that time by both the ticket agent and supervisor that he was being denied transportation since he could not walk and was travelling without an attendant.

After more delay, Pan American arranged with Lufthansa Airlines to transport plaintiff to Boston, attended by an extra flight attendant. He was then transferred to a domestic carrier for the flight to Washington, D.C. Contrary to the assurances given Michael Angel, the Pan American agent in Germany failed to notify Ms. Angel to advise her of the flight change. Ms. Angel learned of this change from another source and was able to make arrangements to meet the appropriate flight.

As a result of the above events, plaintiffs assert a cause for action for breach of contract; violations of tariffs, Civil Aeronautics Board (CAB) and Federal Aviation Administration (FAA) regulations; misrepresentation; gross negligence; and breach of a common carrier's duty to the public, all of which have allegedly caused plaintiffs mental distress, physical hardship, and financial loss. Pan American's motion to stay discovery was granted until resolution of the instant motion.

Pan American argues that it acted in conformity with all applicable regulations, tariffs, and procedures pertaining to international transportation by air carriers of handicapped or incapacitated persons and essentially that this Court does not have jurisdiction to entertain this action under the doctrines of primary jurisdiction of the CAB and the FAA and failure to exhaust administrative remedies.

The doctrine of primary jurisdiction, the defendant argues, is particularly applicable to the area of aviation which is subject to extensive federal regulation by the CAB and FAA under the Federal Aviation Act of 1958 (the "Aviation Act"), 49 U.S.C. § 1301 *et seq.* This statute, *inter alia,* seeks to promote uniformity of the air transportation industry and facilitate resolution of technical questions as to airline safety, aircraft design, technology, and federal transportation policy. Pan American invokes the primary jurisdiction doctrine, asking that the Court stay its pen to permit the expert administrative agencies to consider the important questions presented herein prior to a judicial decree.

Originating in *Texas and P. R. Co.* v. *Abeline Cotton Oil Co.,* 204 U.S. 426, 27 S.Ct. 350, 51 L.Ed. 553 (1907), "primary jurisdiction" provides that courts will not determine a controversy involving a question which is within the jurisdiction of an administrative agency prior to that tribunal's decision where the issue involves the exercise of administrative expertise and where uniformity of ruling is especially important to comply with the purposes of the regulatory scheme. *See Kappelmann* v. *Delta*

*Air Lines, Inc.,* 539 F.2d 165, 169 (D.C.Cir. 1976), *cert. denied,* 429 U.S. 1061, 97 S.Ct. 784, 50 L.Ed.2d 776 (1977). The Supreme Court has noted that "[n]o fixed formula exists for applying primary jurisdiction. In every case the question is whether the reasons for the existence of the doctrine are present and whether the purposes it serves will be aided by its application in the particular litigation." *United States* v. *Western Pacific Ry.,* 352 U.S. 59, 64, 77 S.Ct. 161, 165, 1 L.Ed.2d 126 (1956). *See also Board of Education* v. *Harris,* 622 F.2d 599 (2d Cir. 1979), *cert. denied,* 449 U.S. 1124, 101 S.Ct. 940, 67 L.Ed.2d 110 (1981).

This case does not present a matter that the Court should withhold decision upon pending some action by the CAB or the FAA. Initially, at dispute is the meaning of the tariff existing in June, 1977. In short, plaintiffs argue that the tariff, properly interpreted, would not have prohibited Michael Angel from boarding the Pan American flight leaving Germany. Mr. Justice Brandeis, writing for the Supreme Court in *Great Northern Ry.* v. *Merchants Elevator Co.,* 259 U.S. 285, 42 S.Ct. 477, 66 L.Ed. 943 (1922), expressly held that "the attainment of uniformity does not require that in every case where the construction of a tariff is in dispute, there shall be a preliminary resort to the" administrative agency. *Id.* at 291, 42 S.Ct. at 479. "It is not true," the Justice noted, "that uniformity in construction of a tariff can be attained only through a preliminary report to the [Interstate Commerce] Commission to settle the construction in dispute." *Id.* at 290, 42 S.Ct. at 479. This reasoning applies with equal force in this litigation, for the plaintiffs' chief contention is that the Pan American agent in Germany erred in his interpretation of the tariff then existing when he refused to let Michael Angel board. The parties have briefed and argued the meaning of the tariff before the Court and that question of law is now at issue, without need for factual determinations within the CAB's or the FAA's special expertise.

Additionally, the parties' submissions reflect that uniformity is not critical in constructing guidelines for carriage of the handicapped. Although the tariff relating to transportation of the physically handicapped in effect in 1979 is not at issue here, it demonstrates that airlines have adopted different procedures concerning handicapped passengers, including varying maximum numbers of such persons who might be carried on different types of aircraft. *See* Defendant's Exhibit M. Although uniformity is important, especially in a technically complex area as aviation, the airlines' own conduct belies the notion that a single rule must be promulgated. Accordingly, one of the bases for invoking primary jurisdiction is simply not present in this case.

The defendant next asserts that Michael Angel has not exhausted his administrative remedies, and therefore that this Court should not act pending the decision by the CAB on his complaint. The exhaustion requirement is well-settled as an instrument to avoid premature adjudication of disputes. *See American Dairy of Evansville, Inc.* v. *Bergland,* 627 F.2d 1252 (D.C.Cir. 1980); *National Conservative Political Action Committee* v. *Federal Election Commission,* 626 F.2d 953 (D.C.Cir. 1980).

Plaintiff's complaint has been pending since 1978 at the CAB; it would be unreasonable to dismiss this action now so that he could pursue his remedies at the administrative level. As obvious as is the exhaustion requirement, so is its exception that one need not resort to the administrative agency where to do so would be a futile act. *See Porter County Chapter of Izaak Walton League of America* v. *Costle,* 571

F.2d 359 (7th Cir.) *cert. denied* 439 U.S. 834, 99 S.Ct. 115, 58 L.Ed.2d 130 (1978); *Davis* v. *Bolger,* 496 F.Supp. 559 (D.D.C.1980).

Defendant contends that this action is barred by 49 U.S.C. § 1487, which provides that an action alleging a violation of 49 U.S.C. § 1372 may only be brought by the CAB. § 1372, "Permits to foreign air carriers," is not in issue in this litigation. Rather, plaintiffs allege discrimination in violation of § 1374 which prohibits all forms of discrimination by commercial air carriers. There is a private right of action under § 1374, *see Nader* v. *Allegheny Airlines, Inc.,* 512 F.2d 527 (D.C.Cir. 1975), *rev'd on other grounds* 426 U.S. 290, 96 S.Ct. 1978, 48 L.Ed.2d 643 (1976), and plaintiffs clearly assert that Pan American discriminated against Michael Angel in its interpretation of its own tariffs and procedures and, alternatively, that those tariffs and procedures themselves are discriminatory.

It having been determined that principles of primary jurisdiction and exhaustion of remedies do not bar the plaintiffs from proceeding in this Court, the query remains whether there are material factual questions in dispute and, if not, whether the defendant is entitled to summary judgment as a matter of law. The plaintiffs' case states three independent causes of action: a violation of section 504 of the Vocational Rehabilitation Act, predicated on Pan American's alleged discrimination against a handicapped individual; misrepresentation and gross negligence, based on the airline's statements to plaintiffs (directly to Carolyn Angel and through her, to Michael Angel) that it would transport Michael Angel without an attendant and that it would contact Carolyn Angel concerning Michael's arrival from Germany; and a claim seeking a declaration that under Pan American's tariffs, the airline must permit Michael Angel to board without his needing an attendant.

Section 504 of the Vocational Rehabilitation Act stated in the summer of 1977:

> No otherwise qualified handicapped individual in the United States . . . shall, solely by reason of his handicap, be excluded from the participation in, be denied the benefits of, or be subject to discrimination under any program or activity receiving federal financial assistance.

29 U.S.C. § 794 (1976). The defendant maintains that Pan American has not received direct federal financial assistance since November 1, 1956, when it received a mail related subsidy from the government. Plaintiffs suggest that the airline is the beneficiary of numerous indirect subsidies, sufficient to constitute federal financial assistance and trigger the Act's prohibition against exclusion of handicapped individuals. They point to air traffic controllers provided by the FAA, to airports constructed with federal funds, and to other technical assistance.

In *Gottfried* v. *Federal Communications Commission,* 655 F.2d 297 (D.C.Cir. 1981), the Court of Appeals held that commercial broadcast stations were not considered recipients of federal financial assistance merely by virtue of the licenses granted to them by the federal government. The significance of the *Gottfried* decision to this case is found in its cogent analysis of Section 504. Judge Wright, writing for the Court, discussed Title VI of the Civil Rights Act of 1964, upon which Section 504 was modeled expressly. Referring to the legislative history underlying Title VI, the Court cited a Department of Justice study completed at the request of Congress listing programs that would qualify as recipients of federal financial assistance. *See* 110 Cong.Rec. 13380–13382 (daily ed. June 10, 1964). The only listing for the CAB relates to direct payments to the airlines, which Pan American has not received since 1956. Otherwise, the airlines are not mentioned.

Although the Justice Department did consider that airports would be regarded as recipients of federal financial assistance, this does not vitiate the conclusion that airlines are not within the ambit of Section 504. Subsidies to airports, to be sure, subject those locales to the broad proscription of Section 504, but this does not translate into binding law upon the users of the airports, whether they be commercial airlines or individual passengers. To hold that commercial airlines fall within Section 504 merely because of assistance provided to airports would expand improperly the accepted proposition that Section 504 is limited to direct recipients of federal funds. *See Simpson* v. *Reynolds Metal Co., Inc.,* 629 F.2d 1226 (7th Cir. 1980); *Rogers* v. *Frito-Lay, Inc.,* 433 F.Supp. 200 (N.D.Tex.1977), *aff'd* 611 F.2d 1074(5th Cir.), *cert. denied,* 449 U.S. 889, 101 S.Ct. 246, 66 L.Ed.2d 115 (1980).

The question now arises as to whether plaintiffs should be permitted to proceed claiming that Pan American committed tortious acts with improper application of its tariff. Let us examine those procedures in effect on July 16, 1977, when Michael Angel was denied boarding at Frankfurt, Germany. The inquiry is framed by a reading of a rule, effective May 16, 1977, issued by the FAA, providing that

> [n]o certificate holder may refuse transportation to a passenger on the basis that, because the passenger may need the assistance of another passenger to move expeditiously to an exit in the event of an emergency, his transportation would or might be inimical to safety of flight unless—
> (1) The certificate holder has established procedures (including reasonable notice requirements) for the carriage of passengers who may need the assistance of another person to move expeditiously to an exit in the event of an emergency; and
> (2) At least one of the following conditions exist:
> (i) The passenger fails to comply with the notice requirements in the certificate holder's procedures
> (ii) The passenger cannot be carried in accordance with the certificate holder's procedures.

*See* 49 C.F.R. § 121.586, 42 Fed.Reg. 18392 (April 7, 1977). The CAB has further noted:

> As we read Section 1111 of Federal Aviation Act [49 U.S.C. § 1511] and the FAA's rulemaking thereunder, no disabled or handicapped person can be denied transportation on the grounds of disability other than when done in accordance with rules that have been filed with and accepted by the FAA.

42 Fed.Reg. at 43830 (Aug. 31, 1977). The Court must therefore look to the procedures in effect in July 1977 governing Pan American's carriage of physically handicapped persons; the defendant must demonstrate either that the plaintiff failed to comply with any notice requirements or that the airline could not transport plaintiff without violating its own procedures.

The following Pan American tariff provision PR-3, CAB No. 55, Rule No. 15, was in effect in June and July 1977 when the alleged incidents occurred:

Rule No. 15:  *LIMITATIONS OF CARRIAGE*

I.  *REFUSAL, CANCELLATION OR REMOVAL*

    A.  Carrier will refuse to carry, cancel the reserved space of, or remove enroute any passenger when:

        1.  Such action is necessary for reasons of safety;

        2.  such action is necessary to prevent violation of any applicable laws, regulations, or orders of any state or country to be flown from, into or over;

        3.  the conduct, age or mental or physical condition of the passenger is such as to

            a.  require special assistance of carrier; or

            b.  cause discomfort to make himself objectionable to other passengers; or

            c.  involve any hazard or risk to himself or to other persons or to property. . . .

II.  *RECOURSE OF PASSENGERS:* Subject to the provisions of Rule 37—Denied Boarding Compensation, the sole recourse of any person so refused carriage or removed enroute for any reason specified in the foregoing paragraph shall be recovery of the refund value of the unused portion of his ticket as hereinafter provided in Rule 18.

Def. Motion, Ex. E.

It should also be noted that procedures were filed with the FAA concerning the carriage of handicapped persons by Pan American. Relevant parts of these procedures, found at Section 200, Bulletin 209 (July 1, 1977), shed light on a proper interpretation of Rule No. 15.

> Each person unable to move to an exit under his own power or to attend to his personal requirements must be accompanied by an attendant capable of carrying the incapacitated person. (Procedures at 1).
>
>                 * * *
>
> Incapacitated passengers would include, but not be limited to, passengers who are both blind and deaf, stretcher cases and non-ambulatory wheelchair cases. *(Id.)*

The bulletin limits, according to the type of aircraft in use, the number of persons who will be carried who need assistance to make their way to an exit in an emergency, and requires that such passengers give Pan American 24 hours notice in advance of their intended departure time. *Id.*

Although presenting a complex maze of regulations, this tariff and procedure, as applied to Michael Angel, finds a simple analysis. Plaintiff demonstrates, and defendant accepts for purposes of this motion, that he can move under his own power by crawling and therefore does not need assistance to evacuate an aircraft. Accordingly, under Pan American's own reservations procedure, he need not be accompanied by an attendant as he is both "[a]ble to move to an exit under his own power [and he can] attend to his personal requirements." Implicitly, the reservations procedure defines incapacitated individuals as those who cannot move under their own power because it joins "incapacitated person" in the same phrase as "each person unable to move to an exit under his own power." Moreover, it refers to "non-ambulatory wheelchair cases," who present different problems than "ambulatory wheelchair cases." This interpretation finds support from an Advisory Circular issued by the FAA on March

25, 1977, three months prior to plaintiff's trip to Europe. This statement categorizes handicapped passengers as follows:

a. Ambulatory. A passenger who is able to board the aircraft unassisted and who is able to move about the aircraft unassisted. This includes the blind, deaf, mentally retarded, etc.

b. Nonambulatory. A passenger who is not able to board and deplane from an aircraft unassisted or who is not able to move about the aircraft unassisted.

Advisory Circular No. 120–32, App. B to Plaintiff's Supplemental Memorandum Concerning Pan American's Tariffs and Procedures. Because the facts demonstrate that the plaintiff is capable of entering and exiting an aircraft as well as attending to his personal needs aboard, all under his own power, under the terms of Pan American's reservations' procedure, the plaintiff should have been permitted to board the aircraft in Frankfurt despite the fact that he was travelling alone. Then was he properly denied passage by virtue of the tariff in existence at that time?

Since that tariff provided that a passenger can be excluded if necessary to protect the safety of himself or others, defendant seeks at this stage of the litigation to invoke this "if necessary" discretionary mechanism to justify the refusal of passage to plaintiff. This rationale, however, is not borne out by the facts presented by the plaintiff and assumed by the defendant for purposes of this motion. The plaintiff was told in Germany by Pan American's agent-employees (including a supervisor) that he was denied boarding because he was travelling alone and because he could not walk. Nothing in the record indicates that the agents in Frankfurt even attempted to invoke the discretionary aspect of tariff No. 15 or refer to any passenger's safety aboard the aircraft. The matter as presently viewed in this motion's posture demonstrates no particular safety danger posed by plaintiff; in fact, he was examined by a German doctor at the airport, who issued a certificate in German that he was perfectly capable of flying alone. Angel offered to demonstrate his crawling ability to the agent, who refused to observe him. In an analogous case, the Second Circuit has recently held that whether an airline properly refuses to permit an individual to board

rests upon the facts and circumstances of the case as known to the airline at the time it formed its opinion and made its decision and whether or not the opinion and decision were rational and reasonable and not capricious or arbitrary in the light of those facts and circumstances.

*Williams* v. *Trans World Airlines*, 509 F.2d 942, 948 (2d Cir. 1975). Based upon the facts known to the Frankfurt agents at the time Michael Angel was denied boarding, assumed true by the defendant, the agent acted irrationally and unreasonably, misinterpreting the Pan American tariff and procedures.

The conclusion that plaintiff did not present a safety risk is supported by the study completed by the FAA Civil Aeromedical Institute ("CAMI"), which in recognition that individuals who could not walk did not, automatically, pose a safety risk, concluded "that many non-ambulatory handicapped persons reached the exit with remarkable speed using seat backs for support or in the sitting position, pulling themselves backwards with their arms." 42 Fed. Reg. 18394 (1977).

Were the facts to appear as presented by the plaintiff and as assumed by the defendant, the Court would have no hesitancy in awarding declaratory relief to Michael Angel concerning the application to him of the tariff and reservations procedure in effect in 1977. The defendant, however, erred in characterizing its motion as one for summary judgment, because it neither contended that no material facts were in dispute nor attached the appropriate affidavits and other material pursuant to Fed.R.Civ.P. 56. Instead, Pan American assumed that the plaintiffs' statement of the facts were true, contending that as a matter of law, no claim was presented. Pan American's motion is therefore one for failure to state a claim under Fed.R.Civ.P. 12(b)(6), *see* 2A *Moore's Federal Practice* ¶ 12.08, rather than one for summary judgment. Because no party has developed a factual record nor satisfied the minimal requirements for a summary judgment ruling, the Court must permit discovery and the trial to go forward for ascertainment of the precise factual events leading up to the denial of boarding.

Remaining therefore is the question whether plaintiffs may proceed to trial on their tort claims for misrepresentation and for gross negligence. The defendant seeks judgment as a matter of law on two separate bases: that the claim for misrepresentation ignores the constructive notice provided by the tariffs, and that permitting the plaintiffs to proceed in an action for damages would frustrate the general regulatory scheme over the nation's airlines.

In *Goodman* v. *National Airlines, Inc.*, 201 A.2d 877 (D.C.1964), the District of Columbia Court of Appeals ruled that there can be no misrepresentation regarding a provision of filed tariffs since the parties are bound by the terms and have constructive notice thereof. Defendant argues that because Rule No. 15 was on file and available for public inspection, the plaintiffs had notice of Pan American's procedures concerning transportation of the handicapped. Plaintiffs reject the applicability of *Goodman* in light of *Nader* v. *Allegheny Airlines, Inc.*, 426 U.S. 290, 96 S.Ct. 1978, 48 L.Ed.2d 643 (1976), where the Supreme Court of the United States permitted the plaintiff, after being denied boarding despite a confirmed seat, to litigate a claim for common law misrepresentation notwithstanding an administrative procedure to adjudicate deceptive practices allegedly committed by the airline. Nonetheless, in *Nader* that plaintiff alleged the total absence of disclosure concerning the likelihood that his confirmed ticket might not be honored; no tariff provision was at issue. Despite the seeming unfairness of rigorously binding passengers to the terms of tariffs on file with the CAB, the law in the District of Columbia is clear after *Goodman* that Ms. Angel was on constructive notice as to the tariffs then filed. Moreover, in light of the Court's ruling today, based on the existing record of facts assumed for purpose of the defendant's motion, that the Frankfurt agent improperly denied boarding to Angel, it would be anomalous to hold Pan American liable for the statement by its Washington, D.C. agents who properly interpreted the tariff.

May the plaintiffs, however, proceed on a negligence basis against Pan American for its conduct during the entire incident? In *Nader,* the Supreme Court held that common law remedies which do not frustrate statutory enforcement schemes may proceed to fruition. In that dispute, the defendant claimed that the CAB should have had an opportunity to determine whether, under Section 411 of the Federal Aviation Act, it engaged in a deceptive or unfair practice. Plaintiff contended in *Nader* that the airline's failure to disclose that he might be denied boarding because of a surplus of reservations constituted fraudulent misrepresentation. While the Court in *Nader* rejected the analogy to rate disputes, where conflicting determinations from the CAB and a court might work hardship on an airline, it found no irreconcilable conflict between the common law claim of fraudulent misrepresentation and the statutory mechanism.

This case presents a similar circumstance in that the claim for negligence does not demonstrate jeopardy to any specific part of federal aviation regulations. Plaintiffs will be granted the right to seek to persuade a jury that Pan American acted negligently, in *inter alia,* asserting two conflicting interpretations of the same tariff/procedures and in advising Carolyn Angel, for transmission to Michael Angel, that her son could travel unescorted and that she would be told when her son would arrive when allegedly no notice was given.

On June 6, 1979, the CAB published in the Federal Register a Notice of Proposed Rulemaking: Nondiscrimination on the Basis of Handicap. Regulations were set out there, open to comment, designed at ending discrimination against the handicapped in air transportation. *See* 44 Fed.Reg. 32401 (1979). When the instant motion was argued before the Court, it appeared then and for a considerable time thereafter, prompting stay of this decision, that final CAB rules were imminent. That expectation has not been realized. It should also be noted that on July 13, 1981, the CAB published another Notice of Proposed Rulemaking, seeking elimination of passenger rules tariffs in interstate and overseas air transportation. *See* 46 Fed.Reg. 35926 (July 13, 1981). In this notice, the Board expressly refers to its proposed rules concerning the handicapped, and indicates that the removal of tariff provisions will have no effect on the final rules to be implemented shortly.

Federal law appropriately recognizes the right of the physically handicapped to be free from discrimination. Our society has advanced the rights of the handicapped demonstrably; yet, as those individuals who seek vindication of their rights are all too aware, our nation has not completed the process of ensuring equality. It is hoped that that day is to come soon.

It is this 30th day of July, 1981,

ORDERED that the defendant's motion for summary judgment be and it hereby is denied, and it is

FURTHER ORDERED that discovery terminates in sixty days, with trial to commence October 13, 1981 at 10:00 a. m.

NOTES

1.  Does the *Angel* decision expand the rights of handicapped persons to travel on commercial airlines beyond the limits established by the *Heumann* and *Austin* decisions?

2.  Compare the *Angel* court's approach with respect to the primary jurisdiction issue with the approach taken by *Heumann* court.

## D.  FEDERAL STATUTORY REQUIREMENTS

### 1.  29 U.S.C. § 794

#### b.  Later Judicial Perspectives

p. 494—INSERT the following after the *Leary* case:

## DOPICO v. GOLDSCHMIDT

*United States Court of Appeals for the Second Circuit, 1982*

*687 F. 2d 644*

NEWMAN, Circuit Judge:

This appeal concerns the extent of the efforts that federal law requires of local and federal authorities in pursuing the national policy of making urban mass transportation available to the handicapped. Plaintiffs, individually and representing all wheelchair-bound handicapped persons in New York City, initiated two consolidated class actions in the District Court for the Southern District of New York against local and federal defendants, seeking declaratory and injunctive relief to force defendants to comply with a variety of federal statutes and regulations that implement that policy through a system of federal funding and administrative oversight. The principal local defendants are the New York City Transit Authority, the Metropolitan Transportation Authority, and the New York City Department of Transportation. The federal defendants are officials of the United States Department of Transportation (DOT) and its Urban Mass Transportation Administration (UMTA).

In essence, plaintiffs made two claims. First, they alleged that the local defendants, who are recipients of federal mass transit assistance funds granted by federal agencies, have failed during the past decade to use these funds to make the "special efforts" required by federal law toward making mass transportation services in New York City available to the elderly and the handicapped. Second, they alleged that the federal defendants, who grant such assistance on appropriate application and who must certify local program compliance with federal law, have continued to approve and fund the local defendants' programs even though the federal defendants knew or should have known of the lack of required "special efforts." On motion of defendants, the District Court (Edward Weinfeld, Judge) dismissed the complaint against the local defendants for failure to state a claim upon which relief could be granted, ruling that the statutes upon which the plaintiffs relied either did not create a private right of action or did not permit the kind of relief sought. The Court also granted summary judgment in favor of the federal defendants, ruling that their decisions and actions passed muster under the "arbitrary and capricious" standard of the Administrative Procedure Act, 5 U.S.C. § 706(2)(A) (1976). 518 F.Supp. 1161 (S.D.N.Y.1981). Plaintiffs appealed.

As to the dismissal of the complaint against the local defendants, we affirm several aspects of Judge Weinfeld's ruling, but disagree with his conclusion that section 504 of the Rehabilitation Act of 1973, 29 U.S.C. § 794 (1976), does not permit any of the relief that plaintiffs seek. As to the grant of summary judgment against the federal defendants, we conclude that such a judgment is premature because there is a factual question as to the completeness of the administrative record before the Court. We therefore reverse in part and remand for further proceedings.

*The Regulatory Scheme*

Federal aid to urban mass transit programs is provided primarily under sections 3 and 5 of the Urban Mass Transportation Act ("UMT Act"), 49 U.S.C. §§ 1602, 1604 (1976), and under the Federal-Aid Highway Act ("FAH Act"), 23 U.S.C. §§ 120(a), 142(a),(c) (1976). The UMT Act was enacted in 1964; in 1970 Congress added to it section 16, in response to complaints that the various facilities being subsidized were not accessible to people using wheelchairs. Section 16 declared as "national policy" that the elderly and handicapped have the "same right" as other persons to use mass transit and that "special efforts shall be made in the planning and design of mass transportation facilities and services" to ensure that usable mass transportation is available to them. 49 U.S.C. § 1612(a). Three years later, Congress enacted the Rehabilitation Act of 1973, which includes the authorization of programs to "study and develop solutions to existing . . . transportation barriers impeding handicapped individuals." Rehabilitation Act of 1973, § 2(11), 29 U.S.C. § 701(11) (1976). Specifically involved in this litigation is section 504 of the Rehabilitation Act, 29 U.S.C. § 794, which prohibits recipients of federal funding from excluding from participation in any program, denying the benefits of any program to, or discriminating against otherwise qualified handicapped individuals. The FAH Act also was passed in 1973; section 165(b), as amended in 1975, declares that projects funded under the FAH Act must be planned, designed, constructed, and operated to allow effective use by the handicapped. 23 U.S.C. § 142 note. These enactments form the principal statutory bases for plaintiffs complaint.

Beginning in 1976, the federal defendants began promulgating regulations to implement the directives of these three statutes with regard to use of mass transit programs by the handicapped. Two basic sets of regulations were issued, one in 1976 and the other in 1979. Plaintiffs allege violations of both. The first set was the "special efforts" regulations, appearing in 49 C.F.R. Parts 609 and 613 (1980), and incorporating provisions now appearing at 23 C.F.R. Part 450 (1981). The latter provisions require that a local planning authority annually prepare and submit to the UMTA for its approval a Transportation Improvement Program (TIP). All funded projects must be part of a TIP, the purposes of which include specifying the improvements to be pursued during the program period, setting priorities, and estimating expenses. Each TIP must contain an "annual element" listing the projects to be implemented that year. The "special efforts" regulations added three new criteria to those governing the UMTA's approval of the TIP: (1) the planning process by which the TIP was developed had to show satisfactory "special efforts" in planning services and facilities that could be effectively used by the elderly and the handicapped, 23 C.F.R. § 450.-120(a)(5); 49 C.F.R. § 613.204(a), (2) the annual element of every TIP submitted after September 30, 1976, had to contain projects designed to benefit the handicapped, id. § 613.204(b), and (3) after September 30, 1977, funding recipients had to demonstrate reasonable progress in implementing previously programmed projects, id. § 613.204(c). The regulations did not specify a particular program design that would satisfy the "special efforts" requirement.

The second set of regulations was issued in 1979 and appeared in 49 C.F.R. Part 27 (1980). These superseded the 1976 regulations, requiring far more than mere "special efforts." Instead of the relatively mild 1976 requirement that some progress be made, the 1979 regulations substituted a far more exacting scheme by establishing "accessibility" as a goal and by specifying the criteria for determining its achievement in various types of public transportation and setting a timetable for accomplishing it. The validity of this second set of regulations was placed in question, however, by the District of Columbia Circuit's decision in *American Public Transit Association* v.

*Lewis* (*"APTA"*), 655 F.2d 1272 (D.C.Cir. 1981). That decision held that the new regulations were invalid to the extent that they were based on section 504, since they required extensive and costly modifications beyond that section's authority; the Court "remanded" the regulations to DOT to determine whether, in the absence of section 504, they could properly be based solely on the other statutes to which the regulations referred—section 16 of the UMT Act and section 165(b) of the FAH Act. As a result of the *APTA* case, DOT issued new regulations on July 21, 1981, superseding the 1979 set. *See* 46 Fed.Reg. 37,488 (1981). These are now codified at 49 C.F.R. § 27.77 (1981). They return essentially to the 1976 model, requiring "special efforts" toward providing transportation usable by the handicapped, rather than achieving a predefined goal of "accessibility" by a certain date.

### Plaintiffs' Claims

Plaintiffs allege violations of the three statutes, the 1976 and 1979 regulations, and the Fifth and Fourteenth Amendments. The District Court's opinion provides a thorough account of the factual allegations, which we will summarize here. Plaintiffs' charges pertain to the time period since 1976, when the first set of regulations appeared. Basically, plaintiffs assert the complete inadequacy of the "special efforts" that the local defendants made during that time. Their allegations focus on two main projects proposed in the TIPs for the years in question and intended to satisfy the "special efforts" requirement. The rest was a proposal for specially equipped minibuses; it was accepted by DOT as the "special efforts" for fiscal year 1977–78, but was never implemented. The minibus proposal was replaced in 1980 by a proposal for full-size buses with wheelchair lifts; this amended proposal also has not been implemented. The second project called for a paratransit service system; it was accepted by DOT as the "special efforts" for, in turn, fiscal years 1978–79, 1979–80, and 1980–81, but also has not yet appeared. Plaintiffs claim that the projects were inadequately planned and, in any event, were never implemented, that the money allocated to them each year was neither spent for the designated projects nor set aside for future use, and that the federal defendants continued to provide funding despite these short-comings. They requested various forms of declaratory and injunctive relief, including injunctions requiring the local defendants to comply with the "accessibility" mandate of the 1979 regulations and restraining the federal defendants from granting further funding in the meantime; they also requested the appointment of a special master to determine the amount of money not spent or misspent, to monitor implementation of required plans, and to recommend any necessary additional orders.

### The District Court's Decision

In a comprehensive opinion, the District Court dismissed all claims against the local transit defendants and entered summary judgment in favor of the federal defendants. As to the claim against the local defendants based on section 16 of the UMT Act, the Court ruled, after a careful review of the considerations enumerated in *Cort* v. *Ash*, 422 U.S. 66, 78, 95 S.Ct. 2080, 2087, 45 L.Ed.2d 26 (1975), that it would be inconsistent with the underlying purpose of the Act as a whole to find a private right of action implied under section 16. As to the claim under section 165(b) of the FAH Act, plaintiffs conceded that the section provided no right of action. The Court also concluded that 42 U.S.C. § 1983 did not authorize suit for violation of these provisions because neither section 16 nor section 165(b), each of them only one part of a complex funding statute, created substantive "rights" enforceable through section 1983. Nor, the Court held, had plaintiffs stated a valid equal protection claim under section 1983: measured by the appropriate test–rational relation–defendants' actions were constitutionally unobjectionable.

We affirm these aspects of the District Court's decision, substantially for the reasons elaborated in Judge Weinfeld's opinion. We therefore turn to the two areas where we disagree with the District Court's ruling: the dismissal of the claim against the local defendants under section 504 of the Rehabilitation Act, and the grant of summary judgment in favor of the federal defendants.

I. *The Section 504 Claim Against the Local Defendants*

Section 504 provides that "[n]o otherwise qualified handicapped individual . . . shall, solely by reason of his handicap, be excluded from the participation in, be denied the benefits of, or be subjected to discrimination under any program or activity receiving Federal financial assistance." 29 U.S.C. § 794 (1976). While conceding that current interpretations of section 504 hold that it supports a private right of action, *see e.g., Baker* v. *Bell,* 630 F.2d 1046, 1055 (5th Cir. 1980), *Leary* v. *Crapsey,* 566 F.2d 863, 865 (2nd Cir. 1977) (*per curiam*); *United Handicapped Federation* v. *Andre,* 558 F.2d 413, 418 (8th Cir. 1977); *Lloyd* v. *Regional Transportation Authority,* 548 F.2d 1277, 1284, 87 (7th Cir. 1977), defendants argued, and the District Court held, that section 504 does not permit the relief plaintiffs seek here.

Judge Weinfeld based his decision primarily on a consideration of two cases. In the first, *Southeastern Community College* v. *Davis,* 442 U.S. 397, 99 S.Ct. 2361, 60 L.Ed.3d 980 (1979), the Supreme Court held that section 504 does not impose an "affirmative action obligation" on a state educational institution, *id.* at 411, 99 S.Ct. at 2399 requiring it to make "substantial modifications in [its] programs," *id.* at 405, 99 S.Ct. at 2366, or to incur "undue financial and administrative burdens," *id.* at 412, 99 S.Ct. at 2370, in an effort to accommodate handicapped persons whose disabilities render them not "otherwise qualified" for such programs. The Court ruled against the plaintiff, who suffered from a severe hearing disability that prevented her from participating in the normal training for nurses, because enrolling her would have required a "fundamental alteration in the nature" of the defendant college's registered nursing program. *Id.* at 410, 99 S.Ct. at 2369. In the second case, *APTA, supra,* the District of Columbia Circuit applied *Davis* in the mass transportation context and held that the "extensive modifications of existing systems" required by the 1979 "accessibility" regulations, and the "extremely heavy financial burdens on local transit authorities" that implementing them would impose, were equivalent to the fundamental program alterations held in *Davis* to be beyond the scope of section 504. 655 F.2d at 1278. The Court therefore held that the 1979 regulations were an invalid implementation of that section.

In the present case, the District Court concluded that dismissal was warranted because the plaintiffs were seeking "massive relief involving extra-ordinary expenditures," 518 F.Supp. at 1175, which would amount to the " 'kind of burdensome modifications that the *Davis* Court held to be beyond the scope of section 504,' " *id.* at 1176 (quoting *APTA, supra,* 655 F.2d at 1278). The extreme result of dismissing the claim would be proper only if plaintiffs would not be entitled to any relief, even if they were to prevail on the merits. We do not believe that conclusion can be reached at this preliminary stage of the lawsuit. The complaint does not necessarily seek, nor would a remedy necessarily entail, either "massive relief" of the sort *APTA* feared would be required to achieve accessibility under the 1979 regulations, or "affirmative action" of the sort that *Davis* held was not required by section 504.

A.  *"Massive Relief"*

Judge Weinfeld summarized the central meaning of *Davis* for mass transportation programs to be that section 504 "does not require massive expenditures." 518 F.Supp. at 1176. He then concluded that granting relief for plaintiffs would necessarily entail such a remedy:

> Plaintiffs, if they were to prevail, would compel the local defendants to expend huge resources over the next several decades which would fundamentally alter many transportation services. There is no escaping the fact that plaintiffs in this law suit seek a major overhauling of the transit system in their purpose to compel implementation of programs for the handicapped.

*Ibid.* Even if that view characterizes what plaintiffs seek, it does not necessarily describe less ambitious relief to which they may be entitled.

In the first place, if plaintiffs can prove a violation of section 504, the District Court has inherent power to fashion relief appropriate to the situation. That power is not limited by the fact that plaintiffs may have asked for too much in seeking relief based on the 1979 regulations, *see* Fed.R.Civ.P. 54(c), particularly since other regulations offer guidance in developing a less ambitious solution. Moreover, unlike the Supreme Court in *Davis,* we are not faced with an all-or-nothing choice of remedies. In *Davis* nothing short of fundamental modifications in a professional training curriculum would accomplish the only relief that the plaintiff sought—admission to the nursing program. Here, by contrast, a whole range of prospective relief is imaginable to meet at least some of plaintiffs' concerns, should they be able to prove their allegations. If ordering relief based on the 1979 regulations would exceed the mandate of section 504, then more modest relief must be fashioned within the limits of *Davis.*

It is significant that plaintiffs are not seeking a remedy that would require federal, state, or local authorities to appropriate funds. The large federal subsidies to mass transit that the local defendants already enjoy, which cover from 50% to 85% of total project costs, *see* 23 U.S.C. § 120(a); 49 U.S.C. §§ 1603(a), 1604(e), are extended on the condition that some portion of the money be used for projects that benefit the handicapped. The 1976 "special efforts" regulations suggest, for example, that adequate efforts would consist of allocating an annual average of 5% of a locality's grant under section 5 of the UMT Act to projects for wheelchair users. 49 C.F.R. § 613.204 App. (1980). In 1980, that would have amounted to some $6 million of New York City's total federal capital and operating subsidy for mass transit of $490 million. While this is a considerable sum of money, it is not "massive" either in absolute terms or relative to the City's total receipt of mass transportation assistance, particularly since the very receipt of the money was conditioned on such an expenditure. Among plaintiffs' claims on the merits is that money designated for projects for the handicapped was misspent or not spent at all; if that occurred, it would hardly seem excessive to order that at least some of the money be spent as intended. Relief might also include the earmaking [sic] of subsequently appropriated mass transit funds for new projects to aid the handicapped, to whatever extent federal regulations require.

Judge Weinfeld's focus on the "massive" restructuring necessary to comply with the 1979 "accessibility" regulations obscures the fact that plaintiffs charged violations of the 1976 "special efforts" regulations as well. The latter requirements form a distinct basis for plaintiffs' complaint; they also stand as an independent source of legal obligation during the relevant time period, regardless of the validity of the more extensive 1979 requirements. The 1979 regulations were in force from 1979 to 1981, only the last two of the years covered by plaintiffs' complaint; there is no dispute that the 1976 regulations applied before that. In addition, the 1976 regulations remained in the Code of Federal Regulations throughout the brief life of the 1979 regulations. See 46 Fed.Reg. 17,488 (1981). The earlier requirements were eclipsed—superseded only in the sense of being rendered superfluous for the time being—but were not withdrawn or voided.

Moreover, since the two sets of regulations differ in important respects, the result in APTA does not impair the validity of a cause of action predicated on the 1976 regulations. While the 1979 regulations imposed a requirement that every existing mode of federally funded public mass transportation be made accessible to the handicapped, the 1976 regulations permitted the institution of separate transit services for such persons as an alternative to accessible bus and rail systems. As the APTA opinion noted, the 1976 regulations "allowed each local authority to choose a plan responsive to local needs. For example, a community could provide door-to-door 'special services,' rather than make fixed-route transportation modes accessible." 655 F.2d at 1275. To be sure, the "special efforts" regulations are subject to the same restriction that proved fatal to those issued in 1979: they may not require more than the statute authorities. Unlike the ill-fated 1979 requirements, however, the "special efforts" regulations have never been questioned by a court as going beyond the substantive authorization of section 504. Compare APTA v. Lewis, supra (invalidating 1979 regulations as exceeding authority of section 504), with Leary v. Crapsey, supra (upholding right of action based on section 504 and 1976 regulations) (by implication), United Handicapped Federation v. Andre, supra (same), and Lloyd v. Regional Transportation Authority, supra (same). Even APTA, while attacking the 1979 requirements, seemed to regard the earlier regulations with approval.

In short, these plaintiffs do not necessarily seek the complete overhaul of the New York City transit system that the 1979 "accessibility" regulations seemed to contemplate. Even if they did, those regulations would not be the sole and unalterable measure of the possible relief for the wrongs they allege. While the 1979 regulations may be unenforceable after APTA, the fact that they exceeded the scope of section 504 as interpreted in Davis does not, as the District Court concluded, "appl[y] with equal force to the case at bar," 518 F.Supp. at 1175, and justify dismissing this complaint. APTA only sketches the outer limits in the mass transportation context of the limitations laid down by the Supreme Court in *Davis*. The key issue, therefore, is whether *Davis* not only proscribed forcing "massive" restructuring of transportation programs, but in fact prohibits *any* possible prospective relief in this setting.

B. *"Affirmative Action"*

*Davis* concluded that Congress had understood "the distinction between the evenhanded treatment of qualified handicapped persons and affirmative efforts to overcome the disabilities caused by handicaps," 442 U.S. at 410, 99 S.Ct. at 2369, and plainly had not intended "to impose an affirmative-action obligation on all recipients of federal funds" when it enacted section 504, *id.* at 411, 99 S.Ct. at 2369. The Court acknowledged, however, that the distinction is not always easily drawn: "It is possible to envision situations where an insistence on continuing past requirements and practices might arbitrarily deprive genuinely qualified handicapped persons of the opportunity to participate in a covered program." *Id.* at 412, 99 S.Ct. at 2370. Similarly, *APTA* recognized that its holding that the 1979 statute would not necessarily apply to less extensive remedial measures. "[A]t some point a transit system's refusal to take modest, affirmative steps to accommodate handicapped persons might well violate section 504." 655 F.2d at 1278.

We believe that section 504 does require at least "modest, affirmative steps" to accommodate the handicapped in public transportation. Every court that has considered the question has concluded as much. *See Leary* v. *Crapsey, supra; United Handicapped Federation* v. *Andre, supra; Lloyd* v. *Regional Transportation Authority, supra; Vanko* v. *Finley,* 440 F.Supp. 656 (N.D. Ohio 1977); *Bartels* v. *Biernat,* 427 F.Supp. 226 (E.D.Wis.1977). Even the *APTA* case, decided in the aftermath of *Davis,* acknowledged the need to take action. Moreover, it is difficult to imagine what Congress could have had in mind in including mass transportation within the sweep of section 504 and, more generally, in authorizing programs to "develop solutions to existing architectural and transportation barriers impeding handicapped individuals," 29 U.S.C. § 701(11), if not that some affirmative efforts must be undertaken.

*Davis's* specific conclusion that section 504 imposes no "affirmative action" obligation in the area of requirements for admission to higher education programs is not to the contrary. As Judge Edwards, concurring in *APTA,* noted, *Davis's* roots in the educational context limit the literal transferability of the rule:

> [T]he application of section 504 to public transportation systems raises some questions that are significantly different from those considered by the Supreme Court in the higher education setting in [*Davis*]. In considering the accessibility of public transportation to otherwise qualified handicapped persons, it is much more difficult to avoid "discrimination" without taking some kind of "affirmative action."

655 F.2d at 1281 (Edwards, J., concurring). In the context of public transportation and the handicapped, denial of access cannot be lessened simply by eliminating discriminatory selection criteria; because the barriers to equal participation are physical rather than abstract, some sort of action must be taken to remove them, if only in the area of new construction or purchasing. As plaintiffs pointedly observe, "It is not enough to open the door for the handicapped . . . ; a ramp must be built so the door can be reached." Brief for Appellants at 20–21.

In fact, the very use of the phrase "affirmative action" in this context is unfortunate, making it difficult to talk about any kind of affirmative efforts without importing the special legal and social connotations of that term. The vocabulary of remedies for past discrimination that require or at least set goals for hiring or enrollment of compensatory numbers of a disadvantaged class is inappropriate in a case of this sort. Here, there is no program that "selects" participants. These plaintiffs do not, for example, demand that decisions selecting bus drivers or motormen from the pool of those qualified be weighted in favor of handicapped applicants. Here there is a public service that plaintiffs are entitled to use but that is not practically available to them.

*Davis* used the term "affirmative action" to refer to alteration of the standards or qualifications by which applicants to a program are selected, if those standards unfairly exclude a certain group. Even that use of the term is not in issue in this case. In *Davis*, a ruling in the plaintiff's favor would have required a change in the *nature of the program*, a reconstruction of the college's entire professional training process; in effect, it would have changed the accepted meaning of saying that a person had undergone training as a registered nurse. The central issue in *Davis*, to which questions of expenditures and effort were secondary, was whether "an educational institution [is required] to lower or to effect substantial modifications of [its] standards to accommodate a handicapped person," 442 U.S. at 413, 99 S.Ct. at 2370. The Court's decision that such changes were not required was virtually compelled by its earlier conclusion that the statutory phrase "otherwise qualified" means "one who is able to meet all of a program's requirements in spite of his handicap." 442 U.S. at 406, 99 S.Ct. at 2367. With the issue so defined the only question was whether the ability to hear spoken words was an integral requirement of the nursing program. Concluding that it was, the Court used the phrases "affirmative action" and "substantial modifications" in rejecting a requirement that the college must reconstitute its training program to render unnecessary a nursing student's ability to hear.

Here, plaintiffs do not seek fundamental changes in the nature of a program by means of alterations in its standards. They do not, to adapt the example used above, demand that the physical qualifications for the job of bus driver or motorman be altered so that the handicapped are not excluded. The existing barriers to the "participation" of the wheelchair-bound are incidental to the design of facilities and the allocation of services, rather than being integral to the nature of public transportation itself, just as a flight of stairs is incidental to a law school's construction but has no bearing on the ability of an otherwise qualified handicapped student to study law.

The present controversy, then, is free of two of the more vexing public policy aspects of debates over affirmative action: the problem of reverse discrimination and the associated problem of changes in selection criteria necessary to widen the pool of "qualified" applicants. The issue here is purely economic and administrative—how much accommodation is called for by regulations implementing the Rehabilitation Act. This issue, though difficult, involves a set of questions different from those involved in "affirmative action" cases, for it turns more on considerations of practicality than on matters of entitlement, merit, and restitution. And while it is bounded, after *Davis*, by a general proscription against "massive" expenditures, the question is one of the degree of effort necessary rather than whether any effort at all is required. When

Congress legislates to require accommodating federally funded mass transportation systems to the needs of the handicapped, and regulations specify that fund recipients must use their available funds to make some "special efforts" toward the national policy that Congress has established, courts are obliged to adjudicate claims that the law is not being observed. While we recognize that fashioning relief in this area will be difficult, that difficulty does not justify abandoning the task. We therefore reverse that part of the District Court's ruling that dismissed the complaint under section 504 of the Rehabilitation Act, and remand for consideration of the merits of plaintiffs' claims and for the fashioning of whatever appropriate relief to which they may be entitled.

* * *

*Conclusion*

The judgment of the District Court is affirmed in part, reversed in part, and remanded for further proceedings in accordance with this opinion.

[The opinion of Circuit Judge CARDAMONE, who dissented in part and concurred in part is omitted.]

NOTES

1.   Note the *Dopico* court's differentiation between the specific accessibility problem in *Davis* regarding higher education and the general accessibility problem regarding mass transportation in *Dopico*. This type of differentiation would seem crucial to a proper analysis of almost any Sec. 504 discrimination issue.

2.   The *Dopico* court does a great service to future Sec. 504 analysis by explaining why the use of the phrase "affirmative action" is misleading in the context of Sec. 504.

3.   Relying in part upon the *Dopico* decision, a federal district court in Rhode Island has found a public transit authority to have violated the rights of handicapped persons under Section 504. *Rhode Island Handicapped Action Committee* v. *Rhode Island Public Transit Authority*, C.A. No. 80-0631 (D.R.I. Sept. 20, 1982). The court ruled that Section 504 "is not a hollow promise" in its application to public transportation. *Id.* at 42. Further, the court concluded that "RIPTA's attempts to provide meaningful public transportation for the handicapped of Rhode Island have been inadequate." *Id.* at 44. Consequently, the court issued an injunction ordering the State transit authorities:

1)   to purchase 42 buses with wheelchair lifts and two wheelchair bays;
2)   to maintain no more than a 15% reserve ratio for its lift-equipped buses;
3)   to provide a locking mechanism which will secure electric wheelchair users;
4)   to provide meaningful wheelchair accessible bus service on weekends and in the evenings; and
5)   to repair the kneeling features on all its buses within 90 days of this opinion.

*Id.* at 59–60.

c.   **Regulations under § 504**

p. 497—INSERT the following before **2. UMTA:**

## AMERICAN PUBLIC TRANSPORTATION ASSOCIATION v. LEWIS

*United States Court of Appeals for the District of Columbia Circuit, 1981*
*655 F.2d 1272*

Before MACKINNON, MIKVA and EDWARDS, Circuit Judges.
Opinion for the Court filed by Circuit Judge MIKVA.
Opinion filed by Circuit Judge HARRY T. EDWARDS, concurring in the result.
MIKVA, Circuit Judge:

Petitioners challenge certain regulations promulgated by the Department of Transportation (DOT or Department) on May 31, 1979, to implement section 504 of the Rehabilitation Act of 1973 (Rehabilitation Act), 29 U.S.C. § 794 (Supp. III 1979), section 16 of the Urban Mass Transit Act of 1964 (UMTA), 49 U.S.C. § 1612 (1976), and section 165(b) of the Federal-Aid Highway Act of 1973 (FAHA), 23 U.S.C. § 142 note (1976). These regulations require that every mode of transportation in a mass transit system be made accessible to the handicapped, though waivers can be obtained for rail systems under some circumstances. *See* 44 Fed.Reg. 31,442, 31,477–81 (1979), 49 C.F.R. §§ 27.81–27.107 (1980).

The district court upheld the regulations as a valid exercise of DOT's statutory authority. Although it is possible that the UMTA or the FAHA might support the issuance of such regulations, we find that DOT's view of section 504 of the Rehabilitation Act is inconsistent with the Supreme Court's subsequent analysis of the Act in *Southeastern Community College* v. *Davis,* 442 U.S. 397, 99 S.Ct. 2361, 60 L.Ed.2d 980 (1979). Because we conclude from the administrative record that DOT relied primarily on its understanding of its responsibilities under the Rehabilitation Act in promulgating the regulations, we reverse and remand for further proceedings not inconsistent with this opinion.

### I.  Background

*A.  Events Leading to the Adoption of the 1979 Regulations*

The regulations challenged in this appeal are not the first DOT regulations dealing with mass transit systems and the handicapped. In 1976, DOT issued regulations designed to implement section 504 of the Rehabilitation Act, section 16 of the UMTA, and section 165(b) of the FAHA. *See* 41 Fed.Reg. 18,234 (1976). Each of these statutes deals with the handicapped. Section 504 provides that any program receiving federal funds must not discriminate against the handicapped. Section 16 of the UMTA provides that, as a matter of national policy, handicapped and elderly persons have the same rights as others to use mass transit facilities. This provision imposes an obligation on local planners to make "special efforts . . . in the planning and design of mass transportation facilities and services so that the availability" of such services to the elderly and the handicapped will be "assured." FAHA section 165(b) authorizes the Secretary of DOT to require that a mass transit system, aided by grants from highway funds under the FAHA, "be planned, designed, constructed, and operated to allow effective utilization by elderly or handicapped persons."

The 1976 DOT regulations implemented these provisions by mandating that state and local planners make "special efforts in planning public mass transportation facilities and services that can effectively be utilized by elderly and handicapped persons." 41 Fed.Reg. 18,234 (1976). Approval of project grants was conditioned on "satisfactory special efforts." *Id.* The regulations were accompanied by guidelines issued jointly by the Urban Mass Transit Administration and the Federal Highway Administration to illustrate the kinds of plans that would satisfy the "special efforts" requirement. These guidelines allowed each local authority to choose a plan responsive to local needs. For example, a community could provide door-to-door "special services," rather than make fixed-route transportation modes accessible. *Id.*

On April 28, 1976, two days before the regulations were published in their final form, President Ford issued Executive Order Number 11,914, 41 Fed.Reg. 17,871 (1976). The order directed the Department of Health, Education, and Welfare (HEW) to coordinate implementation of section 504 for all federal agencies and departments by establishing standards and guidelines for determining what practices were discriminatory. The President directed other agencies to promulgate regulations consistent with the guidelines established by HEW.

HEW issued its guidelines in 1978. *See* 43 Fed.Reg. 2132 (1978), 45 C.F.R. §§ 85.1–85.58 (1980). They require that all recipients of federal funds "mainstream" handicapped persons, that is, integrate such persons into the same programs available to others, rather than treat them as a separate group in "special" programs. Under the guidelines, "separate treatment" may be provided only when necessary to ensure equal opportunities. *See* 43 Fed.Reg. at 2134.

In the context of public transportation "mainstreaming" means the physical integration of the handicapped with other members of the travelling public, and the HEW guidelines require that each mode of transportation in a transit system be accessible to the handicapped. *See id.* at 2138–39, 45 C.F.R. §§ 85.56, 85.57. The 1976 DOT regulations clearly violated this requirement; they sanctioned the provision of separate transit services for the handicapped as an alternative to accessible bus and rail systems.

DOT's inconsistent regulations were soon rescinded. Six months after HEW promulgated the guidelines, DOT published its notice of proposed rulemaking, together with proposed rules. *See* 43 Fed.Reg. 25,016 (1976). The notice stated that DOT felt bound by the HEW guidelines to adopt only such options as would constitute "mainstreaming." *Id.* at 25,017. A regulatory analysis, prepared by DOT to explain its rationale and choices, analyzed the various options in terms of their consistency with the HEW guidelines. *See* Department of Transportation Section 504 Regulation Regulatory Analysis, Joint Appendix (J.A.) at 95. Before publication of the final rules, DOT submitted its draft rules to HEW for approval. Based on discussions with HEW, DOT agreed to a number of changes so that former HEW Secretary Califano could find the DOT regulations in compliance with the HEW guidelines. *See* 44 Fed.Reg. 31,468 (1979).

### B.  The 1979 Regulations

The new regulations, formally promulgated by DOT in 1979, differ substantially from the earlier ones, although both sets implement the same statutory provisions. The 1979 regulations require that transit systems receiving any federal funds make each mode of public transportation "accessible" to the handicapped by May 31, 1982, although "extraordinarily expensive" structural changes to, or replacements of, existing vehicles or facilities may be accomplished over periods as long as thirty years. *See* 44 Fed.Reg. 31,442, 31,477–79 (1979), 49 C.F.R. §§ 27.83–27.95 (1980). Some particularly costly structural changes in rail systems may be waived under certain conditions. *Id.* at 31,480, 49 C.F.R. § 27.99.

A transportation mode is generally considered "accessible" when it can be used by a handicapped person in a wheelchair. Every bus purchased after July 2, 1979, must have a wheelchair lift, *id.* at 31,478, 49 C.F.R. § 27.85. The estimated additional cost is $12,000 to $15,000 per bus. At the end of ten years, half of the buses on any system must be accessible to wheelchair users. *Id.*

Subways and other rail systems must be retrofitted with elevators and "gap-closing" equipment that will enable wheelchair users to board trains. *Id.* at 31,478–79, 49 C.F.R. §§ 27.87–27.89. "Key" subway and commuter rail system stations, about forty per cent of all stations, must be accessible, and connector service must be provided between key stations and other stations. *Id.*, At least one car per train must be accessible; to this end, new subway cars acquired after July 2, 1979, must be accessible to wheelchair users, as must new commuter rail cars acquired after January 1, 1983.

The regulations include a special waiver provision for existing subway, commuter rail, and streetcar systems, but not for bus systems. An application for a waiver may be submitted after the metropolitan planning organization, handicapped persons, and their representative groups plan an alternative service that is at least as good as an accessible rail system, and the DOT Secretary has discretionary authority to grant the waiver if these conditions have been met. *Id.* at 31,480, 49 C.F.R. § 27.99.

### C. The Decision Below

DOT's regulations were promulgated on May 31, 1979; on June 29, 1979, the plaintiff, American Public Transit Association (APTA), a voluntary trade association, and eleven of its transit system members, filed suit in district court challenging the validity of the regulations. After hearing argument on cross-motions for summary judgment, the district court entered a judgment affirming the validity of the regulations.

The district court upheld the regulations on the basis of the three statutes cited by DOT: section 16 of the UMTA (local planners must make "special efforts" to provide transportation for the elderly and the handicapped), section 165(b) of the FAHA (transit systems receiving highway funds should be planned, designed, constructed, and operated to allow effective utilization by the elderly and the handicapped), and section 504 of the Rehabilitation Act (no discrimination against qualified handicapped persons in programs receiving federal funds). In addition, the court found that the regulations were supported by DOT's broad power to condition grants to local transit systems under sections 3 and 5 of the UMTA, though these provisions were not cited by DOT in promulgating the regulations.

As the district court recognized, to the extent the regulations enforce section 504, they are suspect under *Southeastern Community College* v. *Davis*, 442 U.S. 397,

99 S.Ct. 2361, 60 L.Ed.2d 980 (1979), a Supreme Court decision interpreting section 504 after the regulations were promulgated. We will first discuss whether the regulations are a valid way of enforcing section 504 of the Rehabilitation Act. Because we conclude that they are not, we then consider whether this court should remand these proceedings to the Department for its reconsideration, rather than determine ourselves the validity of the regulations under other statutes.

II.  Section 504 of the Rehabilitation Act

Section 504 of the Rehabilitation Act was enacted in 1973 and provides in pertinent part:

> No otherwise qualified handicapped individual in the United States . . . shall, solely by reason of his handicap, be excluded from the participation in, be denied the benefits of, or be subjected to discrimination under any program or activity receiving Federal financial assistance or under any program or activity conducted by any Executive agency. . . .

The government argues that the DOT regulations at issue in this appeal are within the scope of the Department's power to enforce this provision. In *Southeastern Community College* v. *Davis*, 442 U.S. 397, 99 S.Ct. 2361, 60 L.Ed.2d 980 (1979), however, the Supreme Court held that section 504 does not give federal agencies the power to impose such onerous affirmative burdens on local programs.

In *Davis*, a deaf woman applied to Southeastern Community College's registered nurse program. After evaluation of the extent of her handicap by an audiologist, the school rejected her application. The audiologist reported that, even with a hearing aid, Davis would be unable to understand speech directed to her except through lipreading. The school concluded that her deafness would preclude her participation in the clinical portion of the nursing program and that she would not be able to perform effectively as a nurse in a variety of situations. Davis argued that the denial of her application was improper for two reasons. First, the school should not have taken her handicap into account in determining whether she was "otherwise qualified" for admission under the standard of section 504. Second, the school should have restructured the program so that her handicap would not bar her participation.

The Court upheld the validity of the school's action against both challenges. On the first, the Court held that an "otherwise qualified" person is one who is able to meet all program requirements, including necessary physical qualifications, despite his handicap. *Id*. at 406–07, 99 S.Ct. at 2367. In response to the second argument, the Court held that section 504 does not require such substantial program modifications.

In analyzing the second issue, the Court noted that "[t]he language and structure of the Rehabilitation Act of 1973 reflect a recognition by Congress of the distinction between the evenhanded treatment of qualified handicapped persons and affirmative efforts to overcome the disabilities caused by handicap." *Id*. at 410, 99 S.Ct. at 2369. The Court concluded that "neither the language, purpose, nor history of § 504 reveals an intent to impose an affirmative action obligation of all recipients of federal funds." *Id*. at 411, 99 S.Ct. at 2369. In reply to the plaintiff's argument that HEW regulations might put a burden on Southeastern not imposed by the statute itself, the

Court responded that if HEW had "attempted to create such an obligation itself, it lack[ed] the authority to do so." *Id.* at 411–12, 99 S.Ct. at 2370.

In holding that section 504 bans discrimination but does not mandate affirmative action to accommodate the handicapped, the Court recognized that the line between impermissible discrimination and optional affirmative action is a fine one. In some situations, "insistence on continuing past requirements and practices might arbitrarily deprive genuinely qualified handicapped persons of the opportunity to participate in a covered program." *Id.* at 412, 99 S.Ct. at 2370. And failure to take affirmative action might be discriminatory when programs could be opened to the handicapped "without imposing undue financial and administrative burdens upon a State." *Id.*

Applying these standards to public transit, we note that at some point a transit system's refusal to take modest, affirmative steps to accommodate handicapped persons might well violate section 504. But DOT's rules do not mandate only modest expenditures. The regulations require extensive modifications of existing systems and impose extremely heavy financial burdens on local transit authorities. Every new bus or subway car must be accessible to wheelchairs regardless of cost; elevators and other modifications must be added to existing subways. The regulations themselves recognize that some changes will be "extraordinarily expensive"; such changes are nevertheless required, though they may be phased in over periods of time longer than the three-year limit otherwise applicable. *See* 44 Fed.Reg. 31,477 (1979), 49 C.F.R. § 27.83 (1980). These are the kind of burdensome modifications that the *Davis* Court held to be beyond the scope of section 504. Thus, if section 504 and the HEW guidelines are the only underpinnings for the 1979 regulations, their validity cannot be sustained.

### III.   The Need for a Proper Statutory Basis

As we explained below, we believe that the primary reason DOT rescinded the newly promulgated 1976 regulations and replaced them with the regulations at issue in this appeal was the perceived need to follow HEW's section 504 guidelines. Every aspect of the rulemaking procedure points to those guidelines as the moving force for change, and, in light of the Supreme Court's decision in *Davis*, section 504 cannot support so burdensome a mandate to local governments. It remains possible, however, that the regulations are a valid exercise of DOT's authority to enforce other provisions of the UMTA and the FAHA; two such provisions were actually cited by DOT in promulgating these rules. We must therefore determine whether the error in relying on section 504 warrants our remanding these proceedings to DOT, rather than considering the validity of the regulations under other statutes.

[2] When an administrative decision is based on inadequate or improper grounds, a reviewing court may not presume that the administrator would have made the same decision on other, valid grounds. *See, e.g., SEC v. Chenery Corp. (II),* 332 U.S. 194, 196, 67 S.Ct. 1575, 1577, 91 L.Ed. 1995 (1947); *SEC v. Chenery Corp. (I),* 318 U.S. 80, 63 S.Ct. 454, 87 L.Ed. 626 (1943). As Judge Leventhal noted in *United States ex rel. Checkman v. Laird,* 469 F.2d 773, 780–83 (2d Cir. 1972) (Leventhal, J., sitting by designation), this rule is necessary to preserve the proper

allocation of responsibilities between administrators and reviewing courts. A court usurps the position of the proper decisionmaker when it "rummages throughout the record," *id.* at 783, to find an alternative basis for the administrator's action: "a court, if it sustains a decision by recourse to reasons outside those specified, opens the door to the improper substituting of the court's judgment and evaluation . . . in place of that of the agency . . . with responsibility." *Id.* at 781.

The government argues that a remand is not necessary in this case for two reasons. First, it maintains that the *Chenery* principle applies only when courts would have to advance alternative factual or policy bases for an agency decision, questions that Congress left to agency discretion. The government maintains that *Chenery* does not apply when the administrator errs in interpreting a statute. The rule is, however, fully applicable to such cases. As the Supreme Court held in *Citizens to Preserve Overton Park* v. *Volpe,* 401 U.S. 402, 416, 91 S.Ct. 814, 823, 28 L.Ed.2d 136 (1971), a reviewing court must always determine whether an administrator properly construed the scope of his statutory authority in making a decision. When it is likely an administrator would not have enforced one statute in the way he enforced another, a decision promulgated on the basis of the wrong statute should be remanded for his reconsideration.

Second, the government argues, and the court below held, that the DOT regulations are valid because they are based on an independent decision of the DOT Secretary to enforce section 16 of the UMTA and section 165(b) of the FAHA, and to exercise his broad authority to condition grants under sections 3 and 5 of the UMTA. It is true that DOT cited two of these provisions, UMTA section 16 and FAHA section 165(b), in promulgating the regulations, but a court's obligation under *Chenery* to give agencies the opportunity to exercise their discretion unfettered by legal error cannot be avoided by relying on the formal citation of additional authority. Instead, this court must determine whether it is likely that DOT's decision to promulgate these regulations was affected by its mistaken reliance on section 504 and the HEW guidelines. *See Massachusetts Trustees* v. *United States,* 377 U.S. 235, 247–48, 84 S.Ct. 1236, 1244–45, 12 L.Ed.2d 268 (1964).

In 1976, the DOT Secretary promulgated regulations implementing section 504 of the Rehabilitation Act, UMTA section 16, and FAHA section 165. Those regulations did not mandate "mainstreaming" in all transportation modes in all transit systems; rather, they provide that each local authority could make transportation services available to the needy in the manner most suited to its particular situation, and they gave examples of several approaches that would satisfy the regulations. *See* 41 Fed.Reg. 18,234 (1976). If the HEW Secretary had not implemented guidelines enforcing section 504 inconsistent with DOT's 1976 regulations, it is quite possible the latter would still be in effect.

Moreover, in deciding what regulations to implement in 1979, DOT stated that it was bound by the HEW guidelines and evaluated alternatives in terms of their consistency with the guidelines. *See, e.g.,* Department of Transportation Section 504 Regulation Analysis, J.A. at 95, 98 ("[R]eliance on special service transit in place of mainline accessibility would not be consistent with the HEW guidelines. Consequently, this analysis of the section 504 requirements for UMTA grantees is based on the view that mainline accessibility is necessary."); Implementation of Section 504 of the Rehabilitation Act of 1973 by the Department of Transportation, J.A. at 196, 197 (DOT document) ("HEW's Guidelines, are, in our view, legally binding on DOT. . . . ").

Furthermore, as discussed above, the DOT regulations were not even promulgated until, after weeks of negotiation and several modifications, the HEW Secretary approved them as consistent with the HEW guidelines. *See* 44 Fed.Reg. 31,442 (1979). Even the formal promulgation of the regulations explains them in terms of the HEW guidelines enforcing section 504. *See id.* at 31,442. In the context of rail systems, DOT explicitly rejected some options because they were inconsistent with the HEW guidelines. *See* 44 Fed.Reg. 31,450 (1979) ("The concept of local option as expressed by many commenters is inconsistent with the assurance of providing program accessibility which section 504 and the HEW guidelines require."). Although no such statement was made in the context of bus systems, subsequent requests for exemptions for such systems have been rejected on the ground that a waiver would be inconsistent with HEW's guidelines. *See, e.g.,* J.A. at 189, 190 (DOT letter rejecting Erie, Pa., request for waiver for bus system: "[B]inding guidelines issued by [HEW] . . . . explicitly require that new transit buses purchased with federal grants be accessible.").

We do not hold that, because the Secretary of DOT followed HEW's section 504 guidelines, he could not have made an independent policy decision to take the same approach in enforcing other statutes. We merely hold that the events surrounding the adoption of the 1979 regulations strongly suggest that he did not do so, and it would be improper for this court to "rummage" through the record to resolve a question— whether the regulations enforce other statutes—that should be made by the Secretary in the first instance.

We therefore remand to give the administrator an opportunity to explain whether these regulations are based on statutes other than section 504. If, on remand from the district court, the Secretary indicates that the regulations do enforce other statutes, he should identify the provisions of the UMTA or the FAHA—or any other act—that are enforced by the regulations, and he should justify the regulations in terms of the cited provisions.

## Conclusion

We find that the regulations challenged here exceed DOT's authority to enforce section 504 of the Rehabilitation Act. Because DOT relied so heavily on the perceived need to enforce section 504 in the manner prescribed by the Secretary of HEW, this case must be remanded to DOT so that it can indicate whether these regulations are also based on some other statutory authority. The decision of the court below is therefore reversed, and we remand to that court for further proceedings not inconsistent with this opinion.

*Reversed and remanded.*

[The concurring opinion of Judge Edwards is omitted.]

NOTE

Is the APTA court's use of the analysis developed by the Supreme Court in *Davis* appropriate in light of the differences that exist between accessibility of handicapped persons to higher education as opposed to mass transportation? An aspect of the Supreme Court's ruling in *Davis* was that to make the program at issue accessible, substantial modifications would be necessary in order to neutralize the detrimental effects of the plaintiff's handicap. In holding that substantial modifications were not required, the Court utilized an analysis based on the unique facts of the *Davis* case. Is it consistent with the intent of Sec. 504 to apply this analysis to the issue of the accessibility of mass transportation?

2.  UMTA

p. 502—INSERT the following after the Note:

DOPICO V. GOLDSCHMIDT

[See pp. 191–199, above.]

E.  FEDERAL AGENCY ENFORCEMENT

2.  The Architectural and Transportation Barriers Compliance Board

p. 520—INSERT the following after Note 2:

3.  The following was excerpted from the July 13, 1982 issue of *Handicapped Rights and Regulations:*

ACCESSIBILITY COMPLAINTS DROP BY 54 IN FY'81
     Complaints to the federal agency in charge of enforcing accessibility law dropped by more than one-third between FY'80 and FY'81, but the numbers are picking up again in FY'82.
     The Architectural and Transportation Barriers Compliance Board received 106 complaints in FY'81, a 33.75% drop from 160 in FY'80 (HRR, Oct. 6, 1981, p. 157). An outreach campaign that was used in FY'79–'80 was halted in FY'81, accounting for some of the decrease, said a board staff member. "Also, the public was not sure whether we'd be around or not," she added, referring to the Administration's plan in the last two years not to fund the board.
     The FY'81 complaints came from 42 states and Puerto Rico, according to the board's annual report. "They included a wide range of accessibility problems, such as inaccessible entrances, lack of ramps and curb cuts, no parking for handicapped persons, and lack of tactile identification for persons with visual impairments and devices for persons with hearing disabilities," said the report.
     The most complaints came from Pennsylvania, District of Columbia and Puerto Rico with eight each, followed by New York with five, and Florida, California and Louisiana with four each. Last year, the most complaints emanated from California. Although the board did not have jurisdiction over all 106 complaints received in FY'81, only two— State Street Mall in Chicago and the Richard B. Russell Building in Atlanta—required legal action. "The others have been resolved or are still pending," said the report. Figures were not available as to how many complaints the board did have jurisdiction

over. Complaints this year have picked up, said the staff member. As of July 9, the board had received 96 complaints, compared to 76 on July 9, 1981. This year, "prompting the most complaints were the lack of handicapped parking spaces, curb cuts, ramps, signage, accessible entrances, elevators and restrooms. Locked doors, overhead hazards, stairs and nonfunctioning platform lifts were the subjects of other complaints," said the board.

The board's funding in FY'81 was $2.3 million, of which $828,000 was used for salaries, $120,000 for public information and education, $368,000 for contracts and research, and $274,000 for such administrative costs as travel, equipment, rent and supplies.

# 5
# Freedom of Choice: Competency and Guardianship

Robert L. Burgdorf Jr.

## SUMMARY OF DOCTRINAL DEVELOPMENTS

WHILE ISSUES OF GUARDIANSHIP AND COMPETENCY have continued to be the subject of much litigation, there has not been much in the way of new doctrinal approaches or major shifts in direction. Most judicial decisions have dealt with procedural matters or application of statutory standards to particular factual situations.

## D.  STANDARDS FOR DETERMINING INCOMPETENCY

### 1.  Statutory Standards

p. 539—INSERT after the Notes:

### IN RE SCHENCK

*Appeals Court of Massachusetts, 1981*
*____ Mass. ____, 427 N.E.2d 23*

Before HALE, C.J., and CUTTER and DREBEN, J.J.
DREBEN, Justice.

This is an appeal from the denial by a probate judge of the petition of a mentally competent ward to discharge a conservator previously appointed with the ward's consent on the ground of her physical incapacity. We reverse and order the conservator discharged.

We take the facts from the findings of the judge as supplemented by undisputed evidence in the record. In 1963, Miss Priscilla Schenck, who since birth has suffered from cerebral palsy, arranged for the appointment of Mr. Henry F. Smith as her conservator. While requiring constant attendance because of her disease, Miss Schenck was at that time and continues to be mentally competent. Miss Schenck has full confidence in Mr. Smith, and the arrangement proved satisfactory until a guardian ad litem appointed in connection with the allowance of the ninth and tenth accounts of the conservator questioned some of the expenditures made by Mr. Smith and sought his removal.

Approving of these expenses and resentful of the activities and costs caused by the guardian ad litem, Miss Schenck filed a petition for discharge of the conservatorship. The evidence at the hearing on her petition included certificates of two physicians attesting to her mental capacity, a deposition of Miss Schenck's present physician, testimony of one of Miss Schenck's companions, testimony of a cousin who is a trustee of several trusts of which Miss Schenck is the primary beneficiary, and testimony of a guardian ad litem appointed in connection with the petition for discharge. It was undisputed, and the judge found, that Miss Schenck is mentally competent. The evidence also showed that Miss Schenck has the ability to make arrangements for the management of her property and fully intends to do so.[2]

Despite this evidence, the judge, finding that Miss Schenck is "entirely dependent upon others to provide for her physical needs as well as managing her estate and dispersing her funds," concluded, "[s]he requires the protection of the Probate Court." The judge ordered the conservatorship to continue.

Such unwanted "protection" by the Probate Court is unwarranted. Apart from any other considerations which may be involved in such interference with the right of a mentally competent person to reassert control of her property, the statutory scheme set forth in G.L. c. 201, §§ 16, 16B and 18, does not permit such "protection" without Miss Schenck's consent.

We first note that G.L. c. 201, §§ 16[3] and 16B[4] provide two different procedures for the appointment of a conservator. Where "mental weakness," "advanced age" or "mental retardation" is the stated ground for such appointment, the petition

---

[2]The report of the guardian ad litem appointed in the discharge proceeding includes the following: "Miss Schenck is fully able to express herself in the course of conversation. She is a charming and intelligent woman who has a clear and concise understanding of the nature of this proceeding. Although Miss Schenck is physically handicapped, she is not confined to her home . . . She maintains sufficient household help for her personal and household needs. She is also able to use a specially equipped electric typewriter . . . Miss Schenck is extremely upset over the proceedings which have been commenced against Mr. Smith for his removal as her conservator. She continues to have the utmost trust and confidence in Mr. Smith . . . I have also reviewed with Miss Schenck the purpose and effect of her discharge from conservatorship and Mr. Smith's . . . ninth and tenth accounts. Miss Schenck is aware of the issues which have been raised in these accounts . . . and stated to me that it is her intent and desire to assent to these accounts if the court allows the petition to discharge her conservatorship proceedings . . . Miss Schenck told me that her bills are usually sent directly to her. She then reviews them and delivers them to Mr. Smith for payment. She also told me that the bills Mr. Smith receives are discussed with her . . . In the event that the court allows Miss Schenck's petition, it is her intention to create a trust under which Mr. Smith . . . will act as trustee for her benefit.

[3]General Laws c. 201, § 16, as amended by St. 1945, c. 728, § 2, provides: "If a person by reason of advanced age or mental weakness is unable to properly care for his property, the probate court may, upon his petition or upon the petition of one or more of his friends, or if a person by reason of physical incapacity is unable to properly care for his property the probate court may, upon his petition or with his written assent, and in each case if after notice as provided in section seventeen and after hearing it appears that such person is incapable of properly caring for his property, appoint a conservator to have charge and management of his property, subject to the direction of the court."

[4]General Laws c. 201, § 16B, as inserted by St. 1974, c. 845, § 9, deals with the appointment of a conservator for a mentally retarded person and permits such an appointment if after hearing the "court finds that the person is mentally retarded to the degree that he is incapable of making informed decisions with respect to the conduct of his financial affairs and that the failure to appoint a conservator would create an unreasonable risk to his property. . . . "

may be filed by someone other than the prospective ward. However, where the ground for the proposed conservatorship is "physical incapacity," the petition must be made upon the petition of the prospective ward "or with his written assent." Thus, § 16 does not authorize an involuntary conservatorship on the grounds of "physical incapacity".

Section 18, as amended by St. 1934, c. 204, § 2, provides that a "conservator may be discharged" when "it appears that the conservatorship is no longer necessary." In view of the undisputed evidence of Miss Schenck's ability to supervise the management of her property, the conservatorship is "no longer necessary" within the meaning of § 18. Although the statute uses the word "may," we do not consider this a case where a judge has discretion to refuse to discharge the conservator. A finding of physical incapacity alone, in the absence of the assent of Miss Schenck, would have been insufficient to impose a conservatorship in the first place. It is also insufficient to order a conservatorship continued once Miss Schenck's assent has been withdrawn, at least in circumstances where she is capable of supervising the management of her property.

Accordingly, we reverse the decree continuing the conservatorship and order the entry of a new decree discharging the conservator. We also order that any additional matters in connection with the conservatorship or its discharge, including the question of compensation for the guardians ad litem, shall be heard by a different judge.

*So ordered.*

NOTES

1.  Can a physical disability ever justify the imposition of a guardianship without the ward's consent?

2.  *In re Gardner,* 621 S.W.2d 92 (Mo. App. 1981), involved an 85-year-old woman who had been adjudged "incapable of managing her property and caring for herself and is therefore incompetent." 621 S.W.2d at 92. The guardianship petition listed the causes of her incapacity as "senility" and "cerebrovascular insufficiency, transient ischemic attacks." *Id.* The Missouri Court of Appeals reversed the judgment of incompetency:

> The most that the evidence here shows is that Audrey did not eat right, did not take her medicine, she got weak, staggered and fell around. Although there is evidence that she had difficulty in keeping her bank account from being overdrawn, there is no evidence that she was incapable of looking after her own affairs or caring for herself.

*Id.* at 93.

Compare the standard applied in the *Gardner* case with those applied in *Schenck, Keiser,* and *Warner.*

### In re Byrne

*Supreme Court of Florida, 1981*
*402 So.2d 383*

BOYD, Justice.

These consolidated cases are before the Court on appeal from judgments of the Circuit Court of the Eleventh Judicial Circuit, in Dade County, which upheld the constitutionality of section 410.104, Florida Statutes (1979). Under the jurisdictional provisions in effect at the time the notices of appeal were filed, jurisdiction of the appeals lay with this Court. Art. V, § 3(b)(1), Fla. Const. (1972).

On June 5, 1979, a social worker visited the appellants in their home and found them completely naked, surrounded by debris and excrement. Herbert Byrne, age 79, had called for help because his niece Norma Turner had fallen and he was unable to get her up. The social worker found that the plumbing was not working, parts of the ceiling were falling, and wires were dangling. A police officer took the appellants to a hospital.

The next day the social worker filed petitions for emergency orders of custody pursuant to section 410.104, Florida Statutes (1979). The court, *ex parte,* immediately issued orders for emergency custody. On the following day, he appointed counsel for the appellants.

On June 8, 1979, the appointed attorneys filed motions to dismiss the petitions on the ground that the emergency procedures provided for by section 410.104 are unconstitutional. The judge held a hearing that same day. The judge denied the motions to dismiss, but found that there was insufficient evidence to establish a need for continued services. On June 13, the court issued an order denying the motion to dismiss and rendered a judgment "acquitting" the appellants from further involuntary custody. This appeal of the denial of the motion to dismiss followed.

Since the time the notices of appeal were filed, Herbert Byrne has died and Norma Turner has been adjudicated incompetent. It is arguable that the controversy has therefore been rendered moot. We retain jurisdiction, however, "since this is a matter of great public importance in the administration of the law and is of general interest to the public." *Sadowski* v. *Shevin,* 345 So.2d 330, 331–32 (Fla. 1977); *see also Clark* v. *State ex rel. Rubin,* 122 So.2d 807 (Fla. 3d DCA 1960).

Section 410.104, Florida Statutes (1979), authorizes the Department of Health and Rehabilitative Services to take elderly persons into custody and transport them to a medical or protective service facility in an emergency situation without their consent. The issue is whether this section comports with due process and is constitutional.

The statute provides as follows:

> (1) Upon probable cause to believe that an individual suffering from the infirmities of aging is being abused, maltreated, or neglected, a representative of the department, accompanied by a law enforcement officer, may enter a premises, after obtaining a court order and announcing their authority and purpose. Forcible entry shall be attained only after a court order has been obtained, unless there is probable cause to believe that the delay incident to obtaining such an order would cause an individual suffering from the infirmities of aging to incur a substantial risk of life-threatening physical harm.
>
> (2) When, from the personal observation of a representative of the department and a law enforcement officer, it appears probable that an individual suffering from the infirmities of aging is likely to incur a substantial risk of life-threatening physical harm or deterioration if not immediately removed from the premises, the department's representative may, when authorized by court order, take into custody and transport, or make arrangements for the transportation of, the individual to an appropriate medical or protective services facility.
>
> (3) When action is taken under this section, a preliminary hearing shall be held within 48 hours, excluding Saturdays, Sundays, and legal holidays, to establish probable cause for grounds for protective placement.

(4) Upon a finding of probable cause, the court may order temporary placement for up to 4 days, pending the hearing for a need for continuing services.

(5) When emergency services are rendered, a report of the exact circumstances, including the time, place, date, factual basis for the need for such services, and the exact services rendered, shall be made and forwarded as provided for in s. 827.09.

§ 410.104, Fla.Stat. (1979).

The section under consideration is part of the Adult Protective Services Act, §§ 410.10–410.11, Fla.Stat. (1979). This statute was enacted to protect adults suffering from the "infirmities of aging" from "exploitation, neglect, abuse, and maltreatment" with "the least possible restriction on personal liberty and the exercise of constitutional rights, consistent with due process. . . ." § 410.101, Fla.Stat. (1979).

The term "infirmities of aging" is defined to mean "organic brain damage, advanced age, or other physical, mental, or emotional disfunctioning in connection therewith, to the extent that the person is substantially impaired in his ability adequately to provide for his own care or protection." § 410.102(1), Fla.Stat. (1979).

Section 410.103, Florida Statutes (1979), provides certain conditions governing the authority of the Department of Health and Rehabilitative Services to provide services:

> (1) CONDITIONS FOR PROVIDING SERVICES.—The Department shall provide protective services in response to complaints concerning, and requests for assistance from or on behalf of, individuals suffering from the infirmities of aging. The department shall provide such services under any of the following conditions:
> (a) The person demonstrates a need for, and requests, such services.
> (b) An interested person requests such services on behalf of a person in need of services.
> (c) The department determines a person is in need of such services.
> (d) A court orders such services.
> (2) VOLUNTARY SERVICES.—An individual shall receive protective services voluntarily unless ordered by the court, requested by a guardian, or provided in accordance with s. 410.104.

Section 410.104(2) authorizes the department to relocate elderly persons without their consent who are "likely to incur a substantial risk of life-threatening physical harm or deterioration if not immediately removed from the premises. . . ." This subsection also provides two procedural safeguards. First, both a representative of the department and a law enforcement officer must personally observe the emergency situation. Second, the relocation may be imposed only when authorized by court order. Even then such relocation cannot be imposed without consent for more than forty-eight hours. § 410.102(6), Fla.Stat. (1979).

Within the forty-eight hour period, a preliminary hearing must be held to determine whether there is probable cause for protective placement. § 410.104(3). At the hearing the allegations of the petition, that the person is suffering from the infirmities of aging and that there is a substantial risk of life-threatening physical harm or deterioration, must be proved. If the allegations are proved, the court may order temporary placement pending a hearing on the need for continuing protective services. § 410.104(4).

We hold that these procedures comport with the constitutional requirements of due process. The appellants' attorney argues that due process requires notice, an opportunity to be heard, and effective assistance of counsel, citing *Specht* v. *Patterson*, 386 U.S. 605, 87 S.Ct. 1209, 18 L.Ed.2d 326 (1967) and *In re Beverly*, 342 So.2d 481 (Fla. 1977). We find these requirements for civil commitment proceedings to be inapplicable to situations such as are reached by the statute under consideration. The purpose of this statute is not to incarcerate or confine mentally incompetent persons by commitment to state custody, but rather to free persons suffering from infirmities of aging from dangerous or oppressive conditions. The stated purpose of the statute—to protect the elderly—is genuine and not a euphemism for punishment. *Compare In Re Gault*, 387 U.S. 1, 87 S.Ct. 1428, 18 L.Ed.2d 527 (1967) (fact that purpose of juvenile delinquency proceedings was rehabilitation and protection of child rather than criminal punishment did not justify denial of all due process rights).

Furthermore, the statute is limited to the situation of an emergency. The state, in such situations, must fulfill its obligation to preserve life whenever it can. *See Satz* v. *Perlmutter*, 362 So.2d 160 (Fla. 4th DCA 1978), *aff'd*, 379 So.2d 359 (Fla. 1980). This responsibility must be balanced against an individual's rights of self-determination and privacy. Under normal conditions, the state may not enter a person's home, take custody, and transport the person to another location without following the strict procedures of criminal prosecution or civil commitment. Due process, however, is not offended by a temporary loss of liberty when a person's life may be threatened. *See Fhagen* v. *Miller*, 29 N.Y.2d 348, 328 N.Y.S.2d 393, 278 N.E.2d 615, *cert. denied*, 409 U.S. 845, 93 S.Ct. 47, 34 L.Ed.2d 85 (1972).

Removing an individual from an environment as unhealthy as the one in this case is essential to making a proper determination of whether the individual should be temporarily or permanently placed elsewhere. The wishes of the individual should be highly regarded and adequately represented, since the statute is designed for his benefit. The legislature recognized that some elderly people may in effect be held hostage by others or by their own environment. They may not know what is best for them or even know what they want after living under such conditions. Thus, relocating such persons and providing them with proper nourishment and medication is necessary to help them to regain a proper perspective on life so they can make a deliberate and unconstrained decision on whether to return.

Appellants' attorney argues that the court's authority to order continuing services is unconstitutionally vague and may lead to an indefinite period of involuntary commitment. We do not believe so. Reading the statute as a whole we find that continuing services should be ordered only until the person is no longer facing a substantial risk of life-threatening harm or deterioration. After that point the department can no longer render any services which are not voluntarily received.

Finally, appellants' attorney argues that the state lacks the authority under the *parens patriae* doctrine to impose services, treatment, and confinement upon competent elderly persons. We first note that under no circumstances can medical treatment be forced upon a person "in contravention of the stated or implied objection of such person." § 410.101, Fla.Stat. (1979). We further note that

> the *parens patriae* notion [is] that the state is the ultimate guardian of those of its citizens who are incapable of caring for their own interest. (Citations omitted). Valid exercise of

the *parens patriae* power presumes an incapability to manage one's affairs that approximates, if it is not identical with, legal incompetence to act.

*In re Beverly,* 342 So.2d at 485, *quoting Lynch* v. *Baxley,* 386 F.Supp. 378, 390–91 (M.D.Ala. 1974). People whose mental and physical capabilities are deteriorating because of old age may be approximating legal incompetency. Thus the state has the authority to exercise its *parens patriae* powers when it appears such persons are incapable of caring for themselves.

We affirm the trial court's order denying the motion to dismiss.

It is so ordered.

ADKINS, OVERTON and MCDONALD, JJ., concur.

SUNDBERG, C. J., and ENGLAND and ALDERMAN, JJ., would dismiss the appeal as moot.

NOTE

What relationship between Mr. Byrne and the Florida Department of Health and Rehabilitative Services is created under the Florida statute? What are the respective rights and authority of each? How does this situation compare with a traditional guardianship?

## G.  THE GUARDIANSHIP PROCEEDING

### 1.  Notice and Hearing

p. 591—INSERT after Note 5:

### RUD v. DAHL

*United States Court of Appeals for the Seventh Circuit, 1978*
*578 F.2d 674*

Before TONE and BAUER, Circuit Judges, and CAMPBELL, Senior District Judge.

PER CURIAM.

This is a suit brought under 42 U.S.C. § 1983, in which plaintiff Rud attacks the facial constitutionality of the Illinois statutory scheme under which he was adjudicated incompetent and a conservator appointed to manage his person and estate. Ill.Rev. Stat. ch. 3, §§ 11–2, et seq. Rud contends that the statutory scheme violates the due process clause of the Fourteenth Amendment in that it permits an adjudication of incompetency to be made without affording the alleged incompetent adequate notice of the nature and consequences of the proceeding and without requiring his presence at the hearing or at least appointment of counsel to protect his rights. Plaintiff seeks declaratory and injunctive relief, but no damages, on behalf of a class composed of all persons adjudicated incompetent in Cook County, Illinois on or after June 17, 1976. The defendants are the Chief Judge of the Probate Division of the Circuit Court of Cook County, another judge of that court, the Clerk of the Circuit Court, and the Associate Clerk in charge of the Probate Division. Defendants moved in the district court for dismissal of the complaint on numerous grounds, including comity, abstention, and failure to state a claim upon which relief could be granted. Without reaching the class certification issue, which plaintiff has not raised on appeal, the district court granted defendants' motion to dismiss for failure to state a claim to relief on grounds of comity and judicial immunity.

We affirm the district court's judgment for the reasons noted below.

## I

Although we agree with plaintiff that, because no monetary damages are sought, the defendants are not immune from suit in the circumstances of this case, *Hansen v. Ahlgrimm*, 520 F.2d 768, 769 (7th Cir. 1975), we affirm the district court's judgment without reaching the comity and abstention issues raised on appeal because plaintiff's complaint fails to state a claim to relief.

For purposes of reviewing the district court's dismissal of plaintiff's complaint, we have, of course treated all of the well-pleaded factual allegations of the complaint as true. *Walker Process Equipment* v. *Food Machinery & Chemical Corp.*, 382 U.S. 172, 86 S.Ct. 347, 15 L.Ed.2d 247 (1965). The relevant facts therein alleged are quite simple. Plaintiff, an 81-year-old resident of a nursing home, was served with a summons to appear at a hearing on a petition to appoint a conservator for him. For reasons left unsaid in the complaint, plaintiff did not respond to the summons and failed to appear at the hearing in person or by counsel. No inquiry was made at the hearing into the reasons underlying his absence, and no counsel was appointed to represent his interests. Nevertheless, he was adjudicated incompetent on the basis of the verified petition and a physician's affidavit that plaintiff was physically and mentally incapable of managing his person and estate because of congestive heart failure, pulmonary fibrosis, generalized arteriosclerosis, and cerebral dementia. As a consequence of the adjudication, the complaint alleges, plaintiff has lost all control over his person and estate.

The complaint further alleges that the Illinois statutory scheme pursuant to which plaintiff was adjudicated incompetent is unconstitutional because (1) the notice provided alleged incompetents of the hearing is not reasonably calculated under all the circumstances to apprise them of the nature and consequences of the proceeding and of the fact that a substantial interest is involved; (2) the adjudication is permitted to proceed in the absence of the respondent and without a valid waiver of his right to be present; and (3) no counsel is appointed to protect the respondent's rights if he fails to personally appear at the hearing. These conclusory allegations of law, of course, need not be taken as true, but they do serve to frame the issues on appeal as to the legal sufficiency of plaintiff's complaint.

## II

We turn first to plaintiff's contention that the Illinois statutory scheme is constitutionally deficient because it does not require that the notice be given of the incompetency hearing in a manner reasonably calculated under all the circumstances to apprise its recipient of the nature and potential consequences of the proceeding.

As plaintiff appears to concede, there is no constitutional infirmity in the mode and manner of service required by the statute or in the manner in which service was made on the plaintiff in this case. The general statutory rule, which was followed in this case, is personal service of the summons and petition on the alleged incompetent, along with personal or mail service of notice of the time, date and place of the hearing on the alleged incompetent's three closest living relatives. Ill.Rev.Stat. ch. 3, § 11–10(a)–(b). Accordingly, if the notice provided plaintiff was inadequate as a matter of due process, it is because of the content of the notice given rather than the failure to give any notice, or the manner in which it was served.

Plaintiff has alleged that the notice provided was substantively deficient because it did not offer any definition of the terms "incompetent" or "conservator," did not state on its face the legal standard governing adjudications of incompetency, and did not specify the legal consequences and practical ramifications resulting from the granting of the petition. Apparently because of these deficiencies, the complaint asserts in conclusory fashion that the notice given alleged incompetents is not "reasonably calculated under all the circumstances to appraise [sic] the alleged incompetent[s] of the pendency and nature of the proceeding and of the fact that a substantial interest is involved, in violation of the Fourteenth Amendment to the United States Constitution." We disagree.

The summons served on plaintiff attached to his complaint states:

> You are summoned to appear at a hearing on a petition, a copy of which is attached, asking that you are adjudged an incompetent and that a conservator be appointed of your estate and person. The day for appearance is June 17, 1976 at 11:30 a. m., Room 1803 Chicago Civic Center, Chicago, Illinois 60602. IF YOU DO NOT APPEAR, THE PETITION MAY BE GRANTED.

On its face, the summons is substantively sufficient to inform the recipient of the pendency, time, date and place of the hearing involved. Moreover, it clearly reveals the nature of the proceeding as one calling into question the recipient's ability to manage his own person and estate, especially when read in conjunction with the petition attached thereto.

As required by statute, the petition states that the petitioner, plaintiff's brother, alleges under oath that plaintiff is incompetent and incapable of managing his estate and person. The reasons given in the petition for plaintiff's incompetency include congestive heart failure, pulmonary fibrosis, generalized arteriosclerosis, and cerebral dementia. The petition, as required by statute, sets forth the approximate value of plaintiff's gross estate and his anticipated annual gross income. It lists, as required by statute, plaintiff's three closest living relatives and their current addresses. Finally, it specifically requests that plaintiff "be adjudged an incompetent," that the petitioner be appointed conservator of plaintiff's estate and person, and that an authorization to appraise the plaintiff's goods and chattels be issued.

We fail to see the substantive deficiencies of the above summons and petition. On their face, the summons and petition reveal the nature of the proceeding to which plaintiff was personally summoned as one calling into question plaintiff's ability to manage his person and estate. The legal standard governing incompetency proceedings—inability to manage one's person and estate—is implicit, as are the legal consequences flowing from such an adjudication—loss of control over one's person and estate in favor of a "conservator" or guardian. Accordingly, we believe that the notice provided plaintiff of the pendency and nature of the proceeding was "reasonably calculated under all the circumstances, to apprise [him] of the pendency of the action and afford [him] an opportunity to present [his] objections." *Mullane* v. *Central Hanover Bank & Trust Co.*, 339 U.S. 306, 314, 70 S.Ct. 652, 657, 94 L.Ed. 685 (1950). That is all due process requires.

Of course, there may be situations in which physical service of notice alone does not afford adequate notice under all the circumstances. *Dale* v. *Hahn*, 486 F.2d 76, 78 (2d Cir. 1973), *cert. denied*, 419 U.S. 826, 95 S.Ct. 44, 42 L.Ed.2d 50 (1974). In this case, however, we are satisfied that the notice given plaintiff was sufficient as a matter of due process to inform plaintiff of the general nature and consequences of the proceeding. Significantly, plaintiff has not even alleged that he did not understand the notice given him. Nor has he favored us with a statement of any circumstances calling the reasonableness of the notice into question. As we believe the notice given him is sufficient on its face as a matter of due process, we hold that his complaint fails to state a claim to relief on the basis of inadequate notice. Given the notice actually provided plaintiff, there are no set of facts that he could prove at trial rendering the notice constitutionally deficient. *Conley* v. *Gibson*, 355 U.S. 41, 45–46, 78 S.Ct. 99, 2 L.E.2d 80 (1957).

## III

We turn next to plaintiff's contention that the Illinois statutory scheme is additionally unconstitutional because it permits an adjudication of incompetency to occur in the absence of the alleged incompetent. We find plaintiff's complaint legally insufficient to state a claim to relief.

Plaintiff, of course, has a constitutional right to be present and be heard at any judicial proceeding, including an incompetency hearing, at which his liberty and property interests may be affected. But, as a general rule, all due process requires is that plaintiff have been afforded an *opportunity* to be present and be heard, and plaintiff was afforded such an opportunity. He was personally served with a summons notifying him of the time, date and place of the hearing, and informing him in bold type that "IF YOU DO NOT APPEAR, THE PETITION MAY BE GRANTED." Having been notified of the pendency and nature of the proceedings, as well as of the consequences of not attending, plaintiff, for reasons not disclosed in the complaint, did not attend the hearing. Nor did plaintiff seek to have the proceeding continued, in the event that he was unable to attend on the scheduled date for reasons outside his control. Accordingly, by failing to attend in person or by counsel, plaintiff waived his right to be present and be heard.

It is true that in some quasi-criminal, as well as criminal proceedings, a defendant's actual presence in court is deemed a constituent element of due process. *Specht* v. *Patterson*, 386 U.S. 605, 87 S.Ct. 1209, 18 L.Ed.2d 326 (1967). This, however, results in large measure from the force of the Sixth Amendment, as incorporated in the due process clause, which by its own terms applies only to criminal proceedings. Apart from *Specht*, which involved a special sentencing proceeding following on the heels of a criminal conviction, the Supreme Court has never held that a civil proceeding requires the presence of the respondent as an element of due process. We are unpersuaded that the Court would extend its *Specht* holding outside the quasi-criminal context in which it arose, notwithstanding the substantial liberty interests implicated by an incompetency proceeding. Accordingly, insofar as the plaintiff's complaint alleges that he was denied due process of law simply because the adjudication proceeded in his absence after he failed to attend, we hold that it fails to state a claim to relief.

## IV

We turn last to plaintiff's contention that the Illinois statutory scheme is constitutionally deficient because it does not require that a guardian ad litem be appointed to represent the alleged incompetent's rights at the hearing.

At the outset, it is essential to recognize that plaintiff is not claiming that the Illinois statutory scheme denies him the right to representation by counsel, if he chooses to be so represented. Nor are we dealing with an indigent unable to afford counsel, who requests the State to appoint one on his behalf. At least the complaint does not disclose any denial of a request for appointed counsel. Rather, plaintiff's complaint is that the State is constitutionally compelled to appoint counsel, whether or not the alleged incompetent requests such an appointment. In effect, plaintiff argues that no adjudication of incompetency can take place in the absence of counsel, or at least a valid waiver of the right to counsel.

Of all of plaintiff's arguments, this one has the most appeal, for, unlike the alleged constitutional requirement that the respondent actually be present at the hearing, the appointment of counsel in respondent's absence bears more directly on the accuracy of the fact-finding process. Moreover, the requirement that counsel be appointed or expressly waived before the adjudication takes place has been extended to certain civil proceedings. *In re Gault,* 387 U.S. 1, 87 S.Ct. 1428, 18 L.Ed.2d 527 (1967) (juvenile court proceeding); *Heryford* v. *Parker,* 396 F.2d 393, 396 (10th Cir. 1968) (involuntary commitment proceeding). However, notwithstanding the significant liberty interests implicated in an incompetency proceeding, we are unpersuaded that the presence of counsel is an essential element of due process at such a proceeding. First of all, the nature of the intrusion on liberty interests resulting from an adjudication of incompetency is far less severe than the intrusion resulting from other types of proceedings in which the presence of counsel has been mandated. Involuntary incarceration, for example, does not result from an incompetency proceeding. Moreover, the technical skills of an attorney are less important, as the procedural and evidentiary rules of an incompetency proceeding are considerably less strict than those applicable in other types of civil and criminal proceedings. Finally, the costs associated with the mandatory appointment of counsel will undermine one of the essential purposes of the proceeding itself—protection of the limited resources of the incompetent's estate from dissipation—for few alleged incompetents will be able to effect a "knowing and intelligent" waiver of undesired counsel. Accordingly, for these reasons and because we doubt that the presence of counsel is *essential* to protect the accuracy of the fact-finding process at incompetency hearings, we decline to require the mandatory appointment of counsel as an essential element of due process. We hold that plaintiff's allegation that the Illinois statutory scheme is unconstitutional because it does not mandate the appointment of counsel for alleged incompetents fails to state a claim to relief.

The district court's judgment is AFFIRMED.

NOTE

Do the notice and hearing requirements for guardianship set out by the court in *Rud* v. *Dahl* differ from those in other civil legal proceedings? Should they?

## IN RE KATIC

*Superior Court of Pennsylvania, 1982*
*439 A.2d 1235*

Before SPAETH, HESTER and SHERTZ, JJ.

SPAETH, Judge:

This is an appeal from an order appointing a guardian for a minor alleged to be incompetent. Since the order was entered *ex parte* and without notice or hearing, the lower court had no jurisdiction over the alleged incompetent. We therefore reverse and remand for further proceedings.

On May 23, 1980, C. Eugene Swiger, Executive Director of the Southwest Communities Mental Health and Mental Retardation Centers, filed a petition asking the lower court to appoint a guardian for the person of Raymond Katic. The petition alleged that Raymond was 13 years old; that he had been under Southwest Communities' supervision since September 1979, and had been "temporarily placed" with Victor and Marilyn Stahl as "host parents"; that he suffered from "profound mental retardation" and a severe hydrocephalus that might require operative procedures on short notice; that he was "so mentally defective and incompetent that he is unable to make proper decisions necessary for his health, safety and welfare, and is accordingly in need of a guardian of his person"; and that if an emergency operative procedure were necessary, his parents' consent could not be obtained because they lived in Oklahoma.

On June 9, 1980, the lower court, *ex parte,* and without notice to Raymond or a hearing, appointed Mr. Swiger guardian of Raymond's person and authorized and directed him "to consent to such necessary operative procedure" as the doctors in charge of Raymond might deem "in the best interests of protecting [Raymond's] health, safety and life."

On June 17, 1980, a request for reconsideration and preliminary injunction was filed on Raymond's behalf. On June 25, the lower court heard argument. It was argued that the order of June 9 should not have been issued without notice to Raymond and a hearing, and also, that the court should consider appointing the Stahls as Raymond's guardians as more personally interested in him and in a better position to make decisions about his welfare. At the conclusion of the argument the lower court denied the request for reconsideration and preliminary injunction, expressing the view that notice was not required. N.T. 6/25/80 at 5, and that "guardianship [should be] based on an agency rather than an individual," *id.,* at 22.

The Probate, Estates and Fiduciaries Code, Act of June 30, 1972, P.L. 508, No. 164, § 2, 20 Pa.C.S.A. § 101, *et seq.*, prescribes the procedure that must be followed before a court may find a person domiciled in Pennsylvania to be incompetent and appoint a guardian of his person or estate. The Code requires that "[n]otice of the petition and hearing shall be given in such manner as the court shall direct to the alleged incompetent . . . and to such other parties as the court may direct." 20 Pa.C. S.A. 5511(a). Thus, while the court may determine the *manner* of giving notice, it may not *dispense* with notice, which must be given to the alleged incompetent, before the hearing. If no notice is given, the court is without jurisdiction to enter a decree of incompetency. In *Hicks Estate*, 414 Pa. 131, 199 A.2d 283 (1964), the proceeding was under the Orphans' Court Act of 1951, P.L. 1163, 20 P.S. § 2080.704, which provided that jurisdiction of the person should be obtained by citation. The petition seeking to have the appellant declared incompetent and to have guardians appointed of her person and her estate did not pray for the issuance of a citation, and no citation was issued and served on the appellant, although her doctor read the petition to her. In reversing the decree of incompetency, the Supreme Court said:

> In the absence of service of citation upon appellant or general appearance on her behalf, all that transpired below was without jurisdiction over her person and was, therefore a nullity. The decree of incompetency, without actual jurisdiction over appellant lacks validity and binding effect. Accordingly, it was error to dismiss the petition and to refuse to vacate the adjudication of incompetency and the orders enlarging the record.

*Id.* at 135, 199 A.2d at 285.
*See also Rosini Estate,* 426 Pa. 220, 223, 232 A.2d 191 (1967).

We must therefore reverse and remand for further proceedings, to be conducted in accordance with the Probate Code.

It is so ordered.

NOTE

Is the underlying dispute here really about the absence of notice to Raymond Katic? What is at stake?

## 2. Right to Counsel and Guardian *ad Litem*

p. 592—DELETE the last sentence in the third full paragraph and replace it with the following:

The Seventh Circuit Court of Appeals has, however, reached a contrary result; see *Rud v. Dahl,* 578 F.2d 674 (7th Cir. 1978), pp. 215–220 above.

## 3. Presence of the Allegedly Incompetent Person at the Hearing

p. 593—ADD to the end of the first paragraph of Subsection 3:

See, however, *Rud v. Dahl,* 578 F.2d 674 (7th Cir. 1978), pp. 215–220 above, where the presence of the alleged incompetent person is held to be unnecessary where the person apparently chooses not to attend.

## 5. Standard of Proof

p. 598—ADD the following to the end of Subsection 5 at the top of the page:

On the other hand, the Supreme Judicial Court of Massachusetts has held that a "preponderance of the evidence" standard should be applied in guardianship proceedings, *In re Guardianship of Roe,* \_\_\_\_ Mass. \_\_\_\_, 421 N.E.2d 40, 47 (1981).

# 6

# FREEDOM FROM RESIDENTIAL CONFINEMENT

Robert L. Burgdorf Jr.

## SUMMARY OF DOCTRINAL DEVELOPMENTS

ISSUES RELATING TO THE CONFINEMENT OF HANDICAPPED PERSONS in residential institutions have been the subject of a great deal of attention by the United States Supreme Court. While several of these cases have significant implications, perhaps the most momentous in the long run may be the Court's decision in *Youngberg* v. *Romeo* (pp. 223–235), because of its indication of the Court's direction on the long-debated issue of a constitutional right to treatment.

## B. RATIONALE FOR CONFINEMENT

p. 640—INSERT before the beginning of Section C:

YOUNGBERG v. ROMEO

*Supreme Court of the United States, 1982*
____ *U.S.* ____, *102 S.Ct. 2452*

Justice POWELL delivered the opinion of the Court.

The question presented is whether respondent, involuntarily committed to a state institution for the mentally retarded, has substantive rights under the Due Process Clause of the Fourteenth Amendment to (i) safe conditions of confinement; (ii) freedom from bodily restraints; and (iii) training or "habilitation."[1] Respondent sued under 42 U.S.C. § 1983 three administrators of the institution, claiming damages for the alleged breach of his constitutional rights.

I

Respondent Nicholas Romeo is profoundly retarded. Although 33 years old, he has the mental capacity of an eighteen-month old child, with an I.Q. between 8 and 10.

---

[1]The American Psychiatric Association explains that "[t]he word 'habilitation,' . . . is commonly used to refer to programs for the mentally-retarded because mental retardation is . . . a learning disability and training impairment rather than an illness. . . . [T]he principal focus of habilitation is upon training and development of needed skills." Brief of American Psychiatric Association as *Amicus Curiae*, at 4, n. 1.

He cannot talk and lacks the most basic self-care skills. Until he was 26, respondent lived with his parents in Philadelphia. But after the death of his father in May 1974, his mother was unable to care for him. Within two weeks of the father's death, respondent's mother sought his temporary admission to a nearby Pennsylvania hospital.

Shortly thereafter, she asked the Philadelphia County Court of Common Pleas to admit Romeo to a state facility on a permanent basis. Her petition to the court explained that she was unable to care for Romeo or control his violence.[2] As part of the commitment process, Romeo was examined by a physician and a psychologist. They both certified that respondent was severely retarded and unable to care for himself. App. 21–22 and 28–29. On June 11, 1974, the Court of Common Pleas committed respondent to the Pennhurst State School and Hospital, pursuant to the applicable involuntary commitment provision of the Pennsylvania Mental Health and Mental Retardation Act, Pa.Stat.Ann. tit. 50 § 4406.

At Pennhurst, Romeo was injured on numerous occasions, both by his own violence and by the reactions of other residents to him. Respondent's mother became concerned about these injuries. After objecting to respondent's treatment several times, she filed this complaint on November 4, 1976, in the United States District Court for the Eastern District of Pennsylvania as his next friend. The complaint alleged that "[d]uring the period July, 1974 to the present, plaintiff has suffered injuries on at least sixty-three occasions." The complaint originally sought damages and injunctive relief from Pennhurst's director and two supervisors; it alleged that these officials knew, or should have known, that Romeo was suffering injuries and that they failed to institute appropriate preventive procedures, thus violating his rights under the Eighth and Fourteenth Amendments.

Thereafter, in late 1976, Romeo was transferred from his ward to the hospital for treatment of a broken arm. While in the infirmary, and by order of a doctor, he was physically restrained during portions of each day.[4] These restraints were ordered by Dr. Gabroy, not a defendant here, to protect Romeo and others in the hospital, some of whom were in traction or were being treated intravenously. 7 Record 40, 49, 76–78. Although respondent normally would have returned to his ward when his arm healed, the parties to this litigation agreed that he should remain in the hospital due to the pending law suit. 5 Record 248, 6 R. 57–58 and 137. Nevertheless, in December 1977, a second amended complaint was filed alleging that the defendants were restraining respondent for prolonged periods on a routine basis. The second amended complaint also added a claim for damages to compensate Romeo for the defendants' failure to provide him with appropriate "treatment or programs for his mental retardation." All claims for injunctive relief were dropped prior to trial because respondent is a member of the class seeking such relief in another action.[6]

An eight-day jury trial was held in April 1978. Petitioners introduced evidence

---

[2]Mrs. Romeo's petition to the Court of Common Pleas stated: "Since my husband's death I am unable to handle him. He becomes violent—kicks, punches, breaks glass; He can't speak—wants to express himself but can't. He is [a] constant 24 hr. care. [W]ithout my husband I am unable to care for him." App. 18.

[4]Although the Court of Appeals described these restraints as "shackles," "soft" restraints, for the arms only, were generally used. 7 Record 53–55.

[6]*Pennhurst State School and Hospital* v. *Halderman*, 451 U.S. 1, 101 S.Ct. 1531, 67 L.Ed.2d 694 (1981) (remanded for further proceedings).

that respondent participated in several programs teaching basic self-care skills. A comprehensive behavior-modification program was designed by staff members to reduce Romeo's aggressive behavior, but that program was never implemented because of his mother's objections. Respondent introduced evidence of his injuries and of conditions in his unit.[10]

At the close of the trial, the court instructed the jury that "if any or all of the defendants were aware of and failed to take all reasonable steps to prevent repeated attacks upon Nicholas Romeo," such failure deprived him of constitutional rights. App. to Pet. for Cert. 110. The jury also was instructed that if the defendants shackled Romeo or denied him treatment "as a punishment for filing this lawsuit," his constitutional rights were violated under the Eighth Amendment. *Id.*, at 73–75. Finally, the jury was instructed that only if they found the defendants "deliberately indifferent to the serious medical [and psychological] needs" of Romeo could they find that his Eighth and Fourteenth Amendment rights had been violated. *Id.*, 15 111–112. The jury returned a verdict for the defendants, on which judgment was entered.

The Court of Appeals for the Third Circuit, sitting en banc, reversed and remanded for a new trial. 644 F.2d 147 (1980). The court held that the Eighth Amendment, prohibiting cruel and unusual punishment of those convicted of crimes, was not an appropriate source for determining the rights of the involuntarily committed. Rather, the Fourteenth Amendment and the liberty interest protected by that amendment provided the proper constitutional basis for these rights. In applying the Fourteenth Amendment, the court found that the involuntarily committed retain liberty interests in freedom of movement and in personal security. These were "fundamental liberties" that can be limited only by an "overriding, non-punitive" state interest. 644 F.2d, at 157–158 (footnote omitted). It further found that the involuntarily committed have a liberty interest in habilitation designed to "treat" their mental retardation. *Id.*, at 164–170.[12]

The en banc court did not, however, agree on the relevant standard to be used in determining whether Romeo's rights had been violated. Because physical restraint "raises a presumption of a punitive sanction," the majority of the Court of Appeals concluded that it can be justified only by "compelling necessity." *Id.*, at 159–160. A somewhat different standard was appropriate for the failure to provide for a resident's safety. The majority considered that such a failure must be justified by a showing of "substantial necessity." *Id.*, at 164. Finally, the majority held that when treatment has been administered, those responsible are liable only if the treatment is not "acceptable in light of present medical or other scientific knowledge." *Id.*, at 166–167 and 173.[14]

---

[10]The District Judge refused to allow testimony by two of Romeo's witnesses—trained professionals—indicating that Romeo would have benefitted from more or different training programs. The trial judge explained that evidence of the advantages of alternative forms of treatment might be relevant to a malpractice suit, but was not relevant to a constitutional claim under § 1983. App. to Pet. for Cert. 101.

[12]The Court of Appeals used "habilitation" and "treatment" as synonymous, though it regarded "habilitation" as more accurate in describing treatment needed by the mentally retarded. See 644 F.2d, at 165 and n. 40.

[14]Actually, the court divided the right-to-treatment claim into three categories and adopted three standards, but only the standard described in text is at issue before this Court. The Court of Appeals also stated that if a jury finds that *no* treatment has been administered, it may hold the institution's administrators

Chief Judge Seitz, concurring in the judgment, considered the standards articulated by the majority as indistinguishable from those applicable to medical malpractice claims. In Chief Judge Seitz's view, the Constitution "only requires that the courts make certain that professional judgment in fact was exercised." 644 F.2d, at 178. He concluded that the appropriate standard was whether the defendants' conduct was "such a substantial departure from accepted professional judgment, practice or standards in the care and treatment of this plaintiff as to demonstrate that the defendants did not base their conduct on a professional judgment." 644 F.2d, at 178.

We granted the petition for certiorari because of the importance of the question presented to the administration of state institutions for the mentally retarded. 451 U.S. 982, 101 S.Ct. 2313, 68 L.Ed.2d 838 (1981).

## II

We consider here for the first time the substantive rights of involuntarily-committed mentally retarded persons under the Fourteenth Amendment to the Constitution. In this case, respondent has been committed under the laws of Pennsylvania, and he does not challenge the commitment. Rather, he argues that he has a constitutionally protected liberty interest in safety, freedom of movement, and training within the institution; and that petitioners infringed these rights by failing to provide constitutionally required conditions of confinement.

The mere fact that Romeo has been committed under proper procedures does not deprive him of all substantive liberty interests under the Fourteenth Amendment. See, e.g., Vitek v. Jones, 445 U.S. 480, 491–494, 100 S.Ct. 1254, 1262–1264, 63 L.Ed.2d 552 (1980). Indeed, the state concedes that respondent has a right to adequate food, shelter, clothing, and medical care. We must decide whether liberty interests also exist in safety, freedom of movement, and training. If such interests do exist, we must further decide whether they have been infringed in this case.

## A

Respondent's first two claims involve liberty interests recognized by prior decisions of this Court, interests that involuntary commitment proceedings do not extinguish. The first is a claim to safe conditions. In the past, this Court has noted that the right to personal security constitutes an "historic liberty interest" protected substantively by the Due Process Clause. Ingraham v. Wright, 430 U.S. 651, 673, 97 S.Ct. 1401, 1413, 51 L.Ed.2d 711 (1977). And that right is not extinguished by lawful confinement, even for penal purposes. See Hutto v. Finney, 437 U.S. 678, 98 S.Ct. 2565, 57 L.Ed.2d 522 (1978). If it is cruel and unusual punishment to hold convicted criminals in unsafe conditions, it must be unconstitutional to confine the involuntarily committed—who may not be punished at all—in unsafe conditions.

---

liable unless they can provide a compelling explanation for the lack of treatment, 644 F.2d at 165, 173, but respondent does not discuss this precise standard in his brief and it does not appear to be relevant to the facts of this case. In addition, the court considered "least intrusive" analysis appropriate to justify severe intrusions on individual dignity such as permanent physical alteration or surgical intervention, id., at 165–166, and 173, but respondent concedes that this issue is not present in this case.

Next, respondent claims a right to freedom from bodily restraint. In other contexts, the existence of such an interest is clear in the prior decisions of this Court. Indeed, "[l]iberty from bodily restraint always has been recognized as the core of the liberty protected by the Due Process Clause from arbitrary governmental action." *Greenholtz* v. *Nebraska Penal Inmates,* 442 U.S. 1, 18, 99 S.Ct. 2100, 2109, 60 L.Ed.2d 668 (1979) (POWELL, J., concurring). This interest survives criminal conviction and incarceration. Similarly, it must also survive involuntary commitment.

## B

Respondent's remaining claim is more troubling. In his words, he asserts a "constitutional right to minimally adequate habilitation." Brief, 8, 23, 45. This is a substantive due process claim that is said to be grounded in the liberty component of the Due Process Clause of the Fourteenth Amendment. The term "habilitation," used in psychiatry, is not defined precisely or consistently in the opinions below or in the briefs of the parties or the amici.[20] As noted previously, at n. 1, *supra,* the term refers to "training and development of needed skills." Respondent emphasizes that the right he asserts is for "minimal" training, see Brief or Respondent at 34, and he would leave the type and extent of training to be determined on a case-by-case basis "in light of present medical or other scientific knowledge," *id.,* at 45.

In addressing the asserted right to training, we start from established principles. As a general matter, a State is under no constitutional duty to provide substantive services for those within its border. See, *Harris* v. *McRae,* 448 U.S. 297, 318, 100 S.Ct. 2671, 2689, 65 L.Ed.2d 784 (1980) (publicly funded abortions); *Maher* v. *Roe,* 432 U.S. 464, 469, 97 S.Ct. 2376, 2380, 53 L.Ed.2d 484 (1977) (medical treatment). When a person is institutionalized—and wholly dependent on the State—it is conceded by petitioner that a duty to provide certain services and care does exist, although even then a State necessarily has considerable discretion in determining the nature and scope of its responsibilities. See *Richardson* v. *Belcher,* 404 U.S. 78, 83–84, 92 S.Ct. 254, 258–259, 30 L.Ed.2d 231 (1971); *Dandridge* v. *Williams,* 397 U.S. 471, 478, 90 S.Ct. 1153, 1158, 25 L.Ed.2d 491 (1970). Nor must a State "choose between attacking every aspect of a problem or not attacking the problem at all." *Id.,* at 486–487, 90 S.Ct., at 1162–1163.

Respondent, in light of the severe character of his retardation, concedes that no amount of training will make possible his release. And he does not argue that if he were still at home, the State would have an obligation to provide training at its expense. See Tr. of Oral Arg. 33. The record reveals that respondent's primary needs are bodily safety and a minimum of physical restraint, and respondent clearly claims training

---

[20]Professionals in the habilitation of the mentally retarded disagree strongly on the question whether effective training of all severely or profoundly retarded individuals is even possible. See, *e.g.,* Favell, Risley, Wolfe, Riddle, & Rasmussen, The Limits of Habilitation: How Can We Identify Them and How Can We Change Them?, 1 Analysis and Intervention in Developmental Disabilities 37 (1981); Bailey, Wanted: A Rational Search for the Limiting Conditions of Habilitation in the Retarded, 1 Analysis and Intervention in Developmental Disabilities 45 (1981); Kauffman & Krouse, The Cult of Educability: Searching for the Substance of Things Hoped For; The Evidence of Things Not Seen, 1 Analysis and Intervention in Developmental Disabilities 53 (1981).

related to these needs. As we have recognized that there is a constitutionally protected liberty interest in safety and freedom from restraint, *supra*, at 2458, training may be necessary to avoid unconstitutional infringement of those rights. On the basis of the record before us, it is quite uncertain whether respondent seeks any "habilitation" or training unrelated to safety and freedom from bodily restraints. In his brief to this Court, Romeo indicates that even the self-care programs he seeks are needed to reduce his aggressive behavior. See Reply Brief of Respondent at 21–22, 50. And in his offer of proof to the trial court, respondent repeatedly indicated that, if allowed to testify, his experts would show that additional training programs, including self-care programs, were needed to reduce Romeo's aggressive behavior. Petition for Certiorari 98–104. If, as seems the case, respondent seeks only training related to safety and freedom from restraints, this case does not present the difficult question whether a mentally retarded person, involuntarily committed to a state institution, has some general constitutional right to training *per se*, even when no type or amount of training would lead to freedom.[23]

Chief Judge Seitz, in language apparently adopted by respondent, observed:

> I believe that the plaintiff has a constitutional right to minimally adequate care and treatment. The existence of a constitutional right to care and treatment is no longer a novel legal proposition. 644 F.2d 176 (Pet. 54).

Chief Judge Seitz did not identify or otherwise define—beyond the right to reasonable safety and freedom from physical restraint—the "minimally adequate care and treatment" that appropriately may be required for this respondent. In the circumstances presented by this case, and on the basis of the record developed to date, we agree with his view and conclude that respondent's liberty interests require the State to provide minimally adequate or reasonable training to ensure safety and freedom from undue restraint. In view of the kinds of treatment sought by respondent and the evidence of record, we need go no further in this case.[25]

---

[23]In the trial court, respondent asserted that "state officials at a state mental hospital have a duty to provide residents . . . with such treatment as will afford them a reasonable opportunity to acquire and maintain those life skills necessary to cope as effectively as their capacities permit." App. to Pet. for Cert. 94–95. But this claim to a sweeping *per se* right was dropped thereafter. In his brief to this Court, respondent does not repeat it and, at oral argument, respondent's counsel explicitly disavowed any claim that respondent is constitutionally entitled to such treatment as would enable him "to achieve his maximum potential." Tr. of Oral Arg. 46–48.

[25]It is not feasible, as is evident from the variety of language and formulations in the opinions below and the various briefs here, to define or identify the type of training that may be required in every case. A court properly may start with the generalization that there is a right to minimally adequate training. The basic requirement of adequacy, in terms more familiar to courts, may be stated as that training which is reasonable in light of identifiable liberty interests and the circumstances of the case. A federal court, of course, must identify a constitutional predicate for the imposition of any affirmative duty on a state.

Because the facts in cases of confinement of mentally retarded patients vary widely, it is essential to focus on the facts and circumstances of the case before a court. Judge Aldisert, in his dissenting opinion in the court below, was critical of the "majority's abandonment of incremental decision-making in favor of promulgation of broad standards . . . [that] lack[] utility for the groups most affected by this decision." 644 F.2d, at 183–184. Judge Garth agreed that reaching issues not presented by the case requires a court to articulate principles and rules of law in "the absence of an appropriate record . . . and without the benefit of analysis, argument or briefing" on such issues. *Id.*, at 186.

### III

#### A

We have established that Romeo retains liberty interests in safety and freedom from bodily restraint. Yet these interests are not absolute; indeed to some extent they are in conflict. In operating an institution such as Pennhurst, there are occasions in which it is necessary for the State to restrain the movement of residents—for example, to protect them as well as others from violence.[26] Similar restraints may also be appropriate in a training program. And an institution cannot protect its residents from all danger of violence if it is to permit them to have any freedom of movement. The question then is not simply whether a liberty interest has been infringed but whether the extent or nature of the restraint or lack of absolute safety is such as to violate due process.

In determining whether a substantive right protected by the Due Process Clause has been violated, it is necessary to balance "the liberty of the individual" and "the demands of an organized society." *Poe* v. *Ullman*, 367 U.S. 497, 522, 542, 81 S.Ct. 1752, 1765–1766, 1776, 6 L.Ed.2d 989 (1961) (Harlan, J., dissenting). In seeking this balance in other cases, the Court has weighed the individual's interest in liberty against the State's asserted reasons for restraining individual liberty. In *Bell* v. *Wolfish*, 441 U.S. 520, 99 S.Ct. 1861, 60 L.Ed.2d 447 (1979), for example, we considered a challenge to pre-trial detainees' confinement conditions. We agreed that the detainees, not yet convicted of the crime charged, could not be punished. But we upheld those restrictions on liberty that were reasonably related to legitimate government objectives and not tantamount to punishment.[27] See *id.*, at 539, 99 S.Ct., at 1874. We have taken a similar approach in deciding procedural due-process challenges to civil commitment proceedings. In *Parham* v. *J. R.*, 442 U.S. 584, 99 S.Ct. 2493, 61 L.Ed.2d 101 (1979), for example, we considered a challenge to state procedures for commitment of a minor with parental consent. In determining that *procedural* due process did not mandate an adversarial hearing, we weighed the liberty interest of the individual against the legitimate interests of the State, including the fiscal and administrative burdens additional procedures would entail.[28] *Id.*, at 599–600, 99 S.Ct., at 2502–2503.

---

[26]In Romeo's case, there can be no question that physical restraint was necessary at times. See n. 2, *supra*.

[27]See also *Jackson* v. *Indiana*, 406 U.S. 715, 738, 192 S.Ct. 1845, 1858, 32 L.Ed.2d 435 (1972) (holding that an incompetent pre-trial detainee cannot, after a competency hearing, be held indefinitely without either criminal process or civil commitment; due process requires, at a minimum, some rational relation between the nature and duration of commitment and its purpose). This case differs in critical respects from *Jackson,* a procedural due process case involving the validity of an involuntary commitment. Here, petitioner was committed by a court on petition of his mother who averred that in view of Romeo's condition she could neither care for him nor control his violence. *Ante*, at 2455. Thus, the purpose of petitioner's commitment was to provide reasonable care and safety, conditions not available to him outside of an institution.

[28]See also *Addington* v. *Texas*, 441 U.S. 418, 99 S.Ct. 1804, 60 L.Ed.2d 323 (1979). In that case, we held that the state must prove the need for commitment by "clear and convincing" evidence. See *id.*, at 431–432, 99 S.Ct., at 1812–1813. We reached this decision by weighing the individual's liberty interest against the state's legitimate interests in confinement.

Accordingly, whether respondent's constitutional rights have been violated must be determined by balancing his liberty interests against the relevant state interests. If there is to be any uniformity in protecting these interests, this balancing cannot be left to the unguided discretion of a judge or jury. We therefore turn to consider the proper standard for determining whether a State adequately has protected the rights of the involuntarily-committed mentally retarded.

B

We think the standard articulated by Chief Judge Seitz affords the necessary guidance and reflects the proper balance between the legitimate interests of the State and the rights of the involuntarily committed to reasonable conditions of safety and freedom from unreasonable restraints. He would have held that "the Constitution only requires that the courts make certain that professional judgment in fact was exercised. It is not appropriate for the courts to specify which of several professionally acceptable choices should have been made." 644 F.2d, at 178. Persons who have been involuntarily committed are entitled to more considerate treatment and conditions of confinement than criminals whose conditions of confinement are designed to punish. Cf. *Estelle* v. *Gamble,* 429 U.S. 97, 104, 97 S.Ct. 285, 291, 50 L.Ed.2d 251 (1976). At the same time, this standard is lower than the "compelling" or "substantial" necessity tests the Court of Appeals would require a state to meet to justify use of restraints or conditions of less than absolute safety. We think this requirement would place an undue burden on the administration of institutions such as Pennhurst and also would restrict unnecessarily the exercise of professional judgment as to the needs of residents.

Moreover, we agree that respondent is entitled to minimally adequate training. In this case, the minimally adequate training required by the Constitution is such training as may be reasonable in light of respondent's liberty interests in safety and freedom from unreasonable restraints. In determining what is "reasonable"—in this and in any case presenting a claim for training by a state—we emphasize that courts must show deference to the judgment exercised by a qualified professional. By so limiting judicial review of challenges to conditions in state institutions, interference by the federal judiciary with the internal operations of these institutions should be minimized.[29] Moreover, there certainly is no reason to think judges or juries are better

---

[29]See *Parham* v. *J. R., supra,* 442 U.S., at 608 n. 16, 99 S.Ct., at 2507 n. 16 (In limiting judicial review of medical decisions made by professionals, "it is incumbent on courts to design procedures that protect the rights of individuals without unduly burdening the legitimate efforts of the states to deal with difficult social problems."). See also *Rhodes* v. *Chapman,* 452 U.S. 337, 101 S.Ct. 2392, 69 L.Ed.2d 59 (1981) ("[C]ourts cannot assume that state legislatures and prison officials are insensitive to the requirements of the Constitution or to the perplexing sociological problems of how best to achieve the goals of the penal function in the criminal justice system. . . ."); *Bell* v. *Wolfish,* 441 U.S. 520, 539, 99 S.Ct. 1861, 1874, 60 L.Ed.2d 447 (1979) (In context of conditions of confinement of pre-trial detainees, "courts must be mindful that these inquiries spring from constitutional requirements and that judicial answers to them must reflect that fact rather than a court's idea of how best to operate a detention facility."); *Wolff* v. *McDonnell,* 418 U.S. 539, 556, 94 S.Ct. 2963, 2974–2975, 41 L.Ed.2d 935 (1974) (In considering procedural due process claim in context of prison, "there must be mutual accommodation between institutional needs of objectives and the provisions of the Constitution that are of general application."). See also Townsend & Mattson, The Interaction of Law and Special Education: Observing the Emperor's New Clothes, 1 Analysis and Intervention in Developmental Disabilities 75 (1981) (judicial resolution of rights of the handicapped can have adverse as well as positive effects on social change).

qualified than appropriate professionals in making such decisions. See *Parham* v. *J. R.*, 442 U.S. 584, 607, 99 S.Ct. 2493, 2506–2507, 61 L.Ed.2d 101 (1979); *Bell* v. *Wolfish, supra,* 441 U.S., at 544, 99 S.Ct., at 1877 (Courts should not " 'second-guess the expert administrators on matters on which they are better informed.' "). For these reasons, the decision, if made by a professional,[30] is presumptively valid; liability may be imposed only when the decision by the professional is such a substantial departure from accepted professional judgment, practice or standards as to demonstrate that the person responsible actually did not base the decision on such a judgment.[31] In an action for damages against a professional in his individual capacity, however, the professional will not be liable if he was unable to satisfy his normal professional standards because of budgetary constraints; in such a situation, good-faith immunity would bar liability. See note 12, *supra.*

## IV

In deciding this case, we have weighed these post-commitment interests cognizable as liberty interests under the Due Process Clause of the Fourteenth Amendment against legitimate state interests and in light of the constraints under which most state institutions necessarily operate. We repeat that the state concedes a duty to provide adequate food, shelter, clothing and medical care. These are the essentials of the care that the state must provide. The state also has the unquestioned duty to provide reasonable safety for all residents and personnel within the institution. And it may not restrain residents except when and to the extent professional judgment deems this necessary to assure such safety or to provide needed training. In this case, therefore, the state is under a duty to provide respondent with such training as an appropriate professional would consider reasonable to ensure his safety and to facilitate his ability to function free from bodily restraints. It may well be unreasonable not to provide training when training could significantly reduce the need for restraints or the likelihood of violence.

Respondent thus enjoys constitutionally protected interests in conditions of reasonable care and safety, reasonably non-restrictive confinement conditions, and such training as may be required by these interests. Such conditions of confinement would comport fully with the purpose of respondent's commitment. Cf. *Jackson* v. *Indiana,* 406 U.S. 715, 738, 92 S.Ct. 1845, 1858, 32 L.Ed.2d 435 (1972); see n. 27, *ante.* In determining whether the state has met its obligations in these respects, decisions made by the appropriate professional are entitled to a presumption of correctness. Such a presumption is necessary to enable institutions of this type—often, unfortunately, overcrowded and understaffed—to continue to function. A single professional may

---

[30]By "professional" decision-maker, we mean a person competent, whether by education, training or experience, to make the particular decision at issue. Long term treatment decisions normally should be made by persons with degrees in medicine or nursing, or with appropriate training in areas such as psychology, physical therapy, or the care and training of the retarded. Of course, day-to-day decisions regarding care—including decisions that must be made without delay—necessarily will be made in many instances by employees without formal training but who are subject to the supervision of qualified persons.

[31]All members of the Court of Appeals agreed that respondent's expert testimony should have been admitted. This issue was not included in the questions presented for certiorari, and we have no reason to disagree with the view that the evidence was admissible. It may be relevant to whether petitioners' decisions were a substantial departure from the requisite professional judgment. See Part III B, *supra.*

have to make decisions with respect to a number of residents with widely varying needs and problems in the course of a normal day. The administrators, and particularly professional personnel, should not be required to make each decision in the shadow of an action for damages.

In this case, we conclude that the jury was erroneously instructed on the assumption that the proper standard of liability was that of the Eighth Amendment. Accordingly, we vacate the decision of the Court of Appeals and remand for further proceedings consistent with this decision.

*So ordered.*

Justice BLACKMUN, with whom Justice BRENNAN and Justice O'CONNOR join, concurring.

I join the Court's opinion. I write separately, however, to make clear why I believe that opinion properly leaves unresolved two difficult and important issues. The first is whether the Commonwealth of Pennsylvania could accept respondent for "care and treatment," as it did under the Pennsylvania Mental Health and Mental Retardation Act of 1966, Pa.Stat.Ann., Tit. 50, § 4406(b) (Purdon), and then constitutionally refuse to provide him any "treatment," as that term is defined by state law. Were that question properly before us, in my view there would be a serious issue whether, as a matter of due process, the State could so refuse. I therefore do not find that issue to be a "frivolous" one, as THE CHIEF JUSTICE does, *post,* at 2466, n. *.[1]

In *Jackson* v. *Indiana,* 406 U.S. 715, 92 S.Ct. 1845, 32 L.Ed.2d 435 (1972), this Court, by a unanimous vote of all participating Justices, suggested a constitutional standard for evaluating the conditions of a civilly-committed person's confinement: "At the least, due process requires that the nature and duration of commitment bear some reasonable relation to the purpose for which the individual is committed." *Id.,* at 738, 92 S.Ct., at 1858. Under this standard, a State could accept a person for "safekeeping," then constitutionally refuse to provide him treatment. In such a case, commitment without treatment would bear a reasonable relation to the goal for which the person was confined.

If a state court orders a mentally retarded person committed for "care *and* treatment," however, I believe that due process might well bind the State to ensure that the conditions of his commitment bear some reasonable relation to each of those goals. In such a case, commitment without any "treatment" whatsoever would not bear a reasonable relation to the purposes of the person's confinement.

In respondent's case, the majority and principal concurring opinions in the Court of Appeals agreed that "[b]y basing [respondent's] deprivation of liberty at least partially upon a promise of treatment, the state ineluctably has committed the community's resources to providing minimal treatment." 644 F.2d 147, 168 (CA3 1980).[2] Neither opinion clarified, however, whether respondent in fact had been totally denied

---

[1] See also Garvey, Freedom and Choice in Constitutional Law, 94 Harv.L.Rev. 1756, 1787–1791 (1981); *Welsch* v. *Likins,* 550 F.2d 1122, 1126, and n. 6 (CA8 1977); *Wyatt* v. *Aderholt,* 503 F.2d 1305 (CA5 1974), aff'g *Wyatt* v. *Stickney,* 325 F.Supp. 781, 785 (MD Ala.1971).

[2] In the principal concurring opinion, Chief Judge Seitz, for himself and three other judges, stated:

The state does not contest that it has placed the [respondent] in Pennhurst to provide basic care and treatment. Indeed, he has a right to treatment under state law, . . . and the fact that Pennhurst has programs and staff to "treatment," as that term is defined under Pennsylvania law. To the extent that the majority addressed the question, it found that "the evidence in the record, although somewhat contradictory, suggests not so much a total failure to treat as an inadequacy of treatment." *Ibid.*

This Court's reading of the record, *ante,* at 2455–2456, and n.7, supports that conclusion. Moreover, the Court today finds that respondent's entitlement to "treatment" under Pennsylvania law was not properly raised below. See *ante,* at 2458, n. 19. Given this uncertainty in the record, I am in accord with the Court's decision not to address the constitutionality of a State's total failure to provide "treatment" to an individual committed under state law for "care and treatment."

The second difficult question left open today is whether respondent has an independent constitutional claim, grounded in the Due Process Clause of the Fourteenth Amendment, to that "habilitation" or training necessary to *preserve* those basic self-care skills he possessed when he first entered Pennhurst—for example, the ability to dress himself and care for his personal hygiene. In my view, it would be consistent with the Court's reasoning today to include within the "minimally adequate training required by the Constitution," *ante,* at 2461, such training as is reasonably necessary to prevent a person's pre-existing self-care skills from *deteriorating* because of his commitment.

The Court makes clear, *ante,* at 2457–2458, and 2462–2463, that even after a person is committed to a state institution, he is entitled to such training as is necessary to prevent unreasonable losses of additional liberty as a result of his confinement—for example, unreasonable bodily restraints or unsafe institutional conditions. If a person could demonstrate that he entered a state institution with minimal self-care skills, but lost those skills after commitment because of the State's unreasonable refusal to provide him training, then, it seems to me, he has alleged a loss of liberty quite distinct from—and as serious as—the loss of safety and freedom from unreasonable restraints. For many mentally retarded people, the difference between the capacity to do things for themselves within an institution and total dependence on the institution for all of their needs is as much liberty as they ever will know.

Although respondent asserts a claim of this kind, I agree with the Court that "[o]n the basis of the record before us, it is quite uncertain whether respondent [in fact] seeks any 'habilitation' or training unrelated to safety and freedom from bodily restraints." *Ante,* at 2459. Since the Court finds respondent constitutionally entitled at least to "such training as may be reasonable in light of [his] liberty interests in safety and freedom from unreasonable restraints," *ante,* at 2461, I accept its decision not to address respondent's additional claim.

If respondent actually seeks habilitation in self-care skills not merely to reduce his aggressive tendencies, but also to maintain those basic self-care skills necessary to his personal autonomy within Pennhurst, I believe he is free on remand to assert that claim. Like the Court, I would be willing to defer to the judgment of professionals as to whether or not, and to what extent, institutional training would preserve respondent's

---

treat patients is indicative of such a purpose. I believe that when the purpose of confining a mentally retarded person is to provide care and treatment, as is undoubtedly the case here, it violates the due process clause to fail to fulfill that purpose.    644 F.2d 147, 176 (CA3 1980).

pre-existing skills. Cf. *ante*, at 2461–2462. As the Court properly notes, "[p]rofessionals in the habilitation of the mentally retarded disagree strongly on the question whether effective training of all severely or profoundly retarded individuals is even possible." *Ante*, at 2458, n. 20.

If expert testimony reveals that respondent was so retarded when he entered the institution that he had no basic self-care skills to preserve, or that institutional training would not have preserved whatever skills he did have, then I would agree that he suffered no additional loss of liberty even if petitioners failed to provide him training. But if the testimony establishes that respondent possessed certain basic self-care skills when he entered the institution, and was sufficiently educable that he could have maintained those skills with a certain degree of training, then I would be prepared to listen seriously to an argument that petitioners were constitutionally required to provide that training, even if respondent's safety and mobility were not imminently threatened by their failure to do so.

The Court finds it premature to resolve this constitutional question on this less-than-fully-developed record. Because I agree with that conclusion, I concur in the Court's opinion.

Chief Justice BURGER, concurring in the judgment.

I agree with much of the Court's opinion. However, I would hold flatly that respondent has no constitutional right to training, or "habilitation," *per se*. The parties, and the Court, acknowledge that respondent cannot function outside the state institution, even with the assistance of relatives. Indeed, even now neither respondent nor his family seeks his discharge from state care. Under these circumstances, the State's provision of food, shelter, medical care, and living conditions as safe as the inherent nature of the institutional environment reasonably allows, serve to justify the State's custody of respondent. The State did not seek custody of respondent; his family understandably sought the State's aid to meet a serious need.

I agree with the Court that some amount of self-care instruction may be necessary to avoid unreasonable infringement of a mentally-retarded person's interests in safety and freedom from restraint; but it seems clear to me that the Constitution does not otherwise place an affirmative duty on the State to provide any particular kind of training or habilitation—even such as might be encompassed under the essentially standardless rubric "minimally adequate training," to which the Court refers. See *ante*, at 2460 and n. 24. Cf. *Romeo* v. *Youngberg*, 644 F.2d 147, 176 (CA3 1980) (C. J. Seitz, concurring). Since respondent asserts a right to "minimally adequate" habilitation "[q]uite apart from its relationship to decent care," Brief for Respondent 23, unlike the Court I see no way to avoid the issue.* Cf. *ante*, at 2460.

---

*Indeed, in the trial court respondent asserted a broad claim to such "treatment as [would] afford [him] a reasonable opportunity to acquire and maintain those life skills necessary to cope as effectively as [his] capacities permit." Petn. for Cert. 94a.

Respondent also maintains that, because state law purportedly creates a right to "care and treatment," he has a *federal substantive* right under the Due Process Clause to enforcement of this state right. See *ante*, at 2458, n. 19. This contention is obviously frivolous; were every substantive right created by state law enforceable under the Due Process Clause, the distinction between state and federal law would quickly be obliterated.

I also point out that, under the Court's own standards, it is largely irrelevant whether respondent's experts were of the opinion that "additional training programs, including self-care programs, were needed to reduce [respondent's] aggressive behavior," *ante,* at 2459—a prescription far easier for "spectators" to give than for an institution to implement. The training program devised for respondent by petitioners and other professionals at Pennhurst was, according to the Court's opinion, "presumptively valid"; and "liability may be imposed only when the decision by the professional is such a substantial departure from accepted professional judgment, practice or standards as to demonstrate that the person responsible actually did not base the decision on such a judgment." *Ante,* at 2462. Thus, even if respondent could demonstrate that the training programs at Pennhurst were inconsistent with generally accepted or prevailing professional practice—if indeed there be such—this would not avail him so long as his training regimen was actually prescribed by the institution's professional staff.

Finally, it is worth noting that the District Court's instructions in this case were on the whole consistent with the Court's opinion today; indeed, some instructions may have been overly generous to respondent. Although the District Court erred in giving an instruction incorporating an Eighth Amendment "deliberate indifference" standard, the court also instructed, for example, that petitioners could be held liable if they "were aware of and failed to take all reasonable steps to prevent repeated attacks upon" respondent. See *ante,* at 2456. Certainly if petitioners took "*all* reasonable steps" to prevent attacks on respondent, they cannot be said to have deprived him either of reasonably safe conditions or of training necessary to achieve reasonable safety.

NOTES

1. In light of the majority opinion and the other concurring opinion, does Chief Justice Burger now stand alone on the issue of a constitutional right to treatment?

2. How extensive is the right to "minimally adequate training" announced by the Court?

3. What are the possible implications of footnote 20?

4. What does the Court mean when it states that "courts must show deference to the judgment exercised by a qualified professional?" How would such deference be applied in such a case?


## C.  PROCEDURAL PREREQUISITES TO INSTITUTIONALIZATION

p. 644—ADD the following to the end of Note 2 at the top of the page:

The Supreme Court, however, has taken a different view, as indicated in the two cases that follow.


p. 644—INSERT before *Lynch* v. *Baxley:*

PARHAM v. J. R.

*Supreme Court of the United States, 1979*
*442 U.S. 584*

Mr. CHIEF JUSTICE BURGER delivered the opinion of the Court.

The question presented in this appeal is what process is constitutionally due a minor child whose parents or guardian seek state administered institutional mental health care for the child and specifically whether an adversary proceeding is required prior to or after the commitment.

I

(a) Appellee J. R., a child being treated in a Georgia state mental hospital, was a plaintiff in this class action[2] based on 42 U.S.C. § 1983, in the District Court for the Middle District of Georgia. Appellants are the State's Commissioner of the Department of Human Resources, the Director of the Mental Health Division of the Department of Human Resources, and the Chief Medical Officer at the hospital where appellee was being treated. Appellee sought a declaratory judgment that Georgia's voluntary commitment procedures for children under the age of 18, Ga. Code §§ 88-503.1, 88-503.2 (1975),[3] violated the Due Process Clause of the Fourteenth Amendment and requested an injunction against their future enforcement.

A three-judge District Court was convened pursuant to 28 U.S.C. §§ 2281 (1970 ed.) and 2284. After considering expert and lay testimony and extensive exhibits and after visiting two of the State's regional mental health hospitals, the District Court held that Georgia's statutory scheme was unconstitutional because it failed to protect adequately the appellees' due process rights. *J. L.* v. *Parham*, 412 F.Supp. 112, 139 (1976).

To remedy this violation, the court enjoined future commitments based on the procedures in the Georgia statute. It also commanded Georgia to appropriate and expend whatever amount was "reasonably necessary" to provide nonhospital facilities deemed by the appellant state officials to be the most appropriate for the treatment of

---

[2]The class certified by the District Court, without objection by appellants, consisted "of all persons younger than 18 years of age now or hereafter received by any defendant for observation and diagnosis and/or detained for care and treatment at any 'facility' within the State of Georgia pursuant to" Ga. Code § 88-503.1 (1975). Although one witness testified that on any given day there may be 200 children in the class, in December 1975 there were only 140.

[3]Section 88-503.1 provides:

> The superintendent of any facility may receive for observation and diagnosis . . . any individual under 18 years of age for whom such application is made by his parent or guardian. . . . If found to show evidence of mental illness and to be suitable for treatment, such person may be given care and treatment at such facility and such person may be detained by such facility for such period and under such conditions as may be authorized by law.

Section 88-503.2 provides:

> The superintendent of the facility shall discharge any voluntary patient who has recovered from his mental illness or who has sufficiently improved that the superintendent determines that hospitalization of the patient is no longer desirable.

Section 88-503 was amended in some respects in 1978, but references herein are to the provisions in effect at the time in question.

those members of plaintiffs' class, n. 2, *supra,* who could be treated in a less drastic, nonhospital environment. 412 F.Supp., at 139.

Appellants challenged all aspects of the District Court's judgment. We noted probable jurisdiction, 431 U.S. 936, and heard argument during the 1977 Term. The case was then consolidated with *Secretary of Public Welfare* v. *Institutionalized Juveniles, post,* p. 640, and reargued this Term.

(b) J. L., a plaintiff before the District Court who is now deceased, was admitted in 1970 at the age of six years to Central State Regional Hospital in Milledgeville, Ga. Prior to his admission, J. L. had received outpatient treatment at the hospital for over two months. J. L.'s mother than requested the hospital to admit him indefinitely.

The admitting physician interviewed J. L. and his parents. He learned that J. L.'s natural parents had divorced and his mother had remarried. He also learned that J. L. had been expelled from school because he was uncontrollable. He accepted the parents' representation that the boy had been extremely aggressive and diagnosed the child as having a "hyperkinetic reaction of childhood."

J. L.'s mother and stepfather agreed to participate in family therapy during the time their son was hospitalized. Under this program, J. L. was permitted to go home for short stays. Apparently his behavior during these visits was erratic. After several months, the parents requested discontinuance of this program.

In 1972, the child was returned to his mother and stepfather on a furlough basis, *i.e.,* he would live at home but go to school at the hospital. The parents found they were unable to control J. L. to their satisfaction, and this created family stress. Within two months, they requested his readmission to Central State. J. L.'s parents relinquished their parental rights to the county in 1974.

Although several hospital employees recommended that J. L. should be placed in a special foster home with "a warm, supported, truly involved couple," the Department of Family and Children Services was unable to place him in such a setting. On October 24, 1975, J. L. filed this suit requesting an order of the court placing him in a less drastic environment suitable to his needs.

(c) Appellee J. R. was declared a neglected child by the county and removed from his natural parents when he was 3 months old. He was placed in seven different foster homes in succession prior to his admission to Central State Hospital at the age of seven.

Immediately preceding his hospitalization, J. R. received outpatient treatment at a county mental health center for several months. He then began attending school where he was so disruptive and incorrigible that he could not conform to normal behavior patterns. Because of his abnormal behavior, J. R.'s seventh set of foster parents requested his removal from their home. The Department of Family and Children Services then sought his admission at Central State. The agency provided the hospital with a complete sociomedical history at the time of his admission. In addition, three separate interviews were conducted with J. R. by the admission team of the hospital.

It was determined that he was borderline retarded, and suffered an "unsocialized, aggressive reaction of childhood." It was recommended unanimously that he would "benefit from the structured environment" of the hospital and would "enjoy living and playing with boys of the same age."

J. R.'s progress was re-examined periodically. In addition, unsuccessful efforts were made by the Department of Family and Children Services during his stay at the hospital to place J. R. in various foster homes. On October 24, 1975, J. R. (with J. L.) filed this suit requesting an order of the court placing him in a less drastic environment suitable to his needs.

(d) Georgia Code § 88-503.1 (1975) provides for the voluntary admission to a state regional hospital of children such as J. L. and J. R. Under that provision, admission begins with an application for hospitalization signed by a "parent or guardian." Upon application, the superintendent of each hospital is given the power to admit temporarily any child for "observation and diagnosis." If, after observation, the superintendent finds "evidence of mental illness" and that the child is "suitable for treatment" in the hospital, then the child may be admitted "for such period and under such conditions as may be authorized by law."

Georgia's mental health statute also provides for the discharge of voluntary patients. Any child who has been hospitalized for more than five days may be discharged at the request of a parent or guardian. § 88-503.3 (a) (1975). Even without a request for discharge, however, the superintendent of each regional hospital has an affirmative duty to release any child "who has recovered from his mental illness or who has sufficiently improved that the superintendent determines that hospitalization of the patient is no longer desirable." § 88-503.2 (1975).

Georgia's Mental Health Director has not published any statewide regulations defining what specific procedures each superintendent must employ when admitting a child under 18. Instead, each regional hospital's superintendent is responsible for the procedures in his or her facility. There is substantial variation among the institutions with regard to their admission procedures and their procedures for review of patients after they have been admitted. A brief description of the different hospitals' procedures will demonstrate the variety of approaches taken by the regional hospitals throughout the State.

Southwestern Hospital in Thomasville, Ga., was built in 1966. Its children and adolescent program was instituted in 1974. The children and adolescent unit in the hospital has a maximum capacity of 20 beds, but at the time of suit only 10 children were being treated there.

The Southwestern superintendent testified that the hospital has never admitted a voluntary child patient who was not treated previously by a community mental health clinic. If a mental health professional at the community clinic determines that hospital treatment may be helpful for a child, then clinic staff and hospital staff jointly evaluate the need for hospitalization, the proper treatment during hospitalization, and a likely release date. The initial admission decision thus is not made at the hospital.

After a child is admitted, the hospital has weekly reviews of his condition performed by its internal medical and professional staff. There also are monthly reviews of each child by a group composed of hospital staff not involved in the weekly reviews and by community clinic staff people. The average stay for each child who was being treated at Southwestern in 1975 was 100 days.

Atlanta Regional Hospital was opened in 1968. At the time of the hearing before the District Court, 17 children and 21 adolescents were being treated in the hospital's children and adolescent unit.

The hospital is affiliated with nine community mental health centers and has an agreement with them that "persons will be treated in the comprehensive community mental health centers in every possible instance, rather than being hospitalized." The admission criteria at Atlanta Regional for voluntary and involuntary patients are the same. It has a formal policy not to admit a voluntary patient unless the patient is found to be a threat to himself or others. The record discloses that approximately 25% of all referrals from the community centers are rejected by the hospital admissions staff.

After admission, the staff reviews the condition of each child every week. In addition, there are monthly utilization reviews by nonstaff mental health professionals; this review considers a random sample of children's cases. The average length of each child's stay in 1975 was 161 days.

The Georgia Mental Health Institute (GMHI) in Decatur, Ga., was built in 1965. Its children and adolescent unit housed 26 children at the time this suit was brought.

The hospital has a formal affiliation with four community mental health centers. Those centers may refer patients to the hospital only if they certify that "no appropriate alternative resources are available within the client's geographic area." For the year prior to the trial in this case, no child was admitted except through a referral from a clinic. Although the hospital has a policy of generally accepting for 24 hours all referrals from a community clinic, it has a team of staff members who review each admission. If the team finds "no reason not to treat in the community" and the deputy superintendent of the hospital agrees, then it will release the applicant to his home.

After a child is admitted, there must be a review of the admission decision within 30 days. There is also an unspecified periodic review of each child's need for hospitalization by a team of staff members. The average stay for the children who were at GMHI in 1975 was 346 days.

Augusta Regional Hospital was opened in 1969 and is affiliated with 10 community mental health clinics. Its children and adolescent unit housed 14 children in December 1975.

Approximately 90% of the children admitted to the hospital have first received treatment in the community, but not all of them were admitted based on a specific referral from a clinic. The admission criterion is whether "the child needs hospitalization," and that decision must be approved by two psychiatrists. There is also an informal practice of not admitting a child if his parents refuse to participate in a family therapy program.

The admission decision is reviewed within 10 days by a team of staff physicians and mental health professionals; thereafter, each child is reviewed every week. In addition, every child's condition is reviewed by a team of clinic staff members every 100 days. The average stay for the children at Augusta in December 1975 was 92 days.

Savannah Regional Hospital was built in 1970, and it housed 16 children at the time of this suit. The Hospital staff members are also directors of the community mental health clinics.

It is the policy of the hospital that any child seeking admission on a nonemergency basis must be referred by a community clinic. The admission decision must be made by a staff psychiatrist, and it is based on the materials provided by the community clinic, an interview with the applicant, and an interview with the parents, if any, of the child.

Within three weeks after admission of a child, there is review by a group composed of hospital and clinic staff members and people from the community, such as juvenile court judges. Thereafter, the hospital staff reviews each child weekly. If the staff concludes that a child is ready to be released, then the community committee reviews the child's case to assist in placement. The average stay of the children being treated at Savannah in December 1975 was 127 days.

West Central Hospital in Columbus, Ga., was opened in December 1974, and it was organized for budgetary purposes with several community mental health clinics. The hospital itself has only 20 beds for children and adolescents, 16 of which were occupied at the time this suit was filed.

There is a formal policy that all children seeking admission to the hospital must be referred by a community clinic. The hospital is regarded by the staff as "the last resort in treating a child"; 50% of the children referred are turned away by the admissions team at the hospital.

After admission, there are staff meetings daily to discuss problem cases. The hospital has a practicing child psychiatrist who reviews cases once a week. Depending on the nature of the problems, the consultant reviews between 1 and 20 cases. The average stay of the children who were at West Central in December 1975 was 71 days.

The children's unit at Central State Regional Hospital in Milledgeville, Ga., was added to the existing structure during the 1970's. It can accommodate 40 children. The hospital also can house 40 adolescents. At the time of suit, the hospital housed 37 children under 18, including both named plaintiffs.

Although Central State is affiliated with community clinics, it seems to have a higher percentage of nonreferral admissions than any of the other hospitals. The admission decision is made by an "admissions evaluator" and the "admitting physician." The evaluator is a Ph.D. in psychology, a social worker, or a mental-health-trained nurse. The admitting physician is a psychiatrist. The standard for admission is "whether or not hospitalization is the more appropriate treatment" for the child. From April 1974 to November 1975, 9 of 29 children applicants screened for admission were referred to noninstitutional settings.

All children who are temporarily admitted are sent to the children and adolescent unit for testing and development of a treatment plan. Generally, seven days after the admission, members of the hospital staff review all of the information compiled about a patient "to determine the need for continued hospitalization." Thereafter, there is an informal review of the patient approximately every 60 days. The patients who were at Central State in December 1975 had been there on the average 456 days. There is no explanation in the record for this large variation from the average length of hospitalization at the other institutions.

Although most of the focus of the District Court was on the State's mental hospitals, it is relevant to note that Georgia presently funds over 50 community mental health clinics and 13 specialized foster care homes. The State has built seven new regional hospitals within the past 15 years, and it has added a new children's unit to its oldest hospital. The state budget in fiscal year 1976 was almost $150 million for mental health care. Georgia ranks 22nd among the states in per capita expenditures for mental health and 15th in total expenditures.

The District Court nonetheless rejected the State's entire system of providing mental health care on both procedural and substantive grounds. The District Court found that 46 children could be "optimally cared for in another, less restrictive, non-hospital setting if it were available." 412 F.Supp., at 124–125. These "optimal" settings included group homes, therapeutic camps, and home-care services. The Governor of Georgia and the chairmen of the two Appropriations Committees of its legislature, testifying in the District Court, expressed confidence in the Georgia program and informed the court that the State could not justify enlarging its budget during fiscal year 1977 to provide the specialized treatment settings urged by appellees in addition to those then available.

Having described the factual background of Georgia's mental health program and its treatment of the named plaintiffs, we turn now to examine the legal bases for the District Court's judgment.

## II

In holding unconstitutional Georgia's statutory procedure for voluntary commitment of juveniles, the District Court first determined that commitment to any of the eight regional hospitals constitutes a severe deprivation of a child's liberty. The court defined this liberty interest in terms of both freedom from bodily restraint and freedom from the "emotional and psychic harm" caused by the institutionalization.[7] Having determined that a liberty interest is implicated by a child's admission to a mental hospital, the court considered what process is required to protect that interest. It held that the process due "includes at least the right after notice to be heard before an impartial tribunal." 412 F.Supp., at 137.

In requiring the prescribed hearing, the court rejected Georgia's argument that no adversary-type hearing was required since the State was merely assisting parents who could not afford private care by making available treatment similar to that offered in private hospitals and by private physicians. The court acknowledged that most parents who seek to have their children admitted to a state mental hospital do so in good faith. It, however, relied on one of appellees' witnesses who expressed an opinion that "some still look upon mental hospitals as a 'dumping ground.'" *Id.*, at 138. No specific evidence of such "dumping," however, can be found in the record.

The District Court also rejected the argument that review by the superintendents of the hospitals and their staffs was sufficient to protect the child's liberty interest. The court held that the inexactness of psychiatry, coupled with the possibility that the sources of information used to make the commitment decision may not always be reliable, made the superintendent's decision too arbitrary to satisfy due process. The court then shifted its focus drastically from what was clearly a procedural due process

---

[7]In both respects, the District Court found strong support for its holding in this Court's decision in *In re Gault*, 387 U.S. 1 (1967). In that decision, we held that a state cannot institutionalize a juvenile delinquent without first providing certain due process protections.

analysis to what appears to be a substantive due process analysis and condemned Georgia's "officialdom" for its failure, in the face of a state-funded 1973 report outlining the "need" for additional resources to be spent on nonhospital treatment, to provide more resources for noninstitutional mental health care. The court concluded that there was a causal relationship between this intransigence and the State's ability to provide any "flexible due process' to the appellees. The District Court therefore ordered the State to appropriate and expend such resources as would be necessary to provide nonhospital treatment to those members of appellees' class who would benefit from it.

### III

In an earlier day, the problems inherent in coping with children afflicted with mental or emotional abnormalities were dealt with largely within the family. See S. Brakel & R. Rock, The Mentally Disabled and the Law 4 (1971). Sometimes parents were aided by teachers or a family doctor. While some parents no doubt were able to deal with their disturbed children without specialized assistance, others, especially those of limited means and education, were not. Increasingly, they turned for assistance to local, public sources or private charities. Until recently, most of the states did little more than provide custodial institutions for the confinement of persons who were considered dangerous. Id., at 5–6; Slovenko, Criminal Justice Procedures in Civil Commitment, 24 Wayne L. Rev. 1, 3 (1977) (hereinafter Slovenko).

As medical knowledge about the mentally ill and public concern for their condition expanded, the states, aided substantially by federal grants, have sought to ameliorate the human tragedies of seriously distrubed children. Ironically, as most states have expanded their efforts to assist the mentally ill, their actions have been subjected to increasing litigation and heightened constitutional scrutiny. Courts have been required to resolve the thorny constitutional attacks on state programs and procedures with limited precedential guidance. In this case, appellees have challenged Georgia's procedural and substantive balance of the individual, family, and social interests at stake in the voluntary commitment of a child to one of its regional mental hospitals.

The parties agree that our prior holdings have set out a general approach for testing challenged state procedures under a due process claim. Assuming the existence of a protectible property or liberty interest, the Court has required a balancing of a number of factors:

> First, the private interest that will be affected by the official action; second, the risk of an erroneous deprivation of such interest through the procedures used, and the probable value, if any, of additional or substitute procedural safeguards; and finally, the Government's interest, including the function involved and the fiscal and administrative burdens that the additional or substitute procedure requirement would entail. *Mathews* v. *Eldridge,* 424 U.S. 319, 335 (1976), quoted in *Smith* v. *Organization of Foster Families,* 431 U.S. 816, 848–849 (1977).

In applying these criteria, we must consider first the child's interest in not being committed. Normally, however, since this interest is inextricably linked with the parents' interest in and obligation for the welfare and health of the child, the private interest at stake is a combination of the child's and parents' concerns.[11] Next, we must examine the State's interest in the procedures it has adopted for commitment and treatment of children. Finally, we must consider how well Georgia's procedures protect against arbitrariness in the decision to commit a child to a state mental hospital.

(a) It is not disputed that a child, in common with adults, has a substantial liberty interest in not being confined unnecessarily for medical treatment and that the state's involvement in the commitment decision constitutes state action under the Fourteenth Amendment. See *Addington* v. *Texas,* 441 U.S. 418, 425 (1979); *In re Gault,* 387 U.S. 1, 27 (1967); *Specht* v. *Patterson,* 386 U.S. 605 (1967). We also recognize that commitment sometimes produces adverse social consequences for the child because of the reaction of some to the discovery that the child has received psychiatric care. Cf. *Addington* v. *Texas, supra,* at 425–426.

This reaction, however, need not be equated with the community response resulting from being labeled by the state as delinquent, criminal, or mentally ill and possibly dangerous. See *ibid.; In re Gault, supra,* at 23; *Paul* v. *Davis,* 424 U.S. 693, 711–712 (1976). The state through its voluntary commitment procedures does not "label" the child; it provides a diagnosis and treatment that medical specialists conclude the child requires. In terms of public reaction, the child who exhibits abnormal behavior may be seriously injured by an erroneous decision not to commit. Appellees overlook a significant source of the public reaction to the mentally ill, for what is truly "stigmatizing" is the symptomatology of a mental or emotional illness. *Addington* v. *Texas, supra,* at 429. See also Schwartz, Myers, & Astrachan, Psychiatric Labeling and the Rehabilitation of the Mental Patient, 31 Archives of General Psychiatry 329 (1974).[12] The pattern of untreated, abnormal behavior—even if nondangerous— arouses at least as much negative reaction as treatment that becomes public knowledge. A person needing, but not receiving, appropriate medical care may well face even greater social ostracism resulting from the observable symptoms of an untreated disorder.[13]

However, we need not decide what effect these factors might have in a different case. For purposes of this decision, we assume that a child has a protectible interest not only in being free of unnecessary bodily restraints but also in not being labeled erroneously by some persons because of an improper decision by the state hospital superintendent.

(b) We next deal with the interests of the parents who have decided, on the basis of their observations and independent professional recommendations, that their

---

[11]In this part of the opinion, we will deal with the issues arising when the natural parents of the child seek commitment to a state hospital. In Part IV, we will deal with the situation presented when the child is a ward of the state.

[12]See also Gove & Fain, The Stigma of Mental Hospitalization, 28 Archives of General Psychiatry 494, 500 (1973); Phillips, Rejection of the Mentally Ill: The Influence of Behavior and Sex, 29 Am. Sociological Rev. 679, 686–687 (1964). Research by Schwartz, Myers, and Astrachan and that of Gove and Fain found "that the stigma of mental hospitalization is not a major problem for the ex-patient." Schwartz, Myers, & Astrachan, Psychiatric Labeling and the Rehabilitation of the Mental Patient, 31 Archives of General Psychiatry 329, 333 (1974).

[13]As Schwartz, Myers, and Astrachan concluded:

Discharge [from a mental hospital] before disturbed behavior is well controlled may advance the patient into an inhospitable world that can incubate the chronicity that was to be avoided in the first place. *Id.,* at 334.

child needs institutional care. Appellees argue that the constitutional rights of the child are of such magnitude and the likelihood of parental abuse is so great that the parents' traditional interests in and responsibility for the upbringing of their child must be subordinated at least to the extent of providing a formal adversary hearing prior to a voluntary commitment.

Our jurisprudence historically has reflected Western civilization concepts of the family as a unit with broad parental authority over minor children. Our cases have consistently followed that course; our constitutional system long ago rejected any notion that a child is "the mere creature of the State" and, on the contrary, asserted that parents generally "have the right, coupled with the high duty, to recognize and prepare [their children] for additional obligations." *Pierce* v. *Society of Sisters*, 268 U.S. 510, 535 (1925). See also *Wisconsin* v. *Yoder*, 406 U.S. 205, 213 (1972); *Prince* v. *Massachusetts*, 321 U.S. 158, 166 (1944); *Meyer* v. *Nebraska*, 262 U.S. 390, 400 (1923). Surely, this includes a "high duty" to recognize symptoms of illness and to seek and follow medical advice. The law's concept of the family rests on a presumption that parents possess what a child lacks in maturity, experience, and capacity for judgment required for making life's difficult decisions. More important, historically it has recognized that natural bonds of affection lead parents to act in the best interests of their children. 1 W. Blackstone, Commentaries *447; 2 J. Kent, Commentaries on American Law *190.

As with so many other legal presumptions, experience and reality may rebut what the law accepts as a starting point; the incidence of child neglect and abuse cases attests to this. That some parents "may at times be acting against the interests of their children" as was stated in *Bartley* v. *Kremens*, 402 F.Supp. 1039, 1047–1048 (ED Pa. 1975), vacated and remanded, 431 U.S. 119 (1977), creates a basis for caution, but is hardly a reason to discard wholesale those pages of human experience that teach that parents generally do act in the child's best interests. See Rolfe & MacClintock 348–349. The statist notion that governmental power should supersede parental authority in *all* cases because *some* parents abuse and neglect children is repugnant to American tradition.

Nonetheless, we have recognized that a state is not without constitutional control over parental discretion in dealing with children when their physical or mental health is jeopardized. See *Wisconsin* v. *Yoder, supra*, at 230; *Prince* v. *Massachusetts, supra*, at 166. Moreover, the Court recently declared unconstitutional a state statute that granted parents an absolute veto over a minor child's decision to have an abortion. *Planned Parenthood of Central Missouri* v. *Danforth*, 428 U.S. 52 (1976). Appellees urge that these precedents limiting the traditional rights of parents, if viewed in the context of the liberty interest of the child and the likelihood of parental abuse, require us to hold that the parents' decision to have a child admitted to a mental hospital must be subjected to an exacting constitutional scrutiny, including a formal, adversary, pre-admission hearing.

Appellees' argument, however, sweeps too broadly. Simply because the decision of a parent is not agreeable to a child or because it involves risks does not automatically transfer the power to make that decision from the parents to some agency or officer of the state. The same characterizations can be made for a tonsillectomy, appendectomy, or other medical procedure. Most children, even in adolescence, simply are not able to make sound judgments concerning many decisions, including their need for medical care or treatment. Parents can and must make those judgments. Here, there is no finding by the District Court of even a single instance of bad faith by any parent of any member of appellees' class. We cannot assume that the result in *Meyer* v. *Nebraska, supra,* and *Pierce* v. *Society of Sisters, supra,* would have been different if the children there had announced a preference to learn only English or a preference to go to a public, rather than a church, school. The fact that a child may balk at hospitalization or complain about a parental refusal to provide cosmetic surgery does not diminish the parents' authority to decide what is best for the child. See generally Goldstein, Medical Case for the Child at Risk: On State Supervention of Parental Autonomy, 86 Yale L. J. 645, 664–668 (1977); Bennett, Allocation of Child Medical Care Decision-making Authority: A Suggested Interest Analysis, 62 Va. L. Rev. 285, 308 (1976). Neither state officials nor federal courts are equipped to review such parental decisions.

Appellees place particular reliance on *Planned Parenthood,* arguing that its holding indicates how little deference to parents is appropriate when the child is exercising a constitutional right. The basic situation in that case, however, was very different; *Planned Parenthood* involved an absolute parental veto over the child's ability to obtain an abortion. Parents in Georgia in no sense have an absolute right to commit their children to state mental hospitals; the statute requires the superintendent of each regional hospital to exercise independent judgment as to the child's need for confinement. See *supra,* at 591.

In defining the respective rights and prerogatives of the child and parent in the voluntary commitment setting, we conclude that our precedents permit the parents to retain a substantial, if not the dominant, role in the decision, absent a finding of neglect or abuse, and that the traditional presumption that the parents act in the best interests of their child should apply. We also conclude, however, that the child's rights and the nature of the commitment decision are such that parents cannot always have absolute and unreviewable discretion to decide whether to have a child institutionalized. They, of course, retain plenary authority to seek such care for their children, subject to a physician's independent examination and medical judgment.

(c) The State obviously has a significant interest in confining the use of its costly mental health facilities to cases of genuine need. The Georgia program seeks first to determine whether the patient seeking admission has an illness that calls for inpatient treatment. To accomplish this purpose, the State has charged the superintendents of each regional hospital with the responsibility for determining, before authorizing an admission, whether a prospective patient is mentally ill and whether the patient will likely benefit from hospital care. In addition, the State has imposed a continuing duty on hospital superintendents to release any patient who has recovered to the point where hospitalization is no longer needed.

The State in performing its voluntarily assumed mission also has a significant interest in not imposing unnecessary procedural obstacles that may discourage the mentally ill or their families from seeking needed psychiatric assistance. The *parens patriae* interest in helping parents care for the mental health of their children cannot be fulfilled if the parents are unwilling to take advantage of the opportunities because the admission process is too onerous, too embarrassing, or too contentious. It is surely not idle to speculate as to how many parents who believe they are acting in good faith would forgo state-provided hospital care if such care is contingent on participation in an adversary proceeding designed to probe their motives and other private family matters in seeking the voluntary admission.

The State also has a genuine interest in allocating priority to the diagnosis and treatment of patients as soon as they are admitted to a hospital rather than to time-consuming procedural minuets before the admission.[14] One factor that must be considered is the utilization of the time of psychiatrists, psychologists, and other behavioral specialists in preparing for and participating in hearings rather than performing the task for which their special training has fitted them. Behavioral experts in courtrooms and hearings are of little help to patients.

The *amicus* brief of the American Psychiatric Association points out at page 20 that the average staff psychiatrist in a hospital presently is able to devote only 47% of his time to direct patient care. One consequence of increasing the procedures the state must provide prior to a child's voluntary admission will be that mental health professionals will be diverted even more from the treatment of patients in order to travel to and participate in—and wait for—what could be hundreds—or even thousands—of hearings each year. Obviously the cost of these procedures would come from the public monies the legislature intended for mental health care. See Slovenko 34–35.

(d) We now turn to consideration of what process protects adequately the child's constitutional rights by reducing risks of error without unduly trenching on traditional parental authority and without undercutting "efforts to further the legitimate interests of both the state and the patient that are served by" voluntary commitments. *Addington* v. *Texas*, 441 U.S., at 430. See also *Mathews* v. *Eldridge*, 424 U.S., at 335. We conclude that the risk of error inherent in the parental decision to have a child institutionalized for mental health care is sufficiently great that some kind of inquiry should be made by a "neutral factfinder" to determine whether the statutory requirements for admission are satisfied. See *Goldberg* v. *Kelly*, 397 U.S. 254, 271 (1970); *Morrissey* v. *Brewer*, 408 U.S. 471, 489 (1972). That inquiry must carefully probe the child's background using all available sources, including, but not limited to, parents, schools, and other social agencies. Of course, the review must also include an interview with the child. It is necessary that the decisionmaker have the authority to refuse to admit any child who does not satisfy the medical standards for admission. Finally, it is necessary that the child's continuing need for commitment be reviewed periodically by a similarly independent procedure.[15]

---

[14]Judge Friendly has cogently pointed out:

> It should be realized that procedural requirements entail the expenditure of limited resources, that at some point the benefit to individuals from an additional safeguard is substantially outweighed by the cost of providing such protection, and that the expense of protecting those likely to be found undeserving will probably come out of the pockets of the deserving. Friendly, "Some Kind of Hearing," 123 U. Pa. L. Rev. 1267, 1276 (1975). See also *Wheeler* v. *Montgomery*, 397 U.S. 280, 282 (1970) (dissenting opinion).

[15]As we discuss more fully later, *infra*, at 617, the District Court did not decide and we therefore have no reason to consider at this time what procedures for review are independently necessary to justify continuing a child's confinement. We merely hold that a subsequent, independent review of the patient's condition provides a necessary check against possible arbitrariness in the *initial* admission decision.

We are satisfied that such procedures will protect the child from an erroneous admission decision in a way that neither unduly burdens the states nor inhibits parental decisions to seek state help.

Due process has never been thought to require that the neutral and detached trier of fact be law trained or a judicial or administrative officer. See *Goldberg* v. *Kelly, supra,* at 271; *Morrissey* v. *Brewer, supra,* at 489. Surely, this is the case as to medical decisions, for "neither judges nor administrative hearing officers are better qualified than psychiatrists to render psychiatric judgments." *In re Roger S.,* 19 Cal. 3d 921, 942, 569 P. 2d 1286, 1299 (1977) (Clark, J., dissenting). Thus, a staff physician will suffice, so long as he or she is free to evaluate independently the child's mental and emotional condition and need for treatment.

It is not necessary that the deciding physician conduct a formal or quasi-formal hearing. A state is free to require such a hearing, but due process is not violated by use of informal, traditional medical investigative techniques. Since well-established medical procedures already exist, we do not undertake to outline with specificity precisely what this investigation must involve. The mode and procedure of medical diagnostic procedures is not the business of judges. What is best for a child is an individual medical decision that must be left to the judgment of physicians in each case. We do no more than emphasize that the decision should represent an independent judgment of what the child requires and that all sources of information that are traditionally relied on by physicians and behavioral specialists should be consulted.

What process is constitutionally due cannot be divorced from the nature of the ultimate decision that is being made. Not every determination by state officers can be made most effectively by use of "the procedural tools of judicial or administrative decisionmaking." *Board of Curators of Univ. of Missouri* v. *Horowitz,* 435 U.S. 78, 90 (1978). See also *Greenholtz* v. *Nebraska Penal Inmates, ante,* at 13–14; *Cafeteria & Restaurant Workers* v. *McElroy,* 367 U.S. 886, 895 (1961).[16]

Here, the questions are essentially medical in character: whether the child is mentally or emotionally ill and whether he can benefit from the treatment that is provided by the state. While facts are plainly necessary for a proper resolution of those questions, they are only a first step in the process. In an opinion for a unanimous Court, we recently stated in *Addington* v. *Texas,* 441 U.S., at 429, that the determina-

---

[16]Relying on general statements from past decisions dealing with governmental actions not even remotely similar to those involved here, the dissent concludes that if a protectible interest is involved then there must be some form of traditional, adversary, judicial, or administrative hearing either before or after its deprivation. That result is mandated, in their view, regardless of what process the state has designed to protect the individual and regardless of what the record demonstrates as to the fairness of the state's approach.

The dissenting approach is inconsistent with our repeated assertion that "due process is *flexible* and calls for such procedural protections as the particular situation demands." *Morrissey* v. *Brewer,* 408 U.S. 471, 481 (1972) (emphasis added). Just as there is no requirement as to exactly what procedures to employ whenever a traditional judicial-type hearing is mandated, compare *Goss* v. *Lopez,* 419 U.S. 565 (1975); *Wolff* v. *McDonnell,* 418 U.S. 539 (1974); *Morrissey* v. *Brewer, supra,* with *Goldberg* v. *Kelly,* 397 U.S. 254 (1970), there is no reason to require a judicial-type hearing in all circumstances. As the scope of governmental action expands into new areas creating new controversies for judicial review, it is incumbent on courts to design procedures that protect the rights of the individual without unduly burdening the legitimate efforts of the states to deal with difficult social problems. The judicial model for factfinding for all constitutionally protected interests, regardless of their nature, can turn rational decisionmaking into an unmanageable enterprise.

tion of whether a person is mentally ill "turns on the *meaning* of the facts which must be interpreted by expert psychiatrists and psychologists."

Although we acknowledge the fallibility of medical and psychiatric diagnosis, see *O'Connor* v. *Donaldson*, 422 U.S. 563, 584 (1975) (concurring opinion), we do not accept the notion that the shortcomings of specialists can always be avoided by shifting the decision from a trained specialist using the traditional tools of medical science to an untrained judge or administrative hearing officer after a judicial-type hearing. Even after a hearing, the nonspecialist decisionmaker must make a medical-psychiatric decision. Common human experience and scholarly opinions suggest that the supposed protections of an adversary proceeding to determine the appropriateness of medical decisions for the commitment and treatment of mental and emotional illness may well be more illusory than real. See Albers, Pasewark, & Meyer, Involuntary Hospitalization and Psychiatric Testimony: The Fallibility of the Doctrine of Immaculate Perception, 6 Cap. U. L. Rev. 11, 15 (1976).[17]

Another problem with requiring a formalized, factfinding hearing lies in the danger it poses for significant intrusion into the parent-child relationship. Pitting the parents and child as adversaries often will be at odds with the presumption that parents act in the best interests of their child. It is one thing to require a neutral physician to make a careful review of the parents' decision in order to make sure it is proper from a medical standpoint; it is a wholly different matter to employ an adversary contest to ascertain whether the parents' motivation is consistent with the child's interests.

Moreover, it is appropriate to inquire into how such a hearing would contribute to the successful long-range treatment of the patient. Surely, there is a risk that it would exacerbate whatever tensions already exist between the child and the parents. Since the parents can and usually do play a significant role in the treatment while the child is hospitalized and even more so after release, there is a serious risk that an adversary confrontation will adversely affect the ability of the parents to assist the child while in the hospital. Moreover, it will make his subsequent return home more difficult. These unfortunate results are especially critical with an emotionally disturbed child; they seem likely to occur in the context of an adversary hearing in which the parents testify. A confrontation over such intimate family relationships would distress the normal adult parents and the impact on a disturbed child almost certainly would be significantly greater.[18]

---

[17]See Albers & Pasewark, Involuntary Hospitalization: Surrender at the Courthouse, 2 Am. J. Community Psychology 287, 288 (1974) (mean hearing time for 21 of 300 consecutive commitment cases was 9.2 minutes); Miller & Schwartz, County Lunacy Commission Hearings: Some Observations of Commitment to a State Mental Hospital, 14 Social Prob. 26 (1966) (mean time for hearings was 3.8 minutes); Scheff, The Societal Reaction to Deviance: Ascriptive Elements in the Psychiatric Screening of Mental Patients in a Midwestern State, 11 Social Prob. 401 (1964) (average hearing lasted 9.2 minutes). See also Cohen, The Function of the Attorney and the Commitment of the Mentally Ill, 44 Texas L. Rev. 424 (1966).

[18]While not altogether clear, the District Court opinion apparently contemplated a hearing preceded by a written notice of the proposed commitment. At the hearing the child presumably would be given an opportunity to be heard and present evidence, and the right to cross-examine witnesses, including, of course, the parents. The court also required an impartial trier of fact who would render a written decision reciting the reasons for accepting or rejecting the parental application.

Since the parents in this situation are seeking the child's admission to the state institution, the procedure contemplated by the District Court presumably would call for some other person to be designated

It has been suggested that a hearing conducted by someone other than the admitting physician is necessary in order to detect instances where parents are "guilty of railroading their children into asylums" or are using "voluntary commitment procedures in order to sanction behavior of which they disapprov[e]." Ellis, Volunteering Children: Parental Commitment of Minors to Mental Institutions, 62 Calif. L. Rev. 840, 850–851 (1974). See also *J. L. v. Parham,* 412 F.Supp., at 133; Brief for Appellees 38. Curiously, it seems to be taken for granted that parents who seek to "dump" their children on the state will inevitably be able to conceal their motives and thus deceive the admitting psychiatrists and the other mental health professionals who make and review the admission decision. It is elementary that one early diagnostic inquiry into the cause of an emotional disturbance of a child is an examination into the environment of the child. It is unlikely, if not inconceivable, that a decision to abandon an emotionally normal, healthy child and thrust him into an institution will be a discrete act leaving no trail of circumstances. Evidence of such conflicts will emerge either in the interviews or from secondary sources. It is unrealistic to believe that trained psychiatrists, skilled in eliciting responses, sorting medically relevant facts, and sensing motivational nuances will often be deceived about the family situation surrounding a child's emotional disturbance.[19] Surely a lay, or even lawtrained factfinder, would be no more skilled in this process than the professional.

By expressing some confidence in the medical decisionmaking process, we are by no means suggesting it is error free. On occasion, parents may initially mislead an admitting physician or a physician may erroneously diagnose the child as needing institutional care either because of negligence or an overabundance of caution. That there may be risks of error in the process affords no rational predicate for holding unconstitutional an entire statutory and administrative scheme that is generally followed in more than 30 states.[20] "'[P]rocedural due process rules are shaped by the risk

---

as a guardian *ad litem* to act for the child. The guardian, in turn, if not a lawyer, would be empowered to retain counsel to act as an advocate of the child's interest.

Of course, a state may elect to provide such adversary hearings in situations where it perceives that parents and a child may be at odds, but nothing in the Constitution compels such procedures.

[19]In evaluating the problem of detecting "dumping" by parents, it is important to keep in mind that each of the regional hospitals has a continuing relationship with the Department of Family and Children Services. The staffs at those hospitals refer cases to the Department when they suspect a child is being mistreated and thus are sensitive to this problem. In fact, J. L.'s situation is in point. The family conflicts and problems were well documented in the hospital records. Equally well documented, however, were the child's severe emotional disturbances and his need for treatment.

[20]Alaska Stat. Ann. § 47.30.020 (1975); Ariz. Rev. Stat. Ann. §§ 36-518, 36-519 (1974); Ark. Stat. Ann. § 59-405 (B) (1971); Cal. Welf. & Inst. Code Ann. § 6000 (West Supp. 1979); D.C. Code §§ 21-511, 21-512 (1973); Fla. Stat. § 394.465 (1) (a) (Supp. 1979); Ga. Code §§ 88-503.1, 88-503.2 (1978); Haw. Rev. Stat. § 334-60 (a)(2) (1976) (only for child less than 15); Idaho Code §§ 66-318, 66-320 (Supp. 1978) (parent may admit child under 14, but child over 16 may obtain release); Ill. Rev. Stat., ch. 91½, §§ 3-502, 3-503 (1978 Supp.); Ind. Code § 16-14-9.1-2 (1976); Kan. Stat. Ann. §§ 59-2905, 59-2907 (Supp. 1978); Ky. Rev. Stat. § 202A.020 (1977); La. Rev. Stat. Ann. § 28:57 (C) (West Supp. 1979); Md. Ann. Code, Art. 59, § 11 (g) (Supp. 1978) (parental consent permissible only to some facilities); Mass. Gen. Laws Ann., ch. 123, § 10 (a) (West Supp. 1979); Mich. Comp. Laws § 330.1415 (1976) (child may object within 30 days and receive a hearing; Miss. Code Ann. § 41-21-103 (1) (Supp. 1978) (certificate of need for treatment from two physicians required); Mo. Rev. Stat. §§ 202.115 (1)(2), 202.115 (2)(2) (1978); Nev. Rev. Stat. §§ 422A.560, 433A.540 (1975); N.Y. Mental Hyg. Law § 9.13 (McKinney 1978) (parent may admit, but child may obtain own release); N.D. Cent. Code § 25-03.1-04 (Supp. 1977); Ohio Rev. Code Ann.

of error inherent in the truthfinding process as applied to the generality of cases, not the rare exceptions." *Mathews* v. *Eldridge*, 424 U.S., at 344. In general, we are satisfied that an independent medical decisionmaking process, which includes the thorough psychiatric investigation described earlier, followed by additional periodic review of a child's condition, will protect children who should not be admitted; we do not believe the risks of error in that process would be significantly reduced by a more formal, judicial-type hearing. The issue remains whether the Georgia practices, as described in the record before us, comport with these minimum due process requirements.

(e) Georgia's statute envisions a careful diagnostic medical inquiry to be conducted by the admitting physician at each regional hospital. The *amicus* brief for the United States explains at pp. 7–8:

> [I]n every instance the decision whether or not to accept the child for treatment is made by a physician employed by the State. . . .
> That decision is based on interviews and recommendations by hospital or community health center staff. The staff interviews the child and the parent or guardian who brings the child to the facility . . . [and] attempts are made to communicate with other possible sources of information about the child. . . .

Focusing primarily on what it saw as the absence of any formal mechanism for review of the physician's initial decision, the District Court unaccountably saw the medical decision as an exercise of "unbridled discretion." 412 F.Supp., at 136. But extravagant characterizations are no substitute for careful analysis, and we must examine the Georgia process in its setting to determine if, indeed, any one person exercises such discretion.

In the typical case, the parents of a child initially conclude from the child's behavior that there is some emotional problem—in short, that "something is wrong." They may respond to the problem in various ways, but generally the first contact with the State occurs when they bring the child to be examined by a psychologist or psychiatrist at a community mental health clinic.

Most often, the examination is followed by outpatient treatment at the community clinic. In addition, the child's parents are encouraged, and sometimes required, to participate in a family therapy program to obtain a better insight into the problem. In most instances, this is all the care a child requires. However, if, after a period of outpatient care, the child's abnormal emotional condition persists, he may be referred by the local clinic staff to an affiliated regional mental hospital.

At the regional hospital an admissions team composed of a psychiatrist and at least one other mental health professional examines and interviews the child—privately in most instances. This team then examines the medical records provided by the clinic staff and interviews the parents. Based on this information, and any additional background that can be obtained, the admissions team makes a diagnosis and determines

---

§ 5122.02 (B) (Supp. 1978); Okla. Stat., Tit. 43A, § 184 (1971); Ore. Rev. Stat. § 426.220 (1) (1977); Pa. Stat. Ann., Tit. 50, § 7201 (Purdon Supp. 1978–1979) (only for child less than 14); R.I. Gen. Laws § 26-2-8 (Supp. 1978) (requires certificate of two physicians that child is insane); S.C. Code § 44-17-310 (2) (Supp. 1978); S.D. Comp. Laws Ann. § 27A-8-2 (1976); Tenn. Code Ann. § 33-601 (a)(1) (1977); Utah Code Ann §§ 64-7-29, 64-7-31 (2) (1953); Wash. Rev. Code § 72.23.070 (2) (1978) (child over 13 also must consent); W. Va. Code § 27-4-1 (b) (1976) (consent of child over 12 required); Wyo. Stat. § 25-3-106 (a)(i) (1977).

whether the child will likely benefit from institutionalized care. If the team finds either condition not met, admission is refused.

If the team admits a child as suited for hospitalization, the child's condition and continuing need for hospital care are reviewed periodically by at least one independent, medical review group. For the most part, the reviews are as frequent as weekly, but none are less often than once every two months. Moreover, as we noted earlier the superintendent of each hospital is charged with an affirmative statutory duty to discharge any child who is no longer mentally ill or in need of therapy.[21]

As with most medical procedures, Georgia's are not totally free from risk of error in the sense that they give total or absolute assurance that every child admitted to a hospital has a mental illness optimally suitable for institutionalized treatment. But it bears repeating that "procedural due process rules are shaped by the risk of error inherent in the truthfinding process as applied to the generality of cases, not the rare exceptions." *Mathews* v. *Eldridge, supra,* at 344.

Georgia's procedures are not "arbitrary" in the sense that a single physician or other professional has the "unbridled discretion" the District Court saw to commit a child to a regional hospital. To so find on this record would require us to assume that the physicians, psychologists, and mental health professionals who participate in the admission decision and who review each other's conclusions as to the continuing validity of the initial decision are either oblivious or indifferent to the child's welfare— or that they are incompetent. We note, however, the District Court found to the contrary; it was "impressed by the conscientious, dedicated state employed psychiatrists who, with the help of equally conscientious, dedicated state employed psychologists and social workers, faithfully care for the plaintiff children. . . ." 412 F.Supp., at 138.

This finding of the District Court also effectively rebuts the suggestion made in some of the briefs *amici* that hospital administrators may not actually be "neutral and detached" because of institutional pressure to admit a child who has no need for hospital care. That such a practice may take place in some institutions in some places affords no basis for a finding as to Georgia's program; the evidence in the record provides no support whatever for that charge against the staffs at any of the State's eight regional hospitals. Such cases, if they are found, can be dealt with individually;[22] they do not lend themselves to class-action remedies.

We are satisfied that the voluminous record as a whole supports the conclusion that the admissions staffs of the hospitals have acted in a neutral and detached fashion in making medical judgments in the best interests of the children. The State, through its mental health programs, provides the authority for trained professionals to assist parents in examining, diagnosing, and treating emotionally disturbed children. Through its hiring practices, it provides well-staffed and well-equipped hospitals and—as the

---

[21]While the record does demonstrate that the procedures may vary from case to case, it also reflects that no child in Georgia was admitted for indefinite hospitalization without being interviewed personally and without the admitting physician's checking with secondary sources, such as school or work records.

[22]One important means of obtaining individual relief for these children is the availability of habeas corpus. As the appellants' brief explains, "Ga. Code § 88-502.11 . . . provides that at any time and without notice a person detained in a facility, or a relative or friend of such person, may petition for a writ of habeas corpus to question the cause and legality of the detention of the person." Brief for Appellants 36–37.

District Court found—conscientious public employees to implement the State's beneficent purposes.

Although our review of the record in this case satisfies us that Georgia's general administrative and statutory scheme for the voluntary commitment of children is not *per se* unconstitutional, we cannot decide on this record whether every child in appellees' class received an adequate, independent diagnosis of his emotional condition and need for confinement under the standards announced earlier in this opinion. On remand, the District Court is free to and should consider any individual claims that initial admissions did not meet the standards we have described in this opinion.

In addition, we note that appellees' original complaint alleged that the State had failed to provide adequate periodic review of their need for institutional care and claimed that this was an additional due process violation. Since the District Court held that the appellees' original confinement was unconstitutional, it had no reason to consider this separate claim. Similarly, we have no basis for determining whether the review procedures of the various hospitals are adequate to provide the process called for or what process might be required if a child contests his confinement by requesting a release. These matters require factual findings not present in the District Court's opinion. We have held that the periodic reviews described in the record reduce the risk of error in the initial admission and thus they are necessary. Whether they are sufficient to justify continuing a voluntary commitment is an issue for the District Court on remand. The District Court is free to require additional evidence on this issue.

IV

(a) Our discussion in Part III was directed at the situation where a child's natural parents request his admission to a state mental hospital. Some members of appellees' class, including J. R., were wards of the State of Georgia at the time of their admission. Obviously their situation differs from those members of the class who have natural parents. While the determination of what process is due varies somewhat when the state, rather than a natural parent, makes the request for commitment, we conclude that the differences in the two situations do not justify requiring different procedures at the time of the child's initial admission to the hospital.

For a ward of the state, there may well be no adult who knows him thoroughly and who cares for him deeply. Unlike with natural parents where there is a presumed natural affection to guide their action, 1 W. Blackstone, Commentaries *447; 2 J. Kent, Commentaries on American Law *190, the presumption that the state will protect a child's general welfare stems from a specific state statute. Ga. Code § 24A-101 (1978). Contrary to the suggestion of the dissent, however, we cannot assume that when the State of Georgia has custody of a child it acts so differently from a natural parent in seeking medical assistance for the child. No one has questioned the validity of the statutory presumption that the State acts in the child's best interest. Nor could such a challenge be mounted on the record before us. There is no evidence that the State, acting as guardian, attempted to admit any child for reasons unrelated to the child's need for treatment. Indeed, neither the District Court nor the appellees have suggested that wards of the State should receive any constitutional treatment different from children with natural parents.

Once we accept that the State's application of a child for admission to a hospital is made in good faith, then the question is whether the medical decisionmaking approach of the admitting physician is adequate to satisfy due process. We have already recognized that an independent medical judgment made from the perspective of the best interests of the child after a careful investigation is an acceptable means of justifying a voluntary commitment. We do not believe that the soundness of this decisionmaking is any the less reasonable in this setting.

Indeed, if anything, the decision with regard to wards of the State may well be even more reasonable in light of the extensive written records that are compiled about each child while in the State's custody. In J. R.'s case, the admitting physician had a complete social and medical history of the child before even beginning the diagnosis. After carefully interviewing him and reviewing his extensive files, three physicians independently concluded that institutional care was in his best interests. See *supra,* at 590.

Since the state agency having custody and control of the child *in loco parentis* has a duty to consider the best interests of the child with respect to a decision on commitment to a mental hospital, the State may constitutionally allow that custodial agency to speak for the child, subject, of course, to the restrictions governing natural parents. On this record, we cannot declare unconstitutional Georgia's admission procedures for wards of the State.

(b) It is possible that the procedures required in reviewing a ward's need for continuing care should be different from those used to review a child with natural parents. As we have suggested earlier, the issue of what process is due to justify continuing a voluntary commitment must be considered by the District Court on remand. In making that inquiry, the District Court might well consider whether wards of the State should be treated with respect to continuing therapy differently from children with natural parents.

The absence of an adult who cares deeply for a child has little effect on the reliability of the initial admission decision, but it may have some effect on how long a child will remain in the hospital. We noted in *Addington* v. *Texas,* 441 U.S., at 428–429, that "the concern of family and friends generally will provide continuous opportunities for an erroneous commitment to be corrected." For a child without natural parents, we must acknowledge the risk of being "lost in the shuffle." Moreover, there is at least some indication that J. R.'s commitment was prolonged because the Department of Family and Children Services had difficulty finding a foster home for him. Whether wards of the State generally have received less protection than children with natural parents, and, if so, what should be done about it, however, are matters that must be decided in the first instance by the District Court on remand,[23] if the court concludes the issue is still alive.

---

[23]To remedy the constitutional violation, the District Court ordered hearings to be held for each member of the plaintiff class, see n. 2, *supra.* For 46 members of the class found to be treatable in "less drastic" settings, the District Court also ordered the State to expend such monies as was necessary to provide alternative treatment facilities and programs. While the order is more appropriate as a remedy for a substantive due process violation, the court made no findings on that issue. The order apparently was intended to remedy the procedural due process violation it found. Since that judgment is reversed, there is no basis for us to consider the correctness of the remedy.

## V

It is important that we remember the purpose of Georgia's comprehensive mental health program. It seeks substantively and at great cost to provide care for those who cannot afford to obtain private treatment and procedurally to screen carefully all applicants to assure that institutional care is suited to the particular patient. The State resists the complex of procedures ordered by the District Court because in its view they are unnecessary to protect the child's rights, they divert public resources from the central objective of administering health care, they risk aggravating the tensions inherent in the family situation, and they erect barriers that may discourage parents from seeking medical aid for a disturbed child.

On this record, we are satisfied that Georgia's medical factfinding processes are reasonable and consistent with the constitutional guarantees. Accordingly, it was error to hold unconstitutional the State's procedures for admitting a child for treatment to a state mental hospital. The judgment is therefore reversed, and the case is remanded to the District Court for further proceedings consistent with this opinion.

*Reversed and remanded.*

MR. JUSTICE STEWART, concurring in the judgment.

For centuries it has been a canon of the common law that parents speak for their minor children.[1] So deeply imbedded in our traditions is this principle of law that the Constitution itself may compel a State to respect it. *Meyer* v. *Nebraska,* 262 U.S. 390; *Pierce* v. *Society of Sisters,* 268 U.S. 510.[2] In ironic contrast, the District Court in this case has said that the Constitution *requires* the State of Georgia to *disregard* this established principle. I cannot agree.

There can be no doubt that commitment to a mental institution results in a "massive curtailment of liberty," *Humphrey* v. *Cady,* 405 U.S. 504, 509. In addition to the physical confinement involved, *O'Connor* v. *Donaldson,* 422 U.S. 563, a person's liberty is also substantially affected by the stigma attached to treatment in a mental hospital.[3] But not every loss of liberty is governmental deprivation of liberty,

---

[1]See 1 W. Blackstone, Commentaries *452–453; 2 J. Kent, Commentaries on American Law *203–206; J. Schouler, A. Treatise on the Law of Domestic Relations 335–353 (3d ed. 1882); G. Field, The Legal Relations of Infants 63–80 (1888).

"It is cardinal with us that the custody, care and nurture of the child reside first in the parents, whose primary function and freedom include preparation for obligations the state can neither supply nor hinder." *Prince* v. *Massachusetts,* 321 U.S. 158, 166.

"The history and culture of Western civilization reflect a strong tradition of parental concern for the nurture and upbringing of their children. This primary role of the parents in the upbringing of their children is now established beyond debate as an enduring American tradition." *Wisconsin* v. *Yoder,* 406 U.S. 205, 232.

"Because he may not foresee the consequences of his decision, a minor may not make an enforceable bargain. He may not lawfully work or travel where he pleases, or even attend exhibitions of constitutionally protected adult motion pictures. Persons below a certain age may not marry without parental consent." *Planned Parenthood of Central Missouri* v. *Danforth,* 428 U.S. 52, 102 (STEVENS, J., concurring in part and dissenting in part).

Cf. *Stump* v. *Sparkman,* 435 U.S. 349, 366 (dissenting opinion).

[2]The child is not the mere creature of the State; those who nurture him and direct his destiny have the right, coupled with the high duty, to recognize and prepare him for additional obligations." *Pierce* v. *Society of Sisters,* 268 U.S., at 535.

[3]The fact that such stigma may be unjustified does not mean it does not exist. Nor does the fact that public reaction to past commitment may be less than the reaction to aberrant behavior detract from this assessment. The aberrant behavior may disappear, while the fact of past institutionalization lasts forever.

and it is only the latter that invokes the Due Process Clause of the Fourteenth Amendment.

The appellees were committed under the following section of the Georgia Code:

> Authority to receive voluntary patients—
> (a) The superintendent of any facility may receive for observation and diagnosis any individual 18 years of age, or older, making application therefor, any individual under 18 years of age for whom such application is made by his parent or guardian and any person legally adjudged to be incompetent for whom such application is made by his guardian. If found to show evidence of mental illness and to be suitable for treatment, such person may be given care and treatment at such facility and such person may be detained by such facility for such period and under such conditions as may be authorized by law.    Ga. Code § 88-503.1 (1975).

Clearly, if the appellees in this case were adults who had voluntarily chosen to commit themselves to a state mental hospital, they could not claim that the State had thereby deprived them of liberty in violation of the Fourteenth Amendment. Just as clearly, I think, children on whose behalf their parents have invoked these voluntary procedures can make no such claim.

The Georgia statute recognizes the power of a party to act on behalf of another person under the voluntary commitment procedures in two situations: when the other person is a minor not over 17 years of age and the party is that person's parent or guardian, and when the other person has been "legally adjudged incompetent" and the party is that person's guardian. In both instances two conditions are present. First, the person being committed is presumptively incapable of making the voluntary commitment decision for himself. And second, the parent or guardian is presumed to be acting in that person's best interests.[4] In the case of guardians, these presumptions are grounded in statutes whose validity nobody has questioned in this case. Ga. Code § 49-201 (1978).[5] In the case of parents, the presumptions are grounded in a statutory embodiment of long-established principles of the common law.

Thus, the basic question in this case is whether the Constitution requires Georgia to ignore basic principles so long accepted by our society. For only if the State in this setting is constitutionally compelled always to intervene between parent and child can there be any question as to the constitutionally required extent of that intervention. I believe this basic question must be answered in the negative.[6]

Under our law, parents constantly make decisions for their minor children that deprive the children of liberty, and sometimes even of life itself. Yet surely the

---

[4]This is also true of a child removed from the control of his parents. For the juvenile court then has a duty to "secure for him care as nearly as possible equivalent to that which [his parents] should have given him." Ga. Code § 24A-101 (1978).

[5]"The power of the guardian over the person of his or her ward shall be the same as that of the parent over his or her child, the guardian standing in his or her place; and in like manner it shall be the duty of the guardian to protect and maintain, and, according to the circumstances of the ward, to educate him or her."

[6]*Planned Parenthood of Central Missouri* v. *Danforth*, 428 U.S. 52, was an entirely different case. The Court's opinion today discusses some of these differences, *ante*, at 604, but I think there is a more fundamental one. The *Danforth* case involved an expectant mother's right to decide upon an abortion—a personal substantive constitutional right. *Roe* v. *Wade*, 410 U.S. 113; *Doe* v. *Bolton*, 410 U.S. 179. By contrast, the appellees in this case had no substantive constitutional right not to be hospitalized for psychiatric treatment.

Fourteenth Amendment is not invoked when an informed parent decides upon major surgery for his child, even in a state hospital. I can perceive no basic constitutional differences between commitment to a mental hospital and other parental decisions that result in a child's loss of liberty.

I realize, of course, that a parent's decision to commit his child to a state mental institution results in a far greater loss of liberty than does his decision to have an appendectomy performed upon the child in a state hospital. But if, contrary to my belief, this factual difference rises to the level of a constitutional difference, then I believe that the objective checks upon the parents' commitment decision, embodied in Georgia law and thoroughly discussed, *ante,* at 613–617, are more than constitutionally sufficient.

To be sure, the presumption that a parent is acting in the best interests of his child must be a rebuttable one, since certainly not all parents are actuated by the unselfish motive the law presumes. Some parents are simply unfit parents. But Georgia clearly provides that an unfit parent can be stripped of his parental authority under laws dealing with neglect and abuse of children.

This is not an easy case. Issues involving the family and issues concerning mental illness are among the most difficult that courts have to face, involving as they often do serious problems of policy disguised as questions of constitutional law. But when a state legislature makes a reasonable definition of the age of minority, and creates a rebuttable presumption that in invoking the statutory procedures for voluntary commitment a parent is acting in the best interests of his minor child, I cannot believe that the Fourteenth Amendment is violated. This is not to say that in this area the Constitution compels a State to respect the traditional authority of a parent, as in the *Meyer* and *Pierce* cases. I believe, as in *Prince* v. *Massachusetts,* 321 U.S. 158, that the Constitution would tolerate intervention by the State.[8] But that is a far cry from holding that such intervention is constitutionally compelled.

For these reasons I concur in the judgment.

MR. JUSTICE BRENNAN, with whom MR. JUSTICE MARSHALL and MR. JUSTICE STEVENS join, concurring in part and dissenting in part.

I agree with the Court that the commitment of juveniles to state mental hospitals by their parents or by state officials acting *in loco parentis* involves state action that impacts upon constitutionally protected interests and therefore must be accomplished through procedures consistent with the constitutional mandate of due process of law. I agree also that the District Court erred in interpreting the Due Process Clause to require preconfinement commitment hearings in all cases in which parents wish to hospitalize their children. I disagree, however, with the Court's decision to pretermit questions concerning the postadmission procedures due Georgia's institutionalized juveniles. While the question of the frequency of postadmission review hearings may properly be deferred, the right to at least one postadmission hearing can and should be affirmed now. I also disagree with the Court's conclusion concerning the procedures due juve-

---

[8]The *Prince* case held that the State may constitutionally intervene in the parent-child relationship for the purpose of enforcing its child-labor law.

If the State intervened, its procedures would, of course, be subject to the limitations imposed by the Fourteenth Amendment.

nile wards of the State of Georgia. I believe that the Georgia statute is unconstitutional in that it fails to accord preconfinement hearings to juvenile wards of the State committed by the State acting *in loco parentis.*

I

### Rights of Children Committed to Mental Institutions

Commitment to a mental institution necessarily entails a "massive curtailment of liberty," *Humphrey* v. *Cady,* 405 U.S. 504, 509 (1972), and inevitably affects "fundamental rights." *Baxstrom* v. *Herald,* 383 U.S. 107, 113 (1966). Persons incarcerated in mental hospitals are not only deprived of their physical liberty, they are also deprived of friends, family, and community. Institutionalized mental patients must live in unnatural surroundings under the continuous and detailed control of strangers. They are subject to intrusive treatment which, especially if unwarranted, may violate their right to bodily integrity. Such treatment modalities may include forced administration of psychotropic medication,[1] aversive conditioning,[2] convulsive therapy,[3] and even psychosurgery.[4] Furthermore, as the Court recognizes, see *ante,* at 600, persons confined in mental institutions are stigmatized as sick and abnormal during confinement and, in some cases, even after release.[5]

Because of these considerations, our cases have made clear that commitment to a mental hospital "is a deprivation of liberty which the State cannot accomplish without due process of law." *O'Connor* v. *Donaldson,* 422 U.S. 563, 580 (1975) (BURGER, C. J., concurring). See, *e.g., McNeil* v. *Director, Patuxent Institution,* 407 U.S. 245 (1972) (defective delinquent commitment following expiration of prison term); *Specht* v. *Patterson,* 386 U.S. 605 (1967) (sex offender commitment following criminal conviction); *Chaloner* v. *Sherman,* 242 U.S. 455, 461 (1917) (incompetence inquiry). In the absence of a voluntary, knowing, and intelligent waiver, adults facing commitment to mental institutions are entitled to full and fair adversary hearings in which the necessity for their commitment is established to the satisfaction of a neutral tribunal. At such hearings they must be accorded the right to "be present with counsel, have an opportunity to be heard, be confronted with witnesses against [them], have the right to cross-examine, and to offer evidence of [their] own." *Specht* v. *Patterson, supra,* at 610.

These principles also govern the commitment of children. "Constitutional rights do not mature and come into being magically only when one attains the state-defined age of majority. Minors, as well as adults, are protected by the Constitution and possess constitutional rights. See, *e.g., Breed* v. *Jones,* 421 U.S. 519 (1975);

---

[1]See *Winters* v. *Miller,* 446 F.2d 65 (CA2), cert. denied, 404 U.S. 985 (1971); *Scott* v. *Plante,* 532 F.2d 939 (CA3 1976); *Souder* v. *McGuire,* 423 F. Supp. 830 (MD Pa. 1976).

[2]See *Knecht* v. *Gillman,* 488 F.2d 1136 (CA8 1973); *Mackey* v. *Procunier,* 477 F.2d 877 (CA9 1973).

[3]See *Wyatt* v. *Hardin,* No. 3195-N (MD Ala., Feb. 28, June 26, and July 1, 1975); *Price* v. *Sheppard,* 307 Minn. 250, 239 N. W. 2d 905 (1976); *Nelson* v. *Hudspeth,* C. A. No. J75-40 (R) (SD Miss., May 16, 1977).

[4]See *Kaimowitz* v. *Michigan Dept. of Mental Health,* 42 U. S. L. W. 2063 (Cir. Ct. Wayne Cty., Mich., 1973).

[5]See generally Note, Civil Commitment of the Mentally Ill, 87 Harv. L. Rev. 1190, 1200 (1974).

*Goss* v. *Lopez*, 419 U.S. 565 (1975); *Tinker* v. *Des Moines School Dist.*, 393 U.S. 503 (1969); *In re Gault*, 387 U.S. 1 (1967)." *Planned Parenthood of Central Missouri* v. *Danforth*, 428 U.S. 52, 74 (1976).

Indeed, it may well be argued that children are entitled to more protection than are adults. The consequences of an erroneous commitment decision are more tragic where children are involved. Children, on the average, are confined for longer periods than are adults.[6] Moreover, childhood is a particularly vulnerable time of life[7] and children erroneously institutionalized during their formative years may bear the scars for the rest of their lives.[8] Furthermore, the provision of satisfactory institutionalized mental care for children generally requires a substantial financial commitment[9] that too often has not been forthcoming.[10] Decisions of the lower courts have chronicled the inadequacies of existing mental health facilities for children. See, *e.g.*, *New York State Assn. for Retarded Children* v. *Rockefeller*, 357 F.Supp. 752, 756 (EDNY 1973) (conditions at Willowbrook School for the Mentally Retarded are "inhumane," involving "failure to protect the physical safety of [the] children," substantial personnel shortage, and "poor" and "hazardous" conditions); *Wyatt* v. *Stickney*, 344 F.Supp. 387, 391 (MD Ala. 1972), aff'd *sub nom.* *Wyatt* v. *Aderholt*, 503 F.2d 1305 (CA5 1974) ("grossly substandard" conditions at Partlow School for the Mentally Retarded lead to "hazardous and deplorable inadequacies in the institution's operation").[11]

In addition, the chances of an erroneous commitment decision are particularly great where children are involved. Even under the best of circumstances psychiatric diagnosis and therapy decisions are fraught with uncertainties. See *O'Connor* v. *Donaldson*, *supra*, at 584 (BURGER, C. J., concurring). These uncertainties are aggravated when, as under the Georgia practice, the psychiatrist interviews the child during a period of abnormal stress in connection with the commitment, and without adequate time or opportunity to become acquainted with the patient.[12] These uncertainties may be further aggravated when economic and social class separate doctor and child, thereby frustrating the accurate diagnosis of pathology.[13]

These compounded uncertainties often lead to erroneous commitments since psychiatrists tend to err on the side of medical caution and therefore hospitalize patients

---

[6]See Dept. of HEW, National Institute of Mental Health, Biometry Branch, Statistical Note 90, Utilization of Psychiatric Facilities by Persons 18 Years of Age, Table 8, p. 14 (July 1973).

[7]See J. Bowlby, Child Care and the Growth of Love 80 (1953); J. Horrocks, The Psychology of Adolescence 156 (1976); F. Elkin, Agents of Socialization in Children's Behavior 357, 360 (R. Bergman ed. 1968).

[8]See B. Flint, The Child and the Institution 14–15 (1966); H. Leland & D. Smith, Mental Retardation; Present and Future Perspectives 86 (1974); N. Hobbs, The Futures of Children 142–143 (1975).

[9]See Joint Commission on Mental Health of Children, Crisis in Child Mental Health: Challenge for the 1970's, p.271 (1969).

[10]See R. Kugel & W. Wolfensberger, Changing Patterns in Residential Services for the Mentally Retarded 22 (1969).

[11]See also *Wheeler* v. *Glass*, 473 F.2d 983 (CA7 1973); *Davis* v. *Watkins*, 384 F.Supp. 1196 (ND Ohio 1974); *Welsch* v. *Likins*, 373 F.Supp. 487 (Minn. 1974).

[12]See J. Simmons, Psychiatric Examination of Children 1, 6 (1974); Lourie & Rieger, Psychiatric and Psychological Examination of Children, in 2 American Handbook of Psychiatry 19 (2d ed. 1974).

[13]See Joint Commission on Mental Health of Children, *supra* n. 9, at 267.

for whom other dispositions would be more beneficial.[14] The National Institute of Mental Health recently found that only 36% of patients below age 20 who were confined at St. Elizabeths Hospital actually required such hospitalization.[15] Of particular relevance to this case, a Georgia study Commission on Mental Health Services for Children and Youth concluded that more than half of the State's institutionalized children were not in need of confinement if other forms of care were made available or used. Cited in *J. L.* v. *Parham,* 412 F.Supp. 112, 122 (MD Ga. 1976).

## II

### Rights of Children Committed by Their Parents

### A

Notwithstanding all this, Georgia denies hearings to juveniles institutionalized at the behest of their parents. Georgia rationalizes this practice on the theory that parents act in their children's best interests and therefore may waive their children's due process rights. Children incarcerated because their parents wish them confined, Georgia contends, are really voluntary patients. I cannot accept this argument.

In our society, parental rights are limited by the legitimate rights and interests of their children. "Parents may be free to become martyrs themselves. But it does not follow they are free, in identical circumstances, to make martyrs of their children before they have reached the age of full and legal discretion when they can make that choice for themselves." *Prince* v. *Massachusetts,* 321 U.S. 158, 170 (1944). This principle is reflected in the variety of statutes and cases that authorize state intervention on behalf of neglected or abused children[16] and that, *inter alia,* curtail parental authority to alienate their children's property,[17] to withhold necessary medical treatment,[18] and to deny children exposure to ideas and experiences they may later need as independent and autonomous adults.[19]

This principle is also reflected in constitutional jurisprudence. Notions of pa-

---

[14]See T. Scheff, Being Mentally Ill: A Sociological Theory (1966); Ennis & Litwack, Psychiatry and the Presumption of Expertise: Flipping Coins in the Courtroom, 62 Calif. L. Rev. 693 (1974).

[15]See Dept. of HEW, National Institute of Mental Health, Biometry Branch, Statistical Note 115, Children and State Mental Hospitals 4 (Apr. 1975).

[16]See generally S. Katz, When Parents Fail (1971); M. Midonick & D. Besharov, Children, Parents and the Courts: Juvenile Delinquency, Ungovernability, and Neglect (1972); Wald, State Intervention on Behalf of "Neglected" Children: A Search for Realistic Standards, 27 Stan. L. Rev. 985 (1975).

[17]See, *e.g., Martorell* v. *Ochoa,* 276 F. 99 (CA1 1921).

[18]See, *e.g., Jehovah's Witnesses* v. *King County Hospital,* 278 F. Supp. 488 (WD Wash. 1967), aff'd, 390 U.S. 598 (1968); *In re Sampson,* 65 Misc. 2d 658, 317 N. Y. S. 2d 641 (Fam. Ct. Ulster County, 1970), aff'd, 37 App. Div. 2d 668, 323 N. Y. S. 2d 253 (1971), aff'd, 29 N. Y. 2d 900, 278 N. E. 2d 918 (1972); *State* v. *Perricone,* 37 N. J. 463, 181 A. 2d 751 (1962). Similarly, more recent legal disputes involving the sterilization of children have led to the conclusion that parents are not permitted to authorize operations with such far-reaching consequences. See, *e.g., A. L.* v. *G. R. H.,* 163 Ind. App. 636, 325 N. E. 2d 501 (1975); *In re M. K. R.,* 515 S. W. 2d 467 (Mo. 1974); *Frazier* v. *Levi,* 440 S. W. 2d 393 (Tex. Civ. App. 1969).

[19]See *Commonwealth* v. *Renfrew,* 332 Mass. 492, 126 N. E. 2d 109 (1955); *Meyerkorth* v. *State,* 173 Neb. 889, 115 N. W. 2d 585 (1962), appeal dismissed, 372 U.S. 705 (1963); *In re Weberman,* 198 Misc. 1055, 100 N. Y. S. 2d 60 (Sup. Ct. 1950), aff'd, 278 App. Div. 656, 102 N. Y. S. 2d 418, aff'd, 302 N. Y. 855, 100 N. E. 2d 47, appeal dismissed, 342 U.S. 884 (1951).

rental authority and family autonomy cannot stand as absolute and invariable barriers to the assertion of constitutional rights by children. States, for example, may not condition a minor's right to secure an abortion on attaining her parents' consent since the right to an abortion is an important personal right and since disputes between parents and children on this question would fracture family autonomy. See *Planned Parenthood of Central Missouri* v. *Danforth*, 428 U.S., at 75.

This case is governed by the rule of *Danforth*. The right to be free from wrongful incarceration, physical intrusion, and stigmatization has significance for the individual surely as great as the right to an abortion. Moreover, as in *Danforth*, the parent-child dispute at issue here cannot be characterized as involving only a routine child-rearing decision made within the context of an ongoing family relationship. Indeed, *Danforth* involved only a potential dispute between parent and child, whereas here a break in family autonomy has actually resulted in the parents' decision to surrender custody of their child to a state mental institution. In my view, a child who has been ousted from his family has even greater need for an independent advocate.

Additional considerations counsel against allowing parents unfettered power to institutionalize their children without cause or without any hearing to ascertain that cause. The presumption that parents act in their children's best interests, while applicable to most child-rearing decisions, is not applicable in the commitment context. Numerous studies reveal that parental decisions to institutionalize their children often are the results of dislocation in the family unrelated to the children's mental condition.[20] Moreover, even well-meaning parents lack the expertise necessary to evaluate the relative advantages and disadvantages of inpatient as opposed to outpatient psychiatric treatment. Parental decisions to waive hearings in which such questions could be explored, therefore, cannot be conclusively deemed either informed or intelligent. In these circumstances, I respectfully suggest, it ignores reality to assume blindly that parents act in their children's best interests when making commitment decisions and when waiving their children's due process rights.

### B

This does not mean States are obliged to treat children who are committed at the behest of their parents in precisely the same manner as other persons who are involuntarily committed. The demands of due process are flexible and the parental commitment decision carries with it practical implications that States may legitimately take into account. While as a general rule due process requires that commitment hearings precede involuntary hospitalization, when parents seek to hospitalize their children special considerations militate in favor of postponement of formal commitment proceedings and against mandatory adversary preconfinement commitment hearings.

First, the prospect of an adversary hearing prior to admission might deter parents from seeking needed medical attention for their children. Second, the hearings themselves might delay treatment of children whose home life has become impossible and who require some form of immediate state care. Furthermore, because adversary

---

[20]Murdock, Civil Rights of the Mentally Retarded: Some Critical Issues, 48 Notre Dame Law. 133, 138 (1972); Vogel & Bell, The Emotionally Disturbed Child as the Family Scapegoat, in a Modern Introduction to the Family 412 (1968).

hearings at this juncture would necessarily involve direct challenges to parental authority, judgment, or veracity, preadmission hearings may well result in pitting the child and his advocate against the parents. This, in turn, might traumatize both parent and child and make the child's eventual return to his family more difficult.

Because of these special considerations, I believe that States may legitimately postpone formal commitment proceedings when parents seek inpatient psychiatric treatment for their children. Such children may be admitted, for a limited period, without prior hearing, so long as the admitting psychiatrist first interviews parent and child and concludes that short-term inpatient treatment would be appropriate.

Georgia's present admission procedures are reasonably consistent with these principles. See *ante,* at 613–616. To the extent the District Court invalidated this aspect of the Georgia juvenile commitment scheme and mandated preconfinement hearings in all cases, I agree with the Court that the District Court was in error.

## C

I do not believe, however, that the present Georgia juvenile commitment scheme is constitutional in its entirety. Although parents seek to commit their children, the State cannot dispense with such hearings altogether. Our cases make clear that, when protected interests are at stake, the "fundamental requirement of due process is the opportunity to be heard 'at a meaningful time and in a meaningful manner.'" *Mathews* v. *Eldridge,* 424 U.S. 319, 333 (1976), quoting in part from *Armstrong* v. *Manzo,* 380 U.S. 545, 552 (1965). Whenever prior hearings are impracticable, States must provide reasonably prompt postdeprivation hearings. Compare *North Georgia Finishing, Inc.* v. *Di-Chem, Inc.,* 419 U.S. 601 (1975), with *Mitchell* v. *W. T. Grant Co.,* 416 U.S. 600 (1974).

The informal postadmission procedures that Georgia now follows are simply not enough to qualify as hearings—let alone reasonably prompt hearings. The procedures lack all the traditional due process safeguards. Commitment decisions are made *ex parte.* Georgia's institutionalized juveniles are not informed of the reasons for their commitment; nor do they enjoy the right to be present at the commitment determination, the right to representation, the right to be heard, the right to be confronted with adverse witnesses, the right to cross-examine, or the right to offer evidence of their own. By any standard of due process, these procedures are deficient. See *Wolff* v. *McDonnell,* 418 U.S. 539 (1974); *Morrissey* v. *Brewer,* 408 U.S. 471 (1972); *McNeil* v. *Director, Patuxent Institution,* 407 U.S. 245 (1972); *Specht* v. *Patterson,* 386 U.S., at 610. See also *Goldberg* v. *Kelly,* 397 U.S. 254, 269–271 (1970). I cannot understand why the Court pretermits condemnation of these *ex parte* procedures which operate to deny Georgia's institutionalized juveniles even "some form of hearing." *Mathews* v. *Eldridge, supra,* at 333, before they are condemned to suffer the rigors of long-term institutional confinement.[21]

---

[21]The National Institute of Mental Health has reported:

"[T]housands upon thousands of elderly patients now confined on the back wards of . . . state [mental] institutions were first admitted as children thirty, forty, and even fifty years ago. A recent report from one state estimates that one in every four children admitted to its mental hospitals 'can anticipate being permanently hospitalized for the next 50 years of their lives.'" Joint Commission on Mental Health of Children, *supra* n. 9, at 5–6.

The special considerations that militate against preadmission commitment hearings when parents seek to hospitalize their children do not militate against reasonably prompt postadmission commitment hearings. In the first place, postadmission hearings would not delay the commencement of needed treatment. Children could be cared for by the State pending the disposition decision.

Second, the interest in avoiding family discord would be less significant at this stage since the family autonomy already will have been fractured by the institutionalization of the child. In any event, postadmission hearings are unlikely to disrupt family relationships. At later hearings, the case for and against commitment would be based upon the observations of the hospital staff and the judgments of the staff psychiatrists, rather than upon parental observations and recommendations. The doctors urging commitment, and not the parents, would stand as the child's adversaries. As a consequence, postadmission commitment hearings are unlikely to involve direct challenges to parental authority, judgment, or veracity. To defend the child, the child's advocate need not dispute the parents' original decision to seek medical treatment for their child, or even, for that matter, their observations concerning the child's behavior. The advocate need only argue, for example, that the child had sufficiently improved during his hospital stay to warrant outpatient treatment or outright discharge. Conflict between doctor and advocate on this question is unlikely to lead to family discord.

As a consequence, the prospect of a postadmission hearing is unlikely to deter parents from seeking medical attention for their children and the hearing itself is unlikely so to traumatize parent and child as to make the child's eventual return to the family impracticable.

Nor would postadmission hearings defeat the primary purpose of the state juvenile mental health enterprise. Under the present juvenile commitment scheme, Georgia parents do not enjoy absolute discretion to commit their children to public mental hospitals. See *ante,* at 614–615. Superintendents of state facilities may not accept children for long-term treatment unless they first determine that the children are mentally ill and will likely benefit from long-term hospital care. See *ibid.* If the superintendent determines either condition is unmet, the child must be released or refused admission, regardless of the parents' desires. See *ibid.* No legitimate state interest would suffer if the superintendent's determinations were reached through fair proceedings with due consideration of fairly presented opposing viewpoints rather than through the present practice of secret, *ex parte* deliberations.[22]

Nor can the good faith and good intentions of Georgia's psychiatrists and social workers, adverted to by the Court, see *ante,* at 615–616, excuse Georgia's *ex parte* procedures. Georgia's admitting psychiatrists, like the school disciplinarians described in *Goss* v. *Lopez,* 419 U.S. 565 (1975), "although proceeding in utmost good faith,

---

[22]Indeed, postadmission hearings may well advance the purposes of the state enterprise. First, hearings will promote accuracy and ensure that the superintendent diverts children who do not require hospitalization to more appropriate programs. Second, the hearings themselves may prove therapeutic. Children who feel that they have received a fair hearing may be more likely to accept the legitimacy of their confinement, acknowledge their illness, and cooperate with those attempting to give treatment. This, in turn, would remove a significant impediment to successful therapy. See Katz, The Right to Treatment—An Enchanting Legal Fiction?, 36 U. Chi. L. Rev. 755, 768–769 (1969); *O'Connor* v. *Donaldson,* 422 U.S. 563, 579 (1975) (BURGER, C. J., concurring).

frequently act on the reports and advice of others; and the controlling facts and the nature of the conduct under challenge are often disputed.'' *Id.*, at 580. See App. 188–190, testimony of Dr. Messinger. Here, as in *Goss*, the ''risk of error is not at all trivial, and it should be guarded against if that may be done without prohibitive cost or interference with the . . . process. . . . '[F]airness can rarely be obtained by secret, one-sided determination of facts decisive of rights. . . .' 'Secrecy is not congenial to truth-seeking and self-righteousness gives too slender an assurance of rightness. No better instrument has been devised for arriving at truth than to give a person in jeopardy of serious loss notice of the case against him and opportunity to meet it.' '' *Goss* v. *Lopez, supra,* at 580, quoting in part from *Anti-Fascist Committee* v. *McGrath,* 341 U.S. 123, 170, 171–172 (1951) (FRANKFURTER, J., concurring).

## III
### Rights of Children Committed by Their State Guardians

Georgia does not accord prior hearings to juvenile wards of the State of Georgia committed by state social workers acting *in loco parentis.* The Court dismisses a challenge to this practice on the grounds that state social workers are obliged by statute to act in the children's best interest. See *ante*, at 619.

I find this reasoning particularly unpersuasive. With equal logic, it could be argued that criminal trials are unnecessary since prosecutors are not supposed to prosecute innocent persons.

To my mind, there is no justification for denying children committed by their social workers the prior hearings that the Constitution typically requires. In the first place, such children cannot be said to have waived their rights to a prior hearing simply because their social workers wished them to be confined. The rule that parents speak for their children, even if it were applicable in the commitment context, cannot be transmuted into a rule that state social workers speak for their minor clients. The rule in favor of deference to parental authority is designed to shield parental control of child rearing from state interference. See *Pierce* v. *Society of Sisters,* 268 U.S. 510, 535 (1925). The rule cannot be invoked in defense of unfettered state control of child rearing or to immunize from review the decisions of state social workers. The social worker-child relationship is not deserving of the special protection and deference accorded to the parent-child relationship, and state officials acting *in loco parentis* cannot be equated with parents. See *O'Connor* v. *Donaldson,* 422 U.S. 563 (1975); *Wisconsin* v. *Yoder,* 406 U.S. 205 (1972).

Second, the special considerations that justify postponement of formal commitment proceedings whenever parents seek to hospitalize their children are absent when the children are wards of the State and are being committed upon the recommendations of their social workers. The prospect of preadmission hearings is not likely to deter state social workers from discharging their duties and securing psychiatric attention for their disturbed clients. Moreover, since the children will already be in some form of state custody as wards of the State, prehospitalization hearings will not prevent needy children from receiving state care during the pendency of the commitment proceedings. Finally, hearings in which the decisions of state social workers are reviewed by other state officials are not likely to traumatize the children or to hinder their eventual recovery.

For these reasons, I believe that, in the absence of exigent circumstances, juveniles committed upon the recommendation of their social workers are entitled to preadmission commitment hearings. As a consequence, I would hold Georgia's present practice of denying these juveniles prior hearings unconstitutional.

## IV

Children incarcerated in public mental institutions are constitutionally entitled to a fair opportunity to contest the legitimacy of their confinement. They are entitled to some champion who can speak on their behalf and who stands ready to oppose a wrongful commitment. Georgia should not be permitted to deny that opportunity and that champion simply because the children's parents or guardians wish them to be confined without a hearing. The risk of erroneous commitment is simply too great unless there is some form of adversary review. And fairness demands that children abandoned by their supposed protectors to the rigors of institutional confinement be given the help of some separate voice.

NOTES

1. What remedial actions are left open within the Court's ruling for a child who has been inappropriately confined in an institution?

2. Does Chief Justice Berger's opinion for the Court give any indication of the adequacy of the record in *Parham?* Could certain additional evidence, concerning, for example, the "dumping" of children by parents, or biases of admitting physicians, have changed the outcome?

3. What are the practical ramifications of a post-admission hearing advocated in Justice Brennan's opinion as contrasted with a pre-admission hearing sought by the *Parham* plaintiffs?

4. Consider the accuracy of the reasoning in footnote 6 of Justice Stewart's concurring opinion in light of *O'Connor* v. *Donaldson*, pp. 618–629 of the *Casebook*.

### SECRETARY OF PUBLIC WELFARE OF PENNSYLVANIA v. INSTITUTIONALIZED JUVENILES

*Supreme Court of the United States, 1979*
*442 U.S. 640*

MR. CHIEF JUSTICE BURGER delivered the opinion of the Court.

This appeal raises issues similar to those decided in *Parham* v. *J. R., ante,* p. 584, as to what process is due when the parents or guardian of a child seek state institutional mental health care.

## I

This is the second time we have reviewed a District Court's judgment that Pennsylvania's procedures for the voluntary admission of mentally ill and mentally retarded children to a state hospital are unconstitutional. In the earlier suit, five children who were between the ages of 15 and 18 challenged the 1966 statute pursuant to which they had been admitted to Haverford State Hospital. Pa.Stat.Ann., Tit. 50, §§ 4402, 4403 (Purdon 1969). After a three-judge District Court, with one judge dissenting, declared the statute unconstitutional, *Bartley* v. *Kremens,* 402 F.Supp. 1039 (ED Pa. 1975), the Pennsylvania Legislature amended its mental health code with regard to the mentally ill. The amendments placed adolescents over the age of 14 in essentially the same position as adults for purposes of a voluntary admission. Mental Health Procedures Act of 1976, § 201, Pa.Stat.Ann., Tit. 50, § 7201 (Purdon Supp. 1978). Under the new statute, the named plaintiffs could obtain their requested releases from the state hospitals independently of the constitutionality of the 1966 statute, and we therefore held that the claims of the named plaintiffs were moot. *Kremens* v. *Bartley,* 431 U.S. 119, 129 (1977). We then remanded the case to the District Court for "reconsideration of the class definition, exclusion of those whose claims are moot, and substitution of class representatives with live claims." *Id.,* at 135.

On remand, 12 new plaintiffs, appellees here, were named to represent classes of mentally ill and mentally retarded children. Nine of the children were younger than 14 and constituted all of those who had been admitted to the State's hospitals for the mentally ill in accordance with the 1976 Act at the time the suit was brought; three other children represented a class of patients who were 18 and younger and who had been or would be admitted to a state hospital for the mentally retarded under the 1966 Act and 1973 regulations implementing the Act. All 12 children had been admitted on the application of parents or someone standing *in loco parentis* with state approval after an independent medical examination.

The suit was filed against several named defendants, the Pennsylvania Secretary of Public Welfare and the directors of three state owned and operated facilities. The District Court, however, certified a defendant class that consisted of " 'directors of all mental health and mental retardation facilities in Pennsylvania which are subject to regulation by the defendant Secretary of Public Welfare.' " 459 F.Supp. 30, 40 n. 37 (ED Pa. 1978).

Representatives of the nine mentally ill children sought a declaration that the admission procedures embodied in § 201[2] of the Pennsylvania Mental Health Procedures Act of 1976, Pa.Stat.Ann., Tit. 50, § 7201 (Purdon Supp. 1978), which subsequently have been expanded by regulations promulgated by the Secretary of Public Welfare, 8 Pa.Bull. 2432 et seq. (1978), violated their procedural due process rights and requested the court to issue an injunction against the statute's future enforcement. The three mentally retarded children presented the same claims as to §§ 402[3] and

---

[2]Section 201 provides in part: "A parent, guardian, or person standing in loco parentis to a child less than 14 years of age may subject such child to examination and treatment under this act, and in so doing shall be deemed to be acting for the child."

[3]Section 402 provides:

      (a) Application for voluntary admission to facility for examination, treatment and care may be made by: (2) a parent, guardian or individual standing in loco parentis to the person to be admitted, if such person is eighteen years of age or younger.

      (b) When an application is made, the director of the facility shall cause an examination to be made. If it is determined that the person named in the application is in need of care or observation, he may be admitted.

403[4] of the Mental Health and Mental Retardation Act of 1966, Pa.Stat.Ann., Tit. 50, §§ 4402, 4403 (Purdon 1969), and the regulations promulgated thereunder.

The District Court certified two subclasses of plaintiffs[6] under Fed. Rule Civ. Proc. 23 and held that the statutes challenged by each subclass were unconstitutional. It held that the State's procedures were insufficient to satisfy the Due Process Clause of the Fourteenth Amendment.

The District Court's analysis in this case was similar to that used by the District Court in *J. L. v. Parham*, 412 F.Supp. 112 (MD Ga. 1976), reversed and remanded *sub nom. Parham v. J. R., ante*, p. 584. The court in this case concluded that these children had a constitutionally protected liberty interest that could not be "waived" by their parents. This conclusion, coupled with the perceived fallibility of psychiatric diagnosis, led the court to hold that only a formal adversary hearing could suffice to protect the children in appellees' class from being needlessly confined in mental hospitals.

To further protect the children's interests, the court concluded that the following procedures were required before any child could be admitted voluntarily to a mental hospital:

1) 48-hour notice prior to any hearing;
2) legal counsel "during all significant stages of the commitment process";
3) the child's presence at all commitment hearings;
4) a finding by an impartial tribunal based on clear and convincing evidence that the child required institutional treatment;
5) a probable-cause determination within 72 hours after admission to a hospital;
6) A full hearing, including the right to confront and cross-examine witnesses, within two weeks from the date of the initial admission. App. 1097a–1098a.

Appellants, all of the defendants before the District Court, appealed the judgment. We noted probable jurisdiction, and consolidated the case with *Parham* v. *J. R., ante*, p.584. 437 U.S. 902.

## II

(a) Much of what we said in *Parham* v. *J. R.* applies with equal force to this case. The liberty rights and interests of the appellee children, the prerogatives, respon-

---

[4]Section 403 provides:

(a) Application for voluntary commitment to a facility for examination, treatment and care may be made by:
(2) A parent, guardian or individual standing in loco parentis to the person to be admitted, if such person is eighteen years of age or younger.
(b) The application shall be in writing, signed by the applicant in the presence of at least one witness. When an application is made, the director of the facility shall cause an examination to be made. If it is determined that the person named in the application is in need of care or observation, he shall be committed for a period not to exceed thirty days.

[6]One subclass consisted of "all juveniles under the age of fourteen who are subject to inpatient treatment under Article II of the 1976 Act." 459 F. Supp., at 41. The other subclass was "mentally retarded juveniles age eighteen or younger." *Id.*, at 42. Appellants argue that the District Court failed to heed our admonition in remanding this case previously that it should " 'stop, look, and listen' before certifying a class in order to adjudicate constitutional claims." *Kremens v. Bartley*, 431 U.S. 119, 135 (1977). Given our disposition of the merits of this appeal, we need not decide whether these subclasses satisfy the requirements of Fed. Rule Civ. Proc. 23.

sibilities, and interests of the parents, and the obligations and interests of the State are the same. Our holding as to what process is due in *Parham* controls here, particularly:

> We conclude that the risk of error inherent in the parental decision to have a child institutionalized for mental health care is sufficiently great that some kind of inquiry should be made by a "neutral factfinder" to determine whether the statutory requirements for admission are satisfied. . . . That inquiry must carefully probe the child's background using all available sources, including, but not limited to, parents, schools, and other social agencies. Of course, the review must also include an interview with the child. It is necessary that the decisionmaker have the authority to refuse to admit any child who does not satisfy the medical standards for admission. Finally, it is necessary that the child's continuing need for commitment be reviewed periodically by a similarly independent procedure.   *Parham* v. *J. R., ante,* at 606–607.

The only issue is whether Pennsylvania's procedures for the voluntary commitment of children comply with these requirements.

(b) Unlike in *Parham* v. *J. R.,* where the statute being challenged was general and thus the procedures for admission were evaluated hospital by hospital, the statute and regulations in Pennsylvania are specific. Our focus here is on the codified procedures declared unconstitutional by the District Court.

The Mental Health Procedures Act of 1976 and regulations promulgated by the Secretary describe the procedures for the voluntary admission for inpatient treatment of mentally ill children. Section 201 of the Act provides that "a parent, guardian, or person standing in loco parentis to a child less than 14 years of age" may apply for a voluntary examination and treatment for the child. After the child receives an examination and is provided with temporary treatment, the hospital must formulate "an individualized treatment plan . . . by a treatment team." Within 72 hours the treatment team is required to determine whether inpatient treatment is "necessary" and why. Pa.Stat.Ann., Tit. 50, § 7205 (Purdon Supp. 1978). The hospital must inform the child and his parents both of the necessity for institutional treatment and of the nature of the proposed treatment. *Ibid.*

Regulations promulgated under the 1976 Act provide that each child shall be reexamined and his or her treatment plan reviewed not less than once every 30 days. See § 7100.108 (a), 8 Pa.Bull. 2436 (1978). The regulations also permit a child to object to the treatment plan and thereby obtain a review by a mental health professional independent of the treatment team. The findings of this person are reported directly to the director of the hospital who has the power and the obligation to release any child who no longer needs institutional treatment.

The statute indeed provides three methods for release of a child under the age of 14 from a mental hospital. First, the child's parents or guardian may effect his release at will. Pa.Stat.Ann., Tit. 50, § 7206 (b) (Purdon Supp. 1978). Second, "any responsible party" may petition the juvenile court if the person believes that treatment in a less restrictive setting would be in the best interests of the child. *Ibid.* If such a petition is filed, an attorney is appointed to represent the child's interests and a hearing is held within 10 days to determine "what inpatient treatment, if any, is in the minor's best interest." *Ibid.* Finally, the director of the hospital may release any child whenever institutional treatment is no longer medically indicated. § 7206 (c).

The Mental Health and Mental Retardation Act of 1966 regulates the voluntary admission for inpatient hospital habilitation of the mentally retarded. The admission process has been expanded significantly by regulations promulgated in 1973 by Pennsylvania's Secretary of Public Welfare. 3 Pa.Bull. 1840 (1973). Unlike the procedure for the mentally ill, a hospital is not permitted to admit a mentally retarded child based solely on the application of a parent or guardian. All children must be referred by a physician and each referral must be accompanied by a medical or psychological evaluation. In addition, the director of the institution must make an independent examination of each child, and if he disagrees with the recommendation of the referring physician as to whether hospital care is "required," the child must be discharged. Mentally retarded children or anyone acting on their behalf may petition for a writ of habeas corpus to challenge the sufficiency or legality of the "proceedings leading to commitment." Pa.Stat.Ann., Tit. 50, § 4426 (Purdon 1969).

Any child older than 13 who is admitted to a hospital must have his rights explained to him and must be informed that a status report on his condition will be provided periodically. The older child is also permitted to object, either orally or in writing, to his hospitalization. After such objection, the director of the facility, if he feels that hospitalization is still necessary, must institute an involuntary commitment proceeding under § 406 of the Act, Pa.Stat.Ann., Tit. 50, § 4406 (Purdon 1969).

What the statute and regulations do not make clear is how the hospital staff decides that inpatient care is required for a child. The director of Haverford State Hospital for the mentally ill was the sole witness called by either side to testify about the decisionmaking process at a state hospital. She described the process as follows:

> [T]here is an initial examination made by the psychiatrist, and is so designated as an admission note on the hospital record. Subsequently, for all adolescents on the Adolescent Service at Haverford State Hospital, there are routine services done, such as an electroencephalogram, a neurological examination, a medical examination, and a complete battery of psychological tests and school evaluation, as well as a psychiatric evaluation. When all their data has been compiled, an entire staff conference is held, which is called a new case conference, at which point the complete case is re-examined and it is decided whether or not the child needs hospitalization, and at the same time, as well, an adequate treatment course is planned. App. 112a.

In addition to the physical and mental examinations that are conducted for each child within the institutions, the staff compiles a substantial "pre-admission background information" file on each child. After the child is admitted, there is a periodic review of the child's condition by the staff. His status is reviewed by a different social worker at least every 30 days. Since the State places a great deal of emphasis on family therapy, the parents or guardians are met with weekly to discuss the child's case. Id., at 113a.

We are satisfied that these procedures comport with the due process requirements set out earlier. No child is admitted without at least one and often more psychiatric examinations by an independent team of mental health professionals whose sole concern under the statute is whether the child needs and can benefit from institutional care. The treatment team not only interviews the child and parents but also compiles a full background history from all available sources. If the treatment team concludes that institutional care is not in the child's best interest, it must refuse the child's admission. Finally, the child's condition is reviewed at least every 30 days. This program meets the criteria of our holding in *Parham*.[9] Accordingly, the judgment of the District Court that Pennsylvania's statutes and regulations are unconstitutional is reversed, and the case is remanded for further proceedings consistent with this opinion.

*Reversed and remanded.*

For the reasons stated in his opinion concurring in the judgment in *Parham* v. *J. R., ante*, p. 621, MR. JUSTICE STEWART concurs in the judgment.

MR. JUSTICE BRENNAN, with whom MR. JUSTICE MARSHALL and MR. JUSTICE STEVENS join, concurring in part and dissenting in part.

For the reasons stated in my opinion in *Parham* v. *J. R., ante*, p. 625 (BRENNAN, J., concurring in part and dissenting in part), I agree with the Court that Pennsylvania's preadmission psychiatric interview procedures pass constitutional muster. I cannot agree, however, with the Court's decision to pretermit questions concerning Pennsylvania's postadmission procedures. See *ante*, at 650 n. 9. In my view, these procedures should be condemned now.

Pennsylvania provides neither representation nor reasonably prompt postadmission hearings to mentally retarded children 13 years of age and younger. For the reasons stated in my opinion in *Parham* v. *J. R.* I believe that this is unconstitutional.

As a practical matter, mentally reatarded children over 13 and children confined as mentally ill fare little better. While under current regulations these children must be informed of their right to a hearing and must be given the telephone number of an attorney within 24 hours of admission, see 459 F.Supp. 30, 49, 51 (ED Pa. 1978) (BRODERICK, J., dissenting), the burden of contacting counsel and the burden of initiating proceedings is placed upon the child. In my view, this placement of the burden vitiates Pennsylvania's procedures. Many of the institutionalized children are unable to read, write, comprehend the formal explanation of their rights, or use the telephone. See App. 1019a (testimony of L. Glenn). Few, as a consequence, will be able to take the initiative necessary for them to secure the advice and assistance of a trained representative. Few will be able to trigger the procedural safeguards and hearing rights that Pennsylvania formally provides. Indeed, for most of Pennsylvania's institutionalized children the recitation of rights required by current regulations will amount to no more than a hollow ritual. If the children's constitutional rights to representation and to a fair hearing are to be guaranteed in substance as well as in form and if the commands of the Fourteenth Amendment are to be satisfied, then waiver of

---

[9]Although the District Court briefly described the situation of each of the children in appellees' class, it did not indicate the process for each of their admissions. We cannot determine on the record before us whether each child's admission conformed to our due process standards. Just as in *Parham*, individual members of Appellees' class are free to argue on remand that their particular commitments violated those standards.

Also, we note that as in *Parham* we are faced only with the issue of what process is due at the initial admission, and thus we are not deciding what postadmission procedures are constitutionally adequate to continue a voluntary commitment. The District Court had no reason to consider that issue, and indeed from our reading of appellees' complaint there does not appear to be any specific challenge to the State's review procedures. However, we leave it to the District Court on remand to determine what further proceedings are necessary.

those constitutional rights cannot be inferred from mere silence or inaction on the part of the institutionalized child. Cf. *Johnson* v. *Zerbst,* 304 U.S. 458, 464 (1938). Pennsylvania must assign each institutionalized child a representative obliged to initiate contact with the child and ensure that the child's constitutional rights are fully protected. Otherwise, it is inevitable that the children's due process rights will be lost through inadvertence, inaction, or incapacity. See 459 F.Supp., at 44 n. 47; *Bartley* v. *Kremens,* 402 F.Supp. 1039, 1050–1051 (ED Pa. 1975).

NOTES

1. Compare the factual situation and procedures at issue in the *Institutionalized Juveniles* case with those in *Parham.* Does the *Parham* rationale resolve the issues in *Institutionalized Juveniles* as the Court indicates? Does confinement of mentally retarded children raise any issues other than the institutionalization of mentally ill children?

2. Consider the implications of footnote 9 of the Court's opinion.

3. How are situations such as those raised in the *Parham* and *Institutionalized Juveniles* cases affected by the Court's ruling in the later case of *Youngberg* v. *Romeo,* pp. 223–235 above?

## D. ALTERNATIVES TO INSTITUTIONALIZATION

p. 701—DELETE the last sentence of Note 5 and replace it with the following:

But see the Supreme Court's resolution of this issue in the appeal of the *Pennhurst* decision, pp. 270–282 below.

p. 701—INSERT after the end of the Notes:

### PENNHURST STATE SCHOOL AND HOSPITAL v. HALDERMAN
*Supreme Court of the United States, 1981*
*451 U.S. 1*

JUSTICE REHNQUIST delivered the opinion of the Court.

At issue in these cases is the scope and meaning of the Developmentally Disabled Assistance and Bill of Rights Act of 1975, 89 Stat. 486, as amended. 42 U.S.C. § 6000 *et seq.* (1976 ed. and Supp. III). The Court of Appeals for the Third Circuit held that the Act created substantive rights in favor of the mentally retarded, that those rights were judicially enforceable, and that conditions at the Pennhurst State School and Hospital (Pennhurst), a facility for the care and treatment of the mentally retarded, violated those rights. For the reasons stated below, we reverse the decision of the Court of Appeals and remand the cases for further proceedings.

I

The Commonwealth of Pennsylvania owns and operates Pennhurst. Pennhurst is a large institution, housing approximately 1,200 residents. Seventy-five percent of the residents are either "severely" or "profoundly" retarded—that is, with an IQ of less than 35—and a number of the residents are also physically handicapped. About half of its residents were committed there by court order and half by a parent or other guardian.

In 1974, respondent Terri Lee Halderman, a minor retarded resident of Pennhurst, filed suit in the District Court for the Eastern District of Pennsylvania on behalf of herself and all other Pennhurst residents against Pennhurst, its superintendent, and various officials of the Commonwealth of Pennsylvania responsible for the operation of Pennhurst. The additional respondents (hereinafter, with respondent Halderman, referred to as respondents) in these cases—other mentally retarded persons, the United States, and the Pennsylvania Association for Retarded Citizens (PARC)—subsequently intervened as plaintiffs. PARC added several surrounding counties as defendants, alleging that they were responsible for the commitment of persons to Pennhurst.

As amended in 1975, the complaint alleged, *inter alia,* that conditions at Pennhurst were unsanitary, inhumane, and dangerous. Specifically, the complaint averred that these conditions denied the class members due process and equal protection of the law in violation of the Fourteenth Amendment, inflicted on them cruel and unusual punishment in violation of the Eighth and Fourteenth Amendments, and denied them certain rights conferred by the Rehabilitation Act of 1973, 87 Stat. 355, as amended. 29 U.S.C. § 701 *et seq.* (1976 ed. and Supp. III), the Developmentally Disabled Assistance and Bill of Rights Act. 42 U.S.C. §§ 6001 *et seq.* (1976 ed. and Supp. III), and the Pennsylvania Mental Health and Mental Retardation Act of 1966. Pa.Stat.Ann., Tit. 50, §§ 4101–4704 (Purdon 1969). In addition to seeking injunctive and monetary relief, the complaint urged that Pennhurst be closed and that "community living arrangements"[1] be established for its residents.

The District Court certified a class consisting of all persons who have been or may become residents of Pennhurst. After a 32-day trial, it issued an opinion, reported at 446 F.Supp. 1295 (1977), making findings of fact and conclusions of law with respect to the conditions at Pennhurst. Its findings of fact are undisputed: Conditions at Pennhurst are not only dangerous, with the residents often physically abused or drugged by staff members, but also inadequate for the "habilitation" of the retarded.[2] Indeed, the court found that the physical, intellectual, and emotional skills of some residents have deteriorated at Pennhurst. *Id.,* at 1308–1310.

The District Court went on to hold that the mentally retarded have a federal constitutional right to be provided with "minimally adequate habilitation" in the "least restrictive environment," regardless of whether they were voluntarily or involuntarily committed. *Id.,* at 1314–1320. The court also held that there existed a constitutional right to "be free from harm" under the Eighth Amendment, and to be provided with "nondiscriminatory habilitation" under the Equal Protection Clause. *Id.,* at 1320–1322. In addition, it found that § 504 of the Rehabilitation Act of 1973, 29 U.S.C. § 794, and § 201 of the Pennsylvania Mental Health and Mental Retardation

---

[1] "Community living arrangements" are smaller, less isolated residences where retarded persons are treated as much as possible like nonretarded persons.

[2] There is a technical difference between "treatment," which applies to curable mental illness, and "habilitation," which consists of education and training for those, such as the mentally retarded, who are not ill. This opinion, like the opinions of the courts below, will use the terms interchangeably.

Act of 1966, Pa.Stat.Ann., Tit. 50, § 4201 (Purdon 1969), provided a right to minimally adequate habilitation in the least restrictive environment.

Each of these rights was found to have been violated by the conditions existing at Pennhurst. Indeed, the court held that a large institution such as Pennhurst could not provide adequate habilitation. 446 F.Supp., at 1318. It thus ordered that Pennhurst eventually be closed, that suitable "community living arrangements" be provided for all Pennhurst residents, that plans for the removal of residents from Pennhurst be submitted to the court, that individual treatment plans be developed for each resident with the participation of his or her family, and that conditions at Pennhurst be improved in the interim. The court appointed a Special Master to supervise the implementation of this order. *Id.*, at 1326–1329.

The Court of Appeals for the Third Circuit substantially affirmed the District Court's remedial order. 612 F.2d 84 (1979) (en banc). Unlike the District Court, however, the Court of Appeals sought to avoid the constitutional claims raised by respondents and instead rested its order on a construction of the Developmentally Disabled Assistance and Bill of Rights Act, 42 U.S.C. § 6000 *et seq.* (1976 ed. and Supp. III).[3] It found that §§ 111 (1) and (2) of the Act, 89 Stat. 502, 42 U.S.C. §§ 6010 (1) and (2), the "bill of rights" provision, grant to mentally retarded persons a right to "appropriate treatment, services, and habilitation" in "the setting that is least restrictive of . . . personal liberty." The court further held that under the test articulated in *Cort* v. *Ash,* 422 U.S. 66, 78 (1975), mentally retarded persons have an implied cause of action to enforce that right. 612 F.2d, at 97. Because the court found that Congress enacted the statute pursuant to both § 5 of the Fourteenth Amendment[4] and the spending power,[5] it declined to consider whether a statute enacted pursuant to the spending power alone "could ever provide the predicate for private substantive rights." *Id.*, at 98. As an alternative ground, the court affirmed the District Court's holding that Pennhurst residents have a state statutory right to adequate "habilitation."

The court concluded that the conditions at Pennhurst violated these federal and state statutory rights. As to relief, it affirmed the order of the District Court except insofar as it ordered Pennhurst to be closed. Although the court concluded that "deinstitutionalization is the favored approach to habilitation" in the least restrictive environment, it did not construe the Act to require the closing of large institutions like

---

[3]As originally enacted in 1975, the definition of "developmentally disabled" included mental retardation. § 6001 (7)(A)(i). As amended in 1978, however, a mentally retarded individual is considered developmentally disabled only if he satisfies various criteria set forth in the Act.

It is perhaps suggestive of the novelty of the Court of Appeals' decision that none of the respondents briefed the Act before the District Court, nor raised it in the Court of Appeals. Rather, the court itself suggested the applicability of the Act and requested supplemental briefs on the issue for purpose of rehearing en banc. Even then the United States, which raised only constitutional claims before the District Court, contended merely that the "most significant implication of the Developmentally Disabled Act is the important light which it sheds upon congressional intent about the nature of the rights of institutionalized mentally retarded persons, and the guidance which it may give in discerning a violation of Section 504 [of the Rehabilitation Act]." Supplemental Brief for United States in No. 78-1490 (CA3), p. 2.

[4]Section 5 of the Fourteenth Amendment provides that "[t]he Congress shall have power to enforce, by appropriate legislation, the provisions of this article."

[5]The spending power is encompassed in Art. I, § 8, cl. 1, of the Constitution which states the "Congress shall have the Power To . . . provide for the . . . general Welfare of the United States."

Pennhurst. *Id.*, at 115. The court thus remanded the case to the District Court for "individual determinations by the court, or by the Special Master, as to the appropriateness of an improved Pennhurst for each such patient" and instructed the District Court or the Master to "engage in a presumption in favor of placing individuals in [community living arrangements.]" *id.*, at 114–115.

Three judges dissented. Although they assumed that the majority was correct in holding that Pennhurst residents have a right to treatment under the Act and an implied cause of action under the Act to enforce that right, they disagreed that the Act imposed a duty on the defendants to provide the "least restrictive treatment" possible. The dissent stated that "the language and structure of the Act, the relevant regulations, and the legislative history all indicate that the States may consider their own resources in providing less restrictive treatment." *Id.*, at 119. It did not believe that the general findings and declarations contained in a funding statute designed to encourage a course of conduct could be used by the federal courts to create absolute obligations on the States.

We granted certiorari to consider petitioners' several challenges to the decision below. 447 U.S. 904. Petitioners first contend that 42 U.S.C. § 6010 does not create in favor of the mentally retarded any substantive rights to "appropriate treatment" in the "least restrictive" environment. Assuming that Congress did intend to create such a right, petitioners question the authority of Congress to impose these affirmative obligations on the States under either its spending power or § 5 of the Fourteenth Amendment. Petitioners next assert that any rights created by the Act are enforceable in federal court only by the Federal Government, not by private parties. Finally, petitioners argue that the court below read the scope of any rights created by the Act too broadly and far exceeded its remedial powers in requiring the Commonwealth to move its residents to less restrictive environments and create individual habilitation plans for the mentally retarded. Because we agree with petitioners' first contention—that § 6010 simply does not create substantive rights—we find it unnecessary to address the remaining issues.

## II

We turn first to a brief review of the general structure of the Act. It is a federal-state grant program whereby the Federal Government provides financial assistance to participating States to aid them in creating programs to care for and treat the developmentally disabled. Like other federal-state cooperative programs, the Act is voluntary and the States are given the choice of complying with the conditions set forth in the Act or forgoing the benefits of federal funding. See generally *King* v. *Smith*, 392 U.S. 309 (1968); *Rosado* v. *Wyman*, 397 U.S. 397 (1970); *Harris* v. *McRae*, 448 U.S. 297 (1980). The Commonwealth of Pennsylvania has elected to participate in the program. The Secretary of the Department of Health and Human Services (HHS), the agency responsible for administering the Act, has approved Pennsylvania's state plan and in 1976 disbursed to Pennsylvania approximately $1.6 million. Pennhurst itself receives no federal funds from Pennsylvania's allotment under the Act, though it does receive approximately $6 million per year in Medicaid funds.

The Act begins with an exhaustive statement of purposes. 42 U.S.C. § 6000 (b)(1) (1976 ed., Supp. III). The "overall purpose" of the Act, as amended in 1978, is:

[*T*]*o assist* [the] states to assure that persons with developmental disabilities receive the care, treatment, and other services necessary to enable them to achieve their maximum potential through a system which coordinates, monitors, plans, and evaluates those services and which ensures the protection of the legal and human rights of persons with developmental disabilities. (Emphasis supplied.)

As set forth in the margin, the "specific purposes" of the Act are to "assist" and financially "support" various activities necessary to the provision of comprehensive services to the developmentally disabled. § 6000 (b)(2) (1976 ed., Supp. III).

The Act next lists a variety of conditions for the receipt of federal funds. Under § 6005, for example, the Secretary "as a condition of providing assistance" shall require that "each recipient of such assistance take affirmative action" to hire qualified handicapped individuals. Each State, in turn, shall "as a condition" of receiving assistance submit to the Secretary a plan to evaluate the services provided under the Act. § 6009. Each State shall also "as a condition" of receiving assistance "provide the Secretary satisfactory assurances that each program . . . which receives funds from the State's allotment . . . has in effect for each developmentally disabled person who receives services from or under the program a habilitation plan." § 6011 (a) (1976 ed., Supp. III). And § 6012 (a) (1976 ed., Supp. III) conditions aid on a State's promise to "have in effect a system to protect and advocate the rights of persons with developmental disabilities."

At issue here, of course, is § 6010, the "bill of rights" provision. It states in relevant part:

Congress makes the following findings respecting the rights of persons with developmental disabilities:

(1) Persons with developmental disabilities have a right to appropriate treatment, services, and habilitation for such disabilities.

(2) The treatment, services, and habilitation for a person with developmental disabilities should be designed to maximize the developmental potential of the person and should be provided in the setting that is least restrictive of the person's personal liberty.

(3) The Federal Government and the States both have an obligation to assure that public funds are not provided to any institutio[n] . . . that—(A) does not provide treatment, services, and habilitation which is appropriate to the needs of such person; or (B) does not meet the following minimum standards. . . .

Noticeably absent from § 6010 is any language suggesting that § 6010 is a "condition" for the receipt of federal funding under the Act. Section 6010 thus stands in sharp contrast to §§ 6005, 6009, 6011, and 6012.

The enabling parts of the Act are the funding sections. 42 U.S.C. §§ 6061–6063 (1976 ed. and Supp. III). Those sections describe how funds are to be allotted to the States, require that any State desiring financial assistance submit an overall plan satisfactory to the Secretary of Health and Human Services, and require that funds disbursed under the Act be used in accordance with the approved state plan. To be approved by the Secretary, the state plan must comply with several specific conditions set forth in § 6063. It, *inter alia,* must provide for the establishment of a State Planning Council, § 6063 (b)(1), and set out specific objectives to be achieved under the plan, § 6063 (b)(2)(A) (1976 ed., Supp. III). Services furnished under the plan must be consistent with standards prescribed by the Secretary, § 6063 (b)(5)(A)(i) (1976 ed., Supp. III), and be provided in an individual manner consistent with § 6011. § 6063 (b)(5)(B) (1976 ed., Supp. III). The plan must also be supported by assurances that any program receiving assistance is protecting the human rights of the disabled consistent with § 6010, § 6063 (b)(5)(C) (1976 ed., Supp. III).[10] Each State must also require its State Planning Council to serve as an advocate of persons with developmental disabilities. § 6067 (1976 ed. and Supp. III).

The Act further provides procedures and sanctions to ensure state compliance with its requirements. The Secretary may, of course, disapprove a state plan. § 6063 (c). If a State fails to satisfy the requirements of § 6063, the Secretary may terminate or reduce the federal grant. § 6065 (1976 ed., Supp. III). Any State dissatisfied with the Secretary's disapproval of the plan, or his decision to terminate funding, may appeal to the federal courts of appeals. § 6068. No other cause of action is recognized in the Act.

As support for its broad remedial order, the Court of Appeals found that 42 U.S.C. § 6010 created substantive rights in favor of the disabled and imposed an obligation on the States to provide, at their own expense, certain kinds of treatment. The initial question before us, then, is one of statutory construction: Did Congress intend in § 6010 to create enforceable rights and obligations?

A

In discerning congressional intent, we necessarily turn to the possible sources of Congress' power to legislate, namely, Congress' power to enforce the Fourteenth Amendment and its power under the Spending Clause to place conditions on the grant of federal funds. Although the court below held that Congress acted under both powers, the respondents themselves disagree on this point. The Halderman respondents argue that § 6010 was enacted pursuant to § 5 of the Fourteenth Amendment. Accordingly, they assert that § 6010 is mandatory on the States, regardless of their receipt of federal funds. The Solicitor General, in contrast, concedes that Congress acted pursuant to its spending power alone. Tr. of Oral Arg. 54. Thus, in his view, § 6010 only applies to those States which accept federal funds.[11]

Although this Court has previously addressed issues going to Congress' power to secure the guarantees of the Fourteenth Amendment, *Katzenbach* v. *Morgan*, 384 U.S. 641, 651 (1966); *Oregon* v. *Mitchell*, 400 U.S. 112 (1970); *Fitzpatrick* v. *Bitzer*, 427 U.S. 445 (1975),[12] we have had little occasion to consider the appropriate test for

---

[10]The provisions of § 6063 were reworded and recodified in 1978. Section 6063 (b)(5)(C) (1976 ed., Supp. III) replaced § 133 (b)(24) of the Act, as added and renumbered, 89 Stat. 491, 506, 42 U.S.C. § 6063 (b)(24), which required a somewhat similar "assurance." The only significant difference between the two provisions is that § 6063 (b)(5)(C) contains a specific reference to § 6010.

[11]The PARC respondents take a somewhat different view. Although they argue that Congress enacted § 6010 under both § 5 and the spending power, they suggest that § 6010 applies only to programs which receive federal money. The PARC respondents are also cross-petitioners in this litigation, arguing that the Act requires Pennhurst to be closed. In their view, the individual placement decisions required by the court below are not authorized by the Act and, in any event, are an improper exercise of judicial authority.

[12]There is of course a question whether Congress would have the power to create the rights and obligations found by the court below. Although the court below held that "section 6010 does not go beyond what has been judicially declared to be the limits of the [F]ourteenth [A]mendment," 612 F.2d, at 98, this

determining when Congress intends to enforce those guarantees. Because such legislation imposes congressional policy on a State involuntarily, and because it often intrudes on traditional state authority, we should not quickly attribute to Congress an unstated intent to act under its authority to enforce the Fourteenth Amendment. Our previous cases are wholly consistent with that view, since Congress in those cases expressly articulated its intent to legislate pursuant to § 5. See *Katzenbach* v. *Morgan, supra* (intent expressly stated in the Voting Rights Act Amendments of 1970); *Fitzpatrick* v. *Bitzer, supra* (intent expressly stated in both the House and Senate Reports of the 1972 Amendments to the Civil Rights Act of 1964); cf. *South Carolina* v. *Katzenbach,* 383 U.S. 301 (1966) (intent to enforce the Fifteenth Amendment expressly stated in the Voting Rights Act of 1965). Those cases, moreover, involved statutes which simply prohibited certain kinds of state conduct. The case for inferring intent is at its weakest where, as here, the rights asserted impose *affirmative* obligations on the States to fund certain services, since we may assume that Congress will not implicitly attempt to impose massive financial obligations on the States.

Turning to Congress' power to legislate pursuant to the spending power, our cases have long recognized that Congress may fix the terms on which it shall disburse federal money to the States. See, *e.g., Oklahoma* v. *CSC,* 330 U.S. 127 (1947); *King* v. *Smith,* 392 U.S. 309 (1968); *Rosado* v. *Wyman,* 397 U.S. 397 (1970). Unlike legislation enacted under § 5, however, legislation enacted pursuant to the spending power is much in the nature of a contract: in return for federal funds, the States agree to comply with federally imposed conditions. The legitimacy of Congress' power to legislate under the spending power thus rests on whether the State voluntarily and knowingly accepts the terms of the "contract." See *Steward Machine Co.* v. *Davis,* 301 U.S. 548, 585–598 (1937); *Harris* v. *McRae,* 448 U.S. 297 (1980). There can, of course, be no knowing acceptance if a State is unaware of the conditions or is unable to ascertain what is expected of it. Accordingly, if Congress intends to impose a condition on the grant of federal moneys, it must do so unambiguously. Cf. *Employees* v. *Department of Public Health and Welfare,* 411 U.S. 279, 285 (1973); *Edelman* v. *Jordan,* 415 U.S. 651 (1974). By insisting that Congress speak with a clear voice, we enable the States to exercise their choice knowingly, cognizant of the consequences of their participation.

Indeed, in those instances where Congress has intended the States to fund certain entitlements as a condition of receiving federal funds, it has proved capable of saying so explicitly. See, *e.g., King* v. *Smith,* 392 U.S., at 333 (Social Security Act creates a "federally imposed obligation [on the States] to furnish 'aid to families with dependent children . . . with reasonable promptness to all eligible individuals,'" quoting the Act). We must carefully inquire, then, whether Congress in § 6010 im-

---

Court has never found that the involuntarily committed have a constitutional "right to treatment," much less the voluntarily committed. See *Sanchez* v. *New Mexico,* 396 U.S. 276 (1970), dismissing for want of substantial federal question 80 N. Mex. 438, 457 P.2d 370 (1968); *O'Connor* v. *Donaldson,* 422 U.S. 563, 587–589 (1975) (BURGER, C. J., concurring). Thus, the Pennhurst petitioners and several *amici* argue that legislation which purports to create against the States not only a right to treatment, but one in the least restrictive setting, is not "appropriate" legislation within the meaning of § 5. Because we conclude that § 6010 creates no rights whatsoever, we find it unnecessary to consider that question.

posed an obligation on the States to spend state money to fund certain rights as a condition of receiving federal moneys under the Act or whether it spoke merely in precatory terms.

## B

Applying those principles to these cases, we find nothing in the Act or its legislative history to suggest that Congress intended to require the States to assume the high cost of providing ''appropriate treatment'' in the ''least restrictive environment'' to their mentally retarded citizens.

There is virtually no support for the lower court's conclusion that Congress created rights and obligations pursuant to its power to enforce the Fourteenth Amendment. The Act nowhere states that is its purpose. Quite the contrary, the Act's language and structure demonstrate that it is a mere federal-state funding statute. The explicit purposes of the Act are simply ''to assist' the States through the use of federal grants to improve the care and treatment of the mentally retarded. § 6000 (b) (1976 ed., Supp. III). Nothing in either the ''overall'' or ''specific'' purposes of the Act reveals an intent to require the States to fund new, substantive rights. Surely Congress would not have established such elaborate funding incentives had it simply intended to impose absolute obligations on the States.

Respondents nonetheless insist that the fact that § 6010 speaks in terms of ''rights'' supports their view. Their reliance is misplaced. '' 'In expounding a statute, we must not be guided by a single sentence or member of a sentence, but look to the provisions of the whole law, and to its object and policy.' '' *Philbrook* v. *Glodgett,* 421 U.S. 707, 713 (1975), quoting *United States* v. *Heirs of Boisdoré,* 8 How. 113, 122 (1849). See *District of Columbia* v. *Carter,* 409 U.S. 418, 420 (1973). Contrary to respondents' assertion, the specific language and the legislative history of § 6010 are ambiguous. We are persuaded that § 6010, when read in the context of other more specific provisions of the Act, does no more than express a congressional preference for certain kinds of treatment. It is simply a general statement of ''findings'' and, as such, is too thin a reed to support the rights and obligations read into it by the court below. The closest one can come in giving § 6010 meaning is that it justifies and supports Congress' appropriation of money under the Act and guides the Secretary in his review of state applications for federal funds. See *United States* v. *Carolene Products Co.,* 304 U.S. 144, 152 (1938).[14] As this Court recognized in *Rosado* v. *Wyman, supra,* at 413, ''Congress sometimes legislates by innuendo, making declara-

---

[14]Respondents also contend that the title of the Act as passed, rather than as codified, reveals an intent to create rights in favor of the disabled. Pub. L. 94-103, 89 Stat. 486 (1975). As passed, the Act contained three Titles. Title I provided for services and facilities to the developmentally disabled and Title II, entitled ''The Establishment and Protection of the Rights of Persons with Developmental Disabilities,'' contained § 6010. Respondents' reliance on this title is misplaced. It has long been established that the title of an Act ''cannot enlarge or confer powers.'' *United States* v. *Oregon & California R. Co.,* 164 U.S. 526, 541 (1896); *Cornell* v. *Coyne,* 192 U.S. 418, 430 (1904). See *United States* v. *Fisher,* 2 Cranch 358, 386 (1805); *Yazoo & Mississippi Valley R. Co.* v. *Thomas,* 132 U.S. 174, 188 (1889). In addition, the location of § 6010 in the Act as passed confirms § 6010's limited meaning. Section 6010 was the preamble of Title II followed by provisions later codified as §§ 6009, 6011, 6012. The congressional findings in § 6010 thus seem to have been designed simply to serve as the rationale for the conditions imposed in the remaining sections of Title II.

tions of policy and indicating a preference while requiring measures that, though falling short of legislating its goal, serve as a nudge in the preferred directions." This is such a case.

* * *

The fact that Congress granted to Pennsylvania only $1.6 million in 1976, a sum woefully inadequate to meet the enormous financial burden of providing "appropriate" treatment in the "least restrictive" setting, confirms that Congress must have had a limited purpose in enacting § 6010. When Congress does impose affirmative obligations on the States, it usually makes a far more substantial contribution to defray costs. *Harris* v. *McRae, supra.* It defies common sense, in short, to suppose that Congress implicitly imposed this massive obligation on participating States.

Our conclusion is also buttressed by the rule of statutory construction established above, that Congress must express clearly its intent to impose conditions on the grant of federal funds so that the States can knowingly decide whether or not to accept those funds. That canon applies with greatest force where, as here, a State's potential obligations under the Act are largely indeterminate. It is difficult to know what is meant by providing "appropriate treatment" in the "least restrictive" setting, and it is unlikely that a State would have accepted federal funds had it known it would be bound to provide such treatment. The crucial inquiry, however, is not whether a State would knowingly undertake that obligation, but whether Congress spoke so clearly that we can fairly say that the State could make an informed choice. In this case, Congress fell well short of providing clear notice to the States that they, by accepting funds under the Act, would indeed be obligated to comply with § 6010. Not only does § 6010 lack conditional language, but it strains credulity to argue that participating States should have known of their "obligations" under § 6010 when the Secretary of HHS, the governmental agency responsible for the administration of the Act and the agency with which the participating States have the most contact, has never understood § 6010 to impose conditions on participating States. Though Congress' power to legislate under the spending power is broad, it does not include surprising participating States with postacceptance or "retroactive" conditions.

Finally, a brief comparison of the general language of § 6010 with the conditions Congress explicitly imposed on the States demonstrates that Congress did not intend to place either absolute or conditional obligations on the States. The Court of Appeals, for example, read § 6010 to impose an obligation to provide habilitation plans for all developmentally disabled persons. But Congress required habilitation plans under § 6011 "only when the Federal assistance under the Act contributes a portion of the cost of the habilitation services to the developmentally disabled person." H.R.Conf.Rep. No. 94-473, p. 43 (1975). If the Court of Appeals were correct, of course, there would be no purpose for Congress to have required habilitation plans at all, or to have limited the requirement to certain programs, since such plans automatically would have been mandated in all programs by the more inclusive requirements of § 6010.

Second, the specific condition imposed in § 6063 (b)(5)(C) (1976 ed., Supp. III) requires each state plan to:

contain or be supported by assurances satisfactory to the Secretary that the human rights of all persons with developmental disabilities . . . who are receiving treatment, services, or habilitation, under programs assisted under this chapter will be protected consistent with section 6010 of this title (relating to rights of the developmentally disabled).

Once again, these limitations—both as to programs assisted under the Act and as to affording protection in a manner that is "consistent with § 6010"—would be unnecessary if, as the court below ruled, all state programs were required to fund the rights described in § 6010.

And third, the court below held that § 6010 mandated deinstitutionalization for most, if not all, mentally retarded persons. As originally enacted in 1975, however, the Act required only that each State use not less than 30 percent of its allotment "for the purpose of assisting it in developing and implementing plans designed to eliminate inappropriate placement in institutions of persons with developmental disabilities." § 6062 (a)(4). Three years later, Congress relieved the States of even that modest duty. Instead of requiring the States to use a certain portion of their allotment to support deinstitutionalization, Congress required the States to concentrate their efforts in at least one of four areas, only one of which was "community living arrangements." § 6063 (b)(4)(A)(ii) (1976 ed., Supp. III). Had § 6010 created a right to deinstitutionalization, the policy choices contemplated by both the 1975 and 1978 provisions would be meaningless.

In sum, the court below failed to recognize the well-settled distinction between Congressional "encouragement" of state programs and the imposition of binding obligations on the States. *Harris* v. *McRae*, 448 U.S. 297 (1980). Relying on that distinction, this Court in *Southeastern Community College* v. *Davis*, 442 U.S. 397 (1979), rejected a claim that § 504 of the Rehabilitation Act of 1973, which bars discrimination against handicapped persons in federally funded programs, obligates schools to take affirmative steps to eliminate problems raised by an applicant's hearing disability. Finding that "state agencies such as Southeastern are only 'encourage[d] . . . to adopt and implement such policies and procedures.' " *id.*, at 410 (quoting the Act), we stressed that "Congress understood [that] accommodation of the needs of handicapped individuals may require affirmative action and knew how to provide for it in those instances where it wished to do so." *Id.*, at 411. Likewise in this case, Congress was aware of the need of developmentally disabled persons and plainly understood the difference, financial and otherwise, between encouraging a specified type of treatment and mandating it.

IV

Respondents also suggest that they may bring suit to compel compliance with those conditions which *are* contained in the Act. Of particular relevance to these cases are § 6011 (a) (1976 ed., Supp. III) and § 6063 (b)(5)(C) (1976 ed., Supp. III), which are quoted *supra*, at 12–13, 26.[20]

---

[20]The Court of Appeals was apparently aware of these conditions since it referred expressly to § 6063 (b)(5)(C) in concluding that § 6010 creates a right to treatment. Its error was in bypassing these specific conditions and resting its decision on the more general language of § 6010.

That claim raises several issues. First, it must be determined whether respondents have a private cause of action to compel state compliance with those conditions.[21] In legislation enacted pursuant to the spending power, the typical remedy for state noncompliance with federally imposed conditions is not a private cause of action for noncompliance but rather action by the Federal Government to terminate funds to the State. See § 6065 (1976 ed., Supp. III). Just last Term, however, in *Maine* v. *Thiboutot*, 448 U.S. 1 (1980), we held that 42 U.S.C. § 1983 provides a cause of action for state deprivations of "rights secured" by "the laws" of the United States. See 448 U.S., at 4. Whether *Thiboutot* controls this case depends on two factors. First, respondents here, unlike the plaintiff in *Thiboutot* who alleged that state law prevented him from receiving federal funds to which he was entitled, can only claim that the state plan has not provided adequate "assurances" to the Secretary. It is at least an open question whether an individual's interest in having a State provide those "assurances" is a "right secured" by the laws of the United States within the meaning of § 1983. Second, Justice Powell in dissent in *Thiboutot* suggested that § 1983 would not be available where the "governing statute provides an exclusive remedy for violations of its terms." *Id.*, at 22, n. 11. It is unclear whether the express remedy contained in this Act is exclusive.

Second, it is not at all clear that the Pennhurst petitioners have violated § 6011 and § 6063 (b)(5)(C) (1976 ed. and Supp. III). These sections, by their terms, only refer to "programs assisted" under the Act. Because Pennhurst does not receive federal funds under the Act, it is arguably not a "program assisted." Thus, there may be no obligation on the State under § 6011 to assure the Secretary that each resident of Pennhurst have a habilitation plan, or assure the Secretary under § 6063 (b)(5)(C) that Pennhurst residents are being provided services consistent with § 6010.

Third, there is the question of remedy. Respondents' relief may well be limited to enjoining the Federal Government from providing funds to the Commonwealth. As we stated in *Rosado* v. *Wyman*, 397 U.S., at 420, welfare claimants were "entitled to declaratory relief and an appropriate injunction by the District Court against the payment of *federal* monies . . . should the State not develop a conforming plan within a reasonable period of time." (Emphasis in original.) There, we rejected the suggestion that the courts could require the State to pay the additional sums demanded by compliance with federal standards. Relying on *King* v. *Smith*, 392 U.S. 309 (1968), we explained that "the State had alternative choices of assuming the additional cost" of complying with the federal standard "or not using federal funds." 397 U.S., at 420–421. Accordingly, we remanded the case so that the State could exercise that choice.

In other instances, however, we have implicitly departed from that rule and have affirmed lower court decisions enjoining a State from enforcing any provisions which conflict with federal law in violation of the Supremacy Clause, *e.g.*, *Carleson* v. *Remillard*, 406 U.S. 598 (1972). In still other cases, we have struck down state laws without addressing the form of relief, *e.g.*, *Townsend* v. *Swank*, 404 U.S. 282 (1971). In no case, however, have we required a State to provide money to plaintiffs, much

---

[21]Because we conclude that § 6010 confers no substantive rights, we need not reach the question whether there is a private cause of action under that section or under 42 U. S. C. § 1983 to enforce those rights. See *Southeastern Community College* v. *Davis*, 442 U.S. 397, 404, n. 5 (1979).

less required a State to take on such openended and potentially burdensome obligations as providing "appropriate" treatment in the "least restrictive" environment. And because this is a suit in federal court, anything but prospective relief would pose serious questions under the Eleventh Amendment. *Edelman* v. *Jordan,* 415 U.S. 651 (1974).[23]

These are all difficult questions. Because the Court of Appeals has not addressed these issues, however, we remand the issues for consideration in light of our decision here.

## V

After finding that federal law imposed an obligation on the States to provide treatment, the court below examined state law and found that it too imposed such a requirement. 612 F.2d, at 100–103. The court looked to § 4201 of the Pennsylvania Mental Health and Mental Retardation Act of 1966, which provides in pertinent part:

> The department of [Public Welfare] shall have power, and its duty shall be:
> (1) To assure within the State the availability and equitable provision of adequate mental health and mental retardation services for all persons who need them, regardless of religion, race, color, national origin, settlement, residence, or economic or social status.   Pa.Stat.Ann., Tit. 50, § 4201 (Purdon 1969).

Respondents contend that, even if we conclude that relief is unavailable under federal law, state law adequately supports the relief ordered by the Court of Appeals. There are, however, two difficulties with that argument. First, the lower court's finding that state law provides a right to treatment may well have been colored by its holding with respect to § 6010. Second, the court held only that there is a right to "treatment," not that there is a state right to treatment in the "least restrictive" environment. As such, it is unclear whether state law provides an independent and adequate ground which can support the court's remedial order. Accordingly, we remand the state-law issue for reconsideration in light of our decision here.

For similar reasons, we also remand to the Court of Appeals those issues it did not address, namely, respondents' federal constitutional claims and their claims under § 504 of the Rehabilitation Act.

## VI

Congress in recent years has enacted several laws designed to improve the way in which this Nation treats the mentally retarded.[25] The Developmentally Disabled

---

[23]We do not significantly differ with our BROTHER WHITE on the remedy for failure to comply with federally imposed conditions. Relying on *Rosado* v. *Wyman,* he argues that Pennsylvania should be given the option of rejecting federal funds under the Act or complying with § 6010. If we agreed that § 6010 was a condition on the grant of federal funds, we would have little difficulty subscribing to that view. We differ only in what he believes that § 6010 imposes conditions on participating States while we believe that the relevant conditions to these cases are §§ 6011 and 6063 (b)(5)(C). If the court on remand determines that there has been a violation of those conditions, it may well be appropriate to apply the principles announced in *Rosado,* as JUSTICE WHITE suggests.

[25]*E.g.,* The Rehabilitation Act of 1973, as amended in 1974 and 1978, 29 U. S. C. § 701 *et seq.;* The Education for All Handicapped Children Act of 1975, 20 U. S. C. §§ 1401–1420; Social Security Amendments of 1974, 42 U. S. C. §§ 1396d (d) and 1397; Community Mental Health Centers Act, 42 U. S. C. § 2689 *et seq.*

Assistance and Bill of Rights Act is one such law. It establishes a national policy to provide better care and treatment to the retarded and creates funding incentives to induce the States to do so. But the Act does no more than that. We would be attributing far too much to Congress if we held that it required the States, at their own expense, to provide certain kinds of treatment. Accordingly, we reverse the principal holding of the Court of Appeals and remand for further proceedings consistent with this opinion.

*Reversed and remanded.*

NOTES

1. The opinion of Justice White, dissenting in part, joined in by Justices Brennan and Marshall, in which he concludes that Section 6010 was intended by Congress to create enforceable rights, is omitted here.

2. What are the implications of footnote 10 of the Court's opinion? Is it not possible that in the 1978 amendments, Congress required the states who receive funding under the Act to comply with "rights" that it had only encouraged in 1975?

3. Consider footnote 12 in light of the *Youngberg* v. *Romeo* decision, pp. 223–235 above.

4. Carefully examine the Court's characterization of Section 504 of the Rehabilitation Act of 1973 and its interpretation of *Southeastern Community College* v. *Davis*. What are the implications of this dicta if it accurately represents a majority viewpoint on the Court? Does Section 504 only "encourage" nondiscrimination? Consider that Section 504 tracks the language of Section 601 of the Civil Rights Act of 1964 (see page 200 of the Casebook). How does this fact bear upon the accuracy of the dicta in *Pennhurst* regarding Section 504?

5. In footnote 20, the Court suggests that relief in this case might have been successfully premised upon Section 6063 rather than Section 6010 of the Act. If so, how significant is the Court's decision regarding Section 6010? Is this "much ado about nothing"?

### HALDERMAN v. PENNHURST STATE SCHOOL & HOSPITAL

*United States Court of Appeal for the Third Circuit, 1982*
*673 F.2d 647, certiorari granted 102 S. Ct. 2956*

Before Seitz, Chief Judge, and Aldisert, Gibbons, Hunter, Weis, Garth, Higginbotham and Sloviter, Circuit Judges.

Opinion of the Court

Gibbons, Circuit Judge, with whom Aldisert, Weis, A. Leon Higginbotham, Jr. and Sloviter, Circuit Judges, join:

This appeal is before us on a remand from the Supreme Court, which on April 20, 1981, reversed our judgment upholding in part and modifying the permanent injunction ordered by the district court.[1]

---

[1] *Pennhurst State School and Hospital* v. *Halderman*, 451 U.S. 1, 101 S.Ct. 1531, 67 L.Ed.2d 694 (1981), reversing 612 F.2d 84 (3d Cir. 1979), which affirmed in part 446 F.Supp. 1295 (E.D. Pa.1977).

I

The Supreme Court's judgment remanded to this court "for further proceedings in conformity with the opinion of the Court." Accordingly it is necessary to examine that opinion, in the light of our prior opinion, to determine what issues must now be addressed. Our judgment, now reversed, rested upon a federal statute and a Pennsylvania statute.

The federal statute we relied upon is the "bill of rights" provision of the Developmentally Disabled Assistance and Bill of Rights Act, 42 U.S.C. § 6010 (1976). Proceeding on the assumption that Congress had constitutional authority under Section 5 of the Fourteenth Amendment to enact that section of the Act, we held that a private cause of action for the enforcement of the rights it defined should be implied. That holding was predicated upon our belief that it was inappropriate for courts faced with a statute which fell within any of several constitutional grants of Congressional lawmaking authority to reject any source of such authority. The Supreme Court, however, adopted a different standard, stating:

> Although this Court has previously addressed issues going to Congress' power to secure the guarantees of the Fourteenth Amendment, . . . we have had little occasion to consider the appropriate test for determining when Congress intends to enforce those guarantees. Because such legislation imposes congressional policy on a State involuntarily, and because it often intrudes on traditional state authority, we should not quickly attribute to Congress an unstated intent to act under its authority to enforce the Fourteenth Amendment. . . . The case for inferring intent is at its weakest where, as here, the rights asserted imposed *affirmative* obligations on the States to fund certain services, since we may assume that Congress will not implicitly attempt to impose massive financial obligations on the States.

451 U.S. at 15–16, 101 S.Ct. at 1539. Applying this newly announced rule of statutory interpretation to Section 6010, the Court held that it was not passed pursuant to Section 5 of the Fourteenth Amendment, but was merely a funding clause enactment. As such, the statute was subject to another rule of statutory interpretation: "if Congress intends to impose a condition on the grant of federal moneys, it must do so unambiguously," for "[b]y insisting that Congress speak with a clear voice, we enable the States to exercise their choice [of participating in a federally funded program] knowingly, cognizant of the consequences of their participation." 451 U.S. at 17, 101 S.Ct. at 1540. Applying this clear statement requirement, the Court held:

> We would be attributing far too much to Congress if we held that it required the States, at their own expense, to provide certain kinds of treatment. Accordingly, we reverse the principal holding of the Court of Appeals and remand for further proceedings consistent with this opinion.

451 U.S. at 31–32, 101 S.Ct. at 1547. The "principal holding" referred to is our holding that Section 6010 conferred substantive rights. The precise holding in the Supreme Court's opinion is that we erred in that single respect.

Turning to our alternative state law grounds for affirming, to the extent we did, the relief ordered by the district court, the Supreme Court observed:

> Respondents contend that, even if we conclude that relief is unavailable under federal law, state law adequately supports the relief ordered by the Court of Appeals. There are,

however, two difficulties with that argument. First, the lower court's finding that state law provides a right to treatment may well have been colored by its holding with respect to § 6010. Second, the court held only that there is a right to "treatment," not that there is a state right to treatment in the "least restrictive" environment. As such, it is unclear whether state law provides an independent and adequate ground which can support the court's remedial order. Accordingly, we remand the state law issue for reconsideration in light of our decision here.[24]

---

24. . . . On remand following our reversal, the Court of Appeals will be in a position to consider the state law issues in light of the Pennsylvania's Supreme Court's recent decision [*In re Joseph Schmidt*, 494 Pa. 86, 429 A.2d 631 (1981)].

451 U.S. at 31, 101 S.Ct. at 1547. Thus the Supreme Court has expressed no view on the question whether state law provides an independent and adequate ground which can support the district court order. We are directed to consider that question in light of the decision in *In re Joseph Schmidt*, announced by the Pennsylvania Supreme Court after our decision but prior to that of the Supreme Court. Implicit in that direction is a holding that the plaintiffs' federal law claims are of sufficient substance to support the exercise of pendent jurisdiction over that Pennsylvania law claim.

Finally, the Court addressed legal contentions advanced by the plaintiffs in support of the district court order which this court found it unnecessary to decide. Respecting the contention that Section 6063 of the Developmentally Disabled Assistance and Bill of Rights Act, which requires that state plans comply with several specific federal conditions, may be enforceable in a private action, the Court noted that the contention raised a number of issues, but concluded:

> These are all difficult questions. Because the Court of Appeals has not addressed these issues, however, we remand the issues for consideration in light of our decision here.

451 U.S. at 30, 101 S.Ct. at 1546. The Court also said:

> For similar reasons, we also remand to the Court of Appeals those issues it did not address, namely, respondents' federal constitutional claims and their claims under § 504 of the Rehabilitation Act [of 1973, as amended in 1974, 1976, and 1978, 29 U.S.C. § 701 et seq.]

451 U.S. at 31, 101 S.Ct. at 1547. We do not understand the remand on these issues as directions that this court *must* consider and decide either constitutional or statutory supremacy issues which, in light of state grounds independent and adequate to support the district court order, may not have to be reached. Rather, we construe the Court's remand as leaving open for our reconsideration, to the extent we find it necessary for such a purpose, any grounds of decision which might support the order appealed from, except our previous holding that Section 6010 was enacted pursuant to Section 5 of the Fourteenth Amendment and thus conferred substantive rights.

The Supreme Court found no fault with the district court's findings of fact, or with the standing of the United States as an intervening plaintiff. Thus there is no need for a repetition of the discussion in Parts II and III of our prior opinion. Moreover the Court did not address those issues respecting scope of relief which are discussed in Part VII of our prior opinion. Thus, assuming the propriety of some legal standard upon which relief could be predicated, there is no occasion, for purposes of this appeal, for a reconsideration of our discussion of the Commonwealth's Eleventh Amendment contention, of objections to the definition of the class, of objections to the use of a master, or of other specific objections to provisions of the injunction which we rejected.

## II

When our prior decision was announced, the highest court of Pennsylvania had not yet definitively construed the effect on the habilitation of mentally retarded persons of that state's Mental Health and Mental Retardation Act of 1966 (hereinafter MH/MR Act of 1966), Pa.Stat.Ann. tit. 50, §§ 4101–4704 (Purdon 1969). We held that the MH/MR Act of 1966 provides a state statutory right to habilitation for such persons, that the plaintiffs could sue to enforce that right and that a federal court has pendent jurisdiction over such a claim, which was properly exercised in this instance. Because the Supreme Court of Pennsylvania had not yet considered whether habilitation under the MH/MR Act of 1966 required the choice by the state of the least restrictive environment, while in our (mistaken) view Section 6010 did, we found it unnecessary to speculate about how that Court would construe the state statute in this respect. Since our decision, however, *In re Joseph Schmidt,* 494 Pa. 86, 429 A.2d 631 (1981), has been decided, and the state court has spoken definitively.

Joseph Schmidt, a mentally retarded adult resided and received treatment from the age of eight at the expense of Allegheny County in a privately operated residential school for mentally retarded children. After 14 years of support for Schmidt in that school, the county petitioned the Court of Common Pleas of Allegheny County for his involuntary commitment to Western Center, a state-operated residential facility. The Commonwealth of Pennsylvania intervened as a respondent, contending that Schmidt's commitment to the Western Center facility would not be appropriate under the MH/MR Act of 1966. The parties did not dispute that neither Allegheny County nor the Commonwealth's Western Center provided a program which would enable Schmidt to receive adequate habilitation. The dispute was over which governmental unit, under the Pennsylvania statutory scheme, was primarily responsible in cases such as his for developing a plan for his habilitation. As in this case, the County contended that it had no obligation under the MH/MR Act of 1966 to provide supportive services which would eliminate the necessity for institutionalization. The Court of Common Pleas rejected the County's contention and ordered it to develop for Schmidt an individual practical life-management plant suitable to his needs. The Pennsylvania Supreme Court reversed, holding that under the MH/MR Act of 1966 the state rather than the county was responsible for developing a suitable placement for a mental patient so severely retarded that there is no alternative for his habilitation less restrictive than long term institutional residential placement. In deciding the allocation of responsibilities between the County and the Commonwealth, however, the Court made it clear that under Pennsylvania law both were bound by the same requirement of normalization. The opinion of the Court states:

> We fully agree with the court below that the legislative scheme was designed to require the county to provide those supportive services where they would eliminate the necessity of institutionalization, even where those services would be required on a long term basis.

With the acceptance of the principle of "normalization" and the resultant legislation, it is clear that the restrictive view urged by the county as to its obligations in the area is out of step. The concept of normalization envisions that the mentally retarded person and his or her family shall have the right to live a life as close as possible to that which is typical for the general population. Consistent with this concept is the requirement that the least restriction consistent with adequate treatment and required care shall be employed.

429 A.2d at 635–36. Addressing the regulations of that Pennsylvania Department charged with the responsibility for administering the MH/MR Act of 1966, the Court observed:

> This [least restrictive alternative] approach to the problem of mental retardation was reflected in the regulations promulgated by the secretary pursuant to § 301 of the Act, 50 P.S. § 4301, on February 10, 1973. Regulations 5200 Appendix IV *County Mental Health and Mental Retardation Program—Service Content of the Program.* The following pertinent excerpts from these regulations are most instructive in the instant inquiry.
>
> The County Program is the means by which minimum services as described in the act shall be readily available to promote the social, personal, physical and economical habilitation or rehabilitation of mentally retarded person with due respect for the full human, social and legal rights of each person. This means that the health, social, educational, vocational, environmental and legal resources that serve the general population shall be marshalled and coordinated by the County Program to meet the personal development goals of mentally retarded persons, in accordance with the principle of normalization. . . .
>
> In keeping with this principle of normalization, the County is responsible to utilize county program funds for the mentally retarded to accomplish the following objectives:
>
> \* \* \*
>
> 4. shaping and maintaining an environment most productive of basic human personality qualities involving parent-child and sibling relationships, environmental adaptation, self-awareness and learning motivation and ability;
> 5. specific training and learning situations designed and implemented to develop all potential;
> 6. community development and restructuring to achieve the maximum normalization for the mentally retarded person wherever he is.
>
> *I.  Responsibility for Planning, Direction and Coordinated Delivery of Services—*
>
> *The Base Service Unit:*
>
> The County Administrator shall be responsible to provide for the establishment of an organizational unit consisting of multidisciplinary professional and non-professional services for persons who are mentally retarded and in need of service from the County Program. . . . The Base Service Unit shall be responsible to perform the following functions in such a way as to carry out the objectives of the County Program as stated above.
>
> \* \* \*
>
> D. Provide for comprehensive diagnosis and evaluation services to:
>
> \* \* \*
>
> 3. Develop a practical life-management plan for the individual and his family and provide the necessary counseling and following-along services;
>
> \* \* \*

These regulations make it clear that the legislative grant of power to the counties under § 301(e)(3) of the Act, 50 P.S. § 4301(e)(3), empowering them to establish additional services and programs "designed to prevent . . . the necessity of admitting or committing the mentally disabled to a facility" was intended to be utilized by the counties to minimize the necessity of institutionalization. It was more than a mere grant of power to be used at the county's option. The power of the department to issue the regulations in question and to require the counties to assume the responsibilities set forth therein was clearly within the purview of section 201 of the Act, 50 P.S. § 4201, which charges the department to create a comprehensive and coordinate program in conjunction with the county governments. Moreover, any question as to the legislative recognition of the concept of normalization and the adoption of the doctrine of least restrictive alternatives in matters relating to the mentally retarded has been removed by the enactment of the Mental Health Procedures Act, Act of 1976, July 9, P.L. 817, No. 143, § 101; 50 P.S. § 7101.

429 A.2d at 636–37.

In the course of announcing that the MH/MR Act of 1966 embodied the least restrictive alternative means standard for achieving habilitation of the mentally retarded, the opinion of the Pennsylvania Supreme Court makes passing reference to the fact that the least restrictive alternative doctrine was first articulated by Chief Judge Bazelon in *Lake* v. *Cameron*, 364 F.2d 657 (D.C.Cir.1966), and subsequently adopted in a series of commitment and treatment related cases. From the context, it is clear that the Court did not suggest that it was giving to the MH/MR Act of 1966 an interpretation not, perhaps, intended by the Pennsylvania legislature, but instead compelled by the federal constitution. Indeed the Attorney General does not suggest that the statutory interpretation of the MH/MR Act of 1966 announced in Schmidt is other than independent of federal law.

The Pennsylvania law ground of decision being entirely independent of federal law, the sole remaining state law question is whether that ground of decision is adequate to support the order appealed from. Except to the extent that we previously required modification of the order, we hold that it is.

This case, unlike *Schmidt*, is a class action. In our prior decision we held that because for some members of the plaintiff class institutionalization might well be the least restrictive available means of habilitation, it was error to order the complete closing of Pennhurst without individualized determinations of need. Addressing the Pennsylvania legislation we observed that

> we do not think that the Pennsylvania legislature, in providing a right to treatment in the Mental Health and Mental Retardation Act of 1966, intended to foreclose all institutionalization. In section 102 of that Act, for example, the legislature expressly included "institution[s]" within the category of "facilities" for which the Department of Welfare was responsible. Pa.Stat.Ann. tit. 50, § 4102. Thus, we see in the MH/MR Act of 1966 exactly the intent ascribed to it by Senator Pechan when he spoke in support of the measure.
>
> > The object of the legislation is to make it possible for every mentally disabled person to receive the kind of treatment he needs, when and where he needs it.
>
> 1966 Pa.Legis.J. 3d Spec.Secc., No. 33, 76 (Sept. 27, 1966). The state statute . . . was focused on *individual* needs.

612 F.2d at 114–15. This interpretation of the MH/MR Act of 1966 was fully confirmed by the *Schmidt* decision. That case involved a dispute between two governmental units over allocation of burdens among them, which in the particular instance of a single individual was resolved in favor of the County. The resolution in *Schmidt* resulted from the Pennsylvania Supreme Court's conclusion that where long term institutional care is in fact the least restrictive means of habilitation, institutionalization is permissible and the state is obliged to provide it. Our prior holding that individual

determinations must be made for each member of the class is entirely consistent with the holding that Joseph Schmidt must be provided a place in a state facility.

But unlike *Schmidt*, we have before us numerous class members who the court found should not be in Pennhurst. For these the court ordered that suitable community living arrangements be provided, and enjoined the county defendants from recommending future commitments to Pennhurst without an individual determination that a community living arrangement or other less restrictive environment would be suitable. These holdings are also consistent with the *Schmidt* opinion, for while the opinion recognizes that under the MH/MR Act of 1966 the state was given responsibility for overall supervision and control of the statutory program, it expressly rejected Allegheny County's contention that the County had no obligation to provide merely ameliorative services until a state placement could be arranged. 429 A.2d at 635. The allocation, in the order appealed from, of responsibility among the county and state defendants based upon individualized determinations as to what is the least restrictive environment in which habilitation can take place, is completely congruent with the *Schmidt* court's interpretation of the MH/MR Act of 1966.

The defendants urge that because the *Schmidt* case did not present any issue of funding of proper care, it should not be regarded as controlling. (Appellants' Joint Brief on Remand, 54, citing 429 A.2d at 633.) Except that this is a class-action, however, we are not persuaded that there is any essential difference in the posture of the *Schmidt* case and this. As in this case, the County attempted to limit its responsibility to petitioning for the commission of mentally retarded persons to a state residential facility. The *Schmidt* court made clear that the Pennsylvania law imposed the obligation on both levels of government to provide habilitation in that environment providing the least restriction on personal liberty consistent with habilitation. Insofar as financial burdens are concerned, it merely referred to Sections 508 and 509 of the MH/MR Act of 1966, which impose funding duties on both levels of government, and which provide mechanisms for the allocation of appropriated funds among the counties.[16] 429

---

[16]Under Section 201(1) of the MH/MR Act of 1966 the Pennsylvania Department of Public Welfare "shall have power, and its duty shall be: (1) To assure within the State the availability and equitable provision of adequate mental health and mental retardation services for all persons who need them, regardless of religion, race, color, national origin, settlement, residence, or economic or social status." Pa.Stat. Ann. tit. 50, § 4201(1) (Purdon 1969). Pennsylvania Counties are obliged.

> Subject to the provisions of sections 508 and 509(5) it shall be the duty of local authorities in cooperation with the department [of Public Welfare] to insure that the following mental health and mental retardation services are available:
> (1) Short term inpatient services other than those provided by the State.
> (2) Outpatient services.
> (3) Partial hospitalization services.
> (4) Emergency services twenty-four hours per day which shall be provided by, or available within at least one of the types of services specified heretofore in this paragraph.
> (5) Consultation and education services to professional personnel and community agencies.
> (6) Aftercare services for persons released from State and County facilities.
> (7) Specialized rehabilitative and training services including sheltered workshops.
> (8) Interim care of mentally retarded persons who have been removed from their homes and who having been accepted, are awaiting admission to a State operated facility.
> (9) Unified procedures for intake for all county services and a central place providing referral services and information.

Pa.Stat.Ann. tit. 50, § 4301(d) (Purdon 1969). Section 508 provides:

> (a) If local authorities cannot insure the availability of any of the services required by section 301, or if they

A.2d at 633. The Commonwealth was ordered to find a placement for *Schmidt* in an institution with a staff-patient ratio suitable to his needs. There is no suggestion in the *Schmidt* opinion that this order would be qualified by the necessity for appropriations. Obviously the *Schmidt* Court anticipated that the adjustment mechanisms of Sections 508 and 509 would be operated in good faith. Nothing in the record which is before us on this appeal suggests that those mechanisms will be dismantled, will be operated other than in good faith, or are inhibited by the provisions of the judgment. On this record we, like the Supreme Court of Pennsylvania, must assume that the Pennsylvania legislature intends compliance with its statutes. Moreover, a Rule 60(b) motion would be the proper vehicle to present a showing that changed circumstances no longer require the use of a federal court master to administer a state program under state laws.

We conclude, therefore, that except as the order appealed from must be modified in accordance with our prior decision, the Pennsylvania MH/MR Act provides adequate support for it independent of federal law.

[Parts III and IV of the court's opinion, holding that relief is not barred by the Eleventh Amendment, and that abstention is not appropriate, are omitted.]

## V

In one respect the MH/MR Act of 1966 does not lend support to the judgment appealed from. As noted in Part II above, and as we held in our prior decision, that Act does not foreclose all institutionalization, and thus does not support that part of the judgment requiring the closing of Pennhurst. Since this is so, even under the *Siler* rule

---

assert that it would be economically unsound to do so, such authorities may make application to the department to be relieved for the period of one year from the duty to insure their availability.

Such application shall specify: (i) the service or services involved and (ii) facts upon which it seeks relief.

(b) If the department after consideration of the application and such independent investigation as it shall deem appropriate determines that the application is justified, it may approve the same, in which event, the department may insure the availability of the service or services specified in the application, for the year specified in the application.

(c) When the department provides said service or services under this section, the liability shall be apportioned in accordance with the appropriate formula determined in accordance with section 509(1).

(d) Local authorities may make successive application hereunder.

Pa.Stat.Ann. tit. 50, § 4508 (Purdon 1969). Section 509 provides, inter alia:

The department [of Public Welfare], subject to the provisions of section 503, shall have the power, and its duty shall be:

(1) From State and Federal funds, to make annual grants to counties to defray part of the cost of county programs authorized by this act and approved by the department, in the amount of ninety per cent of the excess of all such approved expenditures for such programs over the amount paid for the same purpose from any public or private source directly to participating counties, facilities or individuals.

(2) To prescribe the time at which the counties shall submit to the department annual plans and annual estimates of expenditures, and revisions thereof, to carry out mental health and mental retardation programs. Such plans and estimates shall contain such information as the secretary by regulation shall prescribe.

(3) Upon approval of an annual plan and the estimated expenditures for a mental health and mental retardation program, to compute an annual grant in accordance with the formula established in clause (1) of this section.

* * *

(5) In the event that sufficient funds to pay the full amount of the grants to which the counties may be entitled under the provisions of this section have not been appropriated, to distribute State funds among the counties by a formula reasonably designed to achieve the objectives of this act, provided however, that in such event the counties' financial obligations under this act shall be reduced in accordance with the same formula and the counties shall be required to provide only those services for which sufficient funds are available.

* * *

Pa.Stat.Ann. tit. 50, § 4509 (Purdon 1969). The district court was quite aware of these provisions, and the allocation of responsibilities among the respective defendants set forth in the order is consistent with them.

we must consider whether federal law, constitutional or statutory, requires that result. In this one respect federal law issues must be faced, and we reiterate our prior holding that the order directing the eventual closing of and barring all future admissions to Pennhurst went beyond what any federal statute or the Fourteenth Amendment requires.

Since the MH/MR Act of 1966 is sufficient to support the judgment in other respects, the *Siler* rule prevents our consideration of plaintiffs' claims under the Fourteenth Amendment except to the limited extent discussed in the preceding paragraph.

Federal statutory supremacy claims do not implicate the rule against unnecessary constitutional law decisions to the same degree, since a decision on such grounds, while it binds the state legislature, leaves Congress free to act. In our prior opinion we recognized that distinction, and decided one federal statutory supremacy issue, now reversed. Two such issues remain: whether Section 6063 of the Developmentally Disabled Assistance and Bill of Rights Act, which requires that state plans comply with several specific federal conditions, would support the judgment; and whether Section 504 of the Rehabilitation Act of 1973 would support it.

With respect to Section 6063, the Supreme Court noted several issues: whether any plaintiffs have a cause of action to enforce it; whether 42 U.S.C. § 1983 provides such a cause of action; whether Pennhurst's programs fall within Section 6063(b)(5)(C); and whether relief would be limited to an injunction against the federal government. On none of those issues do we have findings of fact by the district judge. Moreover our examination of the record, with which we are obviously less familiar than he is, does not suggest that the facts necessary for decision of the issues presented by Section 6063 have been sufficiently developed.

Although in this court it is settled that Section 504 affords relief for private plaintiffs,[27] and although on this claim the district court did make findings of fact and conclusions of law, in our previous decision we declined to reach the Section 504 issues. Except for the settled question of a private cause of action, the issues presented by Section 504 are at least as complex as are those posed by Section 6063. Moreover the district court's findings of fact were in this case made without the benefit of our recent *en banc* decision discussing allocation of burdens of production and of proof in cases based on antidiscrimination statutes such as Section 504.[29] If we undertook the arduous task of reviewing the district court's findings of fact bearing particularly on the applicability of Section 504 to the several programs for the mentally retarded involved in this case, it is possible that the only outcome would be a remand for reconsideration in light of the appropriate burden of production and proof.

Implicit in our prior decision was a holding that assuming Section 504 applies, as a matter of law it does not require the eventual closing of Pennhurst or the prohibition of all future referrals to that institution. But the remaining relief afforded to the class is supported by the MH/MR Act of 1966. In that circumstance it is clearly unnecessary, and probably inappropriate as well, to reach any more of the merits of the Section 504 claim.

---

[27]*NAACP* v. *The Medical Center, Inc.*, 599 F.2d 1247, 1257–58 (3d Cir. 1979).

[29]*NAACP* v. *The Medical Center, Inc.*, 657 F.2d 1322 (3d Cir. 1981).

It is possible that at some future time the Pennsylvania Legislature may take action which would on state law grounds suggest Rule 60(b) relief from some provisions of the injunction. In that event it will be necessary for the District Court to consider the Section 6063 issues, and perhaps to reconsider its prior Section 504 decision. If the court is presented with that situation these federal statutory supremacy issues which we have left open should be addressed, for they might well afford a basis for avoiding the decision of the plaintiffs' Fourteenth Amendment claims. *Hagans* v. *Lavine*, 415 U.S. 528, 543, 94 S.Ct. 1372, 1382, 39 L.Ed.2d 577 (1974).

## VI

We have reconsidered our prior judgment as directed by the Supreme Court's mandate. Since, to the extent that we affirmed it, the district court's order is supported by the MH/MR Act of 1966, an independent state law adequate to that end, our judgment shall reissue in its original form.

NOTES

1.   Partial dissents of Chief Judge Seitz, joined by Judge Hunter, and of Judge Garth are not included here. Both of these opinions took issue with the appointment of a special master to oversee implementation of relief orders. At 673 F.2d 662 and 673 F.2d 662–670.

2.   In related opinions, the Third Circuit affirmed orders of the district court directing the *Pennhurst* defendants to pay the costs of operation of the special master's office, and holding the Pennsylvania Department of Public Welfare in civil contempt with civil fines of $10,000 per day. See, *Halderman* v. *Pennhurst State School & Hospital*, 673 F.2d 628 (3d Cir. 1982) and 673 F.2d 645 (3d Cir. 1982).

3.   An important development in institutional litigation occurred in 1980 with the passage of the Civil Rights of Institutionalized Persons Act, 42 U.S.C. Sections 1997 *et seq.* The statute gives the United States Attorney General authority to institute civil actions to redress systematic deprivations of constitutional and federal statutory rights of persons residing in state institutions. The Act was prompted by two Circuit Court of Appeals decisions holding that the Attorney General did not have authority to bring suits on behalf of the United States to challenge institutional conditions and practices: *United States* v. *Solomon*, 563 F.2d 1121 (4th Cir. 1977); *United States* v. *Mattson*, 600 F.2d 1295 (9th Cir. 1979). The constitutionality of the Civil Rights of Institutionalized Persons Act was upheld in *Santana* v. *Collazo*, 89 F.R.D. 369 (D.P.R. 1981).

# 7

# HOUSING AND ZONING RESTRICTIONS

Patrick P. Spicer

## SUMMARY OF DOCTRINAL DEVELOPMENTS

THE SIGNIFICANT DEVELOPMENT with respect to the handicapped person's accessibility to housing has been the application of Sec. 504 to this important issue with some degree of success on the part of handicapped persons.

Regarding zoning, while state law continued to have a basically regressive effect on the move toward deinstitutionalization, handicapped persons have used federal statutes to their advantage in making gains in the deinstitutionalization movement.

## A. ZONING RESTRICTIONS

### 1. Single Family Residential Property

p. 711—INSERT the following after Note 4:

GARCIA V. SIFFRIN RESIDENTIAL ASSOCIATION

*Supreme Court of Ohio, 1980*

*63 Ohio St. 2d 259, 407 N.E. 2d 1369*

*Syllabus by the Court*

1. A "family home," as defined in R.C. 5123.18(A)(3), is not a "family" use, as defined in the Canton city zoning ordinance, and is not a permitted use in the R–2 zoned district under such ordinance.

2. The enactment of zoning laws by a municipality is an exercise of the "police power," rather than an exercise of the power of "local self-government," as granted by Section 3, Article XVIII of the Ohio Constitution.

3. R.C. 5123.18(D) and (E) are not "general laws" of the state within the meaning of Section 3, Article XVIII of the Ohio Constitution; therefore, Chapter 1137 of the Canton city zoning ordinance, which prohibits a "family" use as contemplated by R.C. 5123.18 is not unconstitutionally in conflict with a "general law" of the state.

4. R.C. 5123.18(D), (E) and (G) are "special laws" in violation of Section 26, Article II of the Ohio Constitution, and are therefore unconstitutional.

The appellee herein, Siffrin Residential Association (Siffrin), is an Ohio non-profit corporation formed to promote the development of residential, rather than an institutional, type of living environment for certain mentally retarded persons of Stark County, pursuant to the provisions of R.C. 5123.18, which provides for the licensing, inspection and operation of "residential facilities."[1]

In November 1977, Siffrin purchased a residence at 1532 Yale Avenue, N.W., Canton, for the proposed use as a "residential facility" to house eight or fewer "developmentally disabled" female adults. This site is in an area zoned R–2 within Chapter 1137 of the Canton City Ordinances, which zoning classification restricts the sites to one and two-family dwellings.[2]

---

[1]Ohio for a number of years has by law provided for the licensing of facilities for the care of mentally retarded persons. Such licensure provision was contained in R.C. 5123.18. In 1977, the General Assembly enacted a new R.C. 5123.18 which became effective on October 31, 1977. The new section was included within Am. Sub. S. B No. 71.

The portions of R.C. 5123.18 as enacted which are germane to this discussion are as follows:

(A) As used in this section and section 5123.19 of the Revised Code:

(1) "Residential facility" means a home or facility in which a person with a developmental disability resides, except a home subject to Chapter 3721 of the Revised Code or the home of a relative or legal guardian in which a person with a developmental disability resides.

(2) "Developmental disability" means a disability that originated before the attainment of eighteen years of age and can be expected to continue indefinitely, constitutes a substantial handicap to the person's ability to function normally in society, and is attributable to mental retardation, cerebral palsy, epilepsy, autism, or any other condition found to be closely related to mental retardation because such condition results in similar impairment of general intellectual functioning or adaptive behavior or requires similar treatment and services.

(3) "Family home" means a residential facility that provides room and board, personal care, habilitation services, and supervision in a family setting for not more than eight persons with developmental disabilities.

(4) "Group home" means a residential facility that provides room and board, personal care, habitation services, and supervision in a family setting for at least nine but not more than sixteen persons with developmental disabilities.

(B) Every person desiring to operate a residential facility shall apply for licensure of the facility to the chief of the division of mental retardation and developmental disabilities.

* * *

(D) Any person may operate a licensed family home as a permitted use in any residential district or zone, including any single-family residential district or zone, of any political subdivision. Family homes may be required to comply with area, height, yard, and architectural compatibility requirements that are uniformly imposed upon all single-family residences within the district or zone.

(E) Any person may operate a licensed group home as a permitted use in any multiple-family residential district or zone of any political subdivision, except that a political subdivision that has enacted a zoning ordinance or resolution establishing planned unit development districts may exclude group homes from such districts, and a political subdivision that has enacted a zoning ordinance or resolution may regulate group homes in multiple-family residential districts or zones as a conditionally permitted use or special exception, in either case, under reasonable and specific standards and conditions set out in the zoning ordinance or resolution to:

(1) Require the architectural design and site layout of the home and the location, nature, and height of any walls, screens, and fences to be compatible with adjoining land uses and the residential character of the neighborhood;

(2) Require compliance with yard, parking, and sign regulation;

(3) Limit excessive concentration of homes.

(F) This section does not prohibit a political subdivision from applying to residential facilities nondiscriminatory regulations requiring compliance with health, fire, and safety regulations and building standards and regulations.

(G) Divisions (D) and (E) of this section are not applicable to municipal corporations that had in effect on June 15, 1977, an ordinance specifically permitting in residential zones licensed residential facilities by means of permitted uses, conditional uses, or special exception, so long as such ordinance remains in effect without any substantive modification.

[2]The sections of Chapter 1137 of the Canton city zoning ordinance which are pertinent to this discussion are as follows:

1137.02 Permitted Uses.
Principal permitted uses are as follows:

Appellants, Alex J. and Mary L. Garcia, are owners of a residence located adjacent to the proposed facility, in which residence they have lived for approximately 25 years.

In March 1978, Siffrin made application to the Ohio Department of Mental Health and Mental Retardation, pursuant to R.C. 5123.18, for licensure of the home. The department, pursuant to law, issued a notice to the Canton Planning Commission, Canton Board of Zoning Appeals and the Clerk of Canton City Council, prior to the publication of the required legal notice. Letters of objection to the proposed location were filed by Mr. Garcia and another neighbor. Subsequently, a petition was signed by some 50 residents in the neighborhood, objecting to the location of this facility.

The Canton Zoning Department also filed a letter of objection, stating that the proposed use was neither a permitted use nor a conditional use in a R–2 district, and that the home as proposed could only qualify as a "boarding house" or "rooming house," a conditional use in a R–4 residential district.

The Department of Mental Health and Mental Retardation reviewed the objections, including that of the city of Canton, and determined that zoning restrictions imposed by the ordinance were superseded by the effect of R.C. 5123.18 and, more specifically, subsection (D) thereof, which, in pertinent part, states as follows:

> Any person may operate a licensed family home as a permitted use in any residential district or zone, including any single-family residential district or zone, of any political subdivision.

This present cause was thereafter instituted on April 21, 1978, by the filing of the complaint by the Garcias, in the Court of Common Pleas of Stark County (case No. 78–450), seeking to enjoin Siffrin from establishing a "family home" at 1532 Yale Avenue, and requesting that R.C. 5123.18(D) be declared unconstitutional. Appellants also requested that Drs. Moritz and Cannon of the Department of Mental Health and Mental Retardation be enjoined from licensing the home.

The city of Canton filed a complaint against the same defendants, also seeking to enjoin the licensing and establishment of this "family home," and to have R.C. 5123.18(D) declared unconstitutional.

---

(a) Any use permitted in the R-1 District.

(b) Two-family dwellings.

Within the zoning ordinances of Canton we find the following definitions:

1123.24 Dwelling.

"Dwelling" means any building or portion thereof, which is designed for or used for residential purposes; including one and two-family and multi-family, but not including a tent, tourist cabin, trailer, trailer coach, hotels, motels, boarding houses or lodging houses.

1123.25 Dwelling unit.

"Dwelling unit" means a group of rooms arranged, maintained or designed to be occupied by a single-family (see definition of family), and consists of a complete bathroom, complete kitchen or kitchenette; and facilities for living, sleeping and eating. All of the facilities are to be located in contiguous rooms and used exclusively by such family and by any authorized persons occupying such dwelling or with the family.

1123.27 Dwelling, Two-family.

"Two-family dwelling" means a building designed for or used exclusively for residence purposes by two families living independently of each other.

1123.30 Family.

"Family" means one or more persons occupying a dwelling unit and living as a single housekeeping unit, whether or not related to each other by birth or marriage, as distinguished from a group occupying a boarding house, lodging house, motel, hotel, fraternity or sorority house.

Appellee, Ohio Legal Rights Service, moved and was granted leave to intervene as a party-defendant in case No. 78–450. The cases were consolidated and after a hearing, a preliminary injunction was granted to the plaintiffs enjoining the director from issuing a license for this operation.

Upon trial of this matter, evidence was adduced showing that Siffrin is a corporate entity controlled by a board of directors, that the corporation has at least one other "residential facility" in operation; and that the overall operations of this proposed facility, as well as the currently operating facility, are under the control of a director. The staff that was to be brought into this proposed operation in addition to the director, would be a married couple who would reside on the premises, two other women working full-time, and other special purpose training staff as needed to carry out the "habilitation services" and "personal care" as provided by statute and regulations. "Habilitation," as defined in R.C. 5123.68(G), "means the process by which the staff of the institution assists the resident to acquire and maintain those life skills which enable him to cope more effectively with the demands of his own person and of his environment and to raise the level of his physical, mental, social, and vocational efficiency. Habilitation includes but is not limited to programs of formal, structured education and training . . . ."

The director and an admissions committee screen the applicants for the home, and individual month-to-month contracts are entered into with either the individual, member of the family or guardian, or the state of Ohio if the person was institutionalized. The amount charged for the services to be given the individual varies with the physical or educational needs or requirements of the individual. The clients are persons with one or more "developmental disabilities"; all are characterized by deficiencies in adaptive behavior, in socialization, and in life skills, and some have both neurological and organic disabilities or damage.

The budget for this facility would be approximately $61,000, "broken down . . . [into] direct care, indirect staff cost for secretarial, administrative, administrative non-personnel cost, telephone, travel, things of this nature, food, mortgage, utilities, depreciation, insurance, things like this." There is a rather complex funding of residents, including federal and state funds for room and board reimbursement.

Thereafter, on August 18, 1978, Judge DeHoff, of the Court of Common Pleas of Stark County, issued his findings of fact and conclusions of law. Among the findings of fact of the trial court are the following:

20. Under the definitions contained in Chapter 1123 of the Canton City Ordinance, "family" means one or more persons occupying a dwelling unit and living as a single housekeeping unit, whether or not related to each other by birth or marriage, and who do not pay consideration for living there and who do not have an "operator" running the dwelling.

21. Ohio Revised Code Section 5123.18 defines "family home" as a residential facility that provides room and board, personal care, habilitation services, and supervision in a family setting for not more than eight persons with developmental disabilities.

22. Ohio Revised Code Section 5123.18(B) provides that persons desiring to *operate* a family home residential facility must apply for a license. [Emphasis *sic.*]

23. The proposed Siffrin Residential Association for the Developmentally Disabled

of Stark County "family home" will house up to eight female adults, two full-time houseparents and a part-time relief staff employed by the Siffrin Association for the Developmentally Disabled of Stark County and will be administered by a full-time director.

24.   The proposed Siffrin Residential Association for the Developmentally Disabled of Stark County "family home" will operate when at full capacity, on a budget of $65,000 per year.

* * *

26.   Location of the proposed "family home" at 1532 Yale Avenue N.W., Canton, Stark County, Ohio, immediately adjacent to the residence of Alex J. Garcia and Mary Garcia, will cause a diminution of the Garcias' property value.

27.   Location of a group home housing eight mentally retarded adult men at 150 South Rose Avenue, Akron, Ohio, resulted in a thirty-five (35) percent tax valuation reduction to the immediate neighboring property owned by Charles Zindle and Charlotte Zindle.

The conclusions of law of the trial court included the following:

2.   The defendant's, Siffrin Residential Association for the Developmentally Disabled of Stark County, proposed use of the premises located at 1532 Yale Avenue N.W., Canton, Stark County, Ohio, as a "family home" is not a "family" within the meaning of Canton's Zoning Ordinances, effective February 14, 1977, and is not a permitted or conditional use in an R–2 zone.

3.   Amended Substitute Senate Bill No. 71, subsections (D) and (E), Ohio Revised Code Section 5123.18(D),(E), are not "general" laws of the State of Ohio within the meaning of Article XVIII, Section 3, of the Ohio Constitution.

4.   Canton's Zoning Ordinances are enacted pursuant to the constitutional grant of powers of local self-government, Article XVIII, Section 3; are not subject to the "conflict" provision of Article XVIII, Section 3, of the Ohio Constitution; and are not superseded by Amended Substitute Senate Bill No. 71, subsections (D) and (E), Ohio Revised Code Section 5123.18(D), (E).

5.   Amended Substitute Senate Bill No. 71, subsections (D), (E) and (G), Ohio Revised Code Section 5123.18(D), (E), (G) are not uniform in their operation throughout the State of Ohio and are void as special laws prohibited by Article II, Section 26 of the Ohio Constitution.

6.   Amended Substitute Senate Bill No. 71, subsections (D) and (E), Ohio Revised Code Section 5123.18(D), (E), are unconstitutional and in violation of the due process clauses of Article I of the Ohio Constitution and the Fourteenth Amendment to the United States Constitution in that they are arbitrary and capricious.

Judgment was accordingly entered for the Garcias and the city of Canton. Siffrin, Drs. Moritz and Cannon, and the Ohio Legal Rights Service thereafter appealed the decision of the Court of Common Pleas to the Court of Appeals. The members of that court rendered their opinion and judgment in March 1979, reversing the judgment of the trial court.

The Court of Appeals found that the Siffrin operation would be in compliance with the Canton ordinance, in that the facility and its residents could be considered a "family" under the ordinance because they would be "occupying a dwelling unit and living as a single housekeeping unit." Further, the court found that the trial court erred in finding that the establishment of the Siffrin home will occasion a diminution in the value of the Garcias' adjacent property.

The Court of Appeals further found that R.C. 5123.18(D) and (E) are general laws of the state of Ohio within the meaning of Section 3, Article XVIII of the Ohio Constitution.

Further, the Court of Appeals held that the Canton zoning ordinance, being an exercise of the police power pursuant to Section 3, Article XVIII of the Ohio Constitution, is subject to the conflict provision of that section, and held that R.C. 5123.18 was not a ''special'' law, even though under subdivision (G) it excludes certain cities from the zoning overriding features of (D) and (E) and that such statute did have a uniform operation throughout the state, and was therefore not contrary to Section 26, Article II of the Ohio Constitution.

The Garcias and the city of Canton appeal to this court, setting forth the following propositions of law:

1. ''The Siffrin Residential Association's proposed use of the residence at 1532 Yale Ave. N.W., Canton, Ohio, as a 'family home,' defined in O.R.C. Section 5123(A)(3), is not a 'family' use as defined in the Canton city ordinance and consequently is not a permitted use in an R–2 zoned district.''

2. ''Ohio Revised Code Sections 5123.18(D) and (E) are not 'general laws' of the state of Ohio within the meaning of Article XVIII, Section 3 of the Ohio Constitution.''

3. ''Canton's zoning ordinances are enacted pursuant to the constitutional grant of powers of local self-government, Article XVIII, Section 3; are not subject to the 'conflict' provision of Article XVIII, Section 3; and are not superseded by Ohio Revised Code Sections 5123.18(D) and (E).''

4. ''Ohio Revised Code Sections 5123.18(D), (E) and (G) are void as special laws prohibited by Article II, Section 26 of the Ohio Constitution.''

5. ''Ohio Revised Code Sections 5123.18(D) and (E) are unconstitutional and in violation of the due process clauses of Article I of the Ohio Constitution and the Fourteenth Amendment to the United States Constitution.''

6. ''Ohio Revised Code Sections 5123.18(D) and (E) create an arbitrary and discriminatory classification of persons and are unconstitutional under Article I of the Ohio Constitution and the Equal Protection Clause of the Fourteenth Amendment to the United States Constitution.''

7. ''Appellants Garcias are entitled to injunctive relief to prevent operation of the Siffrin Residential Association's 'family home' at 1532 Yale Avenue, N.W., Canton, Ohio pursuant to Ohio Revised Code Section 713.13.''

8. ''Application of the city of Canton's zoning ordinance to prohibit the proposed use of the Siffrin Residential Association's 'family home' in an R–2 district is a constitutional exercise of the city's police powers.''

The cause is now before this court pursuant to the allowance of a motion to certify the record.

Vincent J. Bernabei, Canton, for appellants Garcia.

Harry E. Klide, Director of Law, Ronald E. Stocker, Thomas P. Albu and Thomas M. Bernabei, Canton, for appellant city of Canton.

Zink, Zink & Zink Co., L.P.A., Jeffrey E. Zink, Larry A. Zink and Constance Leistiko, Canton, for appellee Siffrin.

William J. Brown, Atty. Gen., and George Stricker, Jr., Asst. Atty. Gen., for appellees Moritz and Cannon.

John Guendelsberger and Douglas Rogers, Columbus, for appellee Ohio Legal Rights Service.

HOLMES, Justice.

Upon a thorough review of the applicable constitutional provisions, the statutes under consideration, the record, transcripts of proceedings and briefs herein, we reverse the Court of Appeals.

We hasten to add at the outset of our discussion of the legal issues presented here that we are fully in sympathy with, and support of, the purposes of R.C. Chapter 5123 which are specifically set forth within R.C. 5123.67. It may not be reasonably questioned that there is considerable merit in a law which seeks to maximize the assimilation of mentally retarded persons into the ordinary life of the community in which they live, and to provide places for them to live in surroundings and circumstances as close to normal as possible. However, in carrying out these salutory state programs in aid of some of our citizens, the constitutional rights of other members of our citizenry, and the constitutional authority which has been granted to our local governments, must always be guarded and not infringed upon.

In this cause we are not dealing with a state statute which attempts to override a discriminatory exercise of local governmental police power, nor are we indeed dealing with laws of the state which were enacted within the same public purpose area as are the local zoning laws. The state, by passage of R.C. 5123.18, was not seeking to establish a program of statewide land plannning, but instead the state sought by this law to assist developmentally disabled persons by placing these persons in a residential setting. On the other hand, the city of Canton, through its zoning code, seeks to regulate land uses in order to develop the city through comprehensive community-wide planning. Here, the operation of this state law in carrying out the otherwise salutory aims of treating and educating the developmentally disabled obviates laws of local governments which have been enacted for an entirely different purpose. *i.e.,* the planned orderly growth of the community.

Here, based upon the facts within the record, some of which have been alluded to previously, we conclude that residents of these licensed facilities may not reasonably be includable within the definition of "family" as set forth in the Canton zoning code. We do not perceive this facility, and its statutorily mandated purposes and duties, to be likened to what is reasonably thought of to be a single housekeeping unit. We believe the facts show that these clients of Siffrin would not be residing in this dwelling unit as a single housekeeping unit in the same sense as would a group of individuals who had joined together in these premises in order to primarily share the rooming, dining and other facilities. The emphasis in such an instance may be placed upon the dwelling aspect of the unit, and upon the fact that those who are living within that structure are sharing and maintaining a household as a single unit.

We conclude based upon all the evidence that the Siffrin facility would be established not for the prime purpose of eight people sharing a dwelling place, but primarily for the purpose of bringing together a group of developmentally disabled persons for their training and education in life skills, and for the establishment and furnishing of a professional plan of habilitation for each client developed by the licensed operator and implemented through the director of such facility and his staff of interdisciplinary personnel trained and equipped for this purpose. The individualized care and training of these clients who are the resident participants of this program would reasonably appear to be the basis of this program sought to be located at this site.

We do not believe that the operation of this facility constitutes a "family" within the definition of the Canton zoning code.

It being determined that the operation of this facility within the R–2 zoning district of Canton does not comport with the allowable activities for such a district in this community, the question becomes whether this state statute will prevail and override Canton's zoning laws. Municipalities in Ohio are granted the authority to adopt zoning regulations by way of the constitutional home rule provisions of Section 3, Article XVIII of the Ohio Constitution, which provides that:

> Municipalities shall have authority to exercise all powers of local self-government and to adopt and enforce within their limits such local police, sanitary and other similar regulations, as are not in conflict with general laws.

This amendment has repeatedly been interpreted by this court as being a direct grant of authority to a municipality to enact local self-government and police regulations. *Village of Struthers* v. *Sokol* (1923) 108 Ohio St. 263, 140 N.E. 519; *Youngstown* v. *Evans* (1929), 121 Ohio St. 342, 168 N.E. 844.

Whether the passage of zoning ordinances by municipalities constitutes an exercise of constitutionally granted local self-government or police powers presents an interesting question, but a question which in the main has been answered by prior judicial determinations. The Supreme Court of the United States has addressed this issue and held such an ordinance to be an exercise of the municipality's police powers. *Village of Euclid* v. *Ambler Realty Co.* (1926), 272 U.S. 365, 47 S.Ct. 114, 71 L.Ed 303. This court peripherally addressed this subject in *State, ex rel. Euclid-Doan* v. *Cunningham* (1918), 97 Ohio St. 130, 119 N.E. 361, where the court held that ordinances dealing with the regulation of height, mode of construction, and use of tenement houses were an exercise of police power. In *Pritz* v. *Messer* (1925), 112 Ohio St. 628, 149 N.E. 30, this court held that ordinances which divided the municipal territory into districts according to a comprehensive plan which was reasonably necessary for the preservation of the public health, safety and morals would be an exercise of the police power of the municipality.

In *State, ex rel. Toledo* v. *Lynch* (1913), 88 Ohio St. 71, 97, 102 N.E. 670, 673, this court characterized powers of local self-government as those "powers of government as, in view of their nature and the field of their operation, are local and municipal in character." In *State, ex rel. Toledo* v. *Cooper* (1917), 97 Ohio St. 86, 91, 119 N.E. 253, 254, this court additionally stated that such powers are "not only purely local and purely municipal, but purely governmental."

In a functional sense, zoning prescribes and regulates the conduct of individuals in their use of land. Zoning is not functionally a matter of internal municipal organization, as would be ordinances setting forth the form, structure and operation of the municipal government. Rather, the exercise of the zoning power " '. . . aims directly to secure and promote the public welfare, and it does so by restraint and compulsion.' " *Fitzgerald* v. *Cleveland* (1913), 88 Ohio St. 338, 357, 103 N.E. 512, 518.

Upon analysis of their function and purpose, we conclude that zoning ordinances are an exercise of the police power granted to municipalities by Section 3, Article XVIII of the Ohio Constitution.

Zoning ordinances may be valid and constitutional enactments pursuant to Section 3, Article XVIII, without the necessity of further state legislative enabling statutes. *Pritz* v. *Messer, supra*. Such laws, being of the nature of policing regulations of the municipality, unlike the municipality's exercise of its powers of "local self-government" which may be described as being of an administrative nature, are subject to the constitutional provision that they not be "in conflict with general law." *State, ex rel. Klapp* v. *Dayton P. & L. Co.* (1967), 10 Ohio St.2d 14, 225 N.E.2d 230; *Canton* v. *Whitman* (1975), 44 Ohio St.2d 62, 337 N.E.2d 766.

There would seem to be no great controversy here that there is a direct conflict between the local zoning ordinance of Canton and R.C. 5123.18(D). May then this state statute override the Canton zoning ordinance by virtue of the statute being a general law? We think not.

"General laws" are defined to mean statutes setting forth police, sanitary or other similar regulations, and not statutes which by their operation only grant or limit the legislative powers of a municipal corporation to adopt or enforce police, sanitary or other similar regulations. *Village of West Jefferson* v. *Robinson* (1965), 1 Ohio St.2d 113, 205 N.E.2d 382; *Youngstown* v. *Evans, supra*.

These "general laws" are laws operating uniformly throughout the state, *Leis* v. *Cleveland Railway Co.* (1920), 101 Ohio St. 162, 128 N.E. 73, which prescribe a rule of conduct upon citizens generally, and which operate with general uniform application throughout the state under the same circumstances and conditions. *Schneiderman* v. *Sesanstein* (1929), 121 Ohio St. 80, 167 N.E. 158. In the main, the provisions of R.C. Chapter 5123 fall within the definition of a "general law" providing a method by which the mentally retarded may hopefully be acclimated to a useful place in society through the licensure of "residential facilities" and the deinstitutionalizing of these mentally retarded individuals. However, subsections (D), (E) and (G) of R.C. 5123.18 are not reasonably related to the valid purposes and objectives of the regulatory and licensing portions of the other sections of this chapter of law. In this attempt to be supportive of the purposes of this chapter, these sections unreasonably and unlawfully limit the enforcement by municipalities of certain of the police powers authorized by the Ohio Constitution to such municipalities.

It is interesting to note in this regard that subsections (E) and (F) of R.C. 5123.18 specifically preserve some enumerated city planning type of police powers to the municipalities in their control of these "licensed facilities." Subsection (E)(1) provides that the city may enact requirements for architectural design, site layout, height of walls, screens and fences to be compatible with adjoining land uses and residential character of the neighborhood; subsection (E)(2) permits regulation of yard, parking and signs; subsection (E)(3) permits the limitation of "excessive concentration of homes." Subsection (F) provides that the section does not prohibit a political subdivision from applying to "residential facilities" regulations regarding health, fire and safety regulations, and building standards and regulations.

In the view of this majority, these sections of law selectively excise certain of the police powers of local government that have been granted to municipalities by the

Constitution. Thus, such sections, like those considered in *Village of West Jefferson, supra,* are not general laws.

It is our view that subsections (D) and (E) of R.C. 5123.18, as limited by subsection (G) of that section, suffer an additional infirmity, in that they are special laws prohibited by Section 26, Article II of the Ohio Constitution. Such constitutional provision states, in pertinent part, that, "all laws of a general nature shall have a uniform operation throughout the State. . . ."

The requirement of uniform operation throughout the state of laws of a general nature does not forbid different treatment of various classes or types of citizens, but does prohibit nonuniform classification if such be arbitrary, unreasonable or capricious. *Miller* v. *Korns* (1923), 107 Ohio St. 287, 140 N.E. 773.

R.C. 5123.18(G) creates two distinct classes of municipalities with respect to the operation of subsections (D) and (E): first, municipal corporations that had in effect on June 15, 1977, an ordinance specifically permitting in residential zones licensed residential facilities by means of permitted uses, conditional uses, or special exception, so long as such ordinance remains in effect without any substantive modification; and, second, municipal corporations that did not have such a specific ordinance in effect on June 15, 1977. Those cities which acted prior to June 15, 1977, allowably under subsection (G), could have provided that these "family homes" be located only in the less restrictive residential districts such as those districts permitting apartments, rooming houses, boarding houses, dormitories, and the like. Conversely, cities which did not act prior to June 15, 1977, are, under this subsection, required to permit these licensed facilities within any residential district including the most restrictive, single family districts. This classification is based upon a time requirement which is arbitrary in that it establishes June 15, 1977, as a deadline after which even enactment of an ordinance which would permit such licensed residential facilities in residential zones would not relieve a municipality from the effect of the statute.

Additionally, in complying with subsection (G), even though the city of Canton or other municipality had a zoning ordinance in effect at the "deadline" date, which could reasonably be construed to permit facilities of the type in question within certain residential zones, if such ordinance did not *specifically* provide for these licensed residential facilities, the municipality would still come within the purview of the statute.

The desire of the state to make residential zones available to such facilities is a very laudatory one; however, any law enacted to accomplish such purpose must operate uniformly upon all municipalities. The distinction drawn between classes of municipalities by subsection (G) of R.C. 5123.18 is arbitrary and unrelated to the accomplishment of its avowed purpose. It frees some municipalities from state intervention in zoning, while subjecting others to spot zoning by administrative action. Furthermore, it fails to make provision for redemption of the right to exclude such facilities by enactment of remedial legislation after the arbitrary date.

Local option provisions in state statutes do not, *per se,* violate the requirement that all laws of a general nature shall have a uniform operation throughout the state. *Canton* v. *Whitman, supra.* However, R.C. 5123.18(G) should be carefully distinguished from the situation in *Whitman.* In *Whitman,* a municipal corporation could, pursuant to R.C. 6111.13, within a limited time period after enactment of the statute, hold a local election pertaining to fluoridation. In the instant cause, R.C. 5123.18 does not contain any local option provision, and it relates to a date prior to the enactment of the law. The arbitrary fixing of a retrospective date, upon which future rights and powers of a municipality depend, distinguishes this case from *Whitman*.

For these reasons, R.C. 5123.18(D), (E) and (G) are void under Section 26, Article II of the Ohio Constitution, as not being laws of a general nature having uniform operation throughout the state.

Local comprehensive zoning plans have long been held to be a valid exercise of governmental planning and control of land use for the benefit of public health, safety, morals, and general welfare. *Village of Euclid* v. *Ambler Realty Co., supra.* The various zoning provisions, which set forth certain prohibitions, restrictions, or limitations upon the free utilization and enjoyment of one's lands must be a part of a reasonably comprehensive plan for the development of the community. *Village of Belle Terre* v. *Boraas* (1974), 416 U.S. 1, 94 S.Ct. 1536, 39 L.Ed.2d 797; *Village of Euclid* v. *Ambler Realty, supra.*

A zoning ordinance shown to have a substantial relation to the public health, morals or safety, and not to be arbitrary or discriminatory in its operation or effect, will be upheld as a proper constitutional exercise of the police power of local government.

Here we find that the provision of the Canton zoning ordinance which would prohibit the establishment and operation of this residential facility within a R–2 zoned area is a reasonable exercise of the police power granted to municipalities pursuant to Section 3, Article XVIII of the Ohio Constitution.

The overall Canton zoning ordinance seemingly provides for a comprehensive plan for the growth and development of the city. It may be concluded that the specific section here involved has been enacted as a reasonable part of the overall zoning plan, and it has not been shown that such provision is arbitrary, capricious or discriminatory in its operation. We find that such section of the zoning ordinance does not forfeit an owner's rights or deprive him of the reasonable free use of his property. Accordingly, we hold that such section of the ordinance does not violate Section 19, Article I of the Ohio Constitution, nor the Fourteenth Amendment to the United States Constitution, and therefore we find the provision to be constitutionally valid.

There was evidence at the trial of this matter which tended to show that the Garcias and other adjacent property owners would suffer a diminution in property valuation due to the operation of this residential facility in their neighborhood. The evidence in this regard was adduced both through the testimony of a real estate broker dealing in properties in this general vicinity, and by way of testimony of Mrs. Charlotte Zindle, an Akron resident, concerning the lowering of the valuation of her property when a like kind of facility had been established in her neighborhood in Akron.

To counter this evidence of appellants, Siffrin presented evidence from Ken Suchan, a resident of Wooster, an urban planner by profession, who testified that he had no personal experience in real estate sales, nor was he a real estate broker. He testified that, ". . . I wouldn't expect that there would be any difference, any change in—in property values as a result of—of that use being there; and it would, in fact, be almost indistinguishable from the rest of the neighborhood."

Even though the evidence of Mrs. Zindle may not have been probative of the issue of the lowering of real estate values in this Canton neighborhood due to the placement of this facility, the trial court, as trier of the facts, had before it probative evidence offered by both parties which the court could weigh and attribute an amount of significance or weight in determination of the preponderance thereof. The determination of the court found within finding of fact No. 26, *supra*, is in keeping with the evidence, and we hold that it was improper for the Court of Appeals to find that the trial court had erred in this respect.

The appellants assert their standing and right to injunctive relief in the instant matter pursuant to R.C. 713.13. There seems to be no real argument here that the Garcias do in fact have standing. This was acknowledged by the Court of Appeals. We conclude that all the elements of R.C. 713.13 have reasonably been met by the appellants in the presentation of their cause for injunctive relief. The Garcias are the "contiguous" property owners and there was the "imminent threat" that the adjacent property would be utilized in a manner in violation of the zoning ordinance of Canton. Further, it was shown to the satisfaction of the trier of the facts that the Garcias would be "especially damaged" by the placement of this facility adjacent to their residence. Thus, the Garcias did show that they were entitled to the injunctive relief requested.

Based upon all the foregoing, R.C. 5123.18(D), (E) and (G) are hereby held to be unconstitutional. Further, we hold that the provisions of Canton City Code Chapter 1137, insofar as such provides for "R–2 two-family dwellings" that would by their application prohibit the establishment of "licensed residential facilities" in such a district, constitute a constitutional enactment of the city of Canton.

The judgment of the Court of Appeals is hereby reversed.

*Judgment reversed.*

Celebrezze, C. J., and Herbert, William B. Brown and Sweeney, JJ., concur.

Loucher, J., concurs in judgment.

Paul W. Brown, J., dissents.

Paul W. Brown, Justice, dissenting.

For the reasons more fully delineated in my dissent in *Carroll v. Washington Twp.* (1980), 63 Ohio St.2d 249, 408 N.E.2d 191, I must disagree with the majority's resolution in this cause. The majority in the instant cause has again unnecessarily intruded into internal family relations in concluding that a "family home" as defined by R.C. 5123.18(A)(3) is not a family use under the applicable zoning ordinance. Canton zoning ordinance section 1123.30 provides:

> "Family" means one or more persons occupying a dwelling unit and living as a single housekeeping unit, whether or not related to each other by birth or marriage, as distinguished from a group occupying a boarding house, lodging house, motel, hotel, fraternity or sorority house.

Under this broad definition I cannot conclude that the planned home for these developmentally disabled adults would not constitute a family. The majority seems to base its findings upon the premise that under the zoning ordinances the primary purpose for living as a single housekeeping unit must be to share the rooming, dining and other facilities within the dwelling. This requirement, however, appears nowhere within the zoning scheme. So long as the group functions as a single housekeeping unit, their primary purpose in doing so is irrelevant.

The requirement also makes little sense as a judicially created doctrine. Other courts have wisely not seen fit to intrude into the motivations behind the free choice of individuals who seek to live together as single housekeeping unit and create such artificial distinctions, with their attendant possibilities of discriminatory application. *E.g.*, *Des Plaines* v. *Trottner* (1966), 34 Ill.2d 432, 216 N.E.2d 116; *White Plains* v. *Ferraioli* (1974), 34 N.Y.2d 300, 357 N.Y.S.2d 449, 313 N.E.2d 756. More specifically the courts that have addressed the issue presented here, group homes for retarded adults, have concluded that the homes are single housekeeping units. *Freeport* v. *Association for the Help of Retarded Children* (1977), 94 Misc.2d 1048, 406 N.Y.S.2d 221; *Oliver* v. *Zoning Commission* (1974), 31 Conn.Supp. 197, 326 A.2d 841 (where a group home for nine retarded adults was held to constitute a single housekeeping unit, under an almost identical definition of family as that appearing in the Canton ordinances).

Moreover it does not seem so obvious that the individuals who seek to live together here do so primarily to obtain "training and education in life skills." Such training is just as available in institutions whose environment the individuals in this cause have purposely avoided. The primary purpose of these individuals is more likely the avoidance of institutionalization, thus seeking to live in a shared dwelling in a residential neighborhood, in the midst of surroundings as normal as possible.

In *Carroll* v. *Washington Twp.*, *supra*, a case announced this date, it was held that the Ohio Youth Commission's foster home was not a "one family residential dwelling unit." In that case the court stressed the fact that there was no definition of the term "family" contained within the zoning provisions. The court indicated that if the legislative definition could be met it would uphold such a residential use. Yet, in this case, the majority has concluded that the zoning definition focusing upon a single housekeeping unit will not permit the family home sought to be created under R.C. Chapter 5123. Thus, the line to be drawn has conveniently moved in a manner to exclude the family homes, which have been deemed to be so desperately needed. If such a trend should continue the only place for such homes may be factory districts and other non-residential areas. Thus, I conclude as the Court of Appeals did in this cause that the Siffrin home is a permitted use within this R–2 district.

I also do not agree with the majority's home-rule analysis concerning general laws. That opinion concedes the merit inherent in this legislation, but finds itself unable to uphold the constitutionality of R.C. 5123.18(D) and (E). A review of this court's prior case law dealing with this subject, however, leads me to the contradictory conclusion that these provisions are part of a comprehensive licensing scheme and as such constitute portions of a general law.

In *Village of West Jefferson* v. *Robinson* (1965), 1 Ohio St.2d 113, 205 N.E.2d 382, this court established the definition of "general laws" stating in paragraph three of the syllabus that:

> The words "general laws" as set forth in Section 3 of Article XVIII of the Ohio Constitution means statutes setting forth police, sanitary or similar regulations and not

statutes which purport *only* to grant or to limit the legislative powers of a municipal corporation to adopt or enforce police, sanitary or other similar regulations. (Emphasis added.) See, also, *Youngstown* v. *Evans* (1929), 121 Ohio St. 342, 345, 168 N.E. 844.

If the provisions at issue can be fairly characterized as being designed *only* to prescribe the mode and manner in which municipalities must conduct their zoning, they must be struck down as depriving those local governmental bodies of their constitutionally granted authority. R.C. 5123.18(D) and (E), however, do not merely place limits on municipalities, but in a much greater sense are regulatory of this state's citizenry in a licensing context.

Subsections (A) through (C) of R.C. 5123.18 set up a definitional and procedural framework under which a residential facility may be licensed. Subsections (D) and (E) govern the conduct of individuals. Both of these latter provisions begin with the statement that "[a]ny person may operate a [state] licensed . . . home," and, in fact the focus of the entire statutory section is upon individuals who seek to establish the group homes at issue.

The majority relies heavily upon the case of *Village of West Jefferson* v. *Robinson, supra,* in reaching its conclusion that the provisions at issue are not general laws. That case, involving a village that imposed a greater fine for unauthorized peddling than was permitted in the Revised Code, however, is not germane to the instant cause. No state licensure scheme was directly involved there.

On at least five previous occasions this court has held state licensing measures to be general laws. In *Neil House Hotel* v. *Columbus* (1944), 144 Ohio St. 248, 58 N.E.2d 665, regulations of the state Board of Liquor Control governing hours of operation were upheld over a Columbus ordinance. State laws authorizing licensing of watercraft and creating a fee schedule, were upheld over a local ordinance in *State, ex rel. McElroy* v. *Akron* (1962), 173 Ohio St. 189, 181 N.E.2d 26. In *Anderson* v. *Brown* (1968), 13 Ohio St.2d 53, 233 N.E.2d 584, 586, this court ruled that a municipality could not require an additional license for trailer parks where a state statute governed such licenses and provided that they "shall be in lieu of all license and inspection fees. . . ." State laws authorizing the licensing and regulations of bingo operations were upheld over a conflicting municipal ordinance in *Lorain* v. *Tomasic* (1979). 59 Ohio St.2d 1, 391 N.E.2d 726. See, also, *Stary* v. *Brooklyn* (1954), 162 Ohio St. 120, 121 N.E.2d 11.

The case, however, which is most analogous to this cause is *Auxter* v. *Toledo* (1962), 173 Ohio St. 444, 183 N.E.2d 920. There, the state liquor control licensing statute, R.C. 4303.27, providing that, "[e]ach permit issued . . . shall authorize the person named to carry on the business specified at the place . . . described . . ." was upheld over a Toledo ordinance prohibiting the sale of beer without a city license. It involved the same type of legislative grant at issue here, the affirmative right of a state agency to solely govern the carrying out of a particular use at a specific location. The statute at issue in *Auxter* was held to be a general law. Surely this is the proper conclusion, because the General Assembly may in the licensing context do more than grant the license holder a promise of no future interference from the state. Further interference by a municipality may be safeguarded against, under a specific legislative grant permitting a particular use at a specific location governed by a state agency. To hold otherwise, as the majority has done, is to in effect handcuff the General Assembly so that it may not create areas of statewide licensing which are exempt from local municipal control.

In R.C. 5123.67, the General Assembly specifically set forth the purposes for the enactment of the statutory provisions at issue. That statute provides:

> Chapter 5123 of the Revised Code shall be liberally interpreted to accomplish the following purposes:
> (A) To promote the human dignity and to protect the constitutional rights of mentally retarded persons in the state;
> (B) To encourage the development of the ability and potential of each mentally retarded person in the state to the fullest possible extent, no matter how severe his degree of disability;
> (C) To promote the economic security, standard of living, and meaningful employment of the mentally retarded;
> (D) To maximize the assimilation of mentally retarded persons into the ordinary life of the communities in which they live;
> (E) To recognize the need of mentally retarded persons whenever care in a residential facility is absolutely necessary, to live in surroundings and circumstances as close to normal as possible.

R.C. 5123.18(D) and (E) are integral parts of the legislative goal of deinstitutionalization, which may be carried out effectively only through the use of group homes.

The majority has thwarted this goal by reading subsections (D) and (E) in a vacuum without reference to the remainder of R.C. 5123.18, governing licensing, or the remainder of this statutory chapter. Through such a chosen pattern of interpretation, the majority has impliedly found some rationale to distinguish the instant situation from this court's prior line of cases concerning licensing. Perhaps some hidden policy reason requires the exemption of state liquor licenses from local municipal control but not the family home sought to be established here. Because I cannot also conceive of this policy consideration, I must dissent from the majority's determination that R.C. 5123.18(D) and (E) are not general laws.

Due to my conclusion that the contested provisions are general laws, I would find them to allow the operation of the Siffrin home. This court stated in *Canton* v. *Whitman* (1975), 44 Ohio St.2d 62, at page 66, 337 N.E.2d 766, at page 770, that:

> The city may exercise the police power within its borders, but the general laws of the state are supreme in the exercise of the police power, regardless of whether the matter is one which might also properly be a subject of municipal legislation. Where there is direct conflict the state regulation prevails.   Accord *Columbus* v. *Teater* (1978), 53 Ohio St.2d 253, 374 N.E.2d 154.

The majority's holding that subsections (D) and (E) of R.C. 5123.18, as limited by subsection (G) of that statutory section, constitute "special laws" is also unjustified. The conclusion reached that these provisions do not have uniform application flies in the face of the substance of the statute. No single area or type of municipality is singled out, as the statute's mandate is statewide. In *State, ex rel. Stanton* v. *Powell* (1924), 109 Ohio St. 383, at page 385, 142 N.E. 401, at page 403, this court recognized that:

. . . Section 26, Art. II of the Constitution, was not intended to render invalid every law which does not operate upon all . . . political subdivisions within the state. . . . [T]he law is equally valid if it contains provisions which permit it to *operate upon every locality where certain specified conditions prevail.* (Emphasis added.)

R.C. 5123.18(G) merely creates a grandfather clause whereby those municipalities that had pre-existing zoning codes on June 15, 1977, which would specifically allow this type of family home are unaffected by this statute. Grandfather clauses of this type have undisputedly been held valid in other contexts. How R.C. 5123.18(G), which provides that subsections (D) and (E) are redundant and inapplicable where such facilities are already licensed and regulated by local ordinance, adversely affects any municipality is not demonstrated. Simply because some municipalities fall on one side or the other of a valid legislative cut-off does not mean that the cut-off is unreasonable, or that the statute is a "special law" within the meaning of Section 26, Article II of the Ohio Constitution. In *State, ex rel. Lourin* v. *Indus. Comm.* (1941), 138 Ohio St. 618, at page 623, 37 N.E.2d 595, at page 598, it was stated:

. . . [T]he law abounds with situations where a difference of a minute may work a great change in rights and liabilities. Any statute of limitations illustrates this. In the interest of administrative workability, or to effect gradations in legislative policy, certain definite markers must be established, . . . *It is, of course, for the Legislature to determine just where such boundaries shall be set.* (Emphasis added.)

Certainly, the allowance of procedural alternatives effectuating the purposes of R.C. 5123.18 does not prevent the statute from having uniform operation throughout the state.

For the foregoing reasons, I would affirm the Court of Appeals in all respects.

NOTES

1. The *Siffrin* case is an archetypic example of the reluctance of residential communities to accept group homes wherein mentally retarded persons live in noninstitutional settings.

The court in *Siffrin,* as the dissent points out, appears to go out of its way to interpret the state law involved so as to exclude the group home at issue from the residential area in which it was to be located. The court's conclusion that the group home does not meet the definition of a family for the purposes of the zoning ordinance in question, means, again as the dissent points out, that group homes will, at least in the Canton area and in other localities with similar ordinances, be ostracized to commercial and industrial areas, negating one of their most important aspects—location in residential areas.

2. Would the legal theory employed by the plaintiffs in the *11 Cornwell* case, see below, pp. 313–316, or related theories have been of use to the defendants in *Siffrin?*

## 4. Special Situations and Zoning Variations

p. 737—INSERT the following after Note 4:

### McIntyre v. Northern Ohio Properties

*Court of Appeals of Ohio, 1979*
*64 Ohio App. 2d 179, 412 N.E. 2d 434*

JACKSON, Judge.

Plaintiffs, Lawrence and Marie McIntyre, the appellants herein, filed this action alleging that defendant Northern Ohio Properties, Inc. (hereinafter "NOP"), by and through their agent, defendant Steven Holett, an appellee, discriminated against Lawrence McIntyre solely because of his physical handicap, in violation of R.C. 4112.02(H)(1) and 4112.02(H)(4). Plaintiffs sought equitable relief and monetary damages. Upon the motion of the defendants, the trial court ruled that the within matter was to be tried to the court and further dismissed the claim of Marie McIntyre as not cognizable under R.C. Chapter 4112.

The evidence established at trial reveals that plaintiffs were tenants at the Bridlewood Apartments located in North Olmsted, Ohio. Bridlewood is one of several properties managed by defendant Holett, the property manager of NOP. The enforcement of the rules and regulations of the apartments was the responsibility of Mr. Holett.

One of the rules at Bridlewood prohibited residents from wearing "cut offs" (cut off jeans) in the swimming pool. Lawrence McIntyre (hereinafter plaintiff) had lost both of his legs in Vietnam and needed to wear "cut-offs" when swimming in order to protect the stumps of his legs from the cement in the swimming pool. Mr. Todaro, the superintendent of Bridlewood, gave instructions to the lifeguards to permit plaintiff to wear "cut-offs" in the pool.

Plaintiff testified that he used the pool while wearing cut-offs without any problem during the summers of 1974 and 1975. Mr. Holett was not aware of either the specific need of the plaintiff for cut-offs, or the exception granted him by the superintendent of Bridlewood Apartments.

The incident in question occurred on July 27, 1976, as a result of plaintiff's inquiring of Mr. Sloan, the assistant superintendent, about a pool regulation which requires that all guests must be signed in by a resident and accompanied at the pool. Plaintiff's father in law was visiting and plaintiff decided to accompany him to the pool and go swimming in his cut-offs. Mr. Sloan informed him that swimming in "cut-offs" was prohibited.

Defendant Holett, who was on a routine visit to Bridlewood on July 27, 1976, also informed plaintiff that wearing cut-offs in the pool was not permitted and threatened to call the police if plaintiff insisted. However, upon learning from Mr. Todaro that an exception had been made for plaintiff, Mr. Holett testified he ordered Mr. Todaro to inform plaintiff he could wear cut-offs in the swimming pool.

Plaintiff testified he was neither aware of, nor received any information regarding any rule or regulation prohibiting cut-offs in the swimming pool. However, defendant Holett testified that this rule was posted on a sign in the swimming pool area and that a letter was delivered to all residents in May 1976 reminding them that cut-offs were not permitted in the swimming pool.

Plaintiff claims that the conduct of Mr. Holett on July 27, 1976, in refusing to allow him to wear cut-offs in the pool constituted discrimination in violation of R.C. 4112.02(H)(1) and (H)(4), solely because of his physical handicap. Plaintiff alleges that he suffered severe emotional distress and humiliation as a result of the incident and that, because defendant Holett threatened to call the police, he has not utilized the pool since that occasion.

Plaintiff further testified that he did not sustain any monetary damage as a result of the incident, and that he was not otherwise prohibited from using the swimming pool.

Defendants' motion for a directed verdict at the close of plaintiffs' case-in-chief was sustained by the trial court.

Plaintiffs filed a timely notice of appeal and assign three errors for review:

> I. The trial court erred in denying the right of trial by jury to the plaintiff under Ohio's Fair Housing for the Handicapped law.
> II. The trial court erred in directing a verdict based upon the facts elicited at trial.
> III. The trial court erred in dismissing plaintiff's wife as a co-plaintiff as having no standing to sue under the statute.

Plaintiffs maintain in their second assignment of error that the trial court erred in sustaining a motion by defendants for a directed verdict.

First, it is clear from the judgment entry in the case at bar that the trial court utilized the standard provided by Civil Rule 50(A)(4) in ruling on defendants' motion for a directed verdict. However, in a non-jury case such as the case at bar, the motion by defendants should properly have been determined pursuant to provisions of Civil Rule 41(B)(2), involuntary dismissals, non-jury actions, which is governed by a different standard. *See Jacobs* v. *Bd. of County Commrs.* (1971), 27 Ohio App.2d 63, 272 N.E. 635, and *Altimari* v. *Campbell* (1978), 56 Ohio App.2d 253, 382 N.E.2d 1187.

Civil Rule 41(B)(2) provides, in pertinent part:

> Dismissal; non-jury action. After the plaintiff, in an action tried by the court without a jury, has completed the presentation of his evidence, the defendant, without waiving his right to offer evidence in the event the motion is not granted, may move for a dismissal on the ground that upon the facts and the law the plaintiff has shown no right to relief. The court as trier of the facts may then determine them and render judgment against the plaintiff or may decline to render any judgment until the close of all the evidence. . . .

The standard for applying Civil Rule 41(B)(2) has been described as follows:

> This rule was derived from the Federal Rule of the same number. It has been determined in the Federal courts that under this rule the court, in a non-jury case, on a motion for involuntary dismissal, is *not required to review the evidence in the light most favorable to the plaintiff but is required only to determine whether the plaintiff has made out his case be a preponderance of the evidence.* . . .
> It follows that the judge of the Probate Division of the Common Pleas Court, upon the motion for dismissal being made, was entitled to weigh the evidence. *His conclusions may not be set aside unless they are erroneous as a matter of law or against the manifest weight of the evidence.* (Emphasis added and citations omitted.) *Jacobs* v. *Bd. of County Commrs., supra,* 27 Ohio App.2d at 65, 272 N.E. 635.

After carefully reviewing the record in the case at bar, we are persuaded that the trial court correctly sustained the defendants' motion albeit applying an incorrect standard, as plaintiffs failed to satisfy their burden of proof.

The complaint is predicated upon alleged violations of R.C. 4112.02(H)(1) and (H)(4). R.C. 4112.02(H)(1) provides that it shall be an unlawful discriminatory practice:

> (H) For any person to:
> (1) *Refuse to sell, transfer, assign, rent, lease, sublease, finance, or otherwise deny*

*or withhold housing accommodations from any person because of the race, color religion, sex, ancestry, handicap, or national origin of any prospective owner, occupant, or user of such housing;*   (Emphasis added.)

The record in the case at bar is barren of any evidence tending to show that defendants refused to lease "or otherwise deny or withhold housing accommodations" from plaintiffs. The complaint alleges a denial of the use of a swimming pool, which is not a "housing accommodation" as defined in R.C. 4112.01(J). Therefore, Section 4112.02(H)(1) is not applicable under the facts of the case at bar.

R.C. 4112.02(H)(4) provides that it is an unlawful discriminatory practice for any person to:

> *Discriminate against any person* in the terms or conditions of selling, transferring, assigning, renting, leasing, or subleasing any housing or *in furnishing facilities, services, or privileges in connection with the ownership, occupancy, or use of any housing because of* the race, color, religion, sex, ancestry, handicap, or national origin of any present or prospective owner, occupant, or user of such housing;   (Emphasis added.)

When determining whether there has been a violation of R.C. 4112.02(H)(4), the test as applied to the facts in proceedings before this court is whether plaintiff was denied the use of the swimming pool because of his physical handicap.

At best, the record establishes only that plaintiff was denied the use of the swimming pool because "cut-offs" were not permitted to be worn *by any residents* in the swimming pool. Even if plaintiff were to contend that this regulation effectively precluded him from using the swimming pool because of his need to protect his stumps, we are not persuaded that it is sufficient to constitute a discriminatory act under the facts of this case. The evidence establishes the purpose of the rule prohibiting the wearing of "cut-offs" in the pool was to prevent mechanical failure of the pool's filtration system which could be caused by bits of clothing that would detach from cut-offs. The evidence indicates that this rule was applicable to all residents and not specifically directed at plaintiff.

Moreover, R.C. 4112.02(M) supports this conclusion:

> Nothing in division (H) of this section shall be construed to require any person selling or renting property to modify such property in any way or to exercise a higher degree of care for a person having a handicap, *nor shall it be construed to relieve any handicapped person of any obligation generally imposed on all persons regardless of handicap in a written lease, rental agreement, or contract of purchase or sale*, or to forbid distinctions based on the inability to fulfill the terms and conditions, including financial obligations, of the lease, agreement, or contract.   (Emphasis added.)

Therefore, having failed to produce any evidence of a discriminatory act under provisions of the statute by defendants, we find that the judgment of the trial court was not erroneous as a matter of law or against the weight of the evidence. Civ.R. 41(B)(2); *Jacobs, supra.*

The second error assigned is overruled.

Plaintiffs maintain in their first and third assignments of error, respectively, that the trial court erred in denying their right to a jury trial and in dismissing the claim of Mrs. McIntyre as a co-plaintiff in this matter.

As to the latter, whether Marie McIntyre is an "aggrieved person" within the meaning of R.C. 4112.051(A) and thereby has standing to sue under the Ohio Civil

Rights Act is a moot issue. This court having determined that a *prima facie* case of discrimination in violation of R.C. 4112.02(H)(1) and (H)(4) was not established at trial by the plaintiff, the dismissal of Marie McIntyre as a co-plaintiff would not justify as reversal of the judgment and therefore need not be addressed further.

Finally, plaintiffs maintain that the trial court erred when it denied their demand for a jury trial. They rely upon *Curtis* v. *Loether* (1974), 415 U.S. 189, 94 S.Ct. 1005, 39 L.Ed.2d 260, which held, at page 192:

> . . . [W]e think it is clear that the Seventh Amendment entitles either party to demand a jury trial in an action for damages in the federal courts under § 812.

However, the holding in that case was expressly limited to private civil actions brought in federal courts under Section 812 of the Civil Rights Act of 1968. The Supreme Court explained in footnote 6 of the opinion, at page 192:

> . . . [T]he Seventh Amendment issue in this case is in a very real sense the narrower ground of decision. Section 812(a) expressly authorizes actions to be brought "in appropriate State or local courts of general jurisdiction," as well as in the federal courts. *The Court has not held that the right to jury trial in civil cases is an element of due process applicable to state courts through the Fourteenth Amendment. Since we rest our decision on Seventh Amendment rather than statutory grounds, we express no view as to whether jury trials must be afforded in § 812 actions in the state courts.* (Emphasis added.)

Thus, plaintiffs' reliance on *Curtis* v. *Loether, supra,* is clearly misplaced. Accordingly, Ohio law must govern whether plaintiffs have a right to a jury trial under the Ohio Civil Rights Act.

It is well established law in Ohio that the Ohio Constitution preserves the right to a jury trial only in those civil actions where the right existed prior to the adoption of the Constitution. *Belding* v. *State ex rel. Heifner* (1929), 121 Ohio St. 393, 169 N.E. 301. The Franklin County Court of Appeals recognized that:

> Where a statute setting forth a new civil right is adopted, the General Assembly may grant a right to jury trial, but need not do so. No such right is contained in this statute [R.C. 4511.191] and no such right exists. *Bright* v. *Curry* (1973), 35 Ohio Misc. 51, 299 N.E.2d 470. *Raine* v. *Curry* (1975), 45 Ohio App.2d 155, 162, 341 N.E.2d 606.

In the case at bar, provisions of the Ohio Civil Rights Act (R.C. 4112.01 *et seq.*) do not provide for trial by jury in actions brought thereunder. Rather, R.C. 4112.051(E) provides:

> The court may grant such relief as it deems appropriate, including a permanent or temporary injunction, temporary restraining order, or other order, and may award to the plaintiff actual damages, together with the court costs.

Consequently, as the right to a jury trial is not contained in the statute, the trial court did not err in denying plaintiffs' demand for a jury trial. *See* Civil Rule 39(A). Plaintiffs' first and third assigned errors are overruled.

Accordingly, the judgment of the trial court is affirmed.

*Judgment affirmed.*

Krenzler, P. J., and Krupansky, J., concur.

NOTE

Would the result in *McIntyre* have been any different if the plaintiff could have relied upon Sec. 504?

## B.  OTHER HOUSING BARRIERS

p. 752—INSERT the following after Note 4:

### PEOPLE OF STATE OF NEW YORK v. 11 CORNWELL COMPANY

*United States District Court for the Eastern District of New York, 1981*
*508 F. Supp. 273*

Memorandum and Order

GEORGE C. PRATT, District Judge.

Defendant 11 Cornwell Company moves under FRCP 12(b)(1) & 12(b)(6) to dismiss the state's complaint on two grounds: (1) for failure to state a valid claim under 42 U.S.C. § 1985(3); and (2) because the state lacks standing to assert a claim under 42 U.S.C § 1985(3) even if the court determines that one exists. For reasons set forth below, this court concludes that the complaint does state a cause of action under 42 U.S.C § 1985(3) and that the state has standing to assert the claim.

Facts

Plaintiff, the State of New York, brings this action in its *parens patriae* capacity on behalf of its mentally disabled citizens and all other citizens generally. Defendants are residents of Rockville Centre, New York, who have banded together to form the 11 Cornwell Company, and defendant Samuels is the former owner of the property located at 11 Cornwell Street in Rockville Centre.

The complaint alleges that the New York State Office of Mental Retardation and Developmental Disabilities (OMRDD), acting pursuant to state law, negotiated a sale for defendant Samuels' house at 11 Cornwell Street. Upon learning that a sale to OMRDD was imminent, and that the house would be used as a community residence for the mentally retarded, defendants formed a partnership known as the 11 Cornwell Company and purchased the house from defendant Samuels. The complaint alleges that Samuels sold the property to 11 Cornwell Company for a lesser amount than OMRDD had offered to pay, and that the sale took place to prevent the home from being used as a residence for the mentally retarded. It further alleges that 11 Cornwell Company seeks to resell the property, but has refused to negotiate with OMRDD for the sale. Complaint ¶ 11–15.

The state asserts that these allegations, if proved, show that defendants conspired (1) to deny New York State's mentally disabled citizens equal protection of the laws; and (2) to prevent and hinder the state authorities from providing its mentally disabled citizens with equal protection of the laws, both in violation of 42 U.S.C. § 1985(3). Complaint ¶ 16. In addition, the state alleges that defendants' actions violate New York State Executive Law § 296(5)(a), which guarantees mentally disabled persons equal access to housing accommodations in New York State. Complaint ¶ 17, 19. The validity of this pendent state law claim is not now before the court.

### Requisites for a Cause of Action Under § 1985(3)

As outlined above, the state alleges two distinct causes of action under § 1985(3). Since the underlying problem on this motion is whether there is federal jurisdiction and the court concludes that the complaint does state a cause of action under the "preventing or hindering" clause of § 1985, thereby providing federal jurisdiction under 28 U.S.C. § 1343, the court need not at this time address the state's first contention, that the complaint also sets forth a cause of action that defendants conspired to deprive mentally deprived persons of equal protection of the laws.

The relevant portion of § 1985(3) provides that

> If two or more persons in any State or Territory conspire . . . for the purpose of preventing or hindering the constituted authorities of any State or Territory from giving or securing to all persons within such State or Territory the equal protection of the laws . . . the party so injured or deprived may have an action for the recovery of damages, occasioned by such injury or deprivation, against any one or more of the conspirators.

Here the complaint alleges that defendants conspired to prevent the state from securing equal protection for its mentally retarded citizens. The state contends that defendants prevented the OMRDD from purchasing the Samuels' home in order to keep mentally retarded persons from living in the house, and that defendants are intentionally discriminating against a class of persons by seeking to sell the house to someone other than the OMRDD.

Defendants argue that in order to invoke the preventing or hindering clause the state must show that defendants' actions prevented them from performing

> a constitutional duty under the Equal Protection Clause of the Fourteenth Amendment to provide its mentally retarded citizens with community residential facilities. . . . [T]he state can only have such a *duty* if the persons upon whose behalf it is asserted, the potential residents of 11 Cornwell Street, have a constitutional *right* under the Equal Protection Clause to a community residential facility. Defendants' reply memorandum at 6.

In the Developmentally Disabled Assistance and Bill of Rights Act, 42 U.S.C. § 6001 *et seq.*, Congress includes a provision entitled "Congressional Findings Respecting Rights of Developmentally Disabled," which provides in pertinent part:

> (1) Persons with developmental disabilities have a *right* to appropriate treatment, services, and habilitation for such disabilities.
> (2) The treatment, services, and habilitation for a person with developmental disabilities should be designed to maximize the developmental potential of the person and should be provided in the setting that is least restrictive of the person's personal liberty. 42 U.S.C. § 6010 (emphasis added).

The state argues that the DDA thus imposes "an affirmative obligation to provide for the equal protection rights of the developmentally disabled." Plaintiffs' memorandum at 14. Defendant disputes the state's contention that the DDA is properly viewed as a codification of the equal protection rights of the mentally retarded.

The legislative history of the DDA reflects Congress' concern with the deinstitutionalization, where feasible, of previously confined persons and the necessity of focusing on alternatives to institutionalization:

> Since the Committee is well aware that current theory with regard to the treatment and support of the developmentally disabled emphasizes that this treatment should be conducted in the individual's community without unnecessarily institutionalizing him, the Committee has chosen to include a specific requirement that state programs plan for as much deinstitutionalization as is feasible, and earmark moneys for this purpose. . . . It is anticipated that these requirements will prompt some movement of patients from State institutions back into their communities.   H.R.Rep.No.94–58, 94th Cong., 1st Sess. 10, *Reprinted in [1975] U.S. Code Cong. & Ad.News* 919, 928.

In addition to the DDA and other statutes intended to alleviate the plight of mentally disabled citizens, courts have become increasingly sensitive to problems arising from the unnecessary institutionalization of individuals suffering from only slight or nonexistent mental disorders. *E.g., Addington* v. *Texas,* 441 U.S. 418, 99 S.Ct. 1804, 60 L.Ed.2d 323 (1979); *O'Connor* v. *Donaldson,* 422 U.S. 563, 95 S.Ct. 2486, 45 L.Ed.2d 396 (1975); *Halderman* v. *Pennhurst State School & Hospital,* 612 F.2d 84 (CA3 1979) (en banc), *cert. granted,* 448 U.S. 905, 100 S.Ct. 3046, 65 L.Ed.2d 1135 (1980). *See also Vitek* v. *Jones,* 445 U.S. 480, 100 S.Ct. 1254, 63 L.Ed.2d 552 (1980).

The Supreme Court has taken an active role in ensuring that absent a constitutionally permissible justification, so-called mentally ill persons are not involuntarily confined in institutions. In *O'Connor* v. *Donaldson, supra,* the Court emphasized that

> A finding of "mental illness" alone cannot justify a State's locking a person up against his will and keeping him indefinitely in simple custodial confinement. . . . [T]here is . . . no constitutional basis for confining such persons involuntarily if they are dangerous to no one and can live safely in freedom.   422 U.S. at 575, 95 S.Ct. at 2493.

If the state cannot constitutionally confine a person simply because he or she may be mentally disabled, alternatives to institutionalization must be found. Seeking such alternatives is obviously an important state function: "That the State has a proper interest in providing care and assistance to the unfortunate goes without saying." *O'Connor* v. *Donaldson,* 422 U.S. at 575, 95 S.Ct. at 2493.

In this case the complaint alleges that the OMRDD sought to purchase the 11 Cornwell property in order "to acquire and manage residential property so that mentally disabled New York citizens may attain the benefits of normal residential surroundings." Complaint ¶ 16. While defendants argue that the state is not under a constitutional duty to seek community housing for its mentally retarded citizens, this argument flies in the face of the requirement imposed by *O'Connor* and subsequent cases that the state provide alternatives to institutionalization. Community dissatisfaction and displeasure at the prospect of living in the same neighborhood with such persons does not excuse the state from securing for these individuals the freedom from the restrictions imposed by institutional life: "Mere public intolerance or animosity cannot justify the deprivation of a person's physical liberty." 422 U.S. at 575, 95 S.Ct. at 2493.

This court concludes that the state has set forth a cause of action under the preventing or hindering clause of § 1985(3). The complaint alleges a conspiracy to prevent the OMRDD from purchasing the property at 11 Cornwell Street for the purpose of keeping an "undesirable" class of persons from living there. The OMRDD's actions in attempting to buy the home, in light of the relevant case law and statutes, can fairly be characterized as an attempt to give or secure to mentally retarded citizens of New York State equal protection of the laws within the meaning of § 1985(3), by providing them with living conditions that restrict their freedom as little as necessary. If defendants have prevented or hindered the state from buying the home for the reasons alleged by plaintiff, they have therefore violated § 1985(3) and plaintiff is entitled to relief appropriate to the circumstances, including compensatory and punitive damages, for the harm suffered.

Since the court has jurisdiction over the state's § 1985 claim, the court will exercise pendent jurisdiction over plaintiff's pendent claim under New York Executive Law § 296(5)(a). Both causes of action arise out of a common nucleus of operative facts, and it is the court's present intention to consolidate the claims for pretrial and trial purposes.

### The State's Standing to Assert The § 1985 Claim

Defendant also claims that the state does not have standing to assert the § 1985 claim alleged in the complaint. The state answers this argument by asserting it has jurisdiction in both its proprietary and *parens patriae* capacities. Without discussing all of the arguments raised by both sides, the court agrees with the state's view that "representation of mentally disabled persons is the paradigm case for *parens patriae* standing." Plaintiffs' memorandum at 30. *See, e.g., Hawaii* v. *Standard Oil Co.,* 405 U.S. 251, 257, 92 S.Ct. 885, 888, 31 L.Ed.2d 184 (1972) (discussing modern expansion of *parens patriae* concept from common law origin of King "as guardian of persons under legal disabilities to act for themselves"). *See generally O'Connor* v. *Donaldson,* 442 U.S. 563, 95 S.Ct. 2486, 45 L.Ed.2d 396 (1975). The Supreme Court recently reaffirmed that the state's *parens patriae* interest in this area: "The state has a legitimate interest under its *parens patriae* powers in providing care to its citizens who are unable because of emotional disorders to care for themselves." *Addington* v. *Texas,* 441 U.S. 418, 426, 99 S.Ct. 1804, 1809, 60 L.Ed.2d 323 (1979). The court concludes, therefore, that the state has standing to bring this suit on behalf of its mentally retarded citizens.

### Conclusion

Defendants' motion to dismiss the complaint for lack of jurisdiction and for lack of standing to sue is denied. Defendants are directed to file an answer to the complaint within 20 days of receipt of this court's memorandum and order.

The parties are also directed to appear before the court on March 19, 1981 at 9:00 a.m. for a status conference to discuss the future course of this litigation.

So ordered.

NOTE

1. The *Cornwell* decision has two very significant aspects. First, it represents a judicial holding that the Developmentally Disabled Assistance and Bill of Rights Act had as one of its purposes the securing of equal protection of the laws to handicapped persons. Second, the *Cornwell* decision represents one of the uncommon instances in which a state has utilized its *parens patriae* capacity to promote the deinstitutionalization of handicapped persons, through, in *Cornwell*, using *parens patriae* to assert standing to enforce Sec. 1985 and, in turn, the D.D. Act as it has come to be known.

### MAJORS v. HOUSING AUTHORITY OF COUNTY OF DEKALB, GEORGIA
*United States Court of Appeals for the Fifth Circuit, 1981*
*652 F.2d 454*

Before HILL, FAY and ANDERSON, Circuit Judges.

R. LANIER ANDERSON, III, Circuit Judge:

Laura Majors appeals from the judgment of the district court granting summary judgment in favor of the appellee Housing Authority and denying her motion for preliminary injunctive relief. Ms. Majors alleges that she is a handicapped person within the meaning of the Rehabilitation Act of 1973 by virtue of a mental disability which requires the companionship of her pet dog. She further alleges that the Housing Authority has unlawfully discriminated against her by enforcing its ban against pets in its apartments. We find material issues of fact and therefore reverse and remand.

*Facts and Posture of the Case on Appeal*

Ms. Majors, at the time this suit was filed, was a forty-one year old unmarried woman. She has a history of psychological problems. Letters from a physician and several social workers submitted in support of her motion for a preliminary injunction indicate that she has a psychological and emotional dependence upon her pet dog, Sparky, a small poodle. In March, 1978, Ms. Majors applied for housing through the Housing Authority of the County of DeKalb, Georgia. Since she met the financial qualifications, she was admitted to housing; however, she was warned that the Housing Authority did not allow pets within its housing units. Furthermore, the lease included a prohibition against keeping animals in the apartment. Nevertheless, Ms. Majors kept Sparky in her apartment. After several warnings, she was served with a notice of termination.

She then filed a suit for injunctive and declaratory relief alleging that the Housing Authority had violated or threatened to violate § 504 of the Rehabilitation Act of 1973, 29 U.S.C.A. § 794 (Supp.1981) by discriminating against her on account of her mental disability. The Housing Authority's motion for a summary judgment and appellant's motion for preliminary injunctive relief were submitted to the district court upon the following stipulation.

> At the present time both parties stipulate that the case is amenable to a final ruling on the merits and a permanent injunction with one limitation. The primary unresolved factual issue is the question of the Plaintiff's alleged mental disability. Therefore, Defendants

will stipulate for present purposes, the mental disability of Plaintiff and the fact that the mental disability requires that she be permitted to keep the dog in her apartment. Furthermore, the parties stipulate (as the parties' New Joint Case Statement shows) that the only reason behind the threatened eviction is the presence of Plaintiff's dog in her apartment, and that the no pet provisions are uniform throughout all developments owned and operated by Defendant Housing Authority. Furthermore, the parties stipulate (as the New Joint Case Statement shows) that Defendant Housing Authority is a recipient of federal financial assistance and that Plaintiff has previously sent a letter of complaint to the United States Department of Housing and Urban Development complaining of Defendant's alleged discrimination against her. (The letter is attached to Plaintiff's brief of October 29, 1979). The parties stipulate that Plaintiff's lease with Defendant Housing Authority contains a no pet provision and that all of Defendant Housing Authority's leases contain no pet provisions.

Record on Appeal, pp. 120–121. The district court held that Ms. Majors was not an "otherwise qualified handicapped individual" within the meaning of the Rehabilitation Act because she was unable to comply with the lease provision banning animals from the apartment. In so doing, the district court held that the Housing Authority could take into account Ms. Majors alleged handicap in determining whether she was qualified for the program. The district court also held that the no pet rule was "eminently rational, particularly in high density, public housing."

Discussion

Section 504 of the Rehabilitation Act of 1973, 29 U.S.C.A. § 794 (Supp.1981), provides in part:

> No otherwise qualified handicapped individual in the United States, as defined in section 706(7) of this Title, shall, solely by reason of his handicap, be excluded from the participation in, be denied the benefits of, or be subjected to discrimination under any program or activity receiving Federal Financial Assistance or under any program or activity conducted by any Executive Agency or by the United States Postal Service.

The Housing Authority concedes that it is a recipient of federal financial assistance and that Ms. Majors meets the financial qualifications for housing. The central controversy is whether she is an "otherwise qualified handicapped individual" inasmuch as she could not satisfy the no pet rule. For purposes of the summary judgment motion, the Housing Authority has stipulated that Ms. Majors suffers from a mental disability, and under the Act and regulations, a mental disability or disorder may be a handicap. See 29 U.S.C.A. § 706(7) (Supp.1981); 45 C.F.R. § 85.31(b)(1)(ii) (1980). The real question is whether Ms. Majors was an *otherwise qualified* handicapped person. The only Supreme Court decision to address the meaning of "otherwise qualified" is *Southeastern Community College* v. *Davis,* 442 U.S. 397, 99 S.Ct. 2361, 60 L.Ed.2d 980 (1979), in which a deaf person applied for admission to the college's nursing program and was rejected. The district court held that the plaintiff was not an otherwise qualified handicapped individual within the meaning of § 504 because even if accommodations were made in the curriculum for her deafness, her deafness would prevent "her from safely performing in both her training program and her proposed profession." *Davis* v. *Southeastern Community College,* 424 F.Supp. 1341, 1345 (E.D.N.C. 1976). The Fourth Circuit Court of Appeals reversed, 574 F.2d 1158 (4th

Cir. 1978), but the Supreme Court reversed the court of appeals. The Supreme Court stated:

> Section 504 by its terms does not compel educational institutions to disregard the disabilities of handicapped individuals or to make substantial modifications in their programs to allow disabled persons to participate. Instead, it requires only that an "otherwise qualified handicapped individual" not be excluded from participation in a federally funded program "solely by reason of his handicap," indicating only that mere possession of a handicap is not a permissible ground for assuming an inability to function in a particular context.
>
> The court below, however, believed that the "otherwise qualified" persons protected by § 504 include those who would be able to meet the requirements of a particular program in every respect except as to limitations imposed by their handicap. *See* 574 F.2d, at 1160. Taken literally, this holding would prevent an institution from taking into account any limitation resulting from the handicap, however disabling. It assumes, in effect, that a person need not meet legitimate physical requirements in order to be "otherwise qualified." We think the understanding of the District Court is closer to the plain meaning of statutory language. An otherwise qualified person is one who is able to meet all of program's requirements in spite of his handicap.

442 U.S. 405–6, 99 S.Ct. 2366–67 (footnote omitted). Having decided this, the Court went on to determine whether the physical qualifications demanded by the college were necessary. In so doing, the Court concluded that neither the language, purpose, nor history of § 504 reveals an intent to impose an affirmative action obligation on all recipients of federal funds. The Court cautioned that it did not:

> [S]uggest that the line between lawful refusal to extend affirmative action and illegal discrimination against handicapped persons always will be clear. It is possible to envision situations where an insistence on continuing past requirements and practices might arbitrarily deprive genuinely qualified handicapped persons of the opportunity to participate in a covered program. . . . Thus, situations may arise where a refusal to modify an existing program might become unreasonable and discriminatory. Identification of those instances where a refusal to accommodate the needs of a disabled person amounts to discrimination against the handicapped continues to be an important responsibility of HEW.

*Id.* at 412–13, 99 S.Ct. at 2370. The Court held that in this case the college's unwillingness to make major adjustments in its program did not constitute discrimination.

Since the Supreme Court's decision in *Southeastern Community College*, we decided *Tatro* v. *State of Texas*, 625 F.2d 557 (5th Cir. 1980). In *Tatro*, we held that the Rehabilitation Act required the school system to provide a handicapped student with necessary medical services in order that she could participate in a preschool program. The child, Amber Tatro, suffered from a birth defect commonly known as spina bifida. This condition required catheterization of her bladder every three to four hours in order for her to function without the danger of developing kidney infection. The process of cleaning the bladder, known as Clean Intermittent Catheterization (CIC), was a relatively simple procedure which could be performed in five minutes by a person with only thirty minutes training. The local school district had refused to provide this service to the child. The parents filed suit alleging the violation of the Education for All Handicapped Children Act of 1975 (EAHCA), 20 U.S.C.A.

§ 1414(a)(5) (1978) and § 504 of the Rehabilitation Act of 1973. With respect to the claim under § 504, we concluded that the child had been excluded from the school district's program by their refusal to provide the CIC. We distinguished *Tatro* from *Southeastern Community College* on the ground that in the latter case the handicapped person could never realize the principal benefits of the program even with accommodations for her handicap; however, we found that in Amber Tatro's case, she could realize the principal benefits of the pre-school program with the provision of the CIC. Furthermore, we held that the CIC process did not impose an undue financial or administrative burden on the recipient.

Therefore, in *Tatro*, we held that the recipient agency was required to provide some services and accommodations for a handicapped person who could not have participated in the covered program without some accommodation. The holding in *Southeastern Community College*, which the court below and the Housing Authority rely upon—that one must consider the necessary limitations imposed by the handicap itself in determining whether an individual is "otherwise qualified"—must be considered in the context of whether reasonable accommodations will permit the handicapped person to realize the principal benefits of the program. Indeed, the regulations recognize the necessity for reasonable accommodation:

> A recipient shall make reasonable accommodation to the known physical or mental limitations of an otherwise qualified handicapped applicant or employee unless the recipient can demonstrate that the accommodation would impose an undue hardship on the operation of its program.

45 C.F.R. § 85.53 (1980). Furthermore, our decision in *Tatro* recognized that § 504 requires the recipient to provide some services to handicapped persons. It does not, however, require services that impose an undue financial or administrative burden.

With these principles in mind, we turn to the stipulated facts in this case. Defendants have stipulated for purposes of summary judgment that Ms. Majors suffered from a mental disability which requires the companionship of her dog. By enforcing the no pet rule, the Housing Authority has effectively deprived Ms. Majors of the benefit of the housing program. Unlike the circumstances in *Southeastern Community College*, it is possible for Ms. Majors to enjoy the full benefit of the covered program provided that some accommodation is made for her alleged disability. We note further that the qualification in the instant case, *i.e.*, the no pet rule, is different from the qualifications in the *Southeastern Community College* case which were inherent in the program and in the nursing profession. In the summary judgment posture of this case, we must recognize as reasonable the inference that the Housing Authority could readily accommodate Ms. Majors. Even if the "no pet" rule is itself imminently reasonable, nothing in the record rebuts the reasonable inference that the Authority could easily make a limited exception for that narrow group of persons who are handicapped and whose handicap requires (as has been stipulated) the companionship of a dog. Such accommodation falls well within the kind of reasonable accommodation required by the regulation and *Tatro*. Therefore, having determined that on the basis of the stipulated facts there are questions of fact as to whether Ms. Majors is an otherwise qualified handicapped individual, we must remand for an evidentiary hearing.

In summary, having determined that reasonable inferences from the stipulated facts create genuine issues of fact, the case is remanded for a trial on the questions of whether Ms. Majors suffers from a handicap, whether the handicap requires the companionship of the dog and what, if any, reasonable accommodations can be made. It goes without saying that we do not express any opinion on the merits of any of these questions involved. We emphasize that we are presented with a stipulated statement of facts in which the appellee conceded, albeit for the limited purpose of summary judgment, the existence of a mental disorder requiring the companionship of the dog. Furthermore, we have interpreted these stipulated facts with the benefit of a decision of the court rendered after the district court's opinion in this case.

Accordingly, the judgment of the district court is

REVERSED AND REMANDED.

NOTES

1.   The *Majors* court's interpretation of Sec. 504 makes clear that a rational relationship analysis is expressly rejected as a tool in determining whether a certain policy is unlawful discrimination under the statute. Instead the *Majors* court utilizes an analysis that focuses on the individual person's disability and whether reasonable accommodation can be made for the person in light of his or her handicap.

2.   The *Majors* decision demonstrates the far-reaching potential Sec. 504 has for making different aspects of life (in *Majors*, federally subsidized housing) accessible to handicapped persons.

# 8

# EQUAL ACCESS TO MEDICAL SERVICES

Robert L. Burgdorf Jr.

## SUMMARY OF DOCTRINAL DEVELOPMENTS

THERE HAVE BEEN THREE MAJOR AREAS of judicial development in regard to medical services: life-saving medical treatment cases, standards of proof for establishment of discrimination in availability of medical services, and requirements regarding the administration of drugs.

## B. DENIAL TO HANDICAPPED PERSONS OF MEDICAL TREATMENT AVAILABLE TO OTHERS

p. 756—INSERT at the end of Section B:

### IN RE APPLICATION OF CICERO

*Supreme Court of New York, 1979*
*101 Misc.2d 699, 421 N.Y.S.2d 965*

MARTIN B. STECHER, Justice:

By order to show cause dated August 28, 1979, the petitioner, chief executive officer of Misericordia Hospital, petitioned to be appointed guardian of the infant girl born to Lena Vataj on August 20, 1979, for "the sole purpose of consenting to repair of Meningomyelocele," a spinal disorder with which the infant was born.

According to the Nelson Textbook of Pediatrics [10th Ed., W. B. Saunders Company, Philadelphia 1975, pp. 1412 et seq.] spina bifida with meningomyelocele "is a midline defect of skin, vertebral arches and neural tube, usually in the lumbosacral region. . . . (It) is evident at birth as a skin defect over the back, bordered laterally by bony prominences of the unfused neural arches of the vertebrae. The defection is usually covered by a transparent membrane which may have neural tissue attached to its inner surface." Cerebrospinal fluid may accumulate under the membrane causing it to bulge. This is the condition with which the Vataj infant was born.

Failure to repair the opening presents a danger of perforation, highly probable infection, such as spinal meningitis, and death. The likelihood of survival beyond the age of six months is poor, absent treatment. Treatment is recommended within 48 hours of birth. The membrane covering this child's lesion shows signs of progressive erosion making immediate surgery necessary.

The parents have refused treatment and insist on taking the child home. Their attitude, as expressed by the child's father, is "let God decide" if the child is to live or die.* Their rejection of treatment does not appear to stem from the kind of religious conviction with which judges are often faced [cf. *Application of President and Directors of Georgetown College, Inc.*, 118 U.S.App.D.C. 80, 331 F.2d 1000, rehearing den., 118 U.S.App.D.C. 90, 331 F.2d 1010, cert. den. 377 U.S. 978, 84 S.Ct. 1883, 12 L.Ed.2d 746].

Initially, the father consented to surgery but appears to have withdrawn that consent only when the potential enormity of this disorder was fully explained to him by the physicians.

The degree of neural disfunction in a spina bifida case is related to the location of the lesion in the spine. The higher it occurs, the greater the number of organs removed from voluntary control. A cervical or thoracic lesion, for instance, presents a high probability of an invalid life, paralyzed and impaired in most functions. The lower the lesion, the better the opportunity for a useful life providing many of its satisfactions. The Vataj baby has a relatively low lesion. Treated, her extremity deficits will, hopefully, be only at the leg level below the ankles. Additionally, she will lack sphincter control of the bladder and anus; but modern medicine and surgery can ameliorate these conditions too. She should be able to walk with short leg braces and hopefully have a "normal" intellectual development.

Children suffering from this disorder usually run a high risk of hydrocephalus, a disorder in which fluid fails to drain from the cranial areas. Untreated, hydrocephalus results in grossly distorted skull growth and mental retardation. Where a child shows evidence of hydrocephalus at birth, prognosis is poor. Later developing hydrocephalus is treatable by a "shunt" operation, providing a drain for the excess fluid; and, if successfully treated, the distortion may be avoided and the chances of retardation substantially reduced.

The Vataj child shows no present sign of hydrocephalus.

This is not a case where the court is asked to preserve an existence which cannot be a life. What is asked is that a child born with handicaps to be given a reasonable opportunity to live, to grow and hopefully to surmount those handicaps. If the power to make that choice is vested in the court, there can be no doubt as to what the choice must be.

The Supreme Court, under its general equity jurisdiction, may act as *parens patriae* to protect an infant unable to protect her own interests [*Matter of Weberlist*, 79 Misc.2d 753, 755–756, 360 N.Y.S.2d 783, 786]. Additionally, there is statutory authority. The statutory authority for this proceeding is to be found in Article 10 of the Family Court Act which defines a neglected child [F.C.A. Sec. 1012(f)(i)(A)] as one,

---

*There has been some expression of fear on the parents' part that this disorder is so rare that the petitioner and associated physicians regard the child as an object of experimentation. Unfortunately, spina bifida is not that rare. It has been estimated that its incidence varies between 0.5 and 4 per thousand and that in this area the incidence is about 3 per thousand. It would thus appear that of 106,000 births recorded in this city in 1978, approximately 300 cases of this disorder could have been expected to appear in New York City alone.

among others, whose "physical . . . condition . . . is in imminent danger of becoming impaired as a result of the failure of his parent . . . to exercise a minimum degree of care . . . in supplying the child with adequate . . . surgical care, though financially able to do so or offered financial or other reasonable means to do so."**

From the evidence adduced—and there was no contrary or conflicting evidence—and after hearings held on August 30, and September 4, 1979, I find that this infant's physical condition is in imminent danger of becoming impaired unless the recommended surgery is performed; that irrespective of the parents' financial means, thus far undisclosed, the opportunity to have the surgery performed by a competent surgeon is available and that the parents of the child, without justification, refuse to consent to that surgery.

The argument is made that by granting the petition the parental right to choose the treatment, upbringing and welfare of the child is infringed upon by the court. [Cf. *United States* v. *Orito*, 413 U.S. 139 at 142, 93 S.Ct. 2674, 37 L.Ed.2d 513; *Roe* v. *Wade*, 410 U.S. 113 at 152–153, 93 S.Ct. 705, 35 L.Ed.2d 147; *Pierce* v. *Society of Sisters*, 268 U.S. 510 at 534–535, 45 S.Ct. 571, 69 L.Ed. 1070; *Meyer* v. *Nebraska*, 262 U.S. 390 at 399, 43 S.Ct. 625, 67 L.Ed. 1042].

Parental rights, however, are not absolute. Children are not property whose disposition is left to parental discretion without hindrance [*Matter of Parham* v. *J. R.*, 422 U.S. 584, 99 S.Ct. 2493, 61 L.Ed.2d 101; *Matter of Bennett* v. *Jeffreys*, 40 N.Y.2d 543, 387 N.Y.S.2d 821, 356 N.E.2d 277]. Where the child's welfare demands judicial intervention, this court is empowered to intervene [*Matter of Sampson*, supra]. Certainly, every physician who prefers a course of treatment rejected by a parent is not privileged to have the court decide upon the treatment under its *parens patriae* powers [cf. *Matter of Seiferth*, 309 N.Y. 80, 127 N.E.2d 820; *Matter of Hofbauer*, 65 A.D.2d 108, 411 N.Y.S.2d 416; *In re Phillip B.*, 92 Cal.App.3d 796, 156 Cal. Rptr. 48].

But where, as here, a child has a reasonable chance to live a useful, fulfilled life, the court will not permit parental inaction to deny that chance.

There is a hint in this proceeding of a philosophy that newborn, "hopeless" lives should be permitted to expire without an effort to save those lives. Fortunately, the medical evidence here is such that we do not confront a "hopeless" life. As Justice Asch has pointed out [*Matter of Weberlist*, 79 Misc.2d 753, 757, 360 N.Y.S.2d 783, 787], "(t)here is a strident cry in America to terminate the lives of *other* people— deemed physically or mentally defective." (Emphasis in original.) This court was not constituted to heed that cry. Rather, to paraphrase Justice Asch, *supra*, it is our function to secure to each his opportunity for "[l]ife, liberty and the pursuit of happiness."

The petition is granted to the extent of designating Simon Rosenzweig, Esq., of 122 East 42nd Street, New York City, guardian of "Baby Girl" Vataj for the purpose of consenting to the surgery for the repair of the meningomyelocele, the shunt operation for treatment of hydrocephalus, the selection of a hospital in which such surgery

---

**Although "exclusive original jurisdiction . . . under this article" is vested in the Family Court [F.C.A. Sec. 1013] it is clear that the Family Court shares that jurisdiction with the Supreme Court [F.C.A. Sec. 114; N.Y.Constitution,Art. VI, Sec. 7; *see Matter of Sampson*, 37 A.D.2d 668, 323 N.Y.S.2d 253, aff'd 29 N.Y.2d 900, 328 N.Y.S.2d 686, 278 N.E.2d 918].

shall be performed and the selection of such physician or physicians as shall be required to render such treatment to the child.

This constitutes the decision and judgment of the court. The execution of the judgment is stayed until 11 a.m. September 7, 1979.

NOTE

Contrast the medical situation of the infant in the *Cicero* case with that in *Houle*. What different considerations are involved in the two cases?

### IN RE GUARDIANSHIP OF BECKER

*Superior Court of the State of California, Santa Clara County, 1981*
*No. 101981, August 7, 1981*

FERNANDEZ, Superior Court Judge.

Phillip Becker is a Down's syndrome afflicted child who has by parental decision been denied a life prolonging operation and who has parentally been consigned from birth to board and care facilities for his basic needs and for child rearing. Our unique case presents a clear conflict between two legal doctrines. On the one hand the historically venerated "parental rights" doctrine, and on the other hand the more recently emerging doctrine of "best interests of the child." This clash has been dramatically portrayed in the classic dialectic method of arriving at the truth, that is by the statement of a position and then a statement of its opposition. As a consequence of this struggle for the truth between two contending sets of parents numerous sub-issues to the two prime doctrines arise. These issues all need to be addressed and will be in the course of this opinion and in the appendices to it. In order to resolve our unique case, we must first examine the historical and legal underpinnings of the two doctrines.

Custody law and the parental rights doctrine stem from the feudal concept of the child as a chattel who represented important monetary interests. Historically therefore, only the parents' interests were considered in custody matters. Although the law originally gave full status to the concept of the child as a chattel, evolving social standards have arrived at a better reason for parental preference in child custody matters. It is now said that custody by a biological parent will best achieve the goal of protecting the child's interests. Thus the parental rights doctrine is only defensible today by the intuitive psychological generalization that a "blood tie" between parent and child will eventually result in more and better love and hence in a more adequate psychological development of the child.

California has been a stronghold of parental rights. A California court as recently as 1959 stated "the future welfare and best interests of the child are not issues" in proceedings to free a child from parental control."[6] The focus in California in times past has been on parental unfitness. However, a shift in emphasis caused by increased knowledge of child needs and child rearing afforded to the law by the behavioral sciences has caused a change in focus away from the predominant parental preference doctrine and the issue of parental unfitness. The courts of California presently concentrate their attention on the concept of "best interests of the child."

---

[6]*In re Bisenius* (1959) 173 C.A.2d 518, 521–22. In deference to the *Bisenius* court, the question there was abandonment of the child by the mother.

This shift has been occasioned by a growing concern for the welfare of the child and the disappearance of the old belief that a child is property. Thus, the value choice in any modern day judicial proceeding regarding custody should be the maximizing of the "best interests of the child."

California law has embraced the best interests concept in its Civil Code.[10] Eschewed the child as chattel concept by its case law.[11] Determined that, in child custody matters, attention should be directed not at parental unfitness but rather on detriment to the child.[12] This more modern approach is in keeping with a realistic appraisal of the harm that can be caused to children by awarding custody to biological parents who may be perfect strangers to the child and with whom the child has no psychological ties.

It is clear therefore, that under present California law there is a change from the primacy of parental rights in favor of focusing in on the child's well being and determining the child's best interest. Thus as one commentator has pointed out, "Children's needs are best met by helping parents achieve their interests. But in a conflict the legal system should protect the child's interest, for the child is helpless and parents should suffer the consequences of their inadequacy, not the child."[15]

However, in applying the best interest of the child formula, the California Supreme Court has stated:

> Section 4600 expressly recognizes that custody should be awarded to parents in preference to non-parents. As between parents, it permits the court to award custody "according to the best interests of the child," but in a dispute between a parent and a non-parent, the section imposes the additional stipulation that an award to the non-parent requires a finding that "an award of custody to a parent would be detrimental to the child. . . ."[16]

Additionally, the California high court, in speaking of the detrimental finding necessary to sever the parental relationship, has postulated the issue, "What is the least detrimental alternative to the child?"[17] One final word on this subject. Civil Code Section 4600 by its terms further requires a showing to the court that "the award of custody to non-parent is required to serve the best interests of the child."

Who speaks for the child? In our case we have two contending sets of parents who claim the right to speak. They are the biological or de jure parents, the Beckers, and the claimed psychological or de facto parents, the Heaths. We have discussed biological parent rights. What are the legally recognized rights of psychological parents? In the analysis of the rights of the Heaths, as psychological parents, this court must come to some factual conclusions.

Both sides agree that the seminal case regarding psychological parenting rights

---

[10]Civil Code § 4600.

[11]*In re B.G.*, 11 Cal. 3d 679; 114 Ca. Rptr. 444; 523 P.2d 244 (1974).

[12]See *Guardianship of Marino*, 30 C.A.3d 952, 953–959; *In re D.L.C.*, 54 C.A.3d 840; 126 Cal. Rptr. 863.

[15]*Wald*, State Intervention on Behalf of Neglected Children: Standards for Removal of Children From Their Homes, Monitoring the Standards of Children in Foster Care and Terminating Parental Rts., 28 Stan. L. Rev. 625, 672 (hereinafter *Wald*).

[16]*In re B.G.*, *supra*, at 698–699.

[17]See *In re Carmalita B.*, 21 Cal.3d 482, 489; *In re Angelia P.*, [28 Cal.3d 908, 916].

is found in the California Supreme Court decision of, *In re B.G.*[20] The HighCourt relied in its formulation on the concept of authors Goldstein, Freud, and Solnit who defined a psychological parent as a "parent . . . who, on a continuing, day to day basis, through interaction, companionship, interplay, and mutuality, fulfills the child's psychological needs for a parent, as well as the child's physical needs . . . It is the person to whom the child turns to for affection and care."[21] California courts have found psychological parents to be foster parents, aunts, and grandparents. This court knows of no case, whether in California or elsewhere, which has determined that overnight home visiting and weekly visiting of a child in a board and care facility by adults such as the Heaths have done with Phillip constitutes psychological parenting. A review of the decided cases indicates that psychological parenting has only been accorded judicial standing if the claimed psychological parents have had ongoing and continuous care of the child for a considerable period of time.[25]

However, the facts in our case are unique. Phillip Becker is a Down's child who from the age of birth has been in the care of caretakers. He has never received nurturing by his biological parents; he has never received that constancy of affection and love from his biological parents so necessary toward the maturation of a child into happy, healthy adulthood; he has never had the opportunity to develop that basic trust and confidence in his biological parents so essential to good parent-child relationships. Each of these elements are the sine qua non of parenting, and each of these elements are [*sic*] found by this court to be lacking in the relationship between Phillip and Mr. and Mrs. Becker. It is quite evident from the facts at trial that this mentally retarded and emotionally deprived child was ripe for affection and love from any appropriate stranger who bestowed it upon him.

The expert and lay evidence at trial makes clear that a psychological parenting relationship has developed between Phillip and the Heaths. We test the evidence of this by asking and answering the following three questions: 1) Is there a continuity of the relationship between child and adult in terms of proximity and duration? 2) Is there love of the adult for the child? 3) Is there affection and trust of the child toward the adult?

The continuity of the relationship is shown by the visiting and association with Phillip by the Heaths since he was five years old. Their love for him is unquestioned,

---

[20]*In re B.G., supra.*

[21]See *Beyond the Best Interests of the Child*, Joseph Goldstein, Anna Freud, Albert J. Solnit, at 98 (1973) (cited hereafter as *Beyond* or by author). Authors Goldstein, Freud and Solnit were not the first to discuss "psychological parenting." Another legal commentator spoke of psychological parenting in these terms: "The mutual interaction between adult and child, which might be described in such terms as love, affection, basic trust, and confidence, is considered essential for the child's successful development, and is the basis of what may be termed psychological parenthood. It is this psychological parenthood rather than the biological events which may precipitate such a relationship, which many psychologists identify as the sine qua non of successful personality development. While at birth a biological parent potentially has a greater opportunity to achieve this, so can a third party." See 73 *Yale L.J.* at 158.

[25]Generally see *Smith* v. *Organization of Foster Families*, 431 U.S. 816; 97 S.Ct. 2094; 53 L.Ed.2d 14 (1977). Authors Solnit, Freud and Goldstein point out the need of such constancy in parenting in their latest work on this subject (see *Before the Best Interests of the Child*, Goldstein/Freud/Solnit (1979)). Indeed, the authors suggest minimum periods of caretaker care of a child with an adult before psychological parenting may be said to have developed, that is, one or more years for a child under 3, and 2 or more years for a child 3 years or older. (See *Before the Best Interests of the Child* at 188–189).

their testimony in court was charged with their emotional attachment to the child; they offer love and home care, tutoring, and all that Phillip may need in terms of educational, vocational, and basic skills training. Their magnanimity is astonishing and consistent with anyone's ultimate views of good parenting. That Phillip loves them is evidenced by the testimony of witnesses who have described his attachment to the Heaths. These witnesses have also described the adverse psychological effects visited on Phillip by the termination of custodial type visitation of Phillip with the Heaths by the Beckers. The expert testimony has also indicated that Phillip will suffer further psychological damage if his relationship with the Heaths as well as others is terminated. In sum we find that psychological parenting between the Heaths and Phillip exists.

The court has now determined who may speak for the child in these proceedings. Let us examine briefly the procedural framework within which this case arises. It is not an adoption nor a proceeding to terminate all parental rights. It is a proceeding to establish a limited guardianship, with the Heaths as guardians of Phillip under supervision of the court and with the parental ties remaining intact. In California, state interference by way of court action can take many forms, with California having eight separate proceedings dealing with child custody. At least one California court has approved of guardianship of a child to a non-parent over parental objection without severing the parent-child relationship.[32] Legal commentators have suggested that this hybrid form of parenting, custody in a stranger and the non-severance of parental ties, may actually be in a child's best interests, for a child can benefit from two sets of parents.[33] Our case is a test case of this concept. One final note on procedure. Whatever of the eight methods a California Court may use to deal with child custody, the California Supreme Court has held that Section 4600 of the Family Law Act governs any of the proceedings along this custody continuum.[34]

With our doctrines decided, our "parents" determined, and the procedural framework outlined, the court will discuss the conclusions that it has drawn from the evidence. These conclusions or findings will be made in narrative fashion. They need to be made in order that the court may come to its ultimate determination of what is in the best interests of the child, and the least detrimental alternative for him in this custody battle. These conclusions are based on what this court considers to be clear and convincing evidence.[36]

Phillip Becker was born on October 16, 1966. The initial news of the birth elated the family, but within hours of birth Mr. Becker, to his devastation, discovered that the second fruit of the Becker union was a "mongoloid, Down's child with simian characteristics." Within six days of birth, the Beckers placed Phillip in a board and

---

[32]See *Guardianship of Marino, supra*.

[33]See *Wald*, at 672. Simpson, The Unfit Parent: Conditions Under Which a Child May be Adopted Without the Consent of His Parent, 39 *U. Det. L.J.* 347, 391 (1962); Mnookin, Foster Care: In Whose Best Interests?, 43 *Harv. Educ. Rev.* 599, 634 (1973).

[34]See *In re B.G., supra*.

[36]The usual standard in civil cases is by a preponderance of the evidence. However, in custody cases falling under juvenile court law, or where Civil Code Section 232 is being applied, the California Supreme Court has indicated that the evidence must be clear or clear and convincing. (See *In re B.G., supra; In re Angelia P., supra*.)

care facility operated by Neva Lippard and decided to step back so they could "truly understand the situation." They left the question of permanent placement for Phillip open, but never thought of bringing him home. Mrs. Becker felt inadequate to provide Phillip with his needs and undertook no efforts toward the care of Phillip. Mr. Becker's attitude towards his child was one of puzzlement if not anger at having sired a defect. Visits to Neva Lippard's by the Beckers were sporadic and occasional at best. The endings of each visit was [sic] the same; they left the nursery numbed by their crushed expectations for Phillip. The Beckers initially and with growing clarity as the days, months, and years passed, concluded that Phillip would always be retarded, always be a defect, would always need constant custodial care, and would be institutionalized for life. They decided that he should never be close to anyone, or any families nor develop any special attachments. They concluded that Phillip would be happy so long as his physical needs were met and that he did not need his mother for his daily needs or for nurturing. In their view Phillip would always be a burden and of little appreciable value for the rest *of his* life. Their basic opinion of Phillip was that he was a permanently mentally retarded, low IQ Down's child who would never have a hope of living in society.[38]

Their concern for Phillip has a curious ambivalence to it. While they express love for him, they do not display it. While they speak of having an open mind on the issue of surgery, they have not only refused it but have never taken any steps to initiate the basic testing, examination, and review necessary to make such an important decision. In this regard, their actions toward Phillip's health needs, educational needs, and basic skills needs are marked by a puzzling inertia of action on their part. Why wasn't Phillip catheterized or tested at age six to see if he might be a good candidate for surgery? Why was he still in diapers at age six? Why did all his teeth rot? Why didn't he have pre-school? Why wasn't he brought home for overnights at the Beckers' prior to 1981? Why was it necessary for Rebecca Wells to alert the Beckers of care deficiencies when Phillip was transferred from Neva Lippard's hands to the Blanks in 1971? Why doesn't Phillip have real motor skills? Why does Phillip test as a high Down's in social skills and is low in certain basic skills? The list of whys can become endless, but they point out one thing clearly, that Phillip was considered so retarded and defective by the Beckers that the only appropriate placement for him was in a warehouse permanently and with no more than basic care afforded to him.

The available psychological evidence, the demeanor evidence of the witnesses

---

[38]The historic view that mental retardation is permanent and an immutable defect of intelligence is a popular myth. This view has been supplanted by the recognition that a person may be mentally retarded at one age level and not at another. He may change as a result of changes in the level of his intellectual functioning, *or he may move from retarded to non-retarded as a result of a training program which has increased his level of adaptive behavior* to a point where his behavior is no longer of concern to society. (See United States President's Panel on Mental Retardation, Report of the Task Force on Law, 1963. (Judge David L. Bazelon, Chairman. *Cited in: Wyatt* v. *Stickney,* 344 F.Supp. 387, 389, fn. 2 (1972) (the expert testimony at trial is also to this effect). Without doubt the retarded need to be helped to escape their retardation. The Beckers' attitude in this regard was to "wait and see what comes." Again in deference to the Beckers, their low expectations of Phillip may have been based on their own family observations, conversations with friends who had Downs in their family, their reading and study, and so on. Thus, their attitude of once a Downs, always a Downs may have been pre-conditioned by their background and the historical myth.

at trial, as well as the inferences to be drawn from the testimony is that the necessary bonding between biological parent and child has never occurred.

Phillip Becker refused to be quiescent in his storage places. Soon after his transfer to the We-Care facility in 1972, Phillip, although devoid of most basic social or developmental skills, began to demonstrate that he had value.[41] Staff members at We-Care and volunteer workers were attracted to an engaging Down's child. These helpers of the handicapped sensed Phillip's message of value and began to work with him to develop his basic skills and his social deportment. It was during the course of these efforts that the Heaths and Phillip became attached to each other.

Unfortunately, Phillip's upward movement toward societal living was abruptly halted by the issue of surgery for an at birth ventrical [sic] septal defect of the heart. The Beckers, although warned of the defect to Phillip's heart and the possible need for surgery when Phillip was three or four years old, had refused to take any steps towards providing life prolonging surgery for Phillip. In 1977, they refused Doctor Gary Gathman's entreaty for this heart repair work. In 1978 in a dramatic and highly publicized juvenile court hearing pursuant to Welfare and Institutions Code section 300b, the parental decision of no surgery was upheld and Phillip was rejected as a ward of the Juvenile court.[41a]

That hearing must be placed in its proper context. For the issue then was not parenting, but rather child neglect for not authorizing life prolonging surgery. It was a hearing which lasted only two days while our hearing has run the course of 12 long court days.

Although the courts have often been quick to order medical care when a child's illness is life threatening, their response has been mixed when the threat of life has not been imminent.[42] Basically, if surgery has been refused, it is on the grounds that a

---

[41]Whether Phillip had value or lacked value became a central issue in this case. The adversary process highlighted this disagreement as thesis v. anti-thesis was evidenced in the dynamic dialectic of this trial. Whenever the Becker side claimed he couldn't do something, the witnesses for Phillip Becker proved the counter. Thus:

| Becker Thesis | Friends of Phillip Becker Anti-Thesis |
|---|---|
| Phillip can't talk. | Phillip can talk. |
| Phillip can't communicate. | Phillip can communicate. |
| Phillip is a low Down's. | Phillip is a high Downs. |
| Phillip can't write his name. | Phillip can write his name. |
| Phillip can't draw. | Phillip can draw. |
| Phillip can't cook. | Phillip can cook. |
| Phillip is not educable. | Phillip is educable. |
| Phillip can't form loving attachments. | Phillip can form loving permanent attachments. |
| Phillip has few basic skills. | Phillip has many basic skills. |

[41a]See *In re Phillip B.*, 92 C.A.3d 796; 156 Ca. Rptr. 48.

[42]The United States Supreme Court has consistently held that parental rights must give way when parental decisions will jeopardize the health or safety of a child. (See *Prince* v. *Commonwealth of Massachusetts*, 321 U.S. 158, 167. Also, *Wisconsin* v. *Yoder* (1972) 406 U.S. 205, 234 (32 L.ed.2d 15, 35; 92 S.Ct. 1526.) See also *In re Custody of a Minor*, 379 N.E.2d 1053, 1062. However, where the threat of death is not imminent, courts have disagreed on whether surgery should be permitted over parental objection. Cases authorizing surgery where no imminency of death: *In re Sampson*, 65 Misc. 2d 658, 317 N.Y.S.2d

person is constitutionally entitled to be free from a non-consensual invasion of his bodily integrity.[43] Additionally, courts which have refused permission for surgical intervention for a minor have held it may only be performed on an infant if consent is first obtained from the child's natural guardian or of one standing *in loco parentis* to the infant.[44] Such consent is also required when surgery is to be performed upon an incompetent.[45]

Our California courts are peculiarly sensitive in regards to state interference in the parent-child relationship. Our courts take the view that the government through the Superior Court should not run family life. We feel that the law has limited ability to supervise interpersonal relations.[46] In commenting on this legal incapacity, behavioral scientists have postulated the courts' dilemma thus: "Families know their values, priorities and resources better than anyone else. Presumably they, with the doctor, can make the better choices as a private affair. Certainly, they more than anyone else, must live with the consequences . . . If they cannot cope adequately with the child and their other responsibilities and survive as a family, they may feel that the death option is a forced choice. . . . But that is not necessarily bad, and who knows of a better way?"[47] As pointed out by authors Goldstein, Freud, and Solnit: "If parental autonomy is not accorded recognition and if society insists through law that such children (neurologically handicapped or mentally retarded) receive medical treatment rejected by their parents, the state must take upon itself the psychological resources essential to making real the value it prefers for the child it saves. The state would have to demonstrate its capacity for making such unwanted children wanted ones. Minimally, it should fully finance their special-care requirements. In the event parents do not wish to remain responsible for their child, the state would have to find—what is rarely available—adopting parents or other caretakers who can meet not only the child's physical needs but also his psychological requirements for affectionate relationships and emotional and intellectual stimulation."[48]

Is it any wonder therefore that the wardship proceedings of Phillip Becker and the request for surgery floundered on the rock of parental rights? The issue in those proceedings was too narrow, that is, the risks of surgery. The basic issue is and always has been the one of parenting. Because even with the surgery ordered by the Juvenile Court, would Phillip Becker ever escape the grip of institutionalized living? The

---

641 (N.Y. Fam. Ct. 1970), affs. 37 A.D.2d 668, 323 N.Y.S.2d 253, 1971, affs. 29 N.Y.2d 900, 328 N.Y.S.2d 686, 278 N.E.2d 918 (1972); *In re Rotkowitz*, 175 Misc. 948, 25 N.Y.S.2d 624 (N.Y. Dom. Rel. Ct.); *In re Custody of a Minor, supra*. Cases refusing surgery: *In re Seiferth*, 309 N.Y. 80, 127 N.E.2d 820 (1955) (Case is no longer precedent in New York, See *In re Sampson, supra*.); *In re Frank*, 41 Wash. 2d 294, 248 P.2d 553 (1952) (defect was a speech impediment); *In re Hudson*, 13 Wash.2d 673, 126 P.2d 675 (1942) (child had a deformed arm that needed amputation); *In re Green*, 448 Pa. 338, 292 A.2d 387 (1972).

[43]See, *Superintendent of Belchertown* v. *Saikewicz*, 370 N.E.2d 417.

[44]See *In re Hudson, supra*.

[45]See *Pratt* v. *Davis*, 118 Ill. App. 161; also annotation 76 A.L.R. 562.

[46]See *In re Marriage of Jenkins*, 116 C.A.3d 767, 775 (1981).

[47]Kelsey, *Shall These Children Live?* A conversation with Dr. Raymond S. Duff (*Reflections*, 72: 4, 7, 1975) (See *Before The Best Interests of the Child* for quotations source.)

[48]*See Before The Best Interests of the Child*, p. 97. See also Goldstein, *Medical Care for the Child at Risk;* on State Supervention of Parental Authority, 86 *Yale Law Journal* 645 (1977), hereinafter referred to as 86 *Yale L.J.*

answer is No, but this case through the dynamic of the dialectic, has pointed out the future alternatives for Phillip. By positing the two parental theses as found to be true by this court based on the evidence, we will readily see what is the least detrimental alternative for Phillip.

The Beckers' alternative for Phillip is institutional placement for the rest of his life. No life prolonging surgery. Little if any attention to the development of his basic skills, motor skills or social skills. A denial of visits with people who have affection and love for Phillip. A fierce desire to never let Phillip have any permanent attachments to anyone or to have any home life. Their expectations for Phillip and his future are none.

The Heaths' alternative is an abundance of personal affection, love, and care. A placement of Phillip into their home, a situation which the psychological evidence shows Phillip desperately needs. A full time mother; a constant one-to-one training relationship; a private tutor. Attention will be paid to development of his basic skills, his motor skills, and his speech. In short they are willing to do everything necessary to make Phillip a better person. Most important of all they promise to give the issue of surgery for Phillip the most careful and searching consideration possible. This done in the best of parenting fashion by gathering that breadth and quantum of evidence and information necessary to make the correct decision.[50] Their expectations for Phillip's future are great, for they believe that he may be taught to live in and be a part of society. They will always treasure him as if he were their son. They will do everything possible to bring together the two families to the end that Phillip may have a better life by having two sets of parents. All of these promises they make without expectation of financial gain. Their hoped for reward is the love and affection of Phillip and the bestowing upon him of a life worth living.[51] By this succinct recitation of the choices of parenting it must be obvious what is the least detrimental alternative for Phillip Becker.

Before making that finding required by the Family Law Act, of detriment, let

---

[50]The commentators on this subject have suggested an appropriate test for the Court to use in deciding any issue of surgery. Thus parental refusal of medical care would be overcome if: (1) the medical profession is in agreement about what non-experimental medical treatment is appropriate for the child; (2) that the denial of the treatment would mean death for the child; and (3) that the expected outcome is what society agrees to be right for any child—a chance for a normal healthy growth or a life worth living. (See *Before the Best Interests* at 92; also 86 *Yale L.J.* at 652.)

[51]These are surely an astonishing series of promises. This is the kind of "miracle caretaker" that the commentators who have discussed state intervention in child "risk cases" have despaired of ever finding. Thus the dilemma of any court considering medical intervention, that is, who is responsible for follow-up parenting, is resolved by this magnanimous offer. Mr. Becker has cynically observed that there is gain. I can find none other than the satisfaction that any parent would have with the growth and mature development of a child.

One can only marvel that anyone would want to take on the awesome responsibility of trying to raise a near adult child with Down's syndrome and afflicted with a ventrical septal defect, myopia, hearing loss, some spasticity, suffering from lack of basic skills, and presently showing signs of a mysterious narcolepsy. In view of these difficulties, a cynic might suggest that the Heaths will try to salvage the child and then finding the effort too much, abandon Phillip, leaving the Beckers or the state responsible for Phillip. There are four answers to this: (1) Phillip would be no worse off at that time than he is today; (2) the Heaths have made it unmistakably clear in gripping courtroom testimony that they love Phillip and will care for him; I feel certain that they will not give up on Phillip; (3) this case has received so much publicity that public pressure will insure a continuing and ongoing effort by the *de facto* parents to save Phillip; (4) even though the Court deals in a land of broken promises, we must still trust people to keep their word. The Heaths are trustworthy.

us discuss Phillip's rights. For separate and independent of the rights of *de jure* parents and *de facto* parents, there are the rights of the mentally retarded and gravely disabled. It is said that those who are so afflicted are possessed of an inviolable constitutional right to habilitation.[52] This constitutional right is one in which such persons are given a realistic opportunity to be cured or to improve his or her [*sic*] mental condition.[53] Habilitation for the handicapped is the process by which the handicapped person acquires and maintains life skills which enable him to cope more effectively with the demands of his own person and of his environment and to raise the level of his physical, mental, and social efficiency by programs of formal structure—education and treatment.[54] Succinctly, habilitation means that each handicapped person is given a realistic opportunity to lead a more useful and meaningful life and to return to society.[55]

Recently in California, a body of law has been developing aimed at protecting the rights of mentally retarded and gravely disabled minors.[56] Our current view is that minors as well as adults possess constitutional rights.[57] That as to the mentally retarded or gravely disabled minor, the state's interest is that they mature into healthy adults capable of full participation in society.[58] Such a minor is entitled to be free of any injury to his reputation and an interest in not being improperly or unfairly stigmatized as mentally ill or disordered.[59] Thus, our high court has held that an erroneous conclusion by a parent that a child is sufficiently mentally ill to be institutionalized may well affect the health or safety of the child or have the potentiality for significant social burdens triggering intervention by the state for the protection of the child.[60]

This court is aware that the above legal principles have so far only been applied by the courts to mentally handicapped or gravely disabled young people in state institutions. However, Phillip Becker being over 14 years of age and emancipatable, ordinarily having a right to state a preference in a custody proceeding, and having a right in this court's opinion to secure habilitation and avoid the permanent stigmatization of mentally ill or disordered, should be allowed to make a choice and thereby state a preference as to whether he wishes to remain warehoused for the rest of his days or to secure the opportunity for a life worth living by placement in the home environment offered to him by the Heaths. I point out that at sometime in Phillip's adult life he has a right to take that choice, why not now.

California does not provide a method by which a mentally retarded child may state a preference. Other states have used a substituted judgment procedure to allow the

---

[52]See *Wyatt* v. *Stickney,* 344 F.Supp. 387 (1972).

[53]See *Wyatt* v. *Stickney,* 325 F.Supp. 781 (1971).

[54]See *Wyatt* v. *Stickney,* at 395.

[55]See *Wyatt* v. *Stickney,* at 390. Of course, the Federal Court is speaking of handicapped people placed by the state in an institution. But isn't Phillip entitled to similar rights when he is institutionalized by his parents? California subscribes to this view of habilitation for their developmentally disabled population. (See Welfare & Institutions Code Section 4750).

[56]See *In re Roger S.,* 19 Cal.3d 921. For California courts, the age of 14 is significant in this regard.

[57]See *Planned Parenthood of Cent. Mo.* v. *Danforth* (1976) 428 U.S. 52, 74 (49 L.Ed.2d 788, 808, 96 S.Ct. 2831, 2843).

[58]*In re Roger S., supra,* at 935.

[59]See *In re Roger S., supra,* at 929.

[60]See *In re Roger S.*

court to state such a preference for the incompetent.[63] This doctrine requires the court to ascertain as nearly as possible the incompetent person's "actual interests and preferences."[64] The substituted judgment doctrine has been used by the courts in other states to determine a child's preferences and is held to be consistent with the "best interests of the child" doctrine.[65]

In our case the use of the substituted judgment method to arrive at Phillip's preference may best be stated in the form of a platonic dialogue with the court posing the choices to Phillip and Phillip's preference being ascertained from the more logical choice. The dialogue begins:

> The Court: "Phillip I am convinced by the evidence that you have arrived at a crossroad in your life. Whatever path you choose you must follow and will be bound to for the rest of your life. Your first choice will lead you to a room in an institution where you will live. You will be fed, housed, and clothed but you will not receive any life prolonging medical care. If you do receive medical care, it will be basic care only. You will not be given an opportunity to add to your basic skills or to your motor skills and in fact will be treated as if you are a permanently mentally retarded person incapable of learning and not fit to enter into society. You will not be allowed to become attached to any person, in fact efforts will be made to prevent any such attachments. Your biological parents will visit you occasionally, but their love and caring for you will at best be ambivalent. In fact they believe that you will be happy so long as your physical needs are taken care of, and that this kind of care may come from other people, your institutional caretakers."

> "Your second choice, Phillip, will lead you to a private home where you will be bathed in the love and affection of your psychological parents. You will be given all of the benefits of a home environment. You will be given private tutoring and one-on-one training. The purpose of this education and training will be to improve your motor skills and your basic skills in order that some day you may enter into society and be a productive member of our community. Your psychological parents believe that you are educable and will do all in their power to help you receive the education you may need to care for yourself and to secure work when you are an adult. You will have a chance for life-prolonging surgery as well as receiving all the medical care that you need. Even if life-prolonging surgery cannot be performed, your psychological parents will always be there to comfort you and care for you in the dark times of your final illness. Best of all, your psychological parents will do all in their power to involve your biological parents in your habilitation and to unite both families together in ensuring for you a life that is worth living."

In my view, the dialogue would end with Phillip choosing to live with the Heaths.

Sad to say, the foregoing legal analysis has no precedent in California law. There is no way under our present law for a mentally retarded child like Phillip to say: I want habilitation. I want life-prolonging surgery. Those choices belong to his parents or guardians. Phillip's case may pave the way for recognition of a developmentally disabled child's right to choose his fate or destiny by the substituted judgment approach, or by the type of legal proceedings we are presently engaged in.

As to our required finding of detriment. If we define detriment as harm, then

---

[63]See *Superintendent of Belchertown* v. *Saikewicz, id.*

[64]See *In re Custody of a Minor,* 379 N.E.2d 1053, 1065 (1978).

[65]See *In re Custody of a Minor, supra,* at 1065.

Phillip has suffered harm by the parenting of the Beckers. He has suffered severe emotional harm by their severance of all attachments by others to Phillip. He has suffered physical harm by their failure to attend to the basic skills, and motor skills of Phillip. He has suffered medical harm by their refusal from infancy to consider any life-prolonging surgery for him, or to take any interest in seeing that his medical needs are taken care of. He has suffered lasting harm by their stigmatization of Phillip as permanently mentally ill and disordered. If we define detriment as lack of benefits, then simply stated, Phillip can never receive any benefit from custody with the Beckers because they have no expectations for him and will therefore do nothing to allow him to win a place into our society. Clearly the Heaths provide for Phillip his best alternative because their expectations for Phillip are in direct opposition to the Beckers' point of view, and they offer Phillip the best chance he will ever have of securing a life worth living and the chance to grow and avoid the stigmata of the defective. The court finds that it will be in Phillip's best interest to award his custody to the Heaths.

This has been both a wonderful case and an irrational tragedy.[68] It has been wonderful because so many people have come forward to try to make a little boy's life better. They have braved a storm of parental indignation including scathing cross examination and a multi-million dollar lawsuit. The only observable gain is the love and affection of the child and a personal feeling of doing what is right for children.

This case is tragic, because God and nature may already have determined Phillip's future life course. He may very well be entering the dark time of his existence.[68a]

This tragedy is irrational because the contestants are spending thousands of dollars and thousands of hours fighting over rights. That time could be better spent by trying to make the last part of Phillip Becker's life happier than the earlier part. Since the Beckers feel that Phillip can't do and since they have been indifferent to his care, why not give the Heaths a chance to show what Phillip can do and to improve his

---

[68]This case is also a haunting one. It never leaves the mind during every waking moment of this Court. As we in our private life see young and old enjoying living at a wedding and the reception that follows; as we see people at play in the park; as we see people laughing and gay at the theater. The thoughts are always there of the Beckers, Phillip, the Heaths and of what might have been and of what should be, not only for Phillip but for all of the people who suffer grave mental or physical disability. It seems to me that any society must take a stand as to what they intend and what they will do for their infirm. One alternative is that of the Spartans of ancient Greece who cast their defective infants onto Mount Taygetus or into a deep well. Such a solution is unthinkable. Another is to let the weak live but provide to them only warehouse-man's care, food, clothing, shelter and very little else. Allowing the retarded and disabled to vegetate and rust away in some institutional setting. The horrors of these places are illustrated by the description of Willowbrook School for the Mentally Retarded set forth in the opinion of Judge Judd in *New York State Assn. for Retarded Children, In.* v. *Rockefeller*, 357 F.Supp. 752, 755–57 (E.D.N.Y. 1973). Because of the mayhem that may occur in such minimum level institutions, a cynical pragmatist could easily suggest that the Spartan method is far less cruel and inhuman. The third and best alternative is that we as a society set as our goal habilitation for our ill. That we provide them with a sufficiency of care and of programs that will afford them a real opportunity to enter into the mainstream of life. The gains for us as a people are enormous, for those who are sick will be given the realistic hope of a life worth living, and those who are strong will believe that in their weak time, we as a society will care for them as well. Pollyannish perhaps, but a Christian goal and a goal worth striving for. If we can achieve this end for caring for each other, then the Biblical ideal of mutual trust will arise, and the lion may truly lay down with the lamb.

[68a]I have read all of Phillip's admissible medical and nursing records. I note with mounting anguish the developing and growing course of his strangling cyanotic illness; and as I read, I weep uncontrollably at the struggles of this wee lad to survive. My soul reaches out to him and to his laboring heart to try to give it ease, and in this time of grief, I think of Tiny Tim and what might have been but for old Marley's ghost.

physical condition? With our solution to the problem so obvious, why are there so many sacrifices onto the altar of parental rights? We are stretching important legal doctrines to the utmost in order that a little one's life can be made better. Is there any gain by letting false pride rule our hearts? It seems to me that any victories based on such a shaky premise must indeed be Pyrrhic, and any legal defeats must be personally destructive. Let's end the legal struggle now and have two sets of parents working for Phillip's best interest.

Yet despite all our hopes for Phillip, his cause may again flounder. It may flounder because the Heaths' home may not be suitable for him after our Juvenile Department inquiry. It may flounder because the court has somehow created legal error, and the parental rights doctrine may be paramount in this area. It may flounder for any number of other reasons, but one thing is clear to me, this court should state that it does not approve of the Beckers' lack of parenting, and strongly urge that it is time for them to change.

One final word, this is not a hearing to determine surgery for Phillip. That must await another time and a sound parenting decision. This is a hearing for the purpose of giving Phillip Becker another parenting choice. It is a hearing responsive to Phillip's need for habilitation, and responsive to his desire for a chance to secure a life worth living. *I will give him that chance.*

The petition of the Heaths for an order of guardianship of the person of Phillip Becker is granted. Authorization is given for immediate catheterization to determine the feasibility of surgery for his ventricle septal defect.

NOTES

1.   How important was the Beckers' decision regarding medical treatment to the outcome of Judge Fernandez's custody determination? Would the court's reasoning justify the termination of custody of any parents who institutionalize their handicapped child and retain only minimal contact thereafter?

2.   The *Becker* case has been the subject of a huge amount of media attention, including segments on the "Sixty Minutes" TV program and columns by George Will in *Newsweek* magazine. Such publicity has not been well received by the Beckers. The "multi-million dollar lawsuit" referred to by Judge Fernandez was a $60 million breach of privacy action brought by the Beckers against several news organizations, Santa Clara County, Phillip's treating physician, one of the attorneys involved in the case, and several other defendants. (See, Herhold, "Parents file suit over publicity on son's health," *San Jose Mercury,* Mar. 4, 1980.) The defendants in the suit are accused of having disclosed "private" and "confidential" information about the Beckers.

3.   Footnote 41 of the court's opinion illustrates some of the difficulties of trying to predict a child's abilities based upon a single label, such as that of Down's syndrome. How much more difficult it is to try to make such predictions for an infant, as in *Houle* and *Cicero.* What are the legal implications of this inability to accurately predict future functional abilities of a handicapped child?

4.   In spite of the plea of Judge Fernandez to "end the legal struggle now," the Beckers appealed his decision. As this book was going to press, the California Court of Appeals upheld Judge Fernandez's decision. *In re Phillip B.,* 188 Cal. Rptr. 781 (1983).

THE WHITE HOUSE

WASHINGTON

*April 30, 1982*

MEMORANDUM FOR   THE ATTORNEY GENERAL

                      THE SECRETARY OF HEALTH AND HUMAN SERVICES

        SUBJECT:   Enforcement of Federal Laws Prohibiting Discrimination Against the Handicapped

Following the recent death of a handicapped newborn child in Indiana, many have raised the question whether Federal laws protecting the rights of handicapped citizens are being adequately enforced.

Therefore, I am instructing Secretary Schweiker to notify health care providers of the applicability of section 504 of the Rehabilitation Act of 1973 to the treatment of handicapped patients. That law forbids recipients of Federal funds from withholding from handicapped citizens, simply because they are handicapped, any benefit or service that would ordinarily be provided to persons without handicaps. Regulations under this law specifically prohibit hospitals and other providers of health services receiving Federal assistance from discriminating against the handicapped.

I am also instructing the Attorney General to report to me on the possible application of Federal constitutional and statutory remedies in appropriate circumstances to prevent the withholding from the handicapped of potentially life-saving treatment that would be given as a matter of course to those who are not handicapped.

Our Nation's commitment to equal protection of the law will have little meaning if we deny such protection to those who have not been blessed with the same physical or mental gifts we too often take for granted. I support Federal laws prohibiting discrimination against the handicapped, and remain determined that such laws will be vigorously enforced.

NOTES

1.  The Indiana case referred to by the President involved the death of an infant with Down's syndrome at a hospital in Bloomington, Indiana. The child, referred to as Infant Doe in court proceedings, needed surgery to correct a blockage of the esophagus that prevented food from reaching the stomach. When the parents refused to consent to the surgery, the hospital went to court to try to obtain authorization to perform the operation. The trial court upheld the parents' right to withhold treatment, and the Supreme Court of Indiana refused to review the lower court's decision. While an appeal to the United States Supreme Court was being prepared, the infant died of starvation. Court files of the case were ordered sealed. The incident generated much media concern and public outcry. *Congressional Record*–Senate, May 26, 1982, S6143–S6155.

2.  One of the first applications of President Reagan's directive occurred a few weeks after the Indiana incident. It involved a child with spina bifida in Robinson, Illinois, who was allegedly being denied medical treatment that might save the child's life. In reaction to publicity surrounding this incident, the Department of Health and Human Services sent an investigator to check the complaint that surgical treatment was being

withheld. *Congressional Record*–Senate, May 26, 1982, S6155; Ahrens, "Three-week-old with defect pits pro-life 'outsiders' vs. Illinois town," *Washington Times,* May 17, 1982, p. 1.

3. Consider the feasibility of Section 504 being applied in such cases by parties other than the federal grant agencies. Who can invoke the rights guaranteed by the statute in such a case?

## NAACP v. MEDICAL CENTER, INC.

*United States Court of Appeals for the Third Circuit, 1981*
*657 F.2d 1322*

Before ALDISERT, ADAMS, GIBBONS, HUNTER, WEIS, GARTH, HIGGINBOTHAM and SLOVITER, Circuit Judges.

Opinion of the Court

WEIS, Circuit Judge.

The Wilmington Medical Center has been embroiled in litigation for the past five years because of its proposal to construct a new building in the suburbs and renovate one of its buildings in downtown Wilmington, Delaware. In this latest appeal, we hold that disparate impacts of a neutral policy may be adequate to establish discrimination under Title VI of the Civil Rights Act of 1964. Assuming, without deciding, that the plaintiffs presented a prima facie case, we conclude that the Medical Center produced adequate evidence to justify its relocation and reorganization plan. Accordingly, we will affirm the action of the district court in refusing to enjoin implementation of the proposal.

Alleging unlawful discrimination, the plaintiff organizations, representing minority, handicapped, and elderly persons, sought an injunction against the relocation and reorganization of the Medical Center. After we held that the plaintiffs had private rights of action under Title VI of the Civil Rights Act of 1964, 42 U.S.C. § 2000d et seq. (1976), and § 504 of the Rehabilitation Act of 1975, 29 U.S.C. § 794 (Supp. II 1978), see *NAACP* v. *The Medical Center, Inc.*, 599 F.2d 1247 (3d Cir. 1979), the district court brought the matter to trial. The City of Wilmington was added as a party plaintiff, and the complaint was amended to include allegations that the Age Discrimination Act, 42 U.S.C. §§ 6101–6107 (1976 & Supp. II 1978) had been violated. In addition, plaintiffs charged the defendant with intentional discrimination as well as conduct that had a disparate impact on the classes represented by the plaintiffs.

Following a bench trial lasting more than a month, the district court filed a comprehensive and detailed opinion, concluding that the plaintiffs had failed to prove discrimination under any of the three statutes. Judgment was accordingly entered for the defendant. *NAACP* v. *Wilmington Medical Center, Inc.*, 491 F.Supp. 290 (D.Del.1980). The plaintiffs' appeal was heard initially by a panel and then, because of the nature of the issues, was reheard by the court in banc.

The Wilmington Medical Center (WMC) was organized in 1965 by the merger of three non-profit hospitals, General, Memorial, and Delaware, in different areas of Wilmington. WMC furnishes general medical and surgical services, as well as secondary and tertiary hospital care. It provides 1,104 of the 1,471 non-profit, acute general hospital beds in New Castle County. Other institutions in the county include St. Francis Hospital, which has approximately 290 beds, and Riverside Osteopathic Hospital, with a capacity of 100. The concentration of hospital beds in Wilmington proper is higher than is desirable under national standards, while at the same time the southwestern part of the county surrounding Newark, Delaware, is quite underserved.

WMC is the only hospital in the county with a teaching program approved by the American Medical Association. Medical students and residents are important to WMC's delivery of health care to the community. Without their assistance, current levels of care could not be maintained.

Because its physical structures are aging and are not in compliance with Delaware's licensing law, WMC has encountered serious problems. Recruitment for its residency program has been hindered by the fragmenting of its plants, as well as by a lack of conference space and adequate research facilities. The surgical residency program has been placed on probation by its accrediting body and WMC itself is also in danger of losing its certification by the Joint Commission on Accreditation of Hospitals. On two recent occasions, only "probational" accreditation was granted. Loss of accreditation could result in denial of Medicare and Medicaid reimbursements, a situation which would be disastrous to WMC financially, since it relies on these funds for more than one third of its total budget.

WMC has other monetary problems. It provides the largest amount of free care in the county—approximately $8,000,000 annually. Because Medicare and Medicaid do not reimburse it for any portion of fees attributable to subsidization of free care, WMC must depend upon its endowment and the fees assessed upon paying patients and private insurers.

The population shift to the southwestern suburbs and the possibility that another health care institution might be established in that area present another threat to WMC. If it should lose the patronage of people there, most of whom pay for services or are privately insured, the subsidization of a higher percentage of unreimbursed care would become an even more serious drain on its financial resources.

Recognizing the need for remedial action, the WMC Board canvassed the options open to it. After studying about 50 plans for relocation and consolidation, it decided upon Plan Omega. Essentially, this proposal would close the General and Memorial facilities, renovate the Delaware one, and reduce the number of downtown beds to 250. In addition, a new facility of 780 beds would be built in the suburban area 9.35 miles southwest of the Delaware plant. A division of services between the two locations was part of the arrangement.

After the district court ordered a departmental review, HEW found discriminatory effects in the plan. To ensure that Omega would comply with Title VI and the Rehabilitation Act, WMC contracted to make a number of modifications. Because no public transportation to the southwest site is available, WMC agreed to provide shuttle bus service between the Delaware and Southwest divisions for the convenience of patients, visitors, and employees. In addition, WMC committed itself to renovate the Delaware plant, devise inpatient service plans for the two branches to prevent racial identifiability at either location, and operate the two facilities on a unitary basis.

Upon acceptance of these conditions, HEW withdrew its objections to Omega.

Plaintiffs, however, continued their opposition, contending in the district court that the relocation would subject members of the class to inferior health care and disproportionate travel burdens. Moreover, it was alleged that there has been a misallocation of services between the two divisions.

The district court analyzed the case under alternate theories of intentional discrimination and unintended discriminatory effects. The court first determined that there was no evidence of discriminatory purpose. It then applied a disparate effect standard, but concluded after a lengthy review of the evidence that plaintiffs had failed to present a prima facie case.

Rather than ending the inquiry at that point, the court assumed arguendo that a showing of disparate impact had been made. The record was then scrutinized to determine if the defendant had successfully rebutted the plaintiffs' contentions. The court concluded that even if disparate impact had been shown, WMC had demonstrated it had bona fide needs that could not be satisfied by any less discriminatory plan. Finally, the court determined that plaintiffs did not prove that a feasible alternative to Omega was available.

Consideration of the alleged disparate impact was divided into several general categories—access, quality of care, linguistic discrimination, and racial identifiability. Initially, the court found that Plan Omega would bring about vast improvements in the quality of care for all patients, including the classes represented by the plaintiffs. The detrimental effects to minorities and the elderly were determined to be minor and insignificant. With respect to the handicapped, plaintiffs failed to show any adverse impact.

\* \* \*

I

The lengthy recitation of the background makes it clear that this case turns largely on factual matters. There are, however, several discrete legal issues essential to a resolution of the dispute. The first that we shall discuss implicates the nature of the evidence necessary to show a violation of Title VI. If the plaintiff must show intent to discriminate, then our task is a simple one because the trial court found no such evidence and that holding is not contested. We are persuaded, however, that intent is not required under Title VI and proof of disparate impact or effects is sufficient. Our conclusion applies to the other two statutes that have been invoked as well.

Title VI of the Civil Rights Act of 1964, 42 U.S.C. § 2000d (1976), bans discrimination based on race, color, or national origin in any program receiving federal financial assistance. WMC concedes that Medicare and Medicaid payments made to it call Title VI into play.

In *Lau* v. *Nichols,* 414 U.S. 563, 94 S.Ct. 786, 39 L.Ed.2d 1 (1974), the Supreme Court was confronted with a racial discrimination charge growing out of a school system's decision not to provide English language instruction to students of Chinese ancestry. The Court declined to reach an equal protection argument but chose instead to rely on Title VI, interpreting it as follows:

> Discrimination is barred which has that *effect* even though no purposeful design is present: a recipient "may not . . . utilize criteria or methods of administration which have the effect of subjecting individuals to discrimination" or have "the effect of

defeating or substantially impairing accomplishment of the objectives of the program as respect individuals of a particular race, color, or national origin."

*Id.* at 568, 94 S.Ct. at 789 (emphasis the Court's), *quoting* HEW regulation, 45 C.F.R. § 80.3(b)(2).

*Lau* makes it clear that discriminatory impact is enough to constitute a violation of Title VI. WMC, however, argues that *Lau* was overruled by *Board of Education* v. *Harris,* 444 U.S. 130, 100 S.Ct. 363, 62 L.Ed.2d 275 (1979), and *Regents of the University of California* v. *Bakke,* 438 U.S. 265, 98 S.Ct. 2733, 57 L.Ed.2d 750 (1978). We are not convinced, however, that either case did so.

In *Bakke,* the question was whether a state school could properly adopt an admissions policy clearly intended to prefer minorities. It is true, as WMC notes, that five justices expressed reservations in *Bakke* about the holding in *Lau*. In the opinion written by Justice Brennan, in which Justices White, Marshall, and Blackmun joined, it was said, "[W]e have serious doubts concerning the correctness of what appears to be the premise of [*Lau*]." 438 U.S. at 352, 98 S.Ct. at 2779.

The issue did not have to be resolved, however, becuase "even accepting *Lau's* implication that impact alone is in some contexts sufficient to establish a prima facie violation of Title VI, contrary to our view that Title VI's definition of racial discrimination is absolutely coextensive with the Constitution's, this would not assist the respondent in the least." 438 U.S. at 352–53, 98 S.Ct. at 2779. It did not matter, the group wrote, whether Title VI proscribed some acts, such as those at issue in *Lau,* that would survive constitutional scrutiny. As the group read the legislative history of the Civil Rights Act, Congress did not intend to proscribe the particular type of practice challenged by *Bakke*—preferences designed to remedy past discrimination. As stated in another portion of the opinion, "*[A]pplied to the case before us,* Title VI goes no further in prohibiting the use of race than the Equal Protection Clause of the Fourteenth Amendment itself." 438 U.S. at 325, 98 S.Ct. at 2766 (emphasis supplied).

In a separate opinion, Justice Powell used language that may be inconsistent with *Lau,* but he stopped short of advocating that the case be overruled. He wrote, "Title VI must be held to proscribe only those racial classifications that would violate the Equal Protection Clause or the Fifth Amendment." 438 U.S. at 287, 98 S.Ct. at 2746. He then went on to distinguish *Lau,* saying significantly, "[T]he 'preference' approved [in *Lau*] did not result in the denial of the relevant benefit—'meaningful opportunity to participate in the educational program'—to anyone else." 438 U.S. at 304, 98 S.Ct. at 2755.

In determining what weight is to be given to these separate statements, it is important to recognize that the issue presented to the Court in *Bakke* differs substantially from that in the case at bar. It was clear in *Bakke* that whatever the reach of Title VI, the plaintiff had established a prima facie case by showing intentional discrimination. The question facing the Court, then, was whether some forms of intentional discrimination were nevertheless permissible. A majority of the Court concluded that those forms of intentional discrimination that would survive constitutional analysis also were exempt from Title VI. Congress, in enacting the Civil Rights Act of 1964, did not intend to prohibit those racial preferences that are permitted under the Constitution. It does not inexorably follow, however, that Congress also intended the constitutional standard to control every allegation of discrimination. It would be consistent with Congress's expansive, remedial intent to interpret Title VI as prohibiting acts that have the effect of discrimination yet permitting patent preferences designed to remedy past discrimination.

The Powell-Brennan opinions, therefore, may be read as expressing the theory that at least when the charge is intentional discrimination in the nature of a governmental preference, Title VI incorporates the constitutional standard. The case sub judice, however, is not one of a discriminatory governmental preference but one of a neutral program with disparate impact. As we see it, it is still permissible to hold that when the charge is disparate impact, a prima facie case can be established without proof of intent.

The other case on which defendant relies, *Board of Education* v. *Harris, supra,* held that § 702(b) of the Emergency School Aid Act (ESAA) prohibits school districts from maintaining racially identifiable faculties even when the segregation is unintentional. The Court upheld the power of Congress in the exercise of its authority under the spending clause to require the recipients of federal funds to go further in eliminating discrimination than mandated by the Constitution. *Lau* v. *Nichols* was not cited.

In dissent, Justice Stewart argued that since five justices in *Bakke* had stated Title VI prohibited only intentional discrimination, the same premise should govern claims under the ESAA. 444 U.S. at 160, 100 S.Ct. at 379. In this argument, however, he was joined only by Justice Powell. The majority expressly disclaimed any necessity to pass on the standard applicable to Title VI. *Id.* at 149, 100 S.Ct. at 373.

*Fullilove* v. *Klutznick,* 448 U.S. 448, 100 S.Ct. 2758, 65 L.Ed.2d 902 (1980), is another case that considered the constitutionality of a statutory preferential program. A plurality of the Court cited with approval *Lau's* validation of the HEW regulation proscribing actions "*which have the effect*" of discriminating. 448 U.S. at 479, 100 S.Ct. at 2775 (emphasis supplied by Court). Joining in the opinion were Justices White and Powell, who in *Bakke* had taken the position that intent was necessary to establish a Title VI violation.

Although there is ample ground for argument that the Supreme Court has doubts about *Lau's* continued viability, a requiem may be premature and, in any event, should not be sung by this choir. The prerogative of overruling its cases rests with the Supreme Court, and not with us. *Americans United for Separation of Church and State, Inc.* v. *HEW,* 619 F.2d 252, 271 (1980) (Weis, J., *dissenting*), *cert. granted, Valley Forge Christian College* v. *Americans United for Separation of Church and State, Inc.,* 450 U.S. 909, 101 S.Ct. 1345, 67 L.Ed.2d 332 (1981); *United States ex rel. Gockley* v. *Myers,* 450 F.2d 232 (3d Cir. 1971), *cert. denied,* 404 U.S. 1063, 92 S.Ct. 738, 30 L.Ed.2d 752 (1972).[7]

---

[7]*But see Cannon* v. *University of Chicago,* 648 F.2d 1164 (7th Cir. 1981), where it was held that disproportionate impact alone does not establish a violation of Title VI. In *Guardians Ass'n of New York City Police Dep't, Inc.* v. *Civil Service Commission,* 633 F.2d 232, 254 (2d Cir. 1980), a panel of the Court of Appeals for the Second Circuit concluded that only intentional discrimination is actionable under Title VI. An earlier panel of the same court disagreed, however, citing *Lau's* impact test as authority after *Bakke. Board of Education* v. *Califano,* 584 F.2d 576, 589 (2d Cir. 1978), *aff'd on other grounds, Board of Education* v. *Harris,* 444 U.S. 130, 100 S.Ct. 363, 62 L.Ed.2d 275 (1979). Still other panels have either acknowledged that *Bakke* did not expressly overrule *Lau, see Parent Ass'n of Andrew Jackson High School* v. *Ambach,* 598 F.2d 705, 716 (2d Cir. 1979), or have argued in dicta why an effects test probably retains validity. *See Bryan* v. *Koch,* 627 F.2d 612 (2d Cir. 1980).

The question is not one of congressional power but rather of intent. Providing federal funding conditioned on an even-handed application is a positive measure to discourage all forms of discrimination, intentional or not. The use of an effects test, therefore, is consistent with the legislative aim of eliminating discrimination and is in harmony with Title VII of the same Act, and Title VIII, *Resident Advisory Board* v. *Rizzo*, 565 F.2d 126 (3d Cir. 1977), *cert. denied*, 435 U.S. 908, 98 S.Ct. 1457, 55 L.Ed.2d 499 (1978), as well as our previous reference to Title VI in *Shannon* v. *United States Department of Housing & Urban Development*, 436 F.2d 809, 816, 820 (3d Cir. 1970) (Title VI provides redress for discriminatory effects of local housing plans). Moreover this approach parallels regulations adopted by HEW and other departments charged under § 602 of the Civil Rights Act, 42 U.S.C. § 2000d–1, with enforcing the statute.

With due deference to *Lau* v. *Nichols* and congressional intent as we perceive it, therefore, we conclude that plaintiffs in a Title VI case alleging discrimination in the application of federal funds in a facially neutral program need only establish disparate impact. The Rehabilitation Act and the Age Discrimination Act of 1975 provide equally strong cases for application of an impact test since both are patterned after Title VI. We therefore use the same standard.

## II

The next inquiry is whether, applying an effects test, the plaintiffs have established a prima facie case. Before addressing this issue, it is helpful to review the provisions of the agreement between WMC and HEW. Included in the early paragraphs is a statement that the Secretary of HEW desires assurances that operation of the hospital facilities under Plan Omega will be in compliance with Title VI and the Rehabilitation Act.

The agreement obligates WMC to provide free transportation between the Delaware and Southwest divisions, to designate an ombudsman to receive and act upon complaints of discrimination, to adopt a system of inpatient utilization control, and to prevent either division from becoming racially identifiable. It is additionally required that both divisions be operated on a unitary basis, with a single Board of Directors, Executive Committee, medical staff, teaching program and accounting procedure. Any proposed expansion of services at Southwest or reduction at Delaware must be first submitted to HEW for approval. WMC agreed to set aside $2,800,000 for use exclusively in renovating the Delaware facility. WMC also agreed to recognize the need for employment by minority groups, "including in particular urban minority groups." As noted earlier, the court found that WMC would carry out its categorical obligations under this agreement.

### A. The Handicapped

There is no evidence that either facility will not comply with the structural requirements of the Rehabilitation Act. Indeed, the provisions for handicapped with respect to barriers, entry, and free movement within the buildings will be an improvement over existing conditions. The alleged disparate impact upon the handicapped, therefore, rests upon the location of major portions of hospital services and jobs in the Southwest division. The plaintiffs produced no credible evidence, however, establishing the residential distribution of handicapped persons within the county. In the absence of such information, we cannot tell what effect, if any, Plan Omega will have upon disabled persons in the area, and thus agree with the district court that plaintiffs did not establish a prima facie case under § 504.

\* \* \*

NOTES

1. The court concludes that principles of "disparate impact" analysis applicable to other types of discrimination are directly transferable to analysis of discrimination on the basis of handicap. Are there any differences in regard to discrimination against handicapped people that argue against such a conclusion?

2. What are the implications of the court's Section 504 analysis to issues other than the location of hospitals? Should the standards announced by the court in the *NAACP* case be employed in all Section 504 cases?

## C. INFORMED CONSENT

### 2. Application to Handicapped Persons

#### b. Lifesaving or Life-Prolonging Measures

p. 792—ADD before the beginning of Subsection c the following note:

4. A similar factual situation as in *Lane* v. *Candura,* but with a different outcome, occurred in *In re Matter of Schiller,* 148 N.J.Super. 168, 372 A.2d 360 (1977), where a special guardian was appointed to give consent to the amputation of the gangrenous foot of a 67-year-old man found incapable of understanding his condition and, thus, of consenting to or refusing the needed surgery. The court discussed the State's interest in preserving life and the patient's interests in privacy and due process right to be heard, and concluded: "The right of the individual, then, is to have a determination that he or she can make the determination and, if not, to have some competent able person to make it in the best interests of the person." At 372 A.2d 366. How does this standard and delineation of responsibility compare with those in *Lane* v. *Candura* and in *Saikewicz?*

#### d. Electroconvulsive Therapy, Psychosurgery, and Nonconsensual Drug Therapy

p. 846—INSERT before the Additional Reading:

##### MILLS v. ROGERS

*Supreme Court of the United States, 1982*
____ U.S. ____, 102 S.Ct. 2442

Justice POWELL delivered the opinion of the Court.

The Court granted certiorari in this case to determine whether involuntarily committed mental patients have a constitutional right to refuse treatment with antipsychotic drugs.

I

This litigation began on April 27, 1975, when respondent Rubie Rogers and six other persons filed suit against various officials and staff of the May and Austin Units of the Boston State Hospital. The plaintiffs all were present or former mental patients at the institution. During their period of institutionalization all had been forced to accept unwanted treatment with antipsychotic drugs.[1] Alleging that forcible administration of these drugs violated rights protected by the Constitution of the United States, the plaintiffs—respondents here—sought compensatory and punitive damages and injunctive relief.[2]

The District Court certified the case as a class action. See *Rogers* v. *Okin*, 478 F.Supp. 1342, 1352 n.1 (D.Mass.1979). Although denying relief in damages, the court held that mental patients enjoy constitutionally protected liberty and privacy interests in deciding for themselves whether to submit to drug therapy.[3] The District Court found that an involuntary "commitment" provides no basis for an inference of legal "incompetency" to make this decision under Massachusetts law. *Id.*, at 1361–1362.[4] Until a judicial finding of incompetency has been made, the court con-

---

[1]As used in-this litigation, the term "antipsychotic drugs" refers to medications such as Thorazine, Mellaril, Prolixin and Haldol that are used in treating psychoses, especially schizophrenia. See *Rogers* v. *Okin*, 478 F.Supp. 1342, 1359–1360 (D.Mass.1979), aff'd in part and reversed in part, 634 F.2d 650, 653 (CA1 1980). Sometimes called "major tranquilizers," these compounds were introduced into psychiatry in the early 1950s. See Cole & Davis, *Antipsychotic Drugs,* in 2 A. Freeman, H. Kaplan, and B. Sadock, Comprehensive Textbook of Psychiatry II, at 1921–1922 (2d ed. 1975). It is not disputed that such drugs are "mind-altering." Their effectiveness resides in their capacity to achieve such effects. Citing authorities, petitioners assert that such drugs are essential not only in the treatment of individual disorders, but also in the preservation of institutional order generally needed for effective therapy. See Brief for Petitioners 17–41, 54–100. Respondents dispute this claim, also with support from medical authorities. Respondents also emphasize that antipsychotic drugs carry a significant risk of adverse side effects. These include such neurological syndromes as parkinsonisms, characterized by mask-like face, retarded volitional movements, and tremors; akathisia, a clinical term for restlessness; dystonic reactions, including grimacing and muscle spasms; and tardive dyskinesia, a disease characterized in its mild form by involuntary muscle movements, especially around the mouth. Tardive dyskinesia can be even more disabling in its more severe forms. See *Rogers* v. *Okin, supra*, 478 F.Supp., at 1360; *Byck, Drugs and the Treatment of Psychiatric Disorders*, in L. Goodman and A. Gilman, The Pharmalogical Basis of Therapeutics 169 (2d ed. 1975).

[2]The respondents also presented constitutional and statutory challenges to a hospital policy of secluding patients against their will. 478 F.Supp., at 1352. Their complaint additionally asserted claims for damages under state tort law. *Id.*, at 1352, 1383. The District Court held that state law prevented seclusion except where necessary to prevent violence. See *id.*, at 1371, 1374. Neither this decision, nor the denial of relief on the damages claims, is in issue before this Court.

[3]The District Court characterized liberty to make "the intimate decision whether to accept or refuse [antipsychotic] medication" as "basic to any right of privacy" and therefore protected by the Constitution. See 478 F.Supp., at 1366. The court did not derive this right from any particular constitutional provision, although it did observe that the "concept of a right of privacy . . . embodies First Amendment concerns." *Ibid.* In relying on the First Amendment the court reasoned that "the power to produce ideas is fundamental to our cherished right to communicate and is entitled to comparable constitutional protection." *Id.*, at 1367.

[4]Under the common law of torts, the right to refuse any medical treatment emerged from the doctrines of trespass and battery, which were applied to unauthorized touchings by a physician. See, *e.g.*, *Superintendent of Belchertown Hospital* v. *Saikewicz*, 373 Mass. 728, 738–739, 370 N.E.2d 417, 424 (1977); W. Prosser, Torts § 18 (4th ed. 1971). In this case the petitioners had argued—as they continue to argue—that the judicial committment proceedings conducted under Massachusetts law, Mass.Gen.Laws Ann. ch. 123 (1979), provide a determination of incompetency sufficient to warrant the State in providing treatment over the objections of the patient. In rejecting this argument as a matter of state law, the District

cluded, the wishes of the patients generally must be respected. *Id.*, at 1365–1368. Even when a state court has rendered a determination of incompetency, the District Court found that the patient's right to make treatment decisions is not forfeited, but must be exercised on his behalf by a court-appointed guardian. *Id.*, at 1364. Without consent either by the patient or his guardian, the court held, the patient's liberty interests may be overridden only in an emergency.[5]

The Court of Appeals for the First Circuit affirmed in part and reversed in part. *Rogers* v. *Okin*, 634 F.2d 650 (1980). It agreed that mental patients have a constitutionally protected interest in deciding for themselves whether to undergo treatment with antipsychotic drugs. *Id.*, at 653.[6] It also accepted the trial court's conclusion that Massachusetts law recognizes involuntarily committed persons as presumptively competent to assert this interest on their own behalf. See *id.*, at 657–659. The Court of Appeals reached different conclusions, however, as to the circumstances under which state interests might override the liberty interests of the patient.

The Court of Appeals found that the State has two interests that must be weighed against the liberty interests asserted by the patient: a police power interest in maintaining order within the institution and in preventing violence, see 634 F.2d, at 655, and a *parens patriae* interest in alleviating the sufferings of mental illness and in providing effective treatment, see 634 F.2d, at 657. The court held that the State, under its police powers, may administer medication forcibly only upon a determination that "the need to prevent violence in a particular situation outweighs the possibility of harm to the medicated individual" and that "reasonable alternatives to the administration of antipsychotics [have been] ruled out." 634 F.2d, at 656. Criticizing the District Court for imposing what it regarded as a more rigid standard, the Court of Appeals held that a hospital's professional staff must have substantial discretion in deciding when an impending emergency requires involuntary medication. The Court of Appeals reserved to the District Court, on remand, the task of developing mechanisms to ensure that staff

---

Court relied principally on the language of the relevant Massachusetts statutes and on the regulations of the Department of Mental Health. See 478 F.Supp., at 1359, 1361 (citing Department of Mental Health Regulation § 221.02 ("No person shall be deprived of the right to manage his affairs . . . solely by reason of his admission or commitment to a facility except where there has been an adjudication that such person is incompetent"), and Mass.Gen.Laws Ann. ch. 123, § 25 ("No person shall be deemed to be incompetent to manage his affairs . . . solely by reason of his admission or commitment in any capacity. . . .")). The court also appears to have engaged in independent fact-finding leading to the same conclusion: "The weight of the evidence persuades this court that, although committed mental patients do suffer at least some impairment of their relationship to reality, most are able to appreciate the benefits, risks, and discomfort that may reasonably be expected from receiving psychotropic medication." 478 F.Supp., at 1361.

[5]The District Court defined an emergency as a situation in which failure to medicate "would result in a substantial likelihood of physical harm to th[e] patient, other patients, or to staff members of the institution." 478 F.Supp., at 1365.

[6]The Court of Appeals termed it "intuitively obvious" that "a person has a constitutionally protected interest in being left free by the state to decide for himself whether to submit to the serious and potentially harmful medical treatment that is represented by the administration of antipsychotic drugs." 634 F.2d, at 653. Although the Court of Appeals found that the "precise textual source in the Constitution for the protection of this interests is unclear," *ibid.*, it concluded that "a source in the Due Process Clause of the Fourteenth Amendment for the protection of this interest exists, most likely as part of the penumbral right to privacy, bodily integrity, or personal security." *Ibid.* The Court of Appeals found it unnecessary to examine the conclusion of the District Court that First Amendment interests also were implicated.

decisions under the "police power" standard accord adequate procedural protection to "the interests of the patients."[8]

With respect to the State's *parens patriae* powers, the Court of Appeals accepted the District Court's state law distinction between patients who have and patients who have not been adjudicated incompetent. Where a patient has not been found judicially to be "incompetent" to make treatment decisions under Massachusetts law,[9] the court ruled that the *parens patriae* interest will justify involuntary medication only when necessary to prevent further deterioration in the patient's mental health. See 634 F.2d, at 660. The Court of Appeals reversed the District Court's conclusion that a guardian must be appointed to make non-emergency treatment decisions on behalf of incompetent patients. Even for incompetent patients, however, it ruled that the State's *parens patriae* interest would justify prescription only of such treatment as would be accepted voluntarily by "the individual himself . . . were he competent" to decide. *Id.*, at 661.[10] The Court of Appeals held that the patient's interest in avoiding undesired drug treatment generally must be protected procedurally by a judicial determination of "incompetency." If such a determination were made, further on-the-scene procedures still would be required before antipsychotic drugs could be administered forcibly in a particular instance *Id.*, at 661.

Because the judgment of the Court of Appeals involved constitutional issues of potentially broad significance,[13] we granted certiorari. ____ U.S. ____, 101 S.Ct. 1972, 68 L.Ed.2d 293 (1982).

II

A

The principal question on which we granted certiorari is whether an involuntarily committed mental patient has a constitutional right to refuse treatment with

---

[8]It asserted, apparently as a minimum, that "the determination that medication is necessary must be made by a qualified physician as to each individual patient to be medicated." 634 F.2d, at 656.

[9]A number of other States also distinguish between the standards governing involuntary commitment and those applying to determinations of incompetency to make treatment decisions. For a survey as of December 1, 1977, see Plotkin, *Limiting the Therapeutic Orgy: Mental Patients' Right to Refuse Treatment*, 72 Nw.U.L.Rev. 461, 504–525 (1977). The Court of Appeals for the Second Circuit has held that civil commitment does not raise even a presumption of incompetence. See *Winters* v. *Miller*, 446 F.2d 65 (1971).

[10]In imposing this "substituted judgment" standard the Court of Appeals appears to have viewed its holding as mandated by the Federal Constitution. See *ibid.* ("In so holding, we do not imply that the Constitution. . . .). But it followed its ultimate substantive conclusion with a citation to a Massachusetts case: "*Cf. Superintendant of Belchertown* v. *Saikewicz*," 373 Mass. 728, 370 N.E.2d 417 (1977). *Saikewicz* held that a court must apply the "substituted judgment" standard in determining whether to approve painful medical treatment for a profoundly retarded man incapable of giving informed consent. In *Saikewicz* the Massachusetts Supreme Judicial Court appears to have relied on both the Federal Constitution and the law of Massachusetts to support its decision. See *id.*, at 738–741, 370 N.E.2d, at 424–425. But the Massachusetts court characterized its analysis as having identified a "constitutional right of privacy," *id.*, at 739, 370 N.E.2d, at 426, thus creating some doubts as to the extent that the decision had an independent state law basis.

[13]Constitutional questions involving the rights of committed mental patients to refuse antipsychotic drugs have been presented in other recent cases, including *Rennie* v. *Klein*, 653 F.2d 836 (CA3 1980), and *Davis* v. *Hubbard*, 506 F.Supp. 915 (D.Ohio 1980). On the issues raised, see generally Plotkin, *supra;* Shapiro, *Legislating the Control of Behavior Control: Autonomy and the Coercive Use of Organic Therapies*, 47 S.Cal.L.Rev. 237 (1974).

antipsychotic drugs. This question has both substantive and procedural aspects. See 634 F.2d, at 656, 661; *Rennie* v. *Klein*, 653 F.2d 836, 841 (CA3 1980). The parties agree that the Constitution recognizes a liberty interest in avoiding the unwanted administration of antipsychotic drugs.[15] Assuming that they are correct in this respect, the substantive issue involves a definition of that protected constitutional interest, as well as identification of the conditions under which competing state interests might outweigh it. See *Youngberg* v. *Romeo*, ___ U.S. ___, ___–___, 102 S.Ct. 2452, 2460–2461, 72 L.Ed.2d ___; *Bell* v. *Wolfish*, 441 U.S. 520, 560, 99 S.Ct. 1861, 1885, 60 L.Ed.2d 447 (1979); *Roe* v. *Wade*, 410 U.S. 113, 147–154, 93 S.Ct. 705, 724, 727, 35 L.Ed.2d 147 (1973); *Jacobson* v. *Massachusetts*, 197 U.S. 11, 25–27 (1905). The procedural issue concerns the minimum procedures required by the Constitution for determining that the individual's liberty interest actually is outweighed in a particular instance. See *Parham* v. *J.R.*, 442 U.S. 584, 606, 99 S.Ct. 2493, 2506, 61 L.Ed.2d 101 (1979); *Mathews* v. *Eldridge*, 424 U.S. 319, 335, 96 S.Ct. 893, 903, 47 L.Ed.2d 18 (1976).

As a practical matter both the substantive and procedural issues are intertwined with questions of state law. In theory a court might be able to define the scope of a patient's federally protected liberty interest without reference to state law.[16] Having done so, it then might proceed to adjudicate the procedural protection required by the Due Process Clause for the federal interest alone. Cf. *Vitek* v. *Jones*, 445 U.S. 480, 491–494, 100 S.Ct. 1254, 1262–1264, 63 L.Ed.2d 552 (1980). For purposes of determining actual rights and obligations, however, questions of state law cannot be avoided. Within our federal system the substantive rights provided by the Federal Constitution define only a minimum. State law may recognize liberty interests more extensive than those independently protected by the Federal Constitution. See *Greenholtz* v. *Nebraska Penal Inmates*, 442 U.S. 1, 7, 12, 99 S.Ct. 2100, 2106, 60 L.Ed.2d 668 (1979); *Oregon* v. *Hass*, 420 U.S. 714, 719, 95 S.Ct. 1215, 1219, 43 L.Ed.2d 570 (1975); see also Brennan, *State Constitutions and the Protection of Individual Rights*, 90 Harv.L.Rev. 489 (1977). If so, the broader state protections would define the actual substantive rights possessed by a person living within that State.

Where a State creates liberty interests broader than those protected directly by the Federal Constitution, the procedures mandated to protect the federal substantive interests also might fail to determine the actual procedural rights and duties of persons within the State. Because state-created liberty interests are entitled to the protection of the federal Due Process Clause, see, *e.g., Vitek* v. *Jones, supra*, 445 U.S. at 488, 100 S.Ct. at 1261; *Greenholtz* v. *Nebraska Penal Inmates, supra*, 442 U.S. at 7, 99 S.Ct., at 2103, the full scope of a patient's due process rights may depend in part on the

---

[15]In this Court petitioners appear to concede that involuntarily committed mental patients have a constitutional interest in freedom from bodily invasion, see Brief for Petitioners at 43–47, but they deny that this interest is "fundamental." They also assert that it is outweighed in an appropriate balancing test by compelling state interests in administering antipsychotic drugs. *Id.*, at 54–68.

[16]As do the parties, we assume for purposes of this discussion that involuntarily committed mental patients do retain liberty interests protected directly by the Constitution, cf. *O'Connor* v. *Donaldson*, 422 U.S. 563, 95 S.Ct. 2486, 45 L.Ed.2d 396 (1975), and that these interests are implicated by the involuntary administration of antipsychotic drugs. Only "assuming" the existence of such interests, we of course intimate no view as to the weight of such interests in comparison with possible countervailing state interests.

substantive liberty interests created by state as well as federal law. Moreover, a State may confer *procedural* protections of liberty interests that extend beyond those minimally required by the Constitution of the United States. If a State does so, the minimal requirements of the Federal Constitution would not be controlling, and would not need to be identified in order to determine the legal rights and duties of persons within that State.

## B

Roughly five months after the Court of Appeals decided this case, and shortly after this Court granted certiorari, the Supreme Judicial Court of Massachusetts announced its decision in *In the Matter of Guardianship of Richard Roe, III,* ___ Mass. ___, 421 N.E.2d 40 (1981) (*"Roe III"*). *Roe III* involved the right of a noninstitutionalized but mentally incompetent person to refuse treatment with antipsychotic drugs. Expressly resting its decision on the common law of Massachusetts as well as on the Federal Constitution, Massachusetts' highest court held in *Roe III* that a person has a protected liberty interest in " 'decid[ing] for himself whether to submit to the serious and potentially harmful medical treatment that is represented by the administration of antipsychotic drugs.' " ___ Mass., at ___, 421 N.E.2d, at 51 n.9.[18] The court found—again apparently on the basis of the common law of Massachusetts as well as the Constitution of the United States—that this interest of the individual is of such importance that it can be overcome only by "an overwhelming State interest." *Id.,* at ___, 421 N.E.2d, at 51. *Roe III* further held that a person does not forfeit his protected liberty interest by virtue of becoming incompetent, but rather remains entitled to have his "substituted judgment" exercised on his behalf. *Ibid.* Defining this "substituted judgment" as one for which "[n]o medical expertise is required," *id.,* at ___, 421 N.E.2d, at 52, the Massachusetts Supreme Judicial Court required a *judicial* determination of substituted judgment before drugs could be administered in a particular instance,[19] except possibly in cases of medical emergency.

---

[18]Although the Massachusetts court quoted this formulation from the decision of the Court of Appeal in *Mills* v. *Rogers, supra,* 634 F.2d, at 653, the quotation is used to define the right, rather than to identify its legal source. *Roe III* noted that *Mills* v. *Rogers* found the source of this right in the Due Process Clause of the Fourteenth Amendment. The court continued its discussion by stating its reliance on three bases, two of them not cited in *Mills* v. *Rogers:* the "inherent power of the court to prevent mistakes or abuses by guardians, whose authority comes from the Commonwealth," and the "common law" right of persons to decide what will be done with their bodies. ___ Mass., at ___, 421 N.E.2d, at 51, n. 9.

[19]See *ibid.:* "The determination of what the incompetent individual would do if competent will probe the incompetent individual's values and preferences, and such an inquiry, in a case involving antipsychotic drugs [and a noninstitutionalized but incompetent patient], is best made in courts of competent jurisdiction." Having held that a "ward possesses but is incapable of exercising personally" the right to refuse antipsychotic drugs, the Massachusetts Supreme Court viewed the "primary dispute" as over "who ought to exercise this right on behalf of the ward." *Id.,* at ___, 421 N.E.2d, at 51. The Supreme Judicial Court in *Roe III* identified six "relevant" but "not exclusive" factors that should guide the decisions of the lower courts: "(1) the ward's expressed preferences regarding treatment; (2) his religious beliefs; (3) the impact upon the ward's family; (4) the probability of adverse side effects; (5) the consequences if treatment is refused; and (6) the prognosis with treatment." *Id.,* at ___, 421 N.E.2d, at 57. It emphasized that the determination "must 'give the fullest possible expression to the character and circumstances' " of the individual patient and that "this is a subjective rather than an objective determination." *Id.,* at ___, 421 N.E.2d, at 56 (citation omitted).

## C

The Massachusetts Supreme Court stated that its decision was limited to cases involving *noninstitutionalized* mental patients. See ____ Mass., at ____, 421 N.E.2d, at 42, 55, 61–62.[21] Nonetheless, respondents have argued in this Court that *Roe III* may influence the correct disposition of the case at hand. We agree.

Especially in the wake of *Roe III*, it is distinctly possible that Massachusetts recognizes liberty interests of persons adjudged incompetent that are broader than those protected directly by the Constitution of the United States. Compare *Roe III, supra,* ____ Mass., at ____, 421 N.E.2d, at 51 (protected liberty interest in avoiding unwanted treatment continues even when a person becomes incompetent and creates a right of incompetents to have their "substituted judgment" determined) with *Addington* v. *Texas,* 441 U.S. 418, 429–430, 99 S.Ct. 1804, 1811, 60 L.Ed.2d 323 (1979) (because a person "who is suffering from a debilitating mental illness" is not "wholly at liberty," and because the complexities of psychiatric diagnosis "render certainties virtually beyond reach," "practical considerations" may require "a compromise between what it is possible to prove and what protects the rights of the individual"). If the state interest is broader, the *substantive* protection that the Constitution affords against the involuntary administration of antipsychotic drugs would not determine the actual substantive rights and duties of persons in the State of Massachusetts.

Procedurally, it also is quite possible that a Massachusetts court, as a matter of state law, would require greater protection of relevant liberty interests than the minimum adequate to survive scrutiny under the Due Process Clause. Compare *Roe III, supra,* ____ Mass., at ____, 421 N.E.2d, at 51 ("We have . . . stated our preference for judicial resolution of certain legal issues arising from proposed extraordinary medical treatment. . . .") with *Youngberg* v. *Romeo,* ____ U.S. at ____, 102 S.Ct. at 2461 ("[T]here certainly is no reason to think judges or juries are better qualified than appropriate professionals in making [treatment] decisions."), and with *Parham* v. *J.R., supra,* 442 U.S., at 608 n.16, 99 S.Ct., at 2507 (Courts must not "unduly burden[] the legitimate efforts of the States to deal with difficult social problems. The judicial model for fact-finding for all constitutionally protected interests, regardless of their nature, can turn rational decisionmaking into an unmanageable enterprise.").[23] Again on this hypothesis state law would be dispositive of the procedural rights and duties of the parties to this case.

Finally, even if state procedural law itself remains unchanged by *Roe III,* the

---

[21]But cf. *id.,* at ____, 421 N.E.2d, at 50 ("because of the likelihood of . . . the necessity of making similar determinations in other cases, we establish guidelines regarding the criteria to be used and the procedures to be followed in making a substituted judgment determination"), and at ____, 421 N.E.2d, at 62 ("We do not mean to imply that these [involuntarily committed] patients' rights are wholly unprotected or that their circumstances are entirely dissimilar to those we have discussed. We do, suggest, however, that it would be imprudent to establish prematurely the relative importance of adverse interests. . . .").

[23]Even prior to *Roe III,* the Court of Appeals concluded that Massachusetts state law, which it construed as requiring *judicial* determinations of incompetency separate from involuntary commitment proceedings, see 634 F.2d, at 658–659, "in many respects . . . goes well beyond the minimum requirements mandated by the Fourteenth Amendment," *id.,* at 659 (footnote omitted). *Roe III* now has taken the further step of requiring *judicial* procedure in every instance in which a guardian believes drug therapy necessary for a noninstitutionalized incompetent.

federally mandated procedures will depend on the nature and weight of the *state* interests, as well as the individual interests, that are asserted. To identify the nature and scope of state interests that are to be balanced against an individual's liberty interests, this Court may look to state law. See, *e.g., Roe* v. *Wade,* 410 U.S. 113, 148 and n.42, 151 and nn.48–50, 93 S.Ct. 705, 724, 726, 35 L.Ed.2d 147 (1973); *Ingraham* v. *Wright,* 430 U.S. 651, 661–663, 97 S.Ct. 1401, 1407–1408, 51 L.Ed.2d 711 (1977). Here we view the underlying state law predicate for weighing asserted state interests as being put into doubt, if not altered, by *Roe III*.[24]

## D

It is unclear on the record presented whether respondents, in the District Court, did or did not argue the existence of "substantive" state law liberty interests as a basis for their claim to procedural protection under the federal Due Process Clause, or whether they may have claimed state law procedural protections for substantive federal interests. In their brief in this Court, however, respondents clearly assert state law arguments as alternative grounds for affirming both the "substantive" and "procedural" decisions of the Court of Appeals. See Brief for Respondents, esp. at 61, 71–72, 92–95.

Until certain questions have been answered, we think it would be inappropriate for us to attempt to weigh or even to identify relevant liberty interests that might be derived directly from the Constitution, independently of state law. It is this Court's settled policy to avoid unnecessary decisions of constitutional issues. See, *e.g., City of Mesquite* v. *Aladdin's Castle,* ____ U.S. ____, ____, 102 S.Ct. 1070, 1077, 71 L.Ed.2d 152 (1982); *New York Transit Authority* v. *Beazer,* 440 U.S. 568, 582–583 n.22, 99 S.Ct. 1355, 1364, 59 L.Ed.2d 587 (1979); *Poe* v. *Ullman,* 367 U.S. 497, 502–509, 81 S.Ct. 1752, 1755–1759, 6 L.Ed.2d 989 (1961); *Ashwander* v. *Tennessee Valley Authority,* 297 U.S. 288, 341, 347–348, 56 S.Ct. 466, 483, 80 L.Ed. 688 (1936) (Brandeis, J., concurring). This policy is supported, although not always required, by the prohibition against advisory opinions. Cf. *United States* v. *Hastings,* 296 U.S. 188, 193, 56 S.Ct. 218, 220 80 L.Ed. 148 (1935) (review of one basis for a decision supported by another basis not subject to examination would represent "an expression of abstract opinion").

In applying this policy of restraint, we are uncertain here which if any constitutional issues now must be decided to resolve the controversy between the parties. In the wake of *Roe III*, we cannot say with confidence that adjudication based solely on identification of federal constitutional interests would determine the actual rights and duties of the parties before us. And, as an additional cause for hesitation, our reading of the opinion of the Court of Appeals has left us in doubt as to the extent of which state issues were argued below and the degree to which the court's holdings may rest on subsequently altered state law foundations.

---

[24]In *Roe III* the Massachusetts court explicitly considered the implicated state interests, see ____ Mass., at ____, 421 N.E.2d, at 59, and concluded that the trial judge had erred in finding that the State had a "vital" *parens patriae* interest in "seeing that its residents function at the maximum level of their capacity," *ibid.* The Court of Appeals in this case had found and weighed a *parens patriae* interest. 634 F.2d, at 657–661.

Because of its greater familiarity both with the record and with Massachusetts law, the Court of Appeals is better situated than we to determine how *Roe III* may have changed the law of Massachusetts and how any changes may affect this case. Accordingly, we think it appropriate for the Court of Appeals to determine in the first instance whether *Roe III* requires revision of its holdings or whether it may call for the certification of potentially dispositive state law questions to the Supreme Judicial Court of Massachusetts, see *Bellotti* v. *Baird*, 428 U.S. 132, 150–151, 96 S.Ct. 2857, 2867–2868, 49 L.Ed.2d 844 (1976). The Court of Appeals also may consider whether this is a case in which abstention now is appropriate. See generally *Colorado River Water Conservation Dist.* v. *United States*, 424 U.S. 800, 813–819, 96 S.Ct. 1236, 1244–1247, 47 L.Ed.2d 483 (1976).

The judgment of the Court of Appeals is therefore vacated and the case is remanded for further proceedings consistent with this opinion.

*So ordered.*

NOTES

1. How much indication is given in the opinion of the Supreme Court's view as to whether or not there are constitutional liberty interests at stake?

2. The issue avoided by the Court in *Mills* v. *Rogers*—the federal constitutional rights of mental patients in regard to the refusal of medication—was addressed in the case of *Rennie* v. *Klein*, 653 F.2d 836 (3d Cir., 1981), cited in passing in the *Mills* v. *Rogers* opinion. In *Rennie*, the Court of Appeals found that there were not any state law restrictions on the administration of compulsory medication to involuntarily committed mental patients. Thus, the court was forced to face the federal constitutional issues sidestepped in *Mills* v. *Rogers*. The *Rennie* court rejected the argument that involuntary commitment takes away all aspects of a person's liberty rights:

> The record convinces us that there is a difference of constitutional significance between simple involuntary confinement to a mental institution and commitment combined with enforced administration of antipsychotic drugs. It implicates the "right to be free from, and to obtain judicial relief for, unjustified intrusions on personal security." *Ingraham* v. *Wright*, 430 U.S. 651, 673, 97 S.Ct. 1401, 1413, 51 L.Ed.2d 711 (1977). This intrusion rises to the level of a liberty interest warranting the protection of the due process clause of the fourteenth amendment. At 653 F.2d 844.

The court also ruled that the state is constitutionally required to use the "least intrusive means" in treating confined patients. *Id.* at 846–847. The court ruled, however, that these liberty interests could be adequately protected for due process purposes by a system of medical investigation, team reviews, and administrative procedures, that did not require any independent, adversarial hearing, as had been ordered by the district court. *Id.* at 848–851.

## IN RE GUARDIANSHIP OF ROE, III

*Supreme Judicial Court of Massachusetts, 1981*
____ *Mass.* ____, *421 N.E.2d 40*

Before HENNESSEY, C.J., and BRAUCHER, WILKINS, LIACOS and ABRAMS, JJ.
HENNESSEY, Chief Justice.

The ultimate question we address in this case is whether the guardian of a mentally ill person possesses the inherent authority to consent to the forcible administration of antipsychotic medication to his noninstitutionalized ward in the absence of an emergency. We conclude that, absent emergency, antipsychotic medication may be administered forcibly to a ward only when ordered by a judge in accordance with the principles articulated herein. This result is mandated by both constitutional and common law principles. In reaching this conclusion, we note that our decision has distinct limits. As we discuss at length in Part III, *infra*, the guidelines we establish herein are applicable in circumstances in which all of the following factors exist: (1) an incompetent individual is not institutionalized; (2) a party with standing actually seeks to administer medication to the incompetent person in the absence of an emergency, which we define as an unforeseen combination of circumstances or the resulting state that calls for immediate action; and (3) the proposed medication is an antipsychotic drug—a powerful, mind-altering drug which is accompanied by often severe and sometimes irreversible adverse side effects. As a preliminary question, we decide that the appropriate standard of proof to be applied in guardianship proceedings is the usual civil "preponderance of the evidence" standard, and that the appointment of both a temporary and a permanent guardian was warranted under the circumstances of this case. We vacate so much of the order as authorizes the guardian to consent to the forcible administration of anti-psychotic medication and affirm the remainder of the order which appoints Richard Roe, Jr., as guardian of his son, Richard Roe, III.

On April 1, 1980, after a hearing on the petition of Richard Roe, Jr. (the guardian), and his wife, a judge of the Probate Court found that the guardian's son, Richard Roe, III (the ward), was a mentally ill person whose judgment was seriously impaired and who was in need of the immediate appointment of a guardian. At this hearing the ward was represented by a guardian ad litem. The judge appointed the father temporary guardian of the ward, who, since February 19, 1980, had been committed to Northampton State Hospital for observation and report in connection with complaints against him for attempted unarmed robbery and assault and battery. Since the ward was still institutionalized at the time of the hearing, the judge, relying on *Rogers* v. *Okin*, 478 F.Supp. 1342 (D.Mass.1979) (*Rogers I*), aff'd in part, rev'd in part, 634 F.2d 650 (1st Cir. 1980) (*Rogers II*), cert. granted, ____ U.S. ____, 101 S.Ct. 1972, 68 L.Ed.2d 293 (1981), decided that the temporary guardian had the inherent authority to consent to forcible administration of antipsychotic drugs for his ward. On April 4, 1980, prior to the implementation of such medical treatment, the guardian ad litem's motion to stay entry of judgment was allowed by the probate judge for ten days as to the administration of antipsychotic drugs. On April 11, 1980, a single justice of this court continued the stay pending further review.

On May 27 and June 19, 1980, evidentiary hearings on the temporary guardian's petition for appointment as permanent guardian were held in the Probate Court before the same judge. The Commissioner of the Massachusetts Department of Mental Health, represented by the Attorney General, was allowed to intervene in both the Probate Court and this court. On July 30, 1980, the probate judge appointed the temporary guardian to be permanent guardian, stating in his order that upon the vacating of the stay issued by the single justice the permanent guardian would have the authority to consent to the forcible administration of antipsychotic medication to the ward.

In his appeal the guardian ad litem raises several issues. He first contends that the evidence was insufficient to permit the probate judge to make the findings which were used to support the appointments of both the temporary and permanent guardians, and that such evidence must be tested by the "beyond a reasonable doubt" standard of proof. He takes the further position that even if the evidence was sufficient to permit these findings, the challenged findings are insufficient as a matter of law to warrant the guardianship appointments. The guardian ad litem finally contends that even if the evidence was sufficient to support the findings, and the findings are sufficient to warrant the guardianship appointments, it was error for the probate judge to empower the guardian to consent to the forcible administration of antipsychotic drugs for the ward. For reasons we explain below, we hold that both the temporary and permanent guardianship appointments were warranted by the evidence as evaluated under the "preponderance of the evidence" standard of proof, and the findings were legally sufficient, although we agree with the guardian ad litem that to empower the guardian to consent to the challenged medical treatment was error.

[Part I of the court's opinion, in which it concludes that a "preponderance of the evidence" standard is applicable to guardianship proceedings, and that the appointment of a guardian was appropriate in the circumstances of this case, is omitted here.]

*II. The Decision to Administer Antipsychotic Drugs to the Ward*

We begin our discussion of the medical treatment decision by noting that we are directly presented with only one question. We must decide whether the substituted judgment determination to be made in cases such as this may be delegated to the guardian. The probate judge found that the guardian did *not* propose to authorize forcible administration of antipsychotic drugs[7] immediately but rather sought contingent authority to administer such drugs if certain anticipated events took place. Under these circumstances, the question presented by the guardian was hypothetical, and any substituted judgment determination made was premature.[8] However, the judge did in fact authorize the guardian to consent to administration of antipsychotic medication for the ward. We conclude that this was error. Strictly speaking, this conclusion is sufficient to dispose of this case. Nevertheless, because of the likelihood of further proceedings in this case and the necessity of making similar determinations in other cases, we establish guidelines regarding the criteria to be used and the procedures to be followed in making a substituted judgment determination. In Part A, below, we establish that a judicial determination of substituted judgment is to be made. In Part B, we

---

[7]Two drugs—Haldol (haloperidol) and Prolixin (fluphenazine)—were recommended for the ward. Although these drugs are occasionally referred to as "psychotropic" drugs, they are more accurately described as "antipsychotic" drugs. See note 10 *infra*.

[8]It was imprudent to make a determination in these circumstances. A substituted judgment determination may only be made upon direct application of a party with standing who actually seeks the administration of the medication. A premature decision will needlessly burden all involved and will make any substituted judgment determination less accurate. The determination will become more precise as it approaches the time at which it will be implemented because, for example, the ward's choice might change as his medical condition (and other circumstances) change.

identify those factors to be considered in reaching a substituted judgment determination. If the judge determines that the ward, if competent, would accept the medication, he is to order its administration. If the judge determines that the ward's substituted judgment would be to refuse treatment, we set forth in Part C those State interests which are capable of overwhelming the right to refuse antipsychotic medication. If the judge finds that there is a State interest sufficient to override the ward's choice to refuse treatment, but finds that the State interest can be satisfied by means other than forced medication, we then require in Part C(3) that the ward be afforded an extended substituted judgment determination in order to choose from among all acceptable and available means of satisfying the State interest.

### A.  Need for a Court Order

The primary dispute in this case concerns the means by which the ward is to exercise his right to refuse treatment, a right which the ward possesses but is incapable of exercising personally.[9] The guardian's position is that the power to exercise this right on behalf of the ward is vested in the guardian simply by virtue of his appointment as guardian. The ward claims that he is entitled to a judicial determination of substituted judgment. The question is, then, who ought to exercise this right on behalf of the ward? We think that this question is best resolved by requiring a judicial determination in accordance with the substituted judgment doctrine.

We have in the past stated our preference for judicial resolution of certain legal issues arising from proposed extraordinary medical treatment. *Superintendent of Belchertown State School* v. *Saikewicz*, 373 Mass. 728, 759, 370 N.E.2d 417 (1977). *Matter of Spring,* ____ Mass. ____, ____, 405 N.E.2d 115 (1980). See *Rogers* v. *Okin*, 634 F.2d 650, 660 (1st Cir. 1980) (*Rogers II*), cert. granted, ____ U.S. ____, 101 S.Ct. 1972, 68 L.Ed.2d 293 (1981). We reaffirm this preference in the circumstances shown here. While we are mindful that "[t]he judicial model for factfinding for all constitutionally protected interests, regardless of their nature, can turn rational decision-making into an unmanageable enterprise," *Parham* v. *J.R.,* 442 U.S. 584, 608 n.16, 99 S.Ct. 2493, 2507 n.16, 61 L.Ed.2d 101 (1979), the question presented today seems "to require the process of detached but passionate investigation and

---

[9]That such a right exists is indisputable. "[A] person has a constitutionally protected interest in being left free by the state to decide for himself whether to submit to the serious and potentially harmful medical treatment that is represented by the administration of antipsychotic drugs." *Rogers II, supra* at 653. The source of this right according to *Rogers II, supra,* lies in the "Due Process Clause of the Fourteenth Amendment . . . , most likely as part of the penumbral right to privacy, bodily integrity, or personal security." *Id.* Other courts have discussed in individual's First Amendment right to maintain the integrity of his mental processes. See *Scott* v. *Plante,* 532 F.2d 939, 946 (3d Cir. 1976); *Mackey* v. *Procunier,* 477 F.2d 877, 878 (9th Cir. 1973); *Rogers I, supra* at 1366–1367. We ground this right firmly in the constitutional right to privacy, which we have previously described as "an expression of the sanctity of individual free choice and self-determination as fundamental constituents of life." *Superintendent of Belchertown State School* v. *Saikewicz,* 373 Mass. 728, 742, 370 N.E.2d 417 (1977). We find support as well in the inherent power of the court to prevent mistakes or abuses by guardians, whose authority comes from the Commonwealth and the courts. *Buckingman* v. *Alden,* 315 Mass. 383, 389, 53 N.E.2d 101 (1944). *Chase* v. *Chase,* 216 Mass. 394, 397, 103 N.E. 857 (1914). *Hicks* v. *Chapman,* 10 Allen 463, 465 (1865). The third factor upon which we rely is the common law right of every person "of adult years and sound mind . . . to determine what shall be done with his own body." *Schloendorff* v. *Society of N.Y. Hosp.,* 211 N.Y. 125, 129, 105 N.E. 92 (1914) (Cardozo, J.). We have held that the incompetence of a ward does not allow his guardian to exercise vicariously this common law right regarding extraordinary treatment. *Saikewicz, supra.* Cf. G.L. c. 201, §§ 6, 6A; G.L. c. 111, § 70E(1).

decision that forms the ideal on which the judicial branch of government was created,'' *Saikewicz, supra.*

The question presented by the ward's refusal of antipsychotic drugs is only incidentally a medical question. Absent an overwhelming State interest, a competent individual has the right to refuse such treatment. To deny this right to persons who are incapable of exercising it personally is to degrade those whose disabilities make them wholly reliant on other, more fortunate, individuals. In order to accord proper respect to this basic right of all individuals, we feel that if an incompetent individual refuses antipsychotic drugs, those charged with his protection must seek a judicial determination of substituted judgment. No medical expertise is required in such an inquiry, although medical advice and opinion is to be used for the same purposes and sought to the same extent that the incompetent individual would, if he were competent. We emphasize that the determination is *not* what is medically in the ward's best interests—a determination better left to those with extensive medical training and experience. The determination of what the incompetent individual would do if competent will probe the incompetent individual's values and preferences, and such an inquiry, in a case involving antipsychotic drugs, is best made in courts of competent jurisdiction.

There is no bright line dividing those decisions which are (and ought to be) made by a guardian, from those for which a judicial determination is necessary. The tension which makes such a line so difficult to draw is apparent. There is an obvious need for broad, flexible, and responsive guardianship powers, but simultaneously there is a need to avoid the serious consequences accompanying a well-intentioned but mistaken exercise of those powers in making certain medical treatment decisions.

We have recently identified the factors to be taken into account in deciding when there must be a court order with respect to medical treatment of an incompetent patient. ''Among them are at least the following: the extent of impairment of the patient's mental faculties, whether the patient is in the custody of a State institution, the prognosis without the proposed treatment, the prognosis with the proposed treatment, the complexity, risk and novelty of the proposed treatment, its possible side effects, the patient's level of understanding and probable reaction, the urgency of decision, the consent of the patient, spouse, or guardian, the good faith of those who participate in the decision, the clarity of professional opinion as to what is good medical practice, the interests of third persons, and the administrative requirements of any institution involved.'' *Matter of Spring, supra* at ____–____, 405 N.E.2d 115. Without intending to indicate the relative importance of these and other factors in all cases, it is appropriate to identify some of those factors which are weighty considerations in this particular case. They are: (1) the intrusiveness of the proposed treatment, (2) the possibility of adverse side effects, (3) the absence of an emergency, (4) the nature and extent of prior judicial involvement, and (5) the likelihood of conflicting interests.

(1) *The intrusiveness of the purposed treatment.* We can identify few legitimate medical procedures which are more intrusive than the forcible injection of antipsychotic medication.[10] ''In general, the drugs influence chemical transmissions to the brain,

---

[10]The doctors who testified in the proceedings below used the terms psychotropic (''acting on the mind'') and antipsychotic (''tending to alleviate psychosis or psychotic states'') interchangeably. Webster's

affecting both activatory and inhibitory functions. Because the drugs' purpose is to reduce the level of psychotic thinking, it is virtually undisputed that they are mind-altering." *Rogers I, supra* at 1360. A single injection of Haldol, one of the antipsychotic drugs proposed in this case, can be effective for ten to fourteen days. The drugs are powerful enough to immobilize mind and body. Because of both the profound effect that these drugs have on the thought processes of an individual and the well-established likelihood of severe and irreversible adverse side effects, see Part II A(2) *infra*, we treat these drugs in the same manner we would treat psychosurgery or electroconvulsive therapy. Compare Plotkin, Limiting the Therapeutic Orgy: Mental Patients' Right to Refuse Treatment, 72 Nw.U.L.Rev. 461, 466–474 (1977), with *id.* at 474–479. Additionally, "clinicians have encountered great difficulty in scientifically predicting a particular individual's response to a particular drug, and the results frequently appear paradoxical or idiosyncratic." *Id.* at 474–475. The record in this case indicates that if the drugs were mistakenly administered to a nonpsychotic individual, then that individual might develop a "toxic psychosis," causing him to suffer symptoms of psychosis. While the actual physical invasion involved in the administration of these drugs amounts to no more than an injection, the impact of the chemicals upon the brain is sufficient to undermine the foundations of personality.

While antipsychotic drugs can actually lessen the amount and intensity of psychotic thinking, among the most important reasons for their continued use is to control behavior.[11] Plotkin, *supra* at 478. "[T]hese drugs have been intentionally used

---

New Collegiate Dictionary, at 50, 924 (1979). The distinction between the two terms has been subject to confusion in the past. See *Rogers II, supra* at 653 n.1. The specific drugs recommended in this case, Prolixin (fluphenazine) and Haldol (haloperidol), are both classed as "major tranquilizers" or "neuroleptics." Plotkin, Limiting the Therapeutic Orgy: Mental Patients' Right to Refuse Treatment, 72 Nw.U.L.Rev. 461, 474 n.75 and n.77 (1977). See generally Physicians' Desk Reference 1116–1118, 1728–1733 (35th ed. 1981). Their use is characterized by "(1) marked sedation, without sleep; (2) effectiveness in the most intensely agitated and excited patient; (3) progressive disappearance of symptoms in acute and chronic psychoses; (4) extra-pyramidal reaction; and (5) subcortical site of action." Plotkin, *supra* at 474 n.75. We refer to these drugs as "antipsychotic" drugs, "a more generally accepted and less confusing designation than other terminology." American College of Neuropsychopharmacology-Food and Drug Administration Task Force, Neurologic Syndromes Associated with Antipsychotic Drug Use, 289 New England J. Med. 20, 20 (1973).

[11]The obvious potential for misuse of these drugs provides an additional reason to require judicial approval prior to the forcible use of antipsychotic drugs upon incompetent individuals. Another court, which in the past has not required court orders regarding the termination of life support equipment, now requires a court order before administration of treatment which had been "subject to abuse in the past." *In re Grady*, 85 N.J. 235, 252, 426 A.2d 467, 475 (1981). Compare *In re Quinlan*, 70 N.J. 10, 355 A.2d 647, cert. denied sub nom. *Garger v. New Jersey*, 429 U.S. 922, 97 S.Ct. 319, 50 L.Ed.2d 289 (1976), with *In re Grady, supra*. Commentators and courts have identified abuses of antipsychotic medication by those claiming to act in an incompetent's best interests. See Plotkin, *supra;* Baldessarini & Lipinski, Risks vs. Benefits of Antipsychotic Drugs, 289 New England J. Med. 427 (1973); Comment, Advances in Mental Health: A Case for the Right to Refuse Treatment, 48 Temple L.Q. 354, 364 (1975). See also *Mackey v. Procunier*, 477 F.2d 877 (9th Cir. 1973); *Rennie v. Klein*, 476 F.Supp. 1294 (D.N.J.1979); *Pena v. New York State Div. for Youth*, 419 F.Supp. 203, 207 (S.D.N.Y. 1976); *Nelson v. Heyne*, 355 F.Supp. 451, 455 (N.D.Ind.1972), aff'd 491 F.2d 352 (7th Cir.), cert. denied, 417 U.S. 976, 94 S.Ct. 3183, 41 L.Ed.2d 1146 (1974).

The Supreme Court of New Jersey reasoned that a court "must ensure that the law does not allow abuse to continue." *In re Grady, supra*. We agree. The power of the State—and those empowered to act by the State—to administer mind-altering medication must be carefully circumscribed by guidelines and closely scrutinized for abuse. "Whatever powers the Constitution has granted our government, involuntary mind control is not one of them, absent extraordinary circumstances." *Rogers I, supra* at 1367.

for disciplinary purposes, and they have been unintentionally misused as a result of either ignorance or inadequate resources. While psychotropic drugs may play a significant role in the treatment of psychiatric disorders, there is no wisdom in permitting their continued indiscriminate use upon unconsenting persons or upon persons who are uninformed as to their potential consequences." *Id.* at 478–479.

(2) *The possibility of adverse side effects.* Although, as we establish above, the intended effects of antipsychotic drugs are extreme, their unintended effects are frequently devastating and often irreversible. The adverse side effects accompanying administration of antipsychotic drugs have been known since the late 1950's. Baldessarini & Lapinski, Risks vs. Benefits of Antipsychotic Drugs, 289 New England J. Med. 427, 428 (1973). " '[T]oxic' effects regularly accompany the use of antipsychotic drugs to ameliorate schizophrenic symptoms. The most common results are the temporary, muscular side effects (extra-pyramidal symptoms) which disappear when the drug is terminated; dystonic reactions (muscle spasms, especially in the eyes, neck, face, and arms; irregular flexing, writhing or grimacing movements; protrusion of the tongue); akathesia (inability to stay still, restlessness, agitation); and Parkinsonisms (mask-like face, drooling, muscle stiffness and rigidity, shuffling gait, tremors). Additionally, there are numerous other nonmuscular effects, including drowsiness, weakness, weight gain, dizziness, fainting, low blood pressure, dry mouth, blurred vision, loss of sexual desire, frigidity, apathy, depression, constipation, diarrhea, and changes in the blood. Infrequent but serious, nonmuscular side effects, such as skin rash and skin discoloration, ocular changes, cardiovascular changes, and occasionally, sudden death, have also been documented.

"The most serious threat phenothiazines [one type of antipsychotic drug] pose to a patient's health is a condition known as tardive dyskinesia. This effect went unrecognized for years because its symptoms are often not manifested until late in the course of treatment, sometimes appearing after discontinuation of the drug causing the condition. Tardive dyskinesia is characterized by involuntary muscle movements, often in the oral region. The associated rhythmic movements of the lips and tongue (often mimicking normal chewing, blowing, or licking motions) may be grotesque and socially objectionable, resulting in considerable shame and embarrassment to the victim and his or her family. Additionally, hypertrophy of the tongue and ulcerations of the mouth may occur, speech may become incomprehensible, and, in extreme cases, swallowing and breathing may become difficult. To date, tardive dyskinesia has resisted curative efforts, and its disabling manifestations may persist for years.

"There is little doubt that prolonged administration of psychoactive drugs plays a major role in the development of tardive dyskinesia. Individual susceptibility to the condition depends upon a variety of factors including increasing age, sex, and the existence of organic brain syndromes" (footnotes omitted). Plotkin, *supra* at 475–477. Commentators and courts have found that antipsychotic drugs are high-risk treatment.[12] "Tardive dyskinesia is the most important complication of long-term neu-

---

[12]We admit the possibility and express the hope that future medical advances may produce antipsychotic drugs free from the severe adverse side effects we have described above. At the same time, it must be noted that the intended effect of the medication—to alter mental processes—by definition cannot be eliminated from those drugs we have described as "antipsychotic." Nevertheless, we do not foreclose reconsideration of these issues when and if it can be shown that the characteristics of antipsychotic drugs have changed.

roleptic use. What was initially thought to be a rare clinical curiosity has become a significant public health hazard.'' Jeste & Wyatt Changing Epidemiology of Tardive Dyskinesia: An Overview, 138 Am.J.Psych. 297, 297 (1981). "[T]he risks of iatrogenically produced chronic neurologic disability are alarming.'' Baldessarini & Lipinski, *supra* at 428. See generally Jeste & Wyatt, *supra;* American College of Neuropsychopharmacology-Food and Drug Administration Task Force, Neurologic Syndromes Associated with Antipsychotic-Drug Use, 289 New England J. Med. 20 (1973); Crane, Tardive Dyskinesia in Patients Treated with Major Neuroleptics: A Review of the Literature, 124 Am.J.Psych. 40 (Feb. Supp. 1968). See also *Scott v. Plante,* 532 F.2d 939, 945 n.8 (3d Cir. 1976); *Rogers I, supra* at 1360; *Rennie v. Klein,* 462 F.Supp. 1131, 1136–1138 (D.N.J.1978); *In re Boyd,* 403 A.2d 744, 752 (D.C.App.1979).

(3) *The absence of an emergency.* The evidence presented in the proceedings below makes it quite clear that the probate judge was not presented with a situation which could accurately be described as an emergency. We accept the dictionary definition of ''emergency'': ''an unforeseen combination of circumstances or the resulting state that calls for immediate action.'' Webster's Third New Int'l Dictionary, at 741 (1961). Medical evidence showed that the ward apparently had been schizophrenic for four years, without more than slight or temporary improvement, and that without treatment his mental health could deteriorate. Expert testimony indicated that the prognosis for most individuals with untreated schizophrenia was ''gradual worsening.'' In an attempt to elicit an individual prognosis, counsel for the guardian posed a significant question to the expert. ''[I]s there a point in time, Doctor, where the failure to initiate treatment by drug therapy would result in [the ward's] condition being substantially impaired or irreparably impaired in terms of bringing any treatment to him that would help him?'' The doctor responded, ''Well, the longer one waits, the more chance there is of the condition becoming chronic.'' No follow-up questions were asked. We think that the possibility that the ward's schizophrenia might deteriorate into a chronic irreversible condition at an uncertain but relatively distant date does not satisfy our definition of emergency, especially where, as here, the course of the illness is measured by years and no crisis has been precipitated. Cf. *Rogers II, supra* at 654; *Rogers I, supra* at 1364.

We are not called upon here to decide under which circumstances an emergency might relieve a guardian from the obligation of seeking a judicial determination of substituted judgment which would otherwise be required. We do, however, emphasize that in determining whether an emergency exists in terms of requiring ''immediate action,'' the relevant time period to be examined begins when the claimed emergency arises, and ends when the individual who seeks to act in the emergency could, with reasonable diligence, obtain judicial review of his proposed actions. This time period will, of course, be brief—as we noted in *Matter of Spring, supra* at ___, 405 N.E.2d 115, ''expedited decision can be obtained when appropriate.'' We recognize that ''the interests of the patient himself would [not] be furthered by requiring responsible [parties] to stand by and watch him slip into possibly chronic illness while awaiting an adjudication.'' *Rogers II, supra* at 660. However, the evidence shows that this is not such a case—in fact, unless the course of a disease is measured by hours, there need never be such a case in the courts of this Commonwealth. We are certain that every judge recognizes that in any case where there is a possibility of immediate, substantial, and irreversible deterioration of a serious mental illness, even the smallest of avoidable delays would be intolerable.

(4) *The nature and extent of prior judicial involvement.* For the past four years the ward has rejected antipsychotic medication on every occasion on which it has been offered, and there has been no judicial finding of incapacity relative to many of these occasions. It is possible that in some cases, although not in the instant case, a mentally ill ward may retain sufficient competence to make treatment decisions himself, thereby eliminating the need for a substituted judgment determination. It has been held that patients involuntarily committed to State mental hospitals are entitled to a judicial determination of incapacity before they may be forcibly medicated with mind-altering drugs.[14] *Rogers II, supra,* at 661. This is because the "commitment decision itself is an inadequate predicate to the forcible administration of drugs to an individual where the purported justification for that action is the State's *parens patriae* power." *Id.* at 659. Cf. *Boyd* v. *Board of Registrars of Voters of Belchertown,* 368 Mass. 631, 635–636, 334 N.E.2d 629 (1975) ("profound" distinction between commitment and determination of incompetency). A person is presumed to be competent unless shown by the evidence not to be competent.[15] *Lane* v. *Candura,* 6 Mass. App. 377, ____, 376 N.E.2d 1232 (1978). Similarly, in the absence of an independent finding of incompetency to make treatment decisions, we cannot assume that a mentally ill ward lacks the capacity to make a treatment decision of this magnitude. Cf. *In re Grady,* 85 N.J. 235, 265, 426 A.2d 467 (1981).

In a case such as the one before us, some judicial involvement is unavoidable inasmuch as the judge must: (1) appoint the guardian, and (2) determine the ward's competency to make treatment decisions. This significant and inescapable prior judicial involvement eliminates much concern we might otherwise have about requiring a further judicial determination, since one of the factors we consider in deciding whether the guardian is to make the substituted judgment determination is the amount of additional time which will be needed to obtain a judicial determination. While this prior involvement is not conclusive in and of itself, it is a factor to be considered in determining whether a court order must be obtained.

(5) *The likelihood of conflicting interests.* Decisions such as the one the guardian wishes to make in this case pose exceedingly difficult problems for even the most capable, detached, and diligent decisionmaker. We intend no criticism of the guardian when we say that few parents could make this substituted judgment determination—by its nature a self-centered determination in which the decisionmaker is called upon to ignore all but the implementation of the values and preferences of the ward–when the ward, in his present condition, is living at home with other children. Cf. *Matter of Spring,* ____ Mass. ____, ____ n.3 (1980), 405 N.E.2d 115 (1980); *In re Grady, supra,* 85 N.J. at 252, 426 A.2d 467. Nor do we think that the father was not a suitable

---

[14]We express no opinion concerning whether such a finding is sufficient judicial involvement to permit other persons to make subsequent medical treatment decisions for involuntarily committed patients.

[15]This presumption continues even while the person is committed to a public or private institution. G.L. c. 123, § 25.

person to be appointed guardian. Those characteristics laudable in a parent might often be a substantial handicap to a guardian faced with such a decision but who might in all other circumstances be an excellent guardian. Cf. *Ruby* v. *Massey*, 452 F.Supp. 361, 365 n.15 (D.Conn.1978). A judicial determination also benefits the guardian, who otherwise might suffer from lingering doubts concerning the propriety of his decision.

Each individual involved, when called upon to participate in the substituted judgment determination, is assisting in the attempt to determine the ward's values and preferences. The guardian will usually play a major role in this process. The formalities and discipline inherent in a judicial determination will impress upon all involved the need for objectivity and selflessness. We are convinced that in this case, as in other cases, the regularity of the procedure—guaranteed by a judicial determination—will ensure that objectivity which other processes might lack.

*B.  Relevant Factors in the Substituted Judgment Determination*

The immediate question confronting us is resolved by our conclusion that, when a timely determination needs to be made, it is to be made by a judge. However, because of the likelihood that a proper determination will be sought by these or other parties in the future, we set forth below guidelines to be followed in order to ensure accuracy and consistency in proceedings in the Probate Court.

The factors we identify below are to be considered by the probate judge in order to identify the choice "which would be made by the incompetent person, if that person were competent, but taking into account the present and future incompetency of the individual as one of the factors which would necessarily enter into the decision-making process of the competent person." *Superintendent of Belchertown State School* v. *Saikewicz*, 373 Mass. 728, 752–753, 370 N.E.2d 417 (1977). The determination must "give the fullest possible expression to the character and circumstances of that individual." *Id.* at 747, 370 N.E.2d 417. We observe that this is a subjective rather than an objective determination.[16] Cf. *id.* at 746–747, 370 N.E.2d 417. All persons involved in such an inquiry will readily admit that the bounds of relevance therefor are exceedingly broad. In this search, procedural intricacies and technical niceties must yield to the need to know the actual values and preferences of the ward. In this spirit we briefly identify the following relevant factors, cautioning that they are not exclusive, recognizing that certain of them may not exist in all cases, and declining to establish their relative weights in any individual case. They are: (1) the ward's expressed preferences regarding treatment; (2) his religious beliefs; (3) the impact upon the ward's family; (4) the probability of adverse side effects; (5) the consequences if treatment is refused; and (6) the prognosis with treatment.

---

[16]It has been suggested that the substituted judgment determination as it has been formulated in our cases "is only a 'legal fiction' when used for never-competent persons, because it is impossible to ascertain what such persons think is in their own best interests." *Swazey, Treatment and Nontreatment Decisions: In whose Best Interests?, in Dilemmas of Dying 95, 96–97 (C. Wong and J. Swazey, eds. 1981). However, the fact that in such an unfortunate case the substituted judgment doctrine is so difficult to apply provides inadequate justification for denying its benefits in those cases wherein it is more feasible to utilize the doctrine. Cf. Saikewicz, supra,* at 750–751 n. 15, 753–755, 370 N.E.2d 417. "While it may thus be necessary to rely to a greater degree on objective criteria . . . the effort to bring the substituted judgment into step with the values and desires of the affected individual must not, and need not, be abandoned." *Id.* at 751, 370 N.E.2d 417.

(1) *The ward's expressed preferences regarding treatment.* If the ward has expressed a preference while not subjected to guardianship—and presumably competent, *Lane* v. *Candura, supra,* at ____, 376 N.E.2d 1232,—such an expression is entitled to great weight in determining his substituted judgment unless the judge finds that either: (a) simultaneously with his expression of preference the ward lacked the capacity to make such a medical treatment decision, or (b) the ward, upon reflection and reconsideration, would not act in accordance with his previously expressed preference in the changed circumstances in which he currently finds himself. Cf. *In re Boyd,* 403 A.2d 744, 751 (D.C.App.1979).

Even if the ward lacks capacity to make treatment decisions, his stated preference is entitled to serious consideration as a factor in the substituted judgment determination. "Although [the ward] failed to understand his mental condition and his need for treatment, we think his stated preference must be treated as a critical factor in the determination of his 'best interests.'" *Doe* v. *Doe,* 377 Mass. 272, 279, 385 N.E.2d 995 (1979). This respect for the ward's preference and the reasons for this deference have long been recognized in our cases. "A man may be insane so as to be a fit subject for guardianship, and yet have a sensible opinion and strong feeling upon the question who that guardian shall be. And that opinion and feeling it would be the duty as well as the pleasure of the court anxiously to consult, as the happiness of the ward and his restoration to health might depend upon it." *Allis* v. *Morton,* 4 Gray 63, 64 (1855).

(2) *The ward's religious beliefs.* An individual might choose to refuse treatment if the acceptance of such treatment would be contrary to his religious beliefs. If such a reason is proffered by or on behalf of an incompetent, the judge must evaluate it in the same manner and for the same purposes as any other reason: the question to be addressed is whether certain tenets or practices of the incompetent's faith would cause him individually to reject the specific course of treatment proposed for him in his present circumstances. We adopt the approach taken by the court in *In re Boyd,* 403 A.2d 744 (D.C.App.1979). In *Boyd* the court detailed the spectrum of tenacity with which an individual may adhere to religious beliefs and practices, and identified various factors to be considered in determining whether an individual would act consistently with previously held beliefs under unexpected circumstances. *Id.* at 751–752. Compare Developments in the Law—Civil Commitment of the Mentally Ill, 87 Harv.L.Rev. 1190, 1218 n.95 (1974). While in some cases an individual's beliefs may be so absolute and unequivocal as to be conclusive in the substituted judgment determination, in other cases religious practices may be only a relatively small part of the aggregated considerations.

(3) *The impact upon the ward's family.* An individual who is part of a closely knit family would doubtless take into account the impact his acceptance or refusal of treatment would likely have on his family. Such a factor is likewise to be considered in determining the probable wishes of one who is incapable of formulating or expressing them himself. In any choice between proposed treatments which entail grossly different expenditures of time or money by the incompetent's family, it would be appropriate to consider whether a factor in the incompetent's decision would have been the desire to minimize the burden on his family. If this factor would have been considered by the individual, the judge must enter it into the balance of making the substituted judgment

determination. If an incompetent has enjoyed close family relationships and subsequently is forced to choose between two treatments, one of which will allow him to live at home with his family and the other of which will require the relative isolation of an institution, then the judge must weigh in his determination the affection and assistance offered by the incompetent's family. We note, however, that the judge must be careful to avoid examination of these factors in any manner other than one actually designed and intended to effectuate the incompetent's right to self-determination. As we discuss fully in Part C, *infra*, if there are no overriding State interests,[17] then the values and preferences of any institutions or persons other than the incompetent are irrelevant except in so far as they would affect his choice.

(4) *The probability of adverse side effects.* We have described the adverse side effects of antipsychotic medication in Part IIA(2), *supra*. Clearly any competent patient choosing whether to accept such treatment would consider the severity of these side effects, the probability that they would occur, and the circumstances in which they would be endured. The judge must also consider these factors in arriving at a determination of substituted judgment on behalf of an incompetent. *Saikewicz, supra* at 753–755, 370 N.E.2d 417.

(5) *The consequences if treatment is refused.* If the prognosis without treatment is that an individual's health will steadily, inevitably and irreversibly deteriorate, then that person will, in most circumstances, more readily consent to treatment which he might refuse if the prognosis were more favorable or less certain. This general rule, however, will not always indicate whether an individual would, if competent, accept treatment. For example, in regard to the religious beliefs we discussed in Part II B(2), *supra*, "even in a life-or-death situation one's religion can dictate a 'best interest' antithetical to getting well." *In re Boyd, supra* at 750. This factor, as all the rest of the factors, must be utilized to reach an individual determination. While no judge need ignore the basic logic and common values which ordinarily underlie individual preference, he must reach beyond statistical factors and general rules to see "the complexities of the singular situation viewed from the unique perspective of the person called on to make the decision." *Saikewicz, supra* at 747, 370 N.E.2d 417.

(6) *The prognosis with treatment.* We think it can fairly be stated as a general proposition that the greater the likelihood that there will be cure or improvement,[18] the more likely an individual would be to submit to intrusive treatment accompanied by the possibility of adverse side effects. Additionally, professional opinion may not always be unanimous regarding the probability of specific benefits being received by a specific individual upon administration of a specific treatment. Both of these factors—the benefits sought and the degree of assurance that they actually will be received—are entitled to consideration.

Finally, the judge making the substituted judgment determination should ad-

---

[17]Preeminent among the State interests assertable in this context is the State's parens patriae responsibility to protect the interests of dependent children. We recognize that this State interest is capable of overwhelming the right of a patient to refuse medical treatment.

[18]The benefits obtainable from medical treatment today range from immediate and complete cure to only the retardation of accelerating deterioration. We recognize that in many unfortunate situations existing "cures" only prevent significant deterioration.

dress, in the following manner, each of the six factors we have described above, as well as any others relevant in the case before him. He is to make written findings for each factor indicating within each finding those reasons both for and against treatment. Cf. *Saikewicz, supra* at 733–735, 370 N.E.2d 417. Following this he must analyze the relative weight of the findings in that particular case. On this basis he is to conclude whether the substituted judgment of the incompetent would be to accept or reject treatment. If the determination is to accept treatment, the judge is to order its administration.[19] If the determination is to refuse treatment, the judge may order treatment only in accordance with the procedures we discuss in Part C, *infra*.

### C. The Accommodation of Overriding State Interests

There are circumstances in which the fundamental right to refuse extremely intrusive treatment must be subordinated to various State interests.

(1) *The State interests involved*. Among the State interests which we have identified in our prior cases are: "(1) the preservation of life; (2) the protection of the interests of innocent third parties; (3) the prevention of suicide; and (4) maintaining the ethical integrity of the medical profession." *Saikewicz, supra,* at 741, 370 N.E.2d 417. These four State interests are not exhaustive, and other State interests may also deserve consideration. For example, in *Commissioner of Correction* v. *Myers,* \_\_\_\_ Mass. \_\_\_\_, 399 N.E.2d 452 (1979), we held that the State's interest in orderly prison administration was a sufficient countervailing State interest to compel an inmate to submit to hemodialysis. *Id.* at \_\_\_\_–\_\_\_\_, 399 N.E.2d 452. The present case is unlike *Myers* in that the ward is not in custody of a State institution, and therefore those legitimate State concerns dealing with the preservation of institutional order and the maintenance of efficiency are not relevant here. Cf. *Commissioner of Correction* v. *Myers, supra; Rogers I, supra* at 1368–1371.

In the present case the judge found that the State had a vital interest in seeing that its residents function at the maximum level of their capacity and that this interest outweighed the rights of the individual. We disagree. While the State, in certain circumstances, might have a generalized parens patriae interest in removing obstacles to individual development, this general interest does not outweigh the fundamental individual rights here asserted.[20]

---

[19]In his order the judge may appropriately authorize a treatment program which utilizes various specifically identified medications administered over a prolonged period of time. In such a case, the order should provide for periodic review to determine if the ward's condition and circumstances have substantially changed. Any party with standing may seek modification of such an order at any reasonable time. Cf. *Rogers I, supra* at 1363.

[20]The factors which concerned the judge—the natural desire to prevent suffering and the need of each individual to maintain and improve his capabilities—are better viewed as likely foundations of individual preference to be considered in the substituted judgment determination. See Part II B(5), *supra*. Where the medical evidence, unchallenged at every turn and unimpeachable in its sincerity, shows that treatment will maintain or regain competence, this is a weighty factor to be considered by the judge as it would be considered by the affected individual. It is not conclusive, however. If the judge feels that the "best interests" of the ward demand one outcome but concludes that the ward's substituted judgment would require another, then, in the absence of an overriding State interest, the substituted judgment prevails. In short, if an individual would, if competent, make an unwise or foolish decision, the judge must respect that decision as long as he would accept the same decision if made by a competent individual in the same circumstances. Cf. *Lane* v. *Candura,* \_\_\_\_ Mass.App. \_\_\_\_, \_\_\_\_, 376 N.E.2d 1232 (1978) (Mass.App.Ct. Adv.Sh. [1978] 588, 595); *Custody of a Minor,* 377 Mass. 876, \_\_\_\_–\_\_\_\_, 389 N.E.2d

The preservation of life, "the most significant of the asserted State interests," *Saikewicz, supra* at 741, 370 N.E.2d 417, is not assertable in this case, as the proposed treatment is not intended to prolong life. There is no evidence that the ward is suicidal, nor is there evidence that medical ethics are seriously implicated. In the past we have interpreted the phrase "the protection of the interests of innocent third parties" as representing the State's interest in protecting minor children from the emotional and financial consequences of the decision of a competent adult to refuse life-saving or life-prolonging treatment.[21] *Id.* at 741–743, 370 N.E.2d 417. We have identified this as a State interest of considerable magnitude. Equally deserving of such regard is the State interest in preventing the infliction of violence upon members of the community by individuals suffering from severe mental illness. This is a second aspect of the State interest in protecting innocent third parties. Although few would question that this interest is capable of overriding the individual's right to refuse treatment, a substantial question remains as to the likelihood of violence which must be established in order to support forced administration of antipsychotic medication.

(2) *The standard of proof required to justify administration of antipsychotic drugs to an unconsenting, noninstitutionalized individual.* Once it is recognized that the State's interest in the prevention of violence is capable of overriding the individual's right to refuse, it must also be recognized that the character of the government intrusion then changes. The primary purpose of the treatment is not to implement the substituted judgment of the incompetent, nor is it intended to administer treatment thought to be in his best interests. It bears emphasis that public safety then becomes the primary justification for such treatment. Under these circumstances antipsychotic drugs function as chemical restraints forcibly imposed upon an unwilling individual who, if competent, would refuse such treatment. Examined in terms of personal liberty, such an infringement is at least the equal of involuntary commitment to a State hospital. Accordingly, we think that the same standard of proof is applicable in both involuntary commitment and involuntary medication proceedings.

In order to commit an individual to a State hospital without his consent, the likelihood of serious harm must be established beyond a reasonable doubt. *Superintendent of Worcester State Hosp.* v. *Hagberg*, 374 Mass. 271, 275–277, 372 N.E.2d 242 (1978). In G.L. c. 123, § 1, as amended through St.1980, c. 571, § 1 (the statute governing involuntary commitment), the likelihood of serious harm is defined as "(1) a substantial risk of physical harm to the person himself as manifested by evidence of threats of, or attempts at, suicide or serious bodily harm; (2) a substantial risk of physical harm to other persons as manifested by evidence of homicidal or other violent behavior or evidence that others are placed in reasonable fear of violent behavior and serious physical harm to them; or (3) a very substantial risk of physical

---

68 (1979) (Mass.Adv.Sh. [1979] 2124, 2140–2141). We digress concerning this "right to be wrong" only to establish the relationship between the "best interests" standard and the substituted judgment determination. "Extreme cases can be readily suggested. Ordinarily such cases are not safe guides in the administration of the law." *Jacobson* v. *Massachusetts,* 197 U.S. 11, 38, 25 S.Ct. 358, 366, 49 L.Ed. 643 (1905) (Harlan, J.)

[21]This particular aspect of the State interest is inapplicable in the instant case because the ward is unmarried and has no minor children.

impairment or injury to the person himself as manifested by evidence that such person's judgment is so affected that he is unable to protect himself in the community and that reasonable provision for his protection is not available in the community.'' Absent criminal conduct, this statutory definition establishes the earliest moment at which the State may intervene to deny an individual his liberty based upon a prediction of future harmfulness. The State may not justify its intervention on a lower standard merely because it proposes to utilize antipsychotic drugs rather than physical restraints.

(3) *The extended substituted judgment determination.* Since the standard of proof is the same for both involuntary commitment and involuntary administration of antipsychotic medication, in any case where the State's interest in preventing violence in the community has been found sufficient to override the individual's right to refuse treatment, two means are then available for protecting this State interest.[23] In such cases, that lesser intrusive means of restraint which adequately protects the public safety is to be used.[24] The right to the least intrusive means is derived from the right to privacy, which stands as a constitutional expression of the ''sanctity of individual free choice and self-determination as fundamental constitutents of life.'' *Saikewicz, supra* at 742, 370 N.E.2d 417. In order to satisfy the least intrusive means test, the incompetent is entitled to choose, by way of substituted judgment, between involuntary commitment and involuntary medication. Such an extended substituted judgment proceeding differs from the substituted judgment determination we describe in Part II B, *supra,* only in that the outcome is limited to involuntary commitment or involuntary medication.[25]

### III. The Limits of Our Decision

In this opinion we have established that a guardian may be appointed for an individual upon a showing that it is more likely than not that the individual is unable to care for himself by reason of mental illness. In addition we have held that, where no emergency exists, antipsychotic medication may be forcibly administered to a non-institutionalized individual only in accordance with a court order. We have set forth guidelines delineating the circumstances in which a judge is to direct the administration of such treatment. These circumstances are: (1) where a judicial substituted judgment determination indicates that the incompetent individual would, if competent, accept

---

[23]We do not mean to suggest that once an individual has been involuntarily committed he is then subject to involuntary medication because his potential harmfulness had been established by his commitment. We have defined the State interest here as the prevention of violence in the community. By ''community'' we mean those persons likely to encounter the mentally ill individual outside of an institutional setting. This State interest is extinguished when the individual is institutionalized. We do not address the question of whether and to what extent the State interest in *institutional* order and safety may be capable of overwhelming the right of an involuntarily committed individual to refuse medical treatment. Cf. *Baker* v. *Carr,* 369 U.S. 186, 204, 82 S.Ct. 691, 703, 7 L.Ed.2d 663 (1962); *Commissioner of Correction* v. *Myers,* _____ Mass. _____, 399 N.E.2d 452 (1979) (Mass.Adv.Sh. [1979] 2523); *Rogers II, supra; Rogers I, supra.*

[24]We are unwilling to establish a universal rule as to which is less intrusive—involuntary commitment or involuntary medication with mind-altering drugs. Since we feel that such a determination must be individually made, we conclude that the lesser intrusive means is the means of restraint which would be chosen by the ward if he were competent to choose.

[25]We do not perceive any State interest here sufficient to override the incompetent's right to self-determination. Certainly the public safety provides no such interest since it is sufficiently protected by restricting the incompetent's options to these two alternatives.

antipsychotic drugs, or (2) where there exists a State interest of sufficient magnitude to override the individual's right to refuse. If the asserted State interest is the prevention of violent conduct by noninstitutionalized mentally ill individuals, then, upon a showing equivalent to that necessary to commit an individual against his will, the State is entitled to force the individual to choose, by way of substituted judgment, either involuntary commitment or medication with antipsychotic drugs.

While we emphasize those conclusions we have reached and the circumstances in which they are to be utilized, it is prudent to note that our guidelines are not directed toward a single case but rather identify the decisionmaking processes necessary to reach outcomes in a type of case. It is apparent from our decision today that the right of an individual to refuse treatment is not absolute but is, rather, a right to be counterbalanced against State interests. The proper balance to be struck in a given situation can only be determined after examining the specifically defined and precisely articulated interests of those who are or will be actually affected by the decision. The weight to be afforded these interests is impossible to predetermine, and the balance will vary according to the circumstances of those asserting the interests. For these reasons, we decline to strike the balance in any individual case. Specifically, we decline to rule on the right of patients confined against their will to State hospitals to refuse antipsychotic medication. We do not mean to imply that these patients' rights are wholly unprotected or that their circumstances are entirely dissimilar to those we have discussed. We do suggest, however, that it would be imprudent to establish prematurely the relative importance of adverse interests when each may be capable of being controlling and each draws its importance from the circumstances in which it is asserted.

The ward in this case, though institutionalized at the time the temporary guardian was appointed, is currently living at home and has done so for many months. Indeed, the two occasions on which he was institutionalized were for observation and report pursuant to G.L. c. 123, §§ 15(b) and 16(a), and were not involuntary civil commitments. The guardian cannot now institutionalize the ward unless he establishes beyond a reasonable doubt that failure to commit would create a likelihood of serious harm. *Doe* v. *Doe*, 377 Mass. 272, 385 N.E.2d 995 (1979). No antipsychotic medication has yet been administered to him.

In addition to observing that it would be improper to establish the extent to which persons other than a noninstitutionalized individual in a nonemergency situation are entitled to a judicial substituted judgment determination, we wish to emphasize as well that in this case we treat the ward's right to a determination only in so far as it concerns antipsychotic medication. The spectrum of medical care available to individuals and the diverse circumstances in which it may be administered do not permit us to make universal rules in anticipation of cases involving different treatment or different circumstances. Even when a medical treatment decision is confined to a single set of circumstances, it is often difficult to formulate and apply a uniform and predictable standard. Compare *Superintendent of Belchertown State School* v. *Saikewicz*, 373 Mass. 728, 370 N.E.2d 417 (1977), with *Matter of Dinnerstein*, 6 Mass.App. 466, 380 N.E.2d 134 (1978). See also *Matter of Spring*, ____ Mass. ____, ____, 405 N.E.2d 115 (1980).

Our guidelines make clear that if the guardian seasonably petitions the Probate Court for an order directing the administration of antipsychotic medication to the ward, then the petition should receive prompt and full consideration. Since no such request was before the probate judge, his order authorizing involuntary treatment was premature. We therefore vacate the order in so far as it allows the ward to be medicated over his objection. The remainder of the order, appointing Richard Roe, Jr., as guardian of his son, Richard Roe, III, is affirmed.

*So ordered.*

NOTES

1. In light of *Mills* v. *Rogers,* consider how much of the reasoning and procedures set out in *Roe* would be applicable to involuntarily committed persons. How much should the standards differ?

2. *In re Boyd,* 403 A.2d 744 (D.C.App. 1979), mentioned by the *Roe* court, raised the question of substituted judgment in an unusual context. It involved an adjudicated mentally ill woman who had become a Christian Scientist prior to her illness, and had voiced her objection to the use of any medication on religious grounds. The Court of Appeals ruled that such beliefs had to be taken into account in applying the substituted judgment analysis, and remanded the case for reconsideration. If the lower court were to find that Mrs. Boyd would have rejected the medication on religious grounds, then it must respect that decision, unless "a particular, 'compelling state interest' would justify overriding Mrs. Boyd's putative choice." *Id.* at 753.

# 9
# PROCREATION, MARRIAGE, AND RAISING CHILDREN

Robert L. Burgdorf Jr.

## SUMMARY OF DOCTRINAL DEVELOPMENTS

THERE HAVE NOT BEEN ANY IMPORTANT NEW DIRECTIONS in regard to the rights of handicapped persons to enter into marriage. However, significant judicial developments have occurred in regard to sterilization and parental rights. Several courts have found a *parens patriae* authority to order sterilization operations performed when proper procedures have been followed to ensure that sterilization is in the best interest of a legally incompetent handicapped person. And several judicial opinions have recognized and protected the rights of mentally and physically handicapped individuals to retain the custody of their children.

## A. PROCREATION

### 4. Modern Legal Approaches to the Sterilization of Handicapped Persons

#### b. In the Absence of a Statute

p. 904—ADD to the end of Note 4:
The decision in *Ruby* v. *Massey* is reported at 452 F.Supp. 361 (D.Conn. 1978).

#### c. Under *Parens Patriae*

p. 908—INSERT after the Notes:

### WENTZEL v. MONTGOMERY GENERAL HOSPITAL, INC.

*Court of Appeals of Maryland, 1982*
*447 A.2d 1244*

Argued before MURPHY, C. J., and SMITH, DIGGES, ELDRIDGE, COLE, DAVIDSON and RODOWSKY, J. J.

MURPHY, Chief Judge.

This case presents the question whether a trial court of general jurisdiction is empowered to grant a guardian's petition to sterilize an incompetent minor through the performance of a subtotal hysterectomy.

I

The child who is the subject of this litigation, Sonya Star Flanary, is a severely retarded 13-year-old with an I.Q. of about 25 to 30 (the equivalent of a mental age of 1 to 2 years), blind and with pronounced neurological problems. Sonya was born a normal child. At the age of 5 months, she was severely injured in an automobile accident, suffering brain and other physical damage. After an initial paralysis, Sonya's physical condition greatly improved but her mental development was seriously retarded. Unable to cope with the event, Sonya's mother took her to live with her grandmother, Nancy Wentzel, who is now 61 years old. Sonya, her two sisters, and Gail Sheppard, Sonya's aunt, have been living with Mrs. Wentzel since shortly after the accident. This case began when Mrs. Wentzel and Gail Sheppard, who together provide Sonya's principal care, sought the performance of a hysterectomy upon Sonya, which would terminate her menstrual cycle and result in her sterilization. The medical staff of Montgomery General Hospital refused to perform the operation without a court order authorizing the procedure. Consequently, Mrs. Wentzel and Ms. Sheppard filed a petition in the Circuit Court for Montgomery County, seeking appointment as Sonya's guardians with authority to consent to the proposed surgical procedure. The petition recited that Sonya "is currently in need of additional medical care (hysterectomy) and that the medical staff and petitioners request an Order of Court approving said medical procedure for therapeutic reasons."

Pursuant to Maryland Rule R76, the court appointed an attorney to represent Sonya and conducted an evidentiary hearing. The evidence disclosed that Sonya regularly attended a special school, although missing many sessions because of illness. It was established that Sonya had reached puberty and was experiencing pain connected with menstruation. It was shown that Sonya could not care for her most basic hygienic needs, that she would not wear sanitary napkins and was irritable and disoriented during the menstruation process. There was evidence showing that the guardianship petition was motivated by a sincere desire to free Sonya of the pain and other consequences suffered by her during menstruation and because of genuine concern that Sonya was an easy subject for rape and resulting pregnancy. Sonya's mother testified in support of the guardianship petition, stating that sterilization was in Sonya's best interest.

The petitioners produced testimony of a child psychiatrist who, although he had never treated Sonya and had only seen her twice, said that a subtotal hysterectomy would be in Sonya's best interest. The psychiatrist was unable to say, however, that such a procedure was necessary for Sonya's physical or mental health. On cross-examination, the witness admitted that Sonya would not be in any medical danger if the operation were not performed, and he also agreed that some pain and irritation connected with the menstrual cycle is normal. The psychiatrist agreed that no life threatening consequences would occur if Sonya were to have offspring and further that Sonya was perfectly capable of having a normal baby. The evidence disclosed that there was no reasonable expectation that Sonya's mental condition would improve.

It was argued that Maryland Code (1974, 1981 Cum.Supp.), § 13–708 of the Estates and Trusts Article empowered the court to grant the guardianship petition and to authorize the guardians to consent to the operation. Section 13–708, insofar as pertinent, provides:

> (a) The court may grant to a guardian of a person only those powers necessary to provide for the demonstrated need of the disabled person.
>
> (b) Subject to subsection (a) of this section, the rights, duties, and powers which the court may order include, but are not limited to:
>
> (1) The same rights, powers, and duties that a parent has with respect to an unemancipated minor child . . . :
>
> (2) . . .
>
> (3) The duty to provide for care, comfort, and maintenance, including social, recreational, and friendship requirements, and, if appropriate, for training and education of the disabled person;
>
> (4) . . .
>
> (5) . . .
>
> (6) If a guardian of the estate has been appointed, the duty to control the custody and care of the disabled person, . . . ;
>
> (7) . . .
>
> (8) The power to give necessary consent or approval for medical or other professional care, counsel, treatment, or service, except that the court must authorize any medical procedure that involves a substantial risk to life.

The trial judge (Bell, J.) found from the evidence that Sonya was totally lacking in capacity to consent to the operation; that "Sonya cannot care for herself, let alone a baby"; and that "Sonya's menstruation further burdens an already over-burdened family." The court noted the sincerity of the family's belief that the operation was in Sonya's best interest, and it also recognized the possibility that Sonya could become pregnant if sexually abused. The court observed that the psychiatrist did not testify that the operation was necessary for Sonya's medical health or that refusal to authorize it would cause such a mental hardship as would justify the surgery for therapeutic reasons. The court concluded that § 13–708 of the Estates and Trusts Article "could not be interpreted to provide a hysterectomy in a case such as Sonya's." It noted that "the alternative to the hysterectomy is not life threatening." The court said:

> In the absence of such statutory authority and guide lines, this Court cannot find that it has the authority to grant the relief sought.

The court appointed the petitioners as co-guardians of the person and property of Sonya but denied permission to consent to the hysterectomy. The guardians appealed to the Court of Special Appeals. We granted certiorari prior to decision by the Intermediate appellate court to consider the profound issues raised in the case.

II

The guardians claim that the lower court erroneously denied the petition on the ground that it was not empowered, absent express statutory authorization, to order sterilization unless for therapeutic reasons. They maintain that under § 13–708 of the Estates and Trusts Article the court, upon a showing of "demonstrated need," is authorized to approve the sterilization of a minor incompetent for nontherapeutic reasons. The guardians suggest that they have a duty under the statute to plan for the preservation and maintenance of the future well-being of their ward. The evidence in this case, they argue, substantiates the existence of a demonstrated need for the operation because Sonya is mentally and physically unable to care for her own physical needs due to her severe state of mental retardation. It is additionally argued that the medical evidence supports the conclusion that Sonya's sterilization "will preclude future negative trauma both physically and mentally, given the severity of Sonya's mental retardation and her low functioning levels and eliminate the possibility of pregnancy."

The guardians contend that Code (1980 Repl.Vol.) § 1–501 of the Courts and Judicial Proceedings Article confers upon a circuit court full equity powers in civil cases—powers which are not limited by the provisions of § 13–708 of the Estates and Trusts Article. Sterilization would be in Sonya's best interests, the guardians say, because Sonya is unable to communicate effectively with others; to understand or handle her own bodily functions; to know the difference between sexes, much less the needs of a potential child; and to understand the menstrual cycle or pregnancy. Moreover, the guardians point out that they are presently 61 and 33 years old, respectively, and that Sonya's life expectancy far exceeds their own. In these circumstances, it is contended that it is in the best interests of Sonya and those who assume responsibility for her care, both in the present and in the future, that Sonya be sterilized. The guardians maintain that acting under the *parens patriae* doctrine, equity courts have traditionally exercised their powers in the best interests of incompetent minors, and that accordingly the lower court should have granted their petition in order to preserve Sonya's physical and mental well-being. It is emphasized that should Sonya have a child, both she and the child will become wards of the State, if her family cannot care for both. It is argued that this will place a financial burden on the State, and it therefore has a compelling interest justifying granting the guardian's petition authorizing the giving of consent to Sonya's sterilization.

### III

A number of jurisdictions hold that in the absence of express legislative authorization, courts are totally devoid of subject matter jurisdiction to consider petitions seeking sterilization of incompetent minors. *See, e.g., Hudson* v. *Hudson,* 373 So.2d 310 (Ala. 1979); *Guardianship of Tulley,* 83 (Cal. App.3d 698, 146 Cal.Rptr. 266 (1978), *cert. denied,* 440 U.S. 967, 99 S.Ct. 1519, 59 L.Ed.2d 783 (1979); *Matter of S. C. E.,* 378 A.2d 144 (Del.Ch.1977); *A. L.* v. *G. R. H.,* 163 Ind.App. 636, 325 N.E.2d 501 (1975); *Holmes* v. *Powers,* 439 S.W.2d 579 (Ky. 1968); *In Interest of M. K. R.,* 515 S.W.2d 467 (Mo.1974) (en banc); *Frazier* v. *Levi,* 440 S.W.2d 393 (Tex.Civ.App.1969). These cases variously involve evidence of verifiable medical necessity and therapeutic need; likelihood of psychiatric harm absent sterilization; already existing retarded or illegitimate offspring; propensity to, or actually having engaged in sexual relations; and high probability of transmitting disabilities to any offspring. Regardless of the asserted need, these courts have denied sterilization, deferring on jurisdictional grounds to what they consider to be exclusively a legislative prerogative.

Other cases hold that trial courts of general jurisdiction, either by statute, the exercise of inherent equity powers, including application of the *parens patriae* doctrine, or the doctrine of substituted consent, have subject matter jurisdiction to grant petitions authorizing sterilization of incompetent persons in appropriate cases. Some of these cases, independent of statute, impose strict procedural and substantive safeguards upon the determination of such petitions. For example, in *Matter of C. D. M.*, 627 P.2d 607 (Alaska 1981), the parents of a 19-year-old mildly retarded female with Down's Syndrome filed a petition for her sterilization. By statute, guardians were authorized to "give any consents . . . that may be necessary to enable the ward to receive medical or other professional care." 627 P.2d at 612. The evidence showed a high probability that the child's offspring, if any, would be born with Down's Syndrome. Relying upon the equity powers vested in trial courts of general jurisdiction, which encompassed the *parens patriae* power over incompetents, the court concluded that the trial judge, contrary to his holding, had subject matter jurisdiction to act on the petition. However, it withheld approval of the operation because adequate safeguards had not been observed in the proceedings below. The court established the following minimum standards to govern the determination of a petition for sterilization of incompetent persons:

> (1) Those advocating sterilization bear the heavy burden of proving by clear and convincing evidence that sterilization is in the best interests of the incompetent;
> (2) The incompetent must be afforded a full judicial hearing at which medical testimony is presented and the incompetent, through a guardian *ad litem,* is allowed to present proof and cross-examine witnesses;
> (3) The trial judge must be assured that a comprehensive medical, psychological, and social evaluation is made of the incompetent;
> (4) The trial court must determine that the individual is legally incompetent to make a decision whether to be sterilized and that this incapacity is in all likelihood permanent;
> (5) The incompetent must be capable of reproduction and unable to care for the offspring;
> (6) Sterilization must be the only practicable means of contraception;
> (7) The proposed operation must be the least restrictive alternative available;
> (8) To the extent possible, the trial court must hear testimony from the incompetent concerning his or her understanding and desire, if any, for the proposed operation and its consequences, and finally,
> (9) The court must examine the motivation behind the petition. *Id.* at 612–13.

The Supreme Court of Washington reached similar conclusions in *Matter of Guardianship of Hayes,* 93 Wash. 228, 608 P.2d 635 (1980) (en banc). It reversed the judgment of the trial court which had declined to authorize the sterilization of a 16-year-old severely retarded female on the ground of lack of subject matter jurisdiction. In that case, it was shown that the relevant guardianship statute neither authorized nor prohibited sterilization procedures at a guardian's request. The child's mother had petitioned for sterilization because she believed that her daughter was sexually active and because she was concerned about the long-term effects of conventional birth control methods. The court in *Hayes* decried the refusal of other courts to decide this type of case due to an alleged lack of jurisdiction, terming these holdings an "abdication of the judicial function." *Id.* 608 P.2d at 637. It held that a statute was not required to empower the trial court to exercise its jurisdiction, because that power was vested in the court under the state's constitution. The court was unwilling, however, to *sua sponte* approve an order of sterilization absent compliance with most of the safeguards outlined in *Matter of C.D.M.*, *supra*, to which it added a requirement that it be shown by clear, cogent, and convincing evidence that the current state of scientific and medical knowledge does not suggest either (a) that a reversible procedure or other less drastic contraceptive method will shortly be available, or (b) that science is on the threshold of an advance in treatment of the individual's disability. *Id.* 608 P.2d at 641. Furthermore, the court stated that the heavy presumption against sterilization will be even more difficult to overcome in the case of an incompetent minor, whose youth may "make it difficult or impossible to prove by clear and convincing evidence that he or she will never be capable of making an informed judgment about sterilization or of caring for a child." *Id.* The court expressed the belief that only in rare cases would sterilization be in the best interests of the retarded person.

In the case of *In Re Grady*, 85 N.J. 235, 426 A.2d 467 (1981), the parents of 19-year-old Lee Ann, a mentally retarded woman with Down's Syndrome, sought a court order authorizing the performance of a tubal ligation. Lee Ann had been taking birth control pills for four years but her parents wanted her to become less dependent on their supervision. The court attempted to reconcile the conflict between Lee Ann's diverse privacy rights—her right to bodily integrity and to be free from sterilization on the one hand, and on the other, her "right" to be sterilized, *id.* 426 A.2d at 471–73, citing *Griswold* v. *Connecticut*, 381 U.S. 479, 85 S.Ct. 1678, 14 L.Ed.2d 510 (1965); *Eisenstadt* v. *Baird*, 405 U.S. 438, 92 S.Ct. 1029, 31 L.Ed.2d 349 (1972); *Carey* v. *Population Services Int'l*, 431 U.S. 678, 97 S.Ct. 2010, 52 L.Ed.2d 675 (1977); *Planned Parenthood of Missouri* v. *Danforth*, 428 U.S. 52, 96 S.Ct. 2831, 49 L.Ed.2d 788 (1976); *Doe* v. *Bolton*, 410 U.S. 179, 93 S.Ct. 739, 35 L.Ed.2d 201 (1973); *Roe* v. *Wade*, 410 U.S. 113, 93 S.Ct. 705, 35 L.Ed.2d 147 (1973). Stating that courts which decline to assume jurisdiction do not reflect "adequate sensitivity to the constitutional rights of the incompetent person," the New Jersey court resolved the conflict in favor of Lee Ann's "right" to be sterilized, premising its decision on the doctrines of *parens patriae* and substituted consent, citing *In re Quinlan*, 70 N.J. 10, 355, A.2d 647, *cert. denied*, 429 U.S. 922, 97 S.Ct. 319, 50 L.Ed.2d 289 (1976) (court authorized parents of a comatose 22-year-old to consent to removal of extraordinary artificial life support apparatus). As in *Matter of C.D.M.* and *Hayes*, the court enumerated a myriad of factors to be considered in determining whether sterilization was in the best interest of the incompetent person.

In yet another case, *In re Penny N.*, 120 N.H.269, 414 A.2d 541 (1980), the court held that the trial judge had jurisdiction to consider a petition for sterilization, but it refused to order the procedure because sufficient safeguards had not been utilized. There, parents of a 14-year-old girl suffering from Down's Syndrome, severe psychomotor retardation and impaired hearing sought a court order authorizing a hysterectomy. The child had the intelligence level of a 2-year-old, was unable to speak, clothe, or feed herself, and was not toilet trained. In addition, Penny's doctors believed that she was suffering from severe psychological problems which would be aggravated if she began menstruation. In holding that the probate court had jurisdiction to authorize the sterilization, the Supreme Court of New Hampshire relied on a statute that prohibited a guardian from giving "consent for . . . sterilization . . . unless the procedure is first approved by the order of the probate court." *Id.* 414 A.2d at 542. The court, however, remanded the case for further proceedings and the adoption of standards similar to those outlined in *In Re Grady, supra,* stating:

> a probate judge may permit a sterilization after making specific written findings from clear and convincing evidence, that it is in the best interests of the incapacitated ward, rather than the parents' or the public's convenience, to do so. *Id.* 414 A.2d at 543.

*Matter of A. W.,* Colo., 637 P.2d 366 (1981) (en banc), involved a severely mentally retarded 15-year-old female whose parents had petitioned the district court (a court of general jurisdiction) to authorize a hysterectomy. The parents were concerned over the child's fear and fright of the menstrual process and also because of the possibility that she could become pregnant. The evidence showed that the child was physiologically normal and therefore perfectly capable of conceiving a child. The child's physician recommended a hysterectomy to avoid pregnancy and to discontinue the menstrual cycle. The trial court granted the petition on the basis of a Colorado statute generally empowering parents to request medical or surgical care for their child. The Supreme Court of Colorado reversed, concluding "that sterilization of a mentally retarded minor is a special case not covered by the general parental consent statute." 637 P.2d at 368. The court further concluded that a Colorado statute authorizing sterilization of mentally retarded adults, but which was silent as to minors, did not limit the district court's jurisdiction to order sterilization of mentally retarded minors. It held that the district court's broad grant of constitutional authority to determine all civil cases vested it with inherent, nonstatutory powers of adjudication, including the power to consider petitions for sterilization of retarded minors under the *parens patriae* doctrine. The court said:

> Inherent *parens patriae* jurisdiction over incompetents may extend to decisions involving irrevocable consequences for the incompetent individual. Courts have accepted responsibility for deciding whether to authorize a kidney transplant from an incompetent to his gravely ill brother, *Strunk* v. *Strunk,* 445 S.W.2d 145 (Ky. App.1969); whether to consent on behalf of the incompetent to shock treatment, *Price* v. *Sheppard,* 307 Minn. 250, 239. N.W.2d 905 (1976); whether to administer chemotherapy treatment, *Superintendent of Belchertown State School* v. *Saikewicz,* 373 Mass. 728, 738, 370 N.E.2d 417 (1977); and whether to discontinue artificial life support mechanisms, *In re Quinlan,* 70 N.J. 10, 355 A.2d 647, *cert. den.* 429 U.S. 922, 97 S.Ct. 319, 50 L.Ed.2d 289 (1976). *Id.* at 374.

In determining the merits of the sterilization petition, the Colorado court adopted standards to guide the discretion of the trial judge similar to those adopted in *Matter of C.D.M., Hayes,* and *Grady,* all *supra.* Another standard required the trial judge to find by clear and convincing evidence that the sterilization was "medically essential," as to which the court said:

> A sterilization is medically essential if clearly necessary, in the opinion of experts, to preserve the life or physical or mental health of the mentally retarded person. The term "medically essential" is reasonably precise and provides protection from abuses prevalent in this area in the past. The term also avoids confusion as to whose interests are to be

considered. It is not the welfare of society, or the convenience or peace of mind of parents or guardians that these standards are intended to protect. The purpose of the standards is to protect the health of the minor retarded person, and to prevent that person's fundamental procreative rights from being abridged. In some circumstances, the possibility of pregnancy, if supported by sufficient evidences that it would threaten the physical or mental health of the person and that no less intrusive means of birth control would prove save and effective, could justify granting a petition for sterilization as medically essential. *Id.* at 375–76.

Another view of the problem was taken in *Matter of Guardianship of Eberhardy,* 102 Wis.2d 539, 307 N.W.2d 881 (1981). That case involved a petition for sterilization by the guardians/parents of Joan, a 22-year-old mentally retarded woman. The petition was motivated by Joan's parents' belief that she had engaged in sexual activity at a summer camp for the mentally retarded and because Joan's physician recommended sterilization as "she would be unable to care for a child and the chances of a child being severely handicapped were considerable." *Id.* 307 N.W.2d at 883. Joan's parents rejected her usage of an I.U.D. and sought court approval of a tubal ligation. In reversing the judgment of the circuit court that no jurisdiction existed to act on the petition, the Supreme Court of Wisconsin held that the state constitution vested in such courts "jurisdiction in all matters civil and criminal." *Id.* 307 N.W.2d at 885. After an extensive account of Wisconsin's experience with a now repealed eugenic sterilization statute, the court reviewed the dangers and pitfalls involved in a nonstatutory, judicial determination of the merits of a petition for sterilization, *i.e.,* the often subjective nature of the decision, the irreversibility of errors of judgment, the conflicting rights of the parties involved and the inability of courts to deal with the necessary medical technology. Taking all these factors into consideration, the court, although acknowledging the jurisdiction of circuit courts in such cases, concluded that they were not the appropriate forum to resolve such delicate issues of public policy. The court nevertheless stated that if the legislature did not act to develop guidelines and standards for sterilization of incompetents, it would not continue to exercise judicial restraint. *Id.* 307 N.W.2d at 899.

The most recent case on the subject, *In the Matter of Mary Moe,* 385 Mass. 555, 432 N.E.2d 712, decided March 16, 1982, involved a petition to sterilize a severely retarded adult woman. The Supreme Judicial Court of Massachusetts concluded that the trial court—a court of general equity jurisdiction—possessed inherent equitable power to grant a petition for sterilization, shown to be in the best interest of the mentally incompetent ward. In so holding, the court said "that the [trial] court is to determine whether to authorize sterilization when requested by the parents or guardian by finding the incompetent would so choose if competent." 385 Mass. at ____, 432 N.E.2d 712. It indicated that medical necessity was but one relevant factor to be assessed in evaluating whether sterilization was in the best interests of the disabled ward. As to this factor, the court indicated that medical necessity could be demonstrated by proof that pregnancy would threaten the physical or mental health of the incompetent person, with the weight given this factor being dependent upon the facts of the case and the degree of medical necessity. The Massachusetts court concluded that, in applying the standards, the trial judge must exercise the utmost care in reviewing all the evidence presented and in determining whether the ward would consent to sterilization if competent to make such a decision. *Id.* [307 N.W.2d] at 885–886. The judge must enter detailed written findings indicating those persuasive factors that determine the outcome. We are persuaded that a conscientious judge, being mindful of adverse mental and social consequence which might follow the authorization or not of a sterilization operation, will give serious and heedful attention at all stages of the proceeding. 385 Mass. at _____–_____, 432 N.E.2d 712.

## IV

There is no Maryland statute explicitly authorizing courts to approve petitions for the sterilization of any person. Title 13 of the Estates and Trusts Article entitled "Protection of Minors and Disabled Persons" provides in § 13–105 that circuit courts have jurisdiction over guardianship "of the person of a minor and over protective proceedings for minors . . . [and] for disabled persons." As originally enacted by ch. 11 of the Acts of 1974, Title 13 defined a "disabled person" in § 13–101(c) as "a person *other than a minor*" adjudged by a court to be unstable to manage his property because of various enumerated physical, mental and other disabilities. (Emphasis supplied.) A "minor" was defined in § 13–101(i) as a person under the age of 18 years. Chapter 11 of the Acts of 1974 also enacted Subtitle 7 of Title 13, which was entitled "Guardian of the Person"; the new subtitle encompassed §§ 13–701 through 13–704. Section 13–702, captioned "Court appointment of guardian of a minor" simply provided that "the court may appoint a guardian of the person of an unmarried minor." Section 13–704 entitled "Court appointment of guardian of the person of a disabled person" provided that the court may "superintend and direct the care of a disabled person," appoint a guardian therefor and pass orders "directing the disabled person to be sent to a hospital." Neither section delineated with specificity the powers and duties of the guardian.

Title 13 was extensively amended by ch. 768 of the Acts of 1977, which was entitled "An Act Concerning Adult Protective Services." The definition of a "disabled person" was broadened to include a person adjudged by a court "to be unable to provide for his daily needs sufficient to protect his health or safety" because of mental incapacity. The 1977 amendatory act divided the provisions of Subtitle 7 into two parts, the first entitled, "Part I. Minors," which was applicable only to §§ 13–701 through 13–703. The general provision in § 13–702 that the court was empowered to appoint a guardian of the person of an unmarried minor remained unchanged by the amendatory act. Part II of Subtitle 7 was entitled, "Disabled Persons." Included within this Part were new sections—§ 13–705, which authorized appointment of a guardian for a "disabled person," and § 13–708, which enumerated the guardian's rights, duties and powers. As earlier indicated, § 13–708 authorizes the court to grant to guardians only those powers necessary to provide for the "demonstrated need" of the "disabled person" including, but not limited to, the same authority that a parent has with respect to an unemancipated minor child; the care, comfort, training, education and maintenance of the disabled ward; and the power to give necessary consent for medical or other professional care or treatment with the qualification, however, that the guardian must seek court approval before consenting to any medical procedure that involves a substantial risk to life.

From the aforegoing it is evident that § 13–708 does not apply to guardianship of the person of a minor. Thus, the provisions of this section, which permit a guardian of a "disabled person" to consent to a medical procedure where a "demonstrated need" therefor is shown, are not applicable in this case. We think, however, that the statutory formulation of § 13–708 essentially parallels and is the declaratory of the common law *parens patriae* powers of circuit courts over incompetent minors. In enacting § 13–702, expressly recognizing the authority of circuit courts to appoint a guardian of the person of a minor, but without delineating the guardian's powers and duties, the legislature intended that circuit courts would exercise their inherent equitable jurisdiction over guardianship matters pertaining to minors, adopting standards with respect thereto as would be consistent with and in furtherance of the incompetent ward's best interests. *See* § 1–501 of the Courts Article which, in implementation of the provisions of Article IV, § 20 of the Constitution of Maryland, specifies that circuit courts

> are the highest common-law and equity courts of record exercising original jurisdiction within the State . . . [with] full common-law and equity powers and jurisdiction in all civil and criminal cases within [their] count[ies], and all the additional powers and jurisdiction conferred by the Constitution and by law, except where by law jurisdiction has been limited or conferred exclusively upon another tribunal.

The *parens patriae* jurisdiction of circuit courts in this State is well established. The words *"parens patriae,"* meaning "father of the country," refer to the State's sovereign power of guardianship over minors and other persons under disability. *See* 67A C.J.S. *Parens Patriae,* at 159 (1978); Black's Law Dictionary 1003 (5th ed. 1979). It is a fundamental common law concept that the jurisdiction of courts of equity over such persons is plenary so as to afford whatever relief may be necessary to protect the individual's best interests. *See* 27 Am.Jur.2d *Equity* § 69 (1966); 39 Am.Jur.2d *Guardian and Ward* §§ 9, 61 (1968); 59 Am.Jur.2d *Parent and Child* § 9 (1971). Maryland cases are generally in accord. *See Taylor* v. *Taylor,* 246 Md. 616, 229 A.2d 131 (1967); *Thistlewood* v. *Ocean City,* 236 Md. 548, 204 A.2d 688 (1964); *Stirn* v. *Stirn,* 183 Md. 59, 36 A.2d 695 (1944); *Barnard* v. *Godfrey,* 157 Md. 264, 145 A. 614 (1929); *Jenkins* v. *Whyte,* 62 Md. 427 (1884); *Ellis* v. *Ellis,* 19 Md.App. 361, 311 A.2d 428 (1973). Indeed, as we pointed out in *Kicherer* v. *Kicherer,* 285 Md. 114, 400 A.2d 1097 (1979):

> [A] court of equity assumes jurisdiction in guardianship matters to protect those who, because of illness or other disability, are unable to care for themselves. In reality the court is the guardian; an individual who is given that title is merely an agent or arm of that tribunal in carrying out its sacred responsibility.

We conclude, therefore, that as to incompetent minors circuit courts, acting in pursuance of their inherent *parens patriae* authority, have subject matter jurisdiction to consider a petition for an order authorizing a guardian to consent to the sterilization of an incompetent minor. *See Stump* v. *Sparkman,* 435 U.S. 349, 98 S.Ct. 1099, 55 L.Ed.2d 331 (1978).

V

In determining whether a petition to authorize a guardian to consent to sterilization of an incompetent minor is in the minor's best interest, it is essential that the circuit court take into account and be guided by the following minimal standards, which we adopt today in order to safeguard and secure the rights of the ward.

First, the court must appoint an independent guardian *ad litem* to act on the disabled ward's behalf, with full opportunity to meet with the ward and to prese it evidence and cross-examine witnesses at a full judicial hearing. *See* Maryland Rule R78. Second, the court must receive independent medical, psychological and social evaluations by competent professionals and may, if deemed advisable, appoint its own experts to assist in the evaluation of the ward's best interests. Third, the court should personally meet with the minor ward to obtain its own impression of the individual's competency, affording the ward a full opportunity to express his or her personal views or desires with respect to the judicial proceedings and the prospect of sterilization. Fourth, the trial judge must find, by clear and convincing evidence, that the individual lacks competency to make a decision about sterilization and, further, that the incapacity is not likely to change in the foreseeable future. Fifth, the court must be satisfied by clear and convincing evidence that sterilization is in the best interests of the incompetent minor. This determination involves a number of factors, including whether the incompetent minor is capable of reproduction, the child's age and circumstances at the time of the petition, the extent of the child's exposure to sexual contact that could result in pregnancy, the feasibility of utilizing effective contraceptive procedures in lieu of sterilization, the availability of alternative and less intrusive sterilization procedures, and the possibility that scientific advances may occur in the foreseeable future, which could result in improvement of the ward's mental condition. In addition to these factors, the trial court, before authorizing sterilization as being in the best interests of the incompetent minor, must find by clear and convincing evidence that the requested operative procedure is medically necessary to preserve the life or physical or mental health of the incompetent minor. *See Matter of A.W., supra.*

VI

In refusing to authorize sterilization in this case, the trial judge concluded from the evidence that sterilization by hysterectomy to terminate Sonya's menstrual cycle and to prevent her pregnancy was not, within the contemplation of § 13–708's "demonstrated need" formulation, necessary to preserve her life or physical or mental health. While the court noted the absence of any statutory authority or guidance other than that contained in § 13–708, it did not, as we read its opinion, find an absence of subject matter jurisdiction to determine the merits of the petition; it simply found, in light of the evidence in the case, a lack of justification for granting the petition, *i.e.*, that no "demonstrated need" was established.

As we have indicated, § 13–708 has no application to guardianship of the person of an incompetent minor. Consequently, the trial court was wrong in applying the provisions of that section in this case, although the ultimate issue which it considered was for all practical purposes virtually identical to that involved in determining the merits of a petition to sterilize an incompetent minor under common law equitable principles, *i.e.*, whether, in view of the evidence presented, sterilization was shown to be in the best interests of the incompetent minor. We think the trial judge properly concluded that Sonya lacked the mental capacity to herself consent to the operation. Moreover, we think the trial judge was correct in determining that the evidence failed to disclose that sterilization by hysterectomy was in Sonya's best interest as being necessary for her medical or mental health. Manifestly, the fact that Sonya experiences pain and irritation during her menstrual cycle, which she does not understand and with which she has difficulty in coping, does not in itself provide any basis for authorizing a hysterectomy. Nor does the mere fact that Sonya could become pregnant and give birth to a child, for whom she could not care, provide justification to authorize the operation. Indeed, in considering the best interests of an incompetent minor, the welfare of society or the convenience or peace of mind of the ward's parents or guardian plays no part.

Considering Sonya's age and present circumstances, the absence of any evidence, much less clear and convincing evidence, of any medical necessity for the sterilization procedure at this time, no useful purpose would be served by remanding the case to the trial court for further proceedings in light of today's opinion.[3]

We recognize, of course, that declaration of the public policy of this State is normally a function of the legislative branch of government. *Felder* v. *Butler*, 292 Md. 174, 438 A.2d 494 (1981). In view of the profound and recurring nature of the issue here involved, and its obvious importance to the public, the legislature may deem it appropriate at this time to declare the law of the State by enacting a statute governing the granting of consent for sterilization of mentally incompetent minors.

JUDGMENT AFFIRMED, WITH COSTS.

NOTES

1.  The *Wentzel* opinion presents a fairly comprehensive summary of recent precedents dealing with *parens patriae* authority of courts to authorize sterilizations. These cases seem to represent a break with previous rulings that courts do not possess such authority absent a specific statutory authorization. Can this shift of legal doctrine be explained and justified?

2.  In dicta contained in footnote 18 of his partial concurrence and partial dissent in *Parham* v. *J.R.*, 442 U.S. 584, 625, 630–631 (1979), Justice Brennan observed: "[R]ecent legal disputes involving the sterilization of children have led to the conclusions that parents are not permitted to authorize operations with such far-reaching consequences. See, *e.g.*, *A.L.* v. *G.R.H.*, 163 Ind.App. 636, 325 N.E.2d 501 (1975); *In re M.K.R.*, 515 S.W.2d 467 (Mo. 1974); *Frazier* v. *Levi*, 440 S.W.2d 393 (Tex.

---

[3]Maryland Code (1980 Repl. Vol.), Art. 43, § 135(a)(2) provides that a minor has the same capacity to consent to medical treatment as an adult if, *inter alia*, "[t]he minor seeks treatment or advice concerning venereal disease, pregnancy or contraception *not amounting to sterilization*." (Emphasis supplied.) This section prevents a minor, acting alone, from consenting to sterilization; it does not, however, preempt the power of the court, acting within its *parens patriae* jurisdiction, from authorizing the guardian of the person of an incompetent minor to consent to sterilization, where it is shown, by clear and convincing evidence, that such a procedure is in the best interest of the ward.

Civ. App. 1969).'' Is this statement concerning the authority of parents inconsistent with the results in *Wentzel* and the cases it relies upon?

3.  Consider the ages of the persons for whom sterilization was sought in *Wentzel* and the cases discussed. Does the age of the "incompetent" person make any difference? Consider the rights and options concerning sterilization available to nonhandicapped persons and their parents before and after the age of majority. Can a court acting pursuant to its *parens patriae* power have authority over its incompetent ward beyond that parents have over their minor children?

## C.  RAISING CHILDREN

**2.  *Parens Patriae*, Handicaps, and Parental Unfitness**

   **a.  Proceedings and Factual Considerations**

p. 959—INSERT after the end of Note 6:

7.  *In re People in Interest of B.W.*, 626 P.2d 742 (Colo.App. 1981), involved a finding of child neglect and dependency against a woman with Huntington's chorea. Evidence indicated that the woman also had an erratic temper and on one occasion had inflicted first and second degree burns on one of her children by throwing hot coffee on him in the course of an argument. *Id.* at 743. In reaching a conclusion that the decision to remove the children from the mother's custody should be upheld, the court set out the following standards to be applied in determining the impact of a handicapping condition upon parental fitness:

> Of course, the removal of a child from the legal custody of a parent who suffers from a handicap cannot be presumed to be in the best interests of the child based on the fact of the handicap alone. *In re Marriage of Carney*, 24 Cal.3d 725, 157 Cal.Rptr. 383, 598 P.2d 36 (1979). Instead, the court must evaluate a handicapped parent's actual and potential physical capabilities, his adaptation to the disability, how other members of the family have adjusted to the disability, and the special contributions the person may make to the family. *In re Marriage of Carney, supra.* The paramount consideration in this type of proceeding is the best interests of the child.

*Id.* at 743–744.

p. 960—INSERT before *Lewis* v. *Davis*:

### IN RE BABY GIRL WILLIAMS

*Supreme Court of Oklahoma, 1979*
*602 P.2d 1036*

HARGRAVE, Justice.

   This case involves an appeal from an Order terminating parental rights in Baby Girl Williams. Appellant is the natural mother and appellees are the paternal aunt and uncle in whom custody of the child has been temporarily placed.

   Baby Girl Williams was born August 6, 1975, at which time her mother, Judith Williams a/k/a Kellenberger was confined in Eastern State Hospital at Vinita, having been adjudged an incompetent person. The child's father, Billy Williams, was also confined at Eastern State Hospital as an adjudged incompetent, but he is presently absent without leave from that institution. The father is not a party to this appeal.

On August 13, 1975, Baby Girl Williams was placed in the temporary custody of the paternal aunt and uncle, Phyllis Marie Mashburn and Thomas Lee Mashburn, by order of the District Court of Oklahoma County. Pursuant to a petition filed by appellees, a hearing was held February 4, 1976 at which Baby Girl Williams was adjudged a dependent and neglected child and made a ward of the Court. Custody remained in the appellees.

On June 22, 1976, appellees filed a petition praying for termination of the parental rights of Billy Williams and Judith Williams (a/k/a Judith Kellenberger). A hearing was set for August 17, 1976, but was continued in order to give her attorney and guardian more time to bring Judith before the court when her guardian, Marilyn Staats, showed that Judith could not be in attendance at the hearing due to her confinement.

At the continued hearing, of August 31, 1976, the attorney for Judith Williams moved the trial court to grant another continuance or to compel the attendance of Judith Williams before the Court. Ms. Williams' attorney was unable to bring his client before the Court because her incarceration prevented her from attending voluntarily. Prior attempts to compel the attendance of Ms. Williams had been unsuccessful, allegedly due to the Oklahoma County sheriff's refusal to transport the mother from Vinita because of her inability to pay for her transportation. The Court overruled the motion to compel attendance or to grant another continuance and from this denial Judith Williams appeals on Due Process grounds, and denial of her right to confrontation of witnesses.

The appellant's attorney also entered a demurrer for failure of the petition to state a cause of action and for reason that the action was brought pursuant to an unconstitutional statute (10 O.S.Supp.1975 § 1130) that is improperly vague and overbroad, according to appellants. Appellant also argues that the statute puts the burden of proof on the mother to show a change of condition and is thus a denial of her right to due process of law.

On appeal, appellant's major contentions are that 1) the trial court's order terminating the parental rights of Judith Williams was not supported by the evidence, 2) the trial court erred in failing to compel the attendance of the mother at the hearing at which her parental rights were terminated, thereby denying her right to cross-examine witnesses, 3) the trial court was without authority to terminate her parental rights because the statute under which the proceedings were brought is unconstitutionally vague and it places the burden of proof on the mother to show why her parental rights should not be terminated, rather than placing the burden upon the parties seeking termination, and 4) the petition failed to state a cause of action.

We agree with appellant's contention that the trial court's termination of her parental rights is not supported by the evidence. Although the Order determining that Baby Girl Williams is dependent and neglected was not appealed from, that hearing is a procedural step under our statute for terminating parental rights, so its effect must be considered here. The petition filed by appellees below stated only that Baby Girl Williams was dependent and neglected within the terms of the statute because "both of its legal parents have been legally determined to be incompetent and have no legal ways, no means by which to provide for the care of this child.''

The only evidence admitted at the hearing to determine dependent and neglected status (from the record before us) was a letter from the Superintendent of Eastern State Hospital at Vinita. Appellant's guardian had herself requested a written report from the hospital concerning Judith's mental condition. That the Court itself needed the report for further consideration of the case is evidenced by the Court's order of January 27, 1976 compelling the report, which read: ''. . . it further appearing that additional information is needed by the Court in its deliberations regarding Judith Williams' mental condition.'' The order required a written report containing diagnosis and prognosis of Judith Williams' mental condition to be sent before the adjudicatory hearing. What the Court received in response from Eastern State Hospital was a one-paragraph letter from the superintendent, an M.D., stating the psychological name for Judith's condition and stating that most of Judith's life had been spent in mental institutions since 1966 and since Judith was still quite sick, the prognosis as to her functioning outside an institution was poor. This letter was admitted by agreement at the adjudicatory hearing.

Thus, if any standards at all emerged from the hearing which adjudicated the child dependent and neglected, they are only such findings that: 1) the mother is confined in a mental hospital, and 2) the letter from the superintendent at Eastern State Hospital was admitted into evidence. Both of these ''standards'' are related only to the fact that the mother is confined to a mental hospital. Neither of these standards reflects a situation where the parent has wilfully failed to provide for the child or where there is danger of harm to the child. As this Court stated in *Matter of Sherol A.S., 581 P.2d 884 (Okl.1978)*, at page 888:

> [Despite this Court's division] ''on many aspects of our involuntary termination procedure. There is, however, one important point on which we all agree [is]: The purpose of termination is to protect children from HARM suffered by reason of either neglect or the intentional actions of their parents. . . . There is no authority in our Juvenile Code which allows the State to interfere with the family relationship where harm to the children is not involved.'' (citing 10 O.S.1971 § 1130(c)(3).
>
> In that opinion we continue:
> ''. . . The fundamental integrity of the family unit, which has found protection in the Due Process and Equal Protection clauses of the Fourteenth Amendment and the Ninth Amendment, is subject to intrusion and dismemberment by the State only where a 'compelling' State interest arises and protecting the child from harm is the requisite State interest.'' (citations omitted)

No evidence was introduced at the termination hearing on August 31, 1976 to the effect that appellant would *never* be released from custody or that appellant would not, at some time in the future, be able to assume custody of her child. Indeed, the letter from the superintendent at Eastern State Hospital was *not* admitted into evidence at the dispositional hearing and the trial judge specifically stated that he would not consider the letter in his determination. (The trial judge presiding at the termination hearing was a different one from the initial hearing authority.)

In short, the conditions which were found in the case of Judith Williams to be sufficiently compelling to adjudicate her child as dependent and neglected represent merely an unfortunate circumstance that prevents the mother from being able to have physical custody of her child. There is no evidence introduced or even alleged which indicates an intent to abandon her child, any wilful refusal to provide for the child, etc. The appellant's failure to provide support for her child is also attributable to her confinement because of her mental condition, not wilful neglect.

As mentioned above, however, the order determining Baby Girl Williams to be dependent and neglected and made a ward of the court is not appealed from. There is no question that physical custody of her child cannot be with the mother at this time. We do not believe, however, that the mother's physical inability to live with her child and support it justifies the severing of her parental rights to her child forever. (See Justice Simms' dissent in *J. V. v. State of Oklahoma, Okl., 572 P.2d 1283,* at pp. 1291 and 1293; *see also* p. 352 of *Matter of J. L., Okl., 578 P.2d 349 (1978):* ''[S]eparation itself is not necessarily a basis for termination of parental rights.'')

This court has previously held our statute constitutional in providing for termination of parental rights. The decision in *Matter of J. F. C., Okl., 577 P.2d 1300* is dispositive of that issue. In that opinion, this Court noted the statute provides different stages of adjudication and disposition; thus providing the parent with notice of what conduct resulted in the adjudication of dependent and neglected status and that those same conditions must be corrected to prevent termination of parental rights. The entire crux of the argument supporting the constitutionality of our statute is that it provide the parent notice of the conditions which must be corrected.

In *Matter of J. F. C., supra,* at page 1303, in discussing the termination procedure under our statute, this Court stated:

> . . . The adjudication by the court can in itself be looked upon as a set of standards which can be utilized at the hearing in the determination of parental rights. Thus, just as a parent has fair warning of the sanction, the parent is also provided with a standard by which to guide his conduct.

The holding by this Court in *J. F. C., supra,* reversed the trial court order terminating parental rights because clearly against the weight of evidence. In so holding we stated:

> In *Matter of Moore* [Okl., 558 P.2d 371] *supra,* we said the burden of persuasion as to change of conditions was upon the parent after the allegations of the petition to terminate were sustained. To sustain the pleading to terminate trial court must apply the standards of conduct which emerge from the adjudicatory stage. To be affirmed on appeal the record, likewise, must show this Court what those standards were.
>
> * * *
>
> . . . we can find no pleadings or evidence from which we can ascertain what standards evolved from the prior adjudication upon which a standard of conduct could have been set for the present termination of parental rights. For this reason we are reversing trial court's order.

It is clear that in the case at bar, no standards of conduct were set out to provide the court, at the termination hearing, with a criterion for determining whether the parent has corrected those conditions giving rise to the adjudication order. If no standards of conduct are set out at the adjudication stage, the parent is given no notice as to what he or she will be called upon to prove to the court in a later termination hearing. The trial court cannot be heard to terminate the rights of a parent for failure to correct conditions which indicate wilful neglect or harmful conduct to a child when those standards or conditions have never been brought to the attention of the parent in the first place.

For the reason that no standards were promulgated from the adjudication of dependency and neglect to put the mother on notice as to what conditions would have to be shown to be corrected in order to prevent termination of parental rights, we hold that the trial court order terminating parental rights must be reversed. Mere confinement in a mental hospital, while necessitating custody of a child being placed elsewhere, does not constitute failure to give a child the necessary parental care or protection required for his mental or physical health within the purview of our termination statute.

Our termination statute requires a showing that permanent termination is necessary to protect the physical or mental or moral health of the child. Appellee's own testimony established that the child was being well cared for and that there was no immediate threat to the child's welfare if the present custody situation continued into the future. In a situation such as that before this Court, the mother's right to be informed of the conditions she will be required to change must take precedence where there is no immediate threat of harm to the child and no showing that the child is not being well cared for or that the parent is unfit, etc. A termination procedure such as this one is a significant involvement of the rights of a parent to the natural child. The mother's right to know what conditions she is charged with correcting in the adjudicatory stage in order to retain her parental rights has been confirmed by this Court. In the absence of notice of such standards having been established in the adjudicatory stage of the proceeding, the termination cannot be affirmed.

REVERSED.

LAVENDER, C. J., IRWIN, V. C. J., and WILLIAMS, SIMMS, DOOLIN and HARGRAVE, J. J., concur.

OPALA, J., concurs in result.

HODGES and BARNES, J. J., dissent.

NOTE

Does the length of time a person is institutionalized have any impact upon custody determinations and termination of parental rights? How critical to the decision in such cases are the circumstances regarding the interim placement of the child?

### IN RE SWARTZFAGER

*Supreme Court of Oregon, 1981*
*290 Or. 799, 626 P.2d 882*

Before DENECKE, C. J., and TONGUE, LENT, LINDE, PETERSON and TANZER, J. J.

TONGUE, Justice.

This is a proceeding for termination of parental rights based upon a petition which alleged, among other things, (1) that the mother had "failed and neglected without reasonable and lawful cause" to provide for her daughter "for more than one year prior to the date of this petition" (ORS 419.-523(3)), and (2) that "the mother is unfit by reason of conduct or condition seriously detrimental to (the daughter)" because, among other things, "the mother suffers from mental or emotional illness. . . ." (ORS 419.523(2)).

The state appealed to the Court of Appeals from an order by the juvenile court denying the state's petition. The Court of Appeals, by a divided court, affirmed the juvenile court by an opinion holding that although the mother had failed and neglected to provide for the child's needs for the year prior to filing the petition, there was a "reasonable and lawful excuse" for such failure in that during that period she had suffered from systemic lupus erythematosus. 48 Or.App. 205, 616 P.2d 572 (1980). Four members of that court joined in a dissenting opinion stating, among other things, that the mother will never recover her health, but "will always have the same *excuse, and Debbie will never have a chance*" and that under the majority opinion:

> A failure or neglect to provide for a child once initiated can never be subjected to the statutory policy if during any substantial period of time afterwards the parent or parents have an excuse for continuing to act as they initially acted—even if there is no evidence that the parent or parents would have acted differently in the absence of the excuse.

We allowed the state's petition for review because of our concern over the problem raised by that dissenting opinion, as well as what appeared to be a problem arising from the fact that the Court of Appeals did not by its opinion discuss the second contention by the state, namely, that the mother was unfit by reason of mental or emotional illness.

### The Facts

*1. Mother's leaving of Debbie on moving to California*

Mrs. Jones, Debbie's mother, also has two older sons. The younger son lived with her and the older son with her parents. She had twice previously committed herself for psychiatric hospitalization. On one previous occasion both Debbie and the younger son had been placed in foster care while Mrs. Jones was in a hospital and they remained there for over a year.

In February 1977, Mrs. Jones, together with her husband, her younger son Michael, and Debbie were staying with a friend, a Mrs. Davenport, while they were waiting for a check before moving to California. During that time, according to Mrs. Davenport and her daughter, Cathy Valle, Mrs. Jones showed great affection for Michael, but little for Debbie, who she would usually leave when she went out, taking Michael with her, and making Debbie cry quite often.

On or about March 2, 1977, Mr. and Mrs. Jones loaded their belongings in a truck and drove to California, taking Michael but leaving Debbie, then eight years of age, with Cathy Valle. The evidence is conflicting as to the reason why Debbie was left behind. According to Mrs. Davenport, Mrs. Jones said it was because there wasn't room in the truck, although Cathy Valle said that they could have taken her and left some boxes to be shipped to them. Mrs. Jones gave different reasons for leaving Debbie, telling a social worker and a doctor that she left Debbie because Debbie was ill, but testifying that she only did so because she was prevented from taking Debbie by her husband, who threatened to beat her.

According to Mrs. Davenport and Cathy Valle, they were told by Mrs. Jones that she would send for Debbie soon and would send money for her plane or bus fare. According to Mrs. Jones, Cathy Valle was going to drive soon to Mexico and would then bring Debbie to California. This was denied by Cathy Valle.

About a week later, according to Cathy Valle, Mrs. Jones called to say that "they had had some problems" but would send money for Debbie, which they never did. She also testified that she did not hear again from Mrs. Jones; that she tried without success to call Mrs. Jones in California, and finally turned Debbie over to the juvenile authorities. On March 30, 1977, Debbie entered foster care.

Mrs. Jones testified, however, that she sent $200 to Cathy Valle for Debbie's plane fare and later kept trying to call Cathy Valle, but was finally told that the number was disconnected. She said that she contacted the police and welfare authorities for help in locating Debbie, both before and after going to the hospital on May 2, 1977 (as later discussed).

According to social workers assigned to the case, numerous efforts were made by them to communicate with Mrs. Jones by mail, including a letter dated March 31, 1977, informing Mrs. Jones that a petition had been filed, apparently for commitment of Debbie to Children's Services Division, and that only one letter was received from her. That letter, Dated April 12, 1977, stated that she loved Debbie and would "do anything" to get Debbie back; that she had "just gotten a job" and was going to send for Debbie with her first pay check. Apparently, however, that was not done and no letters were received from Mrs. Jones in response to further letters addressed to her.

*2.  The intermittent hospitalization of Mrs. Jones beginning in May 1977—
Psychiatric evaluation of Mrs. Jones and Debbie*

Mrs. Jones became seriously ill sometime between March 2, 1977, and May 2, 1977, when she was admitted to a hospital in California and diagnosed as suffering from systemic lupus erythematosus. Lupus was described as a rheumatological disease primarily of young women and one which can also affect the central nervous system. According to the medical testimony, some of the manifestations that are common include not only severe pain, but "aberrant behavior," hallucinations, schizophrenia, depression and anxiety, and it can also result in memory loss. There was also medical testimony that it is "very probable" that the behavior of Mrs. Jones in abandoning her daughter was "related to the diagnosis of lupus." In addition, there was medical testimony that the psychiatric problems caused by lupus are "not necessarily permanent"; that persons afflicted with lupus may have periods of both remission and exacerbation and that during periods of remission such a person can function normally and responsibly.

According to hospital records, Mrs. Jones was hospitalized for lupus not only from May 2 to 5, 1977, but also from May 15 to 17, 1977; from October 19 to 27, 1977; from December 19, 1977 to January 3, 1978; from February 17 to 21, 1978; from April 5, 1978 to May 16, 1978; from August 3 to 18, 1978, and from December 2 to 8, 1978.

A psychiatrist called by the state as a witness, based upon his "evaluation" of Mrs. Jones in August 1979, testified that she was cooperative and neatly dressed; that he gave her what he described as an "MMPI test," the results of which were not "valid" because she had "preconceived notions" and "presented herself in a sort of a rosy light"; that he had never treated lupus, but that in his opinion Mrs. Jones "is not going to change" and "doesn't learn from her experiences." He also testified that her history shows that she is mentally ill and that although she is functioning as a competent parent to her son and possibly could take proper care of her daughter, it was "improbable," in his opinion, that she would do so, although recognizing that a negative relationship with her daughter does not necessarily make a parent incapable of parenting. In addition, he testified that Debbie is not an ordinary child, but one who had "problems" as a result of "rejection" by her mother, requiring "super-mothering" which Mrs. Jones was not able to do, and that further rejection by her mother would have a seriously detrimental effect on Debbie (who apparently had not been "evaluated" by him).

The state also called as a witness another psychologist, who made evaluations of Debbie, then in a foster home, on March 6, 1978, and August 27, 1979. He testified that she had feelings of rejection as a result of her mother not keeping her promise to send for her; that, in his opinion, she is a "damaged child" who is likely to become involved in delinquent behavior unless provided with adequate stability and security; that lupus cannot cause a mother to favor one child over another (although he had not evaluated Mrs. Jones), and that there are more dangers in returning Debbie to her mother than in placing her in a "neutral setting," although recognizing that if Debbie remains in foster care "she is going to be further damaged." The state also offered in evidence a written evaluation report by another psychiatrist, dated September 9, 1977, describing Debbie as a pleasant cooperative child who needed a stable home environment and wished "strongly [to] be united with her mother or if not her mother then some substitute parents."

Finally, the state offered testimony of a social worker that he had talked to adoption workers and that "the consensus is that Debbie is an adoptable girl."

A Portland doctor, a rheumatologist, who testified on behalf of Mrs. Jones based upon his examination of her hospital records, said that the lupus had involved her central nervous system, but that during periods of remission she could function normally; that if she continues with proper treatment there is some possibility that she will be able to discharge her responsibility as a parent; and that the prognosis "at the present time . . . is reasonably good," but that he could not predict the future; that it was a "good probability" that she would have an exacerbation in the foreseeable future; that she would have "ups and downs" with "a lot of exacerbations and remissions."

The doctor who treated Mrs. Jones since December 1977 testified that when in the hospital she was very sick and upset and not capable of writing a legible letter; that she had psychiatric problems, probably because of lupus, and at times "wasn't making total sense when she talked"; that although she could have made a telephone call, it would have been emotionally difficult for her to do so. That doctor also testified (in October 1979) that Mrs. Jones had then been "in remission" of from eight to ten months, during which she had been able to function competently as a mother to her son, who appeared to be a happy, well cared for child and that during that period she had also taken care of other children who appeared to be happy, well dressed and well cared for; that she loves her daughter and wants her back; that in his opinion she will continue to perform competently as a mother, and that he does not know of any psychiatric problems that would prevent her from being a good parent, although recognizing that her "main problem is the lupus and all the complications of that disease."

### 3. Events since hospitalization of Mrs. Jones

As previously stated, Mrs. Jones was hospitalized for lupus intermittently from early May 1977 to December 1978. Meanwhile, on April 7, 1978, the state filed a petition for termination of her parental rights for failure and neglect to provide for Debbie's needs since March 30, 1977. By letter dated June 21, 1978, Mrs. Jones was informed that she "cannot have any contact with Debbie until a ruling is made regarding the termination of your parental rights. . . ."

A hearing on that petition was continued until September 12, 1978, to give Mrs. Jones an opportunity to appear. When she did not appear at that time an order was entered terminating her parental rights. That order was reversed by the Court of Appeals on July 10, 1979, for the reason that the termination had been ordered as the result of a hearing in her absence. *State ex rel. Juv. Dept.* v. *Jones*, 40 Or.App.401, 595 P.2d 508 (1979).

On August 29, 1979, an amended petition was filed. A hearing was held on that petition on October 5 and 11, 1979.

Meanwhile, and during the previous months of 1979, Mrs. Jones had been living with her son in a two bedroom apartment in an apartment complex after "kicking out" her husband. There she had been "babysitting" several children for working mothers who lived there. She testified that she had friends and relatives nearby in the event that she had problems with lupus; that she had not attempted to contact Debbie because she had been previously told by letter that she could not do so, and that she was in the hospital at the time of the previous termination hearing. Apparently, however, she also did not make any calls or inquiries of social workers regarding Debbie, and she was not in the hospital at that time.

Finally, depositions were offered in evidence of four mothers whose children had been taken care of by Mrs. Jones during 1979. All testified that Mrs. Jones "babysat" as many as six children; that she cared for her children very well; that the children liked her; that Michael, the son of Mrs. Jones, is happy and well cared for, and that although some of the mothers had heard of medical problems of Mrs. Jones, they had not seen her manifest any strange or unusual behavior.

### The Decision by the Trial Court

After hearing this testimony, the trial judge, in an oral opinion, first found that Mrs. Jones was not a "credible witness." The trial judge then went on to find that the state had not proved its allegation of failure or neglect to provide Debbie with support for one year prior to the filing of the (amended) petition because the mother's behavior was excused during that year by the letter which told her not to contact the child. She also found that during the year prior to filing the original petition the state had failed to prove by a preponderance of the evidence "that the mother failed without reasonable and lawful cause to reunite herself with her child."

With reference to the allegation of the petition that Mrs. Jones was unfit as a parent, the trial judge found that:

> I do believe the State has proved by a preponderance of the evidence that the mother was unfit by reason of condition and conduct which were seriously detrimental to Debbie. I cannot make a finding that the mother currently suffers from mental or emotional illness. I do not find that it has been established that she has ever suffered from mental or emotional illness. So I don't believe that one has been proved.

The trial court went on to find that:

> Putting all of that together, I think that I must then look to what's in the best interests of Deborah. And I cannot say that I am convinced that Deborah's best interests will be served by remaining in foster care. To return Deborah to her mother I realize is taking a very large chance. To keep Deborah in foster care is taking an equally large chance. This Court would have to be unconscious, ill-informed, and foolish not to know that there are very few ten-year-olds who are ever adopted.

On October 18, 1979, the trial court entered a written order denying the state's amended petition to terminate the mother's parental rights. As previously stated, the Court of Appeals affirmed by a divided court that decision by the trial court.

### The Trial Court and Court of Appeals did not Err in Denying the Petition for Termination of Parental Rights

The state contends in its petition for review that the decision by the Court of Appeals is "not supported by the record" and "indicates a clear trend" by that court "away from three basic tenets of the juvenile code: 1) the primacy of the children's best interests" (rather than a "focus exclusively on the rights of the parent"); "2) the necessity of meaningful *de novo* review; and 3) the guarantee that persons aggrieved by an order of the juvenile court will have a remedy in the appellate courts."

The state also contends that the amended petition, filed on August 29, 1979, included a new allegation that the mother was unfit as a mother under ORS 419.523(2), which was not addressed by the Court of Appeals in its opinion and that its holding that Mrs. Jones' failure or neglect to provide for Debbie was based upon her testimony, which the trial court found to be not credible, and that of her doctor's, which also was not credible.

Finally, the state contends that even if she was "lawfully excused" by her illness, that finding does not justify denial of the petition because, as stated in the Court of Appeals dissent, she will never recover her health and will always have the same excuse and that Debbie "will never have a chance"; that these comments are equally applicable to the separate allegation that her condition renders her unfit because of an incurable and possibly fatal disease; that this tragedy should not "claim two lives," including Debbie, who is already an "emotionally damaged child"; that to "sentence" Debbie to either living with her mother or in a foster home is to impose two "totally unacceptable alternatives," and that "[i]f this is the best the juvenile court system can offer Debbie . . . , then it has failed utterly."

These are strong words, and well stated. They also express a legitimate concern. In another case involving a petition for termination of parental rights under equally tragic circumstances it was said that:

> . . . the facts of this case . . . illustrate one of the serious social problems of our times. Indeed, this is a particularly tragic case and one calling for the wisdom of a twentieth century Solomon. Perhaps that ancient decree would persuade this mother to yield to the best interests of her child, regardless of constitutional considerations of "due process." Otherwise, the emotional and mental health of this child may well be maimed as surely as if by that proverbial sword.
>
> The courts, however, do not profess to possess either such wisdom or such power. . . . in deciding cases involving such problems, the courts must act within the framework and limitations of the constitution and laws of this state and nation.   Concurring opinion, *State* v. *McMaster,* 259 Or. 291, 304, 486 P.2d 567 (1971).

This is not to say that the primary consideration in the decision of such cases is not the best interests of the child. It does mean, however, that in the application of that primary test the courts can only act upon the authority and within the limitations provided by law. These limitations include not only those imposed by ORS 419.-523, but also fundamental constraints imposed by the nature of our judicial system.

Thus, when the state files a petition to terminate the rights of a parent it undertakes the burden to prove the allegation of its petition. And when the state appeals from adverse findings by a trial judge in such a case, even though the appellate court hears such a case *de novo,* it must, as a practical matter and as in other cases subject to *de novo* review, give considerable weight to the findings by the trial judge who had the opportunity to observe the witnesses and their demeanor in evaluating the credibility of their testimony.

Termination of parental rights for unfitness of a parent or for failure to provide for the needs of a child are controlled by ORS 419.523, which provides:

*   *   *

(2) The rights of the parent or parents may be terminated as provided in subsection (1) of this section if the court finds that the parent or parents are unfit by reason of conduct or condition seriously detrimental to the child and integration of the child into the home of the parent or parents is improbable in the foreseeable future due to conduct or conditions not likely to change. In determining such conduct and conditions, the court shall consider but is not limited to the following:

(a) Emotional illness, mental illness or mental deficiency of the parent of such duration as to render it *impossible to care for the child for extended periods of time.*

(b) Conduct toward any child of an abusive, cruel or sexual nature.

(c) Addictive use of intoxicating liquors or controlled substances.

(d) Physical neglect of the child.

(e) Lack of effort of the parent to adjust the circumstances of the parent, conduct, or conditions to make the return of the child possible or failure of the parent to effect a lasting adjustment after reasonable efforts by available social agencies for such extended duration of time that it appears reasonable that no lasting adjustment can be effected.

(3) The rights of the parent or parents may be terminated as provided in subsection (1) of this section if the court finds that the parent or parents have failed or neglected *without*

*reasonable and lawful cause* to provide for the basic physical and psychological needs of the child for one year prior to the filing of a petition. In determining such failure or neglect, the court shall consider but is not limited to one or more of the following:

(a) Failure to provide care or pay a reasonable portion of substitute physical care and maintenance if custody is lodged with others.

(b) Failure to maintain regular visitation or other contact with the child which was designed and implemented in a plan to reunite the child with the parent.

(c) Failure to contact or communicate with the child or with the custodian of the child. In making this determination, the court may disregard incidental visitations, communications or contributions.

    \*   \*   \*    (Emphasis added)

*1. Failure and neglect to provide for needs of child.*

We first consider the allegations by the state that Mrs. Jones failed and neglected to provide for the basic needs of Debbie for more than one year prior to the date of the original petition, filed on April 7, 1978. We agree with both the trial court and the Court of Appeals that the state failed to prove that such failure and neglect was "without reasonable and lawful cause," as provided by ORS 419.523(3).

Debbie had been placed in foster care on March 30, 1977. The state does not contend that Mrs. Jones was financially able to provide money for the support of Debbie while in foster care, but it contends that she left Debbie when she moved to California and did not then either send for Debbie or inquire concerning her welfare, with the exception of one letter dated April 25, 1977, or respond to numerous letters from social workers.

On May 2, 1977, Mrs. Jones was hospitalized and diagnosed as being afflicted with lupus. She was then repeatedly hospitalized for lupus during both 1977 and 1978. Thus, regardless of whether the medical testimony is to be believed that her behavior during March and April 1977 was the result of lupus, which had not then been diagnosed, there was testimony to support the finding by the trial court and the holding by the Court of Appeals to the effect that during at least a substantial part of the year immediately preceding the filing of the original petition, Mrs. Jones had a "reasonable and lawful" excuse for failing and neglecting to provide for the needs of Debbie, and we agree with that finding and with that holding. Although there was evidence that she might have been able to call or make inquiries relating to Debbie during the intervals between her periods of hospitalization, and during which she may still have been suffering from lupus, we do not believe that such evidence was sufficient to require a contrary finding.

As for the year immediately prior to the filing of the amended petition for termination on August 29, 1979, it must be remembered that by letter dated June 21, 1978, Mrs. Jones had been previously informed that she could not "have any contact with Debbie until a ruling is made regarding the termination of your parental rights."

On this record we agree with the holding by both the trial court and by the majority of the Court of Appeals that the parental rights of Mrs. Jones could not be properly terminated for failure or neglect to provide for the needs of Debbie because of the requirement of ORS 419.523(3) that such failure or neglect must extend for a period of "one year prior to the filing of a petition" and be "without reasonable and lawful cause."

This, of course, does not end the inquiry, because a parent who may have "reasonable and lawful cause" to fail or neglect to provide for the needs of a child may also be a parent who is "unfit by reason of conduct or condition seriously detrimental to the child" within the provisions of ORS 419.-523(2).

2.  *Unfitness of parent.*

The state's amended petition alleged that:

> E.  The mother is unfit by reason of conduct or condition seriously detrimental to Debbie and reintegration of Debbie into the home of the mother is improbable in the foreseeable future due to conduct or condition not likely to change, to wit:
> (1)  The mother suffers from *mental or emotional illness* of such duration as to render it *impossible* for her to care for Debbie for *extended periods of time.*
> (2)  There has been a lack of effort on the part of the mother to adjust her circumstances to make return of the child possible.
> (3)  The parent-child relationship has been alienated as a result of the conduct and condition of the other.  (Emphasis added.)

The trial court, after hearing the testimony, found that Mrs. Jones was "not a credible witness," but that "Allegation E has not been proved by a preponderance of the evidence." For some reason, the Court of Appeals did not discuss in its opinion the contention by the state that Mrs. Jones was "unfit."

With reference to subparagraph (1), there was a conflict in the testimony whether lupus is physical illness, rather than a "mental or emotional illness," as alleged and as provided by ORS 419.523(2)(a). We shall assume, however, that lupus is a "mental or emotional illness" for purposes of that statute. There was also a conflict in the testimony whether, despite the then-existing "remission" from that illness, the probabilities were that she would not only have future "exacerbations" of the disease, but that such exacerbations would be of such a nature and duration to render Mrs. Jones "unfit" as a parent for Debbie.

The testimony was uncontradicted, however, that during the period of from eight to ten months in 1979 immediately prior to the trial of the case, Mrs. Jones had been able to function normally as a mother for her son, who appeared to be happy and well cared for, and had also functioned capably as a "babysitter" for children of working mothers in the apartment complex where she lived. In view of that testimony, we agree with the trial judge that the state had not proved by a preponderance of the evidence that Mrs. Jones suffered from an illness of such a nature or duration "as to render it *impossible* to care for Debbie for *extended periods of time.*"[6]

With reference to subparagraph (2), we also agree with the finding by the trial court in view of the uncontradicted testimony that during that period of from eight to ten months Mrs. Jones had been living with her son in a two bedroom apartment, with the result that the state had not proved its allegation that she had not "adjusted her circumstances to make the return of the child possible."

---

[6]This is consistent with our holding in *State ex rel. Juvenile Dept.* v. *Martin,* 271 Or. 603, 608, 533 P.2d 780 (1975), in which it was held, although under different facts, that the parental rights of a defendant suffering from schizophrenia would not be terminated in view of testimony that during periods of remission he was a good parent and there was "at least a possibility" that with proper treatment he would be able to properly discharge his responsibilities as a parent in the future.

With respect to subparagraph (3), alleging that the "parent-child relationship has been alienated as a result of the conduct and condition of the mother," the evidence was also somewhat conflicting, at least with reference to the extent of the alienation. We note, however, that the alienation of parent-child relationship is not included in ORS 419.523(2) as one of the specifications provided by that statute as a ground for termination of parental rights.

It is true that ORS 419.523(2) provides that the court "shall consider but is not limited to" the grounds specified in subsections (a), (b) and (c) and (2) of that statute. It may or may not be that the alienation of relations between a parent and child may be of such a nature and degree as to justify the state in terminating the parental rights of the mother or father of a child for that reason alone. We believe, however, that the courts should be hesitant in terminating parental rights for what is commonly referred to as "alienation" of relations between parents and their children, regardless of whether the conduct of the parents was primarily responsible for such alienation. It is common knowledge that in this day and age there is at least some degree of "alienation" in the relationships between parents and their children in many American families and that conduct by parents is sometimes the cause of such alienation. Surely the Oregon legislature did not intend for the courts to terminate parental rights in all such families and either place the children in foster homes or put them up for adoption.

We also note that in this case, aside from the testimony of the mother expressing her love for Debbie and her desire for Debbie's return, and also aside from the testimony that Debbie was hurt deeply as the result of being left in Portland by her mother and is considered by a psychiatrist to be a "damaged child," Debbie told another psychiatrist that she wanted to return to her mother and appeared to express affection for her.

On this record we agree with the finding by the judge to the effect that the state had failed to prove that the alienation of relations between Debbie and her mother was of such a nature or degree as to require the termination of the parental rights of Mrs. Jones.

In so holding, we also agree with the observation by the trial judge at the conclusion of the trial that to return Debbie to her mother "is not a satisfactory result," despite the finding that Mrs. Jones is "at this time competent to take care of children." As also noted by the trial court, however, keeping Debbie in a foster home in the hope that she may be adopted, which may be difficult for a ten-year-old child, is also not a satisfactory solution.

We are concerned, as is the state, that in living with her mother Debbie may "never have a chance." In *State* v. *McMaster, supra,* although involving different facts, much the same contention was made that the primary test to be applied in such cases is the best interests of the child and that parental rights should be terminated when the circumstances are such that a child may "never have a chance." In that case this court, after again recognizing (259 Or. at 303, 486 P.2d 567) that "the best interests of the child are paramount," went on to say that:

> The witness was undoubtedly correct when he stated that living in the McMasters' household would not "allow this child to maximize her potential." However, we do not

believe the legislature contemplated that parental rights could be terminated because the natural parents are unable to furnish surroundings which would enable the child to grow up as we would desire all children to do.

For these reasons the decision by both the trial court and the Court of Appeals are affirmed.

NOTES

1.  To what extent do the decisions in *Swartzfager* and *Williams* apply a standard of parental fault rather than a "best interests of the child" analysis? How interrelated are these two concepts? To what degree can either be ignored in proceedings for the termination of parental rights? Can both factors be accommodated?

2.  In *In re Fay G.*, 412 A.2d 1012 (N.H. 1980), the Supreme Court of New Hampshire ruled that a mother could be compelled to undergo an involuntary psychiatric examination in a proceeding for the termination of her parental rights. The court held that such compulsory examination was warranted and not a violation of the mother's constitutional rights to be free from self-incrimination, to privacy, and to freedom from restraint, in light of evidence that the mother had persistently dressed and treated her son as a girl.  *Id.* at 1015.  "Allowing the probate court the discretion to compel a psychiatric examination helps protect the child's welfare by permitting the acquisition of information essential to the disposition of proceedings to terminate parental rights."  *Ibid.*

3.  In *In re Welfare of Frederiksen*, 25 Wash.App. 726, 610 P.2d 371 (1980), the Court of Appeals of Washington upheld a judgment that found the infant of a "chronic undifferentiated schizophrenic" to be a "dependent" child, largely because of evidence of the mother's mental illness and previous neglect of her two older children: "the child of a mother who is suffering from a mental illness, who does not understand the requirements of children and who is incapable of giving that child proper parental care and supplying its basic needs, is a dependent child. There is no need to wait until such a mother commits physical abuse or neglect and actually damages the child's development by failure to meet its physical, mental, and emotional requirements if danger of such a result is clear and present."  *Id.* at 375. How conjectural can a "clear and present" risk be? Is psychiatric testimony the basis for making predictions of such danger? What problems does this present?

p. 963—INSERT after the Note:

## In re McDaniel

*Court of Appeals of Oregon, 1980*
*46 Or.App. 65, 610 P.2d 321*

Before GILLETTE, P. J., and ROBERTS and CAMPBELL, J. J.
CAMPBELL, Judge.

The state appeals from the trial court's order denying its petition to terminate the father's parental rights.

We review the facts de novo on the record, ORS 419.561(4), 19.125(3), giving due regard to the findings of the trial court, which had the opportunity to observe the witnesses. *State ex rel Juv. Dept.* v. *Maves*, 33 Or.App. 411, 576 P.2d 826 (1978).

The petition alleged that the father's parental rights should be terminated under ORS 419.523(2) and (3). We observe at the outset that, at the hearing on the petition, the father's attorney conceded that if the child's best interests were the sole factor to consider, termination would be the proper course. In denying the petition, the trial court stated:

> So it's with a great deal of sadness that I will refuse to terminate this parent's rights because I do believe that it would be in the best interests of the child. And if the issue is: May the Court terminate a parent's right to a child when that relationship has failed for whatever reason and it's not likely to be re-established, then I could very firmly say that this parent's rights should be terminated because I believe the relationship between the father and the child has failed, but I can't say that it's failed due to the father's course of conduct. So I will refuse to terminate the rights.

The court specifically found "that reintegration of this child into the parental home is unlikely in the foreseeable future."

After a review of the record, we concur with the trial court that there is no reasonable likelihood that the child will be reintegrated into the father's home in the foreseeable future, and that the child's best interests weigh heavily in favor of termination. We need not and do not detail the overwhelming evidence leading us to this conclusion. *State ex rel Juv. Dept.* v. *Navarette*, 30 Or.App. 909, 569 P.2d 26 (1977).

The denial of the petition was based on the trial court's finding that the state failed to prove:

> Lack of effort of the parent to adjust the circumstances of the parent, conduct, or conditions to make the return of the child possible or failure of the parent to effect a lasting adjustment after reasonable efforts by available social agencies for such extended duration of time that it appears reasonable that no lasting adjustment can be effected.    ORS 419.523(2)(e).

The court noted that the father arranged on his own for parenting classes and counseling, having received no aid in doing so from Children's Services Division (CSD). The father also continued to request visitation, although sporadically, during the time the child was in foster care. From these findings the court concluded that the father had shown a continuing interest in the child and had made an effort to adjust his circumstances to make possible the return of the child to the home. The court found the father was not at fault for his failure to make a lasting adjustment. The court further found that for a substantial period CSD had given the father no supportive services. In commenting on a letter from a CSD caseworker to the father containing a series of ultimatums regarding actions the father must take to avoid termination proceedings, the court stated that the plan was one which perhaps a lawyer, judge, or juvenile court counselor might be able to understand and act upon, but that in light of the McDaniels' limitations it was reasonable for them to "sit back and wait for things to happen." Rodney McDaniel, Kathy's father, has an eighth grade education. In school he was assigned to a class for the educable mentally retarded (I.Q. 70–85). He is occupationally disabled due to his mental deficiency, and supports his family on Social Security and public assistance grants from the state. Patty McDaniel, Kathy's stepmother, did not finish high school.

We agree with the trial court that the father lacked support from CSD in obtaining the marital and parenting skills he would need for a successful return of the child to the home. CSD did cooperate in arranging visitation, although visitation was hindered by the distance the father and child lived from each other and the CSD offices. We also agree that the father has made an effort to adjust his circumstances. Our review of the evidence convinces us, however, that no amount of effort by CSD and cooperation by the father would offer any reasonable possibility that the child could be permanently reintegrated into the home.

The statutory requirement that available social agencies (here CSD) make ''reasonable efforts'' to help the parent make a lasting adjustment could not have been intended by the legislature as a justification for penalizing the child for CSD's lapses. We refuse so to apply it, particularly in this case when the father, although possessing low intelligence, has shown the ability to seek and find help on his own. Some of the parenting classes and counseling occurred prior to the second of the two placements of the child in the father's home, which failed abysmally, ending after less than three months when the father returned Kathy and one of his other daughters to CSD and insisted that CSD place them in foster care.

Kathy, who was 10 at the time of the hearing, has found a loving, supportive, and family-oriented home with her foster family, and strongly desires to be adopted by her foster parents. Since being placed in that home she has shed her behavioral problems and has made unusually rapid and unexpected improvements in her intellectual development, disproving her earlier rating as mentally retarded. Kathy's foster parents also wish to adopt her. Kathy has but a ''far away attachment'' to her father, has fearful memories of his home, and does not desire to live with him and her stepmother.

This is not a case such as *State ex rel Juv. Dept.* v. *Wyatt,* 34 Or.App. 793, 579 P.2d 889, *rev. den.* (1978), in which fairness dictates that we give the father one more chance to prove his ability as a parent. In this case, delay in terminating the father's parental rights would serve no useful purpose.

Reversed.

NOTES

1.  Compare the attitude toward parental fault and ameliorative efforts in the *McDaniel* case with the *Williams* and *Swartzfager* opinions. Does the situation in *McDaniel* satisfy the standards for terminating parental rights subsequently delineated by the Supreme Court of Oregon in *Swartzfager?*

2.  In regard to the standard of proof required in all of these termination of parental rights cases, see *Santosky* v. *Kramer,* below.

### b.  Constitutional Validity

p. 967—ADD to the beginning of Subsection b, before the *In re William L.* case:

## SANTOSKY V. KRAMER

*Supreme Court of the United States, 1982*
*____ U.S.____, 102 S.Ct. 1388*

Justice BLACKMUN delivered the opinion of the Court.

Under New York law, the State may terminate, over parental objection, the rights of parents in their natural child upon a finding that the child is "permanently neglected." N.Y.Soc.Serv.Law §§ 384–b.4.(d), 384–b.7.(a) (McKinney Supp. 1981–1982) (Soc.Serv.Law). The New York Family Court Act § 622 (McKinney 1975 & Supp.1981–1982) (Fam.Ct.Act) requires that only a "fair preponderance of the evidence" support that finding. Thus, in New York, the factual certainty required to extinguish the parent-child relationship is no greater than that necessary to award money damages in an ordinary civil action.

Today we hold that the Due Process Clause of the Fourteenth Amendment demands more than this. Before a State may sever completely and irrevocably the rights of parents in their natural child, due process requires that the State support its allegations by at least clear and convincing evidence.

### I

### A

New York authorizes its officials to remove a child temporarily from his or her home if the child appears "neglected," within the meaning of Art. 10 of the Family Court Act. See §§ 1012(f), 1021–1029. Once removed, a child under the age of 18 customarily is placed "in the care of an authorized agency," Soc.Serv.Law § 384–b.7.(a), usually a state institution or a foster home. At that point, "the state's first obligation is to help the family with services to . . . reunite it. . . .'' § 384–b.1.(a)(iii). But if convinced that "positive, nurturing parent-child relationships no longer exist," § 384–b.1.(b), the State may initiate "permanent neglect" proceedings to free the child for adoption.

The State bifurcates its permanent neglect proceeding into "fact-finding" and "dispositional" hearings. Fam.Ct.Act §§ 622, 623. At the factfinding stage, the State must prove that the child has been "permanently neglected," as defined by Fam.Ct.Act §§ 614.1.(a)–(d) and Soc.Serv.Law § 384–b.7.(a). See Fam.Ct.Act § 622. The Family Court judge then determines at a subsequent dispositional hearing what placement would serve the child's best interests. §§ 623, 631.

At the factfinding hearing, the State must establish, among other things, that for more than a year after the child entered state custody, the agency "made diligent efforts to encourage and strengthen the parental relationship." Fam.Ct.Act §§ 614.1(c), 611. The State must further prove that during that same period, the child's natural parents failed "substantially and continuously or repeatedly to maintain contact with or plan for the future of the child although physically and financially able to do so." § 614.1(d). Should the State support its allegations by "a fair preponderance of the evidence," § 622, the child may be declared permanently neglected. § 611. That declaration empowers the Family Court judge to terminate permanently the natural parents' rights in the child. §§ 631(c), 634. Termination denies the natural parents physical custody, as well as the rights ever to visit, communicate with, or regain custody of the child.

New York's permanent neglect statute provides natural parents with certain procedural protections. But New York permits its officials to establish "permanent neglect" with less proof than most States require. Thirty-three States, the District of Columbia, and the Virgin Islands currently specify a higher standard of proof, in parental rights termination proceedings, than a "fair preponderance of the evidence." The only analogous federal statute of which we are aware permits termination of parental rights solely upon "evidence beyond a reasonable doubt." Indian Child Welfare Act of 1978, Pub.L. 95–608, § 102(f), 92 Stat. 3072, 25 U.S.C. § 1912(f) (1976 ed., Supp. III). The question here is whether New York's "fair preponderance of the evidence" standard is constitutionally sufficient.

### B

Petitioners John Santosky II and Annie Santosky are the natural parents of Tina and John III. In November 1973, after incidents reflecting parental neglect, respondent Kramer, Commissioner of the Ulster County Department of Social Services, initiated a neglect proceeding under Fam.Ct.Act § 1022 and removed Tina from her natural home. About 10 months later, he removed John III and placed him with foster parents. On the day John was taken, Annie Santosky gave birth to a third child, Jed. When Jed was only three days old, respondent transferred him to a foster home on the ground that immediate removal was necessary to avoid imminent danger to his life or health.

In October 1978, respondent petitioned the Ulster County Family Court to terminate petitioners' parental rights in the three children. Petitioners challenged the constitutionality of the "fair preponderance of the evidence" standard specified in Fam.Ct.Act § 622. The Family Court judge rejected this constitutional challenge. App. 29–30, and weighed the evidence under the statutory standard. While acknowledging that the Santoskys had maintained contact with their children, the judge found those visits "at best superficial and devoid of any real emotional content." *Id*, at 21. After deciding that the agency had made " 'diligent efforts' to encourage and strengthen the parental relationship," *id.*, at 30, he concluded that the Santoskys were incapable, even with public assistance, of planning for the future of their children. *Id.*, at 33–37. The judge later held a dispositional hearing and ruled that the best interests of the three children required permanent termination of the Santoskys' custody. *Id.*, at 39.

Petitioners appealed, again contesting the constitutionality of § 622's standard of proof. The New York Supreme Court, Appellate Division, affirmed, holding application of the preponderance of the evidence standard "proper and constitutional." *In re John AA*, 75 App.Div.2d 910, 427 N.Y.S.2d 319, 320 (1980). That standard, the court reasoned, "recognizes and seeks to balance rights possessed by the child . . . with those of the natural parents. . . ." *Ibid.*

The New York Court of Appeals then dismissed petitioners' appeal to that court "upon the ground that no substantial constitutional question is directly involved." App. 55. We granted certiorari to consider petitioners' constitutional claim. 450 U.S. 993, 101 S.Ct. 1694, 68 L.Ed.2d 192 (1981).

## II

Last Term in *Lassiter* v. *Department of Social Services,* 452 U.S. 18, 101 S.Ct. 2153, 68 L.Ed.2d 640 (1981), this Court, by a 5–4 vote, held that the Fourteenth Amendment's Due Process Clause does not require the appointment of counsel for indigent parents in every parental status termination proceeding. The case casts light, however, on the two central questions here—whether process is constitutionally due a natural parent at a State's parental rights termination proceeding, and, if so, what process is due.

In *Lassiter,* it was "not disputed that state intervention to terminate the relationship between [a parent] and [the] child must be accomplished by procedures meeting the requisites of the Due Process Clause." 452 U.S., at 37, 101 S.Ct., at 2165 (dissenting opinion); see *id.,* at 24–32, 101 S.Ct., at 2158–2162 (opinion for the Court); *id.,* at 59–60, 101 S.Ct., at 2176 (STEVENS, J., dissenting). See also *Little* v. *Streater,* 452 U.S. 1, 13, 101 S.Ct., 2202, 2209, 68 L.Ed.2d 627 (1981). The absence of dispute reflected this Court's historical recognition that freedom of personal choice in matters of family life is a fundamental liberty interest protected by the Fourteenth Amendment. *Quilloin* v. *Walcott,* 434 U.S. 246, 255, 98 S.Ct. 549, 554, 54 L.Ed.2d 511 (1978); *Smith* v. *Organization of Foster Families,* 431 U.S. 816, 845, 97 S.Ct. 2094, 2110, 53 L.Ed.2d 14 (1977); *Moore* v. *East Cleveland,* 431 U.S. 494, 499, 97 S.Ct. 1932, 1935, 52 L.Ed.2d 531 (1977) (plurality opinion); *Cleveland Board of Education* v. *LaFleur,* 414 U.S. 632, 639–640, 94 S.Ct. 791, 796, 39 L.Ed.2d 52 (1974); *Stanley* v. *Illinois,* 405 U.S. 645, 651–652, 92 S.Ct. 1208, 1212–1213, 31 L.Ed.2d 551 (1972); *Prince* v. *Massachusetts,* 321 U.S. 158, 166, 64 S.Ct. 438, 442, 88 L.Ed. 645 (1944); *Pierce* v. *Society of Sisters,* 268 U.S. 510, 534–535, 45 S.Ct. 571, 573–574, 69 L.Ed. 1070 (1925); *Meyer* v. *Nebraska,* 262 U.S. 390, 399, 43 S.Ct., 625, 626, 67 L.Ed. 1042 (1923).

The fundamental liberty interest of natural parents in the care, custody, and management of their child does not evaporate simply because they have not been model parents or have lost temporary custody of their child to the State. Even when blood relationships are strained, parents retain a vital interest in preventing the irretrievable destruction of their family life. If anything, persons faced with forced dissolution of their parental rights have a more critical need for procedural protections than do those resisting state intervention into ongoing family affairs. When the State moves to destroy weakened familial bonds, it must provide the parents with fundamentally fair procedures.

In *Lassiter,* the Court and three dissenters agreed that the nature of the process due in parental rights termination proceedings turns on a balancing of the "three distinct factors" specified in *Mathews* v. *Eldridge,* 424 U.S. 319, 335, 96 S.Ct. 893, 903, 47 L.Ed.2d 18 (1976): the private interests affected by the proceeding; the risk of error created by the State's chosen procedure; and the countervailing governmental interest supporting use of the challenged procedure. See 452 U.S., at 27–31, 101 S.Ct., at 2159–2162; *id.,* at 37–48, 101 S.Ct., at 2164–2171 (dissenting opinion). But see *id.,* at 59–60, 101 S.Ct., at 2176 (STEVENS, J., dissenting). While the respective *Lassiter* opinions disputed whether those factors should be weighed against a presumption disfavoring appointed counsel for one not threatened with loss of physical liberty, compare 452 U.S., at 31–32, 101 S.Ct., at 2161–2162, with *id.*, at 41 and n. 8, 101 S.Ct., at 2167 and n. 8 (dissenting opinion), that concern is irrelevant here. Unlike the Court's right-to-counsel rulings, its decisions concerning constitutional burdens of proof have not turned on any presumption favoring any particular standard. To the contrary, the Court has engaged in a straight-forward consideration of the factors identified in *Eldridge* to determine whether a particular standard of proof in a particular proceeding satisfies due process.

In *Addington* v. *Texas*, 441 U.S. 418, 99 S.Ct. 1804, 60 L.Ed.2d 323 (1979), the Court, by a unanimous vote of the participating Justices, declared: "The function of a standard of proof, as that concept is embodied in the Due Process Clause and in the realm of factfinding, is to 'instruct the factfinder concerning the degree of confidence our society thinks he should have in the correctness of factual conclusions for a particular type of adjudication.' " *Id.*, at 423, 99 S.Ct. at 1808, quoting *In re Winship*, 397 U.S. 358, 370, 90 S.Ct. 1068, 1075, 25 L.Ed.2d 368 (1970) (Harlan, J., concurring). *Addington* teaches that, in any given proceeding, the minimum standard of proof tolerated by the due process requirement reflects not only the weight of the private and public interests affected, but also a societal judgment about how the risk of error should be distributed between the litigants.

Thus, while private parties may be interested intensely in a civil dispute over money damages, application of a "preponderance of the evidence" standard indicates both society's "minimal concern with the outcome," and a conclusion that the litigants should "share the risk of error in roughly equal fashion." 441 U.S., at 423, 99 S.Ct., at 1808. When the State brings a criminal action to deny a defendant liberty or life, however, "the interests of the defendant are of such magnitude that historically and without any explicit constitutional requirement they have been protected by standards of proof designed to exclude as nearly as possible the likelihood of an erroneous judgment." *Ibid.* The stringency of the "beyond a reasonable doubt" standard bespeaks the "weight and gravity" of the private interest affected, *id.*, at 427, 99 S.Ct., at 1810, society's interest in avoiding erroneous convictions, and a judgment that those interests together require that "society impos[e] almost the entire risk of error upon itself." *Id.*, at 424, 99 S.Ct., at 1808. See also *In re Winship*, 397 U.S., at 372, 90 S.Ct., at 1076 (Harlan, J., concurring).

The "minimum requirements [of procedural due process] being a matter of federal law, they are not diminished by the fact that the State may have specified its own procedures that it may deem adequate for determining the preconditions to adverse official action." *Vitek* v. *Jones*, 445 U.S. 480, 491, 100 S.Ct. 1254, 1262, 63 L.Ed.2d 552 (1980). See also *Logan* v. *Zimmerman Brush Co.*, ____ U.S. ____, ____, 102 S.Ct. 1148, 1155–56, 71 L.Ed.2d ____ (1982). Moreover, the degree of proof required in a particular type of proceeding "is the kind of question which has traditionally been left to the judiciary to resolve." *Woodby* v. *INS*, 385 U.S. 276, 284, 87 S.Ct. 483, 487, 17 L.Ed.2d 362 (1966). "In cases involving individual rights, whether criminal or civil, '[t]he standard of proof [at a minimum] reflects the value society places on individual liberty.' " *Addington* v. *Texas*, 441 U.S., at 425, 99 S.Ct., at 1809, quoting *Tippett* v. *Maryland*, 436 F.2d 1153, 1166 (CA4 1971) (opinion concurring in part and dissenting in part), cert. dismissed *sub nom. Murel* v. *Baltimore City Criminal Court,* 407 U.S. 355, 92 S.Ct. 2091, 32 L.Ed.2d 791 (1972).

This Court has mandated an intermediate standard of proof—"clear and convincing evidence"—when the individual interests at stake in a state proceeding are both "particularly important" and "more substantial than mere loss of money." *Addington* v. *Texas,* 441 U.S., at 424, 99 S.Ct., at 1808. Notwithstanding "the state's 'civil labels and good intentions,'" *id.,* at 427, 99 S.Ct. at 1810, quoting *In re Winship,* 397 U.S., at 365–366, 90 S.Ct., at 1073–1074, the Court has deemed this level of certainty necessary to preserve fundamental fairness in a variety of government-initiated proceedings that threaten the individual involved with "a significant deprivation of liberty" or "stigma." 441 U.S., at 425, 426, 99 S.Ct., at 1808, 1809. See, *e.g., Addington* v. *Texas, supra,* (civil commitment); *Woodby* v. *INS,* 385 U.S., at 285, 87 S.Ct., at 487 (deportation); *Chaunt* v. *United States,* 364 U.S. 350, 353, 81 S.Ct. 147, 149, 5 L.Ed.2d 120 (1960) (denaturalization); *Schneiderman* v. *United States,* 320 U.S. 118, 125, 159, 63 S.Ct. 1333, 1336, 1353, 87 L.Ed. 1796 (1943) (denaturalization).

In *Lassiter,* to be sure, the Court held that fundamental fairness may be maintained in parental rights termination proceedings even when some procedures are mandated only on a case-by-case basis, rather than through rules of general application. 452 U.S., at 31–32, 101 S.Ct., at 2161–2162 (natural parent's right to court-appointed counsel should be determined by the trial court, subject to appellate review). But this Court never has approved case-by-case determination of the proper *standard of proof* for a given proceeding. Standards of proof, like other "procedural due process rules[,] are shaped by the risk of error inherent in the truth-finding process as applied to the *generality of cases,* not the rare exceptions." *Mathews* v. *Eldridge,* 424 U.S., at 344, 96 S.Ct., at 907 (emphasis added). Since the litigants and the factfinder must know at the outset of a given proceeding how the risk of error will be allocated, the standard of proof necessarily must be calibrated in advance. Retrospective case-by-case review cannot preserve fundamental fairness when a class of proceedings is governed by a constitutionally defective evidentiary standard.

### III

In parental rights termination proceedings, the private interest affected is commanding; the risk of error from using a preponderance standard is substantial; and the countervailing governmental interest favoring that standard is comparatively slight. Evaluation of the three *Eldridge* factors compels the conclusion that use of a "fair preponderance of the evidence" standard in such proceedings is inconsistent with due process.

### A

"The extent to which procedural due process must be afforded the recipient is influenced by the extent to which he may be 'condemned to suffer grievous loss.'" *Goldberg* v. *Kelly,* 397 U.S. 254, 262–263, 90 S.Ct. 1011, 1017–18, 25 L.Ed.2d 287 (1970), quoting *Joint Anti-Fascist Refugee Committee* v. *McGrath,* 341 U.S. 123, 168, 71 S.Ct. 624, 646, 95 L.Ed. 817 (1951) (Frankfurter, J., concurring). Whether the loss threatened by a particular type of proceeding is sufficiently grave to warrant more than average certainty on the part of the factfinder turns on both the nature of the private interest threatened and the permanency of the threatened loss.

*Lassiter* declared it "plain beyond the need for multiple citation" that a natural parent's "desire for and right to 'the companionship, care, custody, and management of his or her children'" is an interest far more precious than any property right. 452 U.S., at 27, 101 S.Ct., at 2160, quoting *Stanley* v. *Illinois,* 405 U.S., at 651, 92 S.Ct., at 1212. When the State initiates a parental rights termination proceeding, it seeks not merely to infringe that fundamental liberty interest, but to end it. "If the Sate prevails, it will have worked a unique kind of deprivation. . . . A parent's interest in the accuracy and justice of the decision to terminate his or her parental status is, therefore, a commanding one." 452 U.S., at 27, 101 S.CT., at 2160.

In government-initiated proceedings to determine juvenile delinquency, *In re Winship, supra;* civil commitment, *Addington* v. *Texas, supra;* deportation, *Woodby* v. *INS, supra;* and denaturalization, *Chaunt* v. *United States, supra,* and *Schneiderman* v. *United States, supra,* this Court has identified losses of individual liberty sufficiently serious to warrant imposition of an elevated burden of proof. Yet juvenile delinquency adjudications, civil commitment, deportation, and denaturalization, at least to a degree, are all *reversible* official actions. Once affirmed on appeal, a New York decision terminating parental rights is *final* and irrevocable. See n. 1, *supra.* Few forms of state action are both so severe and so irreversible.

Thus, the first *Eldridge* factor—the private interest affected—weighs heavily against use of the preponderance standard at a State-initiated permanent neglect proceeding. We do not deny that the child and his foster parents are also deeply interested in the outcome of that contest. But at the factfinding stage of the New York proceeding, the focus emphatically is not on them.

The factfinding does not purport—and is not intended—to balance the child's interest in a normal family home against the parents' interest in raising the child. Nor does it purport to determine whether the natural parents or the foster parents would provide the better home. Rather, the factfinding hearing pits the State directly against the parents. The State alleges that the natural parents are at fault. Fam.Ct.Act § 614.1.(d). The questions disputed and decided are what the State did—"made diligent efforts," § 614.1.(c)—and what the natural parents did not do—"maintain contact with or plan for the future of the child." § 614.1.(d). The State marshals an array of public resources to prove its case and disprove the parents' case. Victory by the State not only makes termination of parental rights possible; it entails a judicial determination that the parents are unfit to raise their own children.

At the factfinding, the State cannot presume that a child and his parents are adversaries. After the State has established parental unfitness at that initial proceeding, the court may assume at the *dispositional* stage that the interests of the child and the natural parents do diverge. See Fam.Ct.Act, § 631 (judge shall make his order "solely on the basis of the best interests of the child," and thus has no obligation to consider the natural parents' rights in selecting dispositional alternatives). But until the State proves parental unfitness, the child and his parents share a vital interest in preventing erroneous termination of their natural relationship. Thus, at the factfinding, the interests of the child and his natural parents coincide to favor use of error-reducing procedures.

However substantial the foster parents interests may be, cf. *Smith* v. *Organization of Foster Families,* 431 U.S., at 845–847, 97 S.Ct., at 2110–2111, they are not implicated directly in the factfinding stage of a State-initiated permanent neglect proceeding against the natural parents. If authorized, the foster parents may pit their interests directly against those of the natural parents by initiating their own permanent neglect proceeding. Fam.Ct.Act §§ 615, 1055(d); Soc.Serv.Law § 392.7.(c). Alternatively, the foster parents can make their case for custody at the dispositional stage of a State-initiated proceeding, where the judge already has decided the issue of permanent neglect and is focusing on the placement that would serve the child's best interests. Fam.Ct.Act §§ 623, 631. For the foster parents, the State's failure to prove permanent neglect may prolong the delay and uncertainty until their foster child is freed for adoption. But for the natural parents, a finding of permanent neglect can cut off forever their rights in their child. Given this disparity of consequence, we have no difficulty finding that the balance of private interests strongly favors heightened procedural protection.

B

Under *Mathews* v. *Eldridge,* we next must consider both the risk of erroneous deprivation of private interests resulting from use of a "fair preponderance" standard and the likelihood that a higher evidentiary standard would reduce that risk. See 424 U.S., at 335, 96 S.Ct., at 903. Since the factfinding phase of a permanent neglect proceeding is an adversary contest between the State and the natural parents, the relevant question is whether a preponderance standard fairly allocates the risk of an erroneous factfinding between these two parties.

In New York, the factfinding stage of a State-initiated permanent neglect proceeding bears many of the indicia of a criminal trial. Cf. *Lassiter* v. *Department of Social Services,* 452 U.S., at 42–44, 101 S.Ct., at 2167–69 (dissenting opinion); *Meltzer* v. *C. Buck LeCraw & Co.,* 402 U.S. 954, 959, 91 S.Ct. 1624, 1626, 29 L.Ed.2d 124 (1971) (Black, J., dissenting from denial of certiorari). See also dissenting opinion, *post,* at 1406–1408 (describing procedures employed at factfinding proceeding). The Commissioner of Social Services charges the parents with permanent neglect. They are served by summons. Fam.Ct.Act §§ 614, 616, 617. The factfinding hearing is conducted pursuant to formal rules of evidence. § 624. The State, the parents, and the child are all represented by counsel. §§ 249, 262. The State seeks to establish a series of historical facts about the intensity of its agency's efforts to reunite the family, the infrequency and insubstantiality of the parents' contacts with their child, and the parents' inability or unwillingness to formulate a plan for the child's future. The attorneys submit documentary evidence, and call witnesses who are subject to cross-examination. Based on all evidence, the judge then determines whether the State has proved the statutory elements of permanent neglect by a fair preponderance of the evidence. § 622.

At such a proceeding, numerous factors combine to magnify the risk of erroneous factfinding. Permanent neglect proceedings employ imprecise substantive standards that leave determinations unusually open to the subjective values of the judge. See *Smith* v. *Organization of Foster Families,* 431 U.S., at 835, n. 36, 97 S.Ct., at 2105, n. 36. In appraising the nature and quality of a complex series of encounters among the agency, the parents, and the child, the court possesses unusual discretion to underweigh probative facts that might favor the parent. Because parents subject to termination proceedings are often poor, uneducated, or members of minority groups, *id.,* at 833–835, such proceedings are often vulnerable to judgments based on cultural or class bias.

The State's ability to assemble its case almost inevitably dwarfs the parents' ability to mount a defense. No predetermined limits restrict the sums an agency may spend in prosecuting a given termination proceeding. The State's attorney usually will be expert on the issues contested and the procedures employed at the factfinding hearing, and enjoys full access to all public records concerning the family. The State may call on experts in family relations, psychology, and medicine to bolster its case. Furthermore, the primary witnesses at the hearing will be the agency's own professional caseworkers whom the State has empowered both to investigate the family situation and to testify against the parents. Indeed, because the child is already in agency custody, the State even has the power to shape the historical events that form the basis for termination.

The disparity between the adversaries' litigation resources is matched by a striking asymmetry in their litigation options. Unlike criminal defendants, natural parents have no "double jeopardy" defense against repeated state termination efforts. If the State initially fails to win termination, as New York did here, see n. 4, *supra,* it always can try once again to cut off the parents' rights after gathering more or better evidence. Yet even when the parents have attained the level of fitness required by the State, they have no similar means by which they can forestall future termination efforts.

Coupled with a "preponderance of the evidence" standard, these factors create a significant prospect of erroneous termination. A standard of proof that by its very terms demands consideration of the quantity, rather than the quality, of the evidence may misdirect the factfinder in the marginal case. See *In re Winship,* 397 U.S., at 371, n. 3, 90 S.Ct., at 1076, n. 3 (Harlan, J., concurring). Given the weight of the private interests at stake, the social cost of even occasional error is sizable.

Raising the standard of proof would have both practical and symbolic consequences. Cf. *Addington* v. *Texas,* 441 U.S., at 426, 99 S.Ct., at 1809. The Court has long considered the heightened standard of proof used in criminal prosecutions to be "a prime instrument for reducing the risk of convictions resting on factual error." *In re Winship,* 397 U.S., at 363, 90 S.Ct., at 1072. An elevated standard of proof in a parental rights termination proceeding would alleviate "the possible risk that a factfinder might decide to [deprive] an individual based solely on a few isolated instances of unusual conduct [or] . . . idiosyncratic behavior." *Addington* v. *Texas,* 441 U.S., at 427, 99 S.Ct., at 1810. "Increasing the burden of proof is one way to impress the factfinder with the importance of the decision and thereby perhaps to reduce the chances that inappropriate" terminations will be ordered. *Ibid.*

The Appellate Division approved New York's preponderance standard on the ground that it properly "balanced rights possessed by the child . . . with those of the natural parents. . . ." 75 App.Div.2d, at 910, 427 N.Y.S.2d, at 320. By so saying, the court suggested that a preponderance standard properly allocates the risk of *error between* the parents and the child. That view is fundamentally mistaken.

The court's theory assumes that termination of the natural parents' rights invariably will benefit the child. Yet we have noted above that the parents and the child share an interest in avoiding erroneous termination. Even accepting the court's assumption, we cannot agree with its conclusion that a preponderance standard fairly distributes the risk of error between parent and child. Use of that standard reflects the judgment that society is nearly neutral between erroneous termination of parental rights and erroneous failure to terminate those rights. Cf. *In re Winship,* 397 U.S., at 371, 90 S.Ct., at 1076 (Harlan, J., concurring). For the child, the likely consequence of an erroneous failure to terminate is preservation of an uneasy status quo. For the natural parents, however, the consequence of an erroneous termination is the unnecessary destruction of their natural family. A standard that allocates the risk of error nearly equally between those two outcomes does not reflect properly their relative severity.

## C

Two state interests are at stake in parental rights termination proceedings—a *parens patriae* interest in preserving and promoting the welfare of the child and a fiscal and administrative interest in reducing the cost and burden of such proceedings. A standard of proof more strict than preponderance of the evidence is consistent with both interests.

"Since the State has an urgent interest in the welfare of the child, it shares the parent's interest in an accurate and just decision" at the *factfinding* proceeding. *Lassiter* v. *Department of Social Services,* 452 U.S., at 27, 101 S.Ct., at 2160. As *parens patriae,* the State's goal is to provide the child with a permanent home. See Soc.Serv.Law § 384–b.1.(a)(i) (statement of legislative findings and intent). Yet while there is still reason to believe that positive, nurturing parent-child relationships exist, the *parens patriae* interest favors preservation, not severance, of natural familial bonds. § 384–b.1.(a)(ii). "[T]he State registers no gain towards its declared goals when it separates children from the custody of fit parents." *Stanley* v. *Illinois,* 405 U.S., at 652, 92 S.Ct., at 1213.

The State's interest in finding the child an alternative permanent home arises only "when it is *clear* that the natural parent cannot or will not provide a normal family home for the child." Soc.Serv.Law § 384–b.1.(a)(iv) (emphasis added). At the factfinding, that goal is served by procedures that promote an accurate determination of whether the natural parents can and will provide a normal home.

Unlike a constitutional requirement of hearings, see, *e.g., Mathews* v. *Eldridge,* 424 U.S., at 347, 96 S.Ct., at 908, or court-appointed counsel, a stricter standard of proof would reduce factual error without imposing substantial fiscal burdens upon the State. As we have observed, 33 States already have adopted a higher standard by statute or court decision without apparent effect on the speed, form, or cost of their factfinding proceedings. See n. 3, *supra.*

Nor would an elevated standard of proof create any real administrative burdens for the State's factfinders. New York Family Court judges already are familiar with a higher evidentiary standard in other parental rights termination proceedings not involving permanent neglect. See Soc.Serv.Law §§ 384–b.3.(g), 384–b.4.(c), and 384–b.4(e) (requiring "clear and convincing proof" before parental rights may be terminated for reasons of mental illness and mental retardation or severe and repeated child abuse). New York also demands at least clear and convincing evidence in proceedings of far less moment than parental rights termination proceedings. See, *e.g.*, N.Y. Veh. & Traf. Law § 227.1 (McKinney Supp.1981) (requiring the State to prove traffic infractions by "clear and convincing evidence") and *In re Rosenthal* v. *Harnett*, 36 N.Y.2d 269, 367 N.Y.S.2d 247, 326 N.E.2d 811 (1975); see also *Ross* v. *Food Specialties, Inc.*, 6 N.Y.2d 336, 341, 189 N.Y.S.2d 857, 859, 160 N.E.2d 618, 620 (1959) (requiring "clear, positive and convincing evidence" for contract reformation). We cannot believe that it would burden the State unduly to require that its factfinders have the same factual certainty when terminating the parent-child relationship as they must have to suspend a driver's license.

## IV

The logical conclusion of this balancing process is that the "fair preponderance of the evidence" standard prescribed by Fam.Ct.Act § 622 violates the Due Process Clause of the Fourteenth Amendment. The Court noted in *Addington:* "The individual should not be asked to share equally with society the risk of error when the possible injury to the individual is significantly greater than any possible harm to the state." 441 U.S., at 427, 99 S.Ct., at 1810. Thus, at a parental rights termination proceeding, a near-equal allocation of risk between the parents and the State is constitutionally intolerable. The next question, then, is whether a "beyond a reasonable doubt" or a "clear and convincing" standard is constitutionally mandated.

In *Addington,* the Court concluded that application of a reasonable-doubt standard is inappropriate in civil commitment proceedings for two reasons—because of our hesitation to apply that unique standard "too broadly or casually in noncriminal cases," *id.,* at 428, 99 S.Ct., at 1810, and because the psychiatric evidence ordinarily adduced at commitment proceedings is rarely susceptible to proof beyond a reasonable doubt. *Id.,* at 429–430, 432–433, 99 S.Ct., at 1811–1812, 1812–1813. To be sure, as has been noted above, in the Indian Child Welfare Act of 1978, Pub.L. 95–608, § 102(f), 92 Stat. 3072, 25 U.S.C. § 1912(f) (1976 ed., Supp. III), Congress requires "evidence beyond a reasonable doubt" for termination of Indian parental rights, reasoning that "the removal of a child from the parents is a penalty as great, if not greater, than a criminal penalty. . . ." H.R.Rep.No. 95–1386, p. 22 (1978), U.S.Code Cong. & Admin. News 1978, pp. 7530, 7545. Congress did not consider, however, the evidentiary problems that would arise if proof beyond a reasonable doubt were required in all State-initiated parental rights termination hearings.

Like civil commitment hearings, termination proceedings often require the factfinder to evaluate medical and psychiatric testimony, and to decide issues difficult to prove to a level of absolute certainty, such as lack of parental motive, absence of affection between parent and child, and failure of parental foresight and progress. Cf. *Lassiter* v. *Department of Social Services,* 452 U.S., at 30, 101 S.Ct., at 2161; *id.,* at

44–46, 101 S.Ct., at 2168–2169 (dissenting opinion) (describing issues raised in state termination proceedings). The substantive standards applied vary from State to State. Although Congress found a "beyond a reasonable doubt" standard proper in one type of parental rights termination case, another legislative body might well conclude that a reasonable-doubt standard would erect an unreasonable barrier to state efforts to free permanently neglected children for adoption.

A majority of the States have concluded that a "clear and convincing evidence" standard of proof strikes a fair balance between the rights of the natural parents and the State's legitimate concerns. See n. 3, *supra*. We hold that such a standard adequately conveys to the factfinder the level of subjective certainty about his factual conclusions necessary to satisfy due process. We further hold that determination of the precise burden equal to or greater than that standard is a matter of state law properly left to state legislatures and state courts. Cf. *Addington* v. *Texas,* 441 U.S., at 433, 99 S.Ct., at 1813.

We, of course, express no view on the merits of petitioners' claims. At a hearing conducted under a constitutionally proper standard, they may or may not prevail. Without deciding the outcome under any of the standards we have approved, we vacate the judgment of the Appellate Division and remand the case for further proceedings not inconsistent with this opinion.

*It is so ordered.*

NOTES

1. Not included here is the dissenting opinion of Justice Rehnquist, joined by Chief Justice Burger and Justices White and O'Connor. 102 S.Ct. 1403–1414. Among other things, the dissenting opinion points out that the *Santosky* case arose from a factual situation in which the children had received "shockingly abusive treatment," involving broken bones, bruises, malnutrition, cuts, burns, and pin pricks. *Id.* at 1408, n. 10 and accompanying text. Does this change your view of the outcome of the case?

2. The decision in *Santosky* v. *Kramer* necessitates a reevaluation of the continuing validity of all of the termination of parental rights cases decided previously.

p. 992—ADD a new section before Additional Reading:

### c. Custody Determinations Arising Out of Divorce Proceedings

#### IN RE MARRIAGE OF CARNEY
*Supreme Court of California, 1979*
*157 Cal.Rptr 383, 598 P.2d 36*

MOSK, Justice.

Appellant father (William) appeals from that portion of an interlocutory decree of dissolution which transfers custody of the two minor children of the marriage from himself to respondent mother (Ellen).

In this case of first impression we are called upon to resolve an apparent conflict between two strong public policies: the requirement that a custody award serve the best interests of the child, and the moral and legal obligation of society to respect the civil rights of its physically handicapped members, including their right not to be deprived of their children because of their disability. As will appear, we hold that upon a realistic appraisal of the present-day capabilities of the physically handicapped, these policies can both be accommodated. The trial court herein failed to make such an appraisal, and instead premised its ruling on outdated stereotypes of both the parental role and the ability of the handicapped to fill that role. Such stereotypes have no place in our law. Accordingly, the order changing custody on this ground must be set aside as an abuse of discretion.

William and Ellen were married in New York in December 1968. Both were teenagers. Two sons were soon born of the union, the first in November 1969 and the second in January 1971. The parties separated shortly afterwards, and by written agreement executed in November 1972, Ellen relinquished custody of the boys to William. For reasons of employment he eventually moved to the West Coast. In September 1973 he began living with a young woman named Lori Rivera, and she acted as stepmother to the boys. In the following year William had a daughter by Lori, and she proceeded to raise all three children as their own.

In August 1976, while serving in the military reserve, William was injured in a jeep accident. The accident left him a quadriplegic, i.e., with paralyzed legs and impaired use of his arms and hands. He spent the next year recuperating in a veterans' hospital; his children visited him several times each week, and he came home nearly every weekend.[1] He also bought a van, and it was being fitted with a wheelchair lift and hand controls to permit him to drive.

In May 1977 William filed the present action for dissolution of his marriage. Ellen moved for an order awarding her immediate custody of both boys. It was undisputed that from the date of separation (Nov. 1972) until a few days before the hearing (Aug. 1977) Ellen did not once visit her young sons or make any contribution to their support. Throughout this period of almost five years her sole contact with the boys consisted of some telephone calls and a few letters and packages. Nevertheless the court ordered that the boys be taken from the custody of their father, and that Ellen be allowed to remove them forthwith to New York State.[2] Pursuant to stipulation of the parties, an interlocutory judgment of dissolution was entered at the same time. William appeals from that portion of the decree transferring custody of the children to Ellen.

William contends the trial court abused its discretion in making the award of custody.[3] Several principles are here applicable. First, since it was amended in 1972 the

---

[1]He was scheduled to be discharged shortly after the trial proceedings herein.

[2]The court also imposed substantial financial obligations on William. He was ordered to pay all future costs of transporting his sons back to California to visit him, plus $400 a month for child support, $1,000 for Ellen's attorney's fees, $800 for her travel and hotel expenses, and $750 for her court costs.

[3]He also contends the ruling violated his right to equal protection and due process of law. (*Adoption of Richardson* (1967) 251 Cal.App.2d 222, 239–240, 59 Cal.Rptr. 323, see generally Achtenberg, *Law and the Physically Disabled: An Update with Constitutional Implications* (1976) 8 Sw.U.L.Rev. 847; Burgdorf & Burgdorf, *A History of Unequal Treatment: The Qualifications of Handicapped Persons as a "Suspect Class" Under the Equal Protection Clause* (1975) 15 Santa Clara Law. 855; Comment, *The Equal Protection and Due Process Clauses: Two Means of Implementing "Integrationism" for Handicapped Applicants for Public Employment* (1978) 27 DePaul L. Rev. 1169; Note, *Abroad in the Land: Legal Strategies to Effectuate the Rights of the Physically Disabled* (1973) 61 Geo.L.J. 1501.) In the view we take of the case we need not reach the constitutional issues at this time.  [*continued next page*]

code no longer requires or permits the trial courts to favor the mother in determining proper custody of a child "of tender years." (E.g., *White* v. *White* (1952) 109 Cal.App.2d 522, 523, 240 P.2d 1015.) Civil Code section 4600 now declares that custody should be awarded "To either parent according to the best interests of the child." (*Id.*, subd. (a).) Regardless of the age of the minor, therefore, fathers now have equal custody rights with mothers; the sole concern, as it should be, is "the best interests of the child." (See *Taber* v. *Taber* (1930) 209 Cal. 755, 756–757, 290 P. 36, 37.)

Next, those "best interests" are at issue here in a special way: this is not the usual case in which the parents have just separated and the choice of custody is being made for the first time. In such instances the trial court rightly has a broad discretion. (*Gudelj* v. *Gudelj* (1953) 41 Cal.2d 202, 208–209, 259 P.2d 656.) Here, although this is the first actual court order on the issue, we deal in effect with a complete *change* in custody: after the children had lived with William for almost five years—virtually all their lives up to that point—Ellen sought to remove them abruptly from the only home they could remember to a wholly new environment some 3,000 miles away.

It is settled that to justify ordering a change in custody there must generally be a persuasive showing of changed circumstances affecting the child. (*Goto* v. *Goto* (1959) 52 Cal.2d 118, 122–123, 338 P.2d 450.) And that change must be substantial: a child will not be removed from the prior custody of one parent and given to the other "unless the material facts and circumstances occurring subsequently are of a kind to render it essential or expedient for the welfare of the child that there be a change." (*Washburn* v. *Washburn* (1942) 49 Cal.App.2d 581, 588, 122 P.2d 96, 100.1) The reasons for the rule are clear: "It is well established that the courts are reluctant to order a change of custody and will not do so except for imperative reasons; that it is desirable that there be an end of litigation and undesirable to change the child's established mode of living." (*Connolly* v. *Connolly* (1963) 214 Cal.App.2d 433, 436, 29 Cal.Rptr. 616, 618, and cases cited.)

Moreover, although a request for a change of custody is also addressed in the first instance to the sound discretion of the trial judge, he must exercise that discretion in light of the important policy considerations just mentioned. For this reason appellate courts have been less reluctant to find an abuse of discretion when custody is changed than when it is originally awarded, and reversals of such orders have not been uncommon. (E.g., *In re Marriage of Kern* (1978) 87 Cal.App.3d 402, 410–411, 150 Cal.Rptr. 860; *In re Marriage of Russo* (1971) 21 Cal.App.3d 72, 98 Cal.Rptr. 501; *Denham* v. *Martina* (1963) 214 Cal.App.2d 312, 29 Cal.Rptr. 377; *Ashwell* v. *Ashwell* (1955) 135 Cal.App.2d 211, 286 P.2d 983; *Sorrels* v. *Sorrels* (1951) 105 Cal.App.2d 465, 234 P.2d 103; *Bemis* v. *Bemis* (1948) 89 Cal.App.2d 80, 200 P.2d 84; *Juri* v. *Juri* (1945) 69 Cal.App.2d 773, 160 P.2d 73; *Washburn* v. *Washburn* (1942) supra, 49 Cal.App.2d 581, 122 P.2d 96.)

---

William further complains that the trial court erred in declining several offers of evidence of alleged misconduct of Ellen occurring at various times prior to the hearing. We have reviewed the relevant portions of the record and conclude that certain of the offers were properly refused because the evidence in question was too remote (*Prouty* v. *Prouty* (1940) 16 Cal.2d 190, 194), while others should probably have been accepted but failure to do so could not have resulted in prejudice (*People* v. *Watson* (1956) 46 Cal.2d 818, 836, 299 P.2d 243).

Finally, the burden of showing a sufficient change in circumstances is on the party seeking the change of custody. (*Prouty* v. *Prouty* (1940) supra, 16 Cal.2d 190, 193, 105 P.2d 295; *In re Marriage of Kern* (1978) supra, 87 Cal.App.3d 402, 410–411, 150 Cal.Rptr. 860; *In re Marriage of Mehlmauer* (1976) 60 Cal.App.3d 104, 108–109, 131 Cal.Rptr. 325.) In attempting to carry that burden Ellen relied on several items of testimony given at the hearing; even when these circumstances are viewed in their totality, however, they are insufficient for the purpose.

First, Ellen showed that although she had been unemployed when William was given custody in 1972, at the time of trial she had a job as a medical records clerk in a New York hospital. But her gross income from that job was barely $500 per month, and she admitted she would not be able to support the boys without substantial financial assistance from William. (See fn. 2, *ante*.) By contrast, at the time of the hearing William's monthly income from a combination of veteran's disability compensation payments and social security benefits had risen to more than $1,750 per month, all tax-free.

Ellen next pointed to the fact that William's relationship with Lori might be in the process of terminating.[5] From this evidence Ellen argued that if Lori were to leave, William would have to hire a babysitter to take care of the children. On cross-examination, however, Ellen admitted that if custody were transferred to her she would likewise be compelled because of her job to place the children "in a child care center under a baby-sitter nine hours a day," and she intended to do so. During that period, of course, the children would not be under her supervision; by contrast, William explained that because he is not employed he is able to remain at home "to see to their upbringing during the day as well as the night."

Additional claims lacked support in the record. Thus Ellen impliedly criticized William's living arrangements for the boys, and testified that if she were given custody she intended to move out of her one-bedroom apartment into an apartment with "at least" two bedrooms. Yet it was undisputed that the boys were presently residing in a private house containing in effect four bedrooms, with a large living room and a spacious enclosed back yard; despite additional residents, there was no showing that the accommodations were inadequate for the family's needs. Ellen further stated that in her opinion the older boy should be seen by a dentist; there was no expert testimony to this effect, however, and no evidence that the child was not receiving normal dental care. She also remarked that the younger boy seemed to have a problem with wetting his bed but had not been taken to a doctor about it; again there was no evidence that medical intervention in this matter was either necessary or desirable. We obviously cannot take judicial notice of the cause of, or currently recommended cure for, childhood enuresis.[6]

---

[5]Lori candidly testified she had been "thinking about" leaving. She added, however, that "Bill and I have had some problems, just like anyone else in our situation would have, and we are going to get counseling, and hopefully that will settle the matters. And she declared that she loved both of the boys and wanted to continue being their "substitute mother."

[6]In the only testimony on the point Ellen reported that William's cousin, who had been living with the family explained to her the reason the boy wet the bed is "because he wears himself out so much playing that he just doesn't get up at night."

Ellen advanced other grounds for a change of custody that are even more insubstantial. Thus she

In short, if the trial court had based its change of custody order on the foregoing circumstances alone, it would in effect have revived the "mother's preference" rule abrogated by the Legislature in 1972. The record discloses, however, that the court gave great weight to another factor—William's physical handicap and its presumed adverse effect on his capacity to be a good father to the boys. Whether that factor will support the reliance placed upon it is a difficult question to which we now turn.

Ellen first raised the issue in her declaration accompanying her request for a change of custody, asserting that because of William's handicap "it is almost impossible for [him] to actually care for the minor children," and "since [he] is confined to a hospital bed, he is never with the minor children and thus can no longer effectively care for the minor children or see to their physical and emotional needs." When asked at the hearing why she believed she should be given custody, she replied inter alia, "Bill's physical condition." Thereafter she testified that according to her observations William is not capable of feeding himself or helping the boys prepare meals or get dressed; and she summed up by agreeing that he is not able to do "anything" for himself.

The trial judge echoed this line of reasoning throughout the proceedings. Virtually the only questions he asked of any witness revolved around William's handicap and its physical consequences, real or imagined. Thus although William testified at length about his present family life and his future plans, the judge inquired only where he sat when he got out of his wheelchair, whether he had lost the use of his arms, and what his medical prognosis was. Again, when Lori took the stand and testified to William's good relationship with his boys and their various activities together, the judge interrupted to ask her in detail whether it was true that she had to bathe, dress, undress, cook for and feed William. Indeed, he seemed interested in little else.

The final witness was Dr. Jack Share, a licensed clinical psychologist specializing in child development, who had visited William's home and studied his family. Dr. Share testified that William had an IQ of 127, was a man of superior intelligence, excellent judgment and ability to plan, and had adapted well to his handicap. He observed good interaction between William and his boys, and described the latter as self-disciplined, sociable, and outgoing. On the basis of his tests and observations, Dr. Share gave as his professional opinion that neither of the children appeared threatened by William's physical condition; the condition did not in any way hinder William's ability to be a father to them, and would not be a detriment to them if they remained in his home; the present family situation in his home was a healthy environment for the children; and even if Lori were to leave, William could still fulfill his functions as father with appropriate domestic help.

Ellen made no effort on cross-examination to dispute any of the foregoing observations or conclusions, and offered no expert testimony to the contrary. The

---

claimed she wanted to enroll the boys in "some kind of church"—a choice of words scarcely indicative of a deep religious commitment on her part. And she complained that because William had moved several times in the past five years the boys had not had a chance to "get established" in a school or neighborhood—a strange objection coming from one who proposed to move them 3,000 miles. In any event, the record indicated that most of William's moves were job-related and took place prior to the date of his injury, and hence were irrelevant to the family's present situation.

judge then took up the questioning, however, and focused on what appears to have been one of his main concerns in the case—i.e., that because of the handicap William would not be able to participate with his sons in sports and other physical activities. Thus the court asked Dr. Share, "It's very unfortunate that he's in this condition, but when these boys get another two, three years older, would it be better, in your opinion, if they had a parent that was able to actively go places with them, take them places, play Little League baseball, go fishing? Wouldn't that be advantageous to two young boys?" Dr. Share replied that "the commitment, the long-range planning, the dedication" of William to his sons were more important, and stated that from his observations William was "the more consistent, stable part of this family regardless of his physical condition at this point." The judge nevertheless persisted in stressing that William "is limited in what he can do for the boys," and demanded an answer to his question as to "the other activities that two growing boys should have with a natural parent." Dr. Share acknowledged William's obvious physical limitations, but once more asserted that "on the side dealing with what I have called the stability of the youngsters, which I put personally higher value on, I would say the father is very strong in this area." Finally, when asked on redirect examination what effect William's ability to drive will have, Dr. Share explained, "this opens up more vistas, greater alternatives when he's more mobile such as having his own van to take them places. . . ."

We need not speculate on the reasons for the judge's ensuing decision to order the change of custody, as he candidly stated them for the record. First he distinguished a case cited by William, emphasizing "There was no father there or mother that was unable to care for the children because of physical disabilities. . . ." Next he found William and Ellen to be "both good, loving parents," although he strongly chided the latter for failing to visit her sons for five years, saying "She should have crawled on her hands and knees out here if she had to get the children. . . ." The judge then returned to the theme of William's physical inability to personally take care of the children: speculating on Lori's departure, the judge stressed that in such event "a housekeeper or a nursery" would have to be hired—overlooking the admitted fact that Ellen would be compelled to do exactly the same herself for nine hours a day. And he further assumed "There would have to be pick up and probably delivery of the children even though [William] drives his van"—a non sequitur revealing his misunderstanding of the purpose and capabilities of that vehicle.

More importantly, the judge conceded that Dr. Share "saw a nice, loving relationship, and that's absolutely true. There's a great relationship between [William] and the boys. . . ." Yet despite this relationship the judge concluded "I think it would be detrimental to the boys to grow up until age 18 in the custody of their father. *It wouldn't be a normal relationship between father and boys.*" And what he meant by "normal" was quickly revealed: "It's unfortunate [William] has to have help bathing and dressing and undressing. *He can't do anything for the boys himself except maybe talk to them and teach them, be a tutor, which is good, but it's not enough.* I feel that it's in the best interests of the two boys to be with the mother even though she hasn't had them for five years." (Italics added.)

Such a record approaches perilously close to the showing in *Adoption of Rich-*

*ardson* (1967) supra, 251 Cal.App.2d 222, 59 Cal.Rptr. 323. There the trial court denied a petition to adopt an infant boy because of the physical handicap of the proposed adoptive parents, who were deaf-mutes. As here, professional opinions were introduced—and remained uncontradicted—stating that the petitioners had adjusted well to their handicap and had a good realtionship with the child, and that their disability would have no adverse effects on his physical or emotional development. Nevertheless, in language strangely similar to that of the judge herein, the trial court reasoned: "Is this a normally happy home? There is no question about it, it is a happy home, but is it a normal home? I don't think the Court could make a finding that it is a normal home when these poor unfortunate people, they are handicapped, and what can they do in the way of bringing this child up to be the type of citizen we all want him to be." (*Id.* at p. 228, 59 Cal.Rptr. at p. 327.) The Court of Appeal there concluded from this and other evidence that the trial judge was prejudiced by a belief that no deaf-mute could ever be a good parent to a "normal" child. While recognizing the rule that the granting or denial of a petition for adoption rests in the discretion of the judge, the appellate court held that such discretion had been abused and accordingly reversed the judgement. (*Id.* at p. 237, 59 Cal.Rptr. 323).

While it is clear the judge herein did not have the totally closed mind exhibited in *Richardson,* it is equally plain that his judgment was affected by serious misconceptions as to the importance of the involvement of parents in the purely physical aspects of their children's lives. We do not mean, of course, that the health or physical condition of the parents may not be taken into account in determining whose custody would best serve the child's interests. In relation to the issues at stake, however, this factor is ordinarily of minor importance; and whenever it is raised—whether in awarding custody originally or changing it later—it is essential that the court weigh the matter with an informed and open mind.

In particular, if a person has a physical handicap it is impermissible for the court simply to rely on that condition as prima facie evidence of the person's unfitness as a parent or of probable detriment to the child; rather, in all cases the court must view the handicapped person as an individual and the family as a whole. To achieve this, the court should inquire into the person's actual and potential physical capabilities, learn how he or she has adapted to the disability and manages its problems, consider how the other members of the household have adjusted thereto, and take into account the special contributions the person may make to the family despite—or even because of— the handicap. Weighing these and all other relevant factors together, the court should then carefully determine whether the parent's condition will in fact have a substantial and lasting adverse effect on the best interests of the child.[8]

The record shows the contrary occurred in the case at bar. To begin with, the court's belief that there could be no "normal relationship between father and boys" unless William engaged in vigorous sporting activities with his sons is a further

---

[8]A recent statute makes the point in a closely related context: a child may be made a ward of the court because of lack of parental care and control, but "No parent shall be found to be incapable of exercising proper and effective parental care or control solely because of a physical disability. . . ." (Welf, & Inst. Code, § 300, subd. (a); see, e.g., *In re W. O.* (1979) 88 Cal.App.3d 906, 910, 152 Cal.Rptr. 130 [mother's epilepsy no ground for removing children from her custody].

example of the conventional sex-stereotypical thinking that we condemned in another context in *Sail'er Inn* v. *Kirby* (1971) 5 Cal.3d 1, 95 Cal.Rptr. 329, 485 P.2d 529. For some, the court's emphasis on the importance of a father's "playing baseball" or "going fishing" with his sons may evoke nostalgic memories of a Norman Rockwell cover on the old Saturday Evening Post. But it has at least been understood that a boy need not prove his masculinity on the playing fields of Eton, nor must a man compete with his son in athletics in order to be a good father: their relationship is no less "normal" if it is built on shared experiences in such fields of interest as science, music, arts and crafts, history or travel, or in pursuing such classic hobbies as stamp or coin collecting. In short, an afternoon that a father and son spend together at a museum or the zoo is surely no less enriching than an equivalent amount of time spent catching either balls or fish.[9]

Even more damaging is the fact that the court's preconception herein, wholly apart from its outdated presumption of proper gender roles, also stereotypes William as a person deemed forever unable to be a good parent simply because he is physically handicapped. Like most stereotypes, this is both false and demeaning. On one level it is false because it assumes that William will never make any significant recovery from his disability. There was no evidence whatever to this effect. On the contrary, it did appear that the hearing was being held only one year after the accident, that William had not yet begun the process of rehabilitation in a home environment, and that he was still a young man in his twenties. In these circumstances the court could not presume that modern medicine, helped by time, patience, and determination, would be powerless to restore at least some of William's former capabilities for active life.

Even if William's prognosis were poor, however, the stereotype indulged in by the court is false for an additional reason: it mistakenly assumes that the parent's handicap inevitably handicaps the child. But children are more adaptable than the court gives them credit for; if one path to their enjoyment of physical activities is closed, they will soon find another. Indeed, having a handicapped parent often stimulates the growth of a child's imagination, independence, and self-reliance. Today's urban youngster, moreover, has many more opportunities for formal and informal instruction than his isolated rural predecessor. It is true that William may not be able to play tennis or swim, ride a bicycle or do gymnastics; but it does not follow that his children cannot learn and enjoy such skills, with the guidance not only of family and friends but also the professional instructors available through schools, church groups, playgrounds, camps, the Red Cross, the YMCA, the Boy Scouts, and numerous service organizations. As Dr. Share pointed out in his testimony, ample community resources now supplement the home in these circumstances.

In addition, it is erroneous to presume that a parent in a wheelchair cannot share to a meaningful degree in the physical activities of his child, should both desire it. On the one hand, modern technology has made the handicapped increasingly mobile, as demonstrated by William's purchase of a van and his plans to drive it by means of hand

---

[9] The sex stereotype, of course, cuts both ways. If the trial court's approach herein were to prevail, in the next case a divorced mother who became physically handicapped could be deprived of her young daughters because she is unable to participate with them in embroidery, *haute cuisine,* or the fine arts of washing and ironing. To state the proposition is to refute it.

controls. In the past decade the widespread availability of such vans, together with sophisticated and reliable wheelchair lifts and driving control systems, have brought about a quiet revolution in the mobility of the severely handicapped. No longer are they confined to home or institution, unable to travel except by special vehicle or with the assistance of others; today such persons use the streets and highways in ever-growing numbers for both business and pleasure. Again as Dr. Share explained, the capacity to drive such a vehicle "opens more vistas, greater alternatives" for the handicapped person.

At the same time the physically handicapped have made the public more aware of the many unnecessary obstacles to their participation in community life. Among the evidence of the public's change in attitude is a growing body of legislation intended to reduce or eliminate the physical impediments to that participation; i.e., the "architectural barriers" against access by the handicapped to buildings, facilities, and transportation systems used by the public at large (See, e.g., Gov. Code, § 4450 et seq. [requires handicapped access to buildings and facilities constructed with public funds]; Health & Saf.Code, § 19955 et seq. [access to private buildings open to the general public]; Gov. Code, § 4500 [access to public transit systems]; Pub. Resources Code, § 5070.5, subd. (c) [access to public recreational trails]; see also Veh. Code, §§ 22507.8, 22511.5 et seq. [special parking privileges for handicapped drivers].)[10]

While there is obviously much room for continued progress in removing these barriers, the handicapped person today need not remain a shut-in. Although William cannot actually play on his children's baseball team, he may nevertheless be able to take them to the game, participate as a fan, a coach, or even an umpire—and treat them to ice cream on the way home. Nor is this companionship limited to athletic events: such a parent is no less capable of accompanying his children to theaters or libraries, shops or restaurants, schools or churches, afternoon picnics or long vacation trips. Thus it is not true that, as the court herein assumed, William will be unable "to actively go places with [his children], take them places, . . ."

On a deeper level, finally, the stereotype is false because it fails to reach the heart of the parent-child relationship. Contemporary psychology confirms what wise families have perhaps always known—that the essence of parenting is not to be found in the harried rounds of daily carpooling endemic to modern suburban life, or even in the doggedly dutiful acts of "togetherness" committed every weekend by well-meaning fathers and mothers across America. Rather, its essence lies in the ethical, emotional, and intellectual guidance the parent gives to the child throughout his formative years, and often beyond. The source of this guidance is the adult's own experience of life; its motive power is parental love and concern for the child's well-being; and its teachings deal with such fundamental matters as the child's feelings about himself, his

---

[10]Similar legislation has been enacted on the federal level. (See, e.g., Architectural Barriers Act of 1968 (42 U.S.C. §§ 4151–4157) [requires handicapped access to public buildings constructed, leased, or financed by the federal government]; Rehabilitation Act of 1973, § 502 (29 U.S.C. § 792) [creates Architectural and Transportation Barriers Compliance Board to ensure compliance with Architectural Barriers Act and promote removal of "architectural, transportation, and attitudinal barriers confronting handicapped individuals"]; Urban Mass Transportation Assistance Act of 1970, § 8 (49 U.S.C. § 1612) [declares federal policy that mass transit systems be designed for access by handicapped]; see also 49 C.F.R. pt. 609 (1978) [regulations concerning access to mass transit systems receiving federal financial assistance].)

relationships with others, his system of values, his standards of conduct, and his goals and priorities in life. Even if it were true, as the court herein asserted, that William cannot do "anything" for his sons except "talk to them and teach them, be a tutor," that would not only be "enough"—contrary to the court's conclusion—it would be the most valuable service a parent can render. Yet his capacity to do so is entirely unrelated to his physical prowess: however limited his bodily strength may be, a handicapped parent is a whole person to the child who needs his affection, sympathy, and wisdom to deal with the problems of growing up. Indeed, in such matters his handicap may well be an asset: few can pass through the crucible of a severe physical disability without learning enduring lessons in patience and tolerance.

No expert testimony was necessary to establish these facts. As the Court of Appeal correctly observed in a somewhat different context, "It requires no detailed discussion to demonstrate that the support and, even more, the control of the child is primarily a mental function to which soundness of mind is a crucial prerequisite. It is also well known that physical handicaps generally have no adverse effect upon mental functions. . . . It is also a matter of common knowledge that many persons with physical handicaps have demonstrated their ability to adequately support and control their children and to give them the benefits of stability and security through love and attention." (*In re Eugene W.* (1972) 29 Cal.App.3d 623, 629–630, 105 Cal.Rptr. 736, 741, 742.)

We agree, and conclude that a physical handicap that affects a parent's ability to participate with his children in purely physical activities is not a changed circumstance of sufficient relevance and materiality to render it either "essential or expedient" for their welfare that they be taken from his custody. This conclusion would be obvious if the handicap were heart dysfunction, emphysema, arthritis, hernia, or slipped disc; it should be no less obvious when it is the natural consequence of an impaired nervous system. Accordingly, pursuant to the authorities cited above the order changing the custody of the minor children herein from William to Ellen must be set aside as an abuse of discretion.

Both the state and federal governments now pursue the commendable goal of total integration of handicapped persons into the mainstream of society: the Legislature declares that "It is the policy of this state to encourage and enable disabled persons to participate fully in the social and economic life of the state. . . ." (Gov. Code, § 19230, subd. (a).) Thus far these efforts have focused primarily on such critical areas as employment, housing, education, transportation, and public access. (See, e.g., Welf. & Inst. Code, § 19000 [declares policy of rehabilitation for employment]; Gov. Code, § 11135 [bars discrimination against handicapped in state-funded programs]; *id.,* § 19230 et seq. [requires affirmative action programs for handicapped employment state agencies]; *id.,* § 19702 [bars discrimination in state civil service]; Lab. Code, § 1420 [bars discrimination by private employers or labor unions]; *id.,* § 1735 [bars discrimination in employment on public works]; Civ. Code, §§ 54, 54.1 [guarantees access to public transportation, public accommodations, and rented housing]; Ed. Code, § 56700 et seq. [creates special educational programs for physically handicapped students]; Bus. & Prof. Code, § 125.6 [bars discrimination by holders of professional licenses]; Code Civ. Proc., §§ 198, subd. 2, 205, subd. (b) [declares handicapped competent to serve as jurors].)[11] No less important to this policy is the integration of the handicapped into the responsibilities and satisfactions of family life, cornerstone of our social system. Yet as more and more physically disabled persons marry and bear or adopt children—or, as in the case at bar, previously nonhandicapped parents become disabled through accident or illness—custody disputes similar to that now before us may well recur. In discharging their admittedly difficult duty in such proceedings, the trial courts must avoid impairing or defeating the foregoing public policy. With the assistance of the considerations discussed herein, we are confident of their ability to do so.

Lastly, we recognize that during the pendency of this appeal, additional circumstances bearing on the best interests of the children herein may have developed. Any such circumstances may, of course, be considered by the trial court on remand. (See *In re Marriage of Russo* (1971) supra, 21 Cal.App.3d 72, 93–94, 98 Cal.Rptr. 501.)

The portion of the interlocutory decree of dissolution transferring custody of appellant's minor children to respondent is reversed.

Bird, C. J., and Tobriner, Clark, Richardson, Manual, and Newman, J. J., concur.

NOTES

1. The opinion in *Carney* provides a significant judicial statement of the public policy favoring full integration of handicapped individuals into all facets of American life.

2. The Carneys' custody battle was popularized in a made-for-TV movie, "The Ordeal of Bill Carney."

3. Consider the impact on the outcome of the case of Mr. Carney's live-in girlfriend. Would such a situation be as easily accepted today in states other than California? Would the presence of a paid live-in attendant create less of a home-like environment in the eyes of some judges?

## MOYE v. MOYE

*Supreme Court of Idaho, 1981*
*102 Idaho 170, 627 P.2d 799*

Donaldson, Justice.

Appellant Lynnae Denise Moye and respondent Terry Andrew Moye were married December 28, 1974. Two children were born of this marriage, a girl, now

---

[11]Again Congress has enacted similar legislation. (See, e.g., 5 U.S.C. § 7153 [authorizes rules to prohibit discrimination against handicapped by federal agencies and federal civil service]; 20 U.S.C. § 1401 et seq. [promotes education of handicapped children]; Rehabilitation Act of 1973, § 501 (29 U.S.C. § 791) [requires affirmative action programs by federal agencies]; *id.*, § 503 (29 U.S.C. § 793) [requires affirmative action programs by employers who contract with federal government]; *id.*, § 504 (29 U.S.C. § 794) [bars discrimination against handicapped in federally funded programs]; see also 45 C.F.R. pt. 84 (1978) [regulations implementing 29 U.S.C. § 794].)

On these and related topics, see generally *Symposium on Employment Rights of the Handicapped* (1978) 27 DePaul L.Rev. 943–1167; *Symposium on the Rights of the Handicapped* (1977) 50 Temple L. Q. 941–1034, 1067–1085; Jackson, *Affirmative Action for the Handicapped and Veterans: Interpretative and Operational Guidelines* (1978) 29 Lab.L.J. 107.

4½ years old, and a boy, now 2½ years old. The parties separated on October 16, 1978 and on the following October 20, the appellant-mother filed for divorce. Pending the outcome of the divorce proceeding, the mother retained custody of the children under a temporary award made by a lawyer-magistrate.

The divorce proceeding was bifurcated for purposes of trying the custody issue first. Subsequently, the district court, Judge Gilbert C. Norris presiding, granted custody of the children to the respondent-father. The mother immediately appealed the Norris order, but because of the bifurcated nature of the proceedings, which presented problems of finality for purposes of review, this Court on March 2, 1979, remanded the case to the district court for further proceedings.

On April 4, 1979, Judge Norris, citing a personal bias developed because of the publicity of the case, withdrew and submitted the matter for reassignment. Subsequently, Judge Edward J. Lodge assumed jurisdiction of the case. On June 15, 1979, Judge Lodge filed a final decree of divorce which in addition to resolving all other issues at dispute, ordered: "That custody of the minor children is left contingent upon a final decision by the Supreme Court to the State of Idaho, subject to the stipulation to divide custody pending appeal."

Thus, the present posture of the case as it has filtered to this appellate level appears as follows. The Norris order is, at best, an interlocutory order of custody. The Lodge decree is a final judgment which, pursuant to I.A.R. 17(e), incorporates for purposes of appeal the Norris order. Accordingly, review of the Lodge decree, received by this Court for purposes of appeal pursuant to our order of September 17, 1979, necessitates review of the Norris order.

The standard of review is well established:

> Questions of child custody are within the discretion of the trial court, and it has been repeatedly held that this Court will not attempt to substitute its judgment and discretion for that of the trial court except in cases where the record reflects a clear abuse of discretion by the trial court.

*Strain* v. *Strain,* 95 Idaho 904, 905, 523 P.2d 36, 37 (1974); *quoted in Posey* v. *Bunney,* 98 Idaho 258, 261, 561 P.2d 400, 403 (1977). *Accord Blakely* v. *Blakely,* 100 Idaho 107, 594 P.2d 145 (1979); *Koester* v. *Koester,* 99 Idaho 654, 586 P.2d 1370 (1978). *Saviers* v. *Saviers,* 92 Idaho 117, 438 P.2d 268 (1968). *See* I.C. § 32–705.

In the instant action, the appellant-mother's basic contention is that Judge Norris abused his discretion in granting custody to the father because the judge based his order primarily upon the fact that appellant suffers from epilepsy. She also argues that pursuant to the Tender Years Doctrine, she should have received custody.

Upon review, we do not find that the Norris order is in error simply because the mother's physical ailment was a consideration in the judge's formulation of the custody grant. The rule in Idaho is that in determining the custody of a minor child, the child's welfare and best interest is of paramount importance. This rule is substantiated by case law, *Blakely* v. *Blakely, supra, Hawkins* v. *Hawkins,* 99 Idaho 785, 589 P.2d 532 (1978), *Koester* v. *Koester, supra, Cope* v. *Cope,* 98 Idaho 920, 576 P.2d 201 (1978); *Posey* v. *Bunney, supra, Strain* v. *Strain, supra, Adams* v. *Adams,* 93 Idaho 113, 456 P.2d 757 (1969). It follows that the physical condition of a parent is a valid consideration in a "best interests" approach. Accordingly, such a consideration made by a court does not in itself present an incident of error.

Whether there has been abuse of discretion in the custody grant, however, is a matter of inquiry which goes beyond merely looking at a court's consideration of a parent's physical health. An abuse of discretion by the trial court occurs when the evidence is insufficient to support its conclusion that the welfare and interests of a child will be best served by a particular custody award. *Hawkins v. Hawkins, supra; Koester v. Koester, supra; Cope v. Cope, supra; Prescott v. Prescott*, 97 Idaho 257, 542 P.2d 1176 (1975); I.R.C.P. 52(a). It follows that an abuse of discretion may also occur where the court overemphasizes one factor, such as a parent's physical condition, thereby similarly failing to support its conclusion that the welfare and interests of a child will be best served by a particular custody award. In the instant case, we find this latter abuse of discretion.

Specifically, the evidence presented and so found by the trial court, that the appellant-mother suffers from epilepsy which is controlled to a degree through medication, that she requires nine to ten hours of sleep per night, that she has migraine headaches and that she has post-seizure lack of energy, does not, under the circumstances as they appear on the record, sufficiently support the court's conclusion that it is the best interest of the children to vest custody in the respondent-father. The court did make some findings as regards the status of the respondent-father but the court's apparent overemphasis of but one consideration, that being the mother's physical condition, convinces this Court that all other relevant factors impacting upon the best interests of the children were not duly considered or, if they were, it was not so reflected upon the record.[2] We therefore reverse the Norris order and remand to the district court for further proceedings. Pending resolution of the custody issue by the district court, the Lodge decree granting joint custody pursuant to stipulation shall remain in effect except for that portion of the decree requiring that an adult female be with appellant during visitation times, a burden we find to have been imposed without any substantial evidence to support it. We observe further that the Tender Years Doctrine, that custody of a child of tender years should be vested in the mother, has limited impact in Idaho law. To the extent previous case law exists which suggests a preference for the mother as custodian of a child of tender years, the preference exists only when all other considerations are equal. *Prescott v. Prescott, supra.* As we have previously held, the considerations made by the trial court are incomplete and the preference is therefore inapplicable.

Reversed and remanded. Costs to appellant. No attorney fees awarded.

McFADDEN, BISTLINE and SHEPARD, J. J., concur.

BAKES, Chief Justice, dissenting:

I respectfully dissent, well aware of the need to remove the burdensome social stigma which has so undeservedly attached itself to epilepsy and epileptics, a stigma founded solely on fear and ignorance. It is my sincere belief, however, that this case is not the appropriate vehicle to rectify those historical inequities.

One point cannot be overstressed: no one has taken Lynnae Moye's children

---

[2]The Norris order contained ten findings of fact. Six of those findings deal with the mother's physical health. One other finding is that each of the parties loves the children. Only the remaining three concern the status of the father and one, finding number eight, contains what we consider to be irrelevant comments by the court concerning the father's attitude towards dry diapers.

from her because she is an epileptic. Nothing could be farther from the truth. When a district judge awards custody to one of the parents in a divorce case, it is not necessarily because the other parent is not fit. In the ordinary custody case, both parents are loving, capable and determined to raise their children in a proper manner. That does not help the judge who, with the best interests of the child at heart, must pick and probe and scrutinize often petty testimony in an effort to find some articulable difference which will support a painful and difficult choice. When the judge makes that choice, he or she is not taking the children away from the non-custodial parent, nor is that parent found to be unfit. The judge is merely awarding custody to one parent according to the best interests of the child as he views it. This difficult choice is necessitated by the parents' divorce, not by their shortcomings as parents.

Epileptics can and do make excellent parents. As the majority notes, however, a parent's physical health, and therefore epilepsy, is certainly a factor which the trial court can consider in a custody case. This the lower court did. It committed no error in this respect.

Our task on appeal is to determine whether the district court's determination, dictated by the best interests of the children, is supported by the evidence and within the proper bounds of discretion. The lower court in this case properly considered other factors besides the wife's epilepsy. The testimony of several relatives and acquaintances strongly indicated that the father was the more attentive parent and that he extended significantly greater efforts in feeding and caring for the children. This is reflected in the trial court's findings.

### VIII

That defendant is able-bodied and has no apparent moral, physical or mental disabilities, and has demonstrated his ability to look after said children, demonstrating almost a too-zealous attitude about having dry diapers, but the Court considers such zeal is far superior to what the situation would be if he were indifferent to wet diapers.

### IX

That defendant has since the birth of said children personally looked after, cared for and fed said children most of the time when he has been home, and when not home has seen to it that some other responsible person stays with plaintiff most of the time to insure said children are adequately cared for.

The majority dismisses Finding VIII as "irrelevant comments," but in the context of this controversy, Finding VIII manifests the trial court's belief that the father was the more attentive parent. Wet diapers may seem trivial to some members of this Court, but it was certainly one of the many factors which the trial court was entitled to consider. Apparently, one of the Moye children had persistent diaper rash which was exacerbated by wet diapers. The parties apparently felt it was an important problem because they both devoted considerable attention to the diaper issue during the trial. However insignificant it may seem to this Court on appeal, the father's zealous attitude toward dry diapers reflects what the record shows in many other respects was his great concern for the wellbeing of his infant daughter.

The court's final finding reads as follows:

X

That defendant has sufficient income to support and educate said children adequately, and has the ability to provide adequate baby-sitting facilities for the children during the hours he is working.

The phrase "adequate baby-sitting facilities" is perhaps an understatement, since the father had arranged to have his sister-in-law, a licensed practical nurse, take care of the children while he was at work.

There is, on the other hand, not a single finding which in any way indicates it would be in the children's better interest to have custody vested in the appellant. The lack of findings in that regard is supported by a corresponding lack of evidence in the record.

I fear, against hope, that today's opinion will make it very difficult for a parent whose spouse is an epileptic to obtain custody of his or her children, their best interests notwithstanding. While I can understand the majority's desire to rectify an unfounded historical stigmatization, I see no need to reverse a district court's custody order well supported by the record, quite apart from the epilepsy issue. I cannot help but wonder whether today's result would be different had this case not been inaccurately cast as a single-issued *cause celebre*. I would affirm.

It is appropriate to add a final note about an appealability issue ignored by the majority. On January 6, 1979, the plaintiff Lynnae Moye filed her notice of appeal from the district court's custody order. A final decree of divorce had not yet been entered. Thereafter, she requested this Court to enter an order staying execution of the custody order. On March 2, 1979, this Court remanded the case to the district court to consider the motion for stay pending appeal. In that order, this Court observed that "the order appealed from herein may be a non-appealable interlocutory order since there is no Rule 54(b) I.R.C.P. certification, nor any certification to Rule 12, I.A.R., *see Pichon* v. [*L. J. Broekemeier, Inc.*, 99 Idaho 598, 586 P.2d 1042 (1978)]."

On remand, a different district judge entered the final decree of divorce. Rather than appeal from that final judgment, appellant merely moved to augment the appellate record with the final judgment and other appropriate documents.

At this stage of the controversy, therefore, we have only a premature notice of appeal taken from an unappealable order. Ordinarily, a premature appeal taken before any final order is entered must be dismissed. *Kraft* v. *State,* 99 Idaho 214, 579 P.2d 1197 (1978). *Cf.* I.A.R. 17(e) (although this rule provides that an appeal from a final judgment or order includes all orders, judgments and decrees *subsequently* entered, there is no similar provision for premature appeals taken from non-appealable orders). Accordingly, I would advocate dismissal of this appeal were it not for the fact that this Court, in its order of March 2, 1979, merely *remanded* rather than *dismissed* the appeal, thus indicating to the parties that the appeal was still properly pending before the Court. If the Court had dismissed the appeal from the custody order, as it should have, then the appellant would have been free to file a new notice of appeal after the entry of the final divorce decree, thereby appealing from the custody order under I.A.R. 17(e). To the extent that this Court's March 2 order may have misled the parties, I concede, with some hesitation, that this appeal should be entertained.

NOTES

1.   Consider the contention of the dissenting Chief Justice that the *Moye* decision will make it difficult for the spouse of a person with epilepsy to ever be awarded custody of the children in a divorce proceeding. Is this a type of "reverse discrimination" to the benefit of handicapped persons? How realistic is this possibility?

2.   Compare the presence of a handicap with race and sex in terms of their propriety as factors to be considered in making a custody determination.

# 10

# CONTRACTS, OWNERSHIP, AND TRANSFERS OF PROPERTY

**Patrick P. Spicer**

## SUMMARY OF DOCTRINAL DEVELOPMENTS

DEVELOPMENTS IN THE LEGAL AREAS OF contracts, ownership, and transfers of property as they affect handicapped persons have been infrequent since 1979. What few judicial decisions there have been have basically ratified the existing state of the law regarding capacity of handicapped persons to contract and to otherwise control property.

## A. CONTRACTS AND CONVEYANCES

### 1. By Mentally Handicapped Persons

p. 1013—INSERT after Note 2, the following:

UNITED STATES v. MANNY

*United States Court of Appeals for the Second Circuit, 1981*
*645 F.2d 163*

BRIEANT, District Judge:

In these cases, consolidated for appeal, the United States sued in the district court to reduce to judgment and collect unpaid federal estate taxes assessed against the respective estates of Walter Roy Manny, deceased, and James G. Timolat, Jr., deceased, The estate representatives had tendered certain U.S. Treasury bonds, known popularly as "flower bonds," sold under provisions which allow their use at par for the payment of estate taxes. Although the bonds had been accepted, upon further investigation, the Internal Revenue Service ("IRS") assessed a deficiency in each estate and offered to return the bonds.

At issue is whether the flower bonds, purchased in bearer form from third parties, paid for and delivered, but acquired while Manny and Timolat were comatose, through the agency of persons holding powers of attorney to trade in securities, are eligible for redemption at par in payment of federal estate taxes. The district court, 463 F.Supp. 444, held in each case that the bonds were eligible. We affirm.

*  *  *

The Government argues that the agency of the holders of the powers of attorney was "terminated or suspended" when their principals became comatose, and accordingly their "purchases of flower bonds were not effective to make the unwitting principals owners of the bonds at the time of their death" (App. Br. p. 15), and that therefore the district court erred in holding that the bonds were redeemable at par in payment of estate taxes.

A comatose person is mentally incompetent while his coma continues and we think the law of New York is clear that, when an agent under a power of attorney acts during the mental incapacity of a principal who has not been adjudicated incompetent and for whom no court-appointed committee or conservator has been designated, the act is at most voidable, and not void.

*Bankers Trust Co. of Albany, N.A.* v. *Martin*, 51 A.D.2d 411, 381 N.Y.S.2d 1001 (3d Dep't, 1976) was an action in which the judicially appointed conservator of an incompetent sued to enforce a contract of sale made by an attorney in fact for an incompetent person, while the purchasers sued to recover the down payment and their damages. The Court held:

> [A]ppellants alleged four separate causes of action which were all predicated on the allegations that John A. Becker, the owner of the real property and the principal for whom the plaintiff Bankers Trust Company of Albany, N.A., as attorney-in-fact, negotiated the contract of sale, was incompetent at the time and, consequently, the contract was a nullity and unenforceable by any party thereto. . . .
>
> . . . On this appeal, appellants claim . . . that Becker, the owner of the property, was incompetent at the time the contract of sale was executed on his behalf by his attorney-in-fact and that his incompetency revoked the power of attorney and that, consequently, the contract of sale was void. . . .
>
> At the outset we note that the principal was never judicially declared to be incompetent and that the appointment of a conservator is not evidence of the incompetence of the conservatee (Mental Hygiene Law, § 77.25, subd. [b]). There is no claim or proof in the record that the principal was incompetent at the time he executed the power of attorney. Even if Becker, the principal, were incompetent at the time the contract was made by his attorney-in-fact, the contract is not void, but only voidable at the option of the principal upon his regaining competency or by some duly authorized representative. A contract and a power of attorney made by an incompetent person prior to formal adjudication are not void, but only voidable and may be ratified and approved by the incompetent person upon recovering his competency or by a duly authorized person on behalf of the incompetent (*Ortelere* v. *Teachers' Retirement Bd. of City of N.Y.*, 25 N.Y. 196, 303 N.Y.S.2d 362, 250 N.E.2d 460; *Verstandig* v. *Schlaffer*, 296 N.Y. 62, 70 N.E.2d 15; *Finch* v. *Goldstein*, 245 N.Y. 300, 157 N.E. 146; *Blinn* v. *Schwarz*, 177 N.Y. 252, 69 N.E. 542; *Merritt* v. *Merritt*, 43 App.Div. 68, 59 N.Y.S. 357; "Civil Insanity": The New York Treatment of the Issue of Mental Incapacity in Non-Criminal Cases, 44 Cornell L.Rev., p. 76). In *Blinn* v. *Schwarz* (supra) the court held a deed and a power of attorney executed by an incompetent were not void, but only voidable at the option of the incompetent, his committee thereafter appointed, or his personal representative or heir. The court explained that the rule was adopted to protect the incompetent and to give him the benefit of favorable contracts and to relieve him from burdensome contracts. At page 263, 69 N.E. at page 545, the court said:
>
> > We think the rule laid down by these cases is sound, and in the interest of those afflicted with disease of the mind. The deed of a lunatic is not void, in the sense of being a nullity, but has force and effect until the option to declare it void is exercised. The right of election implies the right to ratify, and it may be greatly to the advantage of the insane person to have that right. If the deed or

contract is void, it binds neither party, and neither can derive any benefit therefrom, but, if voidable, the lunatic, upon recovering his reason, can hold on to the bargain if it is good, and let go if it is bad. This option is valuable, for it gives him the power to do so as he wishes, and to bind or loose the other party at will.   51 A.D.2d at 412–13; 381 N.Y.S.2d at 1002–03.

We find no New York case holding that a non-party to such a contract could assert voidability and disaffirm. In *Bankers Trust, supra*, it was the other party to an executory contract, not the incompetent or his legal representative, who tried to disaffirm the transaction. Under *Blinn* v. *Schwarz*, 177 N.Y. 252, 69 N.E. 542 (1904), cited in *Bankers Trust*, quoted above, he was not entitled to do so because disaffirmance is solely the right of the incompetent or his legal representative. The sellers of the bonds in this case could not disaffirm the transaction. *See Estate of Pfohl* v. *Commissioner*, 70 T.C. 630 (1978) reaching the same result, applying New York law.

The Government relies on *In re Berry's Estate*, 69 Misc.2d 397, 329 N.Y.S.2d 915 (Surr.Ct.Queens Co.1972), an accounting proceeding in which beneficiaries of an estate sought to recover funds which decendent's niece, acting under a power of attorney, had transferred, during the lifetime of the decedent, to a trust account for the benefit of the niece's mother. The Surrogate allowed an amendment of the objections to allege that this transfer, which was voidable anyway for self dealing and as *ultra vires*, occurred while the principal was incompetent. In doing so, he held that "if the objectors prove that at the time of the agent's transfer of the funds, and thereafter, that the decedent was mentally incompetent or incapacitated by reason of her alleged comatose or semi-comatose state, then the agency would have been suspended or revoked." 69 Misc.2d at 400; 329 N.Y.S.2d at 918. The Surrogate cited the first *Merritt* case, *Merritt* v. *Merritt*, 27 A.D. 208, 50 N.Y.S. 604, as the "leading case in New York on the proposition that insanity suspends an agency," 69 Misc.2d at 399, 329 N.Y.S.2d at 917, but did not refer to the second *Merritt* case, relied on in *Bankers Trust, supra,* and reported at 43 A.D. 68, 59 N.Y.S. 357, which limits the scope of *Merritt I*. Nor did he cite *Blinn* v. *Schwarz, supra*. To the extent *Berry* may be read to hold that the act of an attorney in fact whose principal has become mentally incompetent is "void" rather than merely voidable, we agree with Judges Duffy and Conner that it is not a correct statement of the law of New York on this subject. *See also Meacham, Law of Agency* § 135 (2d ed. 1914), citing *Merritt II* and *Blinn* v. *Schwarz, supra*.

The Government here, like the Court in *Berry*, relies heavily on general statements of law in the Restatement (Second) of Agency (1958) to the effect that incompetency of the principal "deprives the agent of capacity." Restatement § 122, comment (d) suggests that an agent does not necessarily lose authority to act for the principal where the principal is incapacitated by "temporary mental or physical illness." The difficulty with the Restatement analysis is that at the time of acting the agent cannot tell whether the incapacity will be temporary or permanent. Even in these cases, decedents could have recovered from their comatose conditions and survived. We are persuaded that the Restatement provisions are best construed as depriving agents of capacity only where the incapacity of their principals is known to be permanent from the outset; mental or physical incapacity which does not preclude recovery should render the interim acts of the agent voidable rather than void. This reading is wholly consistent with the weight of New York cases in point and preserves the salutary principle that those temporarily unable to act for themselves should be able to benefit from favorable acts which their agents take during their incapacity. Nor are we certain that the Restatement's analysis would express a federal common law rule. As was held by the late Judge Knight, in the pre-*Erie* case of *Beale* v. *Gibaud,* 15 F.Supp. 1020, 1027 (W.D.N.Y.1936):

> [I]t is claimed that the contract of an insane person is absolutely void and that no one can obtain any rights by virtue thereof. It is said that the federal rule is that a contract of a person of unsound mind is void and not voidable, and support for this contention is claimed to be found in the early case of *Dexter* v. *Hall,* 15 Wall. (82 U.S.) 9, 20, 21 L.Ed. 73 [1872].

After a detailed analysis of *Dexter* v. *Hall* and subsequent state and federal cases, Judge Knight held:

> While we do find the broad assertion in the foregoing cases and some other federal and state cases that a contract made by an incompetent is absolutely void, it is quite clear that this is contrary to the great weight of authority today as is evidenced by many opinions and the textbooks of many well-known authorities on the subject of contracts.
>
> The rule which finds support in many of the authorities today is stated as follows: "While some confusion has arisen by reason of the misuse of the terms 'void' and 'voidable', and some cases have asserted that the contract of an insane person, who has not been so judicially adjudicated, is absolutely void, and not merely voidable, the general rule, supported by the weight of the authority, is that a contract of an insane person, who has not been so judicially adjudicated, is not absolutely void, but voidable." 32 C.J. § 501(c), p. 729.
>
> Black on Contracts (2d Ed.), vol. 2, p. 255; Elliott on Contracts (Accumulative Supp. 1913–1923), § 3820; Page on the Law of Contracts, Supp. 1919–1920, § 1634 et seq.; Bishop on Contracts, § 873; Kent's Commentaries, vol. 2, 451; Chitty on Contracts (18th Ed.), p. 158, by MacFarland & Ragman; all, in effect, declare that the doctrine that conveyances by an insane person are absolutely void is against the "immense preponderance of authority. They are voidable where the person has not been judicially declared incompetent." It is recognized that the insane person may affirm by acts after becoming sane or by failure to disaffirm for a long period of time after becoming sane.

*See also Kevan* v. *John Hancock Mut. Life Ins. Co.,* 3 F.Supp. 288 (W.D.Mo.1933); *Luhrs* v. *Hancock,* 181 U.S. 567, 21 S.Ct. 726, 45 L.Ed. 1005 (1901).

The Government argues, correctly we think, that its rights in the matter should not be affected by any subsequent "ratification" on the part of the executors following death. Although New York cases do seem to speak in terms of "ratification," a voidable contract does not require ratification to come into existence, rather it requires disaffirmance before its existence may be extinguished. A purported act of ratification may preclude a later disaffirmance, but regardless of what the executors did, or did not do, we conclude that at the time of death Manny and Timolat owned legal title to and had possession of the bonds, subject at most to a right to disaffirm upon recovering from their comatose condition, which right later passed to the executors. They could lose the right to disaffirm by inaction, or by action, such as presenting the bonds in decedent's name for redemption, but it is misleading to call such action ratification.

We note that there is no federal requirement in the Treasury Regulations or in the offering circular or elsewhere that in order for bonds to be submitted at par in payment of estate taxes, purchase of the bonds must have been effected of decedent's own volition. Rather, all that is necessary is that he shall have been the actual owner of the bonds, and that the bonds shall have been includable in his estate for federal estate tax purposes. Both requirements are satisfied in these cases.

The judgments appealed from are affirmed.

NOTES

1.   Is there any justification for differentiating between persons adjudicated insane and those who have not but who otherwise appear on the facts to be insane when determining whether a contract executed by a mentally handicapped person should be considered void or voidable?

2.   Should the fact that the incapacity of a principal is known to be permanent from the outset of the agency be conclusive in determining whether the interim acts of the principal's agent are void or merely voidable?

### JOHNSON v. PERRY

*Court of Appeals of Wisconsin, 1978*
*20 Wn. App. 696*

RINGOLD, J.—This is an action brought in November 1975, to quiet title and to obtain judicial confirmation of the forfeiture of a real estate contract. As an affirmative defense the defendant purchaser, Arthur Perry, alleged that he lacked the mental capacity to enter into the contract. Perry's counterclaims alleged: (1) trespass, (2) tortious interference with his contractual relations with his tenants, (3) abuse of process, (4) breach of contract, and (5) misrepresentation, unequal position, duress, lack of capacity, unconscionability and failure of consideration. He sought damages and injunctive relief. The defendant's jury demand was stricken and the cause was tried to the court, which granted the plaintiff's relief and overruled or dismissed all of Perry's affirmative defenses and counterclaims. This appeal followed. We find no error in the trial court rulings and affirm.

Perry purchased the subject property, an apartment building, from the Beau-Dang Corporation in 1969. From 1969 until 1972 he made the $800 monthly payments as required by the real estate contract. Shortly after Perry had purchased the property the seller assigned its interest to Fern Shaffer, who subsequently conveyed her interest by means of quitclaim deeds to the present plaintiffs, her daughters, son-in-law, and their children.

From the record it is not clear when Mrs. Shaffer died, but during the year 1972 the payments were made by Perry to the plaintiffs and he negotiated with the plaintiffs in an effort to reduce the payments. The plaintiffs accepted reduced payments of $500 per month, without agreeing to a modification of the contract. Perry eventually stopped the payments. By February 1974, he was in default under the contract in the amount of $16,800. On April 1, 1974, the plaintiffs directed to Perry a notice of intention to declare a forfeiture and cancel the real estate contract. A declaration of cancellation of the contract and forfeiture of Perry's interest was made on April 29, 1974. Subsequently unlawful detainer actions were commenced to dispossess the tenants of the building, which actions were the basis for several of Perry's counterclaims.

Perry contends that the trial court erred in (1) denying his demand for a jury trial; (2) in permitting the plaintiffs to enforce a real estate contract to which they were not a party; and (3) in failing to find that Perry lacked capacity to enter into the contract. Error is also assigned in the trial court's dismissal of Perry's counterclaims.

\* \* \*

### Perry's Capacity To Contract

Perry was born in February 1910, and formally completed the third grade. He continued to attend school until age 14. Perry did not complete the fourth grade, and worked shining shoes. Later he became a hotel porter. In 1940 he was employed as a laborer in a steel mill. In 1944 he moved to the Seattle area and was employed as a laborer at the Navy yard. In 1945 he went to sea, working as a room steward and as a cook. Sometime early in the 1950's, Perry met Earl F. Goodchild, who at the time was engaged in the real estate business. Mr. Goodchild was referred to Mr. Perry by a friend of Perry's who told Goodchild that this merchant seaman friend had a good pile of money from his trips and he would blow it all and go back out broke.

Mr. Goodchild testified:

> So he said, "I ought to introduce you and see if you could sell him some property so he would have something."
> Q: You were in the business of selling property then?
> A: Yes.
> Q: Did you meet with Mr. Perry?
> A: Yes. The next trip in, I guess it was, he introduced me to Mr. Perry, and we talked a bit, and he said, yeah, he would be interested in buying something. And he said, "What do I do?"
> Well, I said, "You make a down payment and make monthly payments."
> And he said, "Okay, fine. I am going out in a couple of days. Here's $1,500. Buy me something."
> So he gave me the $1,500 in cash and I put it in my pocket. And then he—

The $1,500 was the down payment for the purchase of the Terrace Apartments. During the years Perry owned the Terrace Apartments, he always had someone assist him although he could read and write. In 1969, the Terrace Apartments were sold for $55,000. This money from the sale of the apartments gave Perry the requisite down payment of $50,000 to purchase the apartment house, subject of this action, for $125,000 with the balance at 7½ percent interest with monthly payments of $800 plus taxes and insurance.

Perry's basic defense at the time of trial and on this appeal is lack of capacity on his part to enter into the contract. The trial court had before it the testimony of Mr. Goodchild, Mr. Perry's friends who had helped him manage the apartment houses and collect rentals, and the testimony of a psychiatrist and of a psychologist. The court made finding of fact No. 6:

> None of the affirmative defenses or counterclaims alleged by the defendant Arthur Perry were proven by either clear, cogent and convincing evidence nor by a preponderance of the evidence.

It is often difficult to frame negative findings of fact. We regard this finding as a conclusion of law, and read it in the light of the trial court's oral decision. *Rutter* v. *Rutter,* 59 Wn.2d 781, 784, 370 P.2d 862 (1962).

The trial court well summarizes the issue:

> The evidence in this case I think clearly shows that the defendant Mr. Perry was a man of limited education, limited formal education, I should say. We do have the testimony of the psychiatrist and psychologist as to his I.Q. score on the Wechsler Intelligence Test, and we have their opinions. I think it boils down that he was, in their opinion, based upon an I.Q. test, not capable of understanding all of the ramifications of a business transaction of this type.
>
> The question is: Does that establish a legal defense to this contract?
>
>    *  *  *
>
> I think we must first look at the legal defense of lack of mental capacity. I think if I were to follow the argument of Mr. Sanders we would destroy the law of contracts to a degree that this court is not willing to do. I think there's no question but perhaps the defendant Mr. Perry, by reason of his lack of formal education, his entire life that has been testified to, would not be able to understand all of the nuances as one should at the time of the agreement, and the legal requirements and what legally follows from the failure to make timely payments. I think it would be fair to say that all he knew was for $50,000 he was buying an apartment house; he would have to make monthly payments at a certain sum per month, and that he would have certain expenses, et cetera, and that is what he went into. I don't think that rises to a lack of mental capacity. So, as a legal proposition, I find that the affirmative defense of mental incapacity, as well as the other affirmative defenses have not been sustained.

The rule is stated in *Page* v. *Prudential Life Ins. Co. of America,* 12 Wn.2d 101, 109, 120 P.2d 527 (1942):

> The rule relative to mental capacity to contract, therefore, is whether the contractor possessed sufficient mind or reason to enable him to comprehend the nature, terms, and effect of the contract in issue. *In applying this rule, however, it must be remembered that contractual capacity is a question of fact to be determined at the time the transaction occurred,* . . . that everyone is presumed sane; and that this presumption is overcome only by clear, cogent, and convincing evidence. (Italics ours.)

Perry relies heavily on *Harris* v. *Rivard,* 64 Wn.2d 173, 390 P.2d 1004 (1964) which adopts the standards set in *Page* v. *Prudential, supra.* The trial court in *Harris* determined that one of the contracting parties was incompetent to enter into a contract. The Supreme Court sustained the trial court's findings, holding:

> Ever since the case of *Thorndike* v. *Hesperian Orchards, Inc.,* 54 Wn. (2d) 570, 575, 343 P. (2d) 183 (1959), this court has refused to substitute its opinion for that of the trial court where there is substantial evidence before the court.
>
>    *  *  *
>
> . . . His findings will stand undisturbed.

*Harris* v. *Rivard, supra* at 175–76.

Perry argues, however, that because the testimony of the psychiatrist and psychologist indicates that Mr. Perry is a man with a low I.Q., incapable of understanding all the ramifications of a business transaction of this type and unable to understand the legal requirements of what legally follows in the failure to make timely payments that therefore, as a matter of law, this court should reverse the findings of the trial judge.

Dr. Robert G. Wright, a board-certified psychiatrist, testified that he saw Mr. Perry in 1972 during the time that he was charged with the criminal offense. Dr.

Wright stated that he had referred Mr. Perry for an intelligence test and the results which he obtained were: verbal, 78; performance, 73; a full-scale I.Q. of 74, and in his opinion, Mr. Perry was "borderline functioning." In response to a question as to whether or not within reasonable medical certainty he could say that Mr. Perry was of sufficient mind or reason to comprehend the nature and terms and effect of the contract in February 1969, Dr. Wright responded: "He was not competent at that time to understand the contract."

Dr. Donald Akutawaga, a clinical psychologist, administered the Wechsler Adult Intelligence Test in 1976. He determined from the test that Mr. Perry had a full-scale I.Q. of 74, which is borderline, just above mental deficiency.

Dr. Akutawaga testified that Perry could probably function in normal, everyday types of business transactions, but "I think he would have great difficulty in dealing with anything complex." Dr. Akutawaga doubted that Perry could understand the nature, terms and effects of the real estate contract. The opinions of Drs. Wright and Akutawaga were considered and weighed by the trial court.

A most dangerous precedent would be set were we to accept as a matter of law the results of a standardized intelligence test or the education of a party as a standard by which we will determine the mental capacity of an individual to contract. There was substantial evidence to sustain the trial court's determination that the affirmative defense of lack of capacity to contract had not been proved by clear, cogent and convincing evidence and the finding will not be disturbed.

Affirmed.

WILLIAMS and MUNSON, J. J., concur.

NOTE

The testimony of one of the psychologists in *Perry* indicated that the defendant probably could understand relatively simple transactions but not complex ones. Does such testimony suggest that different standards should be used in determining capacity to contract depending on the nature of the transaction in question?

## 2. By Physically Handicapped Persons

p. 1014—INSERT the following paragraph after the last paragraph in Section A:

In *Cook* v. *Budget Rent-A-Car Corporation*, 502 F. Supp. 494, (S.D.N.Y. 1980) the plaintiff was a handicapped person seeking damages under Sec. 504 on the grounds that the defendant, an automobile rental company, refused to rent him an automobile solely because of his handicap, which the plaintiff claimed in no way affected his driving ability. The court ruled that the defendant was not a recipient of federal funds for purposes of Sec. 504, as the only funds it received from the federal government were by way of automobile rental contracts.

## C. MISCELLANEOUS ISSUES CONCERNING OWNERSHIP OF PROPERTY

p. 1031—INSERT the following paragraph after the last paragraph in Section C and before *Vecchione* v. *Wohlgemuth:*

In *Williams* v. *U.S.*, 694 F.2d 894 (5th Cir. 1981), the court ruled that where a power of appointment was held by an incompetent person over property held in life estate, the value of that property had to be included in calculating the estate tax due on the incompetent person's estate at the time of his or her death.

# II

# VOTING AND
# HOLDING PUBLIC OFFICE

**Patrick P. Spicer**

## SUMMARY OF DOCTRINAL DEVELOPMENTS

THE ONLY DEVELOPMENT OF SIGNIFICANCE in the area of voting rights and the right to hold public office as they relate to handicapped persons has been amendatory legislation passed by Congress regarding voting assistance for handicapped persons.

## A. THE RIGHT TO VOTE

### 4. Special Voting Procedures or Assistance
#### b. Assistance in Marking Ballot

p. 1052—INSERT after NOTE 6, the following:

42 U.S.C. § 1973aa-6

Voting Assistance for Blind, Disabled or Illiterate Persons

Any voter who requires assistance to vote by reason of blindness, disability, or inability to read or write may be given assistance by a person of the voter's choice, other than the voter's employer or agent of that employer or officer or agent of the voter's union.

(Pub. L. 89–110, Title II, § 208, as added Pub. L. 97–205, § 5, June 29, 1982, 96 Stat. 134.)

NOTE

This section was passed by Congress in 1982 as an amendment to the Voting Rights Act, but it does not become effective until January 1, 1984.

### 5. Voting by Residents of State Institutions

p. 1063—INSERT after Note 2:

3. For a discussion of voting rights, state laws, and constitutional analysis, see, Note, "Mental Disability and the Right to Vote," 88 *Yale Law Journal* 1644 (1979).

# 12

# MISCELLANEOUS
# OTHER RIGHTS

Christopher G. Bell

## SUMMARY OF DOCTRINAL DEVELOPMENTS

IN THE AREA OF LICENSES, several state and federal court decisions have been encumbered with speculations about potential safety risks associated with handicapped persons as operators of motor vehicles. Advocates for handicapped people have also been unsuccessful in two federal court challenges to state and private health and medical insurance benefits that provide reduced or no coverage for inpatient psychiatric care in private hospitals. The U.S. Supreme Court refused to require the FCC to apply Section 504 legal standards to applications for license renewals by public and commercial television stations.

## A.   LICENSES

p. 1073—ADD to the end of Note 1:

The Federal Motor Carrier Safety Regulations have been used successfully as a defense to a state law charge of employment discrimination on the basis of handicap. In *Boynton Cab Co.* v. *Department of Industry, Labor and Human Relations,* 96 Wis.2d 396, 291 N.W.2d 850 (Wis. 1980), the Wisconsin Supreme Court held that a taxi cab company's refusal to hire a one-handed driver pursuant to an unwritten policy based upon 49 CFR section 391.41(b) was lawful under the Wisconsin Fair Employment Act. The court determined that the company's policy against hiring one-handed persons as drivers bore a "rational relationship to the safety obligations imposed upon a common carrier of passengers and that the standard . . . was not the result of an arbitrary belief lacking in objective reason or rationale." 291 N.W.2d at 859. The court reasoned that "for Boynton's policy to be reasonable and thus lawful, 'it is enough to show that elimination of the hiring policy might jeopardize the life of one more person than might otherwise occur under the present hiring practice.'" *Id.,* quoting *Hodgson* v. *Greyhound Lines, Inc.,* 499 F.2d 859, 863 (7th Cir. 1974), *cert. denied,* 419 U.S.

The author of this chapter is an Attorney-Advisor with the U.S. Commission on Civil Rights, Washington, DC 20425. The views expressed in this chapter are those of the author alone and do not represent positions of the U.S. Commission on Civil Rights.

1122. What legal arguments can you muster to challenge such a standard if it were applied by a government to deny an "otherwise qualified handicapped individual" a driver's license?

p. 1074—ADD to the end of Note 2:

In *Strathie* v. *Department of Transportation*, 547 F. Supp. 1367 (E.D. Pa. 1982), the United States District Court for the Eastern District of Pennsylvania upheld a Commonwealth of Pennsylvania Department of Transportation regulation prohibiting hearing-aid wearers from being licensed as school bus drivers. In discussing the plaintiff's claim of unlawful discrimination under Section 504 of the Rehabilitation Act of 1973, the court stated:

> Citing empirical studies noting the superior driving abilities of persons with hearing impairments, plaintiff contends that by prohibiting *all* hearing impaired persons from driving school buses, whether the deficiency is corrected by a hearing aid or not, regulation 150 discriminates against him and the class he represents in violation of section 504. . . . I disagree.
>
> On a noisy bus, a hearing-aid wearer might not hear or be able to distinguish the source of sound that would cause danger because sound comes from 360 degrees around him. If a person with impaired hearing wears a hearing aid in only one ear, the right ear for example, all sounds will be presented to that ear whether they emanate from the right, left, ahead, or behind. If the microphone for the device is located at any spot other than in the ear, the deaf person will be misled as to the direction from which the sound is coming. It would seem only stereo hearing aids could hope to overcome this problem.[12] Although that type of hearing aid undoubtedly enables the wearer to localize sounds better than other types, the wearer still may not be able to distinguish the direction from which sound comes as well as a person with normal hearing. Cole deposition at 24. Even with microphones in both ears, the problems of sudden mechanical failure, dislodgment, or hearing aid turn-off in noisy environments still exist. It must be remembered that a hearing aid does not enable a person with a hearing deficiency to hear as if he had no deficiency. The hearing aid merely amplifies within its inherent tonal capacities all sound to a level that the wearer can hear it. The problem shared by people with hearing aids is that in a crowd they hear only a roar of undifferentiated, undeciferable sound— i.e., the magnified sum total of some of what is going on in the vicinity with little or no way to distinguish near from far, tone from tone, or important from trivial. The deaf person may have a cacophonous hubbub or a gentle murmur depending upon how he sets his volume control. In either, the cries of a child or the blare of a horn may be lost. It was this inability to deal with noise that concerned the Department of Transportation. Operating from a concern for the safety of school bus riders, the Department of Transportation adopted regulation 150. Reports from hearings prior to and after enactment state that to be qualified to drive a school bus, an individual not only must be able to drive with great skill and care, he must be able to control the children on the bus and deal with any and all emergencies that may arise. Because even by use of a hearing aid, the wearer may be unable to localize sounds or distinguish particular sounds, a person with a hearing deficiency cannot perform at least two necessary functions of a school bus driver: provide control over and safety to the riders. Additionally, the deficiencies of hearing aids, being subject to turn-off and mechanical failure, might adversely affect a hearing aid wearer's ability to drive a school bus safely. Therefore, plaintiff and the

---

[12]Strathie wears a hearing aid with microphones in both ears. But this too may cause confusion. If the volume control for one ear is higher than its companion, sound will seem to come from the side with the higher volume even though it may actually come from the other.

class he represents are not "otherwise qualified" individuals within the meaning of the Rehabilitation Act. Accordingly, regulation 150 does not discriminate against plaintiff in violation of section 504. *Id.* at 1380–81.

Compare the court's "discussion" with the analysis in *Boynton Cab Co.* v. *Department of Industry, Labor and Human Relations.* How convincing are the courts' respective speculations concerning the future safety of passengers? If you were counsel for a handicapped plaintiff in a similar case, what evidence would you seek to introduce to limit a court's hypothetical musings about potential safety problems?

p. 1074—INSERT after Note 3:

## MONNIER v. UNITED STATES DEPARTMENT OF TRANSPORTATION

*United States District Court for the Eastern District of Wisconsin, 1979*
*465 F.Supp. 718*

Before FAIRCHILD, Chief Circuit Judge, and GORDON and WARREN, District Judges.

### Memorandum and Order

WARREN, District Judge.

Plaintiff, Robert J. Monnier, Sr., a diabetic, has brought this case to challenge the validity of several motor carrier safety regulations promulgated by the Department of Transportation, which regulations prevent diabetics who require insulin treatment from operating trucks inter-city and inter-state. Both the plaintiff and the defendants have moved for summary judgment stating that the issues in this case can be resolved short of trial.

The plaintiff was employed as an over-the-road teamster until August of 1971, when he was terminated pursuant to section 391.41(3), chapters III, sub-chapter B (Motor Carrier Safety Regulations) of Title 49, U.S.Code (49 CFR sections 391.41). That section provides that, in order to be qualified, a driver must have "no established history or clinical diagnosis of diabetes mellitus currently requiring insulin for control." Section 391.49 (49 CFR § 391.49) provides a waiver procedure for those drivers with certain disabilities, not including diabetes. Plaintiff asserts that the agency did not hold a proper hearing and that the agency denied him his constitutional rights. Plaintiff also challenges the failure of the agency to allow him the right to apply for, and receive, a waiver of the disqualification via a hearing at which he can show that he is not impaired by his diabetic condition.

Attached to plaintiff's motion for summary judgment as exhibits, and incorporated within plaintiff's briefs, are the statements of several medical doctors who are of the opinion that the affliction of insulin-dependent diabetes mellitus should not be an absolute bar to a person operating as an over-the-road teamster. Based upon these medical opinions, plaintiff attacks the regulation as depriving plaintiff of his constitutional right to due process because the regulation fails to provide exemption for those diabetics who can prove that the malady would not increase their likelihood of having an accident. Although plaintiff originally asserted that five different grounds for relief were available, he has now stipulated to narrow the issue solely to one of whether a violation of due process occurred.

In conjunction with his motion for summary judgment, plaintiff has submitted his own affidavit in which he states that he was originally diagnosed a diabetic in 1965 and that he began taking insulin by injection in that same year. He further states that as a diabetic, he operated a truck over the highways for at least 100,000 miles a year for five years and that during such time he had only two reportable accidents, both of which were minor. Moreover, plaintiff affirms that he has never fainted, gone into a coma, or become otherwise disabled as a result of his diabetes.

In his brief, plaintiff does not attack the Department of Transportation for excluding persons with diabetes mellitus from driving as an over-the-road motor vehicle driver, but instead attacks the Department of Transportation for failure to create an exemption for those persons with diabetes mellitus who can establish that the ailment in no way constitutes a hazard to·the person's use of a motor vehicle. Pursuant to this argument, defendant refers the Court to several subparagraphs of 49 CFR section 391.41 in which the Department of Transportation has exercised such discretion and thereby provided exemptions when the driver establishes that his handicap in no way limits his driving ability or potential safety record. Plaintiff relies on the statements of several medical doctors who are self-avowed experts on diabetes, who state that in their opinion an exemption should exist for those drivers with the disease who can establish, through competent medical testing, that in their individual case, the disease is controlled and therefore presents no safety risks. Based upon these statements, the plaintiff argues that it was an abuse of discretion for the Department of Transportation to fail to provide an exemption for drivers with diabetes.

During the course of the proceedings in this case, the Federal Highway Administration decided to review its diabetes rule and therefore, on January 7, 1977, Judge Warren stayed proceedings in this case pending completion of that review. Upon completion of the review, the Federal Highway Administration issued a final decision finding that the rule should not be changed. 42 Fed.Reg. 57488 (November 3, 1977). Based upon case law and the extensive record of the administrative hearings, the government has filed a motion for summary judgment asserting that the agency's decision should be affirmed. *Id.* at 719–20.

The Seventh Circuit Court of Appeals' recent decision in *Starr* v. *Federal Aviation Administration*, 589 F.2d 307 (7th Cir. 1978) is persuasive. There the plaintiff was attacking the Federal Aviation Administration's (FAA) Age–60 Rule, which provided that no person over the age of 60 could serve as a pilot in an air carrier for certain operations. In ruling in the case, the court held that it was not "to judge whether Captain Starr [was] fit to fly." *Id.* at 309. Instead the court examined "whether the FAA may establish an 'exemption' policy" that refuses to allow exemptions for a particular class of persons, *i.e.,* those over sixty. The court characterized the real issue in the case to be whether it was an abuse of discretion for the FAA to deny exemptions for those persons over sixty when it is possible for certain individuals to establish that they have no physical limitations which should preclude them from operating the class of aircraft described by the FAA.

The facts in the present case are very similar to those reviewed by the Seventh Circuit Court of Appeals in *Starr, supra*. Plaintiff, Mr. Monnier, may be able to establish that his diabetic condition is so well controlled and so out of the ordinary that his chance of losing consciousness is virtually non-existent. As in *Starr,* our review here is limited to determining whether the Department of Transportation abused its discretion in not granting an exemption for drivers with diabetes. In analyzing the question of whether the Department of Transportation abused its discretion, the Court would note that in certain circumstances a refusal to exercise discretion may itself constitute an abuse of discretion. *Cotonificio Bustese, S.A.* v. *Morgenthau,* 74 App.D.C. 13, 121 F.2d 884 (1941). In reviewing the agency's action, the test to be applied is whether the Department of Transportation's decision to not provide an exemption was arbitrary or capricious. *See* 5 U.S.C. § 706(2)(A); *American Meat Institute* v. *Environmental Protection Agency,* 526 F.2d 442 (7th Cir. 1975); *Giancana* v. *Johnson,* 335 F.2d 372 (7th Cir. 1964). In *Starr* the court, although discussing the statutes applicable to the Federal Aviation Administration, discussed the evidentiary standard which a court should utilize in determining whether the agency's denial of an exemption involved an abuse of discretion. The result should be similar in the present case.

In *Starr* the court relied upon the case of *Tiger International* v. *Civil Aeronautics Board,* 554 F.2d 926 (9th Cir.), cert. denied, 434 U.S. 975, 98 S.Ct. 532, 54 L.Ed.2d 467 (1977) for the proposition that the substantial evidence test is unworkable in a denial of exemption case. In analyzing *Tiger International,* the court in *Starr* stated that the substantial evidence standard is unworkable because:

> In proceedings requesting exemptions from a valid agency rule, . . . the bulk of evidence is petitioner's, since you must show that circumstances justify an exemption in his case. And if an agency's decision to grant or deny an exemption were to be judged under a substantial evidence rule, that agency would be forced to defend its standard rule in every exemption proceeding, thus countermanding the whole purpose of a fixed agency rule—to eliminate the need for intensive hearings and factfindings in every case. Thus . . . where no hearing is required (as in an exemption proceeding), the substantial evidence rule is also not necessary. *Starr* v. *Federal Aviation Administration, supra* at 311.

The Court then went on to define the test to be used stating:

> Under the "arbitrary and capricious test," however, the administrator's discretion is still limited. He is bound by the statutory framework of the program administered by the agency. Thus, a court can review an administrator's decision to insure that he neither included in his analysis factors irrelevant to the congressional purpose of the program he administers, nor ignored factors which Congress has indicated are highly significant. *Id.* at 311.

In reviewing the agency's action in this case, it is important to note that in enacting 49 U.S.C. § 304, the statute granting the Interstate Commerce Commission regulatory authority, Congress granted the Commission authority "to promote the safety of operation and equipment of motor vehicles." 49 U.S.C. § 304(a)(5) and (6). Although the functions under section 304 were originally granted to the Interstate Commerce Commission, in 1966, the authority was transferred to the Secretary of

Transportation) 49 U.S.C. § 1655(e)(6)(C) who in turn delegated them to the Federal Highway Administrator. 49 CFR 1.48(f). The current diabetes rule was originally promulgated on April 22, 1977, based upon an analysis by the Federal Highway Administrator. This rule, effective January 1, 1971, contained the version of 49 CFR § 391.41(d)(3) that is in effect today. Although the Federal Highway Administrator undertook a thorough review of the disease as it applied to over-the-road truck drivers in its original promulgation in 1970, during the course of this case the diabetes rule was fully reconsidered.

Pursuant to this reconsideration, the Administrator published an advanced notice on March 28, 1978, indicating a proposed rulemaking, the purpose of which was to examine the basis for the diabetes rule and to determine whether any changes should be made. 42 Fed.Reg. 16452 (1977). In that document, the Federal Highway Administration discussed the manifestations of diabetes and explained the causes of the disease. Furthermore, the various treatments of the condition and the work environment of over-the-road truck drivers was explained. The report concluded with a discussion of the relationship of the disease to the specific work environment of the interstate truck driver and summarized recent studies indicating a significantly higher accident risk for diabetic drivers versus the general public.

After this review, the Federal Highway Administration solicited written comments and data on the following questions:

> (1) Should insulin-dependent diabetics be restricted from driving commercial motor vehicles in interstate or foreign commerce?
> (2) Should all diabetics be restricted from driving commercial motor vehicles in interstate or foreign commerce?
> (3) Should diabetics who are controlling their condition through use of hypoglycemic agents and diet be restricted from driving commercial motor vehicles in interstate or foreign commerce?
> (4) If exemptions are granted in insulin-dependent diabetics, or the rule changed to relax the present standard, what dosage level of insulin can be documented as a cut-off for establishing a minimum medical standard acceptable to highway safety?
> (5) Since sulfonyluras (orinase, tolinase, dymelor and diabinese) are more prevalent to "hypoglycemic reactions:" should diabetics using these specific hypoglycemic drugs be restricted from driving commercial motor vehicles in interstate or foreign commerce? 42 Fed.Reg. 16459 (1977).

There were 74 respondents who sent comments in response to the Administration's solicitation for comments on the insulin-dependent diabetic rule. Among those groups responding were representatives of the medical profession, the transportation industry, and union organizations. In the report the Federal Highway Administration reviewed the comments of these respondents and indicated that "approximately one out of three respondents were in this category [representatives of the medical profession, the transportation industry, and union organizations] and a ratio of two to one existed for proponents supporting the present rule as written." 42 Fed.Reg. 57488 (1977). Among the reports received by the Federal Highway Administration were the extensive comments of the American Diabetes Association, an organization devoted to ending employment discrimination for diabetics. In commenting upon section 391.41(b)(3), the American Diabetes Association report stated:

We feel that diabetics should have the same chance as any other person of obtaining and performing work for which he is medically and vocationally qualified. However, we feel that the data available to date, presented in the Federal Register on March 28, 1977, support the present Department of Transportation regulation which prohibits insulin-taking diabetics from operating a commercial motor vehicle in interstate and foreign commerce. 49 Fed.Reg. 57489 (1977).

There were numerous other comments which were of the same nature as the comments submitted by the American Diabetes Association. An example of another group submitting information were individual medical professionals. In analyzing the comments of this group, the Federal Highway Administration stated that: "This category represented approximately 17 percent of the respondents and, as a group, favored relaxation or modification of the present rules. None of the opponents submitted supporting documentation . . ." 49 Fed.Reg. 57490 (1977).

In the report in which the Federal Highway Administration re-evaluated and reaffirmed the rule excluding insulin-dependent diabetics from operating motor vehicles in interstate commerce, the Federal Highway Administration noted the receipt of both supporting and opposing comments. As indicated earlier, the scope of the Court's review is to determine whether the agency's decision was arbitrary and capricious. The Supreme Court has held that in reviewing regulations issued under the Interstate Commerce Act, the statute under which 49 CFR section 391.41(b)(3) was promulgated, "we do not weigh the evidence introduced before the Commission; we do not inquire into the wisdom of the regulations that the Commission promulgates; and we inquire into the soundness of the reasoning by which the Commission reaches its conclusions only to ascertain that the latter are rationally supported." *United States* v. *Allegheny Ludlum Steel Corporation,* 406 U.S. 742, 749, 92 S.Ct. 1941, 1946, 32 L.Ed.2d 453 (1972).

The Seventh Circuit Court of Appeals has also set forth the scope of inquiry under the arbitrary and capricious standard, and using language similar to that of the Supreme Court, stated:

> This standard requires us to determine whether "the decision was based on a consideration of the relevant factors and whether there has been a clear error of judgment." We are not to set the effluent limitations ourselves or substitute our judgment for the agency's. Rather, we are to determine whether the limitations set by the agency are "the result of reasoned decisionmaking." *American Meat Institute* v. *Environmental Protection Agency,* 526 F.2d 442, 453. (7th Cir. 1975). [citations omitted].

Furthermore, as indicated by the Court's decision in *City of Chicago* v. *F. P. C.,* 147 U.S.App.D.C. 312, 328, 458 F.2d 731, 747 (1971), cert. denied, 405 U.S. 1074, 92 S.Ct. 1495, 31 L.Ed.2d 808 (1972), a reviewing court in determining whether an agency's rules are rational will not hesitate to give great weight to the judgment of an expert agency on complex scientific questions. Based upon these cases, the question presented to this Court is whether the rule excluding insulin-dependent drivers is rationally based.

In addressing this issue, the Court would note at the outset that plaintiff's contention that the Federal Highway Administration erred in holding an adjudicatory hearing is without support. The Supreme Court indicated in *Florida East Coast Rail-*

*way* v. *United States,* 410 U.S. 224, 93 S.Ct. 810, 32 L.Ed.2d 682 (1973) that such rulemaking may lawfully be done on a notice and comment basis unless the relevant statute either specifies a hearing "on the record" or otherwise indicates that rulemaking must be formal. The text of 49 U.S.C. § 304 does not speak of hearings "on the record," and there is nothing in the history of the statute or its subsequent interpretation to indicate any Congressional intent that rulemaking be formal.

In viewing the question of whether the diabetes rule is rationally based, this Court is led to review the evidence submitted to the administrative agency. Although there were comments submitted to the Federal Highway Administration recommending a liberalization of the rule, the agency's determination, as indicated by the reports of groups such as the American Diabetes Association, is not without support. Furthermore, in commenting upon the evidence submitted to the Federal Highway Administration, the Administration indicated that the reports of many of the proponents of the present rule were supported with documentation and as such were given more weight in the final determination. The Adminstration noted that "In contrast very few of the respondents who supported a relaxation of the current rule directly commented on the data in the Advance Notice of March 1977. Those supporting relaxation also failed to submit any medical reference in support of their position." 42 Fed.Reg. 57491 (1977). Moreover, in the report soliciting comments on 49 CFR section 391.41(b)(3), the Federal Highway Administration not only discussed the physical manifestations of insulin-dependent diabetes and other forms of diabetes, but in addition discussed and set forth the environment of a commercial truck driver and the physical stresses which could affect the metabolism of a diabetic driver. 42 Fed.Reg. 16454–16458 (1977).

In the final analysis, the Court is of the opinion that the Department of Transportation's rule prohibiting insulin-dependent diabetics from driving commercial vehicles in interstate commerce is not arbitrary and capricious. In its reconsideration of the rule, the Federal Highway Administration was presented with numerous comments which directly and unequivocally support the position of the Department of Transportation's rule prohibiting insulin-dependent diabetic drivers from operating motor vehicles in interstate commerce.

In his legal brief, the plaintiff relies upon the statements of several medical experts who are of the opinion that insulin-dependent diabetics can be sufficiently regulated so that they are capable of driving as an over-the-road truck driver. Plaintiff asserts that he should be permitted to establish his personal qualification to operate a motor vehicle as a commercial driver. Therefore, plaintiff asserts, that he should be entitled to a hearing under principles of due process. In discussing this type of a question in *Starr* v. *Federal Aviation Administration, supra,* the Court held that if a rule is reasonable, such as we have determined here, then "it is not an abuse of discretion to reject any individual application for exemption even if the applicant demonstrates that he personally is a superman . . ." *Id.* at 312–313.

Here, in light of the extensive reconsideration given by the Federal Highway Administration to the question of the general competency of an insulin-dependent diabetic to drive a motor vehicle in interstate commerce, there is little doubt that the agency's decision is reasonable. Therefore, this Court will not examine plaintiff's personal physical capabilities any further.

Although waived by plaintiff's brief, the Court would note that plaintiff's other contentions are without merit. Plaintiff contends that the diabetes rule is discriminatory because it disqualifies only insulin-dependent diabetics. The test for determining whether the rule is unconstitutionally discriminatory, is whether there is a rational basis for it. *Massachusetts Board of Retirement* v. *Murgia,* 427 U.S. 307, 96 S.Ct. 2562, 49 L.Ed.2d 520 (1976). As indicated by the evidence presented to the Federal Highway Administration, certain medical authorities were of the opinion that even a well-controlled diabetic could have an insulin reaction and, therefore, lose or have reduced consciousness. Based upon this evidence, there can be little question that there is a rational basis for the limitations of 49 CFR § 391.41(b)(3). Therefore, in light of the broad language of 49 U.S.C. § 304 empowering the Federal Highway Administration to regulate the safety of interstate commerce traffic, and the purpose of the diabetes regulation to protect the public from highway accidents, it is clear to this Court that this regulation is rationally based. Consequently, plaintiff's equal protection argument must fail.

*   *   *

[The court also rejects Monnier's arguments concerning lack of personal notice. The court then determines that summary judgment is appropriate.]

Therefore, it is ordered that defendants' motion for summary judgment must be and hereby is granted.

So ORDERED this 23rd day of February, 1979, at Milwaukee, Wisconsin.

NOTE

Would or should the result in this case be different if the Department of Transportation regulations were challenged today as a discriminatory federally conducted activity in violation of Section 504? Explain.

## B.  INSURANCE

### 2.  Health and Accident Insurance

p. 1083—INSERT after Note 3:

DOE v. COLAUTTI

*United States Court of Appeals for the Third Circuit, 1979*<br>*592 F.2d 704*

Before GIBBONS, VAN DUSEN and ROSENN, Circuit Judges.

Opinion of the Court

ROSENN, Circuit Judge.

This case presents a challenge to limits set by Pennsylvania's medical assistance statute, Pa.Stat.Ann. tit. 62 § 443.1 (Purdon Supp. 1978), for state benefits for hospitalization in private mental institutions.[1] Using the pseudonym "John Doe,"

---

[1]The statute provides, in part:

> The following medical assistance payments shall be made in behalf of eligible persons whose institutional care is prescribed by physicians:

*   *   *

the plaintiff sought declaratory relief and an injunction in the United States District Court for the Eastern District of Pennsylvania against the Pennsylvania Secretary of Public Welfare and others (collectively, the "State"). The injunction would have required the continuation of Doe's benefits for hospitalization in a private psychiatric institution even though the durational limit of the statute had been reached. When the district court denied a motion for a preliminary injunction, Doe appealed. 28 U.S.C. § 1292(a)(1) (1976). We affirm.

I

After an attempted suicide, Doe was admitted in April, 1978, to the Institute of Pennsylvania Hopsital, a private psychiatric institution. Because of his financial circumstances, Doe qualified for benefits under Pennsylvania's medical assistance program. Pa.Stat.Ann. tit. 62 §§ 441.1, 441.2, 442.1 (Purdon Supp. 1978). Under this statute Pennsylvania has set durational limits on the benefits payable for hospitalization in a private mental institution. If a patient hospitalized in such an institution is older than 20 years of age and younger than 65, the law limits his benefits to payments for sixty days of hospital care in any "benefit period." Pa.Stat.Ann. tit. 62 § 443.1(4) (Purdon Supp. 1978). The term "benefit period" is so defined that, after sixty days of hospitalization in a private psychiatric hospital, a patient can receive no further benefits as an inpatient in such an institution until he has passed sixty days in "which he is not an inpatient in a hospital." Pa.Stat.Ann. tit. 62 § 402 (Purdon Supp. 1978). After sixty days of hospitalization at the Institute of Pennsylvania Hospital, Doe was no longer eligible for benefits under the medical assistance program. But he was eligible for care in a *state* mental hospital. *See* Pa.Stat.Ann. tit. 50 §§ 7101–7503 (Purdon Supp. 1978). To avert his transfer from a private to a public mental hospital, Doe, as an individual and as representative of a class, brought this action to invalidate the part of Pa.Stat.Ann. tit. 62 § 443.1 that creates durational limits on benefits for hospitalization in a private psychiatric institution.

Doe contends that the Pennsylvania statute invidiously discriminates against him and against the class of which he is a member—the mentally ill affected by the durational limit. Under Pennsylvania law, a person between 21 and 64 years of age is entitled to benefits for unlimited hospitalization for physical illness in a private general hospital. Pa.Stat.Ann. tit. 62 § 443.1(1) (Purdon Supp. 1978).[3] If a person between 21 and 64 years of age has been hospitalized in a private mental hospital, rather than a general hospital, he is limited to sixty days' benefits in any benefit period. Pa.Stat.Ann. tit. 62 § 443.1(4) (Purdon Supp. 1978). This distinction between hospitalization in a private general hospital and a private mental hospital, Doe argues,

---

(4) The cost of care in any mental hospital or in a public tuberculosis hospital. . . . Care in a private mental hospital shall be limited to sixty days in a benefit period. . . .

[3]The patient must also meet other requirements for eligibility, but those requirements are not relevant to this case. *See* Pa.Stat.Ann. §§ 441.1, 441.2, 442.1 (Purdon Supp. 1978).

It is not clear what are the circumstances under which a mentally ill patient could secure treatment at a general hospital. At the hearing before the district court, one witness testified that, "in general," the mentally ill patient would need to have a medical as well as a psychiatric problem. By its terms, the time limit in § 443.1 does not cover psychiatric care in a general hospital.

discriminates against the mentally ill and conflicts with the Federal Rehabilitation Act of 1973, 29 U.S.C. § 794 (1976), and with the Equal Protection Clause of the fourteenth amendment.

This appeal is from the denial of Doe's motion for a preliminary injunction. In deciding the motion, the district court focused on whether Doe has shown: (1) that he would suffer irreparable harm in the absence of relief *pendente lite,* and (2) that he was likely to succeed on the merits. *See Delaware Port Authority* v. *Transamerican Trailer Transport, Inc.,* 501 F.2d 917, 919–20 (3d Cir. 1974), *quoting A.L.K. Corp.* v. *Columbia Pictures Industries, Inc.,* 440 F.2d 761, 763 (3d Cir. 1971). To prove irreparable harm, Doe introduced testimony that care in private mental hospitals is better than that in public institutions. Doe also presented testimony that he suffered from a schizophrenic disorder, that the chances for his recovery would decline with the passage of time, and that his transfer from one hospital to another would disrupt his relationship with his psychiatrist and would damage his chances for recovery. On the basis of this evidence, the district court concluded that Doe had sufficiently shown irreparable harm. But the district court held that Doe had not demonstrated "a reasonable probability of eventual success in the litigation." *A.L.K. Corp.* v. *Columbia Pictures Industries, Inc.,* 440 F.2d 761, 763 (3d Cir. 1971). We hold that the district court did not abuse its discretion in concluding that even if Doe has shown irreparable harm, his chances of success on the merits are too slight for the issuance of a preliminary injunction. Because of this holding, we need not reach the issue of irreparable harm.

*   *   *

[In Part II of the opinion, the court concludes that the case is not moot despite Doe's transfer to a state psychiatric hospital.]

III

Doe contends that Pa.Stat.Ann. tit. 62 § 443.1 conflicts with § 504 of the Rehabilitation Act of 1973, 29 U.S.C. § 794 (1976), and is therefore unlawful. U.S.Const. art. VI cl. 2. Section 504 reads:

> No otherwise qualified handicapped individual in the United States, as defined in section 706(6) of this title, shall, solely by reason of his handicap, be excluded from the participation in, be denied the benefits of, or be subjected to discrimination under any program or activity receiving Federal financial assistance.

The parties have stipulated that Pennsylvania receives federal financial assistance for mental health programs and for other programs. The state, moreover, has not contested that Doe, a schizophrenic, is "handicapped" under the terms of the Rehabilitation Act. *See* 45 C.F.R. § 84.3(j)(1)(i), (ii), (iii) (1977).

According to Doe, Pennsylvania denies to the mentally ill benefits that it extends to the physically ill. The physically ill are entitled to payments for private general hospital care, however long they remain in the hospital; but the mentally ill, if between 21 and 64 and if in a private mental hospital, are entitled to benefits for only sixty days at a time. In this differentiation, Doe argues, the State has discriminated against the mentally ill by reason of their handicap and has violated section 504 of the Rehabilitation Act.

Doe's position is that the provisions of 45 C.F.R. § 84 (1977), a regulation promulgated under section 504 of the Rehabilitation Act, make clear how the distinction between general hospitalization and psychiatric hospitalization violates federal law.[9] In each instance the provisions prohibit a recipient of federal money from giving the handicapped an "aid, benefit, or service" that is not as good as the aid, benefit, or service provided to the unhandicapped. But the regulation does not explain how to identify the relevant "aid, benefit, or service," which under the statute a recipient of federal funds must provide equally to the handicapped, as to those not handicapped. Doe contends that the State has discriminated against the mentally ill in the provision of "private inpatient care." To the physically ill the State has extended benefits unlimited in time; to the mentally ill, it has afforded only sixty days of benefits. The State, on the other hand, sees care for physical illness as one benefit and care for mental illness as another. In the treatment of their physical illnesses, the mentally ill receive the same benefits as everyone else. A mental patient with heart disease, for instance, is as entitled to benefits for treatment of the heart disease as would be a person not mentally ill.

In resolving this question, we find helpful both an "Analysis of Final Regulation" under the Rehabilitation Act, which appears as an appendix to 45 C.F.R. § 84 (1977), and the structure of the federal Medicaid program, 42 U.S.C. §§ 1396 et seq. (1976). The "Analysis" was prepared by the Department of Health, Education, and Welfare, which administers the Federal Rehabilitation Act.

In discussing the various parts of 45 C.F.R. § 84, this "Analysis" denies that the Rehabilitation Act requires a hospital or other recipient of federal assistance to offer specialized treatment for particular handicaps. The law, as elaborated by the regulation, is construed instead to require that such treatment as a hospital or other recipient gives must be extended to the handicapped on a basis of equality with those not handicapped. The "Analysis" explains, for instance:

> Recipients are not required . . . to provide specialized services and aids to handicapped persons in health programs. If, for example, a college infirmary treats only simple disorders such as cuts, bruises, and colds, its obligation to handicapped persons is to treat such disorders for them.

45 C.F.R. § 84, Appendix A, paragraph 33. Similarly, the "Analysis" construes one part of 45 C.F.R. § 84 to mean that

---

[9]Doe relies especially on the following sections of 45 C.F.R. § 84.4 (1977):

> (b) Discriminatory actions prohibited. (1) A recipient, in providing any aid, benefit, or service, may not, directly or through contractual, licensing, or other arrangements, on the basis of handicap:
> (i) Deny a qualified handicapped person the opportunity to participate in or benefit from the aid, benefit, or service;
> (ii) Afford a qualified handicapped person an opportunity to participate in or benefit from the aid, benefit, or service that is not equal to that afforded others;
> (iii) Provide a qualified handicapped person with an aid, benefit, or service that is not as effective as that provided to others;
> (iv) Provide different or separate aid, benefits, or services to handicapped persons or to any class of handicapped persons unless such action is necessary to provide qualified handicapped persons with aid, benefits, or services that are as effective as those provided to others;
> * * *
> (vii) Otherwise limit a qualified handicapped person in the enjoyment of any right, privilege, advantage, or opportunity enjoyed by others receiving an aid, benefit, or service.

. . . a burn treatment center need not provide other types of medical treatment to handicapped persons unless it provides such medical services to nonhandicapped persons. It could not, however, refuse to treat the burns of a deaf person because of his or her deafness.

*Id.,* paragraph 36. And the "Analysis," in interpreting a provision on drug and alcohol addicts, declares that this provision in the regulation

. . . does not mean that all hospitals and outpatient facilities must treat drug addiction and alcoholism. It simply means, for example, that a cancer clinic may not refuse to treat cancer patients simply because they are also alcoholics.

*Id.,* paragraph 37.

These examples convincingly contradict Doe's interpretation of the regulation under the Rehabilitation Act. If the "aid, benefit, or service" referred to in 45 C.F.R. § 84.4(b) could include the category "private inpatient care," a private cancer center providing hospitalization could not refuse to offer any hospitalization necessary to treat mental illness. Its refusal to treat mental disease would deny "private inpatient care" to the mentally ill solely by reason of their handicap.

Doe attempts to avoid this contradiction by interpreting the examples in the "Analysis" to mean only that a recipient need not provide any new kinds of services or benefits. Here, he argues, the State already supplies some private inpatient care for mental illness, and he does not ask for any new benefit, but only for expansion of an existing benefit. We disagree with Doe's argument. If the "aid, benefit, or service" to which 45 C.F.R. § 84.4(b) refers could include a category such as "inpatient hospital care," the cancer center or burn center hypothesized in the "Analysis" would also be offering an existing program under which the specialized treatment of handicaps would be an expansion—an existing program of "inpatient hospital care." A mentally ill person could seek psychiatric care in a burn center under that center's existing "service" of "inpatient hospital care." Under Doe's broad definition of "aid, benefit, or service," the examples in the "Analysis" all concern existing, rather than new, benefits. Doe's proposed distinction between new and existing services does not hold up.

The structure of the federal Medicaid program also counsels against Doe's interpretation of section 504 in the Rehabilitation Act. States participating in the program are required to provide various medical services, *see* 42 U.S.C. § 1396a(a)(13)(B), (C) (1976), but they need not provide inpatient care at a psychiatric hospital. Indeed, if the patients are between 21 and 64 years of age, the federal government will pay to the states no reimbursements whatsoever for the costs of such care. *See* 42 U.S.C. § 1396d(a)(14), (16) (1976).

The gaps in the requirements of the Medicaid statute were not inadvertent. Congress conferred "broad discretion on the States to adopt standards for determining the extent of medical assistance, requiring only that such standards be 'reasonable' and 'consistent with the objectives' of the Act." *Beal* v. *Doe,* 432 U.S. 438, 444, 97 S.Ct. 2366, 2371, 53 L.Ed.2d 464 (1977) (footnote omitted). In dealing with 21- to 64-year-old inpatients in mental hospitals, Congress not only left participating states free to include or exclude benefits for such patients, but Congress even determined not to reimburse the costs when states did decide to cover these patients. Because Congress so carefully drew these lines in the Medicaid statute, we do not believe, in the absence of any specific evidence supporting Doe's position, that Congress intended section 504 of the Rehabilitation Act to obliterate the distinctions between the medical care a state medical assistance program must cover and the care it need not include.

## IV

In his argument based on the Equal Protection Clause, Doe urges that classifications according to mental illness are "suspect" and demand strict judicial scrutiny. If Pennsylvania's law is measured by this strict standard of review, Doe contends, it must be held unconstitutional. In Doe's view, the law discriminates against the mentally ill by limiting the duration of benefits for private psychiatric hospitalization but granting benefits without time limits for care of physical illnesses in private general hospitals. Doe does not argue, however, that this distinction in benefits is unconstitutional if the appropriate standard for review is less than "strict scrutiny."

Because of the Supreme Court's summary affirmance in Legion v. Weinberger, 414 U.S. 1058, 94 S.Ct. 564, 38 L.Ed.2d 465 (1973), aff'g Legion v. Richardson, 354 F.Supp. 456 (S.D.N.Y.) (three-judge court), Doe's argument under the Equal Protection Clause is not likely to succeed. In Legion the plaintiffs brought a class action in which they challenged the constitutionality of the Medicare and Medicaid laws. As the laws then stood, eligible patients who were older than 65 could receive benefits without limitation of time if they were in a general hospital. If they were in a psychiatric hospital, patients over 65 were entitled to benefits only for a lifetime total of 190 days of care. Contending that most patients over 65 in public mental institutions needed long-term care, the plaintiffs alleged unconstitutional discrimination against the mentally ill who were hospitalized in public mental hospitals. There was a similar argument concerning patients who were 65 or younger. As for these patients, benefits were payable for hospitalization in general hospitals, including psychiatric institutions associated with general hospitals. But patients in state mental hospitals, which would not be associated with general hospitals, were ineligible for benefits. Once again, the plaintiffs asserted that the statutes unconstitutionally discriminated against patients in state mental hospitals.

In examining the challenged laws, a three-judge court applied a test of "rationality":

> Where a statutory classification is not conceived on peculiarly suspect grounds such as wealth or race, all that is constitutionally required is that the challenged classification or restriction bear a reasonable relationship with the objectives sought to be fulfilled by the legislation.

354 F.Supp. at 459 (citation omitted). The court concluded that the laws were rational and satisfied the requirements of equal protection. Id. The Supreme Court summarily affirmed, and this summary affirmance, being a decision on the merits, creates a precedent that is binding upon us. Hicks v. Miranda, 422 U.S. 332, 343–45, 95 S.Ct. 2281, 45 L.Ed.2d 223 (1975).

The Legion case refutes Doe's argument under the Equal Protection Clause. In Legion the Supreme Court sustained a Medicare law under which, for patients over 65, there was a durational limit on benefits for care in a psychiatric hospital, but no limit for care in a general hospital. Pennsylvania's law, for the age group pertinent in this case (21 to 64), makes a similar allocation of benefits. No durational limit applies to hospitalization in a general hospital, but patients in a private psychiatric hospital are subject to a sixty-day limit on benefits. Because Congress could constitutionally set durational limits on benefits for patients over 65 in *all* psychiatric hospitals, it is likely that Pennsylvania may limit benefits for patients from 21 to 64 in *private* psychiatric hospitals.[10] Similarly, the Medicaid law in *Legion,* which granted benefits for those 65 or younger, extended coverage to patients in general hospitals, including private mental hospitals associated with general hospitals, but denied benefits to patients in all other mental institutions. This law excluded patients in public and unaffiliated private mental hospitals from benefits but extended benefits to patients in general hospitals. It was as "discriminatory" as the Pennsylvania law challenged here.

Because the Supreme Court in *Legion* affirmed without opinion, it did not necessarily adopt the reasoning of the three-judge district court, which based its decision on the "rationality" of the challenged law. But the Supreme Court probably implied a rejection of the "strict scrutiny" for which Doe contends, inasmuch as that stringent standard virtually ensures a finding of unconstitutionality. *Cf. Gunther, Foreword: In Search of Evolving Doctrine on a Changing Court,* 86 Harv.L.Rev. 1, 8 (1972) (strict scrutiny of Warren Court "fatal in fact"). Whatever the correct standard for judicial review, the result in *Legion*—the upholding of the particular classifications in the Medicaid and Medicare laws—makes it unlikely that Doe can successfully challenge Pennsylvania's law. As we have observed, *supra,* the laws upheld in *Legion* were no less "discriminatory" than is Pa.Stat.Ann. tit. 62, § 443.1.

Doe's chances for success are made even more remote by the strong arguments against the view that classifications based on mental disease are suspect. The Supreme Court has written that a class is not entitled to special solicitude under the Equal Protection Clause unless the members of the class have "been subjected to unique disabilities on the basis of stereotyped characteristics not truly indicative of their abilities." *Massachusetts Board of Retirement v. Murgia,* 427 U.S. 307, 313, 96 S.Ct. 2562, 2567, 49 L.Ed.2d 520 (1976) (per curiam). Although the mentally ill have been the victims of stereotypes, the disabilities imposed on them have often reflected that many of the mentally ill do have reduced ability for personal relations, for economic activity, and for political choice. This is not to say that the legal disabilities have precisely fit the actual incapacities of the mentally ill individuals whom the law has burdened, but it is important that the legal disabilities have been related, even if imperfectly, to real inabilities from which many of the mentally ill suffer.

The Supreme Court, moreover, has been reluctant to grant extraordinary judicial protections to a class that is "large, diverse, [and] amorphous." *San Antonio School District v. Rodriguez,* 411 U.S. 1, 28, 93 S.Ct. 1278, 36 L.Ed.2d 16 (1973). The concept of "mental illness" is susceptible to much dispute, and the category encompasses a whole range of disorders, varying in character and effects.

Even without judicial recognition of a "suspect classification," many states, and especially Pennsylvania, have in recent years devoted more and more of their

---

[10]As noted *supra,* Pennsylvania would provide Doe with care in a public psychiatric hospital without durational limits. Pa.Stat.Ann. tit. 50 §§ 7101–7503 (Purdon Supp. 1978).

resources to treatment of the mentally ill.[11] Pennsylvania's enactment of the comprehensive Mental Health and Mental Retardation Act of 1966, Pa.Stat.Ann. tit. 50 §§ 4101 *et seq.* (Purdon 1969 and Purdon Supp. 1978), and its allocation of an extraordinarily large portion of its budget to the treatment of the mentally ill are warnings against judicial creation of a new "suspect classification."[12]

## V

Because Doe is not likely to succeed on the merits of his statutory and constitutional arguments, the district court was within its discretion in denying the motion for a preliminary injunction. The order of the district court will be affirmed. Each party is to bear his or its own costs.

## NOTES

1. Chart the parties' varying categories of benefits that are being compared to prove or defeat the claim of discrimination. Which argument is more consistent with the HEW regulations cited by Doe? Is the court correct that Doe's legal argument, taken to its logical conclusion, would require that "a private cancer center providing hospitalization could not refuse to offer any hospitalization necessary to treat mental illness?"

2. Would the result in this case be different if Pennsylvania offered no benefits for private psychiatric hospitalization? Why or why not?

## BERNARD B. v. BLUE CROSS AND BLUE SHIELD

*United States District Court for the Southern District of New York, 1981*
*528 F.Supp. 125*

Opinion

SAND, District Judge.

*Introduction*

Plaintiffs Bernard B., Shirley B., and Lynette D., suing individually and on behalf of an as yet uncertified class, as well as two institutional plaintiffs, challenge a practice which prevailed until November 6, 1980, of excluding from basic Blue Cross

---

[11]In 1966–67, Pennsylvania devoted $142,000,000 to institutional care of the mentally ill and mentally retarded. Of this amount, $125,000,000 had originally come from the State itself, and the rest was from federal and other sources. The State also supported community services for the mentally ill and retarded, paying out a total of $12,900,000, of which $12,500,000 had been supplied from the State's own tax revenues. [1968–1969] Budget of the Commonwealth of Pennsylvania 159–63, 167. By 1976–77, the amounts had multiplied. For institutional care, the State expended $495,000,000, of which $338,000,000 came from the State's own resources. The community services program had reached $91,900,000, and of this amount $91,200,000 represented the State's own contribution. [1978–79] Commonwealth of Pennsylvania Executive Budget 586, 596–97.

[12]Pennsylvania's Mental Health and Mental Retardation Act mandates the Pennsylvania Department of Public Welfare "[t]o assure within the State the availability and equitable provision of adequate mental health and mental retardation services for all perons who need them, regardless of religion, race, color, national origin, settlement, residence, or economic or social status." Pa.Stat.Ann. tit. 50 § 4201 (Purdon 1969). In addition, each county is required to "establish a county mental health and mental retardation program for the prevention of mental disability, and for the diagnosis, care, treatment, rehabilitation and detention of the mentally disabled. . . ." *Id.*, at § 4301. The costs of this county program are in large measure also borne by the State.

and Blue Shield of Greater New York (hereinafter "Blue Cross") insurance coverage psychiatric inpatient care in New York City Health and Hospitals Corporation (hereinafter "HHC") hospitals. Plaintiffs claim that this exclusion was discriminatory in violation of federal and state statutes, and the United States Constitution, because non-psychiatric care in HHC hospitals was covered and psychiatric care in non-HHC hospitals was also covered. Plaintiffs sue Blue Cross under Section 504 of the Rehabilitation Act of 1973, 29 U.S.C. § 794 and under N.Y.Ins.Law § 209(2) (McKinney). They sue Albert B. Lewis, (hereinafter "Superintendent") individually and as Superintendent of the New York State Insurance Department, under § 209(2), and the equal protection and due process clauses of the Fourteenth Amendment, and 42 U.S.C. § 1983. Lastly, plaintiffs sue HHC under the Rehabilitation Act, the Fourteenth Amendment, and § 1983, and also bring a negligence claim against HHC for a failure to warn plaintiffs that the hospital's inpatient psychiatric care was not covered by Blue Cross. Plaintiffs seek declaratory and injunctive relief against all three defendants, plus damages against HHC and Blue Cross, and attorney's fees, costs and disbursements pursuant to 42 U.S.C. § 1988.

The matter comes now before the Court on defendants' motions for summary judgment. Blue Cross and HHC have moved with respect to all claims against them. Blue Cross additionally moves for attorney's fees, costs and disbursements pursuant to the Rehabilitation Act, 29 U.S.C. § 794a(b).

The Superintendent has joined in Blue Cross' motion . . . [a]nd moved with respect to the claims against him.

*Facts*

Bernard and Shirley B., husband and wife, were, at all relevant times, covered by Blue Cross health insurance as an incident of Bernard B.'s private employment. Shirley B. was admitted to an HHC hospital for emergency psychiatric treatment in November of 1978, December of 1978, and January of 1979. Plaintiffs allege that the B's were never informed that Blue Cross did not cover this care. Bernard and Shirley B. received bills totalling $11,600 from the hospital. Blue Cross denied coverage "on the grounds that the contract does not provide benefits for psychiatric care when the admission is to be a governmental hospital." Plaintiffs' Brief at 5–6. Plaintiffs state that HHC has threatened the B's with legal proceedings to collect the $11,600.

Until November 6, 1980, that is, during all three of Shirley B.'s confinements, Blue Cross excluded inpatient psychiatric care in HHC hospitals from its basic coverage. In 1974, Blue Cross had requested permission from the Insurance Department to include such coverage in all contracts of Bernard B.'s category. The Superintendent denied permission.[7] However, Blue Cross had offered the option of such coverage to Bernard B.'s group at an increased premium. The option was declined.

---

[7]The Superintendent's Opinion and Decision stated:

Serious questions arise as to whether community-rated subscribers should be forced to shoulder these additional burdens [for expanded maternity benefits, psychiatric coverage, and hemophiliac care] when the cost of all necessities, including health insurance, has already placed a severe strain on subscribers with low and medium incomes. The problem is further complicated by the fact that there are many other important and beneficial types of medical care that are not now covered by Blue Cross.[2]

["[2]For example, many forcefully advocate that Blue Cross coverage should extend to non-hospital clinics specifically designed for treatment of alcoholism. Others insist that coverage for pre-natal care is equally, if not more, important."] [*continued next page*]

In July, 1980, Blue Cross again sought permission to include the disputed coverage in its minimal hospital coverage. This time the Insurance Department granted permission "on an experimental basis subject to an annual review of the cost and magnitude of the benefit provided," Robins Affidavit ¶ 14. Consequently, "on November 6, 1980, such expanded psychiatric coverage became effective for all Blue Cross community-rated subscribers, including named plaintiffs." Blue Cross' Memorandum at 9 (citation omitted).

\* \* \*

[The court rejects contentions that the claims are moot.]

*Causation*

Both Blue Cross and HHC have raised causation arguments, maintaining that they were not the cause of any injury to plaintiffs and therefore should be granted summary judgment.

Blue Cross advances two causation arguments: first, that it was the failure of Bernard B.'s subscriber group to purchase the option which would have covered inpatient HHC psychiatric care, rather than Blue Cross' failure to include such coverage in its basic plan, which caused the harm complained of; and second, that it was the Superintendent's 1975 denial of the Blue Cross request to include such coverage in its basic plan which was the cause, and Blue Cross cannot be held liable for failing to do that which the Superintendent decreed it could not do.

The first of these arguments is unpersuasive. Even if the decision of the group subscriber not to buy the relevant coverage was a concurrent cause, the fact that the coverage was not a part of the minimum plan but rather had to be bought at extra cost is a cause of Bernard and Shirley B.'s incurring the cost of her hospitalizations. The fact that there was a way to make up for the lack of coverage in the minimum plan, does not alter the fact that if, *arguendo,* plaintiffs had a right to such coverage, Blue Cross'

---

Since the existing source of available financial resources—the consumer's pocketbook—is not limitless, priorities must be established. Any rational determination regarding priorities must be dependent upon the advice of medical and financial experts, as well as the desires and needs of the general public. Such decisions should not generally be established unilaterally in a proceeding directed mainly at premium rate levels, unless, of course, a proposed new benefit either will reduce the overall cost of providing existing coverage or has broad community and expert approval and support.

Viewed in this context, the Department will only approve the proposed benefit for outpatient hemophiliac treatment which will require marginal added costs, if any, since it permits treatment on a less expense outpatient basis under appropriate circumstances rather than in a hospital as presently required.

\* \* \*

While the proposed expanded psychiatric coverage would result in some offsetting savings,[4]

["4 The new benefit might lead some people, who today are treated in high-cost general hospitals because Blue Cross will pay, to receive psychiatric treatment in voluntary private hospitals that have a substantially lower per diem rate."]

there is a considerable net extra cost of $15 million annually. Moreover, the proposed new benefit causes internal inconsistencies and deficiencies. For example, Blue Cross attempts to exclude payment for expensive custodial care by limiting its coverage to facilities having an average stay of 60 days. At the public hearing, it was clearly demonstrated that such a standard is subject to considerable distortions that defeat its very purpose. Furthermore, Blue Cross's proposal excludes State hospitals entirely from its coverage while including municipal and privately owned hospitals. The validity of this exclusion, as well as the degree to which custodial care should be excluded from coverage, should be weighed as a part of the development of a broadly conceived state policy for mental health.

In re Blue Cross and Blue Shield of Greater New York, Opinion and Decision of Benjamin R. Schenck, Superintendent of Insurance, Feb. 19, 1975 (footnote omitted), Appendix I to HHC's Memorandum in Support.

exclusion of such coverage from the minimum plan and placing of that coverage in such a posture that it was a more expensive option and therefore less likely to be purchased and available to the B's, was causally related to Shirley B.'s hospitalizations not being covered by insurance.

As to the second argument, plaintiffs and Blue Cross agree that the issue is whether Blue Cross had sufficient freedom of choice to render it responsible, or whether the State's involvement was "so dominant that it would be unfair to hold a private party responsible," *Cantor* v. *Detroit Edison Co.*, 428 U.S. 579, 592, 96 S.Ct. 3110, 3118, 49 L.Ed.2d 1141 (1976). Certainly, there was extensive state regulation of Blue Cross' actions. However, even if the State's role in the formal decision making process was the dominant one (which we need not now decide), plaintiffs raise an issue as to whether Blue Cross could have "waived" its exclusion of HHC psychiatric inpatient coverage. Blue Cross endeavors to demonstrate that it lacked this option. However, having considered the proofs offered on both sides, we conclude that there remains an issue of material fact, or mixed fact and law, on this point, and we cannot say as a matter of law that Blue Cross has shown such an absence of choice in this area that we should find it without liability on causation grounds.

HHC adds to the causation arguments the assertion that it had no control over whether Blue Cross excluded coverage of HHC inpatient psychiatric care. Plaintiffs on the other hand argue that HHC was causally involved in the injury complained of,

> . . . by entering into "memoranda of understandings" with Blue Cross, through which it agreed to be reimbursed in accordance with the psychiatric exclusion. . . . HHC does not—nor could it—seriously contend that these memoranda do not constitute "contractual arrangements." The effect of HHC's adoption of the psychiatric exclusion is to deny to a class of persons suffering from mental illness (*i.e.* handicapped persons) a benefit available to the class of persons suffering from other illnesses.

Plaintiffs' Brief in Opposition at 37. While HHC claims it had no power over Blue Cross coverage, we cannot say on the record before us that we are persuaded that in fact HHC had no control. HHC seeks to paint a picture of the relationship between itself, Blue Cross, and the Insurance Department, according to which HHC lacked all capacity to initiate or refuse coverage changes. On the proofs before us, we are not convinced of the accuracy of this picture to the extent required on a motion for summary judgment.

### Rehabilitation Act

Plaintiffs bring claims under the Rehabilitation Act against Blue Cross and HHC. These defendants raise several preliminary arguments to the effect that the Rehabilitation Act does not apply to them.

The Rehabilitation Act provides that, "No otherwise qualified handicapped individual . . . shall, solely by reason of his handicap, be excluded from participation in, be denied the benefits of, or be subjected to discrimination under any program or activity receiving Federal financial assistance. . . ." 29 U.S.C. § 794.

HHC maintains: (a) that the McCarran-Ferguson Act, 15 U.S.C. § 1012(b), defeats plaintiffs' Rehabilitation Act claim; and (b) that even if plaintiffs were successful in their Rehabilitation Act claims, this would be no defense to liability for medical services rendered. Blue Cross argues that the Rehabilitation Act does not apply to it, because: (a) Blue Cross is not a recipient of "Federal financial assistance" under the Rehabilitation Act; and (b) the federal funds Blue Cross receives are Medicare funds, and plaintiffs are not claiming as recipients of such funds. We consider these arguments in turn.

The McCarran-Ferguson Act provides in relevant part: "No Act of Congress shall be construed to invalidate, impair, or supersede any law enacted by any State for the purpose of regulating the business of insurance, or which imposes a fee or tax upon such business, unless such Act specifically relates to the business of insurance. . . ." 15 U.S.C. § 1012(b). Plaintiffs do not argue that the Rehabilitation Act falls within the McCarran-Ferguson exception for acts which "specifically [relate] to the business of insurance." Rather, plaintiffs dispute HHC's two assertions that the HHC/Blue Cross agreements constitute "the business of insurance" within the meaning of the McCarran-Ferguson Act, and that the gravamen of plaintiffs' suit is a Blue Cross exclusion which constitutes "the business of insurance" within the meaning of that act.

We find the McCarran-Ferguson Act inapplicable in this case on the basis of *Group Life & Health Insurance Co.* v. *Royal Drug Co.* 440 U.S. 205, 99 S.Ct. 1067, 59 L.Ed.2d 261 (1979). HHC's argument that its agreements with Blue Cross constitute "the business of insurance" flies in the face of *Royal Drug*. Under the *Royal Drug* analysis, while these provider agreements constitute the business of insurance companies, the agreements do not constitute the "business of insurance," *see id.* at 219 n.18, 99 S.Ct. 1077 n.18. The agreements "do not involve any underwriting or spreading of risk, but are merely arrangements for the purchase of goods and services by" Blue Cross. *See id.* at 214, 99 S.Ct. at 1074.

HHC's broader argument, that the gravamen of plaintiff's suit, namely, an exclusion from Blue Cross coverage, constitutes the "business of insurance," raises an issue explicitly left undecided in *Royal Drug*. The Court cautioned, "This is not to say that the contracts offered by Blue Shield to its policyholders, as distinguished from its provider agreements with participating pharmacies, may not be the 'business of insurance' within the meaning of the Act." *Id.* at 230 n.37, 99 S.Ct. at 1082 n.37. However, the Court extensively reviewed the status of Blue Cross, Blue Shield plans under the McCarran-Ferguson Act, and concluded that they were not considered the "business of insurance" under the act at the time it was passed. Moreover, the Court noted that most courts have regarded them as outside of that category for the purposes of the act. *Id.* at 226 n.33, 99 S.Ct. at 1080 n.33. Even if a state treated such plans as insurance, that would not be controlling on the McCarran-Ferguson issue. *See S.E.C.* v. *Variable Annuity Life Insurance Co.,* 359 U.S. 65, 69, 79 S.Ct. 618, 620, 3 L.Ed.2d 640 (1959).

HHC points us to nothing since *Royal Drug* which alters this picture. Accordingly, we find that McCarran-Ferguson Act inapplicable.

HHC's argument that the plaintiffs' claims cannot relieve them of or shift liability for services rendered is likewise unpersuasive. In support of its argument, HHC refers us largely to cases decided under the Hill-Burton Act. We find them inapposite. In the cases before us, plaintiffs assert that the statute under which they

This is not a case of the exclusion of persons from general care because of psychiatric handicap.[8] Instead, it is a matter of covering some benefits in the minimum plan and not others, given limited resources. *See* Superintendent's Opinion at n.7 *supra*. In this particular context, that is, medical insurance, we cannot regard this as discrimination solely by reason of handicap.

The logical consequence of plaintiffs' contention would be to mandate that, if any medical benefits were provided, there could be no benefits excluded regardless of the costs of providing the treatment in question or the preferences of the insured group. We do not believe that Congress intended to prohibit all medical insurance which was less than total in its coverage, for the necessary consequence of such a ruling would be either to end all medical insurance or to require drastic reduction in the amount of allowable benefits for those risks of primary concern to the covered employees. We do not believe that the Rehabilitation Act mandates that the decision between, for example, dental or psychiatric coverage, assuming cost considerations preclude both at a reasonable benefit level, is one which cannot be left to the employer, his employees and the insurer.[9]

Accordingly, plaintiffs' Rehabilitation Act claims must fail.[10]

### Equal Protection

Plaintiffs bring claims under the Fourteenth Amendment against HHC and the Superintendent. The parties dispute the appropriate level of equal protection scrutiny for the mentally handicapped. However, under either an intermediate or minimal level of scrutiny we find that the conduct at issue here passes muster under the equal protection clause.[11]

HHC points us to the articulation of reasons contained in the Superintendent's 1975 decision.[12] There, the Superintendent states that in view of consumers' limited resources, priorities in the provision of benefits must be established. Inpatient psychiatric care in HHC hospitals is one of a number of benefits the Superintendent denies. He approves only a benefit "which will require marginal added costs, if any," stating that as to "the proposed expanded psychiatric coverage . . . , there is a considerable net extra cost of $15 million annually."

That the State has a legitimate interest in regulating medical insurance, including insurance rates, cannot be questioned. New York has an extremely comprehensive system of insurance regulations, including the regulation of Blue Cross practices. The fact that a certain benefit is costly is an appropriate and necessary consideration in deciding whether the cost should be passed on to consumers in the form of higher rates.

---

[8]Nor of course is it a case of exclusion on the basis of an inherently invidious classification such as race.

[9]It is one thing to argue that a disabled person is protected against discrimination solely because of h disability with regard to employment, education or other activities covered by the Rehabilitation Act. It quite another thing to say, in the context of medical insurance, that all forms of medical care must be cove because any exclusion is a discrimination based upon disability.

[10]Although by different reasoning, we reach the same result as did the court in *Doe* v. *Colautti* F.2d 704 (3d Cir. 1979).

[11]Although plaintiffs invite us to apply strict scrutiny, the authorities they advance have : intermediate or minimal scrutiny in the case of the mentally disabled. *See* Plaintiffs' Brief at 54–(

[12]*See* n.7 *supra*.

claim mandates an alteration in medical coverage which would shift liability. If the Rehabilitation Act reaches medical coverage, we find no *a priori* obstacle to relief.

Blue Cross, for its part, advances the argument that it does not fall within the purview of the Rehabilitation Act because it was not the recipient of "Federal financial assistance," 29 U.S.C. § 794. It is undisputed that Blue Cross is the recipient of Medicare, Part A funds. The question is whether Blue Cross' receipt of such funds constitutes federal financial assistance within the meaning of the Rehabilitation Act.

We cannot say that Blue Cross has established that no genuine issues of material fact remain on this point and that it is entitled to judgment as a matter of law. Blue Cross acts as a conduit for Medicare funds, performing various functions and ultimately distributing the funds. Blue Cross additionally receives payment for administrative expenses. Plaintiffs have raised a genuine issue of material fact concerning the intermingling of Medicare and other Blue Cross funds and lumping of expenses such that federal Medicare funds may play a part in enabling Blue Cross to carry on both Medicare and non-Medicare activities. *See* Plaintiffs' Brief in Opposition at 34 and Affidavit cited therein. Although plaintiffs raise this in response to Blue Cross' nexus point, we find it pertinent here as well under the very test Blue Cross advances, that is, whether the contract in question is "in the nature of a subsidy" as opposed to a procurement contract. *See* Blue Cross' Reply Memorandum at 13, *citing Cook* v. *Budget Rent-A-Car Corp.*, 502 F.Supp. 494, 501 (S.D.N.Y.1980).

The same factual issue defeats Blue Cross' nexus argument as well, since this issue raises the possibility of a "material connection," see *Stewart* v. *New York University*, 430 F.Supp. 1305, 1314 (S.D.N.Y. 1976) between the Medicare funds and the Blue Cross activities of which plaintiffs complain. Plaintiffs' Brief in Opposition at 34 n.* further states that,

> Plaintiffs also submit that there is an interplay between Blue Cross reimbursement and non-third party reimbursed services in the municipal hospitals, and that the lack of such reimbursement adversely affects the ability of HHC to provide certain services to all hospital consumers, including Medicare beneficiaries and Blue Cross subscribers.

Thus, even if, as defendant argues, nexus is required, which we do not decide defendant Blue Cross has not established its entitlement to summary judgment on nexus grounds.

This brings us to the merits of plaintiffs' Rehabilitation Act claims. Plaintiff maintain that the exclusion of inpatient care in HHC facilities from minimum Blue Cross coverage, and Blue Cross/HHC agreements to that effect constitute discrimination solely because of handicap. We cannot agree. Medical coverage is structured around the identification of categories of benefits and a calculation of risk and consequent costs for that coverage. The fact that the benefit in question here remains outside the minimum coverage plan is a function of the limited risk coverage. Superintendent's decision of 1975, n.7 *supra*. Reasons other than handicap account the exclusion of the risk. The Second Circuit has identified a "substantial justification" exception to the Rehabilitation Act. *Kampmeier* v. *Nyquist*, 553 F.2d 296 Cir. 1977). The insurance characteristics of the benefit in question here which render it outside the minimum plan constitute "substantial justification."

This type of consideration is central to the activities of the state regulator of insurance practices. The means the State chose here to accomplish its purpose of establishing an affordable insurance package were rational, substantially related to its primary goal, and permissible.

In addition to the Superintendent's decision, plaintiffs challenge the Memoranda of Understanding between Blue Cross and HHC. These Memoranda are agreements that set rates of reimbursement as between HHC and Blue Cross, with no mention of specific benefits. Clearly it is in HHC's legitimate interest to enter into such agreements for payment from an insurer. Plaintiffs argue that HHC thereby acquiesced in the exclusion of HHC psychiatric inpatient benefits. However, HHC's entrance into these agreements and implicit acceptance of certain exclusions is rationally and substantially related to its permissible goal of arranging for insurer payment.

Moreover, although plaintiffs would cast this as a case of discrimination against the mentally handicapped, it is not such a case. At the relevant times, psychiatric inpatient care in non-HHC hospitals was covered. It is only the exclusion of such coverage for HHC care which is challenged. Thus, the line drawing challenged here is not line drawing on the basis of handicap, but on the basis of type of care.[14] There is a rational relationship between this line drawing and the legitimate goals of the Insurance Department and HHC. We cannot find equal protection to mandate in this context that all types of care be offered. *See Legion* v. *Richardson,* 354 F.Supp. 456, 459 (S.D.N.Y.) (three judge court), *aff'd sub nom. Legion* v. *Weinberger,* 414 U.S. 1058, 94 S.Ct. 564, 38 L.Ed.2d 465 (1973).

\* \* \*

*Conclusion*

We grant all three defendants summary judgment on the federal law claims brought respectively against them, and decline to exercise pendant jurisdiction over the state law claims.

So ordered.

## NOTES

1. Like *Doe* v. *Colautti,* the court in *Bernard B.* concludes that there is no classification on the basis of handicap. *Bernard B.* goes further, however, in applying a ''substantial justification'' defense based upon legitimate business and governmental purposes. Are you persuaded by the arguments and the evidence cited by the court in support of its reasoning? Should an articulation of legitimate business or governmental purposes be enough to justify a classification that excludes a subclass of handicapped persons?

2. What is the significance of footnote 9? Is it consistent with the definition of ''handicapped individual'' in Section 7(6) of the Rehabilitation Act of 1973, as amended? (See p. 25 of the Casebook.) If a person is in need of inpatient medical care of any kind, are they *per se* handicapped?

---

[14]*Cf. Schweiker* v. *Wilson,* 450 U.S. 221, 231, 101 S.Ct. 1074, 1081, 67 L.Ed.2d 186 (1981) (''[T]his statute does not classify directly on the basis of mental health. . . . [T]his legislation . . . implies equivalent deprivation on other groups who are not mentally ill, while at the same time benefiting substantial numbers of the mentally ill.'' (Footnote omitted.)).

## E. RECREATIONAL AND ATHLETIC PROGRAMS

p. 1107—INSERT the following at the end of the Note:

Other courts permitting handicapped high school or college students to participate in scholastic athletics over the objection of educational institutions include: *Doe* v. *Marshall*, 622 F.2d 118 (5th Cir., 1980), *cert. denied*, 451 U.S. 993 (1981) (propriety of preliminary injunction permitting emotionally handicapped student to play football was moot because of student's graduation); *Wright* v. *Columbia University*, 520 F.Supp. 789 (E.D.Pa. 1981); *Poole* v. *South Plainfield Board of Education*, 490 F.Supp. 948 (D.N.J. 1980).

p. 1110—INSERT at the end of Note 2:

Faced with a one-eyed college student seeking a temporary restraining order, the court in *Wright* v. *Columbia University*, 520 F.Supp. 789 (E.D.Pa. 1981), distinguished *Kampmeir* on the basis that the college student had introduced evidence that there was little risk to his remaining eye from playing football and that the college student was mature enough to understand and accept the risks, thereby obviating any need to resort to the *parens patriae* doctrine.

p. 1113—INSERT the following new section after Notes:

## F. MASS MEDIA

### COMMUNITY TELEVISION OF SOUTHERN CALIFORNIA v. SUE GOTTFRIED

*United States Supreme Court, 1983*
*103 S.Ct. 885*

JUSTICE STEVENS delivered the opinion of the Court.

The question presented is whether §504 of the Rehabilitation Act of 1973 requires the Federal Communications Commission to review a public television station's license renewal application under a different standard than it applies to a commercial licensee's renewal application. Contrary to the holding of the Court of Appeals for the District of Columbia Circuit, 655 F. 2d 297, we conclude that it does not.

I

On October 13, 1977, respondent Sue Gottfried filed a formal petition with the Federal Communications Commission requesting it to deny renewal of the television license of station KCET–TV in Los Angeles. She advanced two principal grounds for denial: First, that the licensee had failed to discharge its obligation to ascertain the problems, needs, and interests of the deaf and hearing impaired population within its service area; and second, that the licensee had violated, and remained in violation of, §504 of the Rehabilitation Act.[2]

---

[2]In her petition, Gottfried alleged, in part:

"That the Licensee has violated, and remains in violation of Section 504 of the Rehabilitation Act of 1973, and the regulations promulgated thereunder, in that the Licensee has received and is receiving Federal financial

Correspondence attached to Gottfried's petition included complaints about KCET-TV's failure to carry enough programming with special captioning[3] or other aids to benefit the hearing impaired members of the audience. The exhibits emphasized the station's failure to broadcast the ABC evening news in captioned form prior to May 27, 1977, and its subsequent failure to broadcast the captioned program during prime time.

In a verified opposition to the petition, the licensee recounted in some detail its efforts to ascertain the problems of the community it served, including the deaf and the hearing impaired, by a community leader survey and by a general public survey. App. in No. 79–1722 (CADC), pp. 102–105. The licensee also described its programming efforts to respond to the special needs of the hearing impaired,[4] and explained why its two daily broadcasts of the ABC captioned news had usually been scheduled for 11:30 p.m. and 6:30 a.m. The licensee specifically denied that it had violated §504 and averred that the Commission is not an appropriate forum for the adjudication of Rehabilitation Act claims. App. in No. 79–1722 (CADC), p. 113.

On December 12, 1977, Gottfried filed a verified response, criticizing the station's public survey, and commenting further on the station's failure to rebroadcast ABC captioned news programs before May 22, 1977. The response renewed the charge that the station had violated §504,[5] and asserted that the Federal Communications Commission was indeed the proper forum to evaluate that charge.[6]

---

assistance and has discriminated and is discriminating against the Petitioners 'solely by reason of [their] handicap', and said Petitioners have been and are 'excluded from participation in [and have been and are denied] the benefits of, [and have been and are being] subjected to discrimination' under the television services in connection with which Licensee has been and is receiving Federal financial assistance." App. in No. 79–1722 (CADC), p. 26 (brackets in original).

[3]"Captioning" refers to any of several technologies, see Captioning for the Deaf, 63 F.C.C. 2d 378 (1976), that project written text onto a television image so that deaf viewers receive information that is communicated to others by the sound track. See also n. 8, *infra*.

[4]"Contrary to Petitioners' unsupported charges (Petition, p. 3), KCET has responded to the needs of deaf and hearing-impaired persons in its service area. It has done so with three different types of programming: (a) *Captioned ABC Evening News;* (b) a variety of other programs, including children's programs, which were captioned or signed so as to be understandable to the deaf and hearing-impaired; and (c) special programs which have directly addressed needs and concerns of the deaf and hearing-impaired.

\* \* \*

"Over the past three years, KCET has presented more than 960 programs which were either captioned, signed or, in rare instances, which had no spoken words in them at all. All of these programs were understandable to the deaf and hearing-impaired. In many instances, KCET has promoted these programs by listing them as designed for the hearing-impaired audience. During the past three years, in addition to *ABC Captioned News,* these broadcasts have included such programs as 'Zoom', 'Once Upon a Classic,' 'Nova', films of Ingmar Bergman, 'The Tribal Eye', 'Masterpiece Theatre', 'Adams Chronicles', 'President Carter's Clinton, Massachusetts Town Meeting', and many others.

"In addition to programs designed to be understood by the deaf and hearing-impaired, KCET has devoted several special programs to substantive issues affecting those groups." App. in No. 79–1722 (CADC), pp. 106, 109.

[5]The responses stated:

"[T]he station has not been responsive to the needs of the deaf and hearing impaired. In the station's viewing area, the deaf 20 percent of the population are not getting 20 percent of broadcast time; they were not even getting what other deaf in other viewing areas were receiving."
App. in No. 79–1722 (CADC), p. 148.

[6]The responses continued:

"The Commission is a proper forum for the adjudication of claims of discrimination in broadcasting, as it is the

Gottfried also filed separate formal objections to the renewal of seven commercial television station licenses in the Los Angeles area. *E.g.*, App. in No. 79–1722 (CADC), p. 199. The Commission consolidated all eight proceedings and ruled on Gottfried's objections in a single memorandum opinion adopted on August 8, 1978. 69 F.C.C. 2d 451.

The Commission first reviewed its own efforts to encourage the industry to serve the needs of the hearing impaired. In 1970, the Commission had issued a Public Notice to all licensees, advising them of the special needs of the deaf in responding to emergency situations as well as in appreciating general television programming.[7] In 1972, the Commission had granted authority to the Public Broadcasting System to begin experimentation with a "closed" captioning system, which would enable hearing-impaired persons with specially equipped television sets to receive captioned information that could not be seen by the remainder of the viewing audience.[8] In 1976, the Commission had adopted a rule requiring television licensees to broadcast emergency information visually. In that year, however, the Commission had also concluded that there were so many unanswered questions—both technical and financial—concerning the most effective means of improving television service for the hearing impaired, that it remained "the responsibility of each licensee to determine how it could most effectively meet those needs."[9] The Commission summarized its views concerning mandated forms of technology by noting that "there is no requirement that any television licensee—commercial or noncommercial—provide open or closed captioning or any other form of special visual program material other than for broadcasting emergency information." *Id*, at 455.

The Commission then turned to Gottfried's objections to the eight license renewals. It approached the question whether the renewals would serve the public interest, convenience, and necessity from three different perspectives: ascertainment, programming, and §504 of the Rehabilitation Act. It first found that the licensees' efforts to ascertain the special needs of the community were adequate. Next, it held

---

Commission's obligation—even apart from the ACT—to determine how the station has discharged its public trust obligations. The Act and the regulations thereunder, merely give further statutory and regulatory emphasis to that which the Commission is already charged to do under the law."
App. in No. 79–1722 (CADC), p. 148.

[7]The Use of Telecasts to Inform and Alert Viewers with Impaired Hearing, 26 FCC 2d 917 (1970). The Commission described the effect of its 1970 action as follows:

"[I]t was suggested that television stations could make use of visual as well as oral announcements of emergencies, utilize the face of newscasters wherever possible so as to permit lip reading, and feature visualization of materials in news, weather, and sports programs. The Commission hoped that the notice would alert licensees to our concern for the needs of the hearing impaired citizen and make television a truly valuable medium for that segment of the population—estimated by the Department of Health, Education, and Welfare to include 13.4 million persons. We observed, however, that 'it may be necessary to begin rule making looking toward the adoption of minimum requirements.'" 69 F.C.C. 2d, at 454.

[8]"Through the use of an encoder at the transmitting end and a decoder at the receiving end, this closed captioning system could supply visual information—captioning—of the aural portion of the television program to those hearing impaired persons whose television sets were equipped to received the captioned information while the rest of the viewing public would receive the normal visual and aural transmission. This differs from 'open' captioning utilized, for example, by PBS in its rebroadcast of the *ABC Evening News*. Open captioning is transmitted to all viewers who see a printed display of the text of the aural transmission at the bottom of the visual transmission." 69 F.C.C. 2d, at 454.

[9]*Captioning for the Deaf*, 63 FCC 2d 378, 389 (1976).

that the facts alleged by Gottfried did not give rise to a substantial and material question whether any of the eight stations had abused its discretion in its selection of programming matter. The Commission explained that it is more difficult to provide special programming for the hearing impaired than for other segments of the community;[10] in the absence of any Commission requirement for specialized programming techniques, it found "no basis to fault a licensee for failure to provide these options for the deaf and hearing impaired in the station service area." *Id.,* at 458.

The Commission held that §504 of the Rehabilitation Act had no application to the seven commercial licensees because they were not alleged to have received any federal financial assistance. The Commission agreed that KCET–TV might be governed by §504, and that a violation of the Act would need to be considered in a license renewal proceeding, but it saw no reason to consider §504 in the absence of an adverse finding by the Department of Health, Education, and Welfare—"the proper governmental agency to consider such matters." *Id.,* at 459.

On May 29, 1979, the Commission adopted a second memorandum opinion and order denying Gottfried's petition for reconsideration. 72 F.C.C. 2d 273. The Commission again reviewed Gottfried's §504 charge and again concluded that the Rehabilitation Act does not apply to commercial stations and that the allegations against KCET–TV under that Act were premature unless and until the agency with authority to enforce compliance determined that the station had violated its provisions. The Commission also rejected Gottfried's additional argument that it had a duty to adopt regulations to implement §504. Finally, the Commission refused to hold that either its omission of a rule requiring "captioning or other techniques to enable the deaf requiring "captioning or other techniques to enable the deaf and hearing impaired to have full access to television broadcast," or the failure of the licensees to provide such services, was a violation of the "public interest" standard embodied in §309 of the Communications Act of 1934, as amended. The Commission held:

> We find no error and nothing inconsistent in concluding that licensees are serving the public interest although they are not currently providing captioning, in view of the fact that we have not required licensees to undertake such an activity. Furthermore, to judge a licensee's qualifications on the basis of the retroactive application of such a requirement would, in our opinion, raise serious questions of fundamental fairness. Thus, there is no inconsistency or error in our finding that the subject licensees had met their public interest burden even though they did not caption their programming. *Id.,* at 279.

Gottfried appealed the decision of the Commission to the Court of Appeals for the District of Columbia Circuit, pursuant to 47 U.S.C. §402. The Court of Appeals affirmed the portion of the Commission's order that related to the commercial stations but vacated the renewal of the KCET–TV license and remanded for further proceedings. 655 F. 2d 297.

---

[10] "Generally speaking, [special programming for other segments of the community] can be achieved without any additional production techniques other than those utilized for regular programming. Obviously, that is not the situation confronting a licensee who might wish to program for the aurally handicapped. For such programming to be effective, it must offer some specific form of visual communication: sign language interpretations, captioning, or extensive utilization of charts, signs, and facial closeups to permit lip reading. Even sign language and lip reading efforts, according to Gottfried, serve to limit the number of deaf and hearing impaired since many do not effectively understand these methods." 69 F.C.C. 2d, at 458.

The Court held that Congress did not intend the Commission's renewal of a broadcast license to be considered a form of "financial assistance" within the meaning of §504 and therefore that the Rehabilitation Act did not directly apply to the seven commercial stations. The Court was persuaded, however, that the Act reflected a national policy of extending increased opportunities to the hearing impaired and that commercial stations must therefore make some accommodation for the hard of hearing, given the Communications Act's general requirement that licensees serve "the public interest, convenience, and necessity." 47 U.S.C. §§307(d), 309(a), 309(d). In the absence of a more specific statutory directive than that contained in the public interest standard, however, the Court accepted the Commission's judgment that the commercial licenses should be renewed. "Recognizing that the Commission possesses special competence in weighing the factors of technological feasibility and economic viability that the concept of the public interest must embrace, we defer today to its judgment." *Id.*, at 315–316 (footnotes omitted).

The majority of the Court of Appeals reached a different conclusion with respect to KCET–TV. As a recipient of federal financial assistance, the public station was admittedly under a duty to comply with §504. The Court of Appeals did not hold that KCET–TV had violated §504, or that its efforts to provide programming for the hearing impaired were less satisfactory than the efforts of the commercial licensees; nevertheless, it held that a stricter "public interest" standard should be applied to a licensee covered by §504 than to a commercial licensee. Its narrow holding was that the Commission could not find the service of public stations "to be adequate to justify renewal without at least inquiring specifically into their efforts to meet the programming needs of the hearing impaired." *Id.*, at 301.

Judge McGowan dissented in part. He agreed with the majority's view concerning commercial stations that rulemaking would be "a better, fairer, and more effective vehicle for considering how the broadcast industry is required to provide the enjoyment and educational benefits of television to persons with impaired hearing," *id.*, at 301, 316, than case by case adjudication in license renewal proceedings. He felt, however, that the same standard should be applied to public stations until regulations had been issued by the Department of Education dealing specifically with the rights of access of the hearing impaired to television programs.[11] Judge McGowan stated, "[F]orm is favored over substance when commercial stations are, for this reason, spared the expense and uncertainty of renewal hearings, and a noncommercial station is not. Neither, on the record before us, had advance notice during their expired license terms of what was, and therefore could reasonably be, expected of them with respect to the wholly laudable, but technically complex, objective of providing access for the hearing impaired." *Id.*, at 317.

Both the Commission and the licensee petitioned for certiorari. Because of the serious implications of the Court of Appeals' holding on the status of licenses of public broadcasting stations, we granted both petitions. 454 U.S. 1141.

---

[11]Judge McGowan pointed out that on January 19, 1981, the Department of Education had issued a notice of intent to develop such regulations, and invited comments by March 5, 1981. 655 F. 2d at 317. See 46 Fed. Reg. 4954.

## II

All parties agree that the public interest would be served by making television broadcasting more available and more understandable to the substantial portion of our population that is handicapped by impaired hearing.[12] The Commission recognized this component of the public interest even before the enactment of the Rehabilitation Act of 1973, see 26 F.C.C. 2d 917 (1970), and that statute confirms the federal interest in developing the opportunities for all individuals with handicaps to live full and independent lives. No party suggests that a licensee, whether commercial or public, may simply ignore the needs of the hearing impaired in discharging its responsibilities to the community which it serves.[13]

We are not persuaded, however, that Congress intended the Rehabilitation Act of 1973 to impose any new enforcement obligation on the Federal Communications Commission.[14] As originally enacted, the Act did not expressly allocate enforcement responsibility. See Pub. L. 93–112, Title V, §504, 87 Stat. 394. Nevertheless, since §504 was patterned after Title VI of the Civil Rights Act of 1964, it was understood that responsibility for enforcing it, insofar as it regulated private recipients of federal funds, would lie with those agencies administering the federal financial assistance programs. See S. Rep. No. 93–1297, pp. 39–40 (1974). When the Act was amended in 1978, that understanding was made explicit. See Pub. L. 95–602, Title I, §119, 92 Stat. 2982; n. 1, *supra*. It is clear that the Commission is not a funding agency and has never been thought to have responsibility for enforcing §504.[15] Furthermore, there is

---

[12]"Estimates of the number of citizens who have limited hearing and therefore have need for the receipt of news and entertainment material through appropriate television programming range from 8.5 million to 20 million. Many of these persons, it appears, live alone and oftentimes do not receive important new information unless advised by neighbors or friends."
The Use of Telecasts to Inform and Alert Viewers with Impaired Hearing, 26 F.C.C. 2d 917 (1970).

[13]As the Commission has observed:

"In the fulfillment of his obligation the broadcaster should consider the tastes, needs, and desires of the public he is licensed to serve. . . . He should reasonably attempt to meet all such needs and interests on an equitable basis." Report and Statement on Policy Re: Commission's En Banc Programming Inquiry, 25 Fed. Reg. 7291, 7295 (1960). Accord, *In re Applications of Alabama Educational Television Comm'n*, 50 F.C.C. 2d 461, 472 (1975); *In re Applications of Capitol Broadcasting Co.*, 38 F.C.C. 1135, 1139 (1965).

[14]If such an enforcement obligation existed, it would have to derive from the Rehabilitation Act itself, since the general words "public interest" in the Communications Act are not sufficient to create it. In *McLean Trucking Co.* v. *United States*, 321 U.S. 67 (1944), we observed that an agency charged with promoting the "public interest" in a particular substantive area may not simply "ignore" the policies underlying other federal statutes. *Id.*, at 80. But we also emphasized that such an agency is not automatically given "either the duty or the authority to execute numerous other laws." *Id.*, at 79. Thus, in *McLean Trucking* the ICC had an administrative duty to consider the effect of a motor carrier merger on competing motor carriers in determining whether the merger would effectuate over-all transportation policy, *id.*, at 87, yet was "not to measure proposals for all-rail or all-motor consolidations by the standards of the anti-trust laws," *id.*, at 85. Here, the FCC has an administrative duty to consider the needs of handicapped citizens in determining whether a license renewal would effectuate the policies behind the Communication Act but is by no means required to measure proposals for public television license renewals by the standards of §504 of the Rehabilitation Act

[15]In 1976, the President designated the Department of Health, Education and Welfare as the agency responsible for coordinating the implementation of §504. See Exec. Order No. 11,914,45 CFR Part 85, App. A, at 374. In 1980 that Executive Order was revoked and replaced by Executive Order No. 12,250,45 Fed. Reg. 72995, which transferred the coordination and enforcement of authority for §504 from HEW to the Department of Justice. Regulations previously adopted by HEW remain in effect pending the adoption of new regulations by the Department of Justice. See 28 CFR Part 41. 46 Fed. Reg. 40686–40687 (1981).

not a word in the legislative history of the Act suggesting that it was intended to alter the Commission's standard for reviewing the programming decisions of public television licensees.

If a licensee should be found guilty of violating the Rehabilitation Act, or indeed of violating any other federal statute, the Commission would certainly be obligated to consider the possible relevance of such a violation in determining whether or not to renew the lawbreaker's license.[16] But in the absence of a direction in the Rehabilitation Act itself, and without any expression of such intent in the legislative history, we are unwilling to assume that Congress has instructed the Federal Communications Commission to take original jurisdiction over the processing of charges that its regulatees have violated that Act.[17]

The fact that a public television station has a duty to comply with the Rehabilitation Act does not support the quite different conclusion that the Commission must evaluate a public station's service to the handicapped community by a more stringent standard than that applicable to commercial stations. The interest in having all television stations—public and commercial—consider and serve their handicapped viewers is equally strong. By the same token, it is equally unfair to criticize a licensee—whether public or commercial—for failing to comply with a requirement of which it had no notice.[18] As both the majority and the dissenting judge in the Court of Appeals observed, rulemaking is generally a "better, fairer, and more effective" method of implementing a new industry-wide policy than is the uneven application of conditions in isolated license renewal proceedings. That observation should be as determinative in relicensing a public station as it is in relicensing a commercial station.

A federal agency providing financial assistance to a public television station may, of course, attach conditions to its subsidy that will have the effect of subjecting

---

[16]The Commission has explained its policy as follows:

> Normally, we have declined to explore matters currently being litigated before the courts or to duplicate the ongoing investigative efforts of other gorvernment agencies charged with the responsibility of interpreting and enforcing the laws in question. Our restraint in this respect has not been predicated upon the unlikelihood of proving the violation of law. Indeed, conduct which does not contravene law may still run afoul of the public interest standard. . . . By our forebearance we have sought to maintain a proper working relationship with the judiciary and other governmental agencies and to avoid burdening applicants with unnecessary, costly multiple proceedings." 59 F.C.C. 2d 750, 763 (1951)

[17]This is not to say that the Commission may permit a licensee to ignore the needs of particular groups within the viewing public. The point is that the Commission's duties derive from the Communications Act, not from other federal statutes. In *NAACP* v. *FPC*, 425 U.S. 662, 670 n. 7 (1976), for example, this Court noted that the Commission's equal opportunity regulations could be regarded as "necessary to ensure that its licensees' programming fairly reflects the tastes and viewpoints of minority groups." We then reiterated, however, that an agency's general duty to enforce the public interest does not require it to assume responsibility for enforcing legislation that is not directed at the agency:

> "It is useful again to draw on the analogy of federal labor law. No less than federal legislation defining the national interest in ending employment discrimination, Congress in its earlier labor legislation unmistakably defined the national interest in free collective bargaining. Yet it could hardly be supposed that in directing the Federal Power Commission to be guided by the 'public interest,' Congress thereby instructed it to take original jurisdiction over the processing of charges of unfair labor practices on the part of its regulatees." *Id.*, at 671.

[18]We have previously emphasized the desirability of making changes in licensing policies prospective. In *FCC* v. *National Citizens Committee for Broadcasting*, 436 U.S. 775, 811 (1978), we wrote:

> "One of the most significant advantages of the administrative process is its ability to adapt to new circumstances in a flexible manner, see *FCC* v. *Pottsville Broadcasting Co.*, 309 U.S., at 137–138, and we are unwilling to presume that the Commission acts unreasonably when it decides to try out a change in licensing policy primarily on a prospective basis."

such a licensee to more stringent requirements than must be met by a commercial licensee. Or regulations may be promulgated under the Rehabilitation Act that impose special obligations on the subsidized licensee. Conceivably, the Federal Communications Commission might determine that the policies underlying the Communications Act require extraordinary efforts to make certain types of programming universally accessible, thereby placing heightened responsibility on certain stations. But unless and until such a differential standard has been promulgated, the Federal Communications Commission does not abuse its discretion in interpreting the public interest standard, see *FCC* v. *WNCN Listeners Guild,* 450 U.S. 582 (1981); when it declines to impose a greater obligation to provide special programming for the hearing impaired on a public licensee than on a commercial licensee.[19]

The Court of Appeals was unanimous in its holding that the renewal of the seven commercial licensees was consistent with the public interest requirement in §309 of the Federal Communications Act. Neither that Court nor the Commission suggested that there was anything in the record that would justify treating the public licensee differently from the commercial licensees if both classes were to be judged under the same standard. The Court of Appeals' affirmance of the Commission's rejection of Gottfried's objection to the renewal of the commercial licenses therefore requires a like disposition of the objections to the renewal of the KCET–TV license. Accordingly, the judgment of the Court of Appeals is reversed insofar as it vacated the order of the Commission.

*It is so ordered.*

Justice Marshall, with whom Justice Brennan joins, dissenting.

In determining that the "public interest" would be served by renewal of the broadcast license of public station KCET–TV, the FCC refused to consider whether the station had violated the Rehabilitation Act of 1973 during its previous license term. The Court today holds that this refusal to consider the Rehabilitation Act did not constitute an abuse of discretion. In concluding that the FCC was free to disregard the Rehabilitation Act, the Court emphasizes that "the Commission's duties derive from the Communications Act, not from other federal statutes," *ante,* at 12 n. 16, and that there is no evidence that Congress intended to vest the Commission with power to enforce the Rehabilitation Act, *ante,* at 10–11. Because the Court's decision is not supported by either precedent or any sound view of the administrative process, I respectfully dissent.

I

This Court's decisions establish that where an agency has a statutory duty, as does the FCC,[1] to assess the "public interest" in implementing a particular regulatory

---

[19]We note the Commission's argument that, if a differential standard were appropriate, commercial stations would be better able to afford the costs associated with special programming than public television stations which cannot sell advertising and which serve the public in large part by airing programs of specialized interest that lack the mass appeal required for broadcast on network affiliates.

[1]The FCC is directed by statute to grant an application for renewal of a broadcast license only if it finds that the "public interest, convenience, and necessity would be served thereby." 47 U.S.C. §307(d) (1982 Supp.).

scheme, the agency must give at least some consideration to other federal statutes that are pertinent to its administrative decision. Although the open-ended phrase "public interest" "take[s] meaning from the purposes of the regulatory legislation" that defines the particular agency's responsibilities, *NAACP v. FPC,* 425 U.S. 662, 669 (1976), the agency may not focus on those purposes to the complete exclusion of the policies reflected in other relevant statutes.

The principle that an agency may not ignore a relevant Act of Congress was clearly set forth by Justice Rutledge in his opinion for the Court in *McLean Trucking Co. v. United States,* 321 U.S. 67 (1944). In *McLean Trucking* the ICC had approved a proposed consolidation as "consistent with the public interest." *Id.,* at 75–76, quoting 49 U.S.C. § 5(2)(b). While recognizing that the ICC's duties derived primarily from the Interstate Commerce Act and related legislation specifically regulating commerce, Justice Rutledge rejected any suggestion that the ICC could therefore ignore other relevant statutes in deciding whether a proposed transaction would serve the "public interest":

> To secure the continuous, close and informed supervision which enforcement of legislative mandates frequently requires, Congress has vested expert administrative bodies such as the Interstate Commerce Commission with broad discretion and has charged them with the duty to execute stated and specific statutory policies. That delegation does not necessarily include either the duty or the authority to execute numerous other laws. Thus, here, the Commission has no power to enforce the Sherman Act as such. It cannot decide definitively whether the transaction contemplated constitutes a restraint of trade or an attempt to monopolize which is forbidden by that Act. The Commission's task is to enforce the Interstate Commerce Act and other legislation which deals specifically with transportation facilities and problems. That legislation constitutes the immediate frame of reference within which the Commission operates; and the policies expressed in it must be the basic determinants of its action.
>
> But in executing those policies the Commission may be faced with overlapping and at times inconsistent policies embodied in other legislation enacted at different times and with different problems in view. *When this is true, it cannot, without more, ignore the latter. Id.,* at 79–80 (emphasis added).

The Court held that the ICC was obligated to take the Sherman Act into account in deciding whether to approve the proposed consolidation, even though Congress had not given the Commission either the power or the duty to enforce the Act.[2]

Similarly, in *Denver & Rio Grande Western Railroad Co. v. United States,* 387 U.S. 485 (1967), this Court concluded that "the broad terms 'public interest' and 'lawful object' [in § 20a(2) of the Interstate Commerce Act] negate the existence of a mandate to the ICC to close its eyes to facts indicating that the transaction may exceed limitations imposed by other relevant laws." 387 U.S., at 492. JUSTICE BRENNAN

---

[2]The majority errs in attempting to distinguish *McLean Trucking* by quoting Justice Rutledge's statement that the ICC was "not to measure proposals for all-rail or all-motor consolidations by the standards of the anti-trust laws." 321 U.S., at 85, quoted *ante,* at 11 n. 14. The issue here is not whether the FCC should have measured KCET–TV's application by the same standards that would apply in a proceeding to enforce the Rehabilitation Act, but whether the FCC should have given at least some consideration to the policies underlying the Act. *In McLean Trucking* the Court made it clear that the ICC was not free to ignore the policies underlying the anti-trust laws. In addition to the passage quoted in the text, see 321 U.S., at 86 ("Congress . . . neither has made the anti-trust laws wholly inapplicable to the transportation industry nor has authorized the Commission in passing on a proposed merger to ignore their policy.").

explained in his opinion for the Court that "[c]ommon sense and sound administrative policy point to the conclusion that such broad statutory standards require at least some degree of consideration of control and anticompetitive consequences when suggested by the circumstances surrounding a particular transaction." *Ibid.* Accordingly, the Court held that the ICC was required to consider the anticompetitive effect under § 7 of the Clayton Act of a proposed stock issuance by a carrier even though that Act confers no enforcement power on the ICC.

In *Southern Steamship Co.* v. *NLRB,* 316 U.S. 31 (1942), this Court recognized that the National Labor Relations Board must consider federal statutes independent of federal labor law where they are relevant to an issue to be decided by the Board. Although the Court acknowledged the breadth of the Board's discretion, *id.,* at 46, it concluded that the Board had no discretion to disregard pertinent federal laws: "the Board has not been commissioned to effectuate the policies of the National Labor Relations Act so single-mindedly that it may wholly ignore other and equally important Congressional objectives." *Id.,* at 47. The Court ruled that the Board had abused its discretion in ordering the reinstatement of striking seamen without considering whether the strike had violated either a federal law requiring crew members to promise obedience to their superiors or provisions of the Federal Criminal Code proscribing mutiny and revolt aboard ship.

These decisions establish that, however broad an administrative agency's discretion in implementing a regulatory scheme may be, the agency may not ignore a relevant Act of Congress. The agency need not conclusively determine what the statute in question requires or forbids. See *McLean Trucking Co.* v. *United States,* 321 U.S., at 79 (ICC "cannot definitively decide whether the transaction contemplated constitutes a restraint of trade or an attempt to monopolize"). If the agency, after considering the relevant statute, concludes that it should not prevent achievement of the objectives embodied in the regulatory scheme that the agency is specifically empowered to implement, and states reasons for this conclusion, the agency's determination will not lightly be overturned. But the agency cannot simply "close its eyes" to the existence of the statute. *Denver & Rio Grande Western Railroad Co.* v. *United States,* 387 U.S., at 492.

There are good reasons for this Court's insistence that administrative agencies consider relevant statutes. The objectives of Congress would be ill served if each administrative agency were permitted to disregard any statute that it is not specifically authorized to enforce. "No agency entrusted with determinations of public convenience and necessity is an island. It fits within a national system of regulatory control of industry." *Palisades Citizens Association, Inc.* v. *CAB,* 420 F.2nd 188, 191 (DCCA 1969). As the Court observed in *Southern Steamship,* "[f]requently the entire scope of Congressional purpose calls for careful accommodation of one statutory scheme to another." 316 U.S., at 47. There can be no accommodation, careful or otherwise, if an agency refuses even to consider a relevant statute.

## II

In light of the principle established by our prior decisions, the Court of Appeals correctly held that it was an abuse of discretion for the FCC to refuse to consider respondent's allegation that KCET–TV had violated §504 of the Rehabilitation Act.[3]

The relevance of the alleged violation to the Commission's licensing decision is beyond dispute. The chief purpose of the Communications Act was "to make available . . . to *all the people of the United States* a rapid, efficient, Nationwide, and worldwide wire and radio communication service." 47 U.S.C. §151 (emphasis added). See *National Broadcasting Co.* v. *United States,* 319 U.S. 190, 217 (1943). The deaf constitute a substantial segment of the population. *Ante,* at 9 n. 12. If, as this Court has stated, the Commission has an "obligation . . . to ensure that its licensees' programming fairly reflects the tastes and viewpoints of minority groups," *NAACP* v. *FPC,* 425 U.S., at 670 n. 7, then surely it also has an obligation to consider whether a license has denied meaningful programming of any kind to a sizeable minority group.

Since respondent's allegation that KCET–TV had violated the Rehabilitation Act was relevant to the FCC's determination of whether renewal of the station's license would serve the "public interest," the Commission should have given "at least some consideration" to the Act. *Denver & Rio Grande Western Railroad Co.* v. *United States,* 387 U.S., at 492. There is no reason to depart from our traditional insistence that administrative agencies take into account any federal statute that is pertinent to an administrative decision.[4] As the Court noted in *Southern Steamship,* consideration of any pertinent statutes "is not too much to demand of an administrative body." 316 U.S., at 47. The decision of the Court of Appeals demanded no more than this, and the handicapped individuals protected by the Rehabilitation Act are entitled to no less.

## NOTES

1. The Court states: "All parties agree that the public interest would be served by making television broadcasting more available and more understandable to the substantial portion of our population that is handicapped by impaired hearing. . . . No party suggests that a licensee, whether commercial or public may simply ignore the needs of the hearing impaired in discharging its responsibilities to the community it serves." What is the scope of the "public interest" legal standard and how does it differ from

---

[3]Section 504 provides in pertinent part that "[n]o otherwise qualified handicapped individual . . . shall, solely by reason of his handicap, be excluded from participation in, be denied benefits of, or be subjected to discrimination under any program or activity receiving Federal financial assistance." 29 U.S.C. §794 (1976 ed., 1982 Supp.). Respondent alleged that KCET–TV had violated the Rehabilitation Act by, among other things, failing, for most of its license term, to broadcast a captioned version of the ABC Evening News that was made available to it free of charge by the Public Broadcasting Service, and by thereafter failing to broadcast the program during any prime time hours. It is undisputed that KCET–TV conducts a "program or activity receiving Federal financial assistance" within the meaning of §504.

[4]Contrary to the Court's suggestion, *ante,* at 12, a requirement that the Commission take the Rehabilitation Act into account in its licensing decisions involving public stations would not necessarily subject such stations to a more stringent standard than that applicable to commercial stations, which are not covered by the Act. In the exercise of its discretion, there is nothing to stop the Commission from imposing an equally or more demanding standard on commercial stations if it properly explains why such a standard is justified by the purposes of the Communications Act. For example, commercial stations may be better able to afford the costs of special programming. See *ante,* at 13, n. 18. What the Commission cannot do under our prior decisions, is simply ignore the Rehabilitation Act in a licensing proceeding in which that Act is relevant.

the §504 nondiscrimination standard? If a commercial or public television station "simply ignore[d]" the needs of the hearing impaired community, could members of that community challenge such total lack of service in a license renewal proceeding before the FCC after *Gottfried?* How?

2.   The Court refers to §504 being patterned after Title VI of the Civil Rights Act of 1964 as support for its contention that only those agencies administering federal financial assistance programs can enforce §504. Unlike Title VI, however, §504 imposes a separate obligation on the federal government not to discriminate in its operations. Can an argument be made that this obligation was violated by any FCC activity or lack of activity in this case? How would you construct the argument?

3.   The majority's analysis suggests a compartmentalization of enforcement responsibilities by limiting an agency's obligation to enforcing only those statutory policies that it is specifically empowered to enforce and permitting it to essentially ignore national public policy enunciated in other statutes. This analysis is a departure from some current civil rights doctrines. For example, several federal appellate courts have ordered the Internal Revenue Service not to grant nonprofit tax exempt status to religious schools that discriminate in admission on the basis of race. The U.S. Supreme Court has agreed to review the question. *See: Bob Jones University* v. *United States,* 468 F. Supp. 890 (D.S.C.1978), *rev'd,* 639 F.2d 147 (4th Cir. 1980), *cert. granted,* 50 U.S.L.W. 3265 (U.S., Oct. 13, 1981) (No. 81–3); *Goldsboro Christian Schools, Inc.* v. *United States,* 436 F. Supp. 1314 (E.D.N.C. 1977), *aff'd per curiam,* No. 80–1473 (4th Cir. Feb. 24, 1981) (unpublished opinion), *cert. granted,* 50 U.S.L.W. 3265 (U.S., Oct. 13, 1981) (No. 81–1).

# INDEX